UNIVERSITY EDUCATION FOR BUSINESS

A Study of Existing Needs and Practices

By

JAMES H. S. BOSSARD
Professor of Sociology

and

J. FREDERIC DEWHURST
Professor of Industry

Wharton School of Finance and Commerce
University of Pennsylvania

PHILADELPHIA
UNIVERSITY OF PENNSYLVANIA PRESS
1931

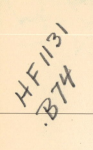

FOREWORD

More critical attention and more constructive thought are being given to education today than at any previous time. This is true of education for the law, for engineering and other professions and also of the aims and methods of teaching languages, the sciences, and many other subjects. This is a most hopeful sign. It makes certain that education in the future will be more effective than it has been in the past, will more definitely influence the lives of individual men and women.

The investigation made by Professors Bossard and Dewhurst throws the searchlight of enquiry upon collegiate and university education for those who are to engage in business upon graduation. Their report, which is presented in full in this volume, is comprehensive and thorough. It was written without any conscious bias on the part of the authors, who have sought to present facts rather than to establish or defend any thesis. It is a fact-finding report, but is so written that it is not so much a report in the common acceptance of the term as a connected, interesting, vital discussion of the information obtained by the authors from collegiate and university schools of business and their graduates, from men of affairs, and from the study of books.

The purpose of the investigation, which was made for, and under the auspices of, the Faculty of Wharton School of Finance and Commerce, was not to secure data that would be helpful only to that School, but to do a piece of work, prepare and publish a volume, that would be significant and useful for all colleges and universities interested in the development of education of those who are to engage in business upon graduation. The Wharton School Faculty will have the benefit of the information contained in this volume in deciding upon its educational aims and methods and upon the curriculum changes found desirable. The same will be true of the faculties of other institutions.

This volume upon University Education for Business appears during the fiftieth year of the activity of the Wharton School, the School having been established in consequence of a gift made March 1, 1881, by Joseph Wharton. The fiftieth anniversary of the founding of the School will be duly celebrated in March, 1931, and it will be gratifying to the faculty, alumni, and other friends of the School that this important contribution to the knowledge

v

of what has thus far been accomplished by collegiate and university schools of business, and of what those who have had experience as business men regard to be essential and useful in educating young men who are to live the life of men of affairs, should appear upon the completion of the first half century of the development of the pioneer collegiate school of business in the United States.

Educational aims, methods, and curricula advance by evolution subject to many influences, but to none other so potent as the changing conditions and requirements of life. All education, whether for the professions or for business, is for life, and education must change, in purpose, content, and method, with changes in the conditions under which men and women live and make their living.

Economic and social conditions have changed greatly during the last half century, and today are possibly more dynamic than ever before. It is manifest that university education for business cannot be static without losing the vital touch with social and economic life that is essential to the accomplishment of results. That part of the present volume that sets forth the reports of business men as to what in their college education has been found valuable and as to what studies and educational methods they, in the light of their practical experience, consider important, reaches the heart of the matter.

The only dependable test of an educational program is its influence upon the lives of those who have pursued the course of studies included in the curriculum. Such a test is not easy to make, but the authors of the present report have succeeded in their task of diagnosing the results of past education for business and the present demands or requirements of business as to the future. The information obtained by the authors and their discussion of it, cannot fail to be appreciated both by educational institutions and by those whom they serve.

EMORY R. JOHNSON

December 19, 1930

PREFACE

This volume embodies the findings of a study of university education for business, made for the faculty of the Wharton School of Finance and Commerce, at the direction of its dean, Professor Emory R. Johnson. It was begun on March 1, 1929, and extended to about September 1, 1930. During this time, covering a period of eighteen months, both of the undersigned devoted virtually their entire time to this task.

The scope of the survey is indicated by the table of contents. It was developed primarily along two lines: one concerning itself with the demands of modern business; the other, with the facilities developed by representative American universities to meet those demands. Both aspects were considered essential, each to an understanding of the other and of the situation as a whole.

Concerning the methodology of the present inquiry, every effort was made to develop an approach as completely objective as possible. To thus analyze the demands of modern business, the following steps were deemed essential: (1) an interpretation of the significance of recent changes in business, as indicated in the contemporary, descriptive literature; (2) an analysis, largely statistical, of the occupational opportunities in business for college men; (3) a study of the training and qualifications for positions in business; (4) a study of the reading interests of business men, as reflected in an analysis of business books and magazines; and (5) a study of the occupational experience and opinions of the graduates of a collegiate school of business. Since the Wharton School of Finance and Commerce of the University of Pennsylvania is the oldest of these schools of business, with more than five thousand living alumni, it was decided to select this group for such a study.

To consider objectively the work of the collegiate schools of business, it was agreed to include an analysis of each of the following topics: (1) collegiate education for business as an organized educational movement; (2) the various types of schools, considered from the standpoint of administrative arrangements; (3) the organization of the curricula of the business schools; (4) the various studies included, with reference to their constituent elements and their place in the curriculum; (5) the problems of faculty and student personnel; (6) teaching methods; and (7) the trends in the curricula.

In connection with this second part of the study, visits were made to most of the member schools of the American Association of Collegiate Schools of Business. The authors wish to take this opportunity of thanking the administrative officers and faculty members of these institutions for their unfailing courtesy, both on the occasion of these visits, and for their prompt response to all inquiries and requests for data concerning the work of the school. The present study owes much to their generous co-operation.

Early in the course of the study, a national advisory committee of leaders prominent in the business life of the nation was chosen. This committee consists of the following members: Henry S. Dennison, Dennison Manufacturing Company, Chairman; Richard L. Austin, Philadelphia Federal Reserve Bank; Chester I. Barnard, New Jersey Telephone & Telegraph Company; Henry Bruere, Bowery Savings Bank, New York; Albert R. Brunker, Wrap-Rite Company; Frederick G. Coburn, Sanderson & Porter; Frederic E. Curtiss, Boston Federal Reserve Bank; Arthur C. Dorrance, Campbell Soup Company; Albert R. Erskine, Studebaker Corporation; Samuel S. Fels, Fels & Company; Philip S. Gadsden, United Gas Improvement Company; William Green, American Federation of Labor; James G. Harbord, Radio Corporation of America; Walter K. Hardt, Integrity Trust Company of Philadelphia; E. N. Hurley, Electric Household Utilities Corporation; Martin J. Insull, Middle West Utilities Company; Henry P. Kendall, The Kendall Company; Morris E. Leeds, Leeds & Northrup; Sam A. Lewisohn, Miami Copper Company; James L. Madden, Metropolitan Life Insurance Company; Arthur Morgan, Morgan Engineering Company; W. Ripley Nelson, Guaranty Trust Company of New York; George W. Norris, Philadelphia Federal Reserve Bank; John W. O'Leary, National Bank of the Republic; Harlow S. Person, Taylor Society; George F. Rand, Marine Midland Trust Company; Andrew W. Robertson, Westinghouse Electric & Manufacturing Company; Lessing J. Rosenwald, Sears, Roebuck & Company; Matthew S. Sloan, New York Edison Company; Philip C. Staples, Bell Telephone Company of Pennsylvania; John A. Stevenson, Penn Mutual Life Insurance Company; William B. Storey, Atchison, Topeka & Santa Fe Railway Company; Percy S. Strauss, R. H. Macy & Company; Merle Thorpe,

Nation's Business; Herbert J. Tily, Strawbridge & Clothier; Ernest T. Trigg, John Lucas & Company, Inc.; John E. Zimmerman, United Gas Improvement Company. To the chairman and members of this committee, preliminary copies of the report were submitted for advice and comment. Acknowledgement is made herewith of the services rendered by the members of this committee and by many other business executives whose advice and criticism aided in the preparation of this report.

The costs of the study were underwritten by the Department of Industrial Research of the University of Pennsylvania and the authors are deeply indebted to Joseph H. Willits, the director of this department, for making the study possible.

The authors are under obligation to various other persons. To a number of publishers, thanks are due for permission to quote selected passages, separate acknowledgment being made in each case. Dr. W. Wallace Weaver, of the department of Sociology of the University of Pennsylvania, and Mr. Ernest A. Tupper, of the department of Industrial Research, aided in the compilation of certain of the data included. Mrs. Barbara Ross, Miss Eleanor V. Preble, and Miss Dorothea Whitaker facilitated the study by the excellence of the secretarial service which they rendered. To numerous other persons, not connected with the colleges of commerce included, and with whom the project was discussed, much credit is due for the information furnished as well as for their suggestive comments. Finally, the authors wish, in particular, to record their appreciation of the helpful attitude of the dean and faculty of the Wharton School of Finance and Commerce. While every possible aid was given by them in the course of this study, there was, on the other hand, no evidence of an attempt at any time to influence or to anticipate the results obtained. In short, the study was conducted under the most favorable circumstances, so that the authors must attribute to their own limitations the defects of the present report, even as they must assume the entire responsibility for its form and content.

JAMES H. S. BOSSARD
J. FREDERIC DEWHURST

December 26, 1930

CONTENTS

PART I

MODERN BUSINESS AND ITS SIGNIFICANCE FOR HIGHER EDUCATION

PART II

STUDY OF A GROUP OF BUSINESS SCHOOL GRADUATES

PART III

THE EVOLUTION OF HIGHER EDUCATION FOR BUSINESS

xi

Part IV

THE CURRICULA OF THE COLLEGIATE SCHOOLS OF BUSINESS

Part V

PROBLEMS OF PERSONNEL AND TEACHING METHODS

UNIVERSITY EDUCATION
FOR BUSINESS

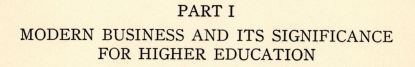

PART I
MODERN BUSINESS AND ITS SIGNIFICANCE
FOR HIGHER EDUCATION

CHAPTER I

THE CHANGING CHARACTER OF AMERICAN BUSINESS[1]

I make no apology for our devotion to business. It represents for the majority of our people the major activity of life. It is more than production. It is more than trade. It is more than transportation and finance. It is more than all of them together. It has made history. It has created law. An eminent jurist has said: "Long before the State arose from its couch, in the morning twilight of history, trade had already completed a good part of its day's work. While the States were fighting one another, trade found out and leveled the roads that lead from one people to another, and established between them a relation of exchange of goods and ideas; a pathfinder in the wilderness; a herald of peace; a torch-bearer of culture."
OWEN D. YOUNG

The half century that has passed since the founding of the first university school of commerce in the United States has witnessed an extraordinarily rapid growth in the production and consumption of economic goods and services and profound changes in the methods of conducting business enterprises. There is probably as little resemblance between the economic world of today and that of Joseph Wharton as there was between the "gilded age" in which he lived and the primitive days before the Industrial Revolution. In his day electric lights, automobiles, radios, airplanes, motion pictures, electric railways, telephones, and a hundred other technical "necessities" of our modern life were unknown and generally unthought of. Agriculture was still the dominant interest of the majority of our population. Manufacturing and the extractive industries, it is true, had been making rapid strides following the Civil War, but until the end of the century our productive energies were still devoted largely to the primary exploitation and development of vast areas of fertile land and varied and abundant resources. We were still settling the country.

---

[1] This study of university education for business represents the joint effort of the authors, and they jointly concur in all of the findings. The authors are individually responsible for the detailed analysis of material and its presentation in the several chapters of the report. Chapter I was prepared and written by J. Frederic Dewhurst.

[3]

GROWTH OF BUSINESS IN RECENT YEARS

The coming of the twentieth century, as pointed out by E. Dana Durand, marked a significant turning point in American industrial history; it ushered in the modern era in our economic development:

> The economic progress of America in the nineteenth century . . . . was very great. In large part it was what might be expected of a new country of very rich natural resources. The growth of agricultural production was fundamentally conditioned by westward expansion, and was in turn a primary cause of the development of the elaborative industries. The latter, too, owed much to new-found mineral resources. The contribution of purely human agencies to progress was notable, but what most distinguished the nineteenth century from the present century is the greater part then played by nature. . . . .
>
> Such economic progress as has been made during the present century the American people owe largely to their own industry, enterprise, ingenuity, and thrift. The start which unusually rich and expanding resources had already given them was, to be sure, an immense help. It is easier to rise from an already high plane than from a low one. But nature has not been showering the people with new gifts in any such fashion as during the earlier history of the century; they have been thrown more and more upon their own capacities.[2]

Despite the fact that the present century has brought no new discoveries of natural resources, no additional areas of virgin land to be developed, the past thirty years have seen a more rapid expansion of American business and a greater improvement in economic well-being then ever before occurred during a similar period in our history. With a population increase during the past three decades of only sixty per cent, the output of minerals has nearly quadrupled and that of manufactured goods has nearly trebled. Power used in manufacturing is nearly four times as great as at the beginning of the century. Railroads are carrying more than three times as much freight in spite of the growing importance of motor transportation. Coal production has more than doubled in the period; the output of petroleum is more than sixteen times as great; while twenty-five times as much of the latest and greatest form of energy, electricity, is being used now as in 1900. The production of steel, entering largely into the manu-

---

[2] E. Dana Durand, *American Industry and Commerce,* Ginn and Co., N.Y., 1930, p. 52.

facture of transportation equipment and machinery, has increased nearly four hundred per cent since the turn of the century. Reflecting the greater use of power driven machinery and the vast improvements in the management of industrial enterprises, the output of goods per worker has increased 80 per cent, while family income has more than doubled during the period. To mention only a few other statistical measures of our astounding economic progress during the present century: a seven-fold increase in bank clearings;[3] a ten-fold increase in life insurance; nearly ten times as many telephones in use; a three-fold gain in the volume of foreign trade with a much greater increase in the export of manufactured goods and the import of raw materials; 25,000,000 automobiles in use as compared with a few thousand in 1900; a multitude of new products—radios, airplanes, vacuum cleaners, electrical refrigerators, etc.,—which were hardly known to exist at the end of the 19th century,—are now in common use.

Pervasive Importance of Business Enterprise

In large measure our impressive material progress during the past three decades can be attributed to the application of the physical sciences to the problems of production and distribution. Intensive rather than extensive development has been the keynote of our recent progress. The scientist and research worker have displaced the explorer and the prospector; discovery has been transferred from the frontier to the laboratory. Instead of merely appropriating and adapting natural materials and forces, we are inventing and creating new substances and new forms of energy. Astonishing as our progress in harnessing the forces of nature has been in recent years, it appears to represent nothing absolutely new; "Acceleration rather than structural change is the key to an understanding of our recent economic developments."[4]

As stated by Wesley C. Mitchell, "What has been happening in

---

[3] Outside New York City. These measure commercial activity more accurately since they eliminate clearings resulting from stock exchange activities.

[4] *Recent Economic Changes in the United States*—Report of the Committee on Recent Economic Changes of the President's Conference on Unemployment, Herbert Hoover, Chairman; including the reports of a special staff of the National Bureau of Economic Research. New York, McGraw-Hill Book Company, Inc., 1929, p. 9.

the United States is the latest phase of cumulative processes which have dominated western life since the Industrial Revolution got under way. . . . . It remains clear that the Industrial Revolution is not a closed episode; we are living in the midst of it, and the economic problems of today are largely problems of its making."[5]

That this continued rapid advance in the technology of produc-tion and distribution, reaching a crescendo in the period described by Julius Klein as "the dramatic decade" following the World War, has borne rich fruits in human well-being is quite apparent without the evidence offered by statistics. Not as widely recog-nized, perhaps, is the fact that the continuing Industrial Revolution is creating a multitude of new social and economic problems which demand for their solution the application of the same scientific methods which resulted in their creation. If other evidence were lacking the speculative crash in the fall of 1929 and its aftermath of unemployment and depression is ample confirmation of the defects in the functioning of our economic system so clearly per-ceived by President Hoover, and expressed in the following words:

> We have probably the highest ingenuity and efficiency in the operation of our industries of any nation. Yet our in-dustrial machine is far from perfect. The wastes of unem-ployment during depression; from speculation and over-pro-duction in booms; from labor turnover; from labor conflicts; from intermittent failure of transportation of supplies of fuel and power; from excessive seasonal operation; from lack of standardization; from losses in our processes and materials— all combine to represent a huge deduction from the goods and services that we might all enjoy if we could do a better job of it.[6]

Inasmuch as our modern commercial organization has been so largely instrumental in the creation of these new problems it is peculiarly the responsibility of business enterprise to share in their solution, to help in doing "a better job of it." Business now oc-cupies a position of dominant and pervasive power, and hence of enormous responsibility in modern life, especially in the United States where the commercialization of human activities has pro-gressed further than at any other time in the history of the world.

A few generations ago business existed for the purpose of

---

[5] *Ibid.*, p. 842.
[6] Herbert Hoover, *Waste in Industry*, McGraw-Hill Book Company, Inc., 1921.

supplying the few and simple wants which we could not satisfy through our own efforts on the farm or in the household. Today business is probably the most potent influence in the creation as well as in the satisfaction of our wants. "But business in its large sense is not only a mechanism for the production of goods, but also a mechanism for the production of habits. Our economic life has always colored our institutions. Now it has even more power to do so."[7]

Instead of supplying us merely with food, clothing, shelter, and tools for our productive work, business now commands our leisure time and influences our aesthetic tastes and fundamental desires and ideas. "A fine sense of discrimination" for the average mortal has become the capacity for choosing among a varied assortment of standardized, packaged, and trade-marked commodities and services. Trade now truly encompasses all of life's activities and desires, and business enterprise, rather than the state, the church, or the school, has become the real arbiter of human destiny.

Small wonder, therefore, that the majority of young men graduating from American universities and colleges are now entering these once despised commercial pursuits which are now emerging upon a professional plane. Perhaps all may not agree with the glowing picture painted by one business executive of the opportunities offered by this new profession:

> Business is today the profession. It offers something of the glory that in the past was given to the crusader, the soldier, the courtier, the explorer, and sometimes to the martyr—the test of wits, of brain, of quick thinking, the spirit of adventure, and especially the glory of personal achievement. Making money is not the chief spur to such men as Dupont, Chrysler, Durant, Filene, Hoover, Heinz, Eastman, Curtis, Gary, Ford, Grace. Money to them is no more than the guerdon. They engage in business, and in the business they engage in, because there are no longer any long, slimy, green dragons holding captive maidens in durance vile; no holy sepulchres to be reft from the infidel, no Pacifics to be viewed for the first time. Business is today the Field of the Cloth of Gold.[8]

---

[7] Lonigan, E., "Wanted: A Criticism of Business," *The New Republic*, June 26, 1929.

[8] Ernest Elmo Calkins, *Business The Civilizer*, Little, Brown & Co., 1928, p. 232.

However, Charles and Mary Beard cannot be accused of a professional bias in stating that "The most admirable and efficient piece of work being done today is the work business is doing. No king or general or priest is accomplishing so much even in terms of his own metier, as the captains of industry—the Vails, Swopes, Youngs, Fords, Altmans, Wanamakers, Filenes, Hoovers, Schwabs, and Lamonts. Business is doing its job, and as much cannot be said of the traditional and historic leaders of mankind."

Business may not yet have become the "Field of the Cloth of Gold," but certainly it offers far greater allure and challenge to the young men of today than the older professions. And although business has reason for pride and gratification in the way it is doing its job, business leaders are the first to recognize that their job has not been completed, that perfection has not yet been attained. It is no small task, therefore, to which the universities, and particularly the collegiate schools of business, have addressed themselves; that of preparing young men to assume and discharge the heavy responsibilities of the business leadership of the future.

Such preparation implies much more than familiarity with the superficial technical routine of business activities, for as Ernest Elmo Calkins so emphatically points out, "Its routine, once the sole concern of business men, is now no more to it than the routine of a hospital to a surgeon, or the routine of a law court to a lawyer." This new profession, if it is to make business not only bigger but also better, demands a broader and sounder understanding of the fundamental forces and problems of our industrial civilization than that involved in purely technical education. Owen D. Young, himself a shining example of the newer and finer type of business leadership, describing the executives of business as "the trustees of our opportunities," says, "We need today more than ever before men to administer this trust, who are not only highly skilled in the technique of business—men who have not only a broad outlook in history, politics, and economics—but men who have also that moral and religious training which tends to develop character. . . . . In no other profession, not excepting the ministry and the law, is the need for wide information, broad sympathies, and directed imagination so great."[9]

---

[9] *Harvard Business Review,* July, 1927.

A foreign observer, André Siegfried, in his keen analysis of our contemporary economic system in *America Comes of Age* also clearly recognizes the growing need for men of broad training in executive positions in business, as indicated in the following passage:

> On the other hand, general culture based not only on experience but on education is becoming more indispensable at the top of the ladder. As a business grows, the problems that must be confronted become broader and require minds that are more alert, keen, and highly trained. The time is past when a youth is initiated into business by sweeping out the office. For the directors, the general secretaries, and the assistants that surround them, America sincerely believes in economic education. This does not mean simply a business college course in bookkeeping, commercial correspondence, economic geography, and so on, but an education that will turn out young men of broad culture. This may seem singular when applied to the American, whom we usually consider deliberately practical; yet the demand for such culture is today nowhere more insistent than in the executive circles of New York, Boston, or Chicago.[10]

Some Distinctive Aspects of Modern Business

An examination of some of the distinctive characteristics of American industry in its modern form may help to indicate something of the type and content of training which appears to be necessary for young men entering upon business pursuits. It is recognized of course that business does not represent a single occupation nor a small group of related occupations or professions like medicine or law. The routes to personal success in business are many and varied, and the collegiate school of business supplies only a small part of the demand for business leadership. Some attempt is made in the following chapter to indicate the principal types of business activity in which the graduates of university schools of commerce normally engage. It is not the purpose of this chapter to analyze the nature of business duties or functions, but merely to indicate some of the more significant aspects of business which appear to deserve consideration in the business curriculum and in the training and guidance of students.

---

[10] Siegfried, André, *America Comes of Age*, Harcourt, Brace and Co., New York, 1927.

Size and Complexity of Business Organization

Probably the most striking feature of modern business enterprise and one from which arises many of the virtues as well as many of the defects of our economic system is the increasing size and complexity of individual and corporate units. The increasing tendency toward large-scale production in manufacturing and the many advantages and economies of this system have been manifest ever since the Industrial Revolution resulted in the transfer of industry from the household to the factory. In the United States, where our vast and uniform market for standardized articles makes mass production extremely profitable, this tendency toward concentration of manufacturing in large units has been carried further than in any other country. The same advantages of economy and efficiency in purchasing, control, and selling have resulted in a similar growth in the size of operating units in merchandising, transportation, and finance.

The most impressive characteristic of this modern trend toward large-scale business, however, is not the growth in the size of individual operating units, which appears to have natural limits beyond which expansion becomes unprofitable, but concentration in the corporate and financial control of large groups of subsidiary operating companies. This consolidation or merger movement may take the form of "horizontal combination" of many companies producing the same or similar products or services, "vertical integration" of units representing sequential steps in production and distribution, or more frequently, certain features of both forms of combination mentioned above. Examples of these types of combination are to be found not alone in such gigantic concerns as the Ford Motor Company, General Motors, General Electric, and Radio Corporation in the field of manufacturing, and in the vast net-works of power and communication lines among the public utilities, but also in mercantile business in the form of chain store and mail order systems, and in finance in the form of chain and group banking and investment systems.

Despite the fact that it has been found advantageous frequently to maintain a considerable degree of autonomy in the operation of individual units in these combinations, the advantages and economies resulting from a coordination or concentration of such functions as purchasing, advertising, research, and finance, are so great that there appear to be no limits to the extent to which corporate combinations of this form may proceed. The comments of Col. M. C. Rorty, Vice-president of the International Telephone and Telegraph Company, are of particular interest in this connection:

> One of the most significant results arising from improvements in the science of management has been an increasing ability to secure from large units or "chains" the type of individual efficiency that a few years ago could be secured only in the small organization working under the direct supervision of a competent employer-owner. Under the older type of organization there was a gain in efficiency with size, up to the point where the reductions in costs, through ability to specialize and functionalize the work of a larger group of workers and the increases in process, purchasing and selling efficiency under larger scale operation, began to be more than offset by a reduced general efficiency due to the inability of the employer-owner to maintain close contacts with the members of the enlarged organization. Recent developments in management methods, and in accounting and statistical control, have apparently broken down these former economic limitations on the size of the individual organization or "chain," with the result that practically all types of business and industry are now open to efficient large-scale corporate control. If this tendency persists, it may represent a fundamental economic change having very far-reaching consequences. The field of operations for the independent owner-manager will be steadily restricted, and the young man of capacity and intelligence will have to look forward more than ever before to a career in which, except by some rare combination of good fortune and adaptability to circumstances, he will continue throughout to be a subordinate worker in a large corporate organization.[11]

Obviously one of the principal economies of large-scale organization results from the functional specialization of the work of individuals all along the line from common labor to the higher corporate management. This means that the college graduates who find employment in these large corporate organizations—and an increasing proportion are entering this field—are faced with the necessity of engaging for many years in functions of a highly specialized nature. Superficially this might be taken to indicate

---

[11] *Recent Economic Changes,* McGraw-Hill Book Company, Inc., 1929, p. 864.

that the university school of commerce should prepare its students for the specialized tasks such as accounting, advertising, traffic administration, production management, in which they will engage after graduation.

But as a matter of fact, such highly specialized training is the last thing these large corporations require in the men they employ. As indicated in the following chapter the larger organizations usually provide training periods during which newly employed college graduates are rotated among various departments before being definitely assigned to their permanent duties. Among the junior and senior executives as well, the management constantly endeavors to maintain the "central management viewpoint" through continued orientation by means of lectures and discussion groups devoted to general management problems. In the highly departmentalized modern business organization technical proficiency on the part of the junior executive staff is the easiest thing to achieve. The most difficult task in training is to keep the individual workers from becoming lost in the maze of routine. University training evidently can best aid in this task of orientation by subordinating specialized technical training to a broader education in economic and business fundamentals; a training which will enable the new employee to see his own particular job in relation to the whole of the business and to understand the place of his own organization in the entire economic system. Of still greater importance is the development of the personal traits and attitudes which will enable graduates to become effective workers in cooperation with others in these large organizations. This type of preparation will help to make possible an harmonious adjustment of the college graduate to the routine of his new job.

Development of Professional and Ethical Attitudes

It is no mere figure of speech to say that business is becoming a profession, perhaps more accurately, a group of professions. Although this growing acceptance of professional responsibility cannot be attributed to modern large-scale organization *per se*, it is partly an outcome of the diffusion of ownership which is frequently a characteristic of the large corporation. This separation of the owners from immediate operating control through widely distributed stockholdings has resulted in the development of a salaried managerial and technical group who have come to assume professional responsibilities.

Patently the leading business occupations conform to certain of the generally accepted criteria of a profession in that they require intellectual training rather than mechanical skill, and in that they employ the scientific method and attitude in approaching the solution of their problems. Nor can it be denied that modern business also recognizes the ethical obligations of professional status, although cynics may doubt whether the profit motive has actually become subordinate to higher ideals of service. Certainly it is clearly apparent that there has been a vast advance in both the practices and ideals of business from the "buccaneering eighties" when "business is business," "the public be damned," and "let the buyer beware" expressed the aspirations and actions of many of our business leaders. It can hardly be said that roguery has disappeared from all business transactions, but it cannot be denied that there is little dependence today on the part of "big business" upon the ruthless methods described by Charles and Mary Beard in *The Rise of American Civilization:*

> Whatever may be said on fine points of legality it is certain that the methods used by the giants of industrial enterprises were artistic in every detail. Undoubtedly in versatility and ingenuity these new lords far outshone the princes of the middle ages who monotonously resorted to the sword, marriage, or poison in the building up of family estates. Related to more complex situations, the modern modes were more varied. If the barons of capitalism did not themselves put on armor and vanquish the possessor of desirable goods in mortal combat at the risk of their lives, they did sometimes hire strong-arm men to help them seize the property of a coveted company; and occasionally they planned real battles among the workingmen in an effort to appropriate a railway or pipe line. Usually, however, they employed less stereotyped means to attain their ends; namely stock manipulations, injunctions, intimidation, rate cutting, rebates, secret agreements, and similar pacific measures.[12]

Today business, and especially big business, is being conducted to an increasing extent "in the open" with an eye to the maintenance of public good-will as a measure of enlightened self-

---

[12] Charles and Mary Beard, *The Rise of American Civilization*, Macmillan Co., 1930, Vol. II, p. 201.

interest. One need not be scornful of the motives involved in such a change of attitude. If the self-interest of business coincides with that of employees and customers so much the better for all concerned. Probably Ernest Elmo Calkins has accurately explained the reasons for this new and enlightened attitude of business in stating, "There is no moral principal involved. The change from 'the public be damned' to 'the public be served' was shrewd business strategy, more profitable than any rule or ruin policy of the past. With few exceptions no monopoly is possible today, even if the paternal influence of the Sherman Act were withdrawn. Monopolies develop their own competition. The only important factor is public good-will, and that is open to all. The way to win it is to deserve it."[13]

This new professional management recognizes its moral responsibility not only to the public it serves but also to the owners of the invested capital and to the workers whose efforts make the enterprise possible. Owen D. Young has expressed this dual responsibility of management in the following words:

> Rather we have come to consider them (managers) trustees of the whole undertaking, whose responsibility is to see to it on the one side that the invested capital is safe and that its return is adequate and continuous; and on the other side that competent and conscientious men are found to do the work and that their job is safe and their earnings are adequate and continuous. Managers may not be able to realize that ideal either for capital or labor. It is a great advance, however, for us to have formulated that objective and to be striving toward that goal.[14]

"To shut our eyes to the broader interests and responsibilities of business," continues Mr. Young, "may have been an attribute of the individualism of the old art. It must be the warning to the group action of the new profession." Surely the universities, and especially the professional schools preparing young men for future business leadership, would be derelict in the discharge of their responsibilities unless they placed primary emphasis upon these broader ethical responsibilities rather than upon the mere

---

[13] Ernest Elmo Calkins, *Business The Civilizer,* Little, Brown and Co., 1928, p. 280.
[14] *Harvard Business Review,* July, 1927.

technique of money-getting. This implies much more than formal courses in "business ethics" and "standards of business conduct." Such training requires, throughout every step of instruction, constant and conscious attention to the ethical and moral values involved in business practices and business judgments. Not only should the students be made cognizant of the formal codes of ethics which have been adopted for the self-discipline of this new profession but they should be led to acquire an instinctive or intuitive appreciation of what constitutes fair and honorable dealing between management and the groups to whom it owes responsibility—capital, labor, and the public.

Growing Importance of Human Relations

One consequence of the increasing scale and widening area of business operations has been the elimination of intimate personal contact between employer and workman and between producer and purchaser. Small plants supplying neighborhood markets have disappeared in most industries, and in their place have risen vast corporate organizations operating dozens or scores of large factories, producing standardized products distributed throughout the country or throughout the world. The owner's relations with the human beings who make his goods and with those who buy his products are carried on through a host of intermediaries or by means of printed orders or advertisements. With the high degree of specialization and functionalization in modern industrial organizations and the resultant mechanization of work, the problem of labor relations becomes even more acute and serious. The nature of this problem is graphically described by Edwin F. Gay in the following words:

> Huge enterprises with a national and international market, owned by corporations with widely scattered unknown stockholders, run by a hierarchy of mostly unknown machine-tenders who, too often, not only are, but feel themselves to be, nameless numbers on a pay-roll—this is what our home industries of a century and less ago have come to be. We have squeezed out personality, and yet nothing to the normal man so drips of personality as the daily work of his hand and brain. This work should be not merely the counter wherewithal to obtain his daily bread; in simpler ages it was, and fundamentally it remains, a part of himself in which mystic

forces inhere, around which songs and poetry and religious feeling gather. "In handiwork of their craft is their prayer."[15]

Not only have problems of labor relations become more important in modern industry, but the growth of national and world markets for goods that were once distributed locally demands greater attention to and a different technique in handling the problems of human relations in distribution. Mass production, especially mass production of new products unknown to consumers, depends for its success upon mass consumption. The sellers' market of a few decades ago has become the buyers' market of today, and increasing attention has to be directed to eliminating the wastes and increasing the effectiveness of distribution.

Thus the revolutionary advances in the application of physical science and engineering to physical substances and forces have created a multitude of human problems which it is the task of the social sciences to solve. In the words of Arnold Bennet Hall, "The power controlling sciences must supplement the power creating sciences if civilization is to endure. We must be as scientific in the solution as we have been in the creation of our problems." Obviously it is peculiarly the function of the collegiate school of business to train its students in these sciences and studies—psychology, economics, sociology, statistics—and in their application to the human problems of business—in advertising, personnel work, labor management, selling, etc. University schools of engineering and technology have contributed much to the technical progress of industry in recent years; the collegiate schools of business have a similar opportunity of helping in the human progress of industry and commerce in the years to come.

Influence of Research and Scientific Method

Of fundamental and pervasive significance throughout the whole structure and functioning of our modern economic system is the influence of organized scientific research in the human as well as the technical aspects of business. Not only are new discoveries

---

[15] Edwin F. Gay, *Social Progress and Business Education,* paper delivered at Northwestern University Conference on Business Education, Chicago, Illinois, June 16-17, 1927.

in the fields of pure science being adapted and applied at a more rapid rate than ever before, but business is now engaged in an organized effort to stimulate and accelerate discovery.

> Business has of course always benefited from discovery, but it has mostly taken discovery where it found it—as a gift. It is now more often the case that, by research, discovery is specifically provided for and so accelerated. Business research does more than invite discovery; it gives to operating management a chance to base its decisions upon fact; and research and the habits of mind it engenders are extending beyond the applied physical sciences into the fields where conditions are determined chiefly by human desires, impulses, and frailties; into industrial psychology, labor management, marketing, sales management, merchandising, advertising.[16]

The most obvious effects of organized research are to be found in the physical sciences with the extensive progress that has been made in the last few years in the utilization of new materials, processes, and types of equipment, the invention and perfection of new products, the better utilization of by-products, and the reduction of waste and increase of efficiency in production. Lower commodity prices, in the face of higher wages and larger profits and a multitude of new, better, and cheaper articles of common consumption, have been the fruits of technological research during the past few years. The results of research in the human aspects of business operations have not been so dramatically apparent nor so rapidly attained in view of the fact that the application of scientific method to these problems is still in an early stage of development. "The sciences which underlie these efforts," says Wesley C. Mitchell in *Recent Economic Changes,*—"psychology, sociology, economics—are far less advanced than physics and chemistry. The experts who are making the application—personnel managers, advertising specialists, sales directors, business economists, and statisticians—are less rigorously trained than engineers."

Moreover, it is clear that business is not yet as thoroughly "sold" on the value and necessity of this sort of research or on the applicability of scientific method to these less tangible human prob-

---

[16] Henry S. Dennison, *Recent Economic Changes,* McGraw-Hill Book Company, Inc., New York, 1929, p. 546.

lems, as it is convinced of the profitability of research in the technical aspects of industry. Yet every fresh advance in the field of technology brings with it problems of human adjustments. New products require new markets and frequently mean the destruction of demand for existing products. New processes and equipment raise new problems of labor relations. The industrial landscape is dotted with the ruins of once prosperous firms that failed to realize before it was too late that the competitive battle was being fought with new weapons.

Obviously collegiate instruction for business should give substantial recognition to the use of the scientific method in solving the problems of industry. Instruction in the basic sciences underlying human and economic relations—psychology, statistics, accounting, economics, sociology—is generally believed to be essential in business training just as instruction in physics, chemistry, and mathematics is essential to an engineering education. Further training in the use of these tool subjects in the investigation of business problems would also seem to be essential in any well organized university course. Whether this training should take the form of special courses designed to attain these ends or the application of the case and problem or project method to existing course material is a question on which there are wide differences of opinion. It is readily apparent, however, that business school students should be graduated not only with a knowledge and appreciation of the significance of the contributions of science and research to business, but also with considerable facility and practice in the application of the scientific method to the actual problems of business administration.

It is equally evident that such facility does not derive from mere familiarity with the outward routine of business transactions nor from a superficial knowledge of the "principles" which are supposed to underlie and explain the phenomena of business.

Growing Importance of Governmental Relations with Business

Any examination of the recent trends in American industrial development cannot fail to reveal the increasing part that government plays in the supervision and regulation of business. However much we may subscribe to the laissez-faire doctrine of "less government in business," it is perfectly apparent that as business grows larger and more complicated it has become more affected with public interest and therefore more subject to public control and regulation. Furthermore, it should be remembered that governmental contact with business does not always take the form of "interference" with its operations. To an increasing extent both the Federal and state governments are cooperating with business firms and trade associations in the solution of their problems. The activities of the Department of Commerce in standardization and simplification of products and processes and in domestic and foreign marketing constitute the outstanding example, of this type of government activity, although other departments of the Federal government and many of the state governments also perform similar services on a smaller scale.

Regulatory bodies such as the state public service commissions, the Interstate Commerce Commission, and the Radio Commission, of course, have long had an important influence upon the policies and practices of the utilities which operate under their supervision. In recent years the Federal Trade Commission has come to exercise a similar function in regulating the competitive practices of commercial firms engaged in interstate commerce, and there is every reason to believe that this sort of regulation will increase rather than decrease in the future. In many other ways as well, the Federal, state, and local governments are regulating and supervising the relations between business firms and their investors, competitors, customers, and employees. Through taxation measures, restrictive legislation, tariffs, embargoes, and subsidies, the activities of government are becoming an increasingly important factor in the operation of business enterprises. Not since the days of the Mercantile System has the state entered so largely and so influentially into the affairs of commerce and industry as at the present time.

Obviously an understanding and appreciation of the nature and functioning of our national and local governments, so vitally important for intelligent citizenship, is doubly necessary as preparation for business life. This need is generally recognized by inclusion in the curricula of courses in business law and political science, although frequently such courses are not well adapted to the particular problems of governmental relations with business. These subjects are essential of course but they treat of only a limited phase of the business man's contact with government. Whatever form such instruction may take, and whether it be given in one course or as part of a dozen courses, it is clear that university students of business should be graduated with a thorough knowledge of the functioning of government in modern economic life and of the restraints and regulations which surround and control the operations of competitive business.

Importance of Foreign and International Relations

During the past three decades the United States has passed from a position of "splendid isolation," both political and economic, to a position of world dominance and world leadership. The turn of the century saw the first substantial foreign loan floated in the American market; today we are the leading creditor nation of the world with approximately fifteen billion dollars invested abroad in commercial and industrial enterprises, exclusive of an equal or larger amount represented in government war debts. Then, the total volume of our foreign trade amounted to only $2,306,822,000; in 1929 the aggregate of our imports and exports totalled nearly ten billion dollars, a very substantial fraction of our entire volume of trade.

But our economic world primacy represents far more than the domination of the dollar. Not only are American investments, American goods, and American factories to be found in all countries of the world, but American business ingenuity and engineering skill are also being "exported" to the remote corners of the world. It is no mere accident that the plans for financial rehabilitation of Europe were drawn by two American business leaders, that the guidance of the new Bank for International Settlements has been entrusted to an American financier, that an American college professor has reorganized the financial systems of a dozen foreign nations, that American capital and engineering management are bringing electric light and power and modern communication systems to the people of a score of foreign countries.

Nor is this growing internationalization of our business entirely one-sided. Many domestic industries depend for their profitable operation not only upon foreign markets for their goods but upon foreign sources for raw materials. Despite the tariff obstacle foreign manufactures are appearing in domestic markets to an increasing extent, while the construction of American plants abroad is being duplicated by the erection of foreign-owned factories behind tariff walls within our borders.

If other evidence were lacking the rapid and violent repercussions of the recent business collapse—following the stock market break—to almost every country of the world would be a forceful demonstration of the intimate interdependence of modern business. "The merchant or manufacturer of today can no longer exist in comfortable isolation even if he wants to," says Julius Klein. "He must know what is going on not simply locally, but in remote parts of the world, if he is to carry on his operations profitably. He must prepare for repercussions upon his establishment from outposts of civilization whose very existence was entirely beyond the comprehension or interest of his immediate predecessors."

That American business executives are fully aware of the significance and importance of foreign developments in their operations is evident from the large amount of space in business periodicals devoted to a discussion of these matters during recent years. This subject is treated at greater length in Chapter IV. The following extract from an editorial, "Keep An Eye Abroad," appearing in a recent issue of *The Business Week* is illustrative of the importance currently attached to these problems:

> For there is one field of business interest in which the principle of unqualified individualism not only breaks down but is disastrous and dangerous. That is the field of international relations.
>
> Great things are happening abroad this year, things of the greatest significance for the future of American business. They may be difficult to understand, for they will probably not be easily interpreted; but it will be worth while for American business to watch them carefully, for they may be more important in many ways than what happens at home.
>
> After more than ten years the World War has reached the final stage of financial liquidation at the Hague Conference, which will set up a new institution of international financial cooperation. At the London Naval Conference the United States and Britain are trying desperately to make the world take a long step toward peace and to reduce the burdens of war preparations. The League of Nations has passed its tenth birthday, and the scope and strength of its influences are being

shown in conferences that have begun to grapple seriously with the problems of removing or lowering the barriers to world trade, and of securing international cooperation in reviving and strengthening the world's sick industries, coal and textiles. Britain is embarking upon a vast experiment in the social control of a basic industry, France is emerging as a great financial force, and Russia's activities and opportunities loom larger than ever before in world affairs.

The more American business understands of these changes the better prepared it will be to meet the problems they will bring. Prosperity begins at home, but it sometimes ends abroad.[17]

Clearly the successful administration of business operations, particularly of large enterprises operating in the world market, demands an understanding of the world-wide economic and political forces that affect the fortunes of American commerce. And it would seem essential that the university curriculum in business should adequately recognize this fact by placing substantial emphasis upon the study of the political and economic institutions of foreign countries. This need is being met in part by courses in economic history, foreign trade, world geography, and in some cases by a study of comparative government, but in general there is still but scant recognition in the business curriculum of the revolutionary change in the world position of the United States.

Summary and Conclusions

1. The past three decades, during which period collegiate preparation for business has come to be a most significant phase of university education, have been characterized not only by a more rapid increase in the volume of business than ever before occured in a similar period but by profound changes in the structure and functioning of business enterprises.

2. The remarkable progress of this century has been chiefly the result of intensification of human effort, rather than continued extensive development of resources, and can be attributed very largely to the successful application of the scientific method to physical and human aspects of production and distribution.

3. The extraordinary advances in technology resulting in vast

---

[17] *The Business Week,* McGraw-Hill Publishing Co., New York, January 18, 1930.

improvements in human well-being have created a multitude of economic and social problems which demand for their solution the application of the same scientific methods which resulted in their creation.

4. The position of dominant and pervasive power and influence which business has come to exercise in our civilization means that adequate professional preparation for business is an educational problem of paramount importance. Educational training for the heavy responsibilities of this new profession should involve primary emphasis upon a broad and sound understanding of the forces and problems confronting our industrial civilization rather than upon mere technical familiarity with the superficial routine of business operations.

5. Certain distinctive characteristics in the organization and functioning of modern business appear to merit special consideration in the planning and administration of collegiate instruction for business. Of particular significance is the increasing size and complexity of business organizations and the consequent functionalization and specialization in the duties and responsibilities of individuals. In view of the fact that there seems to be no limit to the extent to which this tendency toward concentration of corporate control will proceed, it is clear that a preponderant and increasing proportion of university business graduates will enter the employ of large enterprises. The experience of these large organizations with college graduates shows quite distinctly that a general business education, with special emphasis upon the development of personality traits and the power of analysis, is more to be desired than specialized training. Such general training is believed to form a better background for a continuing appreciation by the new employee of the central management problems of these large organizations.

6. Partly as a result of the rapid growth of large organizations and the separation of ownership from control, business is rapidly assuming a professional status. University schools of business should of course recognize their peculiar responsibilities in training students to appreciate and accept the broader moral and ethical obligations of this new profession. This implies not only formal instruction in business standards but the inculcation of an intuitive understanding of what constitutes fair and honorable dealing

between management and the groups to whom it owes responsibility.

7. A knowledge and understanding of human relations has become vitally important with the increasing scale and widening area of business operations and the disappearance of intimate personal relationships which existed in the small establishments of a few generations ago. The business school has a heavy responsibility in training its students in the principles of the sciences underlying human relationships and in their application to the solution of management problems.

8. Application of the methods of science to the solution of the human and technical problems of business is one of the most striking characteristics of our recent economic development. There can be no doubt that the collegiate business training program should ensure not only the students' acquaintance with the significance of the contributions made by physical and social science but also considerable facility in the application of the scientific method to the solution of actual business problems.

9. Examination of the nature of recent economic development in the United States shows clearly the increasing participation of government in the supervision and regulation of business. Obviously it is of primary importance that business students should be graduated with a thorough comprehension of the ways in which the Federal and local governments regulate and control the operations of competitive business.

10. Our "splendid isolation" has disappeared with the rise of the United States to a position of economic world leadership. More than ever before the prosperity of American business is intimately bound up with the prosperity of the entire world. The American business man is as vitally concerned with political, social, and economic developments in many foreign countries as with similar developments in the United States. It seems evident, therefore, that a thorough study of the peoples and institutions of the principal nations of the world and an understanding of international economic and political problems should be provided in the curriculum of university schools of business.

CHAPTER II

OCCUPATIONAL OPPORTUNITIES FOR COLLEGE GRADUATES IN BUSINESS[1]

Students of collegiate schools of business, like those of the other professional schools, regard education as a means to an end. Their motivation in coming to college is vocational. After graduation they expect to engage in business, and although less than half have a specific phase of business in mind for which to prepare themselves when they enter college, the vast majority do enter upon business careers after graduation. Whatever the particular field of business in which they will engage, they believe that chances for rapid advancement to positions of responsibility and importance, as well as financial progress, will have been materially enhanced by the kind of training received in college.

Universities offering courses in business quite frankly recognize the same objectives. Such curricula aim, of course, to prepare the students for "life" by providing the essentials of a cultural and liberal education, but also to earn a living by offering fundamental training in business subjects. Judged by their catalogue statements, collegiate schools of business hope to prepare their students "for managerial positions in business," "for leadership," "for positions of major responsibility," "for executive and other higher positions in business," and so forth. Obviously these are not immediate objectives. Four years in college cannot be expected to prepare young men in their early twenties to step from the classroom into positions of major responsibility. No amount of college education is a substitute for experience and collegiate training for business cannot eliminate, though it should shorten, the necessary period of training and apprenticeship.

The tremendous expansion of commerce and industry in the United States during the past half-century, and more particularly since the war, and the increasing complexity of business tasks make it apparent that there is a large and growing demand for men qualified by talent, training, and experience to fill these executive and other responsible positions in business. So large has this demand become that it not only absorbs each year practic-

[1] Prepared and written by J. Frederic Dewhurst.

[25]

ally all of the nearly seven thousand graduates of university schools of business, but also a large proportion of the graduates of schools of engineering, law, and liberal arts.   In sharp distinction to the situation a half-century ago, when "selfish, huckstering trade" was hardly a respectable calling for an educated person and colleges existed chiefly to train men for the ministry, law, teaching, and medicine, business now attracts more college men than does any other field work.   Probably well over half of all the graduates from American colleges and universities eventually enter this field. But despite this increasing tendency for college men to enter business (or perhaps, more accurately, for men to go to college before entering business), existing opportunities are so numerous that there appears to be little or no danger of an "overproduction" of young men qualified to enter these pursuits.

Is there a Deficiency or Surplus of College Graduates?

The demand for business leaders is not static and bears no fixed relation to the population, as appears to be the case in some of the older professions such as the ministry and medicine.   As long ago as 1909, Dr. Abraham Flexner estimated that the United States needed less than 2,000 new doctors each year.   At that time the medical schools were equipped to graduate nearly 5,000 a year, and in 1926 more than 4,000 medical degrees were granted.   In the legal profession, as well, there is some reason to believe that overcrowding has existed at times in the past, while during the years just prior to the World War there was also a quite noticeable "overproduction" of graduates prepared for certain branches of engineering.   Law and engineering, however, are not highly restricted professions like medicine and dentistry, and many lawyers and engineers leave their original occupations, chiefly to engage in business.

A recent writer in *School Life* cites the existence of a similar situation in certain foreign countries.   "In certain South American countries the predilection of young men for the practice of law or medicine has caused serious consequences.   In 1925 Bolivia summarily stopped the registration of students in law schools, and in the same year all the universities in Ecuador were closed by governmental decree in order to stop the excessive output of lawyers and physicians.   The inclination seems to have arisen in some quarters to predict a similar state of affairs for this country. It is not likely to occur, either in those professions or in any other."[2]

Whether or not a similar state of affairs could exist in this country is a question on which there is a wide range of opinion. The same writer states the opinion that 7,075,248 persons, or more than one out of six of the 41,614,248 individuals reported by the Census of 1920 as being engaged in gainful occupations, held positions "worthy of being filled by persons with college training," and to whom "college training would be clearly advantageous."

TABLE I. NUMBER OF "BUILDERS" REQUIRED IN PRINCIPAL OCCUPATIONS

Occupations	Number of men engaged	Number of builders required	Per cent of builders required
Domestic and personal service.......	1,218,000	120,000	10.0
Mining and quarrying............	1,087,000	120,000	11.0
Clerical occupations..............	1,700,000	250,000	14.5
Agriculture, forestry, and fishing.....	9,869,000	1,500,000	15.0
Mfg. and mechanical industries.....	10,888,000	1,890,000	17.0
Transportation...................	2,851,000	810,000	28.0
Public service....................	749,000	230,000	31.0
Trade...........................	3,575,000	1,390,000	39.0
Professions......................	1,127,000	1,000,000	89.0
Total........................	33,064,000	6,210,000	19.0

Ellsworth Huntington and Leon F. Whitney[3] similarly emphasize a shortage rather than a surplus of men qualified by inherited ability and by (university) education to fill positions of leadership in professional and economic life as "intelligent, reliable, industrious, self-controlled, tactful, and progressive builders." These authors believe, as their data presented in Table I indicate, that more than six million men are required to supply the need for leadership in commercial, professional, and public life. Thus, in their judgment one out of five of the gainfully employed men in the United States should be possessed of the intelligence, education, and personal qualities requisite to leadership. They further contend that only 4,000,000 of these employed men have the "very superior" intelligence necessary for leadership, while an additional 3,000,000 are eliminated because of the lack of

---

[2] "No Danger of Too Many Educated Men," *School Life,* Vol. XIV, No. 9, May 1929.

[3] E. Huntington and Leon F. Whitney, *The Builders of America,* William Morrow & Co., New York, 1927, Chapter II.

temperamental and physical qualities necessary to leadership but infrequently linked with the highest degree of intelligence. Despite the fact that more than one out of ten of the persons of college age in the United States are now attending institutions of higher education, presumably preparing themselves for positions of leadership in society—if one can grant the accuracy of the estimates made by these writers—it is easy to agree with them that, "Not for centuries, and perhaps never, will there be danger that intellectual ability will increase faster than is needed in order to keep pace with the growing demands of civilization. Such demands are the necessary consequence of growth. Today we are in grave danger because civilization is becoming top-heavy; it demands huge numbers of competent people, while the number of such people grows rapidly less. If the future is to be safe, the number who are competent in intellect and temperament must increase at least fast enough to keep pace with the growth of civilization."

In striking contrast to the views expressed by the writers just quoted is the situation depicted by Professor W. B. Pitkin of Columbia University in *The Twilight of the American Mind.*[4] This author, a specialist in vocational psychology, estimates that there are only a paltry 176,200 positions available in the United States which require the grade of intelligence possessed by the highest one percent of the population, *viz.* about equal to that required for graduation from the better class of colleges and universities with good or only fair grades. His estimate of the distribution of such positions among various types of work is as follows:

Banking	4,000
Engineering	15,000
Government service	10,000
Journalism	10,000
Law	5,000
Manufacturing	21,000
Medicine	20,000
Scientific research	40,000
Teaching	27,000
Trade	15,000
Transportation	2,000
Vocational guidance and personnel	6,000
Other	1,200
Total	176,200

He makes no contention of course that men of this high grade of intelligence will be unable to find employment for which they

---

[4] Pitkin, Walter B., *The Twilight of the American Mind,* Simon & Schuster, Inc., New York, 1928.

will be adequately compensated, but that the shortage of positions requiring high intelligence will compel them to accept work far beneath their abilities. In his opinion, furthermore, the whole tendency of our modern socio-economic system is toward an aggravation of this situation, with modern industry making more and more economies in the use of persons of the highest grade of intelligence and education, while our institutions of higher learning are offering greater and greater opportunities for their education and training.

Professor Pitkin does not confuse what he terms an over-production of brains with a surplus of persons qualified for leadership in business or in other social pursuits. Such men are scarce, and will always continue to be scarce, since the capacity for successful leadership depends upon personal and temperamental qualities and traits which are much rarer in their occurrence than is high intelligence, and which are even more infrequently linked with the very highest intelligence. Thus many men of the highest intelligence possess an unfortunate inability to cooperate effectively with others; they are failures at team work. The writer points out a still further reason for the failure of many persons of high intelligence in work of an executive and supervisory nature:

> But there is a still deeper reason for the incompetence of many Best Minds in executive and supervisory work. It lies in the nature of the relation between the leader and the led. As a rule, the successful leader of men, whether in business, in government, in an army, or in education, is a little superior to the majority of those whom he leads, but only a little superior in his intelligence. If he is merely their equal, some of them will occasionally outwit him in an argument, or discover him committing mistakes which they would not have committed, or manifesting a dangerous lack of self-confidence when issuing executive orders to them. Then you see a lack of morale develop among the rank and file as a result of a well founded lack of confidence in the leader's ability. On the other hand, if he is considerably above his subordinates, he is unable to think in their terms, to see their responsibilities and problems as they see them; and worst of all, he is likely to think so rapidly on ordinary matters that, in contrast to him, most of his underlings strike him as dull wits. He grows impatient over them and drops into scolding and noisy complaints. They, on the other hand, do not get his point of view. They cannot comprehend the wisdom of his orders. And so

a different sort of defection is likely to occur; the subordinates feel out of touch with the leader. They may suspect that he privately despises them, looks down on them, is a hoity-toity cuss, and not aglow with the spirit of the organization.[5]

Whether or not one can accept Professor Pitkin's low estimate of the number of positions available for persons of the highest intelligence, much other evidence as well as common observation supports his conclusion that success in business depends not only upon intelligence and education, but upon many other factors as well. Employers of college graduates, while not under-estimating the importance of intelligence and scholarly capacity in the men they employ, have long recognized the value of other indicia such as participation in certain types of campus activities, as measures of potential executive ability. Moreover the occupational records of Wharton School graduates, presented in Chapter VII indicate that superior scholarship alone is not highly correlated with financial success in business. These questions will later be discussed at greater length.

The Number of Opportunities in Business and Public Service

The wide variation in these estimates of the occupational opportunities open to university graduates suggests the possibility that the truth may lie somewhere between these extremes. But any attempt to measure in quantitative terms the occupational opportunities open to graduates of university schools of business administration is fraught with many difficulties. Business is not a highly restricted calling open only to college graduates, like medicine, dentistry, or law. It is not a closed profession, but a broad phase of social activity consisting of a multitude of separate but related occupations calling for a wide range and variety of human talents, training, and experience. Moreover, opportunities for college men even among the "executive and other higher positions" are not limited to the graduates of collegiate schools of business. Each year hundreds of law and engineering graduates are leaving their chosen professions for more attractive openings in business, while the liberal arts colleges are also sending increasing proportions of their graduates into commercial and industrial work.

---

[5] Ibid., p. 75.

A rough approximation of the number and character of positions in business which might be filled to advantage by properly qualified college graduates can be gained by examination of information presented in the Census of Occupations. Unfortunately later data than for 1920 are not yet available; in the interim there has undoubtedly been a substantial increase over the number of such positions shown in Table II, and also many new lines of work not indicated there have since developed. An attempt has been made in this table not only to list the titles of all executive and other higher business positions which might possibly appeal to graduates of university schools of business and for which their natural abilities and education might be expected to prepare them, but also to indicate the occupations and professions open to other classes of university and college graduates. Occupations such as floor-walkers, clerks, overseers, foremen, and inspectors, in which many of the younger graduates are employed during the first few years out of college, were not included in this table since they represent the beginning and intermediate jobs, rather than the "terminal" positions in which they might be permanently employed.

The grand total of 4,184,927 is imposing, but still falls considerably short of the estimates made by Huntington and Whitney. Moreover it represents not more than one out of ten of all persons gainfully employed in 1920. Even so, this estimate probably errs in the direction of an overstatement of the number of positions suitable to the capacity and education of college and university graduates, especially in the case of the 2,612,525 positions in business and public service.

Casual examination of the list of business occupations reveals many positions which may never prove highly attractive to college graduates and for which some other form of preparation than that offered by a university training may be preferable. The questions may well be raised, for instance, as to how many of the 768,300 retail dealers, auctioneers, garage keepers, undertakers, hotel keepers, laundry proprietors and managers, and race track keepers really need a higher education, or whether society would be substantially benefited if these positions were restricted to holders of college diplomas. Many of the builders and building contractors, manufacturers, proprietors and managers of trans-

TABLE II. NUMBER OF PERSONS OVER 19 YEARS OF AGE ENGAGED IN EXECUTIVE
AND OTHER HIGHER OCCUPATIONS

Phase of business and occupation	Number of persons engaged—1920
Distribution	1,085,454
Commercial travelers..	177,555
Employment office keepers......................................	3,007
Proprietors, officials, and managers of elevators...................	8,827
Proprietors, officials, and managers of warehouses.................	6,315
Other proprietors, officials, and managers..........................	16,482
Retail dealers and managers of retail stores*......................	624,733
Auctioneers..	5,013
Sales agents...	40,941
Undertakers..	24,256
Wholesale dealers, importers, and exporters........................	73,237
Theatrical owners, managers, and officials.........................	18,147
Keepers of pleasure resorts, race tracks, etc.......................	3,338
Hotel keepers and managers.....................................	55,515
Laundry managers and officials..................................	4,645
Laundry owners and proprietors..................................	9,009
Canvassers...	14,434
Industry	542,240
Managers and officials of log and lumber camps.....................	2,078
Owners and proprietors of log and lumber camps....................	6,281
Managers of mining establishments...............................	14,432
Officials of mining establishments................................	2,504
Operators of mining establishments...............................	17,266
Builders and building contractors.................................	89,975
Managers and superintendents of manufacturing establishments......	178,701
Manufacturers..	182,924
Officials of manufacturing establishments..........................	48,079
Finance	160,391
Bankers and bank officials.......................................	82,375
Commercial brokers and commission men...........................	27,418
Loan brokers and loan company officials...........................	4,385
Stockbrokers...	29,609
Brokers, not specified, and promoters.............................	16,604
Insurance	134,008
Insurance agents...	118,948
Officials of insurance companies.................................	15,060
Accounting	115,152
Accountants and auditors..	115,152
Public utilities	33,513
Managers, superintendents, and officials of:	
Electric light, gas, and power companies...........................	22,000†
Proprietors, officials, and managers of:	
Telephone and telegraph companies...............................	11,513
Transportation	113,265
Garage keepers and managers....................................	41,791
Proprietors and managers of transfer companies.....................	23,331
Officials and superintendents of steam railroads....................	32,230
Officials and superintendents of street railroads....................	3,440
Agents of express companies.....................................	5,170
Proprietors, officials, and managers of other transportation companies..	7,303
Real estate	148,581
Real estate agents and officials..................................	148,581
Public service	152,964
Marshals and constables	6,888
Sheriffs..	10,632
Officials and inspectors, city and county...........................	55,597

Officials and inspectors, state.................................... 9,126
Postmasters.. 31,448
Other United States officials.................................... 39,273

Other business occupations 126,957
  Agents... 126,957

Non-business occupations open to business graduates 66,598
  Editors and reporters... 33,191
  College presidents and professors................................ 33,407

Non-business occupations and professions 1,505,804
  Architects.. 18,185
  Artists, sculptors, and teachers of art.......................... 33,520
  Authors... 6,622
  Chemists, assayers, and metallurgists............................ 32,841
  Clergymen... 127,270
  Dentists.. 56,152
  Designers, draftsmen, and inventors.............................. 65,429
  Lawyers, judges, and justices.................................... 122,519
  Teachers, school.. 701,815
  Osteopaths.. 5,030
  Physicians and surgeons... 144,977
  Technical engineers... 136,121
  Veterinary surgeons... 13,494
  Librarians.. 14,716
  Actors.. 25,914
  Aeronauts... 1,199

Total occupations in business and public service......................2,612,525
Total occupations open to college graduates...........................4,184,927

* A number of retail dealers were eliminated from this list.
† Estimated.

fer companies, express agents, and real estate agents likewise are probably engaged in work for which a college education would be neither necessary nor advantageous. It is doubtful whether many university men would find lasting satisfaction in permanent employment as city, county, and state officials, as sheriffs, or as marshals and constables, although it is reliably reported that higher education has been carried so far in one of the war-born European countries that most of the policemen are university graduates. Many other occupations included in this list, as well, offer only limited opportunities and possess but small attraction for college graduates and will probably continue in the future, as at present, to be filled satisfactorily by non-college men. The total of 2,612,525 must therefore be regarded as an "outside" maximum rather than as even a rough approximation of the occupational opportunities logically available for college men in industry and commerce and in public service.

However, granting that the majority of these positions—perhaps even three-fourths of them—are not suitable to university graduates, it is still apparent that there is a large "market" for properly qualified college labor in business and public service. Despite the several thousand graduates of collegiate schools of commerce and the many additional thousands graduating in engineering, arts and sciences, and other departments who enter business each year, there seems to be little immediate danger of an oversupply of labor in these occupations. It may be of interest in this connection to examine the data presented in Table III comparing the numbers of baccalaureate and professional degrees granted in various fields in 1928, with the number of persons indicated by the Census of 1920 as being engaged in these fields.

TABLE III. NUMBER OF DEGREES COMPARED WITH NUMBER OF PERSONS OVER 19 YEARS OF AGE ENGAGED IN HIGHER OCCUPATIONS AND PROFESSIONS

Occupation or profession	Number of persons engaged—1920	Number of degrees conferred—1928	Ratio of degrees to persons engaged
Architecture......................	18,185	522	2.8%
Business and public service.........	2,612,525	6,699	0.3
Dentistry........................	56,152	2,725	4.9
Education.......................	735,222	7,187	1.0
Engineering and technology.........	234,491	7,947	3.4
Journalism......................	33,191	435	1.3
Law............................	122,519	8,652	7.1
Medicine........................	144,977	4,342	3.0
Osteopathy......................	5,030	359	7.1
Theology........................	127,270	1,233	1.0
Veterinary medicine..............	13,494	138	1.0
Total—11 occupations..........	4,103,056	40,239	0.9%
All occupations*.................	4,184,927	102,982†	2.5%

* Includes all occupations listed in Table II as being available to college graduate.
† Includes in addition to degrees listed above, degrees in pharmacy and all other baccalaureate degrees granted to both men and women.

The contrast between the situation existing in business and public service and that in other occupations appears to be most striking. In each of the other occupations and professions the number of individuals whose college training specifically prepared them to enter the field each year amounts to at least one per cent of the number of persons engaged, while in law and osteopathy the ratio of degrees to practitioners rises to more than seven per cent. The number of degrees conferred is probably a fairly accurate measure of the number of persons entering such restricted professions as medicine, dentistry, theology, and law. Such is not the case, however, in education, business and public service, engineering and technology, and journalism, as these professions are freely accessible to all qualified persons irrespective of their educational preparation.

It would be absurd, therefore, to assume that the annual "replacement demand" for executive and other higher positions in business and public service is being supplied entirely or even largely by graduates of collegiate schools of business (nearly 7,000), a group which constitutes only a fraction of one per cent of the total number of persons holding these positions. Many of the engineering and technology graduates—perhaps the majority of the 7,947 students receiving such degrees in 1928—eventually will become engaged in business, chiefly in manufacturing, public utilities, and transportation.

Studies made by the National Industrial Conference Board[6] indicate that a large proportion of college men employed as executives in certain manufacturing industries were technical graduates. Thus, 113 rubber manufacturing establishments with total employees numbering 124,738 employed 1,637 men with college training, of whom 761 were technical graduates; 142 chemical manufacturing establishments with 34,895 employees employed 1,635 college graduates, of whom 1,305 were engineering and technological graduates; 149 electrical manufacturing establishments had 8,492 college men among their 153,505 employees, and 7,515 of them had technical training. These figures may not be generally representative of manufacturing industries but they indicate that technical graduates probably constitute a very large proportion of college men in manufacturing.

A considerable proportion of law graduates also enter business occupations, either immediately upon graduation or after some years of practice. In 1928, 27,263 baccalaureate degrees in arts and sciences were conferred upon men by American colleges and universities—nearly as many women also received such degrees—and a large, though indeterminable, proportion of these graduates also entered commercial and industrial pursuits. Various studies of the occupational distribution of these graduates indicate that in most cases at least a third, and in many instances a considerably larger proportion, enter business rather than teaching or other professions.[7]

---

[6] *Technical Education and the Rubber Industry,* N.I.C.B., N.Y., 1924. *Technical Education and the Chemical Industry, Technical Education in the Electrical Manufacturing Industry,* N.I.C.B., N.Y., 1925.

[7] Of 776 men graduating from the Oberlin College of Arts and Sciences during the decade from 1917 to 1926, 233, or 30 per cent, were engaged in business. The author further states "an unusually large proportion of them (Oberlin graduates) enter the professions and especially higher educa-

Based on an arbitrary assumption that approximately 40 per cent of the male recipients of arts and science degrees in 1928 entered commercial pursuits, the accessions to the ranks of business represented by the 6,699 business school graduates would be augmented by 10,905 men. It is not unreasonable to suppose that half of the engineering and technology graduates also entered business, which would account for an additional 3,974, and that one out of five, or 1,730, of the law graduates would eventually enter upon business careers. Thus it seems possible that business careers attracted between 23,000 and 24,000 graduates from the total number granted baccalaureate and professional degrees by American universities and colleges in 1928. Even this total which in view of possible duplication does not include any graduate degree such as that of master of business administration, amounts to less than one per cent of the estimated maximum number of positions in business and public service available for college graduates.

But inasmuch as many of the positions listed under the various designated titles in business and public service really are not appropriate to men of college training, it may be wise in the interest of conservatism to reduce this large total of 2,612,525 by three-fourths and assume there are only 650,000 outstanding attractive opportunities for college men in the fields of business and public service. This total, which amounts to only 2.5 percent of all persons engaged in these fields, is several times as large as Prof. Pitkin's estimate of less than 100,000 positions available for the "Best Minds" in business and government service, but it is less than 14 per cent of the nearly 5,000,000 "builders" estimated by Huntington and Whitney as being required in trade and industry.

It would seem probable, therefore, that this estimate of 650,000 may be an understatement rather than an overstatement of the facts. Based upon these arbitrary but conservative hypotheses, annual accessions of college graduates to business and public service amount to some three or four per cent of the minimum number of positions available to them. This hardly indicates any immediate danger of an oversupply of university graduates in these important fields of work, assuming that the graduates entering

---

tional work, when comparison is made with the graduates of eastern colleges." *Proceedings of the Fifth Annual Meeting of the National Association of Appointment Secretaries,* Boston, Massachusetts, Feb. 1928.

business each year are properly qualified and adapted to the work they undertake. However, should accessions of college graduates continue at the same rate in the future, which would result in "filling" these positions within a period of thirty to fifty years (allowing for "replacement" needs), there is a serious possibility of a future surplus of college graduates in these fields of work.

OCCUPATIONAL OPPORTUNITIES IN SPECIFIC FIELDS

Questions regarding the relative availability of the opportunities offered to college men, and particularly to business school

TABLE IV. EXECUTIVE AND OTHER HIGHER POSITIONS IN BUSINESS AND PUBLIC SERVICE

Phase of business	Number engaged	Per cent of total
Distribution	1,085,454	41.5
Industry	542,240	20.8
Finance	160,391	6.1
Insurance	134,008	5.1
Accounting	115,152	4.4
Public utilities	33,513	1.3
Transportation	113,265	4.3
Real estate	148,581	5.7
Public service	152,964	5.9
Other	126,957	4.9
Total—9 fields	2,612,525	100.0

graduates in various specific fields such as transportation, accounting, merchandising and selling, insurance, real estate, etc., are much more difficult to answer. They depend upon the extent to which these several fields are increasing or decreasing in importance, their attractiveness to university graduates, the nature of the work and the financial returns in each, and the extent to which the various positions are already being supplied from the ranks of available college graduates.

In the absence of extensive quantitative information answers to these questions must be based largely upon surmise and upon such fragmentary data as are available. As indicated in Table IV, more than 41 per cent of the maximum number of available positions are in the field of trade and selling, with industry second in importance and comprising nearly 21 per cent of the total. The six other fields are of subordinate importance, aggregating less than 40 per cent of the total.

Distribution

The general function of mercantile distribution, especially retail merchandising, advertising and salesmanship, is undoubtedly proving to be an unusually attractive field to graduates of university schools of business and to other non-technical graduates. This phase of business has been expanding at an extraordinarily rapid rate during the past two decades, and there have been during this period revolutionary changes in distributive methods accompanying the rapid displacement of old empirical techniques by more scientific practices. The importance and extent of this field, its rapid expansion and changing technique, leave little doubt that the existing demand and need for college men in distribution are considerably in excess of the present supply, even though it must be admitted that a large proportion of the 1,085,454 positions listed under distribution in Table II are not of such a nature as to be attractive to college graduates.

Reflecting opportunities in merchandising and selling, a larger proportion of business and non-technical graduates have entered this field than any other specific phase of business. Slightly over 30 per cent of the graduates of the Wharton School of Finance and Commerce entering business are now engaged in the field of distribution, as represented by advertising, marketing, and foreign trade.[8] Although strictly comparable data for other similar institutions are not extensive, the same tendency seems to prevail elsewhere. Approximately 30 per cent of the students graduating from the University of Kansas School of Commerce between 1925 and 1928 were engaged in mercantile business or in sales work. More than a fourth of the 252 men graduating in the June 1929 class from the Harvard Graduate School of Business Administration were engaged in sales and advertising occupations or in retail stores. Of 142 men graduating from Oberlin College (liberal arts) between 1914 and 1922 who were engaged in business, 47 reported merchandising and selling occupations. A survey of occupations of 2,528 graduates of ten university schools of business made by a committee of the National Electric Light Association showed only 2.8 per cent engaged in retail business, and 0.8 per cent in foreign trade with no other selling occupations designated. However, inasmuch as 67.9 per cent of the total were classified as in "general business" or "miscellaneous and unknown" it is highly probable that a much larger proportion were engaged in distribution.[9]

---

[8] See Table XXXII.
[9] See *Public Utilities, A Survey,* National Electric Light Association, New York, p. 84.

It should be emphasized furthermore that this distribution classification includes only those graduates engaged in the marketing of commodities. Those employed in selling securities, insurance, and real estate—a very considerable number—are classified under these respective categories.

The financial attractiveness of this field has been an important factor in drawing such large numbers into it in recent years. According to information collected from Wharton School graduates, earnings of salesmen, in which work many graduates are employed immediately after graduation, are higher than those of most other non-executive jobs, while sales and advertising managers are generally more highly compensated than managers and superintendents of other departments. In the field of retailing, also, men holding such positions as merchandise manager and buyer reported relatively large incomes.

The curricula of collegiate schools of business generally exhibit ample evidence of the vast and growing importance of this field among the occupations of their graduates. With the exception of accounting, a greater range and variety of courses are offered in merchandising, retailing, advertising, salesmanship, store management, and other aspects of marketing than in any other field of business study. It is apparent that the collegiate school of business stands in a uniquely advantageous position to aid in meeting the pressing social need for the development of more economical and more scientific methods of distribution.

Industry

The number of executive and other higher positions available in the field of industry is second only to that of distribution and is much larger than in other phases of business. For many years college men have been drawn in large numbers into executive and other operating positions in manufacturing, especially in the newer technical branches such as the chemical, electrical manufacturing, and automotive industries. Advancement to executive ranks in manufacturing and other productive enterprises, however, has been largely through the operating and technical departments; in consequence, these higher positions have in the past been filled chiefly by engineering and technical graduates.[10] But the demand for

---

[10] Studies of the National Industrial Conference Board previously referred to showed that 404 establishments in the rubber, chemical, and

men with higher educational training has been so great in recent years that large numbers of business graduates have been employed, especially in the accounting, financial, selling, and personnel departments, and also to a considerable extent in the operating divisions. About 17 per cent of the Wharton School graduates—a larger proportion than in any other field but marketing and finance—reported that they were engaged in operating and production work in manufacturing firms.[11] This proportion is apparently somewhat larger than that for most other business schools although it appears to be generally true that manufacturing attracts a larger number of such graduates than any other fields but marketing and finance.

In manufacturing, business school graduates and technical graduates find themselves in competition for higher executive positions. And members of both groups holding executive positions in this field recognize that their collegiate training was deficient in certain respects in preparing them for their present responsibilities. Commerce graduates complain that they are ill-equipped for an understanding of the technical aspects of manufacturing because of their inadequate knowledge of scientific and technological fundamentals, while the engineers feel that insufficient emphasis was placed upon such courses as economics, accounting, finance, management, and industrial relations in their curricula. The following excerpt from the report of a recent investigation made by the Society for the Promotion of Engineering Education is ample testimony to this fact:

> The engineers were first asked to state whether, in the light of their experience, recent engineering graduates are as well qualified to deal with the economic aspects of engineering problems as they are to deal with their technical aspects. The same question was then asked as to the more experienced graduates. In reply, *over ninety per cent stated that they find recent graduates not as well qualified to deal with the economic as with the technical phases of their work.*

---

electrical manufacturing industries employed a total of 35,447 men classified as "executives," of whom 11,764 were college and university graduates. More than 80 per cent, or 9,581, of these positions were held by technical graduates, the remainder by graduates of business and other non-technical schools.

[11] Exclusive of graduates employed by manufacturing firms in accounting, finance, selling, and advertising.

> Nearly seventy per cent expressed the same view as to graduates of five or more years' experience. . . . .
>
> In response to an inquiry, a majority of recent graduates named economics or related business subjects as the most serious omission from their college curricula. A large proportion also stated that they had pursued the study of these subjects after graduation.[12]

The technical schools are meeting this need to an increasing extent by the introduction of courses in economics and business subjects into the conventional engineering curriculum and by offering regular four year curricula described as "industrial engineering," "commercial engineering," or "industrial administration." In some cases the commerce and engineering schools cooperate in offering a "half-in-half" course comprising fundamental subjects in both fields. More rarely the business school has taken the initiative by allowing students who are preparing for manufacturing to elect specially designed courses in engineering.

Although some of these efforts are meeting with a measure of success, it is still out of all proportion to the need for this type of preparation. Collegiate instruction in engineering, and in business, have developed along traditional and widely separated lines despite the fact that a considerable fraction of the students in both types of institutions are destined for similar occupational goals. This important and well-defined field of industrial operating management is still a "no man's land" for which neither the conventional curriclum in commerce nor that in engineering offers adequate preparation. The task of meeting this demand which, incidentally, is not confined to manufacturing but also exists in certain phases of transportation and public utility operation, is one which faces both the school of commerce and the school of engineering, since certain parts of both curricula are essential in the preparation of men for operating work in these industries.

Finance

Finance and banking has long been a much more important occupational field for college graduates than would be indicated by the number of executive and other higher positions shown in Table IV, for in addition to this total of 160,391, there are a large

---

[12] Italics are my own.

number of such positions available in the financial and credit departments of mercantile and manufacturing firms. Finance has attracted the general college and commerce school graduate rather than the technical graduate to an even greater extent than distribution. Security brokerage and investment banking have always been especially popular, and during the last decade, very lucrative fields of work for college graduates. Earnings of the Wharton School graduates engaged in investment banking were considerably above the average of most other occupations; for men graduating prior to 1923 the median income for this phase of finance was nearly twice as large as the general median for the entire group.

More than a fourth of the Wharton School graduates are now engaged in commercial and investment finance, with a somewhat larger proportion in the former field. Such data as are available indicate that as large or a larger proportion of graduates from other similar institutions are devoting themselves to this kind of work,[13] which appears to be second only in importance to distribution, so far as non-technical graduates are concerned.

Collegiate schools of business have recognized the growing importance of the field of finance by offering varied courses in banking and investments and providing ample opportunities for their students to specialize in these fields. Despite the fact that such large numbers of graduates have been attracted to financial work in recent years, the rapid expansion of this field, and especially of investment banking, indicates that there is little immediate danger of overcrowding these occupations with suitably qualified university graduates.

Insurance

The insurance business, particularly life insurance, has also grown by leaps and bounds since the World War. The total of 134,008 insurance agents and officials shown in Table IV is probably a considerable understatement of the present opportunities in this field. Moreover, there has been a marked tendency toward an elevation of standards in this business and an increasing pro-

---

[13] More than a fourth of the recent graduates of 10 leading schools of commerce who reported a specific phase of business, were engaged in banking. *Public Utilities, A Survey,* National Electric Light Association, New York City, 1929, p. 84.

fessionalization of the business of life insurance underwriting with the result that a larger and larger proportion of the underwriting is being done by university trained men. More than ten per cent of Wharton School graduates are now engaged in this work, and, although the proportion is probably somewhat smaller than this for all business school graduates, there is evidently a substantially increased interest in this field on the part of men graduating from collegiate schools of business and from other non-technical institutions.

Accounting

Accounting was the first, and is now one of the most specific and well defined fields of business for which collegiate schools of business attempt to prepare their students. In some respects it may be described as the original *raison d'etre* for university instruction in business. It was in response to the specific and articulate demand from business for better trained accountants and the gradual elaboration and exfoliation of the field of economic theory that the rather strange marriage of these two fields occurred in the collegiate school of business. At the present time most of the business schools provide an elaborate curriculum in accounting subjects and it is still one of the most important fields of specialization.

A large proportion of commerce students enter accounting upon graduation, in some cases a larger number than enter any other single phase of business. In the study of 2,500 graduates of ten university schools of business previously mentioned, a larger proportion reported accounting as their occupation than any other specific field except banking and public utilities. Of the Wharton School graduates who engaged in business, 8.5 per cent were employed in accounting, a somewhat smaller proportion than were engaged in distribution, finance, manufacturing, or insurance. Among the graduates of most other similar institutions, however, accounting is relatively a more important occupation.

The importance attached to this field in the curricula of commerce schools reflects, of course, not only the vocational importance of the field, but also the fact that a knowledge of accounting is universally regarded as essential in all phases of business. However, in view of the fact that for many years past such large numbers of college men have been entering the rather limited field of accountancy *per se,* there is some question as to whether there has not been some overcrowding in this occupation. It may be somewhat relevent to this question that, among Wharton School graduates, incomes reported by those engaged in accounting were substantially lower than in any other phase of business.

Public Utilities

Of the three remaining business fields—real estate, transportation, and public utilities—the last named attracts an important proportion of the graduates of collegiate schools of business. With the rapid expansion of the telephone and telegraph, and electric light and power businesses during the recent years, these industries have employed an increasing proportion both of technical and non-technical university graduates. In fact it is probable that the American Telephone and Telegraph Company, with its associated system, is today the largest single employer of college labor in the United States. The Bell System has in the past employed from 900 to 1,200 of the men graduating from American colleges and universities each year, of whom a considerable proportion are commerce graduates. The electric and gas utilities also have evinced considerable interest in the problem of higher education as it effects the supply of men available for positions in this industry, as evidenced by the survey of the relation between higher education and the utility industry published last year by the National Electric Light Association.[14] The importance of this industry in the employment of college labor is evidenced by data presented in that publication showing that six per cent of the students graduating in the 1925, 1926, and 1927 classes from ten collegiate schools of business were employed by public utilities—a larger proportion than entered any other specific field except banking. In the same years 17.5 per cent of the men graduating from 21 engineering colleges entered this industry—nearly four times as many as were employed by railroads and a much larger proportion than engaged in manufacturing. These industries, which are expanding so rapidly and are becoming so important as employers of college

[14] *Public Utilities, A Survey of the Extent of Instruction in the Field of Public Utilities in Colleges and Universities, etc.* National Electric Light Association, New York, 1929.

labor, generally speaking receive but scant attention in the curricula, either in business or engineering schools.

Transportation

In marked contrast, the field of transportation has long been an important branch of study both in the technical and commercial curricula. But despite the relatively greater emphasis placed upon these studies and notwithstanding the fact that a number of institutions provide facilities for extensive undergraduate and graduate specialization, comparatively few of the students in either the commercial or engineering schools enter the field upon graduation. The apparent unattractiveness of this type of work, and especially of railroad transportation, to college graduate has become so noticeable in recent years that the attention of many leaders in the industry has been directed to the existence of a serious executive personnel situation. In a recent survey made for the Committee on Transportation of Yale University,[15] General W. W. Atterbury, president of the Pennsylvania Railroad company, is quoted as follows:

> There seems to be a general impression that fewer promising young men than formerly are being taken into the railroad service, and that of those who come a greater number than formerly leave the service after a short period, because of the superior advantages offering in other fields.
>
> If this is true, we will shortly be confronted with a very serious problem, and we should therefore make every effort to ascertain the facts and also the causes and possible remedies.

Concerning this same problem the survey states:

> The fact, then, seems to be that railroading has lost much of its glamour, of the opportunities for outstanding creative effort, for courage and initiative, which were such a marked feature of the nineteenth century of railroad building and welding. At the same time, however, the needs for men capable of attacking the more intricate problems of the present day have become more urgent, but this type of young man does not seem to be forthcoming.[16]

Some question may be raised as to whether the current lack of interest in this industry on the part of university graduates is due

---

[15] Topping, V. and Dempsey, S. J., *Transportation, A Survey of Current Methods of Study and Instruction and of Research and Experimentation,* Privately printed, New Haven, Connecticut, 1926, p. 17.

[16] Ibid., p. 17.

to the absence of glamour or to more mundane considerations. At any rate, there is a rather widespread impression among college students that salaries and opportunities for advancement are somewhat more appealing in other fields of work.

There is general agreement, however, that the need for college trained men in railroading is great. Coupled with this demand are the opportunities afforded by the rapid expansion of other branches of transportation such as motor and air transport. But it must be remembered that the position of the collegiate school of business with respect to these and other phases of transportation, as well as the public utility industries, is somewhat analogous to that with respect to manufacturing. These industries draw their college personnel from both engineering and commerce schools, and in neither type of institution is there generally any extensive effort to train the students specializing in these fields in both the technological and the commercial aspects of the business. Promotion to executive ranks usually proceeds along quite different routes for the two kinds of graduates, and, as in the case of many branches of manufacturing, there is reason to believe that the technically trained man has some advantage over those with general college or business school education.

There has been some attempt on the part of engineering schools to broaden the curriculum by the inclusion of certain business subjects. But there is possibly less need for a composite engineering-commerce course here than in manufacturing owing to the high degree of functionalization, even of executive responsibilities, resulting from the large size of the corporate units in transportation and public utilities.

Real Estate

The real estate business apparently has attracted a small but increasing number of business school graduates in recent years. Although, according to the survey previously referred to,[17] less than one per cent of the 1925, 1926, and 1927 graduates of ten business schools reported that they were engaged in this field, 4.5 per cent of the Wharton School graduates replying to the in-

---

[17] *Public Utilities, A Survey*, National Electric Light Association, New York, 1929, p. 84.

quiry described in Part II were devoting themselves to this phase of business.

That the real estate business has proved profitable for this group of alumni, particularly among recent graduates, is evident from the fact that the median income for those graduating in the last six classes was substantially above that of any other phase of business. Although extensive similar data are not available for other institutions, it seems clear that real estate has become a field which offers occupational opportunities to business school graduates comparable with if not superior to those offered by many other phases of business. The Census shows that nearly 150,000 persons were occupied as real estate agents and officials in 1920. How much this number has increased during the active real estate market of the past decade and what proportion of these positions are really suitable to men with university training it is impossible to ascertain. On the basis of these rather inadequate figures, however, it would seem that on a quantitative basis this field is roughly comparable with accounting and insurance.

Public Service and Other Fields

The occupational opportunities in public service for which graduates of collegiate schools of business are particularly adapted are difficult to appraise. Certainly such institutions generally do not attempt to offer very extensive preparation for specific occupations in this field except by way of preparing students for the study of law, which eventually may lead to political positions in government service. Only an inconsiderable number of students enroll in business schools for the purpose of preparing themselves for government positions—although a few universities do offer opportunities for students to prepare for the diplomatic and consular service—and a similarly small number actually accept such positions upon graduation. Most of this group find employment in the "business" departments of the Federal government or of state and municipal government, or in the foreign service. Even with the great expansion of governmental functions since the World War, however, the number of such non-political positions, for which collegiate training in business offers preparation, is quite limited.

Although the vast majority of business school graduates actually become engaged in the general field of business—for which they prepared themselves—a small proportion enter the teaching profession, either permanently or as a means of further preparation for business. The tremendous growth of commercial education in recent years has of course opened up many teaching opportunities in high schools and universities which have been filled to a great extent by graduates of collegiate schools of business. Indeed many such institutions include among their vocational purposes training for the teaching of commercial subjects. There are some indications that the period of most rapid expansion in this field has now passed so that future opportunities will be limited more largely to replacement demands. These, however, are not inconsiderable in view of the rapid turnover of personnel in this branch of education.

Among the other non-business occupations for which collegiate schools of business attempt to prepare their students, journalism is the most important. Very few graduates of business schools are now entering this field, however, which appears to offer rather restricted opportunities in view of the small number of such positions available and because schools of journalism and other undergraduate courses are also helping largely to supply the demand for college men in this work.

The Question of Specialized Training

In this attempt to appraise quantitatively the occupational opportunities open to graduates of collegiate schools of business, there has been no presumption that such institutions either should or should not attempt to prepare their students specifically for each or any of these fields of work. Decision on this question rests upon many other considerations than that involved in the number and kind of occupational opportunities available in the several fields. Certainly the present practices of schools of commerce recognize definite vocational demands by providing means for specialized training in most of the fields discussed above, albeit a majority of the students usually enroll in the general business course designed to meet the needs of the men who have made no vocational choice. In this connection it is noteworthy that a large proportion of students preparing for a definite field of work fail to enter that field upon graduation, while many who take their first jobs in the work of their choice eventually shift to work of other character.

Moreover a consideration of the nature of the work involved and the training and experience required for many of the occupations in these various phases of business reveals as many similarities as differences. Thus, most of the higher positions available in industry, transportation, banking, and distribution, and many of the positions in other fields of work, involve in some degree the common function of operating management, i.e., the control and direction of human effort in the operation of business enterprises.

In the fields of insurance, real estate, investment banking, and distribution, the men holding most of the responsible positions are concerned either solely or primarily in the selling of goods or services. These two types of activity—management and selling—stand out as the most conspicuous functions which college men and others holding responsible positions in business are called upon to exercise. And both of these functions, whatever the differences in their application in special fields may be, involve "influencing human behavior," which H. A. Overstreet has defined as the "central concern of our lives. That central concern is the same whether we be teachers, writers, parents, merchants, salesmen, preachers, or any other of the thousand and one types into which civilization has divided us. In each case the same essential problem confronts us. If we cannot solve it, we are failures; if we can, we are—in so far, at least—successes. What is this central problem? Obviously, it is to be, in some worthwhile manner, effective within our human environment."[18]

Summary and Conclusions

1. Both students and faculties quite frankly regard collegiate business education as a means to an end—preparation for successful and socially useful careers in business. Inasmuch as this field now attracts a majority of the male graduates of colleges and universities in the United States it is pertinent to compare the number and character of business positions suitable to men of college training with the number of graduates entering these occupations each year.

[18] Overstreet, H. A., *Influencing Human Behavior,* W. W. Norton & Company, Inc., New York, 1925, p. 1.

2.   On this question there is the widest range of opinion, some writers claiming that there are more than 5,000,000 positions in the fields of business and public service available to men of college training, while one estimate places the number of business positions suitable for men of highest intelligence at much less than 100,000.   While it is obviously impossible to arrive at an accurate quantitative estimate, it seems probable that there are at least 650,000 attractive positions in business and public service to which college graduates are adapted.

3.   Accessions of college men to the ranks of business probably amount to some 23,000 annually, of whom graduates of business courses comprise somewhat less than a third.   On this basis less than four per cent of the total available positions are being filled each year.   This would indicate that there is no immediate danger of an oversupply of college men in business, although the future possibility of such a surplus cannot be disregarded.

4.   While there appears to be no danger of a *general* oversupply of college men in business there is a wide variation in the number and attractiveness of opportunities available to graduates of collegiate schools of business in each of the various fields of business. In general it appears that marketing, finance, and industry offer by far the largest number of attractive opportunities.

5.   The field of distribution offers a much larger number of openings and attracts a greater proportion of the graduates of collegiate schools of business than any other phase of business activity.   The rapid expansion of this field, its changing technique, and its financial attractiveness, leave little doubt that the demand for college graduates in distribution far exceeds the existing supply.

6.   The number of executive and higher positions available in industry is second only to that of distribution, but in this field a considerable proportion of such positions is being filled from the ranks of engineering graduates.   While a large proportion of the graduates from both engineering and business schools are being employed in operating phases of manufacturing, it appears that neither type of institution is generally offering adequate training for these responsibilities.   Engineering graduates are inadequately trained in business subjects, while business graduates are ill-equipped for an understanding of the technological aspects

of manufacturing. The problem of meeting this demand for operating executives confronts both the business and the engineering schools, since certain parts of both curricula appear to be a necessary part of such training.

7. Commercial banking and investment finance have long been important occupational fields for college graduates and it is clear that, combined, they attract a larger proportion of business school graduates than any other phase of business except marketing. Financial returns are high, particularly in investment banking, and there appears to be little evidence of an oversupply of college graduates in these fields.

8. Insurance has been growing rapidly in recent years and appears to be attracting an increasing proportion of business school graduates, although the number now engaged in this business is considerably smaller than in distribution, finance, or manufacturing.

9. Accounting was the first, and continues to be one of the most important, fields of specialization in business schools. Accountancy, *per se*, appears to be a rather limited field, however, and there is some evidence that overcrowding exists and that incomes are somewhat lower than in other phases of business.

10. Public utilities are attracting a large and increasing proportion of business graduates despite the fact that the total number of executive positions available in this industry is less than in most of the other distinct fields of business activity. In this field, as in manufacturing and transportation, engineering graduates "compete" with business graduates, reflecting the fact that certain elements of both types of training appear to be desirable.

11. Transportation, like public utilities and manufacturing, draws graduates from both engineering and business schools. Despite the recognized need for college men in transportation, this field appears recently to have offered rather limited attraction as compared with other phases of business.

12. A small but increasing proportion of college graduates are entering the real estate business. Judged by the number of positions available in this field and by its financial attractiveness it appears to offer opportunities comparable with those in many other types of business which hitherto have drawn a relatively larger proportion of college men.

13.   Among the non-business fields, teaching, public service, and journalism appear to be the most important. During recent years a considerable proportion of business graduates have engaged in the teaching of business subjects in high schools and universities, and a number of collegiate schools of business include teacher-training among their vocational purposes. In general, however, probably less than ten per cent of business school graduates enter non-business occupations.

14.   Analysis of the business positions held by graduates shows many similarities in the functions performed by, and hence in the preparation required for, various phases of business. Two types of activity—management and selling—stand out as the most conspicuous functions which college men holding responsible positions in business are called upon to exercise. Whatever the phase of business which graduates may enter, and whether or not specialized training is believed desirable, it is evident that university training for business should recognize the outstanding importance of these functions.

CHAPTER III

TRAINING AND QUALIFICATIONS FOR POSITIONS IN BUSINESS[1]

The ancient prejudice against the college man in business has gradually disappeared. This does not mean that the bachelor's degree has at last become an open-sesame to fame and fortune in the commercial world, or that the graduate's path to business success "has become a board-walk equipped with wheel-chairs and strewn with roses." Nor does it imply that criticism of the college man in business is to be heard no more. If anything, these complaints have increased in volume and intensity with the entrance of larger numbers into commercial pursuits. The college graduate, however, no longer finds it necessary to conceal his past when applying for a job in a business firm. The bachelor's diploma is perhaps not yet accepted universally as a commercial asset by the employer, but at least it is no longer regarded as a liability.

A half century ago what Emerson called "selfish, huckstering trade" attracted but a meager following among college graduates. University education, in so far as it involved vocational preparation, aimed to prepare for the "professions," and the great majority of the graduates, including practically all of the more brilliant ones, entered the ministry, law, medicine, and teaching. Business was not interested in college men and college men were not interested in business.

Today, the great financial, industrial, and mercantile corporations are competing strenuously with one another for the services of the best graduates, not only those from business and engineering schools, but from liberal arts colleges as well. Indeed, the job literally seeks the man in many instances. It is not unusual for men of high scholastic standing, attractive personality, and a good record in campus activities to have received three or four or perhaps as many as a dozen offers weeks before graduation. It must be admitted, however, that this surprising change in the attitude of business is not due entirely to a growing appreciation

---

[1] Prepared and written by J. Frederic Dewhurst.

by employers of the advantages of a college training *per se*. At least partially it is attributable to the fact that a much larger proportion of persons of college age are now attending institutions of higher learning than was true fifty years ago, or even a generation ago. And on the whole this increase in college registration has been from among the better class of high school graduates. As the personnel manager of one of the largest banks said, "It is useless for us to go to the high schools for good men, as we did fifteen years ago. All of the best high school graduates are now going to college, and we have to wait four years longer."

Whatever the causes may be and whether or not the situation is a desirable one it is undoubtedly true that there has come about a real *rapprochement* between business and higher education. When it is considered that more than half of the young men graduating from institutions of higher learning each year are now entering business, as compared with a negligible proportion a few decades ago, it is apparent that a very large part of the recent tremendous growth in university enrollments consists of students who are planning business careers.

This is not tantamount to saying that their undergraduate studies are or should be pursued with that end in view. There is a considerable body of opinion among educators, students, and employers that the best preparation for business and for other similar pursuits is to be found in a liberal training for "living" rather than a professional training for "earning a living." The former is the professed aim of the liberal arts college, and a large proportion of the thousands of graduates from this type of institution do enter directly upon business careers. From engineering and technical schools, also, thousands of young men are entering business each year, and these institutions have recently been adjusting their curricula in recognition of this fact. The latest arrival among professional schools, the university college of commerce or business, which has set for itself the rather definite task of preparing its students not only for life but for earning a living, graduates approximately nine out of ten of its students into business life.

The Needs of Business

This chapter attempts to examine the expressed and implied needs and demands of business as to personnel in terms of the purpose and scope of educational training offered by universities and particularly by collegiate schools of business.

These institutions generally aim to prepare their students for executive and other higher positions, i.e. for leadership in business, although of late there has been a tendency toward some moderation of these claims on the part of schools of business as well as of other branches of higher education. Many educators are inclined to share the doubts expressed by President E. M. Hopkins in a recent address to the students of Dartmouth College: "Consequently, I have come to distrust much of what has been said, including much which I have said myself, in regard to its being the function of higher education to train for leadership. I ask permission to revise this statement to say that the first function of the college is to educate men for usefulness."

Whether or not one can accept the substitution of usefulness for leadership as the goal of university education it is perfectly apparent that employers are inclined to evaluate the effectiveness of such training in terms of the usefulness of college men in business. Graduates, in their turn, are prone to appraise the worth of professional training in terms of their success in business. Both of these criteria may be considered by some as selfish and materialistic, albeit the universities themselves take full cognizance of their importance. Perhaps it may be accepted as a fair statement that, in so far as professional training is concerned, *the primary aim of the university school of commerce is to prepare its students for successful and socially useful careers in business.*

Assuming that this or some similar statement can meet with anything like general agreement among educators, students, and employers, what studies and what methods of instruction are best adapted to realizing this objective? Here one is confronted with a limitless mass of conjecture and opinion, much of it conflicting and most of it difficult to interpret objectively in terms of curriculum content and teaching methods. As William Bennett Munro has said, "Pedagogy is like politics in that anyone can tell you how to do things better than they are being done. Ideas about teaching, like those concerning government, are all created free and equal."

Consequently, ideas about education, however convincingly and honestly they may be expressed, must be examined with care in the light of the sources from which they emanate. Which implies that the competence of the witnesses must be considered. Presumably university teachers of business, being educators, are qualified to testify as expert witnesses on matters pertaining to collegiate business education. Their opinions, as they find composite expression in existing curricula and teaching methods, are presented in Part IV of this study. Even among this group there are such strange and wide differences of opinion concerning the subjects to be required or offered and the instructional methods to be employed that one wonders whether prejudice, self-interest, and expediency do not sometimes influence even their judgment on these questions.

A second group, whose opinions as lay witnesses rather than as experts and whose occupational experience in relation to their professional training are entitled to consideration consists of the former students of collegiate schools of business. The results of an analysis of the undergraduate records, occupational experience, and opinions of a large number of Wharton School graduates are presented in Part II of this study.

It is reasonable to suppose that the employers of college graduates comprise a third group whose views and experience and the nature of whose duties have considerable relevance in any endeavor to appraise the effectiveness of university education for business. Certainly the competence of their opinions as to the traits and qualities necessary for success in their own organizations cannot be questioned even though they may not be qualified to decide upon the best educational methods for developing these traits and qualities.

Evidence from business as to the personal and mental traits and qualities and as to the kinds of training necessary for proficiency in commercial occupations and for success in business is available in the form of:

1. Analysis of the nature of duties and responsibilities involved in executive and other positions held by college men in business.

2. Studies of the relation between success in business, on the one hand, and educational training and the possession of various traits and qualities on the other.

3. Opinions of employers and business executives as

directly expressed or as implied in personnel selection and promotion policies.

4. Implications of corporate training policies for college graduates and junior executives.

DUTIES AND RESPONSIBILITIES OF BUSINESS POSITIONS

Obviously professional education for business, as for other pursuits, aims to provide fundamental training and knowledge as a background for the exercise of the duties and responsibilities which students may be expected eventually to discharge. Whether or not collegiate schools of business should go still further and attempt specific vocational training for the initial and intermediate jobs is still an open question despite the evidence that a large proportion of the students in these institutions are undecided as to their occupations until graduation and that many of those who specialize do not find work in the fields of their choice. A quantitative estimate of the numbers and types of executive and other positions in business and public service open to university graduates was presented in the preceding chapter, while Chapter VII shows the nature of the positions held by a large and representative group of the graduates of the Wharton School of Finance and Commerce.

Types of Work Open to Graduates

The information contained in these two sections shows that, although there is the widest variety of occupations open to business school graduates, the largest number of attractive opportunities and those in which a majority of graduates eventually become engaged consist of positions which entail a substantial amount of executive or managerial responsibility. These positions, whether they pertain to the operation of a department store, a bank, or a factory, involve the common function of administering and coordinating the efforts of human beings, i.e., some measure of leadership. It would seem not unreasonable, therefore, that "training for leadership," given a reasonably cautious interpretation of the meaning of this phrase, be included among the legitimate aims of university education for business.

Another quantitatively important group of positions, many of them also of an executive nature, involve selling activities. Whether or not the college of commerce does or should attempt specific training of its students for this function, large numbers of its graduates find work temporarily or permanently as salesmen of merchandise, insurance, securities, and real estate. Moreover, these positions appear generally to be among the most remunerative in which graduates are employed. Here again, despite technical differences in the commodities and services sold, there exists the common function of dealing with human beings, of "influencing human behavior."

A third group of activities, requiring only limited managerial or selling capacity, but which have become vitally important in the conduct of modern industry, consist of investigational, research, analytical, and accounting work. Included in this group are such positions as auditors, accountants, statisticians, financial analysts, investigators, and research workers. Work of this nature, which is concerned with the investigation and solution of technical and business problems, apparently requires a different type of mind, different traits and qualities, and perhaps a somewhat different type of training than that required for managerial and selling responsibilities.

Of course, such a classification, like most classifications, is inexact and involves much overlapping and duplication. It expresses more accurately, perhaps, the distinction between the kinds of work which business men are called upon to perform rather than the distinction between the duties of specific positions, although it is believed that it is approximately descriptive of the positions available for college men in business.

Qualifications for Management or Leadership

In view of the fact that such a large proportion of the graduates of collegiate schools of business may be expected ultimately to assume responsibilities of a managerial or executive character, it may be of interest to examine the nature of this function as exercised in business enterprises. It is, of course, unnecessary to point out that management is not an abstract function, but is directly related to the particular situation in which it is to be exercised. A man who might be a highly successful manager, or leader, in a given phase of business and with a given group of people, might be a failure under another set of conditions. Good management requires primarily thorough familiarity with all elements and factors relating to the task to be accomplished. Granting this basic technical knowledge, however, a man cannot be an effective leader of other men unless he possesses and exercises certain traits, qualities, and techniques which appear to be common to all leadership.

Before attempting to define these common qualities it is important to distinguish between the management function *per se,* and what A. H. Church calls the "determinative element" in commercial undertakings. The following quotation from *The Science and Practice of Managament* explains a generally recognized distinction between these two aspects of the administration of business enterprises:

> Two elements in any commercial undertaking are (1) determinative element, which decides general policies of what to make and where to sell it, (2) management element, which gives expression to determined policy in buying, making, selling.
>
> The scarcer element is the first—the success or failure of large undertakings usually depends upon the policy determination rather than managerial element.
>
> Success in policy determination, in the broader administrative aspects, depends upon proper synthesis. The strong practical business man of the past was an able synthesizer, usually with inadequate analysis. Synthesis is the artistic element in business; analysis the scientific element. The business administrator can be a better synthesizer, a greater artist, if he can use the scientific tools of analysis and dissection, but the use of the latter does not remove the necessity for the former.
>
> Analysis is becoming more and more necessary as a fact finding aid in the determination of policy but synthesis is no less necessary now than formerly. The aim of synthesis is to determine "what to do," that of analysis, "how to use certain means to the best advantage."[2]

Granting the distinction made here between the determinative and the management elements in the administration of business enterprises it is clear that both functions are frequently exercised by the same individual, especially in smaller organizations. The former function, so far as the financial success of large under-

[2] Church, A. H., *The Science and Practice of Management,* Engineering Magazine Co., 1914, p. 1-25, quoted from *Business Administration* by L. C. Marshall, University of Chicago Press, 1921, p. 764.

takings is concerned, is doubtless the more important, as well as being the scarcer element. But the management function, since it partakes more of the nature of science, and less of the nature of art, is probably more susceptible to description and more capable of being taught.

In order to determine in what respects university training can hope to function in the development of capacity for leadership or management it may be of interest to examine the views of several leading thinkers and writers as to the qualities and traits involved in business leadership. As defined by Ordway Tead, "Leadership is the name for that combination of qualities by the possession of which one is able to get something done by others chiefly because through his influence they become willing to do it."[3] The same author emphasizes certain important aspects of the business leader's work:

> 1. *Planning.* This important aspect of managerial technique involves a special type of thinking, inductive in nature, capacity for which, in his judgment, can be developed by training. Apparently this implies the application of the scientific method in solving managerial problems, involving "(1) recognition of the problem, (2) assembly of the facts, (3) classification of the facts, (4) formulation of a tentative hypothesis, (5) testing of the hypothesis, (6) applying the hypothesis tentatively as long as it works."
>
> 2. *Technical aspects.* The functional organization of modern industry has resulted in the evolution of a new relationship between the operating manager and technical experts such as chemists, engineers, accountants, statisticians. The effectiveness of managers under these new conditions will depend upon their ability "to work with those whom they recognize as experts and leaders in other fields."
>
> 3. *Commanding or order-giving.* Although emphasis upon order-giving can and should be subordinated with the increasing functionalization of modern industry, the need for it will always exist. "But in so far as command-giving must obtain, it is important that suggestions be made and clearly conveyed to leaders as to the best methods of giving orders." Apparently this aspect of management is also capable of being developed by special training.

---

[3] "The Nature and Uses of Creative Leadership," a paper presented by the author at a meeting of the Taylor Society and the Personnel Research Federation, Washington, May 9 and 10, 1927. Printed in the *Bulletin of the Taylor Society,* Vol. XII, No. 3.

4. *Co-ordinating.* This task of providing the means and mechansims for coordination and of insuring effective cooperation of all workers toward a common end is one of the "unique and important contributions of management."

5. *Training.* One of the most important of the executive's tasks is that of teaching the men under his supervision. "The best executive is the best teacher. . . . . He can get nowhere unless he is mindful in the most concrete way of what the teacher does and how he does it and is applying this knowledge in his own hour by hour contacts."[4]

If these can be accepted as important phases of the manager's function it is clear that they involve not only the possession of personal traits and qualities and of skills acquired through experience, but also much material which can be and should be taught in a course which aims to prepare young men for positions of executive responsibility. Of further significance is the author's statement of the "qualifications for face-to-face leadership of people in corporate organizations."

Certainly, among the first in importance is the possession of *physical and nervous energy* by the leader. There is a subtle sense in which strength goes out from the leader, in which power is imparted by the contagion of his own physical and nervous drive. This quality as much as any other seems a factor always present.

Related to it is that combination of physical and psychical qualities spoken of as *enthusiasm.* Here again is a factor seemingly a constant in leaders. Of course, every enthusiast is not a leader, but every leader has a generous endowment of enthusiasm.

Adequate command—even though not perfect command—of the *technical knowledge* or skill as to the project in question is also important.

Intelligence is apparently essential in the psychologist's special use of that word to mean mental alertness. We will probably eventually be able to prove that there is a positive correlation between this quality and effectiveness in leadership.

Imagination is required—namely, that ability to work with the data of past experience in newly conceived combinations. A lively curiosity and sense of excitement in new ideas usually contributes to the finest flowering of imagination.

Knowledge of human nature—whether it be what is called intuitive or however it be acquired—is important. This ability

---

[4] Ibid.

to understand the probable reactions of people and to judge individual differences is an indispensable quality.

In addition, I think that we are going to find that there is required that something which is meant by the phrase *"having faith in people."* An essential aspect of the conception of creative leadership is a belief in the spontaneous and self-generating powers of individuals in groups if they are given a chance to exercise them. The fact that people respond to confidence imposed in them is a familiar truth which the leader must apprehend.

Other characteristics which can be identified are *courage, persistence, initiative, tact, patience, self-confidence, sense of humor,* and *purposiveness.* This last is of great importance. The leader is distinguished as one who believes in his purposes hard enough to work unremittingly for them. To be too continually reflective about the wisdom of the purposes in hand is to be a philosopher rather than a leader.

Over and under and through all these characteristics, I cannot but feel that the thing that distinguishes leaders is the special quality of *their attitude toward those whom they lead.* They are interested in people; they are sympathetic with people; they like people. I suggest tentatively that to be successful they must have positive affection for people, especially for those whom they are leading. I believe I am not unscientific when I say that the creative leader in the industrial environment is a warm-hearted individual—warm-hearted while still remaining, of course, cool-headed.[5]

Obviously some of these qualities, such as physical and nervous energy, intelligence and imagination may be in large measure innate and perhaps cannot be acquired either by educational training or through experience, but others, such as technical knowledge and knowledge of human nature, can either be learned or developed through training. It is interesting to speculate as to whether the usual methods of university instruction actually are conducive to the development of leadership as exemplified by the above named qualifications and duties. Certainly the universities, in stressing scholarship, which to a great extent is the fruit of intelligence, may be placing disproportionate emphasis upon one of the traits or qualifications of leadership and neglecting others.

Moreover, there is considerable difference of opinion as to the extent to which high intelligence is positively correlated with capacity for leadership in commercial undertakings. Professor W.

---

[5] Ibid.

B. Pitkin, while recognizing a vast and growing need for capable executives in business as well as in other walks of life, stresses the point that qualifications for leadership differ with the task to be done and with the kind of group to be led. Further, he doubts that very superior mental ability is a primary determinant of capacity for leadership in any pursuit:

> Now there is an uncommon by-product of health, high energy, and sensitivity which is variously called leadership, social initiative, managerial power, and so on. It is a combination of these many traits and may occur in connection with almost any type of intelligence except the very lowest and the very highest. Never with the lowest because it requires considerable intelligence to penetrate people's motives and to persuade them to follow the leader. Never with the highest because the supremely inquisitive and analytical mind is, like Leonardo da Vinci, like Galileo, like Pasteur, like Newton, too deeply absorbed in natural phenomena and their causes ever to be interested in mere business, in politics, or in social affairs, save by way of diversion. At the same time, the trait complex which we call executive ability or leadership is much rarer than high intelligence; and for the simple statistical reason that it is composed of a larger number of independent variables than intelligence is, hence turns up less frequently in the throw of Nature's dice. Genuine leadership, as distinct from the egocentric's mania for bossing people, which is quite another matter, is always a better than average mind plus better than average health, plus better than average free energy, plus better than average sensitivity to certain things, especially in human reactions. . . . .
> Executives rank considerably below professional workers in their intelligence. But professional workers rank equally far below executives in most traits which enter into executive ability such as self-assertiveness, free energy, initiative, sociability, and so on. We must not forget that we are dealing with radically different powers and orders of usefulness when we are comparing executives and professional people. It is foolish to look down on professionals because they are inferior to executives in some traits, and no less foolish to look down upon executives because they cannot vie with professionals in other traits. It is a fallacy to suppose that a born leader of men must have a great mind. There is scarcely any more connection between mental superiority and social superiority than there is between the ability to turn handsprings and the ability to play the piano.[6]

---

[6] Pitkin, Walter B., *The Twilight of the American Mind*, Simon & Schuster Inc., New York, 1928, pp. 331 and 334.

The question of the relation between scholarship and business success, upon which there is much conflicting evidence, will be discussed in following sections of this chapter and in Part II of the study. At this point it may be worthwhile to note that studies made by the American Telephone and Telegraph Company show a high correlation between undergraduate scholastic records and salaries of men in the Bell System, many of whom presumably are engaged in executive work. On the other hand, the study of Wharton School graduates presented in Chapter VII shows that men of high scholarship are attracted largely to work of a non-executive nature, while graduates holding executive and selling positions had lower than average academic records.

Further evidence as to the importance in executive work of other traits than intelligence is furnished by a study recently made by Dr. Donald A. Laird, Director of the Colgate Psychological Laboratory, in cooperation with the National Association of Office Managers. Members of this organization each rated two sub-executives in his organization having equal opportunities to demonstrate leadership, but one of whom was successful and the other a failure, as to the possession of certain traits and qualities. Although both the poor and the good leaders possessed many traits in common the latter appeared to excell in the possession of the following:

1. The ability wisely to delegate authority.
2. The ability accurately to size up another's capabilities.
3. The ability to "sell" workers and associates on the importance of their jobs.
4. Power to keep a group working toward a common goal.
5. A voice that suggests confidence.
6. A liking for making decisions.
7. Ability to give clear-cut assignments.
8. A knack of saving duplicate effort.
9. A habit of seeking new and improved methods.
10. A habit of planning to save fatigue.
11. A habit of reading widely about one's work.
12. A way of expressing opinions without apologizing for them.
13. Freedom from prejudices.
14. Cheerful acceptance of criticism.
15. Courage to keep up good spirit when things go badly.
16. Willingness to encourage and accept suggestions from subordinates.

17. A knack of inspiring competition among workers.
18. The faculty of mixing easily socially.
19. Good judgment of price values.
20. Ability to praise good work without flattering.
21. Ability to criticize constructively without antagonizing.
22. Recognition of the wisdom of having reasons for orders understood.
23. Ability to keep firm hold of difficult situations without becoming unreasonable.
24. A faculty of concentration in difficult situations.
25. Courage to assume responsibility for one's own blunders without buck passing.
26. A habit of using facts in reaching decisions.
27. A habit of examining one's own decisions critically before accepting them as final.
28. Quickness in making decisions, without going off half-cocked.[7]

The author further points out:

> This paints rather a different picture of executive leadership than the one which has been so popular of late, which has made a pleasing personality and other human-interest traits the chief characteristic of the leader. The record shows in fact that practically half of the men with strong leadership qualities display noticeable dislike of some of their associates, have tempers, are argumentative, do not concern themselves with the home conditions or troubles of other people, and do not inspire others to come to them for confidential advice. They are more apt to interrupt others, to brag and be vulgar. So it is not the smooth-as-silk personality, and far less the toadying nature, that achieves leadership.

Dr. Charles R. Mann, Director of the American Council on Education and author of a study of the needs of engineering education, insists that leadership cannot be appraised by trait analysis, but by a determination of what leaders do. "All of the confusion and ambiguity that inheres in the trait analysis disappears when action is appraised simply as action and jobs are analyzed into things that must be done. This process gives us a common system of units in which to appraise men and work, and makes possible the development of practical and workable methods of solving the eternal problem of finding the right man

---

[7] Laird, Donald A., "What Makes a Leader?" *Forbes Magazine,* October 1, 1929.

for the place, including the problem of discovering competent leaders in all walks of life."[8]

Among other actions, he specifies, tentatively, the following as being "characteristic things leaders do"; "sees a vision of achievement; grasps the significant features of a situation; determines what must be done to realize the vision; concentrates on the necessary work; sticks to the job; inspires others to help him; relates his work to theirs; enjoys the humorous side of things; pursues the vision as it recedes and changes; creates new ways to master difficulties; treats others as he would have them treat him."[9]

Whether or not one can agree that these are the significant and important things that leaders do, it is clear that such an analysis of characteristic executive tasks and actions is necessary as a preliminary to the determination of what qualities, traits, and skills and what kind of knowledge higher education should aim to inculcate and develop. It is important to remember further, than one cannot make such an objective analysis of leadership in the abstract. What is needed is a series of job analyses of various kinds of executive work in various industries and under varying conditions. Such a series of careful job analyses might reveal certain types of skill and knowledge common to and required for all phases of executive work in business.

Whether or not, given a knowledge of these basic traits and characteristics, universities can or should attempt to train students for leadership in business or other walks of life is quite another question. As Dr. H. S. Person, managing director of the Taylor Society, points out, leadership is a response to environment and a product of environmental influences:

> Each of these (environmental situations to which the individual is subjected throughout life) situations plays its particular part in shaping character and ability and in developing leadership capacity out of whatever biological characteristics and plastic primial impulse are raw material for such capacity. In the process of adjustment to these stages of environment there are brought out, or deadened, such simple or compound characteristics of individuality as physical

---

[8] Paper presented at a conference on Business Managment as a Profession, reprinted in supplement to *The Educational Record,* No. 6, January, 1928, p. 9.

[9] Ibid., p. 8.

and nervous energy, courage, initiative, purposiveness, enthusiasm, persistence, patience, imagination, mental alertness, knowledge of human nature, technical and so on, to mention only a part of the list to be found in the enumerations of leadership traits.[10]

Patently, leadership and scholarship are not synonymous. Whether or not there can be general agreement upon the specific traits and characteristics mentioned above, it is clear that executive capacity in business depends upon much more than intelligence and scholastic accomplishment. Perhaps good leaders are born, not made, in which case university training can accomplish little in developing them. But if it is the task of the university to train for leadership, and of the college of commerce to prepare its students for executive positions in business, it would seem the part of wisdom to examine objectively the qualifications and characteristics of such work in the light of existing collegiate standards. Educational standards and methods naturally place primary emphasis upon scholarship and intellectual accomplishment; students are selected and admitted as a result of a sifting through mental alertness and psychological tests and on the basis of previous scholastic records; grades are the sole measure of accomplishment in college; the "good man," in the eyes of his teacher, is the "bright student."

Honor courses, tutorial instruction and other experiments in the individualization of instruction, moreover, are usually adapted to the needs and interests of the exceptional student rather than to those of the man who has displayed definite leadership qualities.

None can deny that the "production of scholars" is an entirely laudable and desirable aim of higher education, and perhaps the only one to which it can adhere; but it should not be confused with the "production of leaders." Of possible interest in this connection is the result of an experiment conducted at the University of Idaho in which each member of the faculty was asked to enumerate the outstanding characteristics of his three best students.[11] All the characteristics mentioned were then arranged in

---

[10] Ibid., p. 16.

[11] Messenger, J. F., "Educating Efficient Underlings," *School and Society,* Vol. XXVIII, No. 716, September 15, 1928, p. 335.

order of frequency with the following result: attention and industry headed the list; next in order were promptness and neatness; interest, accuracy, and good expression; fourth were thoroughness, system, enthusiasm, and confidence. The following were mentioned twice only: ambition, open-mindedness, balance, independence, imagination; and the following once only: appreciation, conscientiousness, discrimination, earnestness, courtesy, thoughtfulness, resourcefulness, stability, originality, leadership, and ability to get along with others.

The low rating attached to such qualities as imagination, resourcefulness, originality, leadership, and ability to get along with others, which appear to be important characteristics of executive leadership, suggests that the qualities which make good scholars do not by themselves make good executives. As suggested by the author of this article,

> The qualities mentioned as most important . . . . *will make efficient workers under direction, but without some additional strong qualities will not make leaders of thought nor action, will not make creators, nor men and women of pronounced success.* . . . . Perhaps the qualities which make leaders are not fostered in regular college work, but are merely native endowments which survive college requirements. Perhaps our job is to educate efficient underlings and trust to nature to produce a few superior human beings. . . . . The fault is not so much in what we do as in what we leave undone. . . . . The small amount of data just presented shows the need of a change of emphasis.[12]

If any such change of emphasis be at all possible it is obvious that the school of business cannot hope to equip men who do not already possess them, with any of the basic and innate traits requisite to executive leadership in business. Health, physical and nervous energy, mental alertness, perhaps also imagination, initiative and resourcefulness, enthusiasm, "sensitivity to human reactions," a sense of humor, and many other qualities are either inborn or the outcome of a long series of environmental influences of which the university is only one. To the extent that they are innate they can be discovered by careful selection, but not developed by training.

---

[12] Ibid., p. 335. Italics are mine.

Many students already possess these qualities in marked degree, albeit there is some doubt as to whether existing methods of instruction stimulate their full and free development. Granting Robert L. Kelly's contention that the American university's function is to help the student "in discovering his own capacities and interests, actual and potential; in revealing to him the implications of those capacities and interests; and in contributing to their realization," it might be desirable for the school of business which is really sincere in attempting education for leadership to provide special training for those students who show real evidence of potential executive capacity.

Granting that such a selection of managerial talent is feasible, it is evident that certain qualifications for leadership can be fostered by university training. Certain aspects of executive work, in particular, would seem to merit considerable attention in the administration of the university curriculum in business:

1. *The use of intelligence, imagination, and technical knowledge in the exercise of business judgment, i.e., in the solution of business problems.* It is a platitude that good judgment is the *sine qua non* of success in business. The executive is confronted constantly with great variety of business problems which he must solve, and solve correctly in a reasonable number of instances, if he wishes to hold his job or remain in business. The solution of these problems requires a special kind of inductive thinking, not at all analogous to the kind of mental discipline which results from solving quadratic equations or from translating Latin idioms, valuable as the latter may be. In addition to being inductive in nature, business problems differ from those in other fields of thought in that they contain a large measure of the unknown, since they involve in substantial degree estimation of the actions and reactions of human beings. Moreover, in many instances, time and cost factors demand their immediate solution.

Obviously the best training in the solution of business problems is to be found in practice with the materials, methods, and situations of business itself. Whether such training should take the form of field investigations, plant visits, supervised research in original source materials, the case or problem method, the cooperative method, or other instructional devices, is a question upon which educators differ widely. The important thing is that the student be permitted, or compelled, to exercise his native intelligence, imagination, and resourcefulness, and his acquired technical knowledge, in dealing with materials, situations, and problems comparable to those which confront the business executive. Such training, carefully administered, should result in better mental discipline for the student than that derived from listening to lectures and memorizing text books. Of course, the use of one of these methods does not preclude that of others; each serves a useful and necessary function in business education. It should be evident, however, that acquisition of technical knowledge and memorization of facts, *per se,* have been given an emphasis out of all proportion to their importance in the actual work of business administration.

2. *An understanding of human nature and human relations and facility in group or cooperative effort.* Since the executive, as well as most other workers in business, accomplishes so much of his work through and with the aid of others, it seems evident that training for business should recognize this important phase or function of management. Just how this can be accomplished is not entirely clear. Courses in psychology and personnel relations undoubtedly contribute to an understanding of the principles of human relations, but they afford little real experience and practice in them. What is needed apparently is some practice in "group functioning," some adaptation of committee and conference methods to the class room. The seminar itself is in some respects, perhaps, the academic prototype of the business conference. Some business schools have already made tentative experiments along these lines by organizing small seminars and research groups in which the students, within the limits established by the instructor, are themselves responsible for organizing and planning their work and for obtaining and criticizing the results. Such experiments, of course, have their dangers and difficulties, and probably could not be widely adopted, but they offer real possibilities for affording students training and experience in cooperative methods of accomplishing results.

3. *Understanding and practice in methods of training and teaching subordinates.* There seems to be general agreement that one of the most important executive functions is that of training subordinates. The executive must be able to issue instructions

which are understandable and comprehensive, to criticize constructively without antagonizing, to stimulate and inspire without driving, to train and develop his subordinates in the most effective ways of getting work done. All of these functions are of the essence of good teaching and the successful executive should be, among other things, an effective teacher. This does not imply necessarily that courses in pedagogy should be added to the business school curriculum or that the teacher should relinquish his class to the students.

But it might involve greater emphasis upon clarity of expression on the part of the students, more insistence upon effective and convincing presentation of facts and conclusions in the class room and in written reports. Too often the student is graded solely on his ability to give the right answer whether or not anyone but himself and the instructor has the remotest idea of what he is talking or writing about.

Obviously these three phases of executive work are closely related. Effectiveness in training subordinates depends upon a knowledge and understanding of human relations and demands facility in oral and written expression. The latter in turn involves clear thinking and good judgment in attacking business problems, including those relating to the human element.

Possibilities of Job Analysis

Obviously not all positions held by college men in business are of an executive nature, nor should the collegiate school of business in its efforts to train for managerial work neglect the needs of those students who do not possess the personal traits requisite for business leadership. For these men business offers many other inviting opportunities for interesting and responsible work and it is equally the task of the university to prepare its students for these fields of usefulness.

Large numbers of graduates—from liberal arts colleges as well as from business schools—enter the field of selling, albeit the university does not accord salesmanship an equal rank with leadership in catalogue announcements and commencement addresses. Does this field of undoubted social usefulness merit special attention in the business school? If so, what are the qualities and qualifications of salesmanship which business school training should seek to develop? Unfortunately, here again there is much confusion among the experts, although there appears to be general agreement that the qualifications for salesmanship are similar in many respects to those for leadership. Certainly both the salesman and the executive must possess technical knowledge of materials and methods; both should have a liking for and ability to get along with people and some understanding of human psychology. Both should have a knowledge of training methods, the latter, to train his subordinates, and the former, to "educate" his customers.

In addition to executive and selling positions, modern industry is making increasing demands for research and analytical capacity. Many students of high intelligence and of marked scholarly capacity, but lacking ability for executive or sales work, are finding interesting opportunities in business for their special talents. It would seem that the collegiate school of commerce is in an excellent position to provide special preparation for this sort of work. Methods of research involving the use of statistics and accounting in the analysis and interpretation of economic data and in the solution of business problems are highly developed in universities as well as in business. Moreover it is probably easier to select the students with special aptitude for this type of work than to discover those with executive or selling capabilities, and the former group can be more effectively trained in the university since the material adapted to their needs is definitely teachable.

It is evidently neither desirable nor feasible for a university to attempt specialized vocational training for each of the myriad industries and occupations into which its graduates may enter. Most collegiate business schools, however, do provide special preparation for each of the main types of business, such as marketing, production, and finance, although many doubts have been expressed as to how far even this kind of specialization is desirable. Aside from general educational aims university preparation for business recognizes two training tasks, viz. (1) that of imparting technical knowledge regarding the principal types of business, and (2) that of training men for the occupational functions they are best qualified to perform. The first takes the form of instruction in insurance, marketing, production, transportation, etc., while the second aims to prepare men for executive work, for sales work, for research work, etc. The first may be thought of as "vertical" or industrial specialization; the second, as "horizontal" or functional specialization. Both aim to impart the knowledge and develop the skills necessary for the performance of future business duties.

Whatever the precise form which the strictly professional phase of collegiate education for business should take it is obvious that it should be based upon some understanding of the duties involved in the positions for which preparation is offered. To discover the nature of these duties and to translate them into terms of curriculum and training methods have been the aims of job analysis. As a basis for job specifications and as an aid in the selection and training of workers, this type of analysis has long served an important purpose in industry, while in recent years its use has been widely advocated as the basis for establishing sound training methods in the professional branches of higher education.

The American Council on Education, under the direction of Dr. Charles R. Mann, has recently been devoting much time and attention to the study of job analysis as an aid to educational planning in institutions of higher learning. Some idea of the purpose and scope of the council's program can be obtained from the following statements by Dr. Mann:

> The need for records of usage, or job specifications, of this type is steadily increasing in business and industrial organizations, on the one hand, and in educational institutions on the other. The social organization is changing rapidly. Professional, political, business, and educational practices are in a state of constant flux in an effort to keep up with the changing times. Such records of usage constitute the ground map of the present situation, making it possible to see clearly where changes are needed. These necessary changes can then be made with full knowledge of their effect on the organization as a whole.
>
> A record of usage, properly drawn in the form herewith presented, contains all the information needed as a sound basis for organizing men for work. If business and the professions write their records of usage approximately in this form, the data from different occupations are comparable. Then these records also give educational institutions the basic facts they

need to discover what activities and modes of procedure are common to many phrases of the world's work. When schools know what these fundamental common elements of human action are, they can release the corresponding personal skills in youth and stimulate constructive thinking about a world that is now organizing for work. This is the kind of school product America must have if it is to achieve the mission to which it is dedicated.[13]

The model form of job specification thus prepared is being tried out by eleven large industrial organizations. Already some 2,000 specifications have been written covering a wide variety of occupations ranging from laborer to educational director and general counsel of a large company. Preliminary analysis of these specifications shows that there are many elements of skill and knowledge that are common to a number of different occupations. These common elements are being tabulated and classified for presentation to schools and colleges as specific suggestions of subject matter that might profitably be woven into curricula. In addition to these common elements, job specifications also contain a large array of concrete cases and problems that enrich the teacher's range of real situations and illustrative material for many regular specialized courses in science, in economics, or in psychology.[14]

The advantages of this method of objective determination of training and educational needs over that so frequently employed in revising university curricula is pointed out by Dr. S. P. Capen, formerly Chancellor of the University of Buffalo, in the following words:

How should the content of professional education be determined by the recommendations of a committee? But every such committee that I have ever heard of, whether it was legislating for a single institution or for a national organization, has contained one or more members who could see nothing but the claims of their own subjects. By making themselves disagreeable these persons are generally able to force the committee to include in the proposed course of study larger amounts of their respective subjects than the other members believe to be justifiable. *In many cases the resultant course of study represents a compromise between the opposing views of specialists, a compromise that suits nobody and that is hard to defend on educational grounds.*

[13] Mann, C. R., "Records of Usage," *Educational Record,* Vol. 9, No. 4, October 1928, pp. 247-248.
[14] Ibid., Vol. 8, No. 1, January 1927, pp. 51-55.

But this is the way that courses of study have always been made. It is the only way we know. Is there any prospect of discovering a more reliable method?

I believe there is. It seems strange that it never occurred to anyone until quite recently that if we wish to find out how to train persons for a given occupation we should study the occupation. I do not mean to subject the occupation merely to crude and casual observation, but really to study it; to resolve it into its elements, to analyze its operations, to record statistically their frequency and importance, and so to discover what information and what qualities the persons need who are going to practice it. Within the last ten years the idea that this may be a useful thing to do and the results may have a bearing on occupational training has gained some currency. The training enterprise of the army during the war is chiefly responsible for the development and spread of this concept. Since the war a number of technical institutions which prepare young people for industry have begun to conduct analytical studies of the occupations for which they train and to modify their curricula as a result of these studies. Is anything to be gained by attacking the professions in the same way?[15]

In its broadest aspects the task of making job analyses to reveal the educational needs of university training for business involves much more than a superficial determination of the duties of executive and other positions for which students are being trained. Such a study should include:

1. A survey of the occupational opportunities available for college men in the various fields of business.
2. Selection of the basic or "terminal" positions for which the school wishes to prepare its students.
3. Determination of the duties involved in each position based upon actual records of the activities of a large number of individuals in each specific occupation.
4. Interpretation of this composite of performance records in terms of personal traits and qualities and acquired knowledge and qualifications needed for the performance of the duties of each position.
5. Determination of the traits and qualities, qualifications, and types of knowledge common to all of the positions or to the broad groups of positions for which training is intended.

---

[15] Capen, S. P., "Tendencies in Professional Education," Ibid, Vol. 5, No. 1, January 1924, pp. 24-27. Italics are mine.

6. Interpretation of these findings in terms of methods of selecting students, curriculum content, and teaching methods.

Obviously such a study, involving the painstaking analysis of scores of executive and other positions of higher business responsibility, could not be lightly undertaken. Moreover, the qualities and training required for intellectual work are not always to be discovered by a mere observation of the individual's activities. What the executive actually does and what he appears to do may be two entirely different things. As indicated by Dean William R. Gray, there is danger of mistaking the outward form for the inward substance, "I have an idea that as some of our rising generation of incipient leaders strive to develop what they believe to be a technique of leadership, they are likely to be deluded into mistaking the form for the substance. It is easy to assume that the manner in which great men conduct themselves in the process of influencing men or events somehow plays an important part in their achievement of great deeds. Perhaps it does, here and there, now and then. But there is reason to believe, here too, that leadership is attained in spite of, rather than because of, some of these outward or surface manifestations of temperament or individuality."[16]

Naturally the most extensive work in job analysis and job specifications has been done in the field of clerical and manual work where these dangers do not appear to as great an extent. Some pioneer analyses of the duties involved in intellectual occupations have been made, however. Especially noteworthy among these are the studies made by Dr. W. W. Charters[17] of The Ohio State University and by the American Council on Education.

Most of the Council's program has not yet been completed, but tentative specifications have been developed for a few positions. Among these the following statement of job specifications for the positions of comptroller, statistician, and purchasing agent are presented merely as illustrations of the experimental and tentative results so far obtained.

---

[16] Gray, Wm. R., "Leadership—Is It Untaught or Unteachable?" *The Management Review,* March, 1928.

[17] Charters, W. W., Lemon A. B., & Monell, L. M., *Basic Material For a Pharmaceutical Curriculum,* McGraw-Hill Book Co., Inc., New York, 1927. This study is an excellent illustration of the technique employed by Dr. Charters.

Duties of Comptroller:[18]

Prepare such financial statistics and reports of the company's operations as may be required and has authority to require from all departments and houses such information as may be necessary to prepare such statistics and reports.

Take charge of the accounting methods of the company in all departments and at all houses.

Audit all accounts of the company.

Represent the company in its relations with public accountants selected to certify to any published reports.

Prepare financial forecasts for use in determining the company's financial policy.

Obtain estimates from the general departments for the succeeding year.

Prepare budgets for the departments and for the company.

Place insurance in such amounts and in such a manner as may be determined to be the company's established policy.

Approve all data on taxes and other statistical reports submitted to the general counsel before filing with public authorities.

Approve all purchase and sales contracts which are on a cost-plus basis.

Prepare and issue general instructions sent out under the authority of the president or vice-president.

Obtain recommendations from the various general departments as to changes in employees' rates of pay and submit summaries to the president and board of directors for their consideration and approval.

Advise on accounting personnel in all departments and at all locations.

Assign work to the following departments:
Accounting Department
General Statistical Department

Approve all extra compensation plans.

Certify to the amount earned by employees under compensation plans.

Duties of Statistician.[19]

Take charge of the general statistical studies of the company.

Analyze and correlate statistics regarding all phases of the business and present these statistics in graphic or summarized form to the executives.

---

[18] "Job Specifications," the *Educational Record Supplement,* American Council on Education, Washington, D.C., October, 1927.

[19] Ibid.

Review all reports being issued and prepare graphic charts for as much of the data as possible, so that the executives can detect important trends of the business accurately and easily.

Suggest the compilation of additional information considered necessary and eliminations of any reports and statistics considered unnecessary.

Cooperate with other departments in such of their studies as are based in part on the statistical records in his office.

Advise officials of the company on the general business condition of this country and other countries.

Keep in contact with state and national agencies, furnishing statistical information.

Make studies of statistics of the company and its subsidiary companies.

Make forecasts and recommendations as a result of these studies to the end that the company may act intelligently and quickly in increasing or decreasing commitments in order to anticipate the expected increase or decrease in sales to customers.

Advise the accountants and statisticians in the various departments of the company and the officials of the subsidiary companies assigned to this work, so that they may at all times be informed as to the trend of affairs with particular reference to the reaction of the trend on their own business.

Make such financial studies as may be necessary to advise as to the probable cause of interest rates.

Advise other departments of the company where statistical studies are being made.

Maintain a general library and a key index to information available within the company.

Maintain files of all sufficiently important statistical reports and analyses prepared by the various departments of the company.

Make studies of foreign exchange conditions in this and other countries to the end that intelligent action may be taken on the transmission of funds from one country to another country.

Duties of Purchasing Agent:[20]

Prepare intelligible specifications covering the quality of material to be purchased and provide the means for checking deliveries against these specifications.

Buy all materials and services required for the company, and

---

[20] Ibid.

be responsible for these until they are delivered to the consuming department.

Obtain the best possible cash discount for the prompt payment of vendors' invoices.

Compare the various items appearing on the invoice with the purchase order to see that the former is correct.

Cooperate with the Industrial Traffic Department so that shipments may be properly routed and delivered when and where required.

Study business conditions and markets.

Investigate new materials and equipment.

Establish relations with supplies and investigate possible new sources of supplies.

Keep a record of quotations.

Keep an adequate record of purchases in files which are readily accessible. (These records should be comprehensive with respect to nature of material purchased, quantities bought, from whom purchased, and price paid.)

Make a complete audit of invoices with respect to prices, terms, footings, and extensions and prepare invoices for prompt payment.

Maintain a complete file of catalogues of material pertaining to the business with which the Purchasing Agent is associated. (These files should be revised from time to time to bring them up to date.)

Dispose of obsolete material and equipment.

Keep the raw material inventory at the lowest possible figure consistent with business and market conditions.

Keep in touch with the general activities of the company and tax service departments.

Interview salesmen who call personally and put them in touch with the technical men of the organization.

Study sales literature received.

File claims.

Interest self in the company's personnel by assisting them in personal purchases and procuring special discounts for them.

Secure such claims as are necessary as the result of the receipt of goods damaged in transit.

Inform all department heads of any developments of materials, devices, equipment, prices, etc.

Cooperate with the production department by having sufficient materials on hand to meet its schedule and by having material available to take care of any of the changes in schedule.

Cooperate with the engineering department by adhering strictly to their specifications, advising them of similar materials or equipment at lower costs or better delivery, and by securing their approval before any change is made in specifications.

Cooperate with the inspection department by ordering the best material consistent with price and service, and by carefully heeding their complaints and informing them of any changes of materials and giving reasons for same.

This analysis of the objectives involved in the duties of these three positions involved the analysis of replies from hundreds of individuals, each of whom submitted a detailed performance record of his activities over a considerable period of time. The final standard record shown above includes the specific types of duties which appeared to be common to all or most of the individuals covered in the analysis. It represents, therefore, something in the nature of model or standard performance records for the positions of comptroller, statistican, and purchasing agent.

Obviously the preparation of this brief generalized statement of the "objectives" or common duties performed by individuals holding these positions, difficult as this may be, represents only an initial step in the direction of devising adequate means of training. This composite record of performance must be interpreted in terms of the traits and qualifications necessary for the performance of these duties, and only then can the proper teaching methods and curriculum be decided upon.

Moreover, as stated in this report, "character, vision, creative imagination are the ultimate aims of education. These do not appear in job specifications and must not be sacrificed to the practical and more elemental need for learning to earn a living." Job specifications and job analyses, no matter how minutely they may be made, cannot establish or determine universal and uniform *desiderata* for life as a whole. They can be useful only in helping to determine the basic needs for vocational or professional duties and even here, no doubt, they have serious limitations.

Furthermore it should be emphasized that although such a study of commercial occupations might necessitate a detailed analysis of the activities of dozens of distinct business positions, its ultimate purpose would be to discover the traits and kinds of training common to all, rather than those peculiar to each.

In other words, the ultimate effects of job analysis upon the curricula of business schools would probably be to reduce the amount of specialization rather than to increase it.

RELATION BETWEEN BUSINESS SUCCESS AND INTELLECTUAL TRAITS

Further evidence of the training and qualities necessary for business is to be found in studies of the relation between records of undergraduate scholarship and other activities and the business success of students after graduation. As this is a matter of considerable interest to employers who are trying to establish sound selection standards for hiring college graduates, as well as to educators, it may be of interest to examine the results of some of these studies.

Business Success and Undergraduate Achievement

Probably the most comprehensive and the most conspicuous analyses of this character have been made by the personnel department of the American Telephone and Telegraph Company which, with its associated companies, is the largest single employer of college graduates in the United States. The president of this company, Walter S. Gifford, in an article appearing a few years ago,[21] presented very convincing evidence that the success of college men in the Bell System, as measured by salary, was closely related to their success in college, as measured by scholarship. On the basis of records obtained directly from the colleges, 3,806 graduates in the employ of the System were classified into four groups *viz.*, those graduating in the first tenth of their class; those graduating in the first third but not the first tenth; those graduating in the middle third; and those graduating in the lower third.

Medians of the salaries received by each of these four groups showed an increasing "spread" as the number of years since graduation increased, with the median salary for the men in the first tenth of their class 55 per cent above the median for the entire group 30 years after graduation; men in the first third were receiving 20 per cent more than the general median, while

---

[21]Gifford, Walter S., "Does Business Want Scholars?" *Harper's Magazine,* May, 1928.

men in the lowest third were below the general average by nearly the same amount. Obviously there were individual exceptions to this general tendency—"men who were poor students who are succeeding well and men who were good students succeeding less well"—but in general, as stated by Mr. Gifford, "From this study . . . . it appears that the man in the first third in scholarship at college, five years or more after graduation, has not merely one chance in three (the normal expectation), but about one in two of standing in the first third in salary. On the other hand, the man in the lowest third in scholarship has, instead of one chance in three, only about one in five of standing in the highest third in salary. There is also nearly one chance in two that he will stand in the lowest third in salary."

Results of another interesting study made by this company comparing success in the Bell System with undergraduate campus activities and outside work were presented in a recent article[22] by Col. R. I. Rees, assistant vice-president of the American Telephone and Telegraph Company. The men whose records were included in this study were divided into three groups: (1) those who had substantial campus achievement, including major class officers, managers of major teams or an important student newspaper, members of senior honorary societies, etc., (2) those who had some achievement as reflected in minor offices and membership on teams and social organizations, and (3) those who had no campus achievement.

Men in the first group tended to exceed the others in salary, with an increasing differential as years after graduation increased. At the end of 25 years the median salary of the "substantial achievement" group exceeded the general median by 20 per cent —about as much as in the case of those who ranked in the first third of their class in scholarship. The group with some campus achievement showed no pronounced divergence in salary during the first 15 years after graduation, but subsequent to that time, exceeded the general median somewhat, while the median salary

---

[22] Rees, Col. R. I., "The Student's College Record as a Forecast of Success," *McGraw-Hill Book Notes,* Fall, 1929. Information presented in this article has been supplemented by data from a paper read by Donald S. Bridgman at a meeting of organizations interested in vocational guidance and personnel at Atlantic City, February 22, 1930. This paper has not been published.

of men with no campus achievement fell below the general average by nearly ten per cent at the end of 25 years.

As indicated by the persons responsible for this analysis the findings are by no means as conclusive and decisive as those relating to scholarship. "On this basis only, it appears that 'substantial campus achievement' does have some rather definite bearing on progress in the Bell System, but that its influence is not so great as that of high grade scholarship."

As to the type of activity, it appeared that men who engaged in "intellectual" activities such as literary, editorial, debating, and managerial work had slightly better salary records than those engaging in athletic and social, and musical and dramatic activities. Comparison of salaries in the Bell System with the earning of expenses in college revealed no significant relationship.

These studies demonstrate beyond peradventure that high scholarship in college is significantly correlated with success in the Bell System. Moreover, so far as teaching, literary and scientific work, and certain other professional pursuits are concerned, there appears to be ample corroborative evidence that real eminence and outstanding achievement in life are closely linked with high scholarship while in college. The studies of Bell System employees represent the first significant attempt to make similar comparisons for business occupations, and they merit all the attention they have received from educators and employers.

As Mr. Gifford suggests, they point to the need for similar studies of scholarship and success in other types of business, as there is no presumption that these findings, in themselves, afford a basis for general conclusions regarding the relationship of these factors. This may be true for two possible reasons. In the first place, it seems probable that the selection methods of this company may have resulted in a preliminary rejection of applicants who did not possess desirable personal attributes. Stated in another fashion this may mean that the findings indicate that, *among graduates with good personalities,* there is a close and positive correlation between scholarship and salary. Perhaps different results would have been obtained if the Bell System had habitually employed a representative cross-section of the students in each institution.

Another possible reason which might preclude the acceptance

of these findings as having general significance may be found in the nature of work in the Bell System. Responsible work in this enterprise undoubtedly does require capacity for management of large groups and facility in personal and public relations, but it is likely that greater emphasis is placed upon careful and systematic planning of work and scientific analysis of data than upon the aggressive and intuitive methods so essential in highly competitive business.

Quite possibly other factors than scholarship or intelligence may be more significant indicators of success in occupations requiring these latter qualities. Significant in this connection is the study of Wharton School graduates described in Chapter VII, which showed that the scholarship of men engaged in selling and executive capacities was lower on the average than that of men in other occupations. While this tentative analysis does not justify final conclusions there was little evidence of a positive correlation between scholastic records and earnings among these graduates. However, the findings of this study regarding the relation between undergraduate non-academic activities and salary did furnish striking confirmation of the conclusions of the Bell System study. Among the Wharton graduates those who had engaged in extra-curricular campus activities had incomes above the general average while undergraduate employment appeared to have, if anything, a negative correlation with earnings.

The conclusions of certain other studies of scholarship and financial success may also be of interest in this connection. In a comparison of scholarship and activities of 90 graduates of the Carnegie Institute of Technology with their salaries a few years after graduation, Beety and Cleeton[23] reported that "neither scholarship nor activities taken alone has predictive significance," although the authors do imply that scholarship and activities combined "suggest possibilities."

So far as mental alertness test ratings were concerned, there appeared to be no significant relation between intelligence and scholarship, and some tendency for men of low intelligence to get high salaries and vice versa. The findings of this study are of course tentative and by no means conclusive, since, unlike the

---

[23] Beety and Cleeton, "Predicting Achievement," *Personnel Journal*, Vol. VI, No. 5, pp. 344-351.

Bell System study, it covers only a small group a short time out of college and engaged in various kinds of activity. The explanation of such negative correlation may be found in the tendency, manifest from the Wharton study, for men of high intelligence to enter more largely into the less lucrative occupations.

Success Compared With Intelligence and Personal Traits

Further interesting evidence of the traits responsible for success is found in a study made by psychologists of Purdue graduates five years after graduation.[24] Comparison of income with various personal and mental traits showed that originality and "front," or good address, were the most conspicuous traits among successful engineers. Aggressiveness, enthusiasm, accuracy in work, and self-reliance followed in the order named, while reasoning power ranked twelfth in a list of 23 traits. Good moral habits, humor, sincerity, and neatness had little or no relation to financial success.

George C. Brandenburg, in a study of two groups of engineers,[25] found similarly that superior personality rather than intelligence was most closely linked with financial success. Enthusiasm, energy, self-reliance, aggressiveness, and accuracy—the personal traits most conducive to success—showed no connection with intelligence nor with moral qualities. Here again the individuals analyzed were engaged in several different phases of engineering, hence the results are not strictly comparable with those obtained from a study of men engaged in a single type of work.

Studies of the relation between intelligence and success in business might be expected to yield somewhat similar results to comparisons of the latter with scholarship. These comparisons must be examined with caution, however, and with full knowledge of their limitations. In the first place, intelligence and scholarship are by no means the same thing. The first is a measure of certain innate traits or capabilities, while the latter is a measure of accomplishment in college. It is quite possible for a student

---

[24] Reported in *The Twilight of the American Mind* by Walter B. Pitkin, p. 110.
[25] Ibid., p. 110.

somewhat below the highest level of intelligence to make excellent grades in college by dint of dogged persistence and hard work, while the truly brilliant man, because of indifference or lack of interest in certain studies, might turn out to be only a mediocre scholar. But these exceptions probably are relatively few; comparisons of scholarship and mental alertness generally show a high correlation between the two. In considering the latter quality, however, it is important to remember that "intelligence," like "personality," is a word which has somewhat different connotations in the minds of different people. Unless we accept in all seriousness the facetious definition that "intelligence is what the intelligence tests test," it is futile to attempt comparisons of this quality with such perfectly concrete and specific concepts as "a salary of ten thousand dollars a year."

Accepting this definition, it may be of interest to describe the results of a study made by W. V. Bingham[26] and W. T. Davis of the Carnegie Institute of Technology, based upon an intelligence examination given to a representative group of 102 successful business men attending the 1922 Babson Statistical Conference at Wellesley Hills. The group consisted of general executives, sales managers, and salesmen, the last named group constituting only one-fifth of the total. There were wide differences in age (executives ranged from 25 to 63), education (half were college graduates), and experience among members of the group. On the basis of extensive personal history data, including among other items, salary, investments, indebtedness, occupational experience, business and social position, 73 of these individuals were rated independently by five men on the staff of the Division of Cooperative Research of the Carnegie Institute of Technology, as being either "very successful," "successful," "below average success," or "business failures."

The scores obtained in the examination showed that the entire group averaged far above the general level of American intelligence and compared favorably with the intelligence ratings of

---

[26] Bingham, W. V., and Davis, W. T., "Intelligence Test Scores and Business Success," *The Journal of Applied Psychology,* Vol. VIII, No. 1, March, 1924. The test used was Personnel Research Text VI, "a spiral-omnibus form of the Army Alpha intelligence examination. The six types of questions used included disarranged sentences, arithemetic, opposites, number completion, analogies, and information."

Army officers. The authors state that, "every individual in the entire group is in the upper half of the population; which suggests that at least this minimum of mental alertness as measured by an intelligence test, is important for business success."

But when the intelligence ratings of the individuals *within this group* were compared with their business success, no significant relationships were discovered. Age and occupational differences appeared to have some relation to the scores obtained on certain of the tests. Intelligence generally was correlated significantly with the years of schooling but had no appreciable relation to business success. The amount of education, moreover, had no significant correlation with business success. This analysis, of course, permits no final conclusions; as indicated by the authors, "Better criteria of success are required, as well as more thorough intelligence examinations. . . . . But the evidence in hand suggests that superiority in intelligence, above a certain minimum, contributes relatively less to business success than does superiority in several non-intellectual traits of personality."

In the following quotation from this article, the authors suggest that the requirements for accomplishment in the university are not identical with those of business:

> University teachers are prone to magnify the importance of intelligence. It is, indeed, likely to be the chief factor in their own success. They tend to estimate the effectiveness of their colleagues in terms of intellectual accomplishment. They rank their students in order of ability to master and manipulate ideas.
>
> In the world of business, on the other hand, success is first of all a matter of getting things done. Ability to persuade and control people is an outstanding asset. Effectiveness within an organization demands such traits as dependability, cooperativeness, energy, promptness of decision. If traits like these are present in high degree, a man may make a notable business success even though his mental alertness test rating on the Army scale is only B or C. Intelligence there must be, above a certain minimum. But this minimum is, perhaps, not so high as is often supposed.

A large proportion of liberal arts, engineering, and business school students find work as salesmen after graduation. Indeed, some branches of selling have come to be staffed almost exclusively by college men, and it has been generally assumed that the general character of this occupation could be vastly improved by bringing into it more men with the training and intelligence represented by completion of a college course. It may be of interest, therefore, to examine the results of a number of investigations regarding the factors responsible for success in selling, made by the Bureau of Personnel Research of the Carnegie Institute of Technology and reported by H. G. Kenagy and C. S. Yoakum in *The Selection and Training of Salesmen.*[27] The work of this bureau, which was commenced in 1916 under the leadership of Walter Dill Scott, has been conducted with the cooperation of a large number of the leading industrial, financial, and mercantile corporations, and has been widely recognized as having made most significant contributions to an understanding of the psychological problems involved in personnel selection and training.

One study[28] reported in this volume has an important general bearing upon questions of education and previous experience as related to selling success. This analysis was based upon personal history items of 152 highly successful salesmen—four from each of 38 nationally known sales organizations—a group of "supersalesmen," who, as stated by the authors, "may be considered the cream of the country's sales force." Although most of the group were comparatively young—the median age was about 38—the amount of schooling appeared to be a variable factor while long experience in selling was not a particularly noticeable factor for success. High school education appeared to be essential for success in most kinds of selling but there was no indication that college training was either necessary or desirable except in the sale of certain complex technical products. "College training has no evident bearing on ability to become a superior salesman, but 26 per cent of our mixed group of high-grade salesmen are college graduates. On the other hand, 35 per cent of the group have had less than high school education. Different amounts of school training seems to be required for different types of selling."[29]

The results of this study were substantiated by others, particu-

---

[27] McGraw-Hill Book Company, Inc., New York, 1925. See Chapters XI, XII, and XIII.

[28] Ibid., p. 216.

[29] Ibid., p. 227.

in a single large organization. Here is was found that although
larly by an investigation of the characteristics of 500 salesmen
educational training in high school or university was desirable,
height and weight were more significantly correlated with success
than graduation from college.

Of still further significance are the results of a number of
elaborate investigations made by this Bureau to determine the
relation between the intelligence ratings of salesmen and their
selling success and length of service, and comparisons of salesmen's test scores with those of other occupations.[30] In general
it appeared to be true that in most branches of selling, including
many in which college graduates are widely employed, there was
no direct relation between intelligence and sales "production."
Moreover, although a certain minimum level of intelligence, varying with the complexity of the work, was required for selling,
there appeared also to be an upper level of intelligence above
which the chances for success decreased. In other words, the
most successful salesmen were neither too "dumb" nor too
"bright."

The same relation held true for length of service. Very intelligent salesmen learned their work quickly and frequently became large producers, but they soon lost interest and quit their
jobs, while those of lesser intelligence learned more slowly, but
tended to remain for a much longer period. Typical of this
situation, an analysis of the intelligence test ratings of 55 salesmen holding similar positions in one company "disclosed the
fact that the successful long-service salesmen were men of average intelligence or below, as measured by the test. . . . . The
average length of service for salesmen scoring over 100 in the
test was less than 15 months, while the average for persons scoring less than 100 was almost five years. That meant that the
company's high turnover had been caused by hiring men whose
intelligence was superior to that required for the job. In this
case, in order to eliminate the turnover, an upper limit score (of
100) was determined upon and instructions were given not to
hire any applicant who made a grade above this limit."[31]

The authors' conclusions regarding the relation between in-

---

[30] Ibid., pp. 249-276.
[31] Ibid., p. 254.

telligence, and success in selling and length of service should be of significance not only to employers, but to educators, in view of the large numbers of college men who enter various branches of selling. One may perhaps question the widespread assumption that "bigger and better brains" are needed for all of life's callings.

> In general, there seems to be no direct relationship between mental alertness, as measured by tests so far devised, and success in selling, except in the lowest grade and highest grade of sales jobs. In the very low grades of selling there is a low negative relationship between these two factors, while in the upper grades of selling there is a low positive relationship. . . . .
>
> Although there may be no direct relationship between intelligence and success, often upper or lower limits of intelligence, or both, are indicated which predict success or failure in selling the products of the particular company. *Such being the case, the sales manager who demands more intelligent salesmen without regard to the complexity of the job he is offering them is almost certainly making a mistake.* In the higher grade jobs such men may make good, but in the lower grades of sales jobs they are frequently failures.[32]

Comparison of intelligence test scores made by various classes of salesmen with those of other occupations reveal interesting disparities. In a comparison of intelligence test scores obtained for 2,800 persons in 17 different occupational and educational groups it was found that major business executives and first year business school graduates had the highest median scores—127 and 125, respectively. The authors state, however, that these two groups were highly selected and that their scores are probably higher than would be found generally. The next highest scores were obtained by sales engineers with a median of 120, college seniors with 118, school superintendents with 109, general business executives with 102, and real estate salesmen with 102. Median scores for other sales groups, including office specialty, insurance, semi-specialty, routine, and house-to-house salesmen, in the order named, ranged from 95 to 65, with retail sales clerks at the bottom of the entire list with a median score of 33.

It is significant that the intelligence levels of college graduates

---

[32] Ibid., p. 256. Italics are mine.

and seniors were higher than those of general business executives or of any of the sales groups except sales engineers. Even this latter group, however, who ranked well above general business executives and all other sales groups, had lower intelligence ratings than design and operating engineers in the same organizations. "Although a higher intelligence is required of sales engineers than of any other sales group, a still higher intelligence is required for purely engineering occupations. Above a certain level, intelligence ceases to become a factor in success as a sales engineer; other qualities condition success or failure."[33]

The difference in intelligence levels of the three principal engineering occupations—sales, operating or management, and design—is particularly interesting in view of the somewhat analogous types of work in which business school graduates are engaged. As has been indicated previously, occupations open to business school graduates fall into three general categories: operating and management positions, selling, and analytical and research work. Although intelligence ratings are not available for men holding these positions, the data on scholarship presented in Chapter VII indicates that average intelligence levels are by far the highest in analytical and research work and somewhat higher in executive work than in selling. Assuming a general equivalence between scholarship and intelligence these results furnish confirmation of the findings cited above concerning the intelligence levels of persons engaged in different phases of engineering.

Although some of the evidence presented in this chapter regarding the relation between scholarship, intelligence ratings, and personal traits, and success in various business pursuits, appears to be conflicting, there can be little doubt that neither scholarship as measured by college grades, nor intelligence as measured by mental alertness tests, taken alone, are reliable indicators of success in business. Personal traits, whether innate or acquired, which enable an individual to get along well with others or to get others to do what he wants them to do appear to be more important aids to success in certain lines of endeavor, notably executive work and selling, than superior intelligence.

If this be true, what implications does it possess for university business training? Obviously it does not mean that the collegiate

---

[33] Ibid., pp. 273-274.

school of business should abandon scholarship as a goal and turn its energies to developing the right personalities for leadership and salesmanship. Perhaps the university should not attempt, and cannot accomplish, more than it is doing now. On the other hand, perhaps the purposes of a university education can be made to embrace both objectives, minimizing in no degree the proper emphasis upon scholarship and mental training, but recognizing the importance of developing the mental and social traits and qualities so necessary for successful and socially useful careers in business.

Opinions of Employers as to Qualities Desired in Graduates

Expressed opinions of employers and business leaders are further evidence that the standards of accomplishment and success in business are far different from those prevailing in the university. Without minimizing the importance of intelligence and scholarly accomplishment the employer attaches primary importance to the possession of desirable traits of personality and character and to the capacity of the individual to work effectively in cooperation with others in the attainment of common ends.

This does not mean that business firms fail to give consideration to the academic records of the college men they employ. On the contrary they are coming more and more to regard the grades received in college not only as the best available objective measure of intelligence, but as a good indication of performance on the last "job" on which the applicant was engaged. The mediocre student who "flunked" several courses and received only "gentlemen's grades" in the remainder has a poor chance of obtaining a position with any of the larger and better firms. Such a record in the employer's judgment, is evidence either of lack of intelligence or of indifference and incompetence.

It cannot be stated too emphatically that good scholarship is demanded, albeit it is by no means the sole *desideratum*. For the business man frequently displays a surprising reluctance to employ the exceptionally brilliant student, especially for executive and selling positions. This is not due to any failure to appreciate unusual intelligence and scholarly diligence *per se*, but because the executive has usually found these qualities linked with emotional instability and other undesirable traits of temperament. Perhaps it is an expression of the popular notion that only a hairsbreadth separates genius and madness.

This somewhat typical attitude has been expressed by Mr. Howard Coonley, president of the Walworth Manufacturing Company, in the following words:

> We find that the man who stands best in his college train-ing as a student very seldom is a good executive. He is often a remarkable specialist. You can pick out in my organization, and that of many others, men who are doing excellent re-search work, who had previously been outstanding students. But the type of mind which made most of them outstanding students does not equip them with the attributes which are required in oustanding executives. If I want to obtain en-gineers I go to an institution which specializes in training engineers of a certain type, but *if I want an engineer executive I always seek a man who has had a general course of en-gineering training.* . . . I do feel very strongly that the college that over-emphasizes studies is not giving the boys the background to make them good citizens. I believe most firmly that if the colleges provided courses that would bring the students closer to our every day life, or encouraged them to cultivate their understanding of life and responsibility rather than brains alone, the world would be far better off. *Such steps in the future would make college requirements very different from those of today.*

Somewhat more emphatically the same experience and opinion are expressed by Dr. James P. Munroe, president of the Munroe Felt and Paper Company:

> It is an undoubted fact that a large proportion of the college men who make good and rise to the very highest posi-tions are those who did not graduate at college, and while the proportion is diminishing, the men who are now at the top of the industries are men who did not graduate. The reason they did not graduate is that they could not stick to the routine of the ordinary college course. They got out. Another reason they are at the top today is because they were socially minded and were awfully fond of going around with other fellows, and in doing that they learned how to get along with men, and that is a thing that the college does not train men to do; so the fellow has to go into student activities and learn how to deal with other men. *The college must find some way of stimulating initiative more than the college now does;*

the college must make the men learn how to get along with men and the members of the faculty.[34]

It is unnecessary to repeat that this opinion is by no means unanimous, but it is sufficiently widespread to suggest the need for a more careful appraisal of the purposes and methods which university training for executive leadership in business should embrace. Not by abandoning scholarship as a goal, but by supplementing emphasis on scholarship with emphasis upon the development of desirable personal traits and qualities, right attitudes toward work and life, disciplined habits of thought, the capacity for working with others and ability in effective expression, can the collegiate school of business achieve the purposes for which it exists.

What are the qualities and traits, the techniques and skills that business demands of the young men graduating from colleges into its ranks? What methods of selection and guidance, what form of curriculum, what teaching methods are best adapted to their development? Employers of college men, as a group, are vitally interested in these questions; their opinions based upon experience with college graduates in their employ are of real significance in answering the first, and hence have an important bearing upon the second, of these inquiries.

Any attempt to arrive at a generalized statement of these opinions, however, encounters formidable difficulties. In the first place, while business men are by no means loath to express their views on these matters, it is difficult to translate them into common terms and sometimes impossible to reconcile the apparently conflicting opinions of one individual. And then, quite naturally, there is the widest divergence of opinion regarding the merits and defects of the college man in business. He is at once "too cocksure" and "lacking in self-confidence," "conceited" and "self-effacing," "afraid to accept responsibility" and "trying to run the whole show," "too impatient to get ahead" and "lacking in ambition," "too skeptical" and "too gullible," he "knows it all" and he "knows nothing," he has "the academic viewpoint" and he has no "breadth of vision."

---

[34] *Proceedings of the Fifth Annual Meeting* of the National Association of Appointment Secretaries. Boston University, Boston, Mass., February 1928, p. 48. Italics are mine.

Obviously much of the criticism of the college graduate is criticism of youth. Moreover, there is no such individual as a "typical college graduate" any more than there is a "typical business executive." Almost every variety of *homo sapiens* is represented in the ranks of each group. It follows, therefore, that the universities cannot be held solely or even largely responsible for the virtues, nor accountable for the defects of the thousands of youths receiving their diplomas each year.

In the opinion of business men, however, collegiate training can accomplish much in helping the students to discover and develop innate capacities and to overcome their weaknesses, and in inculcating in them habits and methods of work and thought which will help them to succeed in their chosen work. In the following pages an attempt has been made to present fairly and accurately the consensus of opinion existing among a large and representative group of executives and employers of college men, most of whom were interviewed in the course of this survey, as to the traits and qualities necessary for success in business.

Desirable Personal Characteristics

Regardless of the fact that no two persons will agree upon the meaning of "personality" there is universal agreement that the possession of the various physical and mental characteristics and attributes which go to make up the "social effectiveness" of the individual is a tremendous asset to the young man entering business. It goes without saying that success in most business occupations, especially in selling and managerial positions, depends upon the ability of the individual to get along well with and to make a good impression upon his associates and colleagues. "Poise and self assurance," "a pleasing personal appearance and manner," "ease in meeting people," "a firm bearing and carriage," "a pleasant disposition," "a manner indicating physical and mental health and energy," "ability to look one squarely in the eye," "a winning smile," "a courteous and respectful manner," these and a dozen other attributes of personality are emphasized repeatedly by employers. It is worth recalling, perhaps, that Purdue psychologists found that "front" and "good address" were the most important characteristics among the most successful graduates of that institution.

The vital importance of personality traits is recognized, of course, not only by employers, but by students and teachers as well. What is not so widely appreciated, however, is that many of these personal attributes can be consciously cultivated. One has only to remember the almost miraculous transformation of the gawky, timid, and self-conscious freshman into the self-assured, sophisticated, and perhaps too standardized product at graduation, to realize the polishing influence of four years of university contacts. This development of the student's personality undoubtedly is, and will continue to be, a by-product of the whole college environment, of extra-curricular as well as of class room influences, and it is questionable to what extent formal attempts at "personality training" would be desirable or fruitful. Certainly the student's teachers can do much in and out of the class room in helping him to develop that self-control and poise, dignity and self-assurance, and kindliness and courtesy in his dealing with others which will ease him over the rough spots ahead of him when he gets his first job.

Cooperative Attitude

It is in the matter of their attitude toward their work and their associates that college graduates in business come in for the severest criticism. In the judgment of employers they are not properly prepared for the shock of adjustment to business life. They are apt to "resent their environment," with the restrictions it puts upon their freedom, and to become intolerant and destructively critical of their superiors and fellow workers. They fail to appreciate the importance and necessity of cooperation and team-work and are unwilling to "buckle down" to mastering the details of the immediate job. They "value education too much and experience too little," "expect too much in too short a time," and are "impatient of the rate of advance." Of somewhat different nature are the criticisms that they are "unwilling to go ahead without instructions," that they lack aggressiveness and interest and ambition, are loath to "accept responsibility for making decisions," that they regard their superiors as they would their instructors, and "lean too heavily upon them for decisions on minute details."

Obviously these criticisms apply to some but not to all college graduates. Many have learned the value and necessity of co-operation in extra-curricular activities and in earning their way through school. Others are able rapidly to adapt themselves to the changed conditions of business life. The problem of adjustment to business routine is a very real one, however, and one which the typical college environment makes still more difficult. In college the student is very nearly the central figure; the entire institution is shaped and adapted to his intellectual, physical, and social needs. Here he is recognized as an individual and treated with kindliness and consideration. His work is far from burdensome, almost entirely free from routine, and interestingly diversified. His social contacts are pleasant ones, his standard of living comparatively high, and his economic responsibility almost nil, unless he is under the unfortunate necessity of earning his way through college.

From this pleasant environment he drops out of sight. In business he becomes a cog in a vast machine in which his interests are subordinated to the purposes of the organization. He has to concentrate on learning the detailed routine of one little job. He is no longer the master of his own time; he must learn to be punctual, to be at his desk eight hours every day instead of attending three or four classes or lectures. Instead of nearly five month's vacation, he now gets two weeks. In place of pleasant campus friendships, he must associate with every type and variety of human being. More important than anything else, he must learn to get along with people, to work cooperatively with others in the attainment of common ends.

If he has not already learned it he must come soon to an appreciation of the fact, as expressed by one executive, that, "The individual who is to participate in the affairs of active life must have what may briefly be called the cooperative attitude. He must be willing, ready, set to go to work with others in mutual enterprises. There are activities, it may be granted, that call for the lone eagle and the single volunteer, but there is no human enterprise of any kind that is to be furthered by the disposition to sulk, to retire needlessly into one's self to play solitaire when bridge is on the program. The futile, needless misunderstandings, the jealousies and animosities, the intrigues and double crossings of untutored men have no place in the make-up of the socially adjusted individual. The importance of the cooperative attitude is well understood by business executives and by all others who are engaged in enterprises in which groups of people are at work."

How can the collegiate school of business foster the cooperative attitude and develop in students the capacity for team-work, and thus lessen the shock which comes to the graduate when he takes his first job? Obviously all of the conditions of business cannot be simulated in the class room, especially as the primary emphasis of university education is upon individual effort, individual accomplishment, and individual recognition. All of which is in direct contrast to the situation in business where the individual is effective chiefly through group achievement. A number of educational experiments, discussed elsewhere in this report, have as their aim the orientation of students in methods of cooperative effort. By required summer work and by alternating periods of employment and study, as at Antioch and Cincinnati, an effort is made to develop in students the proper attitude toward work. Engineering schools have long had successful experience in conducting laboratory and field work in which groups of students work together on a common problem. And a few interesting experiments along similar lines have been made by business schools. Obviously such experiments, even if they prove successful, cannot be expected to do more than supplement existing methods of instruction. Some efforts in this direction, however, seem justified if the college of commerce is to be instrumental in developing and fostering the cooperative attitude on the part of its students.

Disciplined Mental Habits and Analytical Ability

In this requirement employers and educators find themselves in substantial agreement, albeit the former frequently believe that many of the teaching methods in vogue in universities fail to develop the kind of mental capacity necessary in business. Typical of this criticism is the following statement made by the vice-president of a large concern that employs scores of college graduates each year: "The typical graduate has fallen into lazy habits of thought. In college he has had too much of his thinking done for him by his teachers. You should try to develop his initiative, self-reliance, and confidence in his own mental processes by giving him something to accomplish, not something to memorize." Another says, "We don't care how much a college man knows when he comes into our employ; what we are interested in is how rapidly and how efficiently he can acquire new knowledge." The president of a large manufacturing firm emphasizes the importance of mental initiative in the following words, "Mental initiative involves confidence in one's own mental processes, and the desire to exercise them. It is important because it is persistently neglected. We live in a weird sort of civilization in which we permit our serious thinking to be done by experts, and absolve the generality from intellectual responsibility. We thereby lose tremendously. So far as possible, our students ought to be trained to do their own thinking, to acquire their own information, to raise and solve their own problems. We want to decrease the number of those who habitually take their opinions from the club gossip and the newspaper story and never permit themselves the stimulating labor of careful fact assembly, precise discrimination, and sound deduction."

Mr. Earl Dean Howard, who has had long experience as a teacher and as industrial executive describes "sound judgment" as "the most indispensable ingredient of business sense—it is the rarest and best remunerated of human qualities. It appears to arise out of a clear understanding of reality and the relation of cause and effect. It is perhaps synonymous with the scientific habit of mind."

> The real business of education, however, is to do something to the mind and character of the student which will enable him to function more successfully as a business man than he otherwise would. The educated man differs from the uneducated in this: the ideas which come to him or which he is able to generate are more likely to produce desirable and successful utterances and actions. Such utterances and actions, originating in good ideas, lead to better results. The educated man, moreover, should be able to choose from among several ideas the one best suited to the purpose. Mental resourcefulness and sound judgment should be the objectives of education, especially in its later stages, as distinguished from training, the objective of which is mere skill.[35]

---

[35] "Straight Thinking—The Primary Aim in Business Education," *Proceedings of the Stanford Conference on Business Education,* Stanford

In the following words this executive warns against the danger of allowing students to fall into the habit of making superficial judgments based upon facts and principles learned in college:

> Without disparaging the importance of having facts, we all know that a little knowledge, even quite a little knowledge, is a dangerous thing and must always be so unless a man knows how to use it. I want to emphasize ability in the using of facts, rather than the accumulation of facts.
>
> When I start a new man in our business, for the first year I want to forget what he learned in college. I want him to start all over again and learn our business and adjust himself to his environment free from preconceived ideas. I want him to learn to draw conclusions from experience, independent of the principles he learned in school. Principles are dangerous things to some minds. They are opinions—preconceived opinions—substitutes for individual thinking. He has to learn to interpret experience direct, to understand the reality about him, to learn wisdom from that experience rightly interpreted. Until he can do this he belongs in the class for which Napoleon had the greatest contempt—the ideologist. There is no more ineffective person in business than the ideologist who can conceive ideas quite logically but has small ability in applying them to real situations and lacks understanding as to the relative importance of things. . . . .
>
> Therefore, I have come to this conclusion, that we should not have men who speak with authority in the teaching of business. We should have as teachers, instead of men who speak with authority, who impress their ideas on students, who overwhelm them with their importance, and who fill them with second hand opinions and judgments not their own, men expert in directing the thinking of the students. For the future let us have experts in guidance; that is, men who know how to evoke from the student his fundamental ideas—the ideas on which he makes his judgments and the things he really believes in—and then let them guide him to see the error of those ideas. The function of such a guide will be to provide occasion by setting before the student problems or situations or ideas which will give him an opportunity to teach himself, to the end that he will gain confidence in his own judgments, and will acquire the habit of constantly checking them up with experience.
>
> The besetting sin of college men is superficiality. It goes a long way toward canceling the advantages of his wider knowl-

Business Series, No. 1, Stanford University Press, Stanford University, California, 1926, p. 146.

edge gained in school. Unlike the man in actual business, the student does not have to suffer the consequence of his superficial or unsound ideas and judgments. Thus he falls into careless habits of mind which as he grows older tend to become fixed. Habits of mind are much more important than any amount of knowledge or the lack of it. If systematic education, especially in adult years, incurs a sacrifice of the precious ability to learn and profit from experience, we may ask whether the price is not too great.[36]

The insistence of business upon analytical ability in the mental equipment of college men is cogently stated by Paul T. Cherington, another business executive who is also thoroughly familiar with the educational problems of business training: "Preparation for a life of scholarship may call for emphasis on different factors; but preparation for business life calls for ability to deal constructively with concrete facts; and this ability is expected to manifest itself almost immediately. Discriminating skill in the selection of factual materials and capacity for marshalling them to correct conclusions is the combination of qualities which business feels that it has a right to look for in those young people recruited into its ranks from college. Social graces, a mellow scholarship, profound learning in some one branch, even technical facility in business affairs cannot compensate for the lack of this combination of gifts or accomplishments."[37]

Dr. W. J. Donald, managing director of the American Management Association, also recognizes the same need for capacity in solving business problems as indicated in the following passage:

> Fundamentally, there are only two characteristics which should distinguish the college graduate at the time of his employment at the end of his collegiate education: (1) he should have acquired a greater capacity to influence the behavior of and to deal with other men, (2) he should have acquired substantially greater ability to approach the solution of a business problem, however simple, with the use of the tools of scientific method, including a better grasp of ways of arriving at principles of business administration—in other words, ability to think about a business problem.

---

[36] Ibid., pp. 146 and 148.
[37] "College Education for Business," *Journal of Personnel Research,* Vol. IV, No. 2, June 1925, p. 55.

Confirming these opinions, the comment of executives regarding the qualities required in college graduates abound in such phrases as "analytical ability," "power of observation," "ability to solve human and technical problems," "originality in thought," "thinking power," "fertile, creative, imagination," "ability to think objectively and clearly," "reasoning ability," "alertness in thinking," "breadth of vision," "habit of inquiry," "capacity for inductive thinking," "investigational ability," "mental initiative," "resourcefulness in research," "common sense," "sound judgment on business problems."

These few quotations could be duplicated endlessly. They reflect the mature and well-considered judgment of hundreds of thoughtful executives whose organizations have to absorb and assimilate the thousands of college graduates entering the ranks of business each year. A "head crammed with facts and principles about business" is esteemed of far less importance by the employer than a trained capacity for accurate observation, scientific analysis, and sound deduction.

In general it is apparent that the opinions of executives come close to confirming the judgment of educators as to what the ends of higher education should be. The latter recognize that the "learning" of subjects in the curriculum, the memorization of knowledge or information, are in reality of subordinate importance to the development of disciplined habits of thought and work and the capacity for accurate and original reasoning, albeit educational practice appears not always to conform with theory in this respect.

So far as higher education for business is concerned there seems to be no general agreement as to the best methods for developing the student's capacity for attacking and solving business problems. Most of the collegiate schools of business make limited use of the problem and case method, while one institution —the Harvard Graduate School of Business—has been using the case method almost exclusively and with great success for several years. Whether or not this particular method could or should be widely adopted by other institutions, it must be evident that facility in the investigation and solution of business problems can best be developed when use is made of the actual materials and situations existing in business.

Knowledge of Human Nature and Ability to Influence Others

Closely allied to personality and to the cooperative attitude is the requirement that college graduates should possess an adequate working knowledge of human nature to enable them to work effectively with and influence other men. This quality, of course, is of the very essence of executive capacity and it is of no less importance to the beginner in business. Both must understand human motives and human reactions, the leader, so that he may be "able to get something done by others because through his influence they become willing to do it," and the beginner, so that he may work effectively with his associates and superiors. "Managing," according to Mr. Henry S. Dennison, "is understanding, devising, and persuading. . . . . Persuading is the word I have chosen because some idea must be conveyed of so setting forces in motion that a real active carrying out of the plan results. Giving orders is as far as possible from sufficient. Persuading consists in teaching the what and why of each man's part and then by any or several of the devices management uses—pay, threat, or higher spur—inducing him to carry it out. Richly as the business world will reward further advance in understanding and devising, it will need most advance in the art or technique of persuading men. It is the core of the art of leadership."[38]

With equal truth it might be said that this ability to deal with and persuade others is the core of the art of salesmanship. And it is in these two important fields of work—operating and selling —in which the majority of business school graduates are engaged, that this capacity is in such great demand. In large measure this capacity for influencing and persuading others, whether it is exercised by the executive or by the salesman, involves the function of training or teaching. As pointed out by Mr. Sam A. Lewisohn, president of the Miami Copper Company, in *The New Leadership in Industry,* the manager's most important function is educational—teaching his foremen and superintendents to bring about the best adjustments possible between employees and

---

[38] Dennison, Henry S., "The Management Viewpoint in Business Education," *Proceedings of the Stanford Conference on Business Education,* Stanford Business Series, No. 1, Stanford University Press, Stanford University, California; 1926, p. 35.

work. Nor is this important training function limited to the special duties of the personnel manager in this respect. It is equally the responsibility of all of the managerial staff, for as indicated by Dean W. E. Hotchkiss, industry has "come to look upon personnel more as an attitude of mind supported by an accepted but flexible technique than as a division of management."

The importance of the ability to deal with other men and particularly of some understanding of training methods is expressed by Dr. W. J. Donald, in the following words:

> It is becoming more and more generally recognized that the job of an executive is, in very large measure, an educational or training job. It is reported that the executives of one well-known company took the time one day to analyze just what management is in terms of specific activities that must be performed minute by minute and hour by hour in the day. An analysis and classification of these activities led to the conclusion that nine out of ten of them could be classified under education and training. From the president down to the last supervisor, one of the most important functions is that of training their immediate subordinates, not only to do their present work well, but also for promotion. This interpretation of management, which would make of every executive a teacher, might even be carried out to the last employee who may have a certain obligation to improve the efficiency and ability of his fellow employees because it is usually to his own advantage that the work of his fellow employee shall be done as well as his own—shall be done efficiently. If this point of view is accepted, it is easy to reach the conclusion that the college graduate, if he expects promotion into the ranks of junior executive and then later on to more important executive positions, must have acquired an unusual ability to deal with other men, which is in most respects an educational or training activity.[39]

That employers generally recognize the importance of this ability for leadership, i.e., the capacity for influencing, persuading, or training, is evident from their preference for college men who have been engaged in student organizations and in extracurricular activities. In their comments on the qualities desired in college men they employ, executives insist repeatedly upon the ability to "handle men without antagonizing them", "to judge human nature," "to inspire confidence and loyalty in sub-

---

[39] "What College Man Is Wanted?" *Educational Record,* American Council on Education, October, 1927.

ordinates," "to train and stimulate workers," "to get things done without being 'bossy,'" "to teach men the best ways of getting work done," "to issue orders so that they will be understood and willingly complied with," "to be tactful in handling personal problems," "to lead rather than drive subordinates," "to 'get across' to the workers the management's point of view" and so forth. These comments are but a few of many that indicate the importance which business attaches to the capacity for dealing effectively with the human problems of industry. Apparently these needs are vital in all phases of business—in banking and merchandising as well as in manufacturing, in selling as well as managerial positions.

What types of training should preparation for this function involve? Certainly some insight into the nature of these problems is afforded by courses in psychology, in training methods, and in personnel relations, and in the judgment of many executives, formal training of this sort is essential. As for actual practice or experience in leading and influencing others it must be admitted that students find less opportunity for this in the class room than in extra-curricular activities. Interesting possibilities along these lines are suggested by the organization of special professional groups and societies, such as exist in law and engineering schools and in a few of the business schools, which afford students an opportunity to exercise their talents in organizing and administering group activities in the fields of their vocational interests. It would seem, moreover, that some adaptation of present methods of instruction in business subjects is possible to meet the pressing need for this sort of training.

Capacity for Effective Expression

Probably no other single quality or ability is adjudged more important by employers and by the graduates themselves than the power of communicating ideas—facility in oral and written expression. It is significant that not only is the importance of this capacity universally emphasized by executives, but that Wharton School graduates appraise training in the use of English far above any of the other fields of knowledge represented in the curriculum. It is unnecessary to add of course that college faculties, with equal unanimity, recognize the primary importance of training in English, albeit there is too often the tacit assumption that this "problem," like the weather, is one about which nothing much can be done.

Employers, however, are painfully aware of the deficiency in this respect of many of the college men they employ; it is a source of positive wonderment to them that young men who have been subjected for four years to the processes of higher education are unable to write and speak their native tongue correctly, coherently, and effectively.

An executive responsible for employing and training college men in one of the largest public utility systems describes a situation which appears to be rather typical in the following words, "We find the business and engineering graduates we employ well adapted to our business. They are mentally alert, alive to our commercial and technical problems, and willing to learn. But, with few exceptions, they can't write intelligible reports, or even letters, and when it comes to even the simplest sort of public speaking most of them are complete 'busts'! We are now trying to correct these faults by special courses during the training period in report writing and public speaking, but it seems to us that they shouldn't need this sort of training after a university education." Another employer says, "You teach the boys how to think straight and how to write and speak accurately, fluently, and forcefully, and we'll do the rest." One of the largest financial institutions in the United States, and one which employs many college graduates as executives and junior executives, has recently found it necessary to employ a former professor of English to edit and revise all of its letters and reports. In explaining this action the responsible official has this to say, "Of course, this shouldn't be necessary, as most of our men are college graduates, but we believe it will be cheaper in the long run to handle the matter in this way than to attempt to give a course in English to our executives. Our stenographers can take care of the matter of spelling, but we can't expect them to redraft reports and letters that are not intelligible." While there are numerous exceptions to this prevailing situation, these instances are fairly typical of the experience of business firms with the college graduates they employ.

The problem is particularly serious in connection with work of an executive and selling nature, which involves the preparation of reports for superior officers or customers and the writing of letters. Some facility in public speaking is also desirable or essential in many executive and selling positions and here again college graduates are deficient, as attested by their own admissions as well as by the complaints of employers. There is a widespread feeling among the latter group that universities generally are failing to give sufficient attention to training in the use of English, not only in the form of courses in composition and public speaking, but by placing proper emphasis upon precise and effective expression in other courses in the curriculum.

Undoubtedly much of the problem of poor English is to be attributed to the prevailing methods of instruction in other subjects. The futility of expecting the English department, alone and unaided, to correct bad habits of writing and speaking is well expressed by one industrial executive who spent several years teaching collegiate business subjects, "To expect two or three courses in composition and public speaking to correct faults in expression which are allowed to flourish unchecked in other courses and in the daily lives of students is tantamount to expecting that ten minutes of setting up exercises each morning will keep a man healthy throughout a life time of dissipation." Another individual, who graduated from a collegiate school of business a few years ago, expressed the same thought, saying, "Of course I studied English in college, but like everyone else, I looked upon it as a special study which had no bearing on my work in other courses. And it wasn't until I got my first job that I realized how important English is in business."

Most of the engineering and business schools are acutely conscious of the existence of this problem as it affects their students, and they have attempted in various ways to correct the situation. Special courses in business English and in report writing are frequently required in addition to regular work in English, while training in public speaking is also afforded in some instances. Perhaps the greatest promise of real progress in coping with this deficiency, however, is offered by insistent and continuous maintenance of high standards in oral and written work throughout the entire course of study. Without constant attention to the maintenance of these standards formal instruction will be of small avail.

Knowledge of Business Fundamentals

Generally speaking, employers and executives are far less concerned about the kinds of information acquired by the graduates, or the specific courses and subjects studied, than in general evidences of character and mental ability. Technical knowledge of some special phase of business activity is usually adjudged of far less importance than personality, intelligence, and demonstrated capacity for leadership and team-work. In short, the employer is not looking for, nor does he expect to find among graduating students, the finished product; what he wants is "promising raw material" with the native and acquired traits and qualifications which will make possible a rapid and successful adjustment to the particular needs of his organization.

Other things being equal, the choice between two college applicants for the same position, would probably be determined by the special technical knowledge of the business in which the firm was engaged; but since other things are so rarely equal, intensive specialization in a limited phase of business appears to be of dubious vocational value.

An exception to this general statement should perhaps be made in the case of accounting. This field of specialization in collegiate schools of business is more highly developed than any other, and employers have come to expect a greater degree of technical skill in the graduates they employ for this type of work.

With this outstanding exception, however, the opinions of business executives regarding curriculum content are well reflected in the following opinion expressed by an educator, Dr. Frederick P. Keppel:

> Probably the best nucleus around which to develop the qualities we desire will remain the orderly learning of things worth while in themselves and useful as a foundation for further learning, but the teacher of the future will recognize that such learning, good as it may be, is only a by-product. The real objective is a growing human being who is honest with himself and with others, who is as free as it is possible for him to be in this imperfect world from conscious and unconscious inhibitions and taboos and all the rest; whose natural curiosity has not been killed, but encouraged to develop so freely that it will go on working throughout his life. It is far more important that he should have learned the

satisfaction of knowing something thoroughly or doing something well, than that he should have read any particular texts; that he should see what his eyes show him and not what he is told to look for; that he should form his own mind and ideals rather than that they should be formed for him.[40]

Certain subjects, however, are recognized by most executives as being desirable in the preparation of young men for any type of business. Thorough training in English, it goes without saying in view of the previous discussion, is probably the most important and the most frequently emphasized subject. Accounting, and to an increasing extent, statistics, are subjects which most executives believe to be essential in training for any type of business career. These three subjects are widely regarded as essential intellectual tools necessary in the discovery, analysis, interpretation, and communication of business facts, ideas, and problems. In addition there is general agreement that students should possess an adequate understanding of the nature and functioning of business and economic institutions, and of the principal branches of business— production, distribution, and finance.

Executives hold rather generally to the opinion that the teaching of applied subjects and training in specialized fields of business should not be carried too far. Apparently a "knowledge of basic principles," a "perspective of all business," " an understanding of fundamentals," a "coordinated picture of business relationships," a "thorough understanding of economic principles" are required by employers, but only moderate specialization is believed essential or desirable. Typical of this attitude is the opinion expressed by Mr. Owen D. Young that "the best service which education for business can perform . . . . is training in the broad principles of good business management. In this way you will come to turn out not accountants, traffic men, or other sorts of specialists, but attractive candidates for junior executive positions—men who should have the ability to advance rapidly in general responsibility."[41]

The interest of business men in the curriculum is by no means

---

[40] "Strange Things Are Happening," *The Century Magazine,* August, 1928.
[41] *Proceedings of the Stanford Conference on Business Education,* Stanford Business Series No. 1, Stanford University Press, Stanford University, California, 1926.

limited to commercial subjects, however. Most of them emphasize the importance of a general background of liberal studies, stressing particularly history, political and social science, literature, physical science, mathematics, philosophy, and psychology. Interest in psychology and its various applications is especially noticeable. The statement of a prominent public utility official, an engineering graduate, is of interest in this connection, "Engineering deals primarily with physical values; the basic subjects of the engineering curriculum are mathematics and physics and chemistry. Commerce and business are concerned chiefly with human and commercial values. Should not your curriculum be based on business mathematics, which would include accounting and statistics, economics, and psychology? Psychology and economics are the basic sciences explaining human relations just as chemistry and physics are the basic sciences of physical relationships."

In general the opinions of business executives concerning the curriculum are in accordance with those expressed by Wharton School alumni, as indicated in Chapter VIII. The concensus of opinion among both groups is that the business curriculum should consist of a common core of cultural and business studies required of all students, with limited emphasis upon applied subjects in specialized phases of business. So far as business subjects are concerned there is a general belief that those which attempt to show how business should be managed or administered are of decidedly less value than those which attempt a descriptive and analytical study of the nature of and principles underlying the various aspects of business. Employers are particularly reluctant to hire young men fresh from college who, to quote one executive, "come prepared to manage the business for us, or worse still, to tell us how it should be managed but isn't being managed." Whatever the content of the curriculum, however, employers are more interested in results than methods. Studies are regarded as a means to an end, that end being not the acquisition of knowledge by the student, but the development of desirable personal and mental traits and capacities.

CORPORATE TRAINING POLICIES

The corporate training programs so extensively adopted by industrial and financial concerns during the past few years furnish further evidence as to the traits and qualities desired in the younger executive staff. The training methods which proved so successful during the War in preparing new employees for manual and clerical positions have been considerably extended during the past decade to include young men from college employed in the higher ranks of industry, as well as junior executives, and in some cases the senior executive staff.

Many of the larger industrial firms, public utilities, and banks and other financial institutions have developed organized programs of training, covering from a few weeks to a year or more, for the induction of college graduates into their organizations. So far as the graduate himself is concerned, these educational programs appear to have a two-fold purpose, (1) that of orientating the new employee in all departments of the business and familiarizing him with company policies and methods so that he will not become "lost" when finally assigned to a definite job and (2) that of giving him an opportunity to find the work in which he will be most interested and for which the management believes him to be best adapted.

As a rule these programs involve primarily "training on the job" since the new employee is rotated among the various departments, being assigned to actual work for a few weeks in each department rather than being a mere observer. This form of training frequently is also accompanied by assigned readings, lectures, written reports, and class discussions under the direction of a company official, for the purpose of familiarizing the graduate with various aspects of the company's problems and also to test his ability in accurate observation and analysis, quickness to learn new duties, and ability to express himself effectively.

While no particular significance would attach to a detailed study of the precise form of these training programs, their general nature furnishes a striking confirmation of the expressed opinions of employers regarding the qualities they hope to find in college graduates. From the point of view of the new employee they are designed to furnish him with a perspective of the entire business and a comprehension of the relationship of various departments and functions—a background for what Dean Hotchkiss calls "the central management point of view."

This is something which the management evidently believes to be of primary importance but which, in the opinion of executives, is not adequately supplied by the usual college course in business or engineering. Management hopes by means of this training on the jobs to observe the graduate in action under working conditions and to discover whether or not he possesses the qualities desired in candidates for junior executive posts, i.e., adaptability, a co-operative attitude and ability, and capacity for clear thinking and effective expression.

On the other hand, it is quite apparent that the management of concerns offering such training does not expect to find these candidates factually informed on the details of their businesses nor vocationally prepared for specific positions. They regard college graduates as promising raw material equipped by their under-graduate training not with extensive knowledge but with the capacity and willingness to learn, and possessing an attitude toward work which will enable them quickly to discover their aptitudes and interests and to become proficient in the routine of the jobs to which they are assigned.

Executive Training Courses

Courses for junior executives in the larger commercial and in-dustrial establishments naturally follow a somewhat different plan than those designed for beginners. In the former case the employee has not yet been placed in a permanent position, whereas courses for executives are organized for the purpose of developing the potentialities of the younger officials who are performing specific functions. Here again, however, there is usually a conscious effort not to develop specialized technical facility but to broaden the outlook of the individual by acquainting him with the major policies and problems which confront his particular enterprise and the entire industry.

The purpose of such training is expressed by one executive in the following words, "Our problem is not training for technical facility. Our younger executives know the routine of their own jobs; if they don't we don't keep them. What we are trying to do with our training program is to broaden their point of view, to make them see the job ahead of the whole business rather than the job ahead of their own noses, to let them see the problems of our firm as the president or the board of directors would see them.

In a company of our size, with a score of plants scattered around the country and hundreds of sales offices, we can't afford to have 'one-plant men' or 'one-job men.' "

An excellent example of this type of training is found in the courses developed by the General Motors Institute of Technology for junior and senior executives in that organization.[42] The program for junior executives covers two years, and involves attendance at classes six hours a week for three terms of twelve weeks each year. During the two years' course, therefore, the student attends classes for a total of 432 hours, nearly the equivalent of a normal year's work in college. The following courses are now covered in the junior executive program:

First Year

Outline of Industrial Development	4 hours a week for	12 weeks
Effective English (Advanced)	2 " " " "	24 "
Practical Economics	4 " " " "	12 "
Effective Speaking	2 " " " "	12 "
Principles of Psychology	4 " " " "	12 "

Second Year

Fundamentals of Accounting	4 hours a week for	24 weeks
Personal Efficiency	2 " " " "	12 "
Principles of Salesmanship	2 " " " "	12 "
Fundamentals of Cost and Control	4 " " " "	12 "
Principles of Instruction	2 " " " "	12 "

The course for senior executives, which includes a larger content of technical material, covers a period of two years with attendance at classes four hours a week. This course includes the following subjects:

First year

Department Management	2 hours a week for	36 weeks
Materials of Engineering	2 " " " "	24 "
Technique of Executive Control	2 " " " "	12 "

Second year

Factory Organization	2 " " "	24 "
Business Law	2 " "	24 "
Business Cycles and Statistics	2 " " " "	12 "
Modern Industrial Tendencies	2 " " " "	12 "

Analysis of the content of these courses shows that their aim is not to increase further the specialized training of executives, but to enhance their general capacity as executives and to broaden their understanding of fundamental economic and business problems. Of considerable significance is the emphasis placed upon training in such general subjects as English and public speaking,

---

[42] Details on these and other corporate programs are to be found in *Training Plans for Junior Executives*, Metropolitan Life Insurance Company, New York.

psychology, economics, industrial history, and "principles of instruction." This furnishes a striking confirmation in practice of the frequently expressed opinions of employers as to the basic training necessary for business. The business subjects offered in this executive training program give full recognition to the fundamental importance of accounting and statistics as basic tool subjects, also to business law, organization and management, and salesmanship.

Among the great variety of executive training programs to be found in industry few are as elaborate as that of the General Motors Corporation. Many are conducted on an informal voluntary basis, some are designed solely to meet immediate specialized needs, but the great majority recognize the importance of two basic qualities needed by every executive, *viz.*, facility in human relations or the "capacity to influence human behavior," and the capacity for effective oral and written expression. The job of the executive is recognized as involving much more than familiarity with technical processes and methods, and knowledge of business "principles."

Summary and Conclusions

1.   In view of the fact that collegiate schools of commerce aim to prepare their students for successful and socially useful careers in business and that nearly all of their graduates do engage in business, it is clear that the expressed and implied needs and demands of business merit consideration in planning the educational programs of these institutions. The statement of these needs and demands, contained in this chapter, is based upon (1) analysis of the duties and responsibilities involved in executive and other higher business positions, (2) studies of the relation between business success and various factors such as intelligence, scholarship, and personal traits, (3) expressed and implied opinions of employers and executives, and (4) implications of corporate training programs.

2.   Whether or not it is either feasible or desirable for universities to attempt specific "training for leadership," it is evident that a majority of business school graduates eventually become engaged in work of an executive nature. Selling appears to be quantitatively second in importance among the occupations of graduates, while a third distinct group of activities, involving

statistical, analytical, and accounting work, is absorbing increasing numbers.

3. Successful business management demands adequate technical knowledge of the factors involved in the enterprise and sufficient intelligence and imagination for the solution of problems confronting the executive. But more important still, it depends upon the possession of certain personal traits, qualities, and skills which enable the individual to function effectively through and in cooperation with others in the attainment of desired ends. Whether these personal traits and qualifications necessary for leadership are innate, or are susceptible of development, it is clear that they bear little relation to either scholarly capacity or intelligence. Hence, if universities really aim to train students for leadership as well as scholarship this has important implications for teaching methods, course content, and student selection and guidance policies.

4. Although it is questionable how far university training can be successful in developing the capacity for leadership, certain aspects of executive work are definitely teachable and therefore merit considerable attention in collegiate business training: (1) the use of intelligence, imagination, and technical knowledge in the exercise of business judgment, i.e., in the solution of business problems, (2) an understanding of human relations and facility in cooperative effort, and (3) understanding and practice in methods of training and teaching subordinates involving, of course, facility in oral and written expression.

5. The precise form of professional education for business cannot be determined by *a priori* methods, but should be based upon some understanding of the duties and responsibilities involved in the positions for which preparation is offered. This is the aim of job analysis, which involves (1) a survey of available occupational opportunities, (2) selection of the basic positions for which preparation is intended, (3) determination of the duties of each such position on the basis of actual "performance records," (4) interpretation of these duties in terms of necessary personal traits and acquired knowledge and qualifications, and (5) interpretation of findings in terms of curriculum content, teaching methods, and student selection and guidance policies. Obviously such analyses should not be undertaken without full realization of

their limitations and of the dangers and difficulties involved in making and applying them.

6. Comparisons of the financial success of college graduates in business with records of undergraduate achievement yield interesting but conflicting results. Elaborate studies made by the American Telephone and Telegraph Company show a definite and positive correlation between the financial success of college men employed in the Bell System and their undergraduate scholastic records, a similar but less pronounced correlation with achievement in campus activities, but no significant relation with outside employment as undergraduates. Other studies confirm the findings of this analysis regarding the relationship between campus activities, and the lack of significant relationship between outside work, and business success. But there is little corroborative evidence to support a general conclusion that either scholarship or intelligence, above a certain minimum, is significantly correlated with success in business, particularly in selling and managerial activities.

7. The results of various other similar studies show that, although a certain minimum of intelligence and education is required for success in executive and selling work, above this minimum no significant correlation exists between these factors and financial success. Indeed, in the case of salesmen, there appear to be both upper and lower limits, varying according to the complexity of the job, above and below which, respectively, the chances for success decrease. The average intelligence levels of executives and salesmen are somewhat below those of men engaged in many other less lucrative occupations, notably analytical and research work, which apparently attract a relatively larger proportion of men of the highest scholarship. While definite conclusions are not justified, it is clear that neither scholarly capacity as measured by college grades, nor intelligence as measured by mental alertness tests, are as significant determinants of success in managerial and sales positions (in which the majority of college graduates are engaged) as personal traits and other factors.

8. Opinions of employers and business leaders furnish additional evidence that the standards for accomplishment in business are quite different from those prevailing in college. Employers appreciate fully the importance of good college records, albeit they

are sometimes reluctant to engage the most brilliant scholars, but they are still more insistent that the men they employ possess the requisite personal traits and attitudes which make for success in cooperative enterprises.

9. The importance in business of the various physical and mental traits, characteristics, and habits which determine the social effectiveness, or personality, of the individual is widely emphasized by employers and is recognized by students and teachers as well. Not as widely recognized is the fact that personality development is an important by-product not only of the student's extra-curricular activities, but of his class room contacts as well. This being true, it is clear that the student's teachers can do much in developing the traits and attitudes which will help him to become effective in his life after graduation.

10. Employers demand and expect, in the college men they employ, a cooperative attitude, *i.e.* willingness and ability to get along with people and to work effectively with their associates in mutual enterprises. And it is because of their frequent failure in this respect that college graduates come in for the severest criticism. To a considerable extent this difficulty derives from the fact that individual accomplishment is the measure of success in the university, whereas in business the individual is effective chiefly through group achievement. Obviously the conditions of business cannot be simulated in the university, but it seems possible that some class room adaptations of the cooperative methods of business would be feasible and desirable.

11. Educators and employers are in complete agreement that the capacity to exercise sound judgment in attacking and solving the concrete problems of business is of far greater importance than any amount of knowledge of facts and "principles." Many employers, however, are convinced that the orthodox methods of education, in placing primary emphasis upon memorization, are not wholly effective in developing the kind of mental capacity and analytical ability necessary for success in business. Whether or not the adoption of new methods and materials of instruction is desirable, it is apparent that collegiate business education should aim to develop in the student a trained capacity for accurate observation, scientific analysis, and sound deduction in dealing with concrete business situations and problems.

12.   Closely allied to personality traits and to the cooperative attitude is the insistence of employers that college graduates should possess an understanding of human nature and the capacity to work with and influence others. This ability, involving the capacity for training, teaching, and persuading others, is obviously of special importance in executive and selling work.   University schools of business frequently recognize this need by providing courses in psychology, training methods, personnel relations, salesmanship, management, and the like, but unfortunately students generally find less opportunity in the class room for actual practice in leading and influencing others than in extra-curricular activities. Interesting possibilities along these lines are suggested, however, by a few educational experiments which afford students an opportunity to exercise their talents in organizing and administering group activities in the fields of their vocational interests.

13.   The capacity for effective oral and written expression, it goes without saying, is vitally necessary in any field of intellectual endeavor.   College faculties, employers, and graduates all agree that facility in the use of English is of primary importance in business, particularly in managerial and sales positions which involve contact and communication with customers and employees. The development of this facility on the part of students demands much more than formal courses in composition and public speaking, valuable as these courses may be ; what is needed, apparently, is emphatic and continuous insistence upon the maintenance of high standards of expression throughout the entire course of study.

14.   Business executives, generally, are less concerned about the technical knowledge acquired by college men than in other evidences of character, mental ability, and a demonstrated capacity for leadership and team-work.   With the exception of accounting, in which field specialized training is usually expected of graduates, employers do not expect to find young men who are technically proficient in any particular phase of work.   Certain subjects are generally recognized by executives as being desirable in the preparation of young men for any type of business, among which may be mentioned : English, accounting and statistics, economics, and an adequate understanding of the nature and functioning of the principal branches of business—production, distribution, and

finance. Executives hold to the opinion that the teaching of applied subjects in specialized phases of business should not be carried far. The interest of business men in the curriculum is not confined to business subjects; many emphasize the importance of such studies as history, political and social science, mathematics, physical science, literature, and particularly psychology, which is widely regarded as being basic to business in the same sense as the physical sciences are basic to engineering.

15. Corporate training programs, so widely adopted during recent years for the guidance and orientation of new employees and junior executives, furnish striking confirmation of the expressed opinions of employers as to the qualifications desired in the younger executive staff. While these programs take a variety of forms there is usually a conscious effort to broaden the outlook of the individual rather than to develop specialized technical facility. Particularly noticeable is the emphasis frequently placed upon training in written expression and public speaking, in personal efficiency, psychology, methods of training subordinates, and in an understanding of the use of accounting and statistics in operating control. Here again there is evidence that the development of personal and intellectual traits essential to leadership are adjudged of greater importance than specialized technical proficiency in the routine of business operations.

CHAPTER IV

READING INTERESTS OF BUSINESS MEN[1]

A study of the demands and needs of modern business education cannot fail to give some consideration to the nature of the vast and growing literature which caters to the needs of the American business man. Viewed in its quantitative aspects alone, its enormous volume and diversity is potent evidence not only of the pervasive significance of business in our daily lives, but of the amazing revolution in commercial and industrial practices from the rule of thumb methods of a generation ago to the scientific techniques of today.

Then, the business man and books were strangers to each other; business literature consisted of a few dictionaries and encyclopedias of commercial terms and usages, a number of standardized and elementary text books for the beginner, some academic and erudite treatises on economic theory—which the business man could not understand and would not believe—and "a group of works claiming to open up the way to rapid success in any line of business endeavor through the exercise of faith, confidence or what have you?"[2] Now, the business man has discovered literature, or at least the printed word; whether or not he is actually reading them, he is demanding and receiving an amazing number of books, magazines, newspapers, and other printed material bearing on every aspect of business. Not only is there a vast technical literature consisting of dozens of books and one or more periodicals devoted to each minute detailed phase of business and to each specific branch of commerce, industry, and finance, but business books of a more general sort are actually entering the ranks of the best sellers, while even the more serious popular magazines abound with the discussion of economic and business problems.

With this prodigious mass of books and magazines and newspapers almost literally clamoring for his attention, one wonders how the business man finds any time from his reading for his business. The answer is, of course, that the typical executive really

---

[1] Prepared and written by J. Frederic Dewhurst.
[2] Cleland, E., "The Business Man Is Reading," *Nation's Business,* October, 1929.

finds little time for thorough and extensive professional reading, even of the type of articles designed so that "he who runs may read" and captioned: "Reading time—45 seconds."

READING HABITS OF BUSINESS EXECUTIVES

In fact, such meagre evidence as is available seems to indicate that business men read less widely than do persons in other walks of life. A study made by R. B. Parsons[3] of the University of Chicago showed that occupational groups classified as "managerial," "commercial," and "proprietors" (of business establishments), read books and magazines less extensively and devoted much less time to reading than most other occupational groups. While all of these groups read newspapers extensively, less than half read books, and only four out of five read magazines. On the average they devote nearly an hour a day to newspapers, but less than twenty minutes to magazines, and only ten minutes to books. While the findings of this study, which covers only a small group, are not conclusive, they are generally confirmed by other similar surveys and by the testimony of publishers, booksellers, and librarians.

Somewhat similar findings were obtained in a recent analysis made by a large publishing company of the reading habits of about 400 major executives, including presidents and other corporate officers, general managers, and office, sales, production, and purchasing executives employed in manufacturing, transportation, construction, and retail trade.[4]

The principal conclusions of this study were that these executives read both popular and business magazines widely, but not thoroughly, and that only half read non-fiction books. A large majority—more than 90 per cent, in most cases—receive and read business periodicals, chiefly the specialized "industrial publications" devoted to the interests of their particular industries. General periodicals are read by a much smaller proportion of these executives, and it is indicative of the hasty reading habits of this group that the most widely read non-fiction periodicals are two

---

[3] Parsons, R. B., "A Study of Adult Reading"; quoted in *The Reading Interests and Habits of Adults,* by W. S. Gray and R. Munroe, The Macmillan Co., New York, 1929, p. 34.

[4] The source of these data is confidential.

weekly magazines of wide circulation which aim to present a condensed and graphic survey of the outstanding news events of the week.

It is quite apparent that so far as the professional literary interests of this group are concerned their reading is primarily for the purpose of obtaining information having an immediate bearing on their business problems. The subjects of greatest interest to most of the groups and those on which they read most widely are (1) business conditions, i.e., an interpretation and forecast of prices, interest rates, and marketing conditions, (2) governmental and political affairs, such as tariff, taxation, and government regulation of industry, which have a bearing upon the economic situation, (3) new equipment and materials applicable to their industries, and (4) new processes and methods.

Book publishers confirm these conclusions. Although business books are being more and more widely read, the demand is chiefly for informational books relating to the particular kind of business in which the reader is engaged. Books of a more general sort, which attempt an interpretative treatment of the major trends and tendencies and the outstanding problems of American industry, have a much more limited appeal to business executives. As one publishing executive feelingly states, "They like to talk about these problems, but they won't read about them."

Whether or not this situation is a desirable one—and it seems probable that it is not unlike that existing among other professions and occupations—it has a distinct bearing upon any attempt to interpret the content of current business literature in terms of the curriculum needs of collegiate schools of business. Moreover, although the subject matter treated in business magazines and books probably reflects the informational demands—in so far as they can be estimated by the publishers—of the readers of business literature in the aggregate, it has little bearing upon the informational needs of any one individual.

Furthermore, current literature reflects current reader-interest, and fashions in business reading may change as rapidly as fashions in dress. Thus, a few years before the World War what was known as "efficiency" was in vogue, and business men were flooded with articles and books and advice on how to install "efficiency systems." A few years later, when War demands had made efficiency a minor consideration and factories were working overtime, a labor shortage began to develop, and "industrial relations" came into style. Personnel managers displaced efficiency experts, and the editors and writers of business periodicals accordingly turned their attention to this new and pressing problem. After the Armistice came demobilization, depression, and a more adequate labor supply; and the problem of labor relations became less acute. How to sell more goods was the vital question, finding its reflection in a growing literature on advertising, merchandising, installment selling, and similar subjects. And during the golden years prior to October 1929, the interest of business men and the general public in the stock market called forth an unprecedented volume of literature on investment and speculation. However, admitting all these qualifications, it seems fair to assume that an examination and appraisal of the content of current business literature should help to reveal what matters are of major interest and concern to business executives.

ANALYSIS OF ARTICLES IN THE "LITERARY DIGEST"

Before presenting an analysis of the subject matter of business periodicals it may be of interest to reproduce here the results of a study of the topics treated in the *Literary Digest,* made by Franklin Bobbitt and associates[5] of the University of Chicago. The scope and purpose of the investigation and the reasons for selection of this magazine are stated by the authors in the following words:

> For thirty-six years the *Literary Digest* has been going each week to that vast mirror of human interests and activities, the newspaper and periodical press, and selecting and presenting what appear to be the outstanding items. It is, so to speak, the large mirror reduced to one of workable size. In its several departments there has been an attempt at catholicity in presenting the varied aspects of human affairs.
>
> With a view to obtaining quantitative evidence as to the things which enter into man's interests and affairs, all the issue of the *Literary Digest* for the past twenty-one years and a random sampling of the issues for the fifteen years previous to 1905 were analyzed and the topics tabulated. In each case only the major topic of each article was used, the topics being classified in only one place in the tabulations.

[5] Bobbitt, Franklin, and others, *Curriculum Investigations.* Supplementary Educational Monographs, Number 31, The University of Chicago, Chicago, 1926, Chapter VI.

A major reason for analyzing this single periodical for an entire generation was to eliminate the element of transiency of interests. We sought to discover the things that are of relatively permanent interest. *A matter that stands out through an entire period of this length, especially during an era of such profound social changes, is practically certain to be one of the things of mankind's permanent concern.*[6]

The final data comprised 42,308 separate articles which were classified under the 21 natural categories shown in Table V. If the

TABLE V.   TOPICS TREATED IN THE "LITERARY DIGEST."*

	Number of articles	Per cent of total
Literature, language, and the fine arts............	4,079	9.6
Foreign government and international diplomacy....	4,039	9.5
Religion and philosophy........................	3,719	8.8
War and the control of war.....................	3,547	8.4
Personals....................................	3,493	8.3
United States politics and government.............	3,462	8.2
Business, commerce, industry, and agriculture......	2,985	7.1
Communication and transportation...............	2,268	5.4
Family and community social welfare, law and order..	2,248	5.3
Health......................................	1,761	4.2
Development and conservation of resources........	1,641	3.9
Mechanics, invention, and engineering.............	1,204	2.8
Animal and plant life..........................	1,090	2.6
The physical sciences..........................	1,078	2.5
Intimate group glimpses of humanity.............	946	2.2
Capital and labor.............................	854	2.0
Population migrations and racial relations.........	825	2.0
The science of man (not including health).........	804	1.9
Sports, travel, and exploration...................	803	1.9
Physical safety...............................	781	1.8
Education....................................	681	1.6
Total..	42,308	100.0

* Ibid, page 41.

Literary Digest throughout this long period has accurately gauged the serious intellectual interests of the American people, it is apparent that political and military affairs and general cultural and philosophical interests are matters of major importance, as their treatment exceeded by a considerable margin the space devoted to other groups of subjects. General business and economic problems, and matters of social welfare and health appear also to rank high in the interests of the general reader.

Examination of the relative importance of various fields of knowledge as reflected in this table can be facilitated somewhat by regrouping these 21 categories under a generalized classification which corresponds more closely to the usual educational administration of these subjects in colleges and universities. Such a re-

[6] Ibid., p. 40.   Italics are mine.

classification, although admittedly open to considerable difference of opinion, is attempted in Table VI.

This classification brings out even more forcefully the importance which the general reader attaches to affairs of the state—

TABLE VI. MAJOR FIELDS OF KNOWLEDGE REPRESENTED BY TOPICS TREATED IN THE "LITERARY DIGEST."*

Fields and topics	Number of articles	Per cent of total
Political, diplomatic, and military affairs	11,048	26.1
Foreign government and international diplomacy.	4,039	9.5
War and control of war......................	3,547	8.4
United States politics and government.........	3,462	8.2
Literary, philosophical, and artistic interests	7,798	18.4
Literature, language, and the fine arts..........	4,079	9.6
Religion and philosophy.....................	3,719	8.8
Business and economic affairs	5,480	13.0
Business, commerce, industry, and agriculture...	2,985	7.1
Development and conservation of resources.....	1,641	3.9
Capital and labor..........................	854	2.0
Social activities, problems, and interests	5,338	12.6
Family and community welfare, law and order	2,248	5.3
Population migrations and racial relations......	825	2.0
Sports, travel, and exploration................	803	1.9
Physical safety............................	781	1.8
Education................................	681	1.6
Physical sciences and technological developments	4,550	10.8
Communication and transportation............	2,268	5.4
Mechanics, invention, and engineering.........	1,204	2.8
Physical sciences and mathematics............	1,078	2.6
Biological and human sciences	3,655	8.6
Health..................................	1,761	4.1
Animal and plant life......................	1,090	2.6
Science of man...........................	804	1.9
Intimate glimpses of humanity	4,439	10.5
Personals................................	3,493	8.3
Intimate group glimpses of humanity..........	946	2.2
Total..	42,308	100.0

* Ibid., page 41—rearranged from author's data.

political, diplomatic, and military matters.   General intellectual interests, reflected in articles on literary, artistic, and philosophical subjects, claim second place in his attentions, while discussions of economic and social problems apparently attract wider attention than articles dealing with the physical and biological sciences. Obviously it can not be assumed that the relative rank of these subjects and fields in this list represents their intrinsic significance in human affairs.   What it does represent is the apparently successful judgment of the editors of this magazine as to the matters in which their readers are interested.   And there is good reason to believe that the 1,401,425 readers of the *Literary Digest* constitute a group whose occupational and social status,[7] education, intelligence, and discernment are much above the average. It seems fair to assume, therefore, that the pages of this periodical reflect fairly accurately the outstanding intellectual interests and concerns of the better class of American citizens.

In view of the special significance of the social sciences in the curricula of collegiate schools of business it may be of interest to indicate in greater detail the specific topics in these fields which were treated most frequently. The following three tables, VII, VIII, and IX, show the specific topics in each of these fields on which one hundred or more articles appeared in the *Literary Digest* during the 36 years covered by this study, and the persistency[8] with which these topics were treated.

Political, Diplomatic, and Military Affairs

The most striking indication found in Table VII, which gives this information for the field of governmental and political affairs, is the surprising importance of foreign and international political news. Apparently the American public is interested as much, or more, in these matters, as in problems of domestic politics and government. The prominence of war news is easy to understand, but more surprising is the fact that a considerably greater amount of space is devoted to such subjects as Russian and British politics and government and the diplomatic relations of the United States with European countries, than to such outstanding domestic problems as tariff and free trade, public taxation, and state politics and government.

Moreover, interest in these foreign and international problems is neither transitory nor sporadic, since most of the topics show a high persistency, having been discussed throughout almost the entire period covered by the analysis. If the data presented in this

---

[7] The *Literary Digest* and *Time,* of all general non-fiction periodicals, appear to be the most widely read by business executives.

[8] Ibid., p. 45. Author's data were slightly rearranged in Tables VII, VIII, and IX. Persistency index is defined by the author as representing "the percentage of the thirty-six calendar years (1890-1925, inclusive) in which each topic was represented by at least one article." Thus, persistency of 1.00 indicates that the given topic was represented by at least one article in each of the entire 36 years; a persistency of .50 indicates that topic was treated at least once in 18 of the 36 years, etc.

TABLE VII. POLITICAL, DIPLOMATIC, AND MILITARY AFFAIRS
Topics Treated in the "Literary Digest"

	Number of articles	Per cent of total	Persistency
Foreign government and international diplomacy	4,039	36.6	—
Russian politics and government..................	396	3.6	1.00
Great Britain (not including Ireland, Egypt, and Asiatic possessions)...........................	242	2.2	1.00
United States-European diplomacy................	228	2.1	1.00
World War reparations..........................	211	1.9	.25
European big-power diplomacy...................	195	1.8	1.00
German politics and government.................	191	1.7	1.00
China and the powers...........................	184	1.7	1.00
Irish politics and government....................	175	1.6	1.00
Britain in Egypt, India, and the Moslem world......	158	1.4	1.00
Turkish government and diplomacy...............	153	1.4	.97
Europe in Africa (not including Egypt and British South Africa)...............................	141	1.3	.94
Japanese-white race Asiatic relations.............	137	1.2	1.00
Balkan government and diplomacy (not including Turkey).....................................	137	1.2	.89
Church and state and Vatican diplomacy...........	128	1.2	.86
French politics and government...................	112	1.0	.89
International debts..............................	112	1.0	.56
United States-Mexican diplomacy................	103	.9	.44
All other.......................................	1,036	9.4	—
War and the control of war	3,547	32.1	—
Armed strife, revolution and massacre..............	1,752	15.9	.92
Armaments and the science of war.................	530	4.8	1.00
Militaristic jingoism, agitation, and apprehension....	359	3.2	.94
Peace, disarmament, and arbitration..............	314	2.8	1.00
United States national defense....................	231	2.1	.83
The economic cost of war........................	154	1.4	.64
The human cost of war..........................	113	1.0	.61
All other.......................................	94	.9	—
United States politics and government	3,462	31.3	—
The presidency and national-party politics.........	651	5.9	1.00
Regulation of trusts and monopolies...............	440	4.0	1.00
Tariff and free trade............................	227	2.0	.97
Corruption in public office.......................	215	1.9	.94
Government currency, banking, budget reform, and business efficiency............................	200	1.8	.94
State politics and government....................	193	1.7	.89
Public taxation................................	186	1.7	.86
Monroe Doctrine, League of Nations, and foreign alliances....................................	155	1.4	.92
Island administration in the West Indies and the Caribbean Sea...............................	115	1.0	.94
The judiciary and justice........................	106	1.0	.92
Woman suffrage................................	106	1.0	.97
Congressional activity and efficiency..............	106	1.0	1.00
All other.......................................	762	6.9	—
Total.................................	11,048	100.0	—

table are at all significant, it would seem to imply that foreign and international political matters should be accorded generous attention in any undergraduate curriculum and especially in one which attempts to prepare students for an understanding of the fields of business and public service.

Business and Economic Affairs

A similar analysis of the more important subjects appearing in the field of economic and business affairs is shown in Table VIII. Significant, perhaps, of the immediacy of our primary wants is

TABLE VIII. BUSINESS AND ECONOMIC AFFAIRS
Topics Treated in the "Literary Digest"

	Number of articles	Per cent of total	Persistency
Business, commerce, industry and agriculture	2,985	54.5	—
Business finance, banking, stocks and bonds.........	347	6.3	.83
United States domestic and foreign trade............	341	6.2	1.00
Railroad finance and business control..............	298	5.4	.67
General business conditions......................	282	5.2	.97
Economic conditions in foreign lands..............	242	4.4	.86
Personal thrift, banking, and investment...........	219	4.0	.58
Agricultural administration......................	199	3.6	.97
Foreign finance and international exchange.........	198	3.6	.83
Foreign and international trade (not including the United States)...............................	183	3.4	.94
The cost of living...............................	181	3.3	.64
Industrial conservation and business management....	131	2.4	.81
All other.......................................	364	6.7	—
Development and conservation of resources	1,641	29.9	—
Food resources and conservation..................	424	7.7	1.00
Oil, gas, and water-power........................	255	4.6	.83*
Forests, wood and pulp resources, and forest fires.....	162	3.0	.94*
Wearing apparel, fabrics, furs, and leather..........	141	2.6	.94
Coal and heat resources (not including oil, gas, and electricity)...................................	136	2.5	.94
Industrial and rare metals........................	133	2.4	.83*
All other.......................................	390	7.1	—
Capital and labor	854	15.6	—
Strikes and labor violence.......................	200	3.6	.97
Hours, wages, and working conditions..............	146	2.7	1.00
All other.......................................	508	9.3	—
Total...	5,480	100.0	—

* Persistency was in excess of stated index.

the frequency with which articles on food resources and conservation appear. Aside from this, greatest popular interest appears to center in news relating to financial and banking matters, in commerce and marketing, in railroad problems, and in general business conditions in the United States and foreign countries. All of these topics were treated fairly frequently throughout the entire period and appear, therefore, to be matters of permanent importance. Problems of capital and labor come in for generous attention although only half as much space is devoted to them in the aggregate as to the development and conservation of natural resources, while the general field of commerce, industry, and agriculture is by far the most important. Here again, as in the field of political and military affairs, extensive interest is indicated in foreign and international business problems as well as in those of domestic character.

Social Activities, Problems, and Interests

Approximately as much space was devoted to treatment of social problems and interests, shown in detail in Table IX, as was ac-

TABLE IX.   SOCIAL ACTIVITIES, PROBLEMS, AND INTERESTS
Topics Treated in the "Literary Digest"

	Number of articles	Per cent of total	Persistency
Family and community social welfare, law and order	2,248	42.1	—
Liquor problem in America........................	507	9.5	1.00
Crime and crime prevention......................	346	6.5	1.00
Relief of disaster, famine, and war..............	241	4.5	.81
Family stability, marriage, and divorce...........	119	2.2	1.00
Immorality in literature, art, and drama..........	111	2.1	.97
All other..	924	11.3	—
Population migrations and racial relations	825	15.5	—
American negro adjustments.....................	195	3.7	1.00
Immigration from Europe........................	145	2.7	1.00
Jewish racial adjustments.......................	130	2.4	.92
Immigration from Asia..........................	111	2.1	.83
All other..	244	4.6	—
Sports, travel, and exploration	803	15.0	—
Parks, travel, and expositions....................	202	3.8	1.00
Commercialized sports...........................	143	2.7	.67
Outdoor amateur sports.........................	105	1.9	.58
International and foreign games and sports.........	103	1.9	.58*
Hunting and fishing.............................	101	1.9	.64
All other..	149	2.8	—
Physical safety	781	14.6	—
Fire and explosives.............................	139	2.6	1.00
Railroad accidents and safety....................	108	2.0	.86
Automobile accidents, safety, and control..........	108	2.0	.67
All other..	426	8.0	—
Education	681	12.8	—
Curriculum, technique, and method...............	220	4.2	.86
Foreign and international education...............	145	2.7	1.00
College and university administration, efficiency and support...................................	113	2.1	.94
All other..	203	3.8	—
Total..	**5,338**	**100.0**	—

* Persistency in excess of stated index.

corded business and economic affairs. General problems of community social welfare, crime, and delinquency appear to be by far the most important, with the "liquor problem," as might be expected, heading the list by a substantial margin. Problems relating to population and racial relations appear to receive considerably less attention on the whole than those of family and community welfare. However, certain topics in the former category apparently attract widespread interest, notably questions of immigration from Europe and Asia and problems involved in Jewish and negro racial adjustments. Recreational interests and activities are naturally accorded considerable attention, while educational problems appear also to be of considerable interest to the general reader.

ANALYSIS OF CONTENT OF BUSINESS LITERATURE

What does the content of current business literature indicate as to the needs of a collegiate curriculum designed to prepare men for executive and other higher positions in business and public service? In attempting to answer this question it must be remembered that professional reading interests of the business executive are controlled primarily by his desire for information bearing upon the specific and immediate problems which confront him in his endeavor to operate his enterprise successfully and profitably. Naturally the nature of these problems varies from one period to another and from one type of business to another. Thus, under one set of conditions or in one industry, problems of labor, hours, wages, or working conditions may predominate. At another time, questions of price maintenance, governmental regulation, foreign competition or other marketing problems may become acute. Moreover, the problems which confront the individual executive, and hence his needs for information, will depend upon his primary responsibility in the business, i.e. whether it be for sales, advertising, personnel, production management, and so forth.

Therefore, analysis of business literature cannot do more than to show, in the aggregate, the general nature and relative importance of the various types of problems which appear to have confronted business executives during the period covered by such a survey. Obviously, if such an analysis is to reveal a balanced and authentic picture of the relative importance of different kinds of information demanded, it must be confined to periodicals and other literature intended for the needs of general business rather than to trade and industrial journals and books with specialized application to particular trades and industries or to special business functions.

For many years the *Industrial Arts Index*[9] has been recognized as a standard source of information on periodical literature published in the fields of "science and technology, and business and finance." Since all articles on these subjects appearing each month in 233 leading technical and business periodicals, as well as several hundred books and pamphlets, are indexed and classified in this publication, an analysis of these references should provide a fairly comprehensive and accurate picture of the relative importance of current problems arising in different fields of business. *The Industrial Arts Index* for the years 1926-28 was thus analyzed by

[9] The H. W. Wilson Company, New York City.

counting the number of references under each of the topics in the field of business. Since the authors' index involves a complete duplication, only the subject index was used, and in most cases only functional or general business references were counted. That is to say, articles indexed under specific commodities, such as oil, flour, coal, millinery, or specific industries, such as cement manufacturing, canning, shipbuilding, automobile industry, were excluded from the count. However, in the case of marketing, references to such specific items as chain stores were included, and in transportation, similarly, references to air transportation, motor trucks, etc., were also included in the count. Even with these exclusions many articles were counted more than once, but this duplication involves no error since the purpose of the analysis is to discover the importance of the topics, whether one or more are treated in the same article.

The completed analysis covered 26,248 separate references under 368 topical classifications. The references under these separate topical classifications were then assembled into what appeared to be "natural" categories or classes—sixteen in number—the totals for which are shown in Table X. This final classification is by no means perfect as it involves considerable over-lapping between fields, and perhaps many of the separate topics classified under one of the main headings might as well have been classified under another. However, this scheme of classification was found to be a fairly satisfactory means of "condensing" the large number of separate topics included in the *Industrial Arts Index* as well as for the presentation of other data shown in the table.

A similar analysis and classification was made of the items indexed in *Business Books: 1920-1926*,[10] and this information is shown also in Table X. This catalogue includes 2,600 books and other publications, comprising "the major and more valuable part of the book and pamphlet literature of business handled during that period at the Business Branch of the Newark Public Library." This catalogue is generally regarded as containing a thoroughly representative list of the business publications which find the

[10] *Business Books: 1920-1926,* an analytical catalogue of 2,600 titles, by the Business Branch of the Newark, N.J. Public Library, compiled by L. H. Morley and A. C. Kight under direction of John Cotton Dana. The H. W. Wilson Co., New York City, 1927.

TABLE X. NUMBER OF ARTICLES AND BOOKS RELATING TO
PRINCIPAL BUSINESS SUBJECTS

	Industrial Arts Index 1926–1928		Business Books: 1920–1926		Nation's Business 1924–1928		Magazine of Business 1927–1928	
	Number	Per cent	Number	Per cent	Number	Per cent	Number	Per cent
Accounting.........	406	1.5	815	14.1	7	0.2	19	1.1
Advertising and publicity.............	3,049	11.6	428	7.4	80	2.5	84	4.8
Agriculture..........	447	1.7	40	0.7	149	4.6	26	1.5
Business conditions and forecasting.....	301	1.1	41	0.7	71	2.2	48	2.7
Cooperation and business ethics........	277	1.1	54	0.9	115	3.6	40	2.3
Finance and credit....	4,295	16.5	646	11.2	191	5.9	125	7.1
Foreign trade........	164	0.6	131	2.3	143	4.4	73	4.2
General economic problems.............	1,005	3.8	266	4.6	331	10.4	124	7.1
Government and business............	1,870	7.1	272	4.7	699	21.7	40	2.3
Insurance...........	1,178	4.5	150	2.6	55	1.7	16	0.9
Management, operating...............	3,166	12.1	666	11.6	223	6.9	277	15.7
Marketing..........	3,212	12.2	833	14.5	321	10.0	265	15.0
Personnel and labor...	2,267	8.6	431	7.5	187	5.8	116	6.6
Real estate and building...............	340	1.3	67	1.2	25	0.8	24	1.4
Statistics and research.	285	1.1	162	2.8	17	0.5	100	5.7
Transportation and traffic.............	3,317	12.7	138	2.4	304	9.4	209	11.9
Other.............	669	2.5	621	10.8	303	9.4	171	9.7
Totals.............	26,248	100.0	5,761	100.0	3,221	100.0	1,757	100.0

widest use, as the Newark Public Library possesses what is recognized as one of the most comprehensive collections of business literature in the world and one which is used extensively by business firms in and near the New York metropolitan area. The material was analyzed in the same way as that of the *Industrial Arts Index;* the number of references under each of the 4,100 subjects and sub-divisions (excluding references to authors' names and to specific industries) was first counted and totals then compiled for the 16 major classifications.

Only a limited number of business publications are general in their appeal, i.e. directed to the interests of the administrative executive who is responsible for determination of major corporate policies rather than for specific functions such as sales or production. Of these, the *Nation's Business,* a monthly magazine published by the United States Chamber of Commerce, is widely read and appears to be most representative. The separate topical references appearing in the annual indexes of this publication for the five years from 1924 to 1928 were counted, and the totals for major classifications are presented in Table X on a comparable basis with those for the other analyses.

The *Magazine of Business,* formerly published by the McGraw-Hill Publishing Co., but since discontinued and supplanted by *The Business Week,* similarly made its appeal to the general business executive with a discussion of problems common to all types and phases of business.   Table X also presents a similar analysis of the topical references appearing in the annual indexes of this magazine for the years 1927 and 1928.   Neither the *Nation's Business* nor the *Magazine of Business* attempts a profound scientific or technical treatment of the material which they present. Their articles are distinctly popular in nature.   But their editorial boards endeavor to interpret and illuminate the outstanding developments and problems of pervasive interest to business executives.   If this endeavor is successful the pages of these magazines should reflect the more vital concerns and interests confronting American business during the period under review.

On the basis of the number of topics listed in the *Industrial Arts Index,* finance and credit appears to have been by far the most important field, although the total for this subject is considerably less than the combined totals for marketing and advertising, which may be considered to represent the general field of distribution.   References on the subjects of transportation and traffic, and operating management appear to be next in frequency to those on distribution and finance.   The number of references to these subjects, added to the total for personnel and labor, amounts to 19,306, or nearly three-fourths of the grand total.

Articles on the relation of government to business, insurance, and on general economic problems not included under other classifications comprise the bulk of the remaining references.   References to accounting, agriculture, general business conditions, cooperative activities of business, foreign trade, real estate, and statistics and research are comparatively few in number.

The frequency of references on these subjects in the *Industrial Arts Index* cannot, of course, be interpreted as indicating their relative importance in the conduct of business operations, or even their relative importance to the readers of the publications which were indexed, although it does furnish some indication of the relationships involved in the major problems confronting business men during this period.   The subject of accounting, for instance, which received but scant attention in general business periodicals, is of vital and universal importance as indicated by the fact that the catalog of *Business Books: 1920-1926* contained more references to this field than to any other except marketing. In addition to these two subjects, topics in the fields of operating management, finance and credit, personnel and labor, and advertising and publicity, as in the *Industrial Arts Index,* appeared to be the most important.

The *Nation's Business,* widely read by business executives, placed a preponderant emphasis upon governmental activities as related to business, with more than twice as many articles as on the next most important subject—general economic problems. While this may be attributed in part to the sponsorship of this publication by the United States Chamber of Commerce and to the location of its editorial offices in the center of governmental activity, it is probably due chiefly to a recognition of the important and increasing effect which the activities of the Federal government have upon large scale business in the United States. Other subjects treated extensively in *Nation's Business* included marketing, transportation (owing partly to extensive governmental interest in this phase of business), operating management, and labor. The *Magazine of Business* likewise placed considerable emphasis upon the same subjects, with the exception of government and business.

Save for a few striking divergences, these four analyses are generally self-confirmatory as to the relative importance of the various subjects treated in recent business literature. Considering all of the four classes of data analyzed, articles relating to marketing, operating management, and finance and credit, in the order named, appear, on the whole, to have been the most numerous. Furthermore, the importance of the first two of these fields is considerably enhanced if the entire field of distribution is considered as including also advertising and publicity, and if problems of personnel and labor relations are added to those of operating management.

Topics relating to transportation and traffic, and to government and business are apparently next in importance, while the relative rank of the remaining subjects appears to be somewhat in the following order: personnel and labor, general economic problems, advertising and publicity, accounting, foreign trade, statistics and research, insurance, agriculture, cooperation and business ethics, business conditions, and real estate.

TOPICS TREATED IN VARIOUS FIELDS OF BUSINESS

Any possible significance which such an analysis of business literature may have for curriculum-building purposes must rest not only upon an appraisal of the relative importance of these subjects, but upon a detailed examination of the topics treated under each general category. Although such an investigation cannot be attempted here, it may be of interest to indicate briefly the subjects in each of the principal fields which seem to have been of the greatest importance.

Marketing

The topical references in this important field, which includes all aspects of merchandise distribution except those separately listed under advertising and publicity, cover an extremely wide range with primary emphasis, however, upon general problems of distribution as they effect the manufacturer. Various aspects of sales control and stimulation, salesmanship and the training of salesmen, and sales management appear to be of major importance. Of nearly as great importance are questions relating to retail merchandising and the development of chain stores. Other subjects appearing less frequently, but to which considerable space is devoted include pricing policies, price cutting and resale price fixing, installment selling, market surveys and analyses, hand-to-mouth buying, dealer and jobber relations, and questions of inter-commodity competition. As might be expected most of these latter subjects reflect the many problems and questions arising from the striking changes in selling methods and policies which have been taking place during the past decade.

Operating Management

This field includes the general managerial questions involved in the internal operation of business enterprises, as distinct from corporate and financial administration. Articles dealing in a general way with problems of industrial, scientific, or business management, and with organization and administration are by far the most important in this classification. A number of more specific topics in this field appear also to have drawn considerable attention, among which may be mentioned factory location, construction and operation; purchasing policies; design and development of new or improved products; budget control and cost analysis; methods of handling, packing, and shipping materials; standardization and simplification; inventory control; and safety and accident prevention measures.

The effects of recent changes in managerial methods may be seen again in the literature of this field, and particularly the far-reaching influence of the program of simplification and standardization sponsored during the past decade by the United States Department of Commerce. The valuable service rendered by the business and industrial press in disseminating this information is attested by the appearance of such a great variety of articles on subjects that would hardly have been recognized by name a generation ago.

Finance and Credit

The multitude of individual topics classified under this general heading fall into three major categories. Articles relating to investment and speculation were easily the most numerous, reflecting the widespread general interest in this subject which has been manifest during recent years. Included under this heading are numerous discussions of bonds, stocks, dividend policies, stock exchange activities, investment trusts, brokers' loans, savings, speculation, investment, and thrift, which deal not only with the investment problems of the individual but with the effects of the speculative absorption of funds upon the credit problems of business firms.

Next in importance to this general subject, were articles dealing with general banking problems and developments, especially with the growth of new forms and types of commercial banking institutions and services such as bank consolidations, acceptance banking, group and chain banking, finance and industrial loan companies, land banks, and Federal reserve banking.

Substantial interest also centered in the financial and credit problems of the individual business as reflected in articles on corporate finance, collection of accounts, credits and collections, credit management, installment financing, credit departments, foreign credits, and similar topics. Other important fields of interest included money, interest rates, gold shipments, foreign exchange, bank failures, commercial paper, and trust company functions and activities. Obviously developments in all phases of finance and banking have been of vital concern and interest to the business executive, not only in the conduct of his business but as related to the investment of his own funds.

Transportation and Traffic

Although the amount of space devoted to the discussion of railroad problems and rail transportation exceeded considerably that relating to other phases of this business, the interest of business men in new developments is attested by the multitude of articles on air and motor transportation. While numerous references to street railway problems appeared in the *Industrial Arts Index,* this subject, as well as merchant marine and water and ocean transportation, appeared generally to receive but scant attention in recent periodical literature.

Considerable attention was naturally accorded the subject of industrial traffic management and questions of shipping, freight handling, and transporation rates, as these problems are of vital concern in the conduct of business. In the field of transportation, as in those previously discussed, the attention devoted to various subjects cannot be interpreted as a measure of their intrinsic importance. New and startling developments naturally are of more interest to the reader than are those with which he has long been familiar.

Government and Business

The widespread interest of the general reader in political and governmental affairs, as indicated by the analysis of articles appearing in the *Literary Digest,* is accentuated in the case of business executives because of the far-reaching and increasing influence of the Federal and local governments upon business operations. In view of the importance of Federal regulation of various aspects of business, it is not surprising to find more space devoted to this subject—the activities of the Department of Justice in enforcing the Sherman Law, and the activities of various regulatory bodies such as the Interstate Commerce Commission, the Federal Trade Commission, the Oil Conservation Board, the Federal Radio and Power Commissions, and the Supreme

Court decisions relating to these questions—than to any other subject in this general category.

The vital effect of taxes upon business costs and profits finds reflection in the fact that nearly as much importance in current business literature was attached to the question of corporate and personal taxes and taxation policies of the Federal, state, and local governments. The whole question of law and legislation affecting business, particularly banking, and commercial laws, labor laws, and legislation relating to patents and trade marks, to agricultural relief, and to the tariff are all granted generous attention in current business publications.

The business executive is also interested in questions of economy and efficiency in governmental operation, government finance and especially government and municipal ownership and operation in agriculture and in business. It seems patent that the growing interest of business men in governmental and political affairs, evidenced by the number of articles devoted to these subjects in current publications is merely a reflection of the extensive and increasing influence of governmental activity and regulation upon the success and profitability of business operations both in the United States and in foreign countries.

Personnel and Labor

One indication of the changed attitude of employers toward labor problems is found in the substantial attention directed to industrial relations and related questions in current business literature. Much space is devoted to discussion of employment management and employee relations, with special emphasis on hours of labor, working conditions, labor representation, welfare work, and methods used in the selection and training of employees. With respect to the latter, special interest is manifest in these questions as related to foremen and executives. Quite naturally wages and wage payment systems are matters of primary concern, particularly articles dealing with bonus and incentive systems, employee stock ownership, profit sharing, pensions, insurance, and other financial aspects of industrial relations.

Of an importance somewhat subordinate to the subjects already mentioned were topics relating to strikes and other problems of organized labor, industrial accidents, unemployment, employment stabilization and labor turnover, and workmen's compensation. As is true in the case of other groups of subjects in the general classification shown in Table X, there is considerable overlapping with other categories in this instance, particularly with the field of operating management.

General Economic and Social Problems

Despite the predominant interest of executives in matters bearing directly upon the "practical" concerns which confront them in their daily business operations, a surprising amount of attention is devoted by business journals to discussion of general economic and social questions. Although the content of articles in this rather loosely defined field cover the widest range, the greatest interest recently has centered in the implications involved in the trend toward large corporate units and in the consolidation and merger movement generally. Closely related to these are questions of monopoly, restriction of production, and the control of competition and prices.

Foreign economic developments are apparently of substantial interest to readers of business periodicals as these publications abound in discussion of international debts, reparations, foreign competition with American products, the growth of cartels, and the imposition of tariffs, trade embargoes, and other commercial restrictions. Other topics treated extensively include the tariff, immigration, the cost of living, and to a minor extent, socialism, relations of capital and labor, and the distribution of wealth.

Of course, many of the topics classified under other divisions in Table X and especially under "personnel and labor" and "government and business" possess social implications which might justify their being included under this general category. Quite obviously the typical reader of business publications regards them through the eyes of a practitioner rather than as a social scientist; he is interested primarily in learning about new methods and new ideas in business practice which can be applied successfully to his own business and in new developments which may effect his profits, and only secondarily in the more remote social and economic effects of changing conditions. This being true, it is apparent that the nature of topics in this field treated in business publications probably furnishes an inadequate measure of their intrinsic importance.

Advertising and Publicity

Problems of advertising and publicity, like other phases of distribution, are treated extensively in the general publications addressed to business executives as well as in a number of special journals in this field. Special interest exists in the description and discussion of various types of advertisements and advertising campaigns applied to different fields and products, in the question of advertising costs as related to effectiveness and results, and in advertising ethics. Recent applications of advertising in new fields such as finance and insurance and the development of new methods such as radio advertising also have attracted much interest of late. Direct mail advertising, too, attracts considerable attention, particularly the preparation of mailing lists and sales letters.

Accounting

In spite of its fundamental nature and importance, this field apparently does not present as many problems of current importance which merit extensive consideration in general business literature as several of the other fields. In addition to articles relating to general accounting problems and to the management of accounting departments and offices, the principal emphasis is upon cost accounting, especially the part played by cost accounts in relation to budgeting as an executive control function in business operations. Auditing also was treated quite extensively, as were the subjects of depreciation and the preparation of profit and loss and other financial statements.

Other Subjects

The other subjects listed in Table X were treated much less extensively in the publications analyzed than those already mentioned. Articles on foreign and international trade appeared fairly frequently, with primary emphasis on exporting.

Certain aspects of the statistical and research activities of business firms command considerable attention, notably those dealing with the interpretation of index numbers and other current statistical data and the use of charts and maps and other graphic methods in the presentation of business data. The general purposes and functions of commercial and economic research also received some attention. Closely related to these topics are the topics classified under business conditions and forecasting. The principal interest in this field centered in the interpretation and forecasting of business trends, in the description of methods of forecasting, and in discussions of various theories which attempt to account for the business cycle.

The important subject of insurance apparently presented few problems of current significance as it received but scant attention in these publications during the period under review. Articles on this subject covered a rather wide range, with considerable interest displayed in special forms of life insurance for business men.

The few articles on agriculture dealt chiefly with agricultural conditions as they affected the purchasing power of the farmer, although some space was devoted to the market for farm products, farm relief, agricultural credit conditions, and reclamation and drainage projects.

Little interest was displayed in real estate and building judging from the small amount of space devoted to this subject. Topics of greatest interest included construction conditions, the real estate mortgage business, land values, and the design and location of various types of business structure. Numerous technical articles and books dealing with the engineering aspects of construction were of course not included under this classification.

"Cooperative activities of business" included a number of articles pertaining to trade association activities and problems, codes of business ethics, industrial and commercial arbitration, settlement of trade disputes, business conferences and agreements, and other aspects of the self-regulation of business. Primary interest in this field apparently centered in the problems of trade associations and in the development of business standards and ethical codes.

Among the miscellaneous subjects pertaining to business, but not important enough to be classified separately in Table X, the most important had reference to the use of business English, i.e. the preparation of reports, correspondence, sales letters, and particularly to public speaking. The emphasis upon this last subject confirms evidence obtained from other sources as to the importance in business of capacity for effective oral presentation. There were also numerous articles in these publications on the various uses of psychology in business—"character analysis," "industrial psychology," "personality development," and similar subjects.

These subjects, discussed above, comprise more than 98 per cent of the material classified in Table X. It should be emphasized, however, that only the topics appearing in these publications which related to the economic or commercial aspects of business operations were included in the analysis. The *Industrial Arts Index*, particularly, contained a multitude of references to scientific and technological matters which were not properly included within the field of business literature. Moreover, articles dealing with manufacturing or marketing problems of specific industries or commodities, of which there were a great number, likewise were not included.

It is believed, however, that this analysis provides a fairly adequate indication of the major problems of current significance confronting American business executives during the past few years, in so far as these matters have been reflected in typical and representative business publications.

Obviously there can be no assumption that the space devoted to these subjects in current business literature is in any sense an accurate measure of their intrinsic importance in the operation of business enterprises. Even if this were true it would be the height of absurdity to contend that a business curriculum should duplicate the content of business literature. The executive reads primarily for informational purposes; his reading interests are shaped and directed by the nature of the problems and questions which confront him daily.

A university curriculum, on the other hand, has many objectives more important than that of providing students with information. Information is useful in the university mainly for illustrative purposes, and in order to provide students with fundamental "background" knowledge of various fields upon which they can base an understanding of trends, developments, and inter-relationships. As to the nature of these important current developments and problems, however, business literature should furnish some indication. In this respect, therefore, it seem probable that .

examination of the content of business publications may be of some use in building a curriculum for a collegiate school of business.

READING AND STUDY COURSES FOR BUSINESS MEN

Like almost every other aspect of modern life, economic and social, the reading done by business men has been "organized." A generation ago, when business literature first began to appear in noticeable volume and correspondence schools commenced to flourish, a varied assortment of special sets of business books known as "executives' libraries," "business men's reading courses," etc., appeared in the market in response to a real and extensive demand from business men for information and ideas on the problems and practices of business.

This demand has continued, albeit in somewhat diminished volume, to the present day, and apparently reflects a real need on the part of younger executives and others, particularly those who have not had the advantage of a higher education, for a better understanding of the fundamentals of business. Obviously, much of this material, shallow in nature and superficial in content, is quite inadequate to meet the needs and demands for which it is prepared. Admitting this, however, the titles and content of the books included in such "libraries" and courses do cast some light upon the character of the information and training which the readers of these books believe they need. The publisher is striving to print something that will sell, i.e., fill a real or fancied need. The buyer wants something which will help him to succeed in business. Both may be wrong, but their opinions, recognized as opinions, are of some significance in a study of this sort.

Like general business literature, these courses usually place primary emphasis upon practical and applied information relating to the major functions of business. Usually some attempt is made at the outset to orient the reader in the general field of business by a volume of some such title as *"Economics and the Individual,"* or *"Practical Economics."* Then follow studies of business administration, organization of business, business management, of similar subjects. The major functions of business—production, marketing, finance, and accounting, usually are accorded separate treatment, even in the shorter courses. The more exhaustive courses include a variety of volumes on the more specialized and detailed phases of business such as insurance, foreign trade, credits and collections, advertising, business correspondence, factory management, transportation, foreign exchange, labor problems, real estate, and a host of other subjects quite similar to those offered in collegiate schools of business.

In addition to these specific business subjects, many reading courses devote much space to discussion of the individual's personal development. Some of them presume to tell him how to "build character," "develop mental ability" or "will-power," utilize his time to the best advantage, or keep himself physically fit, but these are in the minority. Somewhat less ambitious, but responding to very real and evident needs, are volumes devoted to public speaking, to leadership, and to the technique of thinking in business, i.e., the solving of business problems. Representative of the better type of such courses, and one which has found an extensive market among business executives, is "The Business Executive's Library."[11] The titles of the seven books included in this library—*Practical Economics; Fundamentals of Business Organization; Forecasting, Planning, and Budgeting in Business Management; Personal Leadership in Industry; The Business Man and His Bank; How to Think in Business; and Public Speaking for Business Men*—are in themselves suggestive of what appear to be the major problems and concerns which confront the general administrative executive.

Much more elaborate in scope, but of a somewhat different nature, is the correspondence course which has been long and successfully offered by the Alexander Hamilton Institute. During the 20 years of its existence, the Institute states that 400,000 persons have enrolled for the course—certainly a potent indication of the demand for information and training in the field of business. The fundamental aim of the course is to provide a general business training, the purpose being stated by the Institute in the following words:

---

[11] McGraw-Hill Book Co., Inc., New York. The authors of these books in the order designated are as follows: Henry P. Shearman, Webster Robinson, Percival White, David R. Craig and W. W. Charters, William H. Kniffin, Mathew T. McClure, and William G. Hoffman.

1. Better understanding of sound business principles.
2. Ability to plan effectively.
3. Increased confidence in handling business problems.
4. Ability to make quicker and more accurate decisions.
5. More leisure for recreation and constructive thought.
6. Increased ability to handle men.
7. Insurance against mistakes.

For many years the content remained basically the same except for an expansion in the attention devoted to the fields of marketing and advertising, to investment finance, and to business organization and management. During the past year a significant change has been made in the organization of this work, with provision for a degree of specialization in the following "four fundamental fields":

1. *Production and operations*—including office administration, plant management, and cost finding.

2. *Marketing*—including advertising, merchandising, transportation, foreign trade, and correspondence.

3. *Finance*—including credits and collections, corporate finance, insurance, and commercial credit.

4. *Accounting*—including statistics and record keeping.

Although thus recognizing the increasing functionalization of executive duties with the growth of large-scale enterprises, the course still appreciates the need for basic training in the fundamentals of business and economics.

Significant in the classification shown above is the consolidation under each of these "fundamental fields" of subjects and departments frequently existing separately in university business schools. Thus the field of production includes also that of operating management of other types of business and cost finding; marketing includes advertising, transportation, and foreign trade; finance includes also insurance; and the field of accounting, in accordance with the usual departmental administration of this function in most business organizations, includes also statistics.

The Institute, under the new plan, offers a short course in "The Business Fundamentals," involving the study of the following texts: *Business and the Man, Commercial Law, Marketing and Merchandising, Business Correspondence, Business Organization,*

Corporation Finance, Accounting Principles, Insurance, Investments, and *Economics—The Science of Business.* In addition there is offered the general business course, using the texts indicated below, and three special management courses, viz., marketing, finance, and production. The following ten text-books are used in the general business course and in each of the three specialized courses, and therefore represent the judgment of the Institute as to the subjects or studies which are of pervasive importance in all phases of business:

Business Organization	Business Correspondence
Commercial Law	Insurance
Marketing	Real Estate
Accounting Principles	Personnel Management
Corporation Finance	Budgetary Control

The titles of the additional texts used, and the course or courses in which each is included, are shown below:

Texts	Courses		
Credit and Collections	Marketing	Finance	General
Salesmanship	"	"	"
Advertising Principles	"		"
Advertising Campaigns	"		"
Sales Management	"		"
Foreign Trade	"		"
Retail Advertising	"		
Marketing Geography	"		
Financial and Business Statements	Production	"	"
Investments	"	"	"
Banking		"	"
Corporate Consolidation and Reorganization		"	"
Financial and Business Forecasting		"	"
The Stock and Commodity Exchanges		"	
Factory Management	"		"
Cost Finding	"		"
Office Administration	"		"
Transportation	"		"
Production Control and Time and Motion Study	"		
Purchasing and Storing	"		
Economics			"

Obviously the general plan of these curricula does not differ greatly from the program of business subjects followed in many collegiate schools of commerce. Certain features, however, are of particular interest. It is noteworthy, for instance, that the ten "core" subjects required in all four of the curricula include certain fields such as insurance, real estate, personnel management, and budgetary control, which are not now universally required in most collegiate schools. Credits and collections and salesmanship are evidently adjudged to be of substantial importance in both the marketing and finance curricula since they are required in both. Study of financial and business statements, and of investments are included in the production management as well as the finance course. Transportation is included in the production course but not in the other specialized curricula.

Manifestly no profound significance may be attached to the content and scope of this or other correspondence courses offered to business men. They constitute only one among the many objective indications of what the educational needs and demands of business may be. Like general business literature, this material merely represents the best judgment of the publishers as to what the business men for whose eyes it is intended think they need and are willing to purchase.

Summary and Conclusions

1. In view of the prodigious increase in the volume and diversity of current literature devoted to the needs of business and the increasing attention in general periodicals to discussion of business and economic problems, it is evident that an analysis of the content of this literature should help to indicate the outstanding current problems in this field which should merit attention in the collegiate business curriculum.

2. Despite the vastness of the literature catering to the needs of business executives, it is clear that, as a class, they read widely, but not thoroughly or reflectively, devoting only a few minutes a day to professional and technical articles in books and magazines. Reading interests of this group appear generally to be highly specialized, being concerned chiefly with informational articles bearing on business conditions as they affect their own industries, governmental affairs affecting the economic situation, new equipment and materials, and new processes and methods.

3. Analysis of the topics treated in a weekly magazine appealing to the general reader, the *Literary Digest,* during a period of 36 years, shows that political, diplomatic, and military affairs, particularly foreign and international aspects of these questions, were of primary importance, with 26 per cent of all articles devoted to them. Literary, philosophical, and artistic interests, con-

stituting more than 18 per cent of the total, were second in importance, while business and economic affairs, and social problems and interests followed, with 13 per cent of all articles devoted to each of these two fields. The remaining articles treated of scientific and technological matters, of the biological and human sciences, and of personal items. This analysis, reflecting widespread and vital interest in developments within the fields of political science, economics, and sociology, would seem to imply that any university curriculum, especially one which aims to prepare young men for business and public service, should direct substantial attention to these subjects.

4. An appraisal of the relative importance attached to various fields in current business literature was obtained from the topical references in the *Industrial Arts Index* and *Business Books: 1920-1926,* and from articles appearing during recent years in two general business magazines, *Nation's Business* and the *Magazine of Business.* This analysis shows that, on the whole, articles relating to marketing, to operating management, and to finance and credit, in the order named, were the most numerous. The relative rank of the remaining subjects was approximately in the following order: transportation and traffic, government and business, personnel and labor, general economic problems, advertising and publicity, accounting, foreign trade, statistics and research, insurance, agriculture, cooperation and business ethics, business conditions, and real estate.

5. The topics which seem to have been among the most important in each of the principal fields mentioned above, as indicated by the number of articles appearing thereon, are as follows:

> *Marketing:* Salesmanship; training of salesmen; sales management; retail merchandising; chain stores; pricing policies; price cutting; resale price fixing; installment selling; market analysis; hand-to-mouth buying; inter-commodity competition.
>
> *Operating Management:* Industrial and scientific management; factory location, construction, and operation; purchasing policies; design of new products; budget control and cost analysis; handling, packing, and shipping materials; standardization and simplification; inventory control; and safety and accident prevention.

Finance and credit: Investment and speculation; dividend policies; investment trusts and broker's loans. Banking developments; bank consolidations; acceptance banking; group and chain banking; industrial loan companies; land banks; and Federal reserve banking. Corporate finance; credits and collections; credit management; installment financing; and foreign credits. Money; interest rates; gold shipments; foreign exchange; bank failures; commercial paper; and trust company functions.

Transportation and traffic: Railroad problems; air transsportation; motor transportation; street railway problems; shipping; freight handling; and transportation rates.

Government and business: Government regulation of business; activities of regulatory commissions; taxes and taxation policies; banking, commercial, labor legislation; Federal agricultural relief; governmental budget, economy, and efficiency; and government ownership and operation.

Personnel and labor: Employee management; hours of labor; working conditions; labor representation; welfare work; selection and training of employees; wages; wage payment systems; bonus and incentive systems; employee stock ownership; profit sharing; pensions; insurance; strikes; problems of organized labor; unemployment; employment stabilization; labor turnover; and workmen's compensation.

General economic and social problems: Consolidation and merger movement; monopoly; restriction of production; control of competition and prices; foreign economic developments; international debts and reparations; cartels; tariffs and trade embargoes; immigration; cost of living; capital and labor; socialism; and questions of the distribution of wealth.

Advertising and publicity: Advertisements and advertising campaigns; advertising costs; advertising ethics; radio advertising; direct mail advertising; preparation of mailing lists; and application of advertising to new fields and new products.

Accounting: General accounting problems; management of accounting offices; cost accounting; auditing; budgeting; depreciation; valuation; and financial statements.

6. The nature and content of the great variety of organized reading and study courses, designed for busines men, furnishes another indication of the kind of training demanded by the younger executives who have not had the advantages of a university education. These courses usually aim to furnish practical and applied information on the general background of economics and on the major functions of business, such as production, mar-

keting, finance, and accounting, while the more exhaustive courses involve treatment of the more specialized and detailed phases of business. Of much greater significance, however, is the emphasis which most of these courses place upon the personal development of the individual—personal leadership, public speaking, the technique of thinking in business, personal efficiency—thus confirming the opinions expressed by business executives and graduates of collegiate schools of business that personal and mental traits are far more important determinants of success than mere knowledge of the practices and principles of business.

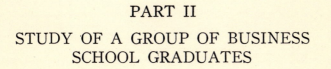

PART II

STUDY OF A GROUP OF BUSINESS SCHOOL GRADUATES

CHAPTER V

OCCUPATIONAL PREFERENCES AND UNDER-GRADUATE TRAINING[1]

More than six thousand men have been granted the degree of Bachelor of Science in Economics by the Wharton School of Finance and Commerce since its founding at the University of Pennsylvania in 1881. Despite its long history, characterized by a very considerable growth of student and faculty personnel and the addition of many new subjects to the curriculum during the half century of its existence, the fundamental aim and purpose of the school have remained the same, i.e., to afford its students liberal training in subjects of general educational value and professional training for careers in business and public service. Thus, this large group of alumni, drawn from every part of the United States and from many foreign countries, with the widest variety of social and economic antecedents, and with an extensive range in present maturity and experience, possesses a common background of training at this institution.

Purpose and Scope of Inquiry

Such a group offers an unusual opportunity for a study of alumni experience and opinion in relation to undergraduate training for business. Of course it would be absurd to attempt an evaluation of the effectiveness of university training for business or for any other vocation solely upon the basis of the opinions and occupational experience of the graduates. It would be as reasonable to assume that the patient is the best judge of the success or failure of the doctor's efforts or that his physical condition upon leaving the hospital was conclusive evidence of the efficacy of medical treatment. The patient might have recovered without the aid of doctors, nurses, and hospitals; he may have recovered in spite of their ministrations. Nature is the silent partner of every physician, and nature likewise contributes an unknown share to the success or failure of our educational experiments.

---

[1] Prepared and written by J. Frederic Dewhurst.

[153]

WHARTON SCHOOL OF FINANCE AND COMMERCE

UNIVERSITY OF PENNSYLVANIA

ALUMNI RECORD SHEET

Undergraduate Occupational History

1. Did you defray any part of your undergraduate college expenses through employment? (Check) Yes ☐ .No ☐

2. If "Yes" please state explicitly the nature of such employment in each year and the approximate percentage of expenses thus defrayed:

Year	Nature of employment	Percentage defrayed
First		
Second		
Third		
Fourth		

3. When you *entered* college did you have some specific phase of business in mind for which you expected to prepare yourself? (Check) Yes ☐ No ☐.

4. If "Yes," what was this phase of business?...................

5. If "Yes" to item 3, check on the following list the chief reason for your preference for that phase of business at that time. (Check only one reason.)   (Check)
   a. Special interest in it.............................. ☐
   b. Special ability for it.............................. ☐
   c. Family connection with it......................... ☐
   d. Urge or influence of family or others............. ☐
   e. Economic possibilities without reference to any of the
      above .... ☐
   f. Other (Please state)............................. ☐

6. If "No" to item 3, did you decide on some specific phase of business?
   a. By the beginning of your Junior year? (Check) Yes ☐ No ☐.
   b. Before you graduated? (Check) Yes ☐ No ☐.

7. At the time you made your decision, had you had experience in that phase of business? (Check) Yes ☐ No ☐.

8. Are you now following that specific occupation? (Check) **Yes** ☐ No ☐.

9. If "No," are you in a closely allied field? (Check) Yes ☐ No ☐.

10. Check the *chief* reason or basis on which you chose your **first** occupation after leaving college. (Check only one reason.)

(Check)

a. Special interest in it.............................. ☐
b. Special ability for it.............................. ☐
c. Family connection with it.......................... ☐
d. Urge or influence of family or others.............. ☐
e. Attractive beginning salary without reference to a, b, c, or d.. ☐
f. Opportunity for advancement without reference to a, b, c, or d.. ☐
g. Geographic location................................ ☐
h. Only position available............................ ☐
i. Other (Please state) .... ☐

11. Did you have any pre-college experience in the work of **your** *present* occupation? (Check) Yes ☐ No ☐.

Occupational History Since Graduation

12. Please give fully the information requested below concerning your present position:

a. Name and address of firm.................................
b. Business of firm...
c. Official title and description of your position...............
....
d. How many employees are directly under your supervision and authority? ....
e. Indicate approximately your present annual earned income by using one of the following symbols:....(Check)

A	B	C	D	E	F	G	H

A—Less than $2000
B—$2000 to $2999
C—$3000 to $3999
D—$4000 to $4999

E—$5000 to $5999
F—$6000 to $8999
G—$9000 to $11,999
H—$12,000 and over

13. Please give specifically and fully the information asked below consecutively for each of the positions you have held since graduation, whether or not your successive positions were held with the same or different firms:

Name of firm	Business of firm	Position held	Period of employment		First and last salary in each position (Use symbols indicated above)	
			From	To	First	Last

Educational Training Since Graduation

14. Please give below the information requested concerning any courses of instruction (such as night school, correspondence school, post-graduate college work, or courses given by employer) you may have taken since graduation:

Courses studied	Name and type of institution offering courses	Approximate number of hours devoted to course

15. What specific need caused you to enroll in the above courses? (Check only one reason.)

         (Check)

a. Desire for advancement .... ☐
b. Prepare for other occupation or position........... ☐
c. Desire to establish business or personal contacts.... ☐
d. General education interest other than above........ ☐
e. Other (Please state)............................. ☐

Appraisal of Undergraduate Training

16. Below you will find seven outstanding fields of knowledge usually covered in the curricula of existing collegiate schools of business. This classification is intended merely to provide a simplified grouping for the multitude of separate courses offered and topics treated in such institutions. Please consider these fields in the light of the explanations given, rather than in terms of specific courses which you may have studied. Using the scale of rating indicated below,* please express your judgment of the importance which each group should occupy in a curriculum for the Wharton School. In addition to this rating, the reader may underscore specific subjects listed under each group which he thinks should be emphasized. The fields of knowledge previously referred to are given below:

Please read over the descriptions of all fields before attempting to rate any one field.

*Scale of Rating

A—Of primary importance   D—Of subordinate importance
B—Highly desirable   E—Of doubtful value
C—Desirable

I. MEDIA OF COMMUNICATION

    A. ENGLISH LANGUAGE........... (Check)

A	B	C	D	E

        Studies and practice in the oral and written use of the English language, including such subjects as Composition, Business English, Public Speaking, Report Writing, etc.

    B. FOREIGN LANGUAGES.......... (Check)

A	B	C	D	E

        Studies of modern foreign languages such as French, Spanish, German, Italian, etc.

II. METHODS OF MEASUREMENT...... (Check)

A	B	C	D	E

    Study of methods of measurement and mathematical analysis including such subjects as Algebra, Trigonometry, Business Mathematics, Statistics, Accounting, etc.

III. BACKGROUND OF THE PHYSICAL SCIENCES .... (Check)

A	B	C	D	E

    Fundamental descriptive studies of the physical and technological background upon which human and business activities are developed. This would include such subjects as Physical Geography, Geology, Chemistry, Physics, Biology, etc.

IV. SOCIAL SETTING OF BUSINESS LIFE. (Check) 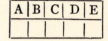 Studies of the structure, functioning and historical development of the political and socio-economic institutions, practices, and customs within which business functions. This includes most of the work usually given in Political Science, Sociology, and Business Law.

V. DESCRIPTIVE ANALYSIS OF BUSINESS ACTIVITIES................(Check)

A	B	C	D	E

Studies which describe and interpret the basic activities in which business men are engaged and their interrelations. The emphasis in these studies is placed upon an understanding of the phenomena of business rather than upon the administration of business activities. This includes material which appears in whole, or in part, in many different courses now given in the Wharton School. Among these courses are Economics, Manufacturing, Transportation, Merchandising, Money and Banking, Financial Organization of Society, Business Cycles, etc.

VI. ADMINISTRATION OF BUSINESS ACTIVITIES ....(Check)

A	B	C	D	E

Studies which aim specifically to train in the managerial administration of various kinds of business activities. This involves courses given under the title of Sales Administration, Industrial Management, Corporate Organization and Control, Steamship Traffic Management, Bank Administration, etc.

VII. Studies Broadly Interpretative . (Check)
This includes courses dealing in
a broad, cultural way with man's
history, thought, philosophy, behavior, literary and artistic pursuits, such as Philosophy, Psychology, Literature, Art,
Architecture, Logic, Ethics, etc.

A	B	C	D	E

17. Please indicate below the nature of any extra-curricular campus activities in which you engaged and positions you held while an undergraduate:

Athletic ....

Literary, dramatic, and musical organizations ....

....

....

Publications ....

Class positions ....

Fraternity and fraternity activity ....

....

18. In what ways have your campus activities been of direct value to you in your business and social life since graduation? ......

....

....

....

....

19. What further comment would you make on the basis of your experience since graduation as to

a. The courses offered by the Wharton School? ....

....

....

b. The emphasis given to various subjects? ....

....

....

c. The methods of instruction employed? ....

....

....

Students come to an educational institution with a diverse heritage of intelligence and inborn capacity and from a wide variety of environmental backgrounds. And they have but four brief years during which the university helps to influence their development. They then enter upon business careers or other occupations where personal traits, native ability, and opportunity probably play a larger part than formal education in determining their future progress. But they have received their certificates of competence; they are the finished products of the educational process. As such they are entitled to the right to testify. Not as experts in education, but as lay witnesses, their opinions concerning their college training and their occupational experience since graduation are entitled to consideration in any attempt to appraise collegiate training for business or for any other occupation.

The success of such a study of alumni experience and opinion depends upon the voluntary cooperation of a large number of individuals, and the accompanying questionnaire was prepared as one which would meet the minimum need for information and also ensure an adequate number of replies. To avoid misinterpretation questions were phrased as simply and explicitly as possible and were so devised that replies could be made with a minimum of effort. Although the desirability of obtaining much more complete information was recognized, it was apparent that if adequate sampling of alumni experience and opinions was to be obtained the inquiry would have to be limited to a comparatively short questionnaire. The questions were devised to supply four classes of information which might help to illuminate and aid in solving the teaching and curriculum problems of the Wharton School and, perhaps, similar problems of other business schools:

1. *Undergraduate occupational history.* These questions were intended to disclose the kind of vocational motivation which influenced students to matriculate in this institution, their occupational preferences and the reasons therefor, the amount of business experience obtained either before matriculation or during the college term, and the reasons for choosing the first job after graduation. Such information presumably has a bearing upon the type of curriculum which might be offered, the extent of

vocational specialization which should be encouraged or permitted, and the possible success of such educational experiments as the cooperative plan, which attempts to coordinate classroom instruction with student employment.

2. *Occupational history since graduation.* This inquiry was expected to furnish an approximate record of the occupational careers of the alumni and some information concerning the positions they now hold. It cannot be assumed, of course, that the effectiveness of a university course can be measured by the business success of its graduates. But so far as the vocational aspects of business school education are concerned, some idea of the nature of the problems can be obtained from a knowledge of the positions held by graduates and of the kinds of business work in which they have been and are engaged.

3. *Educational training since graduation.* The purpose of these questions was to discover the extent to which the graduates have supplemented university study by further formal educational training since graduation, the nature of courses studied, and the reasons for taking such work. Such information may help to reveal deficiencies or needs in the undergraduate curriculum and might indicate the possibility of a continuing relationship between the university school of business and its graduates.

4. *Appraisal of undergraduate training.* By this inquiry it was hoped to obtain a reliable and adequate reflection of the mature judgment of the graduates concerning the relative importance of various broad fields of study offered in the curriculum, the effectiveness of teaching methods and materials, and the value of extracurricular activities. Obviously a university should be administered primarily to meet the needs, and only secondarily to meet the wishes, of its students and graduates. By offering elective courses and permitting specialization, however, university curricula generally do respect the wishes of the undergraduate. Therefore, it seems evident that the more mature opinions of these same students after graduation merit some attention in considering curriculum and teaching problems.

Representativeness of Replies

Copies of the questionnaire were mailed in May, 1929, to all graduates of the 41 classes from 1888 to 1928 inclusive, a total of 5,751. Nearly two-fifths of the entire group, including members of every class, graduates of all courses, and men now holding a great variety of positions, eventually returned questionnaires with the information requested. Because many were received too late for inclusion, the present analysis is based upon replies from 1,670 alumni, or 29 per cent of the entire number. The earlier classes are well represented, as is indicated in Table XI,

TABLE XI. NUMBER OF GRADUATES REPLYING TO QUESTIONNAIRE

Classes	Total number of graduates	Number of replies	Proportion replying
1928	573	236	41.2%
1927	569	185	32.5
1926	498	147	29.5
1925	579	156	26.9
1924	570	188	33.0
1923	522	135	25.9
1921–22	721	212	29.4
1919–20	445	124	27.9
1917–18	223	55	24.7
1914–16	336	85	25.3
1911–13	216	43	19.9
1905–10	235	50	21.3
1899–04	105	25	23.8
1888–98	159	29	18.2
All classes	5,751	1,670	29.0%

although, as might be expected, a larger proportion of replies were received from the more recent graduates. Owing to the small size of many of the earlier graduating classes, their replies were grouped together for purposes of analysis as shown in the table. It is of course impossible to determine how representative are the opinions and experience of these 1,670 men, but it seems reasonable to assume that a sample of this size would show but slight variation from the entire group. A comparison of the scholarship records of a number of men selected at random from those replying to the questionnaire with records for all students in the same classes showed a close correspondence. But it seems likely that the graduates who have met with the least success in their business careers would be more reluctant to reply, especially to questions regarding present salary and business position. This would probably be more true of the earlier than of the later classes. It seems logical to assume then that this inquiry records the opinions and experience of graduates of average scholarship, but, perhaps, of better-than-average business success.

Occupational Motives for Entering College

Vocational motives are predominant, doubtless, in the minds of students enrolling in the Wharton School as in other business, engineering, and professional schools. There is ample evidence that the great majority of students enrolling in this school do so primarily to prepare for a vocation, although many other motives are present to a minor extent. In reply to a question concerning the reasons for coming to college submitted to the 1928 graduating class,[2] 70 per cent indicated that the "decisive reason in your own mind why you first came to college" was "to prepare for a vocation," although many of this group also cited additional reasons. Thirty per cent stated that they came primarily to get a "liberal education," but since they enrolled in a school of business rather than a liberal arts college, doubtless they also were actuated by vocational motives, differing from the other group in their opinions as to the best means of preparing for life and work after graduation. These reasons mentioned above were the most important, although some students frankly attributed their decision to enter college to the desire for prestige, to be with old friends or to make new ones, for "college life" and athletics, to please parents, or because it was "the thing to do." Inasmuch as these students enrolled in an institution offering training for business, law, and public service it is to be expected that their vocational choices would fall within these fields.

Analysis of the replies received from 1,670 Wharton School graduates who returned the questionnaire showed that 947, or 56.7 per cent of the total number, before they entered college, had selected a specific phase of business for which they wished to prepare themselves. By the beginning of the junior year an additional 12.9 per cent had made a selection, while all but 17.8 per cent had decided on an occupation before graduation. The tendency toward an early occupational choice was more pronounced among the earlier classes. Of the six classes graduating between 1899 and 1904, 84 per cent had made a decision before matriculation, while the average proportion was 60.8 per cent for

---

[2] This information was not obtained from the alumni questionnaire described above but as part of a general examination given to the 1928 graduating class.

all classes from 1888 to 1922, as compared with only 54.2 per cent for the last six graduating classes.

The contrast between these two groups of alumni—those of the last six classes, and those graduating prior to 1923—is significant. Examination of other data obtained from the questionnaires showed similar differences between the earlier and the later graduates. Apparently the year 1923, which witnessed a substantial increase in the size of the graduating class, was somewhat in the nature of a dividing line between the pre-war and war period and the post-war era, in the development of the Wharton School. For this reason, in many of the subsequent tabulations, the replies have been classified into two groups, the first including those graduating in the classes from 1888 to 1922, and the second, classes from 1923 to 1928.

Reasons for Occupational Preference

An examination of the reasons given for occupational preference helps to explain why a larger proportion of the earlier classes made a specific choice of a business occupation before entering college. Table XII shows the principal reasons accounting for

TABLE XII. REASONS FOR OCCUPATIONAL PREFERENCES

	All classes	1888–1922	1923–1928
Number of graduates	1,670	623	1,047
Number stating preference	947	379	568
Proportion of all graduates stating a preference	56.7%	60.8%	54.2%
Proportion giving various reasons:			
Special interest and ability	26.9	26.1	27.3
Family connection and influence	24.0	30.7	20.0
Economic possibilities	4.0	2.9	4.6
Other reasons	1.8	1.1	2.3

the occupational choices reported by men who had selected a specific phase of business before entering college.

All but a small percentage attribute their vocational choices to special interest and ability or to family connection or influence; the latter reason has become noticeably less important among the later classes. Evidently, in recent years, a relatively smaller number of students have been preparing for the responsibilities of family business. One-fifth of the students in the last six classes were probably preparing for a position in a family firm, as compared with 30.7 per cent of the classes graduating prior to 1923. This change is only partly due to the rise of corporations and the decline of family firms, but also to the fact that a larger proportion of the student body in recent years has been drawn from families of the employee, rather than the employer class. This tendency may have some bearing upon the question as to whether or not intensive specialization should be encouraged in an undergraduate school of business.

Previous Occupational Experience

A moderately large proportion—42.9 per cent—of those making a vocational choice before entering college reported previous experience in the phase of business selected. Table XIII shows

TABLE XIII. PROPORTION OF GRADUATES EXPRESSING PREFERENCE WHO HAD PREVIOUS EXPERIENCE IN FIELD CHOSEN

Reason for choice	All classes	1888–1922	1923–1928
Special interest and ability..........................	37.9%	40.1%	36.6%
Family connection and influence......................	54.2	53.3	44.9
Economic possibilities.............................	16.7	17.6	16.3
Other reasons.....................................	31.8	*	23.5
All reasons..	42.9%	45.7%	41.0%

* Too few cases to be significant.

the percentage of the graduates who had had experience in the phase of business selected by them before entering college, classified according to reasons for their choice of a particular occupation.

It is evident that a relatively smaller number of recent graduates had had previous experience in the kind of business chosen at the time of entrance. This is chiefly attributable to a decline in the importance of family connection and influence as a determinant of occupational choice. Only a small fraction of those drawn to their chosen occupations by attractive earnings and opportunities had had previous experience.

PHASE OF BUSINESS SELECTED

The vocational preferences of its students are of course a matter of considerable importance to the collegiate school of business in administering the curriculum. In most four-year schools considerable latitude is allowed the student in the choice of courses, presumably for the purpose of permitting vocational specialization. In some cases this tendency has gone to the point of establishing separate schools offering complete curricula in particular areas of the general field of business. Specialization, entirely aside from its vocational aims, serves certain general educational purposes, and its advantages and disadvantages cannot be appraised solely on the grounds of its usefulness in training for specific business professions or occupations.

However, so far as the vocational function of specialization is concerned, it would seem fair to examine it in the light of the vocational preferences of students and the extent to which they followed their original choices in selecting a field of special study

TABLE XIV. OCCUPATIONAL PREFERENCES OF GRADUATES UPON
ENTERING COLLEGE

	All classes	1888–1922	1923–1928
Number of graduates	1,670	623	1,047
Proportion not expressing preference	43.3%	39.2%	45.8%
Proportion having preference	56.7	60.8	54.2
Accounting	9.5	8.8	9.9
Marketing	9.2	8.8	9.5
Manufacturing	7.2	10.1	5.5
Commercial finance	6.1	7.2	5.4
Investment finance	3.0	2.4	3.3
Insurance	2.3	1.9	2.6
Foreign trade	2.3	1.8	2.7
Advertising	2.0	2.4	1.8
Real estate and building	1.6	1.5	1.7
Transportation	1.1	0.9	1.1
Public utilities	0.1	0.2	0.1
Other*	12.3	14.8	10.6

* Includes law, teaching, and other non-business and business occupations.

in college and an occupation after graduation. It will be remembered that somewhat less than half of all those replying did not state a preference for a particular phase of business at the time of enrollment. The distribution of occupational choices among the principal phases of business designated by the 56.7 per cent of all graduates who stated a preference is shown in Table XIV.

Accounting and marketing have been the largest single fields of interest to students entering this school. Practically a third of the graduates having a vocational preference, or 18.7 per cent of all graduates replying, planned to enter one or the other of these fields, while manufacturing, commercial finance, investment finance, and insurance, together, accounted for an equal additional number. Differences in business preference between the earlier and later classes are significant. Although manufacturing and commercial finance are attracting fewer of the students in recent classes, accounting, marketing, investment banking, insurance, and foreign trade are fields which are evidently proving more popular. It must be remembered, however, that nearly half of all students had no definite occupational preference when they entered school, hence the total number selecting these eleven major fields of business was only 44.4 per cent of all the men included in the survey.

RELATION BETWEEN OCCUPATIONAL PREFERENCE AND
COURSE OF STUDY

The Wharton School provides the opportunity for specialized training by permitting each student, prior to the beginning of his second year, to select from a number of groups of courses one which conforms to his occupational objectives. For the ensuing three years the student follows the program prescribed for his "group." It may be of interest to consider the question of vocational preference in relation to the undergraduate fields of study followed by the men replying to this questionnaire.

In Table XV is shown the distribution of the 1,047 alumni in the last six classes among the phases of business for which they expressed a preference, compared with the distribution of this group of students among the various course groupings. Some combinations of courses and of vocational preferences were made for the sake of comparability.

The most noteworthy fact evident in this table is that almost half of the total number had formed no preference for a specific phase of business at the time of entering school, while nearly as many (although not necessarily the identical students), enrolled in the general course, which is adapted to the needs of men who have not selected a field of specialization. The general course also appeals to a considerable number of students who, although they may have a definite preference for a specific phase of business, wish to escape some of the more restricted course requirements of other groups.

This tendency for the general course or its equivalent to absorb half or more of the students is true not only of this institution but of other similar undergraduate schools of business. Moreover, the organization of the curriculum and the educational administration of most university schools of business does not as yet encourage—although offering ample opportunity for—very extensive vocational specialization. This is in sharp contrast to the situation in most of the engineering schools, where students are usually required to select one of the principal branches of engineering early in their undergraduate careers.

TABLE XV. COMPARISON OF OCCUPATIONAL PREFERENCE AND FIELD OF SPECIALIZATION

Occupational preference and field of specialization	Proportion of total	
	Expressing preference	Selecting specialized curriculum
Phase of business not selected.......................	45.8%	
General curriculum................................		41.9%
Accounting field..................................	9.9	
Account.ng curriculum.............................		11.4
Commercial finance and real estate field.............	7.1	
Banking and real estate curriculum..................		5.2
Marketing and advertising field.....................	11.3	
Merchandising curriculum..........................		8.9
Manufacturing field...............................	5.5	
Manufacturing and labor management curriculum.......		3.3
Investment finance field...........................	3.3	
Corporation finance and investments; and brokerage curricula.......................................		1.9
Insurance field...................................	2.6	
Insurance curriculum..............................		2.6
Foreign trade field................................	2.7	
Preparation for foreign trade curriculum.............		3.5
Transportation field...............................	1.1	
Commerce and transportation curriculum.............		1.5
Other fields......................................	10.7	
Journalism; preparation for law; public service and civic work, and social economy curricula..............		19.8
Total..	100.0%	100.0%

RELATION OF OCCUPATIONAL PREFERENCE, FIELD OF SPECIALIZATION, AND PRESENT OCCUPATION

The existence of detailed occupational and educational data for the persons covered in this survey makes it possible to discover with what consistency students expressing business choices before they entered school adhered to these early preferences during their subsequent college and business careers. A total of 742 men, distributed as shown in Table XVI, had expressed definite preferences for the ten fields of business there indicated. The second column shows the percentage of each group who, during their college career, pursued the specialized course groupings corresponding to their vocational choices, while the third and fourth columns respectively, show the proportion whose first job and whose present job, is in the same phase of business as that originally selected at the time of entering college.

Less than half of this group followed their original preferences in their undergraduate fields of specialization, while not more than the same proportion adhered to their original choice in the occupations followed after graduation. A far larger proportion of the students stating a preference for accounting fol-

TABLE XVI. DISTRIBUTION OF STUDENTS STATING PREFERENCE FOR
SPECIFIC PHASE OF BUSINESS

Phase of business*	Number stating preference	Proportion of number stating preference who:		
		Followed corresponding field of specialization†	Held first position in same business	Hold present position in same business
Accounting............	159	72.2%	47.8%	42.1%
Marketing............	154	35.7	57.8	58.5
Manufacturing........	121	28.9	52.1	46.3
Commercial finance.....	101	56.4‡	37.6	47.5
Investment finance.....	50		50.0	52.0
Insurance.............	39	54.8	79.5	84.6
Foreign trade..........	39	63.2	23.1	20.5
Advertising...........	34	60.9	32.4	38.2
Real estate...........	27	33.3	55.5	59.2
Transportation........	18	54.5	50.0	33.3
Total—10 fields........	742	48.5%	49.0%	48.9%

* First and present jobs are classified according to kind of business work being done by the individual, viz., an accountant or auditor in a manufacturing firm was classified under accounting rather than manufacturing; an advertising manager in a bank, under advertising; a treasurer in a department store, under commercial finance, etc.

† As specialized course groupings have only been offered since 1920, the percentages in this column are calculated on the basis of classes graduating in 1922 and subsequent years.

It was impracticabe to segregate fields of specialization in finance.

lowed the corresponding course than did those who selected any other phase of business. Insurance shows the largest proportion holding their first and present jobs in the field of their original choice, while a fairly large proportion of those in marketing and real estate also adhered to their original preference. Of those selecting foreign trade, only a fifth are now working in that field, while two-thirds of those originally preferring transportation have gone into other phases of business.

In general there seems to be little close relationship between the extent to which men adhere to their original preference in selecting their college course and the extent to which they followed their preference in selecting work after graduation. Thus, although only 29 per cent of those preferring manufacturing took the manufacturing course, 46 per cent are now engaged in this field, while in advertising, on the other hand, 61 per cent took the course, but only 38 per cent are now engaged in this work.

The likelihood of a student's entering the specific phase of business for which he expressed a preference is apparently increased only slightly by his following the special course in the field of his choice. Table XVII shows the proportion of those students who expressed an original preference for a specific phase of business and who followed their preference by taking the corresponding course of study, who are now employed in these same

TABLE XVII. DISTRIBUTION OF STUDENTS HAVING PREFERENCE AND TAKING COURSE IN SPECIFIC PHASE OF BUSINESS*

Phase of business	Number with preference in field who followed curriculum	Per cent of number stating preference and following specialized curriculum who:	
		Held first position in same business	Hold present position in same business
Accounting............	83	45.7%	50.6%
Marketing............	40	62.5	62.5
Manufacturing........	26	65.4	57.6
Commercial finance†.... ⎫ Investment finance†.... ⎭	62	64.5	71.0
Insurance.............	17	88.3	94.0
Foreign trade..........	19	21.1	21.1
Advertising...........	14	35.7	35.7
Real estate...........	7	57.2	71.5
Transportation........	6	50.0	50.0
Total.................	274	55.1%	58.0%

* Since specialized course groupings have only been offered since 1920, data in this table do not cover earlier classes.
† These fields were not segregated.

fields. Only 58 per cent of this entire group, who indicated such pronounced interest in the fields of their choice, are now engaged in the phase of business which they originally selected.

Too much signficance cannot be attached to the data for real estate and transportation owing to the small numbers reported in these fields. Insurance again makes the best showing with 16 out of 17 men, or 94 per cent now engaged in the field of their choice and preparation. When the facts shown in this table are considered in the light of the data previously given they seem to indicate that (1) only about half of 1,670 graduates had a definite preference for a specific phase of business at the time of enrollment, (2) only half of this number, or a fourth of the entire group, in addition to expressing a definite preference, followed this preference by enrolling in the special course provided for their needs (approximately the same proportion eventually found work in the field of their choice), (3) only three-fifths of this latter number or one-sixth of the entire group of 1,670 graduates, in addition to expressing a definite preference and following the corresponding course of study, eventually found work in the fields which they originally selected.

This lack of close relationship between original occupational preference, educational specialization, and present position is made even more apparent by examination of Table XVIII, which shows the proportion of graduates now engaged in each of the major

TABLE XVIII. VOCATIONAL PREFERENCE AND COURSE FOLLOWED BY GRADUATES NOW ENGAGED IN VARIOUS PHASES OF BUSINESS

Phase of business	Number holding present position in	Proportion of number having present position in each field who:		
		Followed corresponding field of specialization	Had original preference for field	Held first position in same field
Accounting............	114	65.3%	59.3%	69.9%
Marketing............	345	26.6	26.8	64.6
Manufacturing.........	224	33.3	24.7	64.3
Commercial finance.....	205	{40.2*	23.8	55.9
Investment finance......	148		17.7	57.1
Insurance.............	138	29.1	23.9	66.6
Foreign trade..........	20	57.1	40.0	65.0
Advertising...........	47	24.2	27.7	38.3
Real estate...........	61	36.6	26.7	53.3
Transportation........	20	33.3	30.0	55.0
Total	1,322	38.0%	27.7%	61.5%

* Not segregated for various fields of specialization in finance.

business fields who held their first jobs in the same field, who followed the undergraduate course designed for that field, and who had an original preference for that field.

The total of 1,322 contains many graduates who originally preferred some other field than that in which they are now engaged or who had formed no definite preference at the time of entering school, hence the disparities are very great. Although 61.5 per cent of the group held their first position after graduation in the same business as that in which they are now engaged, only 38 per cent took the course designed to prepare them for this business, and only 27.7 per cent originally had this phase of business in mind at the time of entering college. Those now engaged in accounting show by far the greatest persistency, 65.3 per cent of this group having taken the course, and 59.3 per cent having expressed original preference for this occupation. In none of the other major fields of business—marketing, manufacturing, finance, and insurance—does the "record of persistency" seem exceptional. In most cases only about a fourth of those now holding positions in these fields expressed a preference for them originally, but a somewhat larger proportion followed the corresponding course of study.

Summary and Conclusions

1. The information presented in this and in the four succeeding chapters was based upon replies to a questionnaire received from a representative group of 1,670 Wharton School graduates, constituting 29 per cent of all those graduating in the classes from 1888 to 1928.

2. Although many motives actuated students in entering this institution, the vast majority enrolled for the expressed purpose of preparing for business. Nearly 57 per cent, before they entered college, had selected a specific phase of business for which they wished to prepare themselves, while all but 18 per cent had formed a preference before graduation.

3. Slightly less than half of those who had formed a preference before matriculation attributed their choice to special interest and ability; 40 per cent were influenced primarily by family connections or advice; the remainder, by economic possibilities and other considerations.

4. A fairly large proportion—42.9 per cent—of those having a specific preference before matriculation had had previous experience in the field of their choice while in the case of those whose preference was influenced by family advice, the proportion was much larger.

5. The largest single group, constituting a fifth of those making a definite occupational choice, selected the field of marketing (including advertising) ; accounting was next in importance, followed by manufacturing, commercial finance, investment finance, and insurance, in the order named. These fields attracted nearly 70 per cent of all students who had made a decision as to their future occupations before entering college.

6. Comparison of the distribution of occupational preferences among different fields of business with the enrollment of students among the various specialized curricula in the Wharton School shows that the proportion of students enrolled in the general

business course (more than two-fifths of the total) was nearly as large as the proportion who expressed no preference for a specific phase of business at the time of matriculation. Relatively fewer students enrolled in each of the following specialized curricula than expressed a preference for the corresponding fields of business: commercial finance, marketing and advertising, investment finance and brokerage, and manufacturing and labor management. The reverse was true in the case of the insurance, foreign trade, and transportation curricula, in each of which as large or larger relative numbers were enrolled as expressed corresponding preferences.

7. Examination of the educational and occupational experience of the individuals who expressed a preference for a specific field of business shows that less than half of this entire group (a) followed the specialized curriculum designed to meet their needs, or (b) held their first position in the field of their choice, or (c) hold their present position in the business for which they had original preference.

8. Of those who followed the specialized curriculum corresponding to their original preference, only 55 per cent held their first positions, and only 58 per cent, their present positions, in the fields of business for which they prepared themselves.

9. Thus, of the entire group of 1,670 alumni, (a) somewhat more than half had formed an occupational preference upon entering college, (b) less than half of this latter group, or one-fourth of the original number, followed the corresponding courses of study, (c) less than two-fifths of this last named group, or only one-sixth of the original number expressed an original preference for an occupation for which they prepared themselves in college and in which they are now engaged.

10. Further evidence bearing on this point is obtained from study of 1,322 graduates now holding positions in the ten most important fields of business. Only 61 per cent of this group held their first positions in the same business; only 38 per cent followed the curriculum corresponding to their present occupation; and only 28 per cent had an original preference for the field in which they are now engaged.

11. The evidence presented seems to indicate that the specialized courses offered by this institution have not been wholly

effective as a means of vocational preparation, whatever the other educational and pedagogical advantages of specialization may be. Neither are the original preferences of the students at the time of enrollment very reliable indicators of what their future work will be. It should be stated, however, that in the case of the 24 per cent of all graduates whose occupational preferences were based upon family connection, there was a considerably greater tendency for the students to follow the course of study corresponding to their preference and to find work in the field chosen. This is to be expected in view of the fact that many of this group became employees in family firms. As indicated previously, however, the proportion of students in this group has become noticeably smaller in recent years.

CHAPTER VI

UNDERGRADUATE EMPLOYMENT AND CAMPUS ACTIVITIES[1]

Undergraduate Employment

The time has long since passed when the advantage of university education was limited to the children of wealthy parents. Today the greater availability of university facilities, especially in the larger cities, has made it possible for young men and women in moderate circumstances to share in the benefits of a

TABLE XIX. GRADUATES DEFRAYING SOME PART OF
THEIR COLLEGE EXPENSES

Class	Number replying	Number defraying expenses	Proportion defraying expenses
1928	236	133	56.4%
1927	185	93	50.3
1926	147	67	45.6
1925	156	74	47.4
1924	188	91	48.4
1923	135	59	43.7
1921–22	212	97	45.8
1919–20	124	52	41.9
1917–18	55	18	32.7
1914–16	85	37	43.5
1911–13	43	19	44.2
1905–10	50	14	28.0
1899–04	25	13	52.0
1888–98	29	9	31.0
Total	1,670	776	46.5%

higher education. By summer work or part-time employment during the school term a substantial proportion of the undergraduates in American institutions contribute a share to the expenses of their education. Replies from 1,670 Wharton School graduates indicate that nearly half of the entire group earned at least a part of their college expenses. As indicated in Table XIX, considerable numbers of all classes defrayed some part of their expenses through employment, although in later years the proportion of students who worked has increased. In 1928 for example, over 56 per cent, and in the preceding year more than half the class, helped to earn their expenses. In none of the last ten classes did less than 40 per cent defray some part of their expenses, while the average for the group was close to 50 per

[1] Prepared and written by J. Frederic Dewhurst.

cent, considerably above the average for the earlier classes.

Most of the students who were employed worked during the summer vacations and school terms for the entire four years. More than half of the total number defraying expenses, or over a fourth of the total, reported that they were employed for all four years, while an additional 9.8 per cent worked during three of the school years. Relatively fewer of the first year men engaged in outside work, although more than a third reported employment in that year. Forty per cent of the entire group worked

TABLE XX. UNDERGRADUATE EXPENSES DEFRAYED BY GRADUATES

	All classes	1888–1922	1923–1928
Number of graduates	1,670	623	1,047
Defraying no part of expenses......	53.5%	58.4%	50.6%
Defraying some part of expenses....	46.5	41.6	49.4
Defraying more than 10 per cent....	44.4	39.8	47.1
" " " 20 " "	37.2	34.7	38.7
" " " 30 " "	28.1	26.2	29.3
" " " 40 " "	23.1	22.2	23.7
" " " 50 " "	19.4	19.4	19.4
" " " 60 " "	14.8	14.4	15.2
" " " 70 " "	11.4	10.1	12.2
" " " 80 " "	8.7	8.3	9.0
" " " 90 " "	6.2	6.1	6.3

in the junior year, with somewhat smaller proportions in the sophomore and senior years.

Expenses Defrayed by Employment

Although nearly half of the graduates defrayed some part of their expenses, only a very small fraction—less than six per cent—entirely supported themselves while at the university. The percentages of students who defrayed various proportions of their expenses are shown in Table XX. Nearly a fourth of the group defrayed more than 40 per cent of their expenses by outside work, and almost a fifth earned enough money to pay more than half their expenses. That a somewhat larger share of college expenses has been borne by the students in the more recent classes, than by the earlier graduates, is evident from the data shown in the table.

Nature of Work Engaged In

The work engaged in by the students covered a considerable range of activities. As indicated in Table XXI, the largest single group, constituting nearly 30 per cent, were employed in clerical capacities, notably as bank clerks working at night, as billing clerks, bookkeepers, and at similar tasks. A considerable number in both the earlier and later classes earned part of their expenses by serving as stewards in fraternity houses and by waiting on table in boarding houses and campus restaurants. Although practically none of the men graduating prior to 1923 were reported as engaged in selling, this field has proved a most important source of income to recent undergraduates. Many of the men in the classes graduating between 1923 and 1928 were employed

TABLE XXI. NATURE OF UNDERGRADUATE EMPLOYMENT
IN WHICH STUDENTS ENGAGED

	All classes	1888–1922	1923–1928
Number of graduates	1,670	623	1,047
Number defraying expenses	776	259	517
Clerical......................	28.7%	27.2%	29.9%
Stewards and waiters...........	12.4	9.8	13.8
Selling........................	11.8	0.8	17.1
Laborer.......................	9.7	4.2	12.4
Camp and settlement work......	8.4	9.2	3.5
Tutoring and teaching..........	6.8	13.2	4.0
Newspaper work...............	4.9	8.7	3.1
Orchestra work................	3.2	2.6	3.5
Factory work..................	2.8	5.3	1.7
Chauffeur.....................	2.4	0.0	3.5
Coaching athletics.............	2.3	1.1	2.8
Other.........................	6.6	7.9	4.7
Total	100.0%	100.0%	100.0%

as salesmen in retail stores and a considerable number worked part-time during the school term and in summer vacations selling household articles from door to door. A few, although not as many as popular experience might lead one to expect, earned their way through college by selling magazine subscriptions. Manual labor not only served as a means of keeping athletes from "getting soft" during summer months, but was an important source of earnings, especially among recent graduates. Jobs as counsellors at boys' summer camps, grading papers, tutoring fellow students, and newspaper reportorial work, all contributed substantially toward the expenses of students in the earlier classes, but have been less important in recent years. Factory work was also a more important means of livelihood to the earlier graduates, perhaps partly reflecting the fact that a much larger proportion of this group were planning to enter manufacturing.

It is evident that much of the work engaged in by these students contributed little in the nature of the practical experience and contact with business operations which might have been valuable to them in later life. Most of the work was of a necessitous nature in which the student was interested primarily in making money to pay expenses and only secondarily in getting experience. Nearly half of the working graduates from the last six classes, however, were engaged in clerical work, selling, and factory work —commercial occupations which might be expected to yield at least a modicum of practical business experience.

It is difficult, of course, to appraise the advantages and disadvantages of outside work, either to the student or to the university. Moreover, it is particularly hard to generalize, since the kind of experience which proves profitable to one student may be equally undesirable for another. Certainly the nature of the problems presented by outside employment is not in many respects dissimilar from that of other forms of extra-curricular activity. Athletics and campus activities, like outside work, absorb some of the time which might more profitably be spent in study; both tend to distract the student from his purely academic interests. But both possess compensations—the stimulating effects of human contacts and experience in working cooperatively with others.

Relation Between Scholarship and Outside Work

One objective test which can be used to measure the possible effects of outside employment upon academic work is a comparison of the scholarship records of students engaging in such work with records of those who have not. Although it has been impracticable to prepare complete and accurate measures of scholarship for all graduates included in this survey, some data are available for purposes of such a comparison. A study of a number of student course records selected at random showed that the total number of D's received by a student during his college career was a fairly accurate measure of scholarship. Undergraduate course record cards of all graduates replying to the questionnaire were examined and the number of D's[2] determined for each student.

[2] D (Distinguished) is the highest term or semester course grade, corresponding on a numerical scale to a grade of 90 to 100 per cent. Other

All graduates for whom a four-year record was available were therefore ranged according to the number of D's each received, and classified as being in the highest tenth, highest third, middle third, lowest third, or lowest tenth. Members of each class were classified separately in this fashion so as to avoid the effects of any changes in grading standards which may have occurred over a period of time. Since this information was available for each student it was thus possible to compare the average scholarship of various groups of students. Table XXII shows the scholarship of students classified by the extent to which they contributed to their undergraduate expenses by working. As

TABLE XXII. SCHOLARSHIP OF STUDENTS WHO DEFRAYED
UNDERGRADUATE EXPENSES

Scholarship class	Proportion of following groups included in each scholarship class:			
	All students	Students not defraying expenses	Students defraying some part of expenses	Students defraying more than half of expenses
Highest tenth..........	10.0%	8.4%	13.6%	15.0%
Highest third..........	33.3	32.8	36.0	33.5
Middle third..........	33.3	31.0	35.1	35.3
Lowest third..........	33.3	36.2	28.9	31.2
Lowest tenth..........	10.0	10.7	8.2	12.1

pointed out previously, scholarship was based on the number of D's received by 937 students for whom complete records were available.

Cursory examination of the table would indicate that the scholarly standing of the students who were employed during their college years was somewhat higher than that of the men who did not work. Of the half of the entire group of 1,670 students who defrayed some part of their expenses, 13.6 per cent were in the highest tenth of their classes, and 36 per cent in the highest third, as compared with 8.4 per cent and 32.8 per cent, respectively, for students who defrayed no part of their expenses. In the lowest tenth and lowest third reverse conditions prevail; larger proportions of the students who were not employed and smaller proportions of those who were employed, are found in these scholarship classes. The distribution of the small group of students who defrayed more than half of their expenses dis-

___

grades given in the Wharton School are G (good), 80 to 90 per cent; P (passed), 70 to 80 per cent; N (not passed, or conditioned), below 70; F (failed), below 70.

plays a curious contrast. In general, this group appears to have had a higher-than-average record, there being 33.5 per cent in the highest third, and only 31.2 per cent in the lowest third. A very large proportion—15 per cent—ranked in the highest tenth; on the other hand, more than 12 per cent were found in the lowest tenth—a larger proportion than in the case of students who defrayed no expenses. Explanation of this anomaly is not readily apparent, unless it be that the effects of very burdensome outside work are highly selective, revealing a few brilliant and able men whose energy permits them to make good records, and another

TABLE XXIII. STUDENT PARTICIPATION IN CAMPUS ACTIVITIES

	All classes	1888–1922	1923–1928
Number of graduates	1,670	623	1,047
Proportion participating in:			
No activities...................	34.4%	35.2%	34.0%
Athletic........................	44.0	41.7	45.3
Dramatic and musical...........	21.6	25.8	19.1
Publications...................	18.1	19.1	17.6
Class activities................	19.7	23.4	17.5
Other activities................	1.7	1.0	2.2

group who are unable to stand up under the double pressure of academic duties and outside work.

Whatever the effects, beneficial or detrimental, of outside work upon the student, there can be little doubt that so far as this group is concerned, the scholarship of those who were employed was distinctly higher than that of those who did not work. The distribution of grades among the small group who earned more than half their expenses indicates the probability that scholarship is adversely affected when students have to work enough to defray the major part of their expenses.

Student Participation in Campus Activities

As compared with slightly less than half of the student body who engaged in outside work, a substantial majority of the alumni replying to the questionnaire engaged in one or more of the various forms of extra-curricular campus activities. In response to the question concerning participation in such activities, 405 of the 1,670 did not reply, and an additional 170 reported no participation. Assuming that all who did not reply were non-participants, practically two-thirds of the entire group devoted time and energy to some form of non-academic student activity while they were in college.

As will be seen in Table XXIII, athletics was by far the most important extra-curricular interest, with more than twice as many students participating as in any other form of activity; in recent years nearly half of the students have engaged in some form of athletic activity. Next in importance to athletics, dramatic and musical activities attracted 21.6 per cent of all students,

TABLE XXIV. NUMBER OF TYPES OF CAMPUS ACTIVITIES
PARTICIPATED IN BY STUDENTS

	All classes	1888–1922	1923–1928
Number of graduates	1,670	623	1,047
Proportion participating in:			
No activities......................	34.4%	35.2%	34.0%
One type of activity...............	35.3	31.6	37.4
Two types of activity..............	18.9	20.5	17.9
Three types of activity............	8.4	9.5	7.7
Four types of activity.............	1.3	2.2	0.8
More than four types of activity.....	1.7	1.0	2.2
Total	100.0%	100.0%	100.0%

while nearly as many men engaged in campus publication work and in class activities.

The more recent graduates have evidently participated in campus activities to a slightly greater extent than the earlier classes, but this recent increase is almost entirely attributable to a pronounced increase in student participation in athletics. To other student interests, notably dramatic and musical work and class activities, relatively smaller proportions of recent classes have been attracted.

Obviously considerable numbers of students participated in more than one type of activity. Table XXIV shows that the entire group is divided roughly into three nearly equal portions, a third who engaged in no activities,[3] a third who engaged in only one type of activity, and nearly a third who participated in two or more types of student activities.

Opinions as to Value of Campus Activities

In view of the very substantial participation by this group of students in a great variety of extra-curricular campus activities it may be of interest to examine their opinions of the ways in

---

[3] This group was composed largely of students who were employed.

which "campus activities have been of direct value in social and business life since graduation." Replies to this question ranged all the way from the opinion that "activities have not only been of no value but have proved positively detrimental," through the rather faint praise to the effect that "activities filled up spare time and were more wholesome than loafing or dissipation," to an apparently sincere belief that "they have been more valuable than all the courses taken in college."

A surprisingly large proportion of the 1,153 graduates who replied to this question—31 per cent—indicated their opinion that no direct value had been derived from these activities, and this proportion has been increasing somewhat in recent years. As shown in Table XXV, nearly half of the group believed that

TABLE XXV. OPINIONS OF GRADUATES AS TO DIRECT VALUE
OF CAMPUS ACTIVITIES

	All classes	1888–1922	1923–1928
Number of graduates replying	1,153	434	719
Proportion indicating following values:			
No direct value	31.2%	29.5%	32.3%
Making social and business friends	47.4	49.5	46.2
Development of character and cooperative spirit	28.8	27.0	29.9
Understanding of human nature	9.4	6.5	11.1
Other values	6.8	7.8	6.1

campus activities were instrumental in making social and business friendships which proved helpful and valuable in life after leaving college. Nearly 29 per cent of the group stated that campus activities had been instrumental in developing character and a spirit of fair play and cooperation in their relations with others. A smaller number believed that an improved understanding of human nature resulted from participation, reflected in greater tolerance for the opinions of others, better ability in meeting men and situations, surer poise, and the development of other personal qualities.

Relation Between Scholarship and Campus Activities

In view of the relatively high scholarship standing of the students who helped to earn their way through college, it may be significant to compare the scholarship of students engaging in various campus activities with that of those who did not participate and with that of those who defrayed some part of their expenses. Table XXVI, in which such comparisons are made, shows very striking differences in the scholarship displayed by participants in various types of activities. Those reporting no participation in campus activities, comprising approximately a third of all graduates, had scholarship records slightly better than the average and above that of those engaging in campus activities. It will be remembered that the students who helped to defray their expenses, including a large proportion of those not engaging in campus activities, had scholarship records above the average for the entire group. By far the highest scholarship was displayed by those reporting participation in dramatic and other activities (exclusive of athletics), while those engaging solely

TABLE XXVI. SCHOLARSHIP OF STUDENTS PARTICIPATING
IN CAMPUS ACTIVITIES

Campus activity	Proportion of students in each type of activity who were in following scholarship classes:				
	Highest tenth	Highest third	Middle third	Lowest third	Lowest tenth
All students	10.0%	33.3%	33.3%	33.3%	10.0%
No participation...........	13.0%	36.6%	29.8%	33.6%	10.3%
Participation in any activity.	9.2	33.3	34.2	32.5	9.2
Dramatic and other (excluding athletic).............	13.4	44.3	36.1	19.6	3.1
Publications, only..........	7.5	37.4	32.8	29.8	11.9
Athletic and other..........	11.6	34.8	29.9	35.3	11.6
Athletics, only.............	5.7	25.5	37.7	46.8	9.0

in athletics had the poorest academic standing. Over 44 per cent of the former ranked in the highest third of their classes, and less than a fifth in the lowest third. But in the case of the athletes the situation was almost reversed, with almost a fourth of this group in the highest third and nearly 47 per cent in the lowest third. Curiously, although athletic activities had the smallest proportions in the first tenth and first third, and the largest proportion in the lowest third, only nine per cent—less than the average for all students—were in the lowest tenth.

The distribution of grades for those engaging in both athletic and other activities was close to the average for the entire group, with somewhat larger proportions in the highest and lowest tenths of their classes. Students engaging solely in campus publication work also had somewhat better than average scholarship despite the small percentage of this group in the highest tenth. Whatever the explanation for these contrasts may be, it seems clear that participation in dramatic, musical, publication, and other "intellectual" activities was coupled with very high scholastic standing, while the exact opposite was true in the case of athletic activities.

SUMMARY AND CONCLUSIONS

1.   Nearly half (46.5 per cent) of the graduates replying to this questionnaire—and a somewhat larger proportion of the recent classes—reported that they defrayed some part of their college expenses through employment during the college terms or summer vacations.   Almost a fifth of the entire number of graduates defrayed more than half of their expenses, but less than six per cent entirely supported themselves while at the university.

2.   More than half of those defraying expenses, or a fourth of the entire number, were employed during all four years, while a third of the entire group worked during three of the four years.

3.   While the employment engaged in covered a wide range,—including clerical work, waiting on table, selling, common labor, summer camp counselling, tutoring and teaching, athletic coaching, and many other occupations—nearly half of those in recent classes defraying expenses were engaged in commercial and industrial occupations which furnished some measure of practical business experience.

4.   A study of the academic records of these graduates showed that the scholarship of those defraying some part of their expenses was distinctly higher than that of the group who did not engage in outside work.   However, there was evidence that scholarship was adversely affected among the students who defrayed more than half of their expenses.

5.   Approximately two-thirds of all students reported participation in some form of campus activity, while nearly half of this number, or a third of the entire group, engaged in two or more distinct types of activities.   Athletics was by far the most popular, engaging the interests of twice as many students as were attracted to the next most important phases—dramatic and musical activities, publications, and class activities.

6.   Nearly a third of those engaging in activities expressed the opinion that they were of no direct value in "social and business life since graduation."   Almost half believed that their

chief value was in making social and business friends; much smaller numbers stated that activities had been helpful in the development of character, a cooperative attitude, and an understanding of human nature.

7. The scholarship of students participating in campus activities was somewhat below that of those who did not engage in them, and distinctly lower than the records of men who helped to defray their expenses by outside work. Among the men engaging in various kinds of extra-curricular activities there were wide differences in scholarship; those engaging solely in athletics, had the poorest academic records, while those participating in dramatic, musical, and publication work had records much above the average for other students.

8. If the records of this group of 1,670 graduates can be considered as representative it is patent that "going to college" means considerably more to the typical student then attendance at classes and lectures and preparation of assignments. Obviously a considerable part of the student's time and energy—in some cases, the major portion—is expended in activities not directly related to his academic responsibilities. Such activities, moreover, are an integral and important part of the environment which helps to shape and mold the student's development while in college; they are closely related to his academic success, as measured by scholarship, and there is substantial evidence that they are also related to his success in life after graduation. In view of these facts, the question may well be raised as to whether a university should not concern itself to a considerable extent in the extra-curricular activities of its students, as well as in those activities which are directly related to his classroom accomplishment.

CHAPTER VII

OCCUPATIONAL EXPERIENCE OF GRADUATES[1]

One of the primary tasks of the university school of business is that of preparing its students to enter upon successful and socially useful careers in business and similar fields of endeavor. Although the social usefulness of such training cannot be measured solely by the subsequent progress and status of the graduates, an examination of the character of work they are called upon to perform, of the types of positions they hold, and of the nature of their duties and responsibilities should help to indicate how the school of business may best discharge its responsibilities. It was with this object in mind that the graduates to whom the present inquiry was directed were asked to furnish detailed information upon their occupational experience since graduation.

Reasons for Choosing First Occupation After Graduation

It will be remembered that more than half of this group of graduates, by the time they entered college, had formed a preference for a specific phase of business for which they expected to prepare themselves. Almost half of those stating such a preference attributed their choice to special interest or ability, while nearly as large a number were motivated by family connection with the business they expected to enter, or by the urge or influence of family or others. Table XXVII shows that these two reasons were predominant in causing students to choose their first occupations after leaving college, although other reasons had also become important. Special interest and ability accounted for the occupational choice of about a third of all students, both of the earlier and later classes, but family connection and influence have become noticeably less important in recent years. A substantial portion of the men, especially in recent classes, chose their occupations because of economic possibilities, reflected in a favorable opportunity for rapid advancement or an attractive beginning salary, while nearly one out of ten took the only job offered. Only a few men chose their positions because of geo-

---

[1] Prepared and written by J. Frederic Dewhurst.

graphic location, a rather surprising fact in view of evidence indicating that the geographic distribution of graduates on their present jobs is much the same as that of their original homes.

GEOGRAPHIC DISTRIBUTION OF STUDENTS AND GRADUATES

A comparison of the geographic sections in which students attending the Wharton School during the years from 1922 to 1929 lived before matriculation, with those in which the recent graduates included in this inquiry are now residing is shown in Table XXVIII. Particularly noteworthy is the close correspondence in the geographic distribution of both students and graduates and

TABLE XXVII. REASONS FOR CHOOSING FIRST OCCUPATION AFTER GRADUATION

	All classes	1888–1922	1923–1928
Number of graduates	1,670	623	1,047
Number of graduates giving reasons	1,357	505	852
Proportion giving each of following reasons:			
Special interest and ability	34.2%	33.3%	34.8%
Family connection and influence	29.5	34.8	26.3
Economic possibilities	16.3	11.9	18.9
Only position available	9.3	10.1	8.8
Geographic location	2.8	2.4	3.1
Other reasons	7.9	7.5	8.1
Total	100.0%	100.0%	100.0%

the fact that such large proportions of both groups were located in the three Middle Atlantic states. Pennsylvania alone has contributed nearly half of the student body in recent years, while a slightly smaller number of the graduates report their present employment in this state. New York has apparently attracted many of the students who came to the school from other sections, since more than a fifth of the graduates are employed there, as compared with less than a sixth who reported that state as their residence. Philadelphia, with 28 per cent of recent graduates, and New York City, with 14 per cent, together employ more than two out of five of the men graduating since 1923.

The influence of proximity is seen in the fact that nearly half of the students from the middle west came from Ohio, and almost as many graduates were employed there, while more than half of the students from the south reported their homes in the nearby states of Maryland, West Virginia, Virginia, and Delaware, and in the District of Columbia. Thus, although every state in the Union and many foreign countries are represented among the student and alumni body of the Wharton School, the great majority, constituting three-fourths of the entire number, originally resided in Pennsylvania and the contiguous states, and an equal number have found employment in these same sections.

This tendency toward geographic concentration of the graduates in the Middle Atlantic states has become more pronounced during recent years. Only 63 per cent of those replying to the questionnaire who were graduated prior to 1923 reported their present location as Pennsylvania, New York, and New Jersey,

TABLE XXVIII.   GEOGRAPHIC DISTRIBUTION OF STUDENTS AND GRADUATES*

	Students, 1922–1929		Graduates, 1923–1928	
Number of students and graduates	3,166		1,052	
Proportion in each geographic section:				
Middle Atlantic states		69.0%		70.7%
Pennsylvania	45.5		42.8	
New York	15.5		20.7	
New Jersey	8.0		7.2	
New England states		5.8		4.3
Southern states		8.7		8.7
Middle Western states		12.1		13.1
Mountain states		1.3		1.0
Pacific Coast states		1.0		1.4
United States territories		0.4		0.7
Foreign countries		1.7		0.1
Total		100.0%		100.0%

* The geographical classification follows mainly that of the U. S. Census, except that "Southern states" includes Delaware, Maryland, District of Columbia, Virginia, North Carolina, South Carolina, Georgia, Florida, Kentucky, Tennessee, Alabama, Mississippi, Arkansas, Louisiana, Oklahoma, Texas; and "Middle Western states" includes Ohio, Indiana, Illinois, Michigan, Wisconsin, Minnesota, Iowa, Missouri, North Dakota, South Dakota, Nebraska, and Kansas.

while 70.7 per cent of the later classes are now employed in these three states. New York City has been especially attractive to recent graduates, 14 per cent of this group reporting that they were employed there, as compared with only seven per cent of the men graduating prior to 1923. Relatively fewer of the later graduates, on the other hand, have found employment in the more distant sections—the middle west, the south, and the Pacific Coast states. This tendency for the school to draw its student personnel more extensively from nearby sections and for its graduates to find employment in this region is to be expected in view of the recent rapid growth of collegiate schools of commerce in other parts of the country and the heavy concentration of business and finance, with consequent employment opportunities, in the Middle Atlantic states.

OCCUPATIONS OF GRADUATES

The wide diversity in the positions held and in the nature of the work performed by the graduates replying to this inquiry reflects the fact that, far from being a restricted and specialized vocation or profession, business represents a pervasive and ever broadening phase of social activity demanding multifarious types of human interest and ability. Athough the standards of business conduct are gradually being raised to a professional level, business occupations are in no sense restricted professions, like those of medicine and law. Like engineering, business is an "open profession" to which all persons may have access, whether or not they have had the advantages of university education. Indeed, until quite recently, a college education was popularly believed to be more of a liability than an asset in the rough and tumble of business life and even now the great majority of responsible positions in business are held by men who never attended college.

But business, more and more, is making urgent demands upon the universities in recruiting personnel destined ultimately to fill its positions of authority and responsibility. The graduates of two types of professional schools—law and engineering—were the first college men to enter the ranks of business in large numbers and members of these groups now hold many of the higher executive positions in business. More recently the university school of commerce has been graduating thousands of young men each year into the ranks of business, while the liberal arts college also is now sending many of its graduates into commercial life. What part should the university take—more particularly, what rôle should the school of business play—in the task of preparing its young men for these important pursuits? In part, perhaps, the answer may be found in more careful study of the responsibilities and duties which the graduates of universities have been called upon to discharge.

An attempt has been made in the data presented in Table XXIX to show how the graduates of this institution are now distributed among the different types of business enterprises in which they are employed, and also the nature of the duties they perform.

The classification used in this table may perhaps demand some explanation. The first column shows the number and propor-

tion of the graduates who were employed in each of the principal types of enterprise irrespective of the function or kind of
work performed by the individual, while in the second column,
the distribution is based upon the nature of the individual's
duties. Thus, under the accounting classification, the total number of graduates employed by public accounting firms is shown in
the first column, while the second column shows the number engaged in accounting work, including many who are employed
by manufacturing, mercantile, financial, and other enterprises.

TABLE XXIX. PHASE OF BUSINESS AND NATURE OF WORK IN
WHICH GRADUATES ARE EMPLOYED

Phase of business	Phase of business		Nature of work	
	Number	Per cent	Number	Per cent
Accounting.................	58	3.5	114	6.9
Advertising................	28	1.7	47	2.8
Marketing.................	257	15.6	345	20.8
Manufacturing..............	410	24.9	224	13.5
Commercial finance.........	128	7.8	205	12.4
Investment finance..........	152	9.2	148	8.9
Insurance..................	142	8.6	138	8.3
Foreign trade...............	20	1.2	20	1.2
Real estate.................	66	4.0	61	3.7
Transportation.............	23	1.4	20	1.2
Public utilities..............	47	2.9	26	1.6
Law.......................	85	5.2	85	5.1
Education..................	84	5.1	84	5.1
Other.....................	147	8.9	142	8.5
Total	1647	100.0	1659	100.0

In the same way, the first column under advertising shows the
total number of men employed by advertising agencies, and the
second column shows the total number engaged as advertising
managers, copy-writers, and in other kinds of advertising work,
whether they were employed by advertising agencies or by other
business institutions. The marketing classification, in the first
column, includes all the graduates, whether they be sales managers, treasurers, comptrollers, accountants or advertising
managers, who were employed by retail stores, mail order houses,
wholesale firms, or other types of mercantile business. In the
second column, under this classification, is shown the total number
of men engaged in marketing functions, i.e., salesmen, sales managers, market analysts, etc., irrespective of whether they were
employed by marketing, manufacturing, or other kinds of firms.
One exception to this functional classification should be noted
here: men engaged in selling insurance, securities, or real estate

were shown respectively, in both columns, under these three classifications rather than under marketing. In accordance with this method of classification the number of men indicated in the second column as engaged in manufacturing, as to nature of work, includes only the "residual" group employed in strictly operating and management functions in industrial establishments. All men employed by manufacturing establishments in functional positions, such as sales managers, salesmen, accountants, treasurers, traffic managers, and export managers, were classified under the special functions which they performed.

Nearly nine out of ten of the men replying were employed by

TABLE XXX. GRADUATES ENGAGED IN SELLING
AND MARKETING FUNCTIONS

Commodities or services	Total engaged in selling and marketing		Salesmen; sales correspondents; sales representatives		Other positions of a selling nature	
	Number	Per cent	Number	Per cent	Number	Per cent
Commodities........	325	58.0	92	43.2	233	67.1
Securities..........	108	19.4	62	29.1	46	13.5
Insurance..........	72	12.8	45	21.1	27	7.7
Real estate.........	41	7.3	7	3.3	34	9.7
Other..............	14	2.5	7	3.3	7	2.0
Total	560	100.0	213	100.0	347	100.0

business firms and were engaged in business occupations; the small remaining fraction were engaged chiefly as lawyers and teachers, most of the latter being on the faculties of university schools of business. Almost two-thirds of those entering business were employed by manufacturing, mercantile, financial, and insurance *firms,* while 1,174 graduates, or 71 per cent of those replying, were engaged in the *functions* of marketing, manufacturing, commercial and investment finance, insurance, and accounting. Marketing is by far the most important single kind of work in which these men were engaged, and the importance of this general function is still further increased when it is realized that a large proportion of those in real estate, investment finance, and insurance were engaged as salesmen, sales managers, and in other positions primarily of a selling nature. Furthermore, advertising, in which 47 graduates were engaged, may also be considered a marketing function.

It may be of interest in this connection to indicate in greater

TABLE XXXI. NATURE OF WORK IN WHICH GRADUATES ARE ENGAGED BY CLASSES

Proportion of number in each class engaged in each of following kinds of work

Classes	All graduates	Per cent	Accounting	Advertising	Marketing	Manufacturing	Commercial finance	Investment finance	Insurance	Foreign trade	Real Estate	Transportation	Public utilities	Other
All	1,659	100.0	6.8%	2.9%	20.6%	13.4%	12.3%	8.9%	8.3%	1.2%	3.6%	1.2%	1.6%	19.3%
1928	231	100.0	6.8%	3.0%	19.1%	14.8%	10.2%	7.6%	8.9%	1.7%	1.7%	2.5%	3.4%	20.3%
1927	184	100.0	10.3	2.2	17.3	14.6	10.3	10.8	6.5	.5	2.7	2.2	3.2	19.4
1926	146	100.0	6.8	2.0	21.9	11.6	17.8	10.9	8.8	1.2	2.0	1.2	.7	15.1
1925	156	100.0	7.1	3.2	23.1	10.3	10.9	9.0	8.3	1.9	3.8	.6		21.8
1924	188	100.0	11.2	3.7	23.4	12.8	11.7	7.4	10.6	1.9	3.2	.7	1.6	11.7
1923	135	100.0	5.9	2.2	23.0	12.6	11.7	7.4	10.4	1.6	6.7	1.1	.7	20.0
1921-22	212	100.0	7.4	2.4	24.2	13.2	10.4	9.0	8.0	.5	3.3	.9	1.9	16.5
1919-20	123	100.0	4.8	4.0	21.1	8.1	12.7	7.3	5.6	2.4	4.8		2.4	25.8
1917-18	55	100.0	3.6	7.3	20.0	21.9	13.7	7.3	7.1		7.3			14.5
1914-16	85	100.0	2.4	3.5	28.2	20.0	14.5	7.1	3.6	1.2	3.5			17.6
1911-13	43	100.0	4.7	4.7	9.3	16.3	9.4	7.1	11.6	4.7	4.7	2.3		18.0
1905-10	50	100.0	2.0		14.0	18.0	11.6	11.6	12.0		6.0			18.0
1899-04	23	100.0			8.0	16.0	18.0	8.0			4.0			56.0
1888-98	28	100.0			6.9	10.3	13.9	13.9	6.9		3.4	3.4		41.3

detail the distribution among different types of business of the 560 graduates whose duties were chiefly or partially of a selling nature, exclusive of those engaged in advertising. The group shown in Table XXX includes salesmen, sales representatives, and sales correspondents, and also sales managers and others who were engaged primarily in selling and marketing functions, including all those engaged in general functions in mercantile concerns.

As indicated in Table XXXI, there is some divergence in the occupational distribution of members of the various classes. Thus, few or none of the members of the very earliest classes are now engaged in accounting, advertising, and foreign trade. Only during the past decade have any graduates entered the public utility field, the importance of which appears recently to have been increasing rapidly. Accounting also has been employing larger proportions of the more recent classes although this disparity is probably due to the fact that many of the older graduates who originally entered this field have been promoted to higher positions not strictly of an accounting nature. Since 1914 marketing has maintained a position of outstanding importance employing larger proportions in every class than any other field. Manufacturing, on the other hand, appears to have been a relatively less important field during the past decade than during the two preceding decades, although in the last two classes a substantial increase has occurred in the proportion entering this field. Investment finance has attracted a larger proportion of the men graduating since 1925 than of the ten preceding classes, although a large number of the earliest graduates are engaged in this field.

Except for these few general tendencies and certain apparently erratic differences among individual classes, the occupational distribution of graduates appears to be fairly uniform. Marketing is the most important single field, and manufacturing, commercial finance, investment finance, insurance, and accounting employ all but a small fraction of the remaining graduates.

Lack of comparable data from most other similar institutions makes it impossible to state whether this occupational distribution is generally representative of the graduates of university schools of business. Some fragmentary data are available, however, which indicate similar tendencies elsewhere. Statistics of the

1929 graduating class of the Graduate School of Business Administration of Harvard University show that 252 graduates were employed as follows: 65 in marketing, sales, and advertising; 60 in investment finance; 39 in commercial finance; 20 in manufacturing; 4 in accounting; and 64 in other activities. Finance and marketing, as in the case of the Wharton School graduates, absorbed a large proportion of the total, but very few were engaged in accounting and none in insurance—fields which are important among the latter group.

Relation of Occupations to Preferences and Courses Offered

The distribution of graduates among the various types of business activity cannot in itself be considered a measure of the potential opportunities offered by business to college graduates, and more particularly to graduates of collegiate schools of business. Students are actuated by many causes in choosing their occupations. Early preference, based upon natural aptitudes, previous experience, or the advice of parents and friends, interest aroused by the courses taken in college, and the opportunities available at graduation or later in life all help to determine the nature of the work in which the graduates eventually become engaged.

Early preferences, except in the case of those expecting to enter family business, appear to have been of only limited significance in determining the future occupational choices of graduates. In the first place nearly half of all students entered school without any definite preference, while less than half of those expressing such preference eventually found work in the specific field they had chosen. Although the economic possibilities of the opportunities, irrespective of the nature of the work offered, influenced a considerable number of students in choosing occupations at graduation, it seems likely that the student's academic experience and the courses he studied had some influence upon his choice of an occupation, especially if he entered college without a definite preference. The extent of these influences is of course impossible to measure but some significance may attach to the comparison, shown in Table XXXII, of early preferences, present occupations, and the number of semester hours in various business subjects offered in the Wharton School curriculum.

Although there is little relationship between preferences and courses offered, a general correspondence appears to exist between the occupational importance of these fields as indicated by the number of graduates engaged in each, and the importance attached to them in the curriculum as measured by the number of semester hours offered in each. Marketing, commercial and investment finance, manufacturing, insurance, and accounting, in which fields nearly nine out of ten of the graduates are engaged, are the most important subjects in the curriculum, representing in the aggregate slightly more than 70 per cent of the hours offered in business courses. Among some of the individual fields, a very close relationship exists, notably in the case of insurance

TABLE XXXII. OCCUPATIONAL PREFERENCES AND PRESENT OCCUPATIONS OF GRADUATES, AND SEMESTER HOURS OFFERED IN BUSINESS SUBJECTS

Phase of business	Preferences		Occupations		Semester hours	
	Number	Per cent	Number	Per cent	Hours	Per cent
Accounting...........	159	21.4	114	8.5	31.0	11.0
Advertising..........	34	4.6	47	3.5	10.0	3.5
Marketing...........	154	20.7	345	25.6	35.0*	12.4
Manufacturing.......	121	16.3	224	16.6	32.0†	11.3
Commercial finance....	101	13.6	205	15.2	36.5	12.9
Investment finance....	50	6.7	148	11.0	38.5‡	13.7
Insurance............	39	5.2	138	10.2	29.0	10.3
Foreign trade........	39	5.2	20	1.5	16.0	5.7
Real estate..........	27	3.6	61	4.5	16.0	5.7
Transportation.......	18	2.4	20	1.5	34.0	12.1
Public utilities.......	2	0.3	26	1.9	4.0	1.4
All fields (11)	744	100.0	1,348	100.0	282.0	100.0

* Includes also certain courses in commerce.
† Includes also courses in management and personnel relations.
‡ Includes also courses in brokerage and security markets.

and advertising, but in other instances important divergences occur. Marketing and manufacturing, for example, which employ a large proportion of the graduates, appear to possess considerably greater importance as occupations than is attached to them in the curriculum. Comparatively few graduates, on the other hand, are engaged in foreign trade and transportation, while the number of course hours offered in these fields represents a very substantial part of the total.

There is little conclusive evidence in the data of this table to show whether or not the courses offered to the students, or those they are required to study, are important determinants of their future occupations. It is undoubtedly true, however, that the existence in an institution such as the Wharton School of a well organized and comprehensive department of instruction in a particular field serves to attract many students specifically interested in preparing themselves for that field who might otherwise attend another institution. Furthermore, the large number of students—43 per cent of the total—who enter the school without any definite vocational preference are probably influenced somewhat in their choice of an occupation by the existence of such a department. This appears to have been true in the case of insurance, which attracted twice as large a proportion of the graduates as had originally expressed an intention to enter that field. Investment finance, public utilities, and real estate also proved distinctly more attractive to the alumni upon graduation than at the time of entering the university. Relatively fewer of the graduates, on the other hand, reported that they were engaged in the fields of accounting, advertising, foreign trade, and transportation than had expressed a preference for these fields at the time of matriculation.

Labor Mobility Among Graduates

Although the distribution of graduates among the principal kinds of business work has been fairly constant from class to class, except for a general increase in the importance of investment and banking and public utilities, the group has been characterized by considerable "labor mobility" accompanied in many individual instances by a complete shift from one phase of business to another. Analysis of the occupational records of 1,322 graduates employed in the ten fields of business specified in the preceding section shows that nearly 40 per cent are now engaged in a different kind of work than that of their first positions after graduation.

To a considerably greater extent, of course, there has been shifting from one job to another not involving a change in the field of activity. Indeed, the average duration of the first jobs held by alumni after graduation was less than two years. Even the class of 1928, whose members had been out of college less than a year at the time this inquiry was made, showed a job turnover involving a change of employer of 24 per cent, i.e., nearly a fourth of the total number had worked for two or more employers. Of the preceding class, with less than two years' employment, 44 per cent had made at least one change of employer and 17.9

per cent had had three or more employers. These data are shown by classes in Table XXXIII. More than half of those graduating prior to 1926, with the exception of the 1888-98 classes, had worked for two or more employers, and more than a fourth had held three or more jobs. Whether or not this represents an excessive amount of job turnover which might be reduced by more adequate vocational guidance is impossible to determine without much more extensive investigation. Many alumni, in their comments, however, complained of difficulty in making satisfactory

TABLE XXXIII. NUMBER OF EMPLOYERS WORKED FOR BY
GRADUATES SINCE LEAVING COLLEGE

Classes	Number of graduates reporting	Proportion having worked for following number of employers:						
		One or more	Two or more	Three or more	Four or more	Five or more	Six or more	Seven or more
		%	%	%	%	%	%	%
1928	236	100.0	24.2	5.6	0.8	0.4	—	—
1927	185	100.0	44.0	17.9	5.9	1.1	—	—
1926	147	100.0	46.6	20.6	9.6	4.1	1.4	0.7
1925	156	100.0	55.8	26.3	15.4	4.5	1.9	—
1924	188	100.0	56.9	25.5	13.8	9.0	3.2	—
1923	135	100.0	63.0	30.4	10.4	6.0	2.2	2.2
1921–22	212	100.0	62.6	39.9	20.0	6.3	2.4	—
1919–20	124	100.0	65.0	43.9	24.4	11.4	3.3	0.8
1917–18	55	100.0	67.3	47.3	27.3	18.2	12.7	1.8
1914–16	85	100.0	79.5	56.6	37.3	25.2	14.4	2.4
1911–13	43	100.0	69.8	48.9	23.3	7.0	4.7	—
1905–10	50	100.0	57.1	42.8	30.6	20.4	10.2	2.0
1899–04	25	100.0	79.2	58.4	50.1	25.1	12.6	12.6
1888–98	29	100.0	44.8	31.0	24.1	17.2	3.4	3.4

adjustments in business and emphasized the need for vocational advice and guidance prior to graduation.

Some of the larger employers of college graduates, notably the American Telephone and Telegraph Company and its associated companies, have recognized this need by publishing complete descriptions of the nature of duties which new employees are expected to perform and of the various routes which lead to positions of responsibility in the business. Perhaps vocational adjustment could be made more satisfactory for the individual if, during the latter part of his undergraduate years, he were able to receive some instruction in the nature of work men engaged in various kinds of business work are expected to perform.

POSITIONS HELD BY GRADUATES

Any attempt to ascertain the nature of specific business positions held by the graduates, as contrasted with an analysis of the fields

TABLE XXXIV. PRESENT POSITIONS HELD BY GRADUATES BY CLASSES

Positions	All classes	1881–1898	1899–1904	1905–1910	1911–1913	1914–1916	1917–1918	1919–1920	1921–1922	1923	1924	1925	1926	1927	1928
All positions	1,659	28	23	50	43	85	55	123	212	135	188	156	146	184	231
Corporate officers	271	8	8	17	17	27	21	35	43	16	21	22	16	7	13
Presidents	65	5	3	9	5	8	7	7	7	3	4	7	2		2
Vice-Presidents	85	1	2	2	7	9	7	14	18	4	7	5	4	1	4
Secretary-Treasurers	37		2	1	3	1	5	4	5	4	1	4	4	3	
Secretaries	56	1		1	2	8	3	4	8	4	6	6	3	3	6
Treasurers	28	1	1	4		1	3	6	5	5	3		3		1
Proprietors or partners, n.o.s.	97	2	1	7	6	11	4	9	15	13	10	3	5	8	3
Managers	326	3	2	7	6	20	9	19	55	37	44	26	39	29	30
Advertising managers	14			1	1	1		1		1	2	3	1	1	2
Auditors	17					1	1	2	5	1		1	2	1	3
Cashiers	13			1	1			1	3	1	1	1	2	4	1
Department managers, n.o.s.	21				1	5	2		5	4	4		4	3	2
General managers	39	1	1	1	1		1	1	8	6	4	3	3	1	1
Merchandise managers	10							2	1	2	1	2	3	1	
Office managers	23		1	1	1		1	1	4	1	3	2	3	4	
Sales managers	44			4	1	5	1	4	4	5	4	4	4	4	5
Store managers	11				1			1	4	3	2	1	4	1	1
Superintendents	15				1	2	1	1	4	1	4	2	1		
Supervisors	18	2		1	2	2	1	2	1	1	3		2	2	3
Managers, other	101			1	2	7	2	5	16	12	14	8	10	11	11
Assistant managers	150			1	3	3	6	6	16	15	24	11	18	18	29
Assistant cashiers	10				1	1	1		2		2	1	1	1	
Assistant general managers	14					1	1	1	2		2	1	3	2	4
Assistant sales managers	15				1		1		1	3	3	1	3	1	2
Assistant treasurers	15			1		1	1	1	3	2	2		1	1	2
Assistant managers, other	96				1	1	3	5	8	8	17	8	11	13	21

TABLE XXXIV (*Cont.*)

Positions	All classes	1881–1898	1899–1904	1905–1910	1911–1913	1914–1916	1917–1918	1919–1920	1921–1922	1923	1924	1925	1926	1927	1928
Other business positions	549	5	2	9	5	15	6	28	54	28	65	68	51	97	116
Accountants	77					2		2	10	7	16	7	6	15	12
Brokers, traders, and dealers	38	4		5	3	1		7	2	2	2	2	3	4	3
Clerks	61				1			4	2		4	9	3	17	21
Engineers and inspectors	16						1		3		3	1	2	3	3
Sales correspondents	13								3			1	2	1	6
Sales representatives	29		1					3	7		3	7	2	3	3
Salesmen	171			3		4	4	9	17	13	25	17	22	28	29
Statisticians	58					3		2	3	5	6	9	6	9	15
Training course	16						1		1			1		4	9
Business positions, other	70	1	1	1	1	5		1	6	1	6	14	5	13	15
Non-business positions	258	9	10	9	6	9	9	26	29	26	22	25	16	24	38
Lawyers	85	7	7	2	4	1	2	9	11	13	10	13	2	1	3
Students	61								1		1	2	10	22	25
Teachers	85	1	2	7	2	4	4	12	14	11	6	10	2	1	9
Non-business positions, other	27	1	1			4	3	5	3	2	5		2		1
Unemployed	8	1									2	1	1	1	2

TABLE XXXV. FIRST POSITIONS HELD BY GRADUATES BY CLASSES

Positions	All classes	1888–1898	1899–1904	1905–1910	1911–1913	1914–1916	1917–1918	1919–1920	1921–1922	1923	1924	1925	1926	1927	1928
All positions	1,659	29	24	50	43	84	55	123	211	135	188	156	146	184	231
Corporate officers	88	5	1	8	1	6	2	8	11	8	9	10	10	5	4
Presidents	14		1		1	1		1	2		2	1	2		
Vice-Presidents	23	3		2		1		1	3		2	3	3		1
Secretary-Treasurers	16					1		4	3	4	2	2	2		1
Secretaries	24	1		2		2	1	1	1	2	1	4	2	2	
Treasurers	11	1		4		1	1	1	2	2	2		1	3	2
Proprietors or partners, n.o.s.	46	3	3	4	1	3	1	3	11	3	7	3	1	4	3
Managers	194	3	3	7	3	9	12	18	23	17	20	19	18	21	21
Advertising managers	14		1	1	1	1		1	1	1	2	1	1	1	1
Auditors	22		1			1	1	4	2	1	2	1	1	1	2
Cashiers	8	1	1	1		1		3	4	1	2	2	2	6	2
Department managers, n.o.s.	14				1	1		1	1	1	1	2	1	1	2
General managers	21		1	1		1	2	1	1	3	4	2	2	1	1
Merchandise managers	5												2	1	5
Office managers	19			4	1	2	2	2	2	2	2	2	2	4	1
Sales managers	18								3	2	1	1	1	1	
Store managers	7						1		1	2	1	2	1		
Superintendents	7	1							1	1	1	2		1	
Supervisors	10			1		3	2	1	1		1	1	3	1	3
Managers, other	49	2	1	1	1	3	4	7	7	4	5	6	4	2	5
Assistant managers	107	1		1	2	6	5	4	11	12	10	13	12	11	20
Assistant cashiers	9	1			1	1	1		3	1	1	2	2	3	4
Assistant general managers	13				1	1	1		2	1	1	1		3	1
Sales managers	8					1	1		1	1	1	1	1	1	1
Assistant treasurers	8							1		1	1	1		1	
Assistant managers, other	69			1		4	2	3	5	9	7	9	9	6	14

TABLE XXXV. (*Cont.*)

Positions	All classes	1888-1898	1899-1904	1905-1910	1911-1913	1914-1916	1917-1918	1919-1920	1921-1922	1923	1924	1925	1926	1927	1928
Other business positions															
Accountants	973	7	9	23	33	47	22	69	128	70	122	88	88	122	145
Brokers, traders, and dealers	126		1	3	1	4	5	12	15	11	24	10	10	13	17
Clerks	31	1		2	3	1		3	2	3	5	3	1	2	5
Engineers and inspectors	250	5	4	8	11	14	3	20	28	16	26	18	16	40	41
Sales correspondents	19			1	1			1	2	2	3		2	6	1
Sales managers	9						1	2	1	1	1	2			1
Sales representatives	12							1	1	1	1	3	1	2	2
Salesmen	266		2	6	12	13	7	15	40	20	35	25	30	32	29
Statisticians	49			1			1	4	7	3	5	6	3	6	13
Training courses	80				1	2	1	6	9	7	10	8	13	8	15
Business positions, other	131	1	2	2	4	13	3	5	23	6	13	13	12	13	21
Non-business positions															
Lawyers	251	10	11	8	3	13	14	21	27	25	20	23	17	21	38
Physicians	63	7	6	5	1	1	1	5	5	10	7	10	1		4
Students	62								2		1	3	12	17	27
Teachers	77	1	2	3	2	6	4	9	16	12	6	6	2	2	6
Non-business positions, other	49	2	3			6	9	7	4	3	6	4	2	2	1

TABLE XXXVI. PRESENT POSITIONS HELD BY GRADUATES ACCORDING TO PHASE OF BUSINESS IN WHICH FIRM IS ENGAGED

Positions	Total	Accounting	Advertising	Marketing	Manufacturing	Commercial finance	Investment finance	Insurance	Foreign trade	Real estate	Transportation	Public utilities	Other
Total	1,659	58	28	257	410	128	152	142	20	66	23	47	328
Corporate officers	271		8	69	101	19	15	18	5	15	2		19
Presidents	65		8	16	26	3	4	6	1	3	2		3
Vice Presidents	85		3	25	25	11	6	3	1	5			5
Secretary-Treasurers	37		3	5	19	3	2	3		4			2
Secretaries	56		1	13	19	1	1	5		2			3
Treasurers	28		1	10	12	1	2	1	3	1			6
Proprietors or partners, n.o.s.	97	18	2	24	16	2	4	10	1	15			5
Managers and superintendents	326	2	5	88	109	25	14	23	3	11	4	19	23
Advertising managers	14			4	10		1					4	2
Auditors	17	2		3	3		1			2		1	3
Cashiers	13			7	1	8	1	4					
Department managers, n.o.s.	21		1	13	3	4	1	1	1	1	1		3
General managers	39			8	15	3	1	1	1	2	1	3	1
Merchandise managers	10			2	1		1					3	1
Office managers	23		1	9	6	1	2	2	1	1	1		2
Sales managers	44		1	10	27		2					7	1
Store managers	11			2				3					6
Supervisors	18			2	3			3		1	1		
Superintendents	15			2	8			10					
Managers, other	101		2	28	32	9	5		1	4	1	3	3
Assistant managers	150		2	31	42	23	13	17	2	4	2	6	8
Assistant cashiers	10			6	4	6	2	2			1	1	
Assistant general managers	14			2	11	1	1						
Assistant sales managers	15			3	3	1	1						
Assistant treasurers	15		1			2	1	2	2		1		3
Assistant managers, other	96		1	20	24	13	8	13		4	1	5	

TABLE XXXVI (*Continued*)

Positions	Total	Accounting	Advertising	Marketing	Manufacturing	Commercial finance	Investment finance	Insurance	Foreign trade	Real estate	Transportation	Public utilities	Other
Total	1,659	58	28	275	410	128	152	142	20	66	23	47	328
Other business positions	550	38	11	45	135	58	106	72	7	21	14	22	21
Accountants	77	38		6	16	6	1	2		3	1	5	1
Brokers, traders, dealers	38			1	1		26			8			8
Clerks	61			4	11	14	4	11	1	1	5	3	1
Engineers and inspectors	16				4	1	1	1			2	5	
Sales correspondents	13			1	6	1	1	2	1		1	1	
Sales representatives	29			2	14	2	5	2	1		1	1	1
Salesmen	171		2	16	50	8	45	41	1	7	1		
Statisticians	58		1	5	16	15	14	3			1		3
Training courses	16			1	4	2	2	1				5	
Business positions, other	71		8	9	13	9	7	9	3	2	2	2	7
Non-business positions	257				7	1		2	2		1		244
Lawyers	85					1		2	1		1		81
Students	61				1				1				60
Teachers	84												83
Non-business positions, other	27				6								20
Unemployed	8												8

of work in which they are engaged, is confronted with innumerable difficulties. "What's in a name? That which we call a rose, by any other name would smell as sweet" applies with double force when names are used by individuals to describe and dignify their own positions in the eyes of their fellow men. Titles may mean little, especially when they are self-assigned, and even if the title is an accurate description of an individual's position, the actual responsibilities of the position vary widely from one industry to another and from one firm to another. However, taken in conjunction with other measures such as earnings, numbers of employees under supervision, and type of business, titles should furnish some indication of the responsibility and authority which attaches to the work of the individual. Table XXXIV shows the present positions held by the 1,659 graduates furnishing this information, while Table XXXV shows the first positions held by graduates. Table XXXVI shows the distribution of present positions among different types of business firms. Totals are shown only for those individual positions in which ten or more graduates are now employed.

More than half of the entire group are now employed in positions implying executive responsibility, *viz.*, corporate officers, proprietors or partners, managers, and assistant managers. Apparently many of the graduates found it unnecessary to "start in at the bottom of the ladder," when it is considered that 26 per cent of the group reported that they held positions involving executive responsibility on their first employment after graduation. It is necessary to state, however, that most of such positions were with small firms and many of these graduates were employed by business establishments operated by their families.

Earnings and Managerial Responsibility of Various Positions

Some idea of the wide range in compensation and responsibility attaching to various positions reported under the same title may be gained from Tables XXXVII and XXXVIIII. Information is presented for each position in which 14 or more individuals were engaged, showing the calculated median income and income distribution, the median number of employees under supervision, and the distribution of this item. The highest earnings were

TABLE XXXVII. ANNUAL EARNED INCOME REPORTED FOR PRINCIPAL
POSITIONS HELD BY GRADUATES

Position	Number of graduates reporting income	Median income	Proportion reporting following amounts of earned income:							
			Less than $2000	2000 or more	3000 or more	4000 or more	5000 or more	6000 or more	9000 or more	12,000 or more
			%	%	%	%	%	%	%	%
Corporate officers										
Presidents............	54	$11,000	—	100.0	98.1	96.3	88.9	77.8	57.4	46.3
Vice-president and general managers......	14	8,400	—	100.0	100.0	100.0	100.0	78.6	42.9	28.6
Vice-president and sales managers..........	14	9,000	—	100.0	85.7	71.4	71.4	64.3	50.0	35.7
Vice-presidents.......	41	7,690	2.4	97.6	92.7	75.6	70.7	61.0	41.5	26.8
Secretary-treasurers...	33	5,500	—	100.0	84.8	75.8	60.6	39.4	21.2	18.2
Secretaries...........	55	4,940	5.5	94.5	80.0	65.5	49.1	32.7	16.4	12.7
Treasurers...........	27	5,830	—	100.0	92.6	81.5	59.3	48.1	37.0	18.5
Proprietors or partners	96	6,530	4.2	95.8	85.4	68.6	59.4	53.1	35.4	27.1
Managers										
Advertising managers..	14	4,500	7.1	92.9	85.7	64.3	35.7	21.4	7.1	—
Auditors.............	17	2,640	23.5	76.5	35.3	11.7	5.9	—	—	—
Department managers, n.o.s..............	21	3,080	28.6	71.4	52.4	23.8	19.0	14.3	9.5	4.8
General managers.....	38	5,000	2.6	97.4	86.8	60.5	50.0	42.1	36.8	26.3
Office managers.......	23	3,100	21.7	78.3	52.2	30.4	30.4	13.0	8.7	4.3
Sales managers.......	43	5,070	—	100.0	93.0	79.1	51.2	34.9	23.3	16.3
Supervisors..........	18	3,250	11.1	88.9	55.6	33.3	16.7	11.1	11.1	11.1
Managers, others......	23	3,500	8.7	91.3	65.2	34.8	26.1	21.7	4.3	—
Assistant Managers										
Assistant general managers..............	14	2,750	28.6	71.4	42.9	35.7	28.6	21.4	7.1	7.1
Assistant sales managers	15	4,250	6.7	93.3	66.7	53.3	40.0	26.7	13.3	—
Assistant treasurers....	15	3,920	6.7	93.3	86.7	46.7	13.3	13.3	—	—
Other business positions										
Accountants..........	75	2,540	30.7	69.3	33.3	10.7	5.3	4.0	1.3	1.3
Brokers, traders, dealers	27	{over 12,000	3.7	96.3	88.9	85.2	81.5	77.8	66.7	55.6
Clerks...............	61	1,420	70.5	29.5	6.6	—	—	—	—	—
Engineers............	14	3,330	7.1	92.9	64.3	21.4	7.1	7.1	—	—
Sales representatives...	28	4,000	3.6	96.4	67.9	50.0	35.7	21.4	10.7	7.1
Salesmen.............	170	3,360	20.6	79.4	57.6	36.5	25.3	16.5	5.9	2.4
Investigators.........	19	3,167	15.8	84.2	52.6	36.8	26.3	21.1	10.5	—
Statisticians..........	28	2,730	21.4	78.6	39.3	14.3	14.3	10.7	3.6	3.6
Training courses......	16	2,130	43.7	56.3	6.3	—	—	—	—	—
Non-business positions										
Lawyers.............	32	2,910	18.7	81.3	46.9	40.6	31.3	21.9	18.8	18.8
Lawyer and partners...	49	5,300	18.4	81.6	69.4	59.2	53.1	42.9	28.6	22.4
Teachers.............	83	3,300	10.8	89.2	57.8	31.3	22.9	14.5	1.2	—

reported by brokers, traders, and dealers; the median income for
this group was more than $12,000, reflecting no doubt the active
securities and real estate markets of the past few years. With the
exception of these individuals, however, graduates holding positions as corporate officers reported the largest earnings, substantially above those reported for managers and assistant managers.
Among the groups holding executive positions in business the
highest salaries were received by those engaged in selling and
advertising. Thus, the median income for vice-president and sales

TABLE XXXVIII. NUMBER OF EMPLOYEES UNDER SUPERVISION
FOR PRINCIPAL POSITIONS HELD BY GRADUATES

Positions	Number of graduates reporting number of employees	Median number of employees	Proportion reporting following number of employees under supervision:							
			None	1 or more	5 or more	20 or more	50 or more	100 or more	500 or more	1000 or more
			%	%	%	%	%	%	%	%
Corporate officers										
Presidents............	54	48	1.9	98.1	87.0	70.4	48.1	31.5	7.4	3.7
Vice-president and general managers......	14	200	—	100.0	100.0	78.6	78.6	64.3	7.1	—
Vice-president and sales managers.........	12	20	8.3	91.7	83.3	41.7	33.3	16.7	—	—
Vice-presidents.......	41	23	7.3	92.7	82.9	51.2	36.6	24.4	4.9	2.4
Secretary-treasurers...	34	15	2.9	97.1	67.6	41.2	23.5	14.7	2.9	—
Secretaries...........	50	18	10.0	90.0	70.0	46.0	24.0	14.0	2.0	2.0
Treasurers...........	26	33	—	100.0	84.6	61.5	34.6	23.1	—	—
Proprietors or partners	89	6	7.9	92.1	51.7	19.1	9.0	5.6	—	—
Managers										
Advertising managers..	13	7	23.1	76.9	53.8	15.4	7.7	—	—	—
Auditors.............	14	3	35.7	64.3	42.9	14.3	7.1	7.1	—	—
Dept. managers, n.o.s..	21	8	4.8	95.2	57.1	19.0	—	—	—	—
General managers.....	33	33	—	100.0	87.9	57.6	39.4	24.2	6.1	3.0
Office managers.......	21	16	4.8	95.2	52.4	19.0	9.5	4.8	—	—
Sales managers.......	40	15	2.5	97.5	75.0	37.5	10.0	2.5	—	—
Supervisors..........	16	10	12.5	87.5	62.5	25.0	—	—	—	—
Managers, others.....	19	13	—	100.0	84.2	21.1	5.3	—	—	—
Assistant managers										
Asst. general managers.	11	18	9.1	90.9	81.8	45.5	18.2	18.2	—	—
Asst. sales managers...	14	13	7.1	92.9	64.3	35.7	14.3	7.1	—	—
Assistant treasurers....	12	11	16.7	83.3	66.7	25.0	8.3	—	—	—
Other business positions										
Accountants.........	61	—	65.6	34.4	19.7	6.6	1.6	—	—	—
Brokers, traders, dealers	21	5	28.6	71.4	47.6	14.3	14.3	9.5	—	—
Clerks..............	53	—	66.0	34.0	15.1	1.9	—	—	—	—
Engineers...........	13	5	38.5	61.5	46.2	30.8	30.8	15.4	7.7	—
Sales representatives...	23	—	73.9	26.1	8.7	4.3	—	—	—	—
Salesmen............	132	—	75.8	24.2	7.6	4.5	1.5	0.8	—	—
Investigators.........	15	—	53.3	46.7	20.0	6.7	6.7	—	—	—
Statisticians.........	28	2	32.1	67.9	28.6	—	—	—	—	—
Training courses......	12	—	83.3	16.7	8.3	8.3	—	—	—	—
Non-business positions										
Lawyers.............	22	—	50.0	50.0	13.6	4.5	4.5	4.5	4.5	—
Lawyer and partners ..	43	3	11.6	88.4	25.6	4.7	—	—	—	—
Teachers............	46	—	56.5	43.5	26.1	13.0	10.9	10.9	—	—

manager was $9,000, second only to that of president and exceeding that of vice-president and general manager.[2] Sales managers earned more than general managers and were more highly paid than any other members of the managerial group, while advertising managers, assistant sales managers, salesmen, and sales

---

[2] The United States Personnel Board, in 1928, collected data on salaries paid executives in a large number of corporations. Median salaries for principal comparable positions were as follows: presidents, $20,000; vice-presidents, $9,292; secretaries and treasurers, $7,749; advertising managers, $5,978; sales managers, $5,137. *Report of Wage and Personnel Survey,* House Document No. 602, 70th Congress, 2nd Session, G.P.O., Washington, D.C., 1929, p. 210.

representatives all reported relatively large earnings among their respective grades. Auditors in the managerial group, and accountants among other business positions, reported comparatively small earnings.

Although these data reveal significant differences in the earnings received by graduates holding different positions in business, still more conspicuous is the wide range of income earned by individuals holding identical positions. Many of the men holding major executive positions reported earnings in the lower income brackets while groups whose median earnings were much below those of corporate officers and managers had many individuals in the upper salary levels. Thus, of the 238 graduates holding positions as corporate officers, 24, or ten per cent, reported earnings of less than $3,000 annually, although the median earnings for this group ranged from $5,500 for secretary-treasurer to $11,000 for president. Sales managers, with a median income considerably less than those of most groups of corporate officers, had more than a sixth of their number earning more than the median income for presidents.

Another objective measure which may possess some significance in appraising the importance represented by these positions is the number of employees reported by graduates as being directly under their supervision. This question was more susceptible to misinterpretation and misstatement than that concerning salary and for that reason too great reliance cannot be placed in the results. This information, presented in Table XXXVIII, indicates that graduates holding official and managerial positions discharge a considerable measure of executive responsibility in supervising the work of others.

The responsibilities of the position of vice-president and general manager, in this respect, were evidently much greater than that of other positions. The median number of employees under supervision of these officials was 200 as compared with 48 for presidents,[3] and 33 for treasurers and for general managers. Smaller numbers of employees were reported under the super-

---

[3] This question asked for the number of employees "directly under your supervision"; presidents and other corporate officers, through department heads, probably have indirect supervision over larger numbers than are reported in Table XXXVIII.

vision of all other members of the official and managerial groups, while for only four of the other positions listed—brokers, engineers, statisticians, and law partners—was the median number of employees larger than zero. As in the case of the salary distribution there was a much wider range among the individual members of any one group than the disparity between the medians for the several groups. More than a fifth of the vice-presidents and general managers, for instance, reported that they had less than 20 employees under their supervision, although the median number for the group was 200, while over 10 per cent of the

TABLE XXXIX. ANNUAL EARNED INCOME OF GRADUATES ACCORDING TO NUMBER OF EMPLOYEES UNDER SUPERVISION

Number of employees under supervision	Number of graduates reporting	Proportion in each group	Median income
None...................	374	28.4%	$ 2,560
1 to 4...................	298	22.7	3,490
5 to 19.................	316	24.0	4,510
20 to 49................	145	11.0	5,360
50 to 99................	66	5.0	7,750
100 to 499..............	98	7.4	8,120
500 to 999..............	12	0.9	over 12,000
1,000 or more...........	7	0.6	over 12,000
Total	1,316	100.0%	$ 3,730

general managers reported less than five employees under their supervision.

As would be expected in view of the fact that the major executive positions, with few exceptions, were the most highly paid and involved the greatest responsibility for supervision of personnel, there was an approximate relation between compensation and the number of employees under supervision. Table XXXIX shows that the small numbers of graduates responsible for large groups of employees received much higher average earnings than those without such responsibilities. More than a fourth of the entire group of 1,316 for whom this information was available reported no employees under their supervision. The median salary for these graduates was only $2,560, half the salary of those supervising 20 to 49 employees, and less than a third of that of those reporting between 50 and 99 employees, while the small number having supervision over more than 500 employees had a median income in excess of $12,000. It is significant that only a fourth of the entire group were responsible for 20 or more employees and only 19 men reported 500 or more employees. The conclusions based upon these data seem to be justified despite the fact that, for reasons already stated, information in reply to this question is probably not accurately representative of the entire group.

However, it is quite obvious that a most important, if not the most important, factor in determining the earnings and executive responsibility of individuals is their maturity, as measured by the

TABLE XL. ANNUAL EARNED INCOME OF GRADUATES BY CLASSES

Classes	Number of graduates	Number reporting income	Median income	Proportion reporting following amounts of earned income:							
				Less than $2000	$2000 or more	$3000 or more	$4000 or more	$5000 or more	$6000 or more	$9000 or more	$12000 or more
				%	%	%	%	%	%	%	%
1928	236	205	$1,850	58.5	41.5	21.7	6.3	3.9	2.9	1.5	1.0
1927	185	163	2,240	39.9	60.1	18.4	7.4	4.3	3.1	—	—
1926	147	138	3,080	17.4	82.6	52.2	25.4	17.4	10.9	3.6	2.9
1925	156	150	2,860	17.3	82.7	44.7	24.7	17.3	10.7	6.0	4.7
1924	188	185	3,740	3.2	96.8	75.1	41.1	25.4	14.6	4.3	2.7
1923	135	131	4,140	2.3	97.7	78.6	52.7	35.6	25.2	13.0	6.1
1921–22	212	210	4,860	1.3	98.7	87.1	64.8	47.6	32.4	16.2	11.0
1919–20	124	117	5,970	1.7	98.3	93.2	79.5	65.8	49.6	30.8	18.8
1917–18	55	49	7,070	2.0	98.0	95.9	81.6	67.3	55.1	40.8	22.4
1914–16	85	80	7,800	—	100.0	93.8	83.8	72.5	61.3	42.5	35.0
1911–13	43	42	12,000	—	—	100.0	97.6	95.2	76.2	57.1	50.0
1905–10	50	48	10,370	—	—	100.0	95.8	89.6	81.2	60.4	37.5
1899–04	25	22	12,000 (over)	13.6	86.4	86.4	86.4	81.8	77.3	59.1	50.0
1888–98	29	26	12,000	—	—	100.0	96.2	92.3	84.6	65.4	61.5
All classes	1,670	1,417	$3,730	16.2	83.8	63.0	45.3	35.1	26.4	15.9	11.20

number of years they have been out of college. This fact becomes apparent from an examination of Table XL, showing median earned income and the distribution of graduates of each class or group of classes among different salary levels. With only two exceptions—that of the 1925 class and the 1905 to 1910 group of classes—income increases as the length of time since graduation increases. Median income of the 1928 class, which had been employed less than a year at the time of the inquiry, was only $1,850, slightly less than half that of the 1924 class, whose members had been working for five years. Median income was more than twice as large again for the members of the 1914 to 1916 classes, while half of the 1911 to 1913 graduates reported annual earned income of more than $12,000. Graduates of the six immediately preceding classes reported a smaller income, but the earnings of the earliest classes were $12,000 or more.

The distribution of graduates among the various income levels shows a wide dispersion in individual earnings in each class. All but the two most recent classes have some of their members earning $12,000 or more; a proportion which is quite small among the last six classes, but which increases to 62 per cent of those graduating between 1888 and 1898. Practically none of the older graduates—those graduating prior to 1914—was earning less than $3,000, and only a very small number reported less than $4,000 income. On the other hand, each of the last 12 classes had at least a few individuals receiving less than $2,000 annually, although this proportion is very small prior to the 1925 class. In general, as the number of years since graduation increases, there is a fairly steady decline in the numbers at lower income levels and a corresponding increase of the higher salary groups.

A similar picture of the influence of increasing maturity and experience upon executive responsibility is revealed by the data have reached positions of responsibility involving the supervision of large numbers of employees, while nearly half of the graduates who have been out of college ten years or longer reported at least 20 employees under their supervision. In none of the classes, however, with the exception of 1928, did more than half of the graduates replying to this question report that they had no responsibility for supervising the work of others. Evidently some

TABLE XLI. NUMBER OF EMPLOYEES UNDER SUPERVISION OF
GRADUATES BY CLASSES

Classes	Number of graduates	Number reporting number of employees	Proportion reporting following number of employees under supervision:							
			None	1 or more	5 or more	20 or more	50 or more	100 or more	500 or more	1000 or more
			%	%	%	%	%	%	%	%
1928	236	159	50.9	49.1	27.7	9.4	3.1	1.9	1.2	—
1927	185	134	44.0	56.0	32.8	14.9	7.5	3.7	0.7	—
1926	147	126	30.2	69.8	43.7	15.9	7.9	7.1	—	—
1925	156	122	36.9	63.1	36.1	18.0	9.0	5.7	0.8	0.8
1924	188	158	31.6	68.4	48.7	21.5	10.1	5.1	0.6	0.6
1923	135	117	22.2	77.8	47.9	29.1	15.4	10.3	0.9	—
1921–22	212	175	17.7	82.3	57.7	31.4	17.1	10.9	1.1	—
1919–20	124	100	21.0	79.0	57.0	27.0	12.0	6.0	—	—
1917–18	55	51	19.6	80.4	64.7	41.2	29.4	17.6	3.9	3.9
1914–16	85	73	12.3	87.7	79.5	46.6	31.5	21.9	4.1	2.7
1911–13	43	39	5.1	94.9	76.9	53.8	41.0	28.2	10.3	—
1905–10	50	41	9.8	90.2	70.7	46.3	22.0	19.5	2.4	—
1899–04	25	21	4.8	95.2	66.7	38.1	33.3	19.0	14.3	4.8
1888–98	29	20	—	100.0	65.0	40.0	35.0	25.0	—	—
All classes	1,670	1,336	28.2	71.8	49.0	25.3	14.1	9.1	1.5	0.7

measure of responsibility for the management of labor falls to the lot of the majority of the graduates of this institution, and in most cases, this occurs fairly early in their careers.

Earnings of Graduates in Different Fields of Work

It is natural to expect the responsibility and compensation of graduates to increase in proportion to the years of experience and maturity gained since graduation. Admitting that this factor appears to be of the greatest importance in explaining income differences it may be of interest to examine the effects of certain other influences. The information shown in Table XLII indicates that there are noticeable differences in the compensation reported by graduates engaged in different kinds of work.[4] No data are shown for public utilities, foreign trade, and transportation, since so few graduates were engaged in these fields that the calculated medians were unreliable.

The absolute values of the calculated median incomes are not highly significant in themselves for reasons already stated; for each kind of work, they include both the older graduates, with relatively high incomes, and the younger graduates, with low incomes. But the relation between the median incomes for different

TABLE XLII. ANNUAL EARNED INCOME OF GRADUATES ACCORDING TO NATURE OF WORK

Nature of work	Number of graduates	Median incomes		
		All classes	1888–1922	1923–1928
Accounting............	114	$2,770	$4,700	$2,410
Advertising............	47	4,350	8,630	3,380
Marketing............	345	4,170	6,940	3,330
Manufacturing........	224	3,640	7,410	2,740
Commercial finance....	205	3,700	5,550	2,780
Investment finance.....	148	4,680	12,000	2,240
Insurance............	138	3,600	7,130	2,900
Real estate............	61	5,300	7,000	4,300
Law................	85	4,250	8,250	2,400
Education............	84	3,300	4,500	2,480
All graduates*	1,659	$3,730	$6,430	$2,830

* Includes also graduates engaged in other kinds of work not specified above.

groups appears to reveal real differences in the earnings of men in different kinds of work in view of the fact that occupational

---

[4] The classification used in this table describes the nature of the work or function performed by the individual, not the type of firm by which he is employed. It is identical with that used in Table XXIX.

distributions were fairly uniform among different classes. Thus the accounting group earned the lowest income—lower even than that of teachers,—while real estate and investment finance appear to have been the most lucrative fields of work. Graduates engaged in the advertising and marketing fields also received considerably higher than average incomes while manufacturing, commercial finance, and insurance had approximately equal earnings, only slightly below the average for the entire group. Of the non-business fields represented, those engaged in law received earnings much higher than the average, while the median income of teachers was nearly $400 less than that of all graduates reporting this information.

The situation revealed in this table was also found to be generally true when the individual classes were considered separately. These data are represented in Table XLIII, for the six most important business fields only, in view of the small numbers engaged in real estate and advertising. In most of the classes earnings were highest among those engaged in investment finance and marketing, and somewhat lower in manufacturing, commercial finance, and insurance.

TABLE XLIII. ANNUAL EARNED INCOME OF GRADUATES ACCORDING TO NATURE OF WORK BY CLASSES

Nature of work	Median annual earned income of graduates in each field by classes							
	1928	1927	1926	1925	1924	1923	1921–22	1919–20
All fields	$1,850	$2,240	$3,080	$2,860	$3,740	$4,140	$4,860	$5,970
Accounting..........	$1,570	$2,000	$2,500	$2,500	$3,250	*	$4,330	*
Marketing..........	2,170	2,600	3,420	3,500	4,000	4,440	5,460	7,500
Manufacturing.......	1,970	2,150	3,200	3,200	3,700	4,000	4,710	8,000
Commercial finance...	1,710	2,070	2,730	2,920	3,830	5,330	4,380	5,170
Investment finance...	1,750	2,460	3,670	3,570	4,000	4,880	7,500	*
Insurance...........	1,750	2,250	3,130	3,170	3,780	3,750	4,830	*
Law...............	†	†	†	1,670	2,670	3,670	5,130	8,250
Education...........	1,800	*	*	2,500	2,600	2,790	3,190	5,000

* Number too small to be representative.
† Graduates of these classes were students in law schools.

An adequate explanation for these apparent disparities in the financial returns of different kinds of work is not entirely apparent. The low average for accounting may be due partially to the fact that many men ultimately leave this field for other kinds of work, notably commercial finance. It should be emphasized, however, that this group includes not only all men holding positions as accountants and auditors, irrespective of the business in which the employing firm is engaged, but also all graduates, including proprietors and partners, attached to public accounting firms. The relatively poor economic status of this group is all the more significant when it is considered that this field was one of the first, and is now one of the most highly organized, departments of instruction in collegiate schools of business, attracting a considerable proportion of the students enrolling in these institutions. That teaching has long been a comparatively poorly paid occupation is a matter of traditional knowledge, particularly among teachers. The group represented here, with a median income of $3,340, moreover, is probably somewhat more highly paid than the average, as most of them are teaching business and economic subjects in universities, a type of work which is compensated more highly than most kinds of teaching.

Investment finance and real estate have been conspicuously profitable fields of work, reflecting especially the active security markets and rapid expansion in building and real estate operations in the decade following the World War. It is not surprising, therefore, to find the graduates engaged in these types of business receiving large incomes. The fields of distribution and advertising have also expanded noticeably during the past few years and have attracted increasing numbers of college graduates to positions of major responsibility. It will be remembered from the analysis of compensation of graduates in specific business positions that sales and advertising managers were more highly paid than comparable managerial positions in other fields; likewise salesmen earned more than those in other non-executive business positions.

Whether these great disparities in earnings are due entirely to real differences in the nature of duties and responsibilities or to a surplus or deficiency in the supply of college graduates trained for the several fields, the very existence of such disparities is a matter which should concern both the students and faculties of university schools of business. Obviously the sole, or even the primary, aim of such a school cannot be that of ensuring that its graduates earn the largest possible amount of money. Individuals, however, whether or not they are college graduates, and in the case of the latter, whether they have been graduated from schools of business, law, medicine, or liberal arts, are inclined to measure their success in life in terms of dollars. Universities, talking of the "dollars and cents value of a college education," point with pride to the large earnings of their graduates. And students in tens of thousands flock to the universities because they believe that a college diploma will materially enhance their chances for success in their work after graduation.

It would seem therefore, that the university and especially the professional school which prepares its students for more or less specialized occupations, has a definite responsibility to appraise the relative attractiveness of the occupational opportunities open to its graduates. There may "always be room at the top of the ladder" in any field of work, but some ladders are more crowded than others.

EARNINGS COMPARED WITH ACTIVITIES AND SCHOLARSHIP

In the light of the data already presented on the reasons given by graduates for choosing their occupations and concerning undergraduate employment and participation in extra-curricular campus activities, the information presented in Table XLIV may be of some interest. More than a fourth of the men graduating in the last six classes and well over a third of the earlier graduates chose their first occupations because of family connection or influence. This group, most of whom are employed in family busi-

TABLE XLIV. ANNUAL EARNED INCOME OF GRADUATES ACCORDING TO REASONS FOR CHOOSING OCCUPATION, UNDERGRADUATE EMPLOYMENT, UNDERGRADUATE ACTIVITIES AND SCHOLARSHIP RECORDS.

	All classes	1888–1922	1923–1928
Reason for choosing occupation:			
Family connection or influence..............	$4,200	$7,200	$3,050
Other reasons.............................	3,620	6,120	2,770
Undergraduate employment:*			
Defraying some part of expenses............	3,350	5,920	2,640
Defraying 50% or more of expenses.........	3,690	6,130	2,650
Defraying no part of expenses..............	3,870	6,490	3,030
Undergraduate activities:			
Dramatic, literary, etc. (excluding athletic)....	3,750	6,410	2,790
Athletic (excluding all other)................	3,370	6,240	2,720
Athletic and other........................	4,460	8,280	3,190
No participation..........................	3,890	5,540	2,900
Scholarship records:†			
Highest tenth of class......................	2,880		2,500
Highest third of class......................	3,170		2,710
Middle third of class.......................	3,430		2,900
Lowest third of class.......................	3,000		2,600
Lowest tenth of class......................	3,690		3,180

* All graduates choosing occupation because of family connection or influence were excluded from this tabulation.
† Scholarship records were not available for classes prior to 1921; therefore no data are presented for the 1888–1922 group.

nesses, reported consistently higher incomes than those choosing their jobs for other reasons, there being a difference of $600 in median income between the two groups.

Since many of the students with family business connections found it unnecessary to engage in outside work as undergraduates, they were eliminated in the second comparison shown in this table. The highest incomes were earned by those students who reported that they defrayed no part of their undergraduate expenses, a rather surprising fact in view of the relatively low scholarship records made by this group as undergraduates.[5] Graduates who defrayed some part of their college expenses, comprising 46.5 per cent of all, had a median income of only $3,350, much less than the average for the entire group, despite their relatively better scholarship records. Curiously enough, the median income of the men who defrayed more than half of their college expenses, and who did have higher than average scholarship records, was above that of all graduates who worked while in college but below that of those who were not employed. Apparently any relation between undergraduate employment and earnings after graduation is inverse rather than direct.

Participation in undergraduate campus activities appears to have some relation to earnings after graduation. Sharp differences exist in the median incomes reported for each of the four groups shown in the table. By far the highest income was that of men who engaged in both athletic and "intellectual" activities, while those engaging solely in athletics had the lowest income. Incidentally the latter group also had the lowest scholarship record. Those engaged in dramatic and other activities but eschewing athletics, who had by far the best scholarship records, had incomes only slightly above the average for all graduates. Graduates reporting no participation in campus activities, had a median income somewhat above the general average.

SCHOLARSHIP COMPARED WITH EARNINGS AND OCCUPATIONS

The comparison of earnings with scholarship, also shown in Table XLIV, tells another interesting, albeit for the educator, a rather disconcerting story. Men who ranked in the highest tenth

---

[5] See Table XXII.

of their classes in scholarship failed to have a correspondingly high rank in earnings; in fact the median income of this group was below the general median and substantially lower than the median income of graduates whose scholarship was in the lowest tenth. Incomes of those in the highest third, however, were slightly higher than of those in the lowest third, although the disparities are hardly great enough to be very significant.

Superficially it would seem that the teacher, attempting to stimulate his students to greater efforts in their class room activities, could obtain little comfort from these comparisons. Moreover, they are at striking variance with the results of certain other similar studies. For instance, the experience of the American Telephone and Telegraph Company, previously referred to, showed that the success of college graduates in the Bell System[6] was closely related to their undergraduate scholarship records, with the men of high scholastic standing advancing more rapidly in salary than those with poor academic records. The results of this and similar studies suggests that further analysis is necessary to explain the relationship between scholarship and earnings shown in Table XLIV. In view of the marked disparities in earnings of graduates engaged in different occupations it may be of interest to examine the distribution of scholarship among men engaged in the principal kinds of work.

TABLE XLV. SCHOLARSHIP RECORDS COMPARED WITH KINDS OF WORK IN WHICH GRADUATES ARE ENGAGED

Kind of work*	Number of graduates	Proportion of graduates in each of the following scholarship classes:				
		Highest tenth	Highest third	Middle third	Lowest third	Lowest tenth
All graduates	933	10.0%	33.3%	33.3%	33.3%	10.0%
Accounting	66	16.7	39.4	36.4	24.2	9.1
Advertising	30	16.7	36.7	26.6	36.7	0.0
Marketing	206	5.8	32.0	28.2	39.8	14.1
Manufacturing	134	7.5	28.4	37.3	34.3	8.2
Commercial finance	111	9.9	34.2	33.3	32.5	7.2
Investment finance	73	6.8	31.5	30.1	38.4	11.0
Insurance	69	7.2	21.7	40.6	37.7	13.0
Real estate	34	8.8	29.4	38.2	32.4	5.9
Public utilities	20	35.0	60.0	25.0	15.0	5.0
Law	41	17.0	46.4	39.0	14.6	7.3
Education	38	26.3	60.5	21.1	18.4	5.3

* Because of small numbers engaged in foreign trade and transportation comparisons for these fields are not available.

[6] See Chapter II.

Apparently the curious relation between scholarship and earnings is at least partially explained by the data presented in Table XLV. It will be remembered that the highest incomes were reported by graduates engaged in investment finance, real estate, marketing, advertising, and law. With the exception of the two last named occupations, however, the scholarship of men engaged in these fields was not above the average. Indeed, in marketing and investment finance it appears to be distinctly below that of most other fields. The best scholarship records were displayed by men entering education, law, public utilities, and, to a less extent, accounting, and advertising. Among these fields, the earnings of accountants and teachers were very low as compared with other occupations, the earnings of lawyers were relatively high, and those of men employed by public utilities, not far from the average. It is interesting to note the high scholarship of the graduates engaged in public utility work, a large proportion of whom are employed by the Bell System. The most obvious conclusion from this analysis is that the explanation of income differences is related more closely to occupations than to scholarship. Further studies, which unfortunately cannot be made at this time, are necessary to show whether or not, *within* each occupation, scholarship will show a close and positive correlation with earnings.

Some further light may be thrown on this question, however, by the data on scholarship of graduates holding the positions shown in Table XLVI. In view of the lack of comparable scholarship records for all graduates it is necessary to limit this analysis to a few of the leading positions—those specific positions in each of which at least 20 men were engaged for whom scholarship data were available.

Here again there appears to be little evidence that scholarship is the chief criterion of success in business. Graduates holding the highest executive positions—corporate officers—were distinctly below the average in scholarship, with less than 7 per cent in the highest tenth and only 27 per cent in the highest third of their classes, and 37 per cent in the lowest third. The same situation holds true in the case of managers and superintendents, with only 29 per cent in the highest and 39 per cent in the lowest thirds, while the minor executive positions—assistant managers—have a somewhat higher scholarship standing. Among the non-executive business positions, accountants and statisticians, who hold poorly paid positions, have higher than average scholarship records, while salesmen, whose earnings are much above those of most other non-executive occupations, have scholarship records considerably below the average.

TABLE XLVI. SCHOLARSHIP RECORDS COMPARED WITH PRINCIPAL POSITIONS HELD BY GRADUATES

Positions	Number of graduates	Proportion of graduates holding each position in each of the following scholarship classes:				
		Highest tenth	Highest third	Middle third	Lowest third	Lowest tenth
All graduates	933	10.0%	33.3%	33.3%	33.3%	10.0%
Corporate officers........	118	6.8	27.1	35.6	37.3	10.2
Presidents...........	23	8.7	30.4	26.1	43.5	13.0
Vice-presidents.......	38	2.6	34.2	42.1	23.7	7.9
Secretaries..........	25	8.0	28.0	28.0	44.0	4.0
Proprietors and partners..	47	4.3	32.0	29.7	38.3	14.9
Managers and superintendents................	193	6.2	29.0	32.2	38.8	9.8
Office managers.......	20	5.0	35.0	35.0	30.0	10.0
Sales managers........	25	8.0	28.0	32.0	40.0	24.0
Assistant managers.......	94	17.0	33.0	33.0	34.0	11.7
Other business positions..						
Accountants.........	47	21.3	38.3	40.4	21.3	10.6
Clerks............	43	16.3	32.6	39.5	27.9	7.0
Salesmen*...........	127	3.9	26.0	32.3	41.7	10.2
Statisticians..........	33	9.1	48.5	18.2	33.3	3.0
Non-business positions						
Lawyers............	41	17.1	46.4	39.0	14.6	7.3
Teachers............	38	26.3	60.5	21.1	18.4	5.3

* Includes also sales correspondents and sales representatives.

SUMMARY AND CONCLUSIONS

1. Since one of the primary aims of collegiate business education is the preparation of students for successful and socially useful careers in business and similar pursuits, it is believed that a detailed examination of the occupational careers since graduation of 1,670 business school graduates, presented in this chapter, should help to indicate something of the nature of the task which confronts the university school of business.

2. The motives actuating graduates in choosing their first jobs after graduation were much the same as those which accounted for the original occupational preferences of students at the time of entering college. More than a third chose the first position because

of "special interest and ability," while nearly 30 per cent attributed their choice to "family connection or influence." Approximately half of the remaining group were attracted by favorable "economic opportunities," while nearly one out of ten accepted the only job available.

3. Although students come to the Wharton School from, and its graduates are employed in, every state of the Union and many foreign countries, approximately 70 per cent of both groups are located in the nearby states of Pennsylvania, New York, and New Jersey. More than two out of five of the men graduating since 1923 are employed in Philadelphia (with 28 per cent), and New York City (with 14 per cent), and this tendency towards geographic concentration in nearby metropolitan centers, especially New York, is becoming more pronounced among later classes.

4. Nearly nine out of ten of the graduates were engaged in business and two-thirds of this group were employed by manufacturing, mercantile, financial, and insurance companies. As to the nature of work, or function, in which graduates were engaged, marketing was by far the most important, followed in the order named by manufacturing, commercial finance, investment finance, insurance, and accounting. If the marketing function be considered as including men engaged in selling securities, insurance, and real estate as well as commodities, it appears that 33 per cent of the total number of graduates are engaged in work of this nature.

5. Comparison of the occupational distribution of these graduates with other data obtained in this inquiry shows that much larger proportions are engaged in marketing, investment finance, insurance, real estate, and public utilities than expressed an original preference for these fields at the time of entering college. In the case of accounting, advertising, foreign trade, and transportation, on the other hand, relatively fewer men are employed in these fields than expressed an early preference for them. The numbers now engaged in manufacturing and in commercial finance are in fairly close correspondence with the proportion expressing preference for these fields. The number of hours offered in various fields of study appeared to have some relation to the occupational importance of each field, although here again wide disparities exist. Thus the fields of accounting, investment finance, foreign trade,

real estate, and especially transportation appeared to be quantitatively more important as courses in the curriculum than as occupations, while the reverse   situation held true in the case of marketing, manufacturing, commercial finance, and public utilities.

6.   Occupational records showed that alumni had experienced considerable "turnover" in jobs and occupations. Since graduation nearly 40 per cent have made a complete shift to work of a different nature than that of their first positions, while a much larger proportion have changed employers. Nearly a fourth of the members of the 1928 class, who had been employed less than a year at the time of this survey, had worked for two or more employers, while more than half of those graduating prior to 1926 had held at least two jobs, and more than a fourth had had three or more employers. Whether or not this turnover is excessive is not apparent, but many alumni suggest the need of vocational advice and guidance before graduation.

7.   More than half of the entire group—and a much larger majority of the earlier classes—are now holding positions of an executive nature, *viz.*, corporate officers, proprietors and partners of firms, managers, and assistant managers. Nearly half of the remainder (i.e., those not employed as executives), as well as a considerable proportion of the executives, are engaged in selling activities.

8.   There was naturally a general tendency for income and the number of employees under supervision of graduates to vary with the nature of the position, although there were many disparities among positions and a wide range of salary and responsibility among men holding similar positions. Thus, with the exception of the group designated as brokers, traders, and dealers, whose median income was above that of all other positions, the earnings of corporate officers were above those of managers, and salaries of the latter group exceeded those of men holding non-executive positions in business. In the same way, responsibility for supervision of employees was greater among corporate officers (with a median of 200 employees for vice-president and general manager) and managers (median of 33 employees for general manager), than among those holding non-executive positions.

9.   Between these two measures of status there was a close relation: thus, the median income of graduates having 500 or more

employees under supervision was over $12,000; of those having 100 to 499 employees, $8,120; 50 to 99 employees, $7,750; 20 to 49 employees, $5,360, etc. The median income of graduates with no supervisory responsibility was lowest—$2,560.

10. Executive responsibility and earnings also generally varied directly with the number of years out of college. Thus, the median income of the 1928 class, one year after graduation, was $1,850; of the 1924 class, five years out of college, $3,740; of classes nine or ten years out, $5,970; of those 13 to 15 years out, $7,800; of those 19 to 24 years out, $10,370; and of the earliest classes, over $12,000. In the same way, responsibility for supervision over employees was generally greater among the earlier, than among the later, classes.

11. Comparison of earnings in different fields of work showed striking disparities; investment finance and real estate appeared to be the most lucrative, while the lowest incomes were reported by those engaged in accounting and education. Earnings of graduates engaged in advertising, marketing, and law were considerably above the average. Median incomes of men engaged in manufacturing, commercial finance, and insurance were nearly equal and somewhat above those of the entire group. It seems probable that these disparities indicate real differences in the opportunities available in different fields, which should be of significance to both the students and faculties of university schools of business.

12. As might be expected the median income of graduates who selected their first occupation because of "family connection or influence" was much higher than that of other students. Participation as undergraduates in outside work and in campus activities appears to have an interesting relationship to present earnings of graduates. Despite the fact that students defraying their college expenses had higher-than-average scholastic records, the median income of this group of alumni was distinctly below that of those who defrayed no part of their college expenses. Men who engaged in both athletic and "intellectual" activities in college reported earnings considerably above those of other graduates, while those who engaged solely in athletics had the lowest median income. Incidentally athletes also had the poorest scholastic records.

13. Comparison of earnings with undergraduate scholarship records gave negative results, with some slight indication that large

earnings were linked with low scholarship and vice versa. Explanation of this phenomenon is apparently to be found in the fact that men of high scholarship were more largely attracted into certain types of analytical and research work which afford them intellectual satisfaction but, unhappily, smaller material rewards than are to be found in other occupations. Selling and executive work, on the other hand, in which relatively high incomes are received, were more alluring to graduates of lesser intellectual attainment. Although definite conclusions must await more comprehensive studies, this analysis suggests the possibility that scholarly attainment, as measured by grades received in college, is only remotely related to financial success in certain important fields of endeavor. If it be true, as seems likely, that personal traits and other factors are more important determinants of success than scholarship this has important implications for collegiate business education.

CHAPTER VIII

OPINIONS OF GRADUATES AS TO COLLEGE TRAINING[1]

A considerable portion of the questionnaire addressed to the graduates was devoted to an attempt to obtain from each person replying full and frank comment on the courses and methods of instruction employed in the Wharton School as well as an expression of his judgment regarding the relative importance which various fields of knowledge should occupy in a curriculum for such an institution. During its entire history this school has provided a four year undergraduate program, about half of the work consisting of business courses and the remainder, of social sciences and other liberal studies. The faculty of the Wharton School have offered the courses in business and in social sciences, while liberal arts courses have been taught by the faculty of The College (of liberal arts and science). Required courses in a wide range of liberal and business subjects constitute a considerable proportion of the student's work; his remaining studies consist of restricted and free electives to be chosen from among courses offered by both undergraduate schools.

Appraisal of Various Studies

As will be remembered, each graduate was asked to express his judgment regarding the importance which each of the following eight fields of knowledge should occupy in a curriculum for the Wharton School:

> *English language*—Studies and practice in the oral and written use of the English language.
> *Foreign languages*—Studies of modern foreign languages.
> *Methods of measurement*—Study of methods of measurements and mathematical analyses.
> *Background of the physical sciences*—Fundamental descriptive studies of the physical and technological background upon which human and business activities are developed.

---

[1] Prepared and written by J. Frederic Dewhurst.

[223]

Social setting of business life—Studies of the structure, functioning, and historical development of the political and socio-economic institutions, practices, and customs within which business functions.

Descriptive analysis of business activities—Studies which describe and interpret the basic activities in which business men are engaged and their interrelations. The emphasis in these studies is placed upon an understanding of the phenomena of business rather than upon the administration of business activities.

Administration of business activities—Studies which aim specifically to train in the managerial administration of various kinds of business activities.

Studies broadly interpretative—This includes courses dealing in a broad, cultural way with man's history, thought, philosophy, behavior, and literary and artistic pursuits.

Graduates were asked to express their judgment as to the importance which should be attached to these fields by indicating whether each field was (A) Of primary importance, (B) highly desirable, (C) Desirable, (D) Of subordinate importance, (E) Of doubtful value. It was not the purpose of this inquiry to obtain anything in the nature of a criticism of existing courses or methods of instruction, based upon the past experience of the student, but rather to obtain his mature opinion concerning the relative importance of the educational and informational content of each of these fields as described in the questionnaire. In order to avoid any possible misinterpretation of this question the designated fields were so described and delimited that they would cut across rather than coincide with traditional departmental boundaries.

The rating scale was purely qualitative, it being possible, as will be seen by referring to the questionnaire, for the person replying to rate every field as "of primary importance," or at the other extreme, as "of doubtful value." In a few cases questionnaires were returned with such extreme ratings, but in general there was a fairly wide variation of opinion as to the importance of the various designated fields. There was apparently considerable interest in this question, and all but a few of the graduates furnished complete replies.

It is noticeable from an examination of Table XLVII that of the total number of 12,944 "ratings" made by this group more than a third were in the highest of the five classes, i.e. "of primary importance." Somewhat less than a fourth each were in the "highly desirable" and "desirable" classes, while less than a fifth of the total were in the two lowest classifications combined—"of subordinate importance" and "of doubtful value." In other words, there was a decided preponderance of ratings at the upper or "desirable" end of the scale, apparently reflecting common opinion that nearly all of the designated fields were essential or desirable in a well rounded business school curriculum aiming to provide both liberal and vocational education.

This uneven distribution of appraisals must be kept in mind in attempting to interpret alumni opinion concerning any one of these eight fields. Thus if any given one of the eight fields were estimated to be of "average" or typical importance by the group of graduates it would receive 12.5 per cent of the ratings of each category, i.e., "highly desirable," "desirable," etc. Stated in other terms, about a third (4,418 out of a total of 12,944) of the total number of ratings given to this field of "average" importance would normally be in the highest category "of primary importance"—while less than seven per cent (804 out of a total of 12,944) of the ratings would classify it as "of doubtful value."

TABLE XLVII. APPRAISAL OF IMPORTANCE OF FIELDS OF KNOW-
LEDGE BY GRADUATES

Fields of knowledge	Total	Number and proportion of graduates rating each specified field as:									
		Primary importance		Highly desirable		Desirable		Subordinate importance		Doubtful value	
		No.	%	No.	%	No.	%	No.	%	No.	%
English language.	1,636	1,241	28.0	271	8.8	101	3.2	14	0.9	0.9	1.0
Foreign language.	1,598	51	1.2	181	5.9	535	17.2	453	30.4	378	45.0
Methods of measurement........	1,610	437	9.9	502	16.3	474	15.2	137	9.2	60	7.1
Background of physical sciences	1,612	131	3.0	259	8.4	611	19.7	432	29.0	179	21.3
Social setting of business life....	1,631	512	11.6	617	20.0	402	12.9	76	5.1	24	2.9
Descriptive analysis of business activities......	1,633	1,038	23.5	380	12.3	163	5.2	38	2.5	14	1.7
Administration of business activities...........	1,610	614	13.9	432	14.0	347	11.2	150	10.1	67	8.0
Studies broadly interpretative..	1,614	394	8.9	442	14.3	478	15.4	191	12.8	109	13.0
Total ratings	12,944	4,418	100.0	3,084	100.0	3,111	100.0	1,491	100.0	804	100.0

Inspection of Table XLVII as well as Table XLVIII showing the distribution among the different categories of the grades or ratings given each of the eight fields, shows quite forcefully that alumni appraisals of separate fields are in no instance in close conformity with the average distribution of ratings for all fields.

Of outstanding significance is the very high importance accorded the study of English language by nearly all of the graduates. More than three-fourths of the total number of graduates believed that training in the written and oral use of the mother tongue

TABLE XLVIII. DISTRIBUTION OF TOTAL RATINGS FOR EACH FIELD
OF KNOWLEDGE

Fields of knowledge	Total	Proportion of total ratings for each field in each of following classes:				
		Primary importance	Highly desirable	Desirable	Subordinate importance	Doubtful value
English language.........	100.0%	75.9%	16.6%	6.2%	0.8%	0.5%
Foreign languages........	100.0	3.2	11.3	33.5	28.3	23.7
Methods of measurement..	100.0	27.2	31.2	29.4	8.5	3.7
Background of physical sciences..............	100.0	8.1	16.1	37.9	26.8	11.1
Social setting of business life.................	100.0	31.4	37.8	24.6	4.7	1.5
Descriptive analysis of business activities........	100.0	63.5	23.3	10.0	2.3	0.9
Administration of business activities..............	100.0	38.1	26.8	21.6	9.3	4.2
Studies broadly interpretative.................	100.0	24.4	27.4	29.6	11.8	6.8
All fields	100.0%	34.1%	23.8%	24.1%	11.5%	6.5%

should occupy a position of primary importance in a curriculum, while only a negligible fraction believe this field should be accorded a secondary position. Opinions of this group concerning the vital importance of English in university training for business furnish emphatic confirmation of the testimony of educators, business men, and employers, and of other evidence already cited.

At the opposite extreme from the position of English, foreign languages were rated by the graduates as of far less importance than any of the other eight designated fields of instruction. Foreign languages were rated as of primary importance only 51 times out of a total of 4,418 such ratings, while 831 of the 1,598 alumni—a far larger proportion than in the case of any other field —believed that they were of subordinate importance or of doubtful value in a business curriculum. The contrast between the importance attached to the study of English and to foreign languages is evident from the fact that less than a sixth of the graduates believed the latter to be of primary importance or highly desirable, while more than nine-tenths of all graduates believed that the former was of primary importance or highly desirable.

These opinions concerning the value of foreign language study find confirmation in a recently published study of engineering education. The following quotation from the report of this investigation may be of interest in this connection:

> Four of the groups of engineers were asked to indicate the extent to which they have used foreign languages in their business and professional activities, which languages they have employed, and their views on the question:
> *Are modern foreign languages, as generally taught to engineering students, justified by their cultural value in proportion to the time expended?*
> The replies to the first question make it plain that the leading men of the engineering fraternity in America make relatively little use of foreign languages. . . . .
> The modern language question elicited numerous comments. Many state that language study is properly a part of preparatory education. Those who advise that the engineering student should get a working knowledge of at least one foreign language stress facility in reading more often than ability to converse. . . . . Naturally, there is a body of comment definitely opposing required foreign language study in the engineering curriculum. Many frankly characterize such work as waste of time with the usual type of teaching. It is often stated that languages are not mastered well enough to be of real value and that the environment needed for their mastery is lacking in America. A number of comments voice a preference for other media of culture, many definitely advising that the time should be given to English and public speaking.
> Taken as a whole, the formal and informal opinions do not seem to place a value on the foreign languages which would justify their general retention as required work. A thorough reading knowledge of at least one language other than English, gained principally in preparatory work and extended where necessary through elective study in college, would seem to meet with general approval. Little can be said, however, in favor of scattering the student's effort among a number of languages without fair mastery of any. It is worth noting that a number of those who offered comments would place Latin on a par with the living tongues.[2]

[2] *Opinions of Professional Engineers Concerning Educational Policies and Practices, Bulletin Number 13 of the Investigation of Engineering Education,* Society for the Promotion of Engineering Education, New York, 1927.

The field designated as "descriptive analysis of business activities," comprising studies which describe and interpret the basic activities in which business men are engaged, and in which emphasis is placed upon an understanding of the phenomena of business activities, was accorded a position in the opinion of graduates second in importance to that of English language. A position third in importance among the fields of knowledge to be covered by the curriculum was assigned to studies dealing with the "social setting of business life," i.e. studies of the structure, functioning, and historical development of the political and socio-economic institutions, practices, and customs within which business functions.

The surprising thing here is not that these two fields of background studies should rank high in the estimation of the graduates, but that they should both be assigned positions of greater relative importance than the group of business studies, so avidly sought by many undergraduates, which aim to teach the "administration of business activities,"—studies which aim specifically to train in the managerial administration of various kind of business activities. This field was rated somewhat above the average, but not greatly higher, and if common experience can be depended upon, undergraduates have far greater faith in the efficacy and usefulness of applied business coures than do these same students after a few years' experience in business. Numerous comments made by alumni to this questionnnaire further confirm the impression that, in the light of their experience since graduation, they now attach far greater value to basic and fundamental courses aiming to reveal principles, than to the applied business courses devoted specifically to teaching how to manage or administer business activities.

Alumni rated the remaining three designated fields—"methods of measurement," "studies broadly interpretative," and "background of the physical sciences,"—in the order named, somewhat below the average, but above the position accorded to foreign languages. However majority opinion rated all of these fields, with the exception of foreign languages, as desirable components of the curriculum.

Ratings of Various Fields of Knowledge

By assigning arbitrary numerical values to the scale of rating used in appraising the various fields, opinions of graduates concerning the relative importance of these fields can be shown more precisely and on a more comparable basis. The importance of each field can thus be expressed as a percentage of a possible maximum value of 100. Values or weights were assigned to each category in the rating scale as follows:

Of primary importance.............	4	Of subordinate value...............	1
Highly desirable.................	3	Of doubtful value.................	0
Desirable.....................	2		

By using these weights an average appraisal[3] was obtained for each of the eight designated fields.

Comparisons of the average appraisals of various fields calculated on this basis are shown in Table XLIX.

TABLE XLIX.   AVERAGE RATINGS OF FIELDS OF KNOWLEDGE BY GRADUATES

Fields of knowledge	All classes	1888–1922	1923–1928
English language.............................	92%	91%	92%
Foreign languages...........................	35	37	34
Methods of measurement......................	67	69	66
Background of physical sciences................	46	49	44
Social setting of business life..................	73	76	71
Descriptive analysis of business activities........	87	87	86
Administration of business activities............	71	76	69
Studies broadly interpretative.................	63	59	65
All fields of knowledge	67%	68%	66%

[3] The method can be illustrated by calculating the average appraisal of foreign languages on the basis of data presented in Table XLVII. In the following tabulation are shown the number of men rating this field as "Of primary importance", "Highly desirable", etc., the weights assigned to, and the weight-products of, each rating:

	Number	Weights	Weight-products
Of primary importance.........................	51	4	204
Highly desirable...............................	181	3	543
Desirable.....................................	535	2	1,070
Of subordinate value..........................	453	1	453
Of doubtful value.............................	378	0	0
Totals.....................................	1,598	10	2,270

Obviously the maximum value (100.0%) would have been derived if the entire 1,598 graduates had rated this subject as "of primary importance" in which case the weight-product would have been 4 × 1598 = 6392. Dividing the sum of the actual weight-products (2270) by the maximum weight-product (6392) the result—35%—represents the weighted average appraisal of the importance of foreign languages in terms of a possible maximum rating of 100%.

The figures shown here generally confirm the conclusions already presented, English ranking above, and foreign languages considerably below, all other fields, while other subjects ranged between a low value of 46 per cent for physical sciences and a high rating of 87 per cent for "descriptive analysis of business activities." Three groups of courses—foreign languages, physical sciences, and broadly interpretative studies were rated below the average appraisal of 67 per cent.

Of particular interest is the contrast between the importance ascribed to various fields by the earlier classes and by the later classes. There has evidently been an appreciable decline in recent classes in the appraisal of the importance of studies related to the administration of business activities, social setting of business life, background of physical sciences, and foreign languages, while "broadly interpretative studies" and English have been held in higher esteem.

Despite the tendencies mentioned above, there has been substantial uniformity in the importance accorded the various fields, which is especially surprising in view of the fact that the scale of rating was purely qualitative, depending for its interpretation upon the meaning assigned by each individual to the terms used. Among the entire group of classes, English has consistently held the highest rank among the various fields, while physical sciences and foreign languages have been evaluated substantially below the other fields. Descriptive analysis of business activities has also maintained a high standing second only to English, except among the earliest group of classes.

Minor variations from class to class in the rating accorded various fields are probably not very significant. Possibly they reflect the variable experiences of different groups of alumni with courses actually studied by them as undergraduates in the various designated fields, despite the fact that they were asked to "consider these fields in the light of the explanations given, rather than in terms of specific courses which you may have studied." Then too, these variations may reflect something in the nature of "wishful thinking." The more recent graduates, who have had ample opportunity to study specialized courses in the field of business administration, think less highly of them than the earlier graduates, who did not have this opportunity. The cultural, or "broadly interpretative" studies are held in lower esteem by the earlier classes, whose courses presumably included a somewhat larger proportion of these general studies than has been true in recent years. Apparently here, as in other human judgments and desires, the greenness of other pastures varies directly with their remoteness.

Variation in Ratings According to Scholarship and Earnings

It may be of some significance to compare the appraisals of these various fields made by graduates with high and low scholarship records, of high and low salaries, and engaged in various kinds of business work. Table L shows the ratings given the various fields according to scholarship and salary standing and Table LI gives similar information according to occupations.

The variations shown in Table L are so slight that it seems safe to conclude that salary and scholarship account for no substantial differences in ratings of these fields. Men in the highest tenth of their classes tend to rate nearly all fields somewhat higher than those with poorer scholastic records but these differences

TABLE L. APPRAISAL OF FIELDS OF KNOWLEDGE BY GRADUATES ACCORDING TO SCHOLARSHIP AND SALARY

Fields of knowledge	Scholarship				Salary	
	Highest tenth	Lowest tenth	Highest third	Lowest third	Below $3000	Above $9000
English language..........	94%	92%	91%	90%	92%	92%
Foreign languages.........	38	36	34	33	31	39
Methods of measurement...	69	68	67	64	68	69
Background of the physical sciences..............	47	45	45	44	45	47
Social setting of business life	74	71	73	73	71	74
Descriptive analysis of business activities.........	86	86	86	87	86	86
Administration of business activities.............	74	70	69	72	70	74
Studies broadly interpretative.................	62	64	64	63	64	62

are fairly uniform. In the case of salary groups, foreign languages and administration of business activities are rated higher by graduates receiving over $9,000 than by those earning less than $3,000, but the former group is composed chiefly of members of the older classes who, it will be remembered, accorded these two fields a higher rating than was given by the more recent graduates.

Variations in Appraisals According to Nature of Employment

Some interesting but not altogether unexpected differences occur in the ratings of various fields by men engaged in the various kinds of business. Accountants naturally attach a greater value to "methods of measurement," which includes such subjects as mathematics and accounting, than do men in other occupations. It is also noticeable that accountants attach less value than does any other group to the broadly interpretative "cultural" studies. Graduates engaged in manufacturing also appraise courses in methods of measurement above the average, and they naturally assign a considerably higher value to the physical sciences than does any other group.

Graduates engaged in advertising show rather noticeable divergences in their appraisals of several of the fields. Methods of measurement were rated by this group much below the average, while their rating of the broadly interpretative studies was 76 per cent, as compared with an average of only 63 per cent for this field. Foreign languages were rated 44 per cent by this group—far higher than the appraisal accorded these studies by graduates engaged in any other occupation except foreign trade and transportation. Apparently the advertising business demands of its votaries far wider acquaintance with the humanities than is true in the case of other business occupations.

TABLE LI. APPRAISAL OF FIELDS OF KNOWLEDGE BY GRADUATES ACCORDING TO NATURE OF PRESENT EMPLOYMENT

Nature of employment	English language	Foreign language	Methods of measurement	Physical sciences	Social setting of business	Descriptive analysis of business activities	Administration of business activities	Broadly interpretative studies
Accounting	92%	33%	82%	45%	76%	85%	70%	55%
Marketing	89	35	64	44	71	90	78	60
Manufacturing	90	32	72	51	71	83	73	61
Commercial finance	91	32	72	42	73	87	75	58
Investment finance	91	35	65	47	70	92	69	67
Insurance	93	32	65	45	81	89	66	66
Foreign trade	87	49	62	40	75	84	75	63
Advertising	95	44	52	43	73	88	72	76
Real estate	93	34	72	41	77	89	77	65
Transportation	86	52	73	46	74	89	81	60
Public utilities	94	30	73	43	70	87	67	66
Law	95	41	59	47	76	77	60	73
Education	94	39	73	52	78	89	67	63
All	92%	36%	67%	46%	73%	87%	71%	63%

The relatively high rating given to foreign languages by men engaged in foreign trade is to be expected. The high appraisal of this field by those engaged in transportation, coupled with a relatively low rating for English, is probably attributable to the fact that a considerable number of those engaged in this field are Orientals.

It is noteworthy that men engaged in the two non-business fields—law and education—both rate English and foreign languages above the average. Lawyers attribute more importance to the broadly interpretative studies than do those employed in most other fields, and quite naturally they attach relatively less importance to courses in the administration of business and the descriptive analysis of business activities.

Although there are certain other variations in the evaluation of the fields by graduates engaged in different occupations they do not appear to be significantly large. Indeed the most striking conclusion to be drawn from this comparison of appraisals by occupations, as in the comparison by classes, is the remarkable uniformity in the judgment of the graduates regarding the relative importance which each of these eight fields of study should occupy in a curriculum for a university school of business. In all cases English was accorded the first position. The descriptive analysis of business activities and the social setting of business, accorded second and third places, respectively, were generally considered of somewhat greater importance than the administration of business activities. Methods of measurement and the broadly interpretative cultural studies were believed to be of nearly equal importance, ranking slightly below the business administration courses. Physical sciences and foreign languages are rated considerably below the other fields, the latter being accorded an importance only 35 per cent of the possible maximum, as compared with 92 per cent for the English language.

These relative values evidently represent the consensus of opinion of this large group of graduates as to the relative importance which should be attached to the designated fields of study in a well balanced curriculum for a four-year undergraduate school of business. Although they were asked to express their opinions "in the light of explanations given, rather than in terms of specific courses" which they may have studied, it is of course impossible to determine how large an influence their academic experience may have exercised upon their judgments. Their varying occupational careers since graduation, as has been shown, have been responsible for some differences in the appraisals of various fields but this does not appear to have been a predominant influence in most cases. In general there seems to be widespread agreement in the judgment of this group of alumni on the relative importance of these fields.

Opinions Concerning Undergraduate Instruction

In the preceding inquiry graduates were asked to express their judgment as to the relative importance of the several fields of knowledge usually represented in the curricula of collegiate schools of business without reference to the specific courses which they may have studied as undergraduates. The purpose of the present investigation, on the other hand, was to secure specific comments, criticisms, and suggestions from graduates as to the instruction offered them as undergraduates. They were invited to comment freely on (1) the courses offered by the school, (2) the emphasis given to various subjects in the curriculum, and (3) the methods of instruction employed. Since specific questions were not asked in this inquiry the replies covered the widest range of possible opinion. It was practicable, however, to distill out of this mass of criticism and comment certain broad inferences reflecting rather widespread agreement among the graduates as to certain aspects of educational methods and policies. Moreover, despite the fact that replies were received from graduates of the past 41 classes, during which period many changes have occurred in course content, faculty personnel, and teaching methods, there was a remarkable uniformity of agreement among both younger and older men as to what were the desirable and undesirable aspects of their undergraduate training.

Opinions Regarding Curriculum Content

In Table LII is shown the distribution of alumni opinion concerning the relative emphasis given to various types of courses in the curriculum. Many of the alumni, as was to be expected, failed to reply to these questions. However, the comments of more than

a thousand graduates, or 61 per cent of all those returning questionnaires, would seem to furnish sufficient data from which to
draw certain general conclusions. As indicated in the table, nearly
a fourth—but a smaller proportion of the recent graduates—expressed general approval of the curriculum as it was constituted
at the time they were undergraduates. Of the remainder, the
largest single group, constituting 15 per cent of all those replying,
advocated greater emphasis upon the general cultural courses.
Only 2.5 per cent of the group maintained the opposite position,
i.e., that the curriculum was deficient in applied business courses.
More than six per cent of the graduates who replied believed that

TABLE LII. SUGGESTIONS OF GRADUATES AS TO EMPHASIS PLACED ON VARIOUS
TYPES OF COURSES

	All classes	1888–1922	1923–1928
Number of graduates.....................	1,670	623	1,047
Number of graduates replying............	1,023	358	665
Proportion of those replying making follow-ing suggestions:			
General approval....................	23.4%	26.5%	21.6%
More general cultural courses; less spec-ialization in applied business courses...	15.0	12.3	16.5
More specialization in applied business courses; fewer general cultural courses	2.5	2.0	2.9
More electives; fewer required courses..	6.2	2.8	8.1
More required courses; fewer electives..	3.0	3.9	3.0
More emphasis on English............	12.2	14.0	11.3
" " " accounting.........	5.0	6.1	4.4
" " " economics..........	3.0	2.2	3.4
" " " marketing..........	1.7	3.3	0.8
" " " mathematics.......	1.4	1.7	1.2
" " " business law.......	1.3	2.0	0.9
" " " senior research......	1.3	1.4	1.2
Less emphasis on foreign languages.....	3.9	3.1	4.4
" " " senior research......	1.4	—	2.1
Other comments....................	18.4	18.7	18.2
Total	100.0%	100.0%	100.0%

course requirements should allow the inclusion of more elective
courses, while only half of that number believed the curriculum
would be strengthened by the addition of more required studies.
This opinion was held even more emphatically by the alumni of
recent classes.

A substantial proportion of all men replying—a larger fraction
than expressed an opinion on any other specific subject—emphasized the need of more English courses in the curriculum, thus
confirming the high rating according this subject in the appraisal
of various fields of knowledge. In addition to English, which was

mentioned by 125 graduates, only six other subjects, as indicated in the table, were designated by as many as ten men as justifying greater emphasis in the curriculum. Only two subjects—foreign languages and senior research—were specified by as many as ten or more of the graduates as justifying a less important position in the curriculum than that held at present. Other comments included a wide range of miscellaneous criticisms and observations, but consisted principally of suggestions as to the addition or elimination of certain specific courses from the curriculum. Not more than ten men out of the total of 1,023, however, specifically advised the addition or elimination of any one course except those specified in the table.

Opinions Regarding Methods of Instruction

A significant picture of alumni comment on the methods of instruction employed in the school is given in Table LIII. Replies to this question covered the widest possible range, but there seemed to be general agreement among substantial numbers as to the desirability of certain changes in teaching methods. Greater alumni interest in the problems raised by this question was evidenced by the fact that more replies were received than in response to the previous inquiry on curriculum content. A fairly large proportion —21.8 per cent—expressed general approval of teaching methods.

Some significance might be attached to the fact that a larger proportion of the older than of the younger graduates expressed

TABLE LIII. COMMENTS AND SUGGESTIONS OF GRADUATES AS TO METHODS OF INSTRUCTION

	All classes	1888–1922	1923–1928
Number of graduates.....................	1,670	623	1,047
Number of graduates replying............	1,128	381	747
Proportion of those replying making following suggestions:			
General approval.....................	21.8%	31.2%	17.0%
More field work and practical experience	9.3	6.6	10.7
More emphasis on analysis, less on memorization of detailed, specific facts....	11.8	7.6	14.0
Greater use of problem and case method	5.4	5.8	5.2
More independent study and research..	9.3	8.4	9.8
Greater individualization of instruction.	8.7	10.0	8.0
Smaller classes......................	10.3	11.3	9.8
More lectures by experienced men......	4.6	3.1	5.4
More mature and experienced instructors..............................	8.9	7.6	9.5
Other comments.....................	9.9	8.4	10.6
Total	100.0%	100.0%	100.0%

their general satisfaction with the methods of instruction employed when they were undergraduates. This can hardly be interpreted as indicating any undesirable change in the methods of instruction employed in this institution, however. It seems more probable that the explanation of this discrepancy may be found in the mellowing effect of age upon judgment; the older graduates, as intervening years blur early memories, tend to become more lenient and more temperate in their criticisms. Confirming this observation, it is worth noting that only 61 per cent of the earlier classes, as compared with 71 per cent of those graduating since 1923, replied to this question.

A considerable fraction of those replying, especially in the case of graduates of the last six classes, expressed a belief that greater emphasis in teaching should be placed upon analysis and interpretation of facts, and less upon mere memory work. Further amplification of this same thought is seen in the suggestions made by considerable numbers of graduates that greater emphasis be placed upon independent study and research and upon the problem and case method. The need for more field work and practical experience in dealing with business situations is voiced by more than ten per cent of the recent graduates. Considerable numbers emphasize the desirability of smaller classes and more personal contact between teachers and students, while another substantial fraction believe that the teaching personnel should be strengthened by the addition of older and more experienced members.

Educational Training Since Graduation

Some interest may attach at this point to a consideration of the extent to which graduates have availed themselves of the opportunity of pursuing studies after graduation and the nature of such studies. Answers to the question concerning educational work revealed the fact that a surprisingly large number of alumni have supplemented their undergraduate study by formal educational training since graduation. More than half of the 1,670 graduates replying to the questionnaire reported that they had pursued such a course during the years since they left college. As indicated in Table LIV, the largest single group, comprising 21 per cent of those taking post-graduate work, was enrolled in law courses. This is not surprising in view of the fact that a considerable number of students, as undergraduates, pursued the special group of courses designed for pre-law preparation.

In addition to law, vocational courses in the field of business seem to have been the most popular. Finance, with more than a tenth of the total number enrolled, was the most important business subject studied by students after graduation, while accounting, selling, insurance, and marketing all attracted considerable numbers. Many of the graduates who entered the employ of large

TABLE LIV. EDUCATIONAL COURSES TAKEN BY GRADUATES SINCE GRADUATION

	All classes	1888–1922	1923–1928
Number of graduates.....................	1,670	623	1,047
Number taking courses since graduation....	933	338	595
Proportion studying courses in:			
Law..............................	20.8%	18.3%	22.2%
Finance............................	11.1	11.8	10.8
Accounting.........................	8.3	7.7	8.6
Training course.....................	6.1	2.7	8.1
Selling............................	5.9	4.7	6.5
Insurance..........................	5.9	4.1	6.9
General business....................	5.4	6.5	4.7
Marketing..........................	3.0	3.9	2.5
Other courses......................	33.5	40.3	29.7
Total	100.0%	100.0%	100.0%

corporations, especially those graduating during the past few years, reported attendance in the apprentice training courses maintained by such companies. Indicative of the great development of these courses in recent years is the fact that 8.1 per cent of the recent graduates reported attendance in these courses as compared with only 2.7 per cent of those graduating prior to 1923.

"Other courses" includes a great variety of vocational and nonvocational studies ranging from psychology to plastic art, but most of all, studies followed in university graduate schools by a considerable number of graduates who entered the teaching profession directly after graduation. In general, the courses followed by graduates since leaving college reflect primarily vocational interests, although an appreciable number pursued work in history, literature, language, and other cultural fields.

The reasons given by 796 graduates for taking courses since graduation, as shown in Table LV, reveal the predominance of vocational motives. Only 13 per cent enrolled in courses because of their general educational interest in the subject, whereas more than a third were impelled to study because of desire for advance-

TABLE LV. REASONS GIVEN BY GRADUATES FOR TAKING COURSES
SINCE GRADUATION

	All classes	1888–1922	1923–1928
Number of graduates....................	1,670	623	1,047
Number giving reasons..................	796	281	515
Proportion giving following reasons:			
Desire for advancement..............	40.1%	43.1%	38.2%
Prepare for another position..........	22.5	16.1	26.8
General educational interest..........	13.4	17.3	11.1
Desire to establish business or personal contacts........................	2.3	2.3	2.3
Other reasons......................	21.7	21.2	21.6
Total	100.0%	100.0%	100.0%

ment, and an additional fifth because they wished to prepare for another position. It is interesting to note that general educational interest was a more important motive for post-graduate education among the older graduates, than among those leaving college since 1923. A much larger proportion of this latter group studied courses in order to prepare themselves for other positions.

As disclosed in Table LVI, the largest single group of alumni pursued their post-graduate courses in university graduate schools. This group, which constituted a much larger relative proportion of the earlier classes, consisted chiefly of those who pursued courses of graduate study while engaged as teachers at the Wharton School or similar institutions. Corporation schools also enrolled a considerable number—more than a fourth of the recent graduates, but only a sixth of those leaving college before 1923—including not only employees taking apprentice training courses, but those taking special courses offered by large corporate institutions. Only a small fraction continued their training in evening and extension schools, despite the many facilities for this type of study offered by universities in the larger cities, where most of the graduates are

TABLE LVI. TYPES OF INSTITUTIONS PROVIDING EDUCATIONAL
TRAINING FOR GRADUATES

	All classes	1888–1922	1923–1928
Number of graduates....................	1,670	623	1,047
Number taking courses.................	933	338	595
Proportion studying courses in:			
University graduate schools..........	28.4%	37.3%	23.4%
Corporation schools.................	22.5	15.7	26.4
University law schools...............	20.8	18.3	22.2
Evening and extension schools........	7.8	5.9	8.9
Association and other schools.........	20.5	22.8	19.1
Total	100.0%	100.0%	100.0%

now employed. Slightly over 20 per cent of the group pursued courses offered by other institutions than universities or corporations, including those maintained by trade and professional associations and institutes, correspondence schools, and other private educational institutions.

It is patent that universities, through graduate, law, and other professional schools, and through evening and extension courses, are already helping substantially to meet the educational needs of students after graduation. Whether or not their facilities can or should be extended still further to meet the demands of their graduates for further training is a question which may well be considered in view of the fact that such a large proportion of the alumni continue educational work after graduation. It is worthy of note in this connection that many of the graduates in replying to this questionnaire expressed the definite opinion that some sort of continuing educational relationship between the university and its graduates would be highly desirable. This question becomes still more pertinent when it is remembered that more than a third of this group of Wharton School students are working and living in the immediate vicinity of Philadelphia.

Summary and Conclusions

1. The sixteen hundred graduates whose judgement concerning the importance which should be attached to various fields of knowledge in a business school curriculum and whose views regarding course content and methods of instruction have been analyzed in this chapter, constitute a group which should be adequately representative of Wharton School alumni opinion on these important questions.

2. Replies to the question concerning the importance which each of eight fields of study in the curriculum should possess, showed that the English language was accorded a position far above that of any other field, with an average rating of 92 per cent of the possible maximum of 100. Foreign languages received an average rating of only 35 per cent—much below other fields. Ratings of the remaining six fields were as follows: descriptive analysis of business activities, 87 per cent; social setting of business life, 73 per cent; administration of business activities, 71 per

cent; methods of measurement, 67 per cent; broadly interpretative studies, 63 per cent; and physical sciences, 46 per cent.

3. These average ratings appeared to be fairly uniform among different salary, scholarship, and age groups, except that there was some tendency for the older graduates to attach greater importance to foreign languages, methods of measurement, physical sciences, social setting of business life, and administration of business activities, and less importance to broadly interpretative studies than did the younger graduates.

4. Among occupational groups there were noticeable variations in the ratings of various fields. Thus, the English language was adjudged of greater importance by graduates employed in law, teaching, public utilities, and advertising than by those in other occupations. Men in advertising and foreign trade valued foreign languages more highly than did other occupational groups. Methods of measurement received the highest rating from accountants and the lowest rating from advertising men. The reverse was true in the case of the broadly interpretative studies which were given the highest rating by the latter group and the lowest by accountants. Vocational interests were also manifested in the relatively high ratings accorded the physical sciences by alumni in manufacturing, and descriptive analysis of business activities, by those in investment finance. These and other differences among occupations in the appraisal of these fields may have some significance in planning curricula designed for specialized vocational training.

5. Despite the wide range of expressed and implied opinion reflected in the ratings accorded various subjects in the curriculum and in the answers received to other questions concerning educational problems and policies there appear certain general principles which express widespread and consistent agreement among this group of graduates as to what the purpose, methods, and content of university instruction for business should be. These principles are expressed in the seven following paragraphs.

6. Of primary importance among the aims of university education is the training of students in habits of work and methods of thought rather than the acquisition of information. As a means of developing power in thinking, emphasis should be placed upon the observation, analysis, and interpretation of facts and

data, rather than upon their memorization. Information is useful only as it enables the student to strengthen his judgment and train his mind in deriving principles from it, and these principles are useful only as they can be applied in understanding and explaining business phenomena and in solving concrete problems.

7. Of equal importance, and closely related to this primary aim, is the training of students in clear and effective oral and written expression. Training in writing and speaking the English language should not be confined to formal courses in composition and public speaking, but should be made an important part of classroom work in all fields of study. The importance of the English language as a means of communicating ideas, as a means of persuasion, and hence as an essential tool in all business and other human relations cannot be over-emphasized.

8. The methods of instruction should be shaped and adapted to accomplish these two ends, *viz.*, training in analysis and training in expression. Major emphasis should be placed upon teaching methods involving the use of cases and problems, field and laboratory work involving actual observation and experiences, seminar and research work and other individualized methods of instruction involving the investigation and critical appraisal of original material and formal written or oral presentation of findings. Minor emphasis should be placed upon mere reading, memorization, and class-room repetition of printed factual material and informational lectures.

9. Lectures delivered by distinguished members of the faculty and by men of similar qualifications from other walks of life serve a highly desirable purpose in stimulating thought and in presenting the more subtle implications and less tangible aspects of the courses studied. But if lectures are to be purely factual in content and informational in purpose they might better be replaced by assigned readings in original source materials.

10. The character, training, and academic and business experience of the teaching staff is a more important determinant of the success or failure of undergraduate instruction than either the content of courses or methods of instruction. The most effective teachers are those who not only know their own fields at first hand and also are familiar with related fields, but who have a primary interest in undergraduate instruction and whose temperments

permits them to serve as sympathetic guides and counsellors to their students. Small classes, organized as seminars or discussion groups or individual conferences as in senior research are the most effective means of enabling able teachers to influence the mental and moral development of their students.

11. The curriculum should be so designed that every student will be required to follow an integrated, coordinated, and coherent course of study consisting of a common core of required subjects, basic in character and of pervasive significance, with a moderate number of elective subjects to be studied chiefly in the later years.

12. The content of the curriculum should recognize the educational necessity of a broad background of general and cultural knowledge, appreciation of the social and ethical aspects of the material studied, and thorough training in the fundamentals of economics and business, with only moderate emphasis upon study of the applied and specialized techniques of business practice.

13. Nearly 56 per cent of the entire group of 1,670 alumni— and a larger proportion of recent classes—have pursued educational work since graduation. This group consisted chiefly of those studying in law schools, of teachers in universities following post-graduate work in business and economics, and of newly engaged employees enrolled in corporation schools. In most cases vocational interests were the dominating motives in causing these men to pursue further study although more than an eighth of the number reported that they were actuated by general educational interest. In view of the fact that such a large proportion of recent graduates, more than a third of whom live in or near Philadelphia, have continued to study after graduation, the question may well be considered as to whether some sort of continuing educational relationship between the school and its graduates might not be desirable.

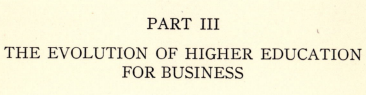

PART III

THE EVOLUTION OF HIGHER EDUCATION
FOR BUSINESS

CHAPTER IX

THE DEVELOPMENT OF COLLEGIATE EDUCATION FOR BUSINESS[1]

HISTORY AND BACKGROUND

Education as a National Tool[2]

The acceptance of education as a national tool is one of those pervasive factors in the history of the people of the United States without which their collective achievements could not possibly be accounted for or understood. Whether it has been the sharpening of the religious consciousness, the awakening of a civic sense, preparation for the professions, or training for commercial pursuits, education has been emphasized, inevitably and well nigh universally, as the outstanding means to the accomplishment of the stated purpose.

Going to school has come to be an American habit. From the youngest child in the nursery school to the oldest recruit in the newest class for adult education, almost every American family is represented in some one or more of the various institutionalized forms of our educational system. Perhaps close to one-third of our entire population are today enrolled in more or less formal schools or courses of some kind of instruction.

The Growth of School Enrollments[3]

The past generation particularly has witnessed an extraordinary growth of interest in, and opportunities for, education of all kinds. The twenty-five million students enrolled today in the elementary schools are not far from twice the total of 1890.

The expansion in the field of secondary school education has proceeded at an unprecedented rate. In 1880, a total of 110,000 boys and girls were enrolled in the public high schools of the United States. By 1900, this number had increased to 519,000; by 1910 to 915,000; by 1920 to 2,200,000; and by 1925 to 3,650,000.

---

[1] Prepared and written by J. H. S. Bossard.
[2] Title suggested by Cubberley, Ellwood P., *The History of Education*, Houghton Mifflin Company, Boston, 1920, p. 711.
[3] Cf. Bossard, James H. S., *School and Society*, August 17, 1929, pp. 216 ff.

Allowance for the enrollment of private secondary schools increases this last figure by more than a third of a million. For three decades and more "each annual report of the growth of the secondary school population has shown, not only an absolute increase in numbers, but an increase in the rate of growth. . . . . Regardless of the theories of educators or the views of statesmen, the American people are apparently committed to the universal extension of the opportunities of secondary education."[4]

Higher education has followed a similar course, although growth in numbers here has been more recent in point of time, occurring chiefly since the close of the World War. The number of students in colleges, universities, and professional schools of college grade in 1890 was 157,000. By 1900, this number had grown to 238,000; by 1910, to 356,000; and by 1915, to 403,000. Following the temporary disorganization of the collegiate situation during the war, the registration rose in 1920 to 597,000. In 1927-1928, the last year for which complete returns are available at the present writing, the million mark was almost reached.

The Federal Bureau of Education[5] has shown the increase in the percentage of young people in the age groups, 19 to 22 inclusive, going to universities, colleges, and professional schools since 1890. In 1890, the number enrolled was 2.43 per cent of those four single age groups. In 1905, the percentage was 3.03 per cent; in 1915, it was 4.16 per cent; in 1920, 6.32 per cent; in 1922, 7.51 per cent; in 1924, 9.03 per cent; in 1926, 10.41 per cent; and in 1928, 11.77 per cent.

The Development of Commercial Education

Coincident with this remarkable expansion of our educational system has been an equally phenomenal growth of American business, reference to which has been made in a preceding chapter. The result was inevitable. Business looked to education as the tool to produce the trained personnel which its development and its growing responsibilities demanded.

---

[4] Counts, George S., "Education in 1927," *American Journal of Sociology,* Chicago, Illinois, July, 1926, p. 179.

[5] Office of *Education Bulletin* (1929) No. 38, United States Department of the Interior, *Statistics of Universities, Colleges and Professional Schools: 1927-1928,* U. S. Government Printing Office, Washington, p. 3.

To meet these demands and opportunities of the business world, there has emerged a variety of educational developments, designed for differing purposes and functioning at separate levels. These various educational activities, having the common aim of preparation for business careers, are usually grouped together under the general term of commercial education. Commercial education may be defined, then as "that education and training which prepares specifically for an understanding of the relationship and the performance of activities in business."[6]

The history of commercial education in the United States is characteristically American, involving a series of enterprises, chiefly private, growing up, in several cases almost simultaneously, in response to public need. Its beginnings, in point of time, go back to the fourth decade of the nineteenth century, but its development has been chiefly since 1890. This has been in keeping with the evolution of American business.

Chief Forms of Commercial Education

The chief forms which commercial education has taken include the private commercial school, better known as the business college; the commercial departments of the high schools, public and private; the private school of commerce, such as those conducted by the Y.M.C.A.; the correspondence school; the corporation school, conducted by business enterprises; and the collegiate school of business or commerce. Each of these, growing up in answer to definitely voiced demands, has its own particular history and its own peculiar place in the evolution of commercial education.

Table LVII gives some indication of the development and relative numerical importance of some of the forms of commercial education. Unfortunately data are not available year by year, and the latest data available for all forms represented in the table are for 1924. The table covers, then, a twenty-five year period.

Present Status of Commercial Education

Approximately 1,000,000 pupils in the public and private high schools, private business colleges, and universities are definitely

---

[6] Malott, J. O., *Biennial Survey of Education, 1924-1926,* Bulletin No. 25, Department of the Interior, Government Printing Office, Washington, 1928, p. 251.

TABLE LVII. ENROLLMENTS IN COMMERCIAL CURRICULA IN
DIFFERENT TYPES OF SCHOOLS

Year	Public high schools (commercial)	Private high schools and academies	Private business and commercial schools	Colleges and universities	Total
1895	25,539	8,819	96,135	97	130,590
1897	33,075	11,574	77,746	*	
1899	38,134	10,609	70,186	*	
1900	68,890	15,649	91,549	*	
1903	79,207	15,455	137,979	1,100	233,741
1904	85,313	13,479	138,363	1,537	238,692
1905	90,309	13,394	146,086	1,710	251,499
1906	95,000	13,868	130,085	1,193	240,146
1907	*	*	137,364	*	
1910	81,249	10,191	134,778	4,321	230,539
1911	110,925	11,956	155,244	4,194	282,319
1912	128,977	14,173	137,790	*	
1913	154,042	15,940	160,557	*	
1914	161,250	17,457	168,063	*	
1915	208,605	17,706	183,268	9,323	418,902
1916	243,185	17,228	192,388	11,653	464,454
1918	278,275	23,801	289,579	17,011	608,666
1920	*	*	336,032	36,855	
1924	430,975	18,210	188,363	47,552	685,100

* Figures not available.

preparing to enter business occupations, according to the latest estimates of the Federal Bureau of Education. The total number has been increasing rapidly. Two-thirds of those enrolled in business curricula are women. The number of women taking business subjects is increasing more rapidly than men. The greatest number of women in business subjects, however, are in the secondary schools.

Collegiate Education for Business

The collegiate school of business, with which this study is concerned primarily, must be considered, then, as a phase of development of commercial education, i.e., as the expression of the collegiate level of the adjustment of the educational system to the growing demands of the modern business world. That it has not generally been considered in this relationship, nor been coordinated with it, does not alter the fact of its obvious kinship. Nevertheless, while laterally the collegiate school of business is a phase of commercial education, historically its antecedents are in the field of higher education, and its development must be considered also against that background.

By Way of Perspective[7]

All education is purposive, originally in rather direct relation to the conditions of life in which it originates. This is perhaps

[7] Cf. Cubberley, op. cit., Part IV.

another way of saying that all education, in a certain sense, is vocational. To prepare for commerce, or engineering, or scientific agriculture in the United States in recent times implies the same usage of education as a tool and the same utilitarian, nay, even vocational, motive as preparation for public life in ancient Greece, as training for a career in the church in the Middle Ages, or subsequently, the cultivation of "cultural" pursuits by the leisured sons of an established nobility.

As modern civilization increased in complexity and the ramifications of our social and industrial life widened, institutions of learning were called upon to broaden their work and to develop new types of instruction in order to maintain, if not increase, their general effectiveness. We are interested particularly at this point in this broadening process in the field of higher education.

The development of the Industrial Revolution, the breakdown of the age-old system of apprenticeship training, the developments attained by pure science, and the international rivalries and competition which loomed so large as the nineteenth century progressed, were perhaps the outstanding stimuli to the increase within the past half century in the number of kinds of specialized training in the field of higher education. While the passage of the Morrill Act (1862) is hailed generally as the beginning of this movement in the United States, a general survey shows that real interest did not manifest itself until after 1880, and that its phenomenal advance comes after the turn of the century. Today, training for medicine, law, ministry, dentistry, pharmacy, engineering, scientific agriculture, social work, education, architecture, commerce, etc., each represent important divisions in the field of higher education whose separate significance has come to be recognized and whose particular needs are being provided for with increasing adequacy. College education for business represents, then, by way of perspective, a phase of this process of differentiated training in the field of higher education.

The First Collegiate School of Business

The first collegiate school of business in the United States was established at the University of Pennsylvania, on the basis of a gift from Mr. Joseph Wharton, of Philadelphia. This school, known originally as the Wharton School of Finance and Economy and subsequently renamed the Wharton School of Finance and Commerce, was established in 1881. At the present writing, then, the history of higher education for business in this country covers a scant half century.

The Growth of the Movement

While the growth of the movement for this period as a whole has been phenomenal, progress during the earlier decades was both slow and painful. For seventeen years the Wharton School remained the lone pioneer of a new educational idea, not imitated at other American colleges and universities, and handicapped by, and depreciated in, its own academic home. The story of those earlier years has been told elsewhere[8] and need not be repeated at this point. In 1898, the second and third collegiate schools of business made their appearance. The College of Commerce and Politics was organized at the University of Chicago and the University of California established its College of Commerce. In presenting the further growth of this movement, two indices for its quantitative measurement will be utilized: (1) the increase in the number of colleges and universities providing instruction in business subjects; and (2) the data on student enrollments.

The Increase in the Number of Colleges and Universities Providing Business Instruction. One indication of the growth of collegiate education for business is the increase in the number of new schools, divisions, departments, or courses in commerce during the period since 1881. Marshall lists 182 as having been established by the opening of the year 1925.[9] Arranged by date of establishment they seem to group themselves into four definite periods:

a. *The Period of the Pioneers.* This covers the years from 1881 to the close of the century. Reference has been made to the three institutions, Pennsylvania, Chicago, and California— which established schools or colleges of commerce during this period. The geographical distribution of the three pioneers might

---

[8] James, E. J., "Origin and Progress of Business Education in the United States," address at Conference at University of Illinois, 1913; and McCrea, Roswell, C., "The Work of the Wharton School of Finance and Commerce," Journal of Political Economy, XXI, 1913.

[9] Marshall, L. C., and others, *The Collegiate School of Business,* University of Chicago Press, Chicago, 1928, pp. 4-9.

be noted—one in the east, one in the middle west, and one on the Pacific coast.

b. *The Period of Steady Growth.* This covers the opening years of the twentieth century up to the year of the outbreak of the World War. Twenty-five universities developed schools or divisions for business instruction during these fourteen years (1900-1913). Included in this list are Wisconsin, Dartmouth, Vermont, New York, Illinois, Washington and Lee, Harvard, Northwestern, Pittsburgh, Denver, Georgia, Marquette, and Boston.

c. *The War Period.* The years 1914-1918 witnessed a decided acceleration of the movement for collegiate instruction in business. Thirty-seven additional institutions gave some recognition to the idea. Among the better known of the schools established during this period are those at Columbia, Ohio State, Washington, Oregon, and Missouri.

d. *The Post-War Period.* During the years since the World War, "a veritable craze for business education has swept over the country." From 1919 to 1924, inclusive, a total of 117 colleges and universities, according to Marshall[10] developed a more or less definite set-up for instruction in the field of business.

No effort has been made in connection with this study to make a complete enumeration of the colleges and universities now giving instruction in business. That the rate of expansion has not abated since 1924 is evidenced by the statement of Federal Bureau of Education, in its last biennial report[11] to the effect that approximately 400, or half of the colleges and universities, offered some business courses. It might be added, as a significant item in this connection, that 358 higher institutions offered courses in accounting in 1928.[12]

The Data on Student Enrollments. It is difficult, if not impossible, to secure comparable data on student enrollments in this connection, due to incompleteness of figures, differences of classification, and variations in university organization. However, there are several sources of data which are useful in this connection as indicating the growth of the movement.

---

[10] *Ibid.,* pp. 5-9.
[11] *Bulletin,* 1929, No. 26, p. 3.
[12] Malott, J. O., *Ibid.,* p. 3.

(1)   There are the data gathered by the Federal Bureau of Education concerning "men and women who are majoring in the commercial curricula (of the colleges and universities) by taking the various subjects designed to prepare them for business occupations." The totals by designated years are as follows:

1915	9,323
1916	11,653
1918	17,011
1920	36,855
1922	45,356
1924	47,552
1926	57,728

This shows an increase of more than five-fold within a period of eleven years.

(2)   A second source of information on this point is to be found in the data on student enrollment compiled by Mr. H. S. Wright, Grand Secretary-Treasurer of Delta Sigma Pi, and published in the November, 1928, issue of *Deltasig*. Ignoring for the moment any questions concerning the justification of comparing registration figures, Mr. Wright's figures of total registration figures for "universities offering courses in Commerce and Business Administration during a nine-year period" are as follows:

TABLE LVIII. REGISTRATION STATISTICS: COMMERCE STUDENTS IN UNIVERSITIES OFFERING COURSES IN COMMERCE AND BUSINESS ADMINISTRATION

College year	Number of institutions	Men	Women	Total
1919–20	45	33,905	2,551	36,456
1920–21	55	41,454	2,667	44,121
1921–22	62	44,723	2,731	47,454
1922–23	70	49,624	2,838	52,462
1923–24	72	51,496	4,566	56,062
1924–25	78	51,943	5,117	57,060
1925–26	83	57,083	5,672	62,755
1926–27	87	60,221	6,074	66,295
1927–28	89	61,057	6,439	67,496

How comprehensive Mr. Wright's figures are may be indicated by the reminder that a total of 89 schools are included in the enumeration of the year 1927-28.

Reference has been made to the difficulties of comparison of the data on student enrollment in commerce secured from different colleges and universities. Chief among these difficulties is the difference in the number of years spent in schools of commerce at different institutions. As will be discussed more fully later in this report, some schools operate on a four-year basis, others on a two or three-year basis.   Since pre-commerce registration is not included, it is improper obviously to compare the registration of a two year college of commerce with one covering the entire four years.

(3)   A comparison of first degrees granted in commerce, year by year, eliminates the objections that can be raised to a comparison of registration data and offers one more index of the growth of collegiate education for business.   These figures, obtained from the Biennial Survey of Education by the Federal Bureau of Education, are as follows:

TABLE LIX. FIRST DEGREES GRANTED IN COMMERCE: 1914–1928

Academic year	Men	Women	Total number
1914–15	615	*	
1915–16	789	*	
1917–18	610	30	640
1919–20	1,397	162	1,559
1921–22	3,205	357	3,562
1923–24	4,573	375	4,948
1925–26	4,972	463	5,435
1927–28	5,474	1,147	6,621

* Figures not available

BUSINESS AND OTHER ASPECTS OF HIGHER EDUCATION: A COMPARATIVE STUDY

To appreciate its full significance, the growth of collegiate education for business needs to be compared both with the growth of higher education as a whole and with the developments in its specific fields or aspects.

Collegiate education for business, measured in terms of changes in student enrollments, clearly has grown more rapidly than collegiate education as a whole.   Whereas the total student enrollment for colleges, universities, and professional schools in 1926 was two and a half times that in 1915, the total student enrollment in commerce in 1926 was more than six times that of 1915.

More interesting and significant, however, is a comparison of the development of collegiate education for business with other aspects of higher education.

A Study of First Degrees Granted to Men

To compare the growth and relative importance of education for business with other fields of higher education generally entered by men, the following table has been compiled showing the number of first degrees granted to men, and in certain specified fields. The data are for the universities, colleges, and professional schools included in the biennial reports of the Bureau of Education of the United States Department of the Interior, and are taken from successive reports of that bureau. The period covered is from 1914-15 to 1927-28.

TABLE LX. A STUDY OF FIRST DEGREES GRANTED TO MEN IN COLLEGES, UNIVERSITIES, AND ALSO IN CERTAIN PROFESSIONAL COURSES: 1915–28

Year	Total baccalaureate degrees male	Total arts and science male	Total engineering male	Total commerce male	Total theology male	Total law male	Total medicine male
1914–15	19,040	11,229	4,289	615	1,794	4,347	3,645
1915–16	20,586	12,358	4,282	789	2,023	4,220	3,316
1917–18	14,720	9,092	3,079	610	816	2,272	2,339
1919–20	23,272	14,272	4,400	1,397	546	3,094	2,691
1921–22	26,296	15,616	6,823	3,205	752	4,801	2,438
1923–24	36,258	19,550	7,461	4,573	1,293	6,447	3,458
1925–26	41,106	23,775	7,376	4,972	1,324	7,510	3,902
1927–28	45,912	27,263	7,607	5,474	1,179	8,209	4,155

The foregoing table indicates the relative numerical importance (for male students) of the several types of education included, from the standpoint of the country as a whole. Since not all colleges and universities offer facilities for training in engineering and commerce, but do in the arts and sciences, it is interesting to raise the question of the relative numerical importance of these three fields which male students enter so largely, on the basis of first degrees granted, at a number of representative institutions offering facilities in all three fields. The following table presents this data for 26 institutions, all members of the American Association of Collegiate Schools of Business, and offering facilities for training in these three fields.

The University of Pennsylvania: A Study in Certain Degrees Granted

It would seem permissible, by way of comparison with a general comparative study, to present data on this point for a single institution in which facilities for collegiate education for business have existed over a relatively long period of time. The University of Pennsylvania is selected for this purpose. The data cited are for first degrees granted. The period covered is thirty years.

It is clear, on the basis of the data presented, that education

TABLE LXI. FIRST DEGREES GRANTED TO MEN IN SELECTED FIELDS
AND AT SELECTED SCHOOLS: 1925–26

College or university	Arts and science	Commerce	Engineering
California..............	537	181	155
Cincinnati.............	78	23	54
Columbia..............	421	72	43
Denver................	57	42	15
Georgia...............	39	28	11
Illinois................	253	306	239
Iowa..................	241	83	58
Kansas................	215	35	64
Kentucky..............	68	25	66
Minnesota.............	203	93	196
Missouri..............	117	36	98
Nebraska..............	159	102	62
New York University.....	259	678	45
North Carolina.........	118	70	26
North Dakota..........	53	38	35
Ohio State.............	152	184	166
Oklahoma.............	136	36	35
Pennsylvania...........	202	499	73
Pittsburgh.............	186	111	77
Southern California......	68	43	35
Syracuse...............	78	160	55
Texas.................	166	101	55
Tulane................	39	17	34
University of Washington.	155	120	110
Washington University...	41	51	59
Wisconsin.............	319	83	171
	4,360	3,217	2,037

TABLE LXII. A STUDY OF FIRST DEGREES GRANTED AT THE
UNIVERSITY OF PENNSYLVANIA: 1900–1929

Year	Arts and science			Engineering						Commerce	Certain professional degrees	
	A.B.	B.S.	Total	B.S. in chemistry	B.S. in chem. eng.	B.S. in civil eng.	B.S. in mech. eng.	B.S. in elec. eng.	Total	B.S. in economics	M.D.	LL.B.
1899–1900	16	27	43	11	0	4	7	8	30	10	180	83
1900–1901	27	27	54	6	2	7	11	12	38	17	160	79
1901–1902	21	27	48	10	2	11	5	3	31	17	151	80
1902–1903	25	24	49	9	3	11	5	5	33	18	109	80
1903–1904	24	33	57	9	3	8	27	10	57	29	96	91
1904–1905	28	39	67	5	2	17	15	5	44	23	116	65
1905–1906	27	31	58	13	5	23	17	8	66	27	94	61
1906–1907	20	39	59	16	5	22	29	14	86	26	114	73
1907–1908	27	35	62	11	9	40	20	15	95	32	142	61
1908–1909	25	45	70	20	4	39	28	23	114	61	108	62
1909–1910	28	46	74	16	4	44	16	21	101	66	134	74
1910–1911	23	58	81	7	15	56	31	30	139	73	151	65
1911–1912	35	68	103	14	11	50	37	24	136	66	124	69
1912–1913	34	44	78	5	20	38	27	23	113	77	99	70
1913–1914	25	36	61	16	18	35	39	17	125	79	74	69
1914–1915	34	37	71	10	23	35	28	38	134	110	57	71
1915–1916	47	24	71	6	18	32	25	19	100	147	74	70
1916–1917	55	28	83	9	19	30	24	20	102	154	159	84
1917–1918	53	6	59	6	9	19	13	10	57	69	115	22
1918–1919	53	5	58	5	13	20	15	11	64	137	123	13
1919–1920	79	8	87	16	28	34	21	17	116	308	131	33
1920–1921	82	4	86	8	16	27	27	17	95	345	109	31
1921–1922	118	2	120	8	40	34	23	16	121	376	118	69
1922–1923	98	2	100	12	20	24	23	24	103	522	123	40
1923–1924	119	1	120	5	23	21	23	20	92	570	132	58
1924–1925	142	3	145	12	14	23	31	25	105	579	131	62
1925–1926	164	2	166	3	12	20	24	17	76	498	133	61
1926–1927	209	0	209	7	7	8	15	21	58	569	129	97
1927–1928	219	2	221	4	9	18	12	17	60	573	136	116
1928–1929	281	0	281	1	13	14	18	23	69	607	134	110

for business has forged ahead to a place of relative importance in the field of higher education, and in an amazingly brief period of time. For the country as a whole first degrees in commerce to men has reached almost the total number of first degrees granted in engineering, and about one-fifth the total number of first degrees to men in arts and science. Taking only schools where facilities for all three kinds of training exist, commerce ranks above engineering, and approaches by three-fourths the total of male first degrees in arts and science. At such institutions as Illinois, New York, Ohio State, Pennsylvania, and Syracuse, the first degrees granted to men in commerce exceeds the number in arts and science or engineering.

The Range of Collegiate Instruction In Business

In citing the data on student enrollments and degrees granted, no mention has been made thus far of the various channels or media through which collegiate instruction in business is carried on.

1. First and foremost is the day school. This represents the basic development and includes the major part of the total student enrollment. It is this development which is implied ordinarily when the term collegiate school of business is used.

2. Second in point of numerical importance is the work of the evening schools. Wright's data for 1927-28 reveal an evening school at 21 of the 89 institutions included, with a total registration of 30,307. In other words, the evening school enrollment amounts to almost 70 per cent of the day school enrollment, including the previously designated allowance for the pre-commerce enrollment at the two and three year schools.

Evening school instruction in commerce subjects is confined chiefly to eight schools, located in larger cities—New York, Northwestern, Boston, Pittsburgh, Pennsylvania, Cincinnati, Temple, and Duquesne. At each of these schools except Pennsylvania, the evening school enrollment exceeds that of the day school.

Evening courses in commerce represent a very important part of collegiate education for business, and perhaps a still more important aspect of the university's relation to the public. The evening school must be considered an integral part of the work of any university which is located in or near an urban center and which conceives of its functions in any sort of a broad and liberal spirit. It is unfortunate that so many university administrators and educators have not recognized this fact.

Nor is the evening school simply an extension of the day school into evening hours. The evening school of commerce has its distinctive clientele, with its own particular needs and demands. It has its own problems, and these merit serious and separate attention. The limitation of the present study to the undergraduate day school of business is due, not to any lack of appreciation of the importance of the problems of the evening school, but to a realization of their distinctive nature. Circumstances did not permit the addition of so large an element to the present study.

3. The work of the extension schools or classes in commerce and business must not be overlooked. A report of the Federal Bureau of Education shows that 51 institutions reported a total of 384 extension classes in these subjects for 1928. Of these 51 institutions, 46 reported enrollments, showing a total of 16,229 students. Chief among the institutions doing extension work in commerce and business are the University of California with 5,838 enrollments, the University of Minnesota with 3,124, New York University with 1,600, and the University of Southern California with 1,402. These figures include duplicates.[13]

4. Graduate instruction in business studies has taken a variety of forms in the United States. There are, to begin with, those schools which are exclusively for graduate students. There are two of these, at Harvard and Stanford, with enrollments in 1927-28 of 751 and 28, respectively. Then there are schools, such as Dartmouth and Michigan, which combine a year of graduate instruction with the senior year of the undergraduate course. Their respective registrations for 1927-28 were 91 and 96, most of which number, however, were undergraduates. Another type of school is that which, while primarily an undergraduate school, increasingly emphasizes an additional year in its general program of training. Such is the case at Chicago, for example. It is a very thin line, if any, which separates this type of arrangement from that existing at other universities where facilities for graduate work in business exist. In the case of such institutions as

---

[13] Malott, J. O., in Commercial Education Circular, No. 34, August, 1929.

Columbia, Illinois, Pennsylvania, etc., there are larger numbers of graduate students in the business field than at any of the graduate institutions except Harvard.

The term graduate work applied to collegiate education for business is rather a misnomer, as is much other graduate work now given in the United States, if by graduate work one implies instruction of an advanced nature based on an undergraduate foundation in that field. Much of the so-called "graduate" work in business thus far has consisted of undergraduate courses slightly stepped up for students in the graduate schools. The general development of graduate work in business must await the more satisfactory organization and adjustment of the work of the undergraduate schools.

PRESENT STATUS OF COLLEGIATE EDUCATION FOR BUSINESS

Reference has been made to the report of the Federal Bureau of Education to the effect that approximately four hundred, or half of the colleges and universities, offered some business courses. Many of these institutions, of course, are small and their efforts at business instruction must not be taken too seriously. "Approximately one-half of the colleges and universities offering curricula in business," writes Malott[14] "have only one or two courses in each of three or four subjects in this field. . . . . For example, of the 127 higher institutions offering courses in foreign trade and foreign service in 1928, 65 reported only one course in this field. . . . . Although 358 higher institutions offered courses in accounting in 1928, approximately only 10 per cent of that number offered a major in this subject." Nevertheless, the very attempts of these institutions to provide such courses, whatever their number and quality may be, indicate the extent of interest in and the need for this type of education, as well as the passing stage of development of the movement. Moreover, while such schools seldom prepare for proficiency in specialized opportunities, they do provide the student with some orientation in the general field of business.

A total of 57,728 students are reported as majoring in business subjects in 132 colleges and universities in 1926, taught by 2,575

[14] Bulletin, 1929, No. 26, p. 3.

instructors of business subjects. These figures represent an increase of student enrollment over 1924 of 21 per cent, and of instructors of 16 per cent.[15]

Wright, in his report previously referred to, deals with total enrollment in business schools rather than majors in business curricula. For 89 selected colleges of commerce, he reports a total registration for 1927-28 in the day schools of 37,195. Mr. Wright estimates the pre-commerce enrollment of the two and three year schools at 6,442. This estimate is based on the ratio of distribution by classes in twenty universities operating four year schools of commerce in different sections of the country. On the basis of this estimate, the total commerce and pre-commerce enrollment for these 89 schools of business is 43,537. The enrollment of the evening schools at those universities which offer such facilities was 30,307 for the academic year 1927-28. The combined total of these figures is 73,944.

To this total must be added the enrollment of the extension classes. Mention has been made of the fact that 51 institutions reported such classes and that 46 of them reported a total of 16,229 students. This total, however, includes duplications.

With due allowance for incompleteness of data and for a reasonable growth since the years for which data are available, it seems reasonable to conclude that close to 100,000 students are today receiving collegiate instruction in business through some one or more of the agencies maintained for this purpose.

Enough has been said to make it clear that academic training for business is an integral part of modern educational plans. The collegiate school of business is neither an isolated incident nor an experimental fad. Laterally it takes its place in the lustily growing field of commercial education, comprehending now a million students; historically, it is but another evidence of that vocational bent of higher education which has resulted in specialized training for the ministry, for law, for medicine, for engineering, and for social service administration; philosophically, it represents a fruition of the educational creed of modern civilization—that it is the function of the university to serve the need of the community.

---

[15] Malott, Ibid., p. 3.

Summary

Six points stand out in the present chapter. Stated briefly they follow:

1. The acceptance of education as a national tool is a pervasive factor in the history of the people of the United States. Data on school enrollment indicate how extensive this acceptance is.

2. The phenomenal growth of American business created a large demand for trained personnel. Naturally, business is looking to education to produce such personnel. The various educational activities which have grown up to meet this demand constitute the field of commercial education.

3. Commercial education has taken many forms—the business college, the commercial department of the high school, the corporation school, the private school of commerce, and the collegiate school of business. Each form has its own place and history.

4. Collegiate education for business in the United States covers a scant half century, the first collegiate school of business having been established by Joseph Wharton at the University of Pennsylvania.

5. This movement has grown very rapidly, several hundred such schools or divisions or departments now existing, with close to a hundred thousand students now receiving collegiate instruction in business.

6. Academic training for business is an integral part of modern educational plans. Its growth in recent years has been phenomenal, both at and below the college level. The collegiate school of business is neither an isolated experiment nor an experimental fad. It is a phase of the movement for commercial education, as well as of the adjustment of colleges and universities to the public needs.

CHAPTER X

COLLEGIATE SCHOOLS OF BUSINESS: THEIR ORGANIZATION AND OBJECTIVES[1]

THE AMERICAN ASSOCIATION OF COLLEGIATE SCHOOLS OF BUSINESS

Another measure of the status of collegiate education for business is to be found in the formation of the American Association of Collegiate Schools of Business, organized in 1916 for the promotion and improvement of higher education for business in North America. The standards of admission formulated by this organization represent the current code of acceptable practice in this field of higher education. This Association in 1930 had 42 members, and no doubt there are additional schools which could meet its modest requirements for admission.

Basis of Membership

The following is a statement of the standards of admission as revised in May, 1925:[2]

1. The College or School shall require for admission at least fifteen units of secondary work as defined by the North Central Association of Colleges and Secondary Schools or its equivalent.

2. The School shall require for the undergraduate degree the completion of a minimum quantitative requirement of 120 semester hours of credit or the equivalent. A portion of this work may be taken in some other college, as a Liberal Arts College of approved standing.

3. The School shall have been established as a bona fide division of a College or University whose credits are accepted at full value by members of the Association of American State Universities; and its affairs shall be administered under the control and with the active support of such College or University.

4. The School shall have been established and operated in accordance with the standards indicated herein for a period of at least three years; but a School which has been

---

[1] Prepared and written by J. H. S. Bossard.

[2] Marshall, L. C. and others, *The Collegiate School of Business,* University of Chicago Press, Chicago, 1928, pp. 13-14.

in operation for not less than three years, and which may have failed, in that period, to meet all the requirements herein stated, may, at the discretion of the Executive Committee, be admitted to membership whenever such requirements have been fulfilled by the School.

5. The Faculty of the School shall include at least three teachers of full professional rank, giving full time, or nearly all their time to instruction in courses offered in the curriculum of the School; in general, the majority of all teachers on the faculty shall give the greater part of their time to such instruction.

6. Those holding full professional rank shall have the Doctor's degree, or their professional or technical training and experience shall be such as will enable the Executive Committee of this Association to give them a rating equal to those who have received the Doctor's degrees. In general, all teachers of business subjects in collegiate schools of business above the grade of assistant shall have a Master's degree, or their training and experience shall be such that the Executive Committee of this Association gives them a rating equal to those who have the Master's degree.

7. The School shall maintain a scale of teachers' salaries which, in the judgment of the Executive Committee, is adequate to the successful conduct of the work of a high grade school of business.

8. The School shall have so apportioned the teaching load of members of its staff that the teaching burden will not be excessive. In general, teachers should not teach elementary work in excess of 15 hours a week and advanced work in excess of 12 hours a week.

9. All collegiate schools shall offer a reasonable amount of work in at least five groups of study, such as business finance, accounting, business law, marketing, and statistics.

10. At least 40 per cent of the 120 credit hours or its equivalent required for the Bachelor's degree must be taken in commercial and economic subjects; a liberal proportion of the courses in this group shall be professional in character in that they deal with problems of management or administration.

11. At least 40 per cent of the 120 credit hours or its equivalent required for the Bachelor's degree shall be taken in subjects other than economics and commerce providing that general economics and economic history may be counted in either the liberal or commercial groups.

12. The School shall have such library facilities as are in the judgment of the Executive Committee adequate.[2]

The Member Schools

The membership of the Association consists of the following 42 schools.

1. University of Alabama—School of Commerce and Business Administration
2. Boston University—College of Business Administration
3. University of California—College of Commerce
4. University of Chicago—School of Commerce and Administration
5. University of Cincinnati—College of Engineering and Commerce
6. Columbia University—School of Business
7. Dartmouth College—Amos Tuck School of Administration and Finance
8. University of Denver—School of Commerce, Accounts and Finance
9. University of Florida—College of Commerce
10. University of Georgia—School of Commerce
11. Georgia School of Technology—School of Commerce
12. Harvard University—Graduate School of Business Administration
13. University of Illinois—College of Commerce and Business Administration
14. Indiana University—School of Commerce and Finance
15. University of Iowa—College of Commerce
16. University of Kansas—School of Business
17. University of Kentucky—College of Commerce
18. Marquette University—Robert A. Johnston College of Business Administration
19. University of Michigan—School of Business Administration
20. University of Minnesota—School of Business Administration
21. University of Missouri—School of Business and Public Administration
22. University of Nebraska—College of Business Administration
23. New York University—School of Commerce, Accounts and Finance
24. University of North Carolina—School of Commerce
25. University of North Dakota—School of Commerce
26. Northwestern University—School of Commerce
27. Ohio State University—College of Commerce and Administration
28. University of Oklahoma—College of Business Administration
29. University of Oregon—School of Business Administration
30. University of Pennsylvania—Wharton School of Finance and Commerce

31. University of Pittsburgh—School of Business Administration
32. University of Southern California—College of Commerce and Business Administration
33. Southern Methodist University—Dallas School of Commerce
34. Stanford University—Graduate School of Business
35. Syracuse University—School of Business Administration
36. University of Texas—School of Business Administration
37. Tulane University—College of Commerce and Business Administration
38. University of Virginia—McIntire School of Commerce
39. University of Washington—College of Business Administration
40. Washington University—School of Business and Public Administration
41. Washington and Lee University—School of Commerce and Administration
42. University of Wisconsin—School of Commerce

The Collegiate Business Degrees

Reference to the formation of the American Association of Collegiate Schools of Business, a development in accord with the customary practice of professional schools, recalls among other things the question of degrees granted and the possible desirability of some sort of standardization.

Eleven different baccalaureate degrees are awarded by the member schools of the Association. The various degrees and number of colleges conferring them, arranged in order of numerical importance are as follows:

TABLE LXIII. THE RANGE AND FREQUENCY OF BACCALAUREATE BUSINESS DEGREES

Degree	Number of schools awarding
Bachelor of Science in Commerce	11
Bachelor of Science	9
Bachelor of Science in Business Administration	6
Bachelor of Business Administration	5
Bachelor of Commercial Science	2
Bachelor of Science in Business	2
Bachelor of Arts	2
Bachelor of Philosophy	2
Bachelor of Science in Commerce and Business Administration	1
Bachelor of Science in Economics	1
Commercial Engineer	1

Such diversity is perhaps an inevitable result of the extensive development of collegiate education for business within a comparatively short time. It would seem that some sort of standardization of the business degree would be feasible within the not remote future. Certainly it would seem desirable.

Aims and Objectives of Collegiate Schools of Business

Just what do these business curricula and schools aim to do? What are their objectives? Is there any agreement as to fundamental purposes?

An analysis of the formal announcements of the 42 schools belonging to the American Association of Collegiate Schools of Business shows that four distinct objectives are mentioned. Brief discussion of each follows:

1. *Training in the general fundamentals of business and business administration.* Twenty-eight of the member schools state this as one, and usually the outstanding one, of its objectives. While various phrases are utilized, the general ideas involved are substantially the same: viz., that there are certain principles of business, its organization and administration; that these are essentially of a non-specialized nature; that they are of fundamental and general importance to all persons entering business, regardless of their particular specialty; and that those general principles or fundamental studies can be taught to the average college student.

Some half dozen institutions point out, by way of postscript, that their emphasis is upon "science and theory" rather than upon "art and practice"; that the purpose is not to teach details, since these change from time to time and from one industry to another.

2. *Training for certain specialized fields.* This is the second, outstanding objective announced by American Collegiate schools of business. Fifteen schools specifically include this in their statement of aims. Obviously, it is a part of the program of other schools, even though no express mention is made of it. The fields for which specialized training is available include accounting, which is mentioned more frequently than any other; salesmanship; advertising; foreign trade; statistics; employment management; banking; real estate; traffic; transportation; etc.

The statement of aims most frequently found combines reference to both of the objectives just mentioned. The importance of training in the fundamentals or principles of business is indicated as of primary importance, but certain opportunities for additional specialized training for certain particular business callings are mentioned as being available to the student.

3. *Training for business leadership.* Some such phrase expresses the current hope of most of the higher education for business. Reference to "the education needed by the modern business executive," "the functions of the business manager and the fields of study which prepare for these functions," "the essential unity of management," "the solution of management problems," "advancement to managerial positions," and "leadership in business" literally abound in college of commerce catalogues. Eighteen of the schools in the American Association made definite reference to training for executive positions.

4. *Cultural and ethical foundation.* Ten institutions, in their formal declarations of intent, lay stress upon their functions in this respect. "To give a cultural background"; "to prepare students to become better citizens"; to give an understanding of modern social and economic problems"; "to teach economics and commerce from the broad, social point of view"; "to foster a high standard of business conduct"; these are the indicative phrases used.

The foregoing analysis of catalogue statements shows substantially the same results as the questionnaire sent (1925-26) by the Commission on "Correlation of Secondary and Collegiate Education with Particular Reference to Business Education" to presidents of colleges and universities maintaining schools of business, and to the deans and instructing staffs of a large number of these schools. Of the replies obtained, 86 per cent agreed that preparation for executive positions in business is an appropriate aim; 88 per cent approved of preparation for professional careers, e.g., accountants, statisticians, etc.; and 88 per cent indicated the importance of introducing persons with a social point of view into business.[3]

In connection with the question of aims or objectives, two further facts would seem to warrant emphasis. One is the matter of the fundamentals of business training. Most schools mention this as an important function; no conversation on collegiate education for business proceeds far without reference to it. From the standpoint of curriculum construction, then, it would seem to be highly important to identify these fundamental sciences underlying education for business, arrange them in a progressive sequence

---

[3] Marshall, et al., op. cit., pp. 105-109.

and integrate them with the rest of the curriculum. Here, in other words, is a basic problem in collegiate education for business.

A second matter suggesting itself in this connection is the importance of a more definite determination of the objectives of any particular school of business. The question of what the objectives of collegiate business education ought to be is an alluring one. Dean Heilman, of Northwestern University, has pointed out that "this subject has three distinct aspects. First, the objectives from the standpoint of the general public; second, from the standpoint of our own students; third, from the standpoint of the entire system of higher education in America, of which we are a part."[4] Perhaps there is no one generally acceptable objective or group of objectives for all schools. Once the play of varying sets of conditioning factors, to which Dean Heilman has referred is recognized, objectives become a relative matter. Certainly there are already the beginnings of specialization of function among the different schools.

What does seem important, especially at this stage of the development of higher education for business, is that each school consciously and rather definitely has some objective or objectives to seek to accomplish. What the particular objective or objectives shall be is important, but perhaps still more important is that there be some one or more. Only thus can progress be made in the development of a unified and well integrated curriculum. All this is but equivalent to saying that before one can make much progress in doing a thing, one needs to decide what it is that one wishes to do.

Types of Collegiate Schools of Business

On a Formal or Administrative Basis

Collegiate schools of business have been classified customarily from the standpoint of their formal or administrative organization. On this basis, the day schools, with which this study is concerned chiefly, arrange themselves into six rather definite types. These types will be considered at this point, the discussion

---

[4] Heilman, R. E., "A Revaluation of the Objectives of Business Education," Proceedings of the tenth annual meeting of the American Association of Collegiate Schools of Business, The Ronald Press, 1928, p. 1.

being confined to the members of the American Association of Collegiate Schools of Business.

1. *The two-year undergraduate school.* Twelve of the member schools are organized, at the present writing (1930), on a two-year basis, students being admitted to the school or college of commerce after having completed the first two years, usually in the college of liberal arts. The idea involved is the building of a two-year professional course upon a two-year liberal arts preparation, with a distinct administrative cleavage maintained. These twelve institutions are Chicago, Columbia, Indiana, Iowa, Kansas, Minnesota, Missouri, North Dakota, Northwestern, Texas, Washington University, and Wisconsin. It will be observed that all of these, with one exception, are situated in the middle west.

2. *The three-year undergraduate school.* Up to this time, only two institutions have developed a three-year school for business, an arrangement which is generally found in European universities. These institutions are the University of Georgia and Washington and Lee.

3. *The four-year undergraduate school.* These institutions admit students directly from secondary schools and maintain a control over the students during the four years of collegiate grade. Twenty-three of the member schools are of this kind, including Alabama, Boston, California, Denver, Florida, Georgia Tech, Illinois, Kentucky, Marquette, Nebraska, New York, North Carolina, Ohio, Oklahoma, Oregon, Pennsylvania, Pittsburgh, Southern California, Southern Methodist, Syracuse, Tulane, Virginia, and the University of Washington.

4. *The five-year undergraduate school.* Since 1920, the work of the College of Commerce of the University of Cincinnati has been conducted wholly on the cooperative plan, extending over a five-year period. The School of Commerce of the Georgia School of Technology, which maintains a regular four-year course in Commerce, also offers a five-year co-operative plan. In this connection, mention should also be made of the fact that the College of Business Administration of Boston University now maintains control of its students for a fifth year, which is devoted to supervised employment. In other words, to the four years of class attendance there is now added a fifth year of satisfactory

supervised employment before the baccalaureate degree is given.

5. *The undergraduate-graduate school.* Two institutions, Dartmouth College and the University of Michigan, maintain schools of business whose two years of instruction extend into both the undergraduate and graduate levels. They are undergraduate in the sense that they admit only such students as have completed three years of work of college grade. Since the school's project includes a year of graduate work and since holders of baccalaureate degrees are admitted, they are also graduate schools.

Mention should be made at this point of the fact that the School of Commerce and Administration of the University of Chicago now conceives of itself as an undergraduate-graduate school, placing its emphasis upon a three-year program beginning with the junior year. Since the work of this school still is mostly on the traditional two-year basis, Chicago was included among the two-year undergraduate schools. There is a similar tendency in the school of business at Columbia University.

6. *The graduate school.* Harvard and Stanford maintain graduate schools of business to which selected holders of baccalaureate degrees are admitted, whether of an arts college, engineering school, business school, or other recognized branch of university education.

Certain qualifications are necessary, however, in referring to the above as graduate schools of business. They are not graduate schools of business in the sense that they presuppose or require an undergraduate training or curriculum in business studies, rather must they be thought of as schools offering instruction in business subjects at the graduate level. It has been pointed out previously that these are not the only schools which offer graduate work in business. Such universities as Columbia, Chicago, Illinois, and Pennsylvania have each a considerable number of graduate students in business courses.

The two-two vs. the four-year school

Most of the member schools of the American Association (35 out of the 42) are organized either on a two-two or four-year basis. Some interest has been shown in discussing the relative merits of these two plans. Without wishing to become involved in any controversy concerning this matter, certain facts which have a bearing upon it and which appear in the course of this study, may be cited here.

From the foregoing summary, it will be observed that the four-year plan is the more customary, outnumbering the two-two plan at the rate of two to one. Comparing the situation in 1930 with that of 1925-26, the year of the Marshall study, it appears that in the interval the schools of business at the Universities of Chicago and Wisconsin changed from a four to a two-two plan. On the other hand, the schools at Oklahoma and Pittsburgh shifted from a two-two to a four-year basis. Of the four schools admitted since 1925-26, three—Alabama, Florida, and Marquette—are organized on a four-year basis, and Washington and Lee on a three-year basis.

From discussion of this problem with various administrative officers and teachers directly concerned, it appears that four factors are responsible chiefly for the development of the two-two plan, the relative force of these factors and their particular combination at any one institution depending on regional circumstances. These factors are (a) the development of Junior colleges, with the consequent enrollment of numerous students at the beginning of the junior year; (b) a compromise with the liberal arts faculty in the interests of academic harmony; (d) a welcome lightening in the administrative load of the business school; and (d) a conviction that business education should be developed on a broad cultural base. A decided majority of the faculty members at the two-two schools with whom the matter was discussed were not wholly happy with the arrangement, the feeling ranging from passive dissatisfaction to restive antagonism. At only two of the twelve institutions does the weight of opinion seem to be definitely and largely on the side of this type of organization. On the other hand, almost all of those functioning in a four-year school are satisfied with that arrangement, having no thought of change. (The point was raised at one school during the year and decided negatively.)

From the point of view of the larger interests of collegiate education for business, certain questions concerning the two-two plan insistently present themselves. Is it wise, pedagogically speaking, to develop a two-year liberal arts hurdle for the student who wishes to secure a collegiate business education? It must be admitted that some students do not know upon entering college what they wish to do, and that two years of general cultural training under these circumstances may be desirable. But the question that at once suggests itself is this: what help are such students given during these two years to facilitate a wise decision? Is the decision facilitated or merely postponed? It might be recalled that commerce teachers complain that students are not advised disinterestedly by arts teachers during these two years. Moreover, a large proportion of students have decided at the time of entering college upon a business course. Is it justifiable, and wise, to say to these: We know you have come to us for a business education. Before allowing you to study business subjects, we insist that you spend two years studying non-business subjects which we have arranged for you? Is this good pedagogy? Does this make for maximum motivation of the student?

A second question presenting itself is this: Is it wise to thus segregate cultural and business studies? Is it good practice educationally to say to a student in substance: We will devote two years to your culture and two years to your business training. Does this sharpen the line in his mind, between these groups of studies, or does it integrate them in that manner which all will admit to be highly desirable? Since both the two-two and the four-year school emphasize the importance of cultural studies, and seemingly in about the same amount, is it better to administer the cultural and business doses successively, by two-year periods, or concomitantly? These are questions which instructors both in two-year and in four-year schools repeatedly raised in the course of the present study.

It might be added here that this same problem has long agitated the engineering schools, and has come to be settled by almost unanimous consent of the unified, four-year plan. The following is the summary of the study of this problem, as made by the Society for the Promotion of Engineering Education:

> The unified plan of engineering education has valid historical sanctions, is firmly fixed in status, and is consistent with the objectives of the engineering colleges; it makes the most of the student's motivation, aids in the try-out of his educational and professional choices, and lends itself to adjustments of program to fit individual needs; it fits into the requirements of the public and industry and makes for time

economy; it exercises a wholesome influence on secondary education and insures the requisite sequence of studies; and it subtracts nothing vital from the cultural ideals of education, but affords opportunity for a closer linking up of cultural and vocational interests. The circumstances which led to the adoption of the divided plan in other branches of professional training are almost wholly lacking in the case of engineering. A general abandonment of the present unified program would be a disrupting influence in educational organization and would have little support from the engineering profession. There has been no demonstration of the superiority of the divided plan on either cultural or technical grounds, when programs of equal total length are compared; and no convincing case has been made for its general adoption.

Defense of engineering education as a unified process should not be mistaken as a plea for uniformity. There is no inherent reason why all engineering colleges should be organized on the same plan or offer similar programs of studies. Standardized uniformity is sterile, but diversity makes for progress which is more often spread through experiment and example than imposed through mass movement. A comparison of engineering curricula of the unified type with present curricula in medicine and dentistry indicates that the engineering colleges enjoy greater freedom from standardization. Local circumstances may make a division between the engineering curriculum and the introductory general studies advantageous in particular institutions and it is well that the plan should be fully tried out. The actual trials thus far made have not achieved assured success and the more notable advances of recent years have been achieved in institutions which maintain a unified program.[5]

On the Basis of the Spread of Business Courses

The classification of collegiate schools of business on the basis of formal or administrative organization is assumed usually to be synonymous with differences on the basis of the curricula of these schools. Actually, this is not true, which fact introduces an important complicating element into the discussion of the two-two vs. the four-year plan. What is equally important, if not more so, than a classification on the basis of administrative organization is one based on curricula, i.e., on differences in the spread of business courses.

[5] Second Report of the Board of Investigation and Coordination, The Society for the Promotion of Engineering Education, June, 1927, pp. 11-12.

As a matter of fact, most of the institutions with two-year (upper division) schools of business reach down, into the lower years, prescribing business subjects, and "pre-business" schedules in the sophomore, and at times even in the freshman year. On the other hand, some of the four-year schools show freshman and sophomore schedules only slightly, if at all, different from those required in other schools or colleges of the same university. It would seem expedient, therefore, to classify the member schools on this other basis of the spread of, or academic period covered by, the business subjects. This classification is presented herewith.

1. *The two-year graduate business course.* This includes Harvard and Stanford, and does not differ from the grouping based on administrative organization.

2. *The two-year senior graduate course.* The business schools at Dartmouth and Michigan are in this class, there being no difference from the other classification.

3. *The junior-senior business course.* An analysis of the announcements of member schools shows that only one, that at the University of Missouri can be so classified. Five semester hours of general economics is the only requirement prior to the junior year which is suggestive in any way of the business studies. In the case of the other "two-year" schools of business, there is a reaching down below the junior year, with an advising or requiring of business courses which spreads the business subjects over three, and at times over four, years. The subjects usually projected into the lower years by these schools include general economics, economic history, commercial geography, mathematics of finance and investment, accounting, money and banking, statistics, and commercial correspondence.

4. *The sophomore-junior-senior business course.*

(a) There is the school at Washington and Lee which definitely announces a three-year schedule, i.e., the study of business subjects does not begin until the sophomore year.

(b) There are those schools which, while organized formally as two-year schools, actually project the study of business subjects into the sophomore year. Obvious illustrations are the schools at Columbia, Northwestern, Washington University, and Texas. Columbia, for example, includes economic geography and elements of business administration in the sophomore year of the pre-commerce course.   Northwestern has a pre-commerce course which includes economics, accounting, and money and banking in the sophomore year.   Both Washington University and Texas place accounting in the sophomore year.

(c)   Finally, there must be included those schools which, while organized on a four-year basis, nevertheless show but a three-year spread of business studies.   California might be cited as an illustration.   While business subjects may be taken conceivably by the freshman, they are not included in the program suggested ordinarily for the freshman year, with the possible exception of the course in real estate, where economic history and commercial geography are included in the designated freshman studies. Other illustrations would be Ohio State and Virginia.

5.   *The four-year undergraduate business course.*

(a)   It has been pointed out that most of the member schools are organized on a four-year basis.   Of these, nineteen actually distribute the business subjects over a four-year period.   The business subjects usually scheduled in the freshman year include accounting, business mathematics, economic history, economic resources, principles of economics, and elements of business organization.

(b)   Some of the schools organized on a "two-year" basis actually extend, through pre-business curricula or through requirements for full admission, the study of business subjects over the four years.   Indiana's pre-business freshman year includes two terms of accounting and one term in the mathematical theory of investment.   North Dakota's new pre-commerce course includes economic geography and accounting and such other business subjects as may be added through the electives allowed. Chicago, Kansas, and Minnesota include so many business subjects among the pre-commerce requirements that it is unlikely that most of them will be taken in the sophomore year.   Actually, there is a four-year spread.

(c)   Also, as a matter of actual fact, the five-year cooperative courses at Cincinnati and Georgia Tech, as well as the five-year program at Boston University, involve but four years of business studies and should be included at this point in the above classification.

On the Basis of Departmental Make-up

Because of a certain looseness of organization and the non-existence or vagueness of departmental lines, an accurate classification of schools on the basis of departmental make-up cannot be made. It does seem possible, however, to distinguish three rather definite types of schools on the basis of the general fields of instruction which are included as constituent elements in the business schools as now organized.

1. The relatively complete or isolated college unit, which embraces within the folds of its organization virtually all the fields of instruction represented in the curriculum of that school. Not only are the various business subjects or departments, together with economics and the other social sciences, included, but this type of school also gives its own English courses, its own work in psychology or mathematics or language or whatever the subject may be. In other words, all courses and studies represented on the curriculum are "given" by the school, controlled by its responsible administrative officer, specifically developed for the purposes of the school and integrated into its general program. Member schools of this type include Boston, Denver, and Tulane.

Conversation with deans and other faculty members at these schools indicates a general and pronounced satisfaction with this type of organization. Two distinct advantages are emphasized. One is that it facilitates the development of a unified and integrated curriculum. Courses can be added and shaped as they fit into the program of the business school, not as they reflect the half-hearted gesture of an unsympathetic or indifferent arts department. The second advantage emphasized is that it permits the selection of a more interested teaching force. There can be no doubt but that many teachers of arts courses given in business schools show, whether consciously or not, the so-called contempt of the scholar for "mere business." This is neither good pedagogy nor good business. With the control of these subjects by the business school, teachers can be selected who are interested in and sympathetic with the work for which the school exists.

Conflicting arguments, from the standpoint of departmental and general university administration, can be advanced. These will be touched upon in the succeeding chapter. Sufficient is it here to point out that this plan of the independent, isolated school is being tried in the field of business education, and that those functioning under such an arrangement seem completely satisfied with it.

2. At the opposite pole is the school organized on the basis of a restricted inclusion only of those subjects, courses, or departments which are strictly of a business nature. Courses usually associated with the departments of general economics are not even included except as some technical (managerial, for example) aspect is being considered.

Oregon is an illustration of this type. While the School of Business Administration there recognizes the importance of a "broad knowledge of economics, law and liberal arts," its curricula are built around one idea—the development of business executives —and the work offered by the school itself consists of courses in business from the administrative and managerial aspect. In other words, instead of comprehending the entire range of business education, this school conceived of itself as contributing a specialized and technical aspect of that training.

3. Occupying the middle ground between these two types are the majority of the member schools with an organization that comprehends more than the specialized and technical business studies, but extends rarely beyond the domain of the social sciences. Economics, geography, political science, and sociology, usually are the social studies included—obvious evidence of the historical antecedents of the business school. Perhaps half of the undergraduate member schools are clearly of this type. In these schools one finds the tendency, at differing degrees of development, for separate programs, like public and social administration, to spring up alongside of the business curricula.

In this chapter only a brief outline of the growth and organization of collegiate education for business has been attempted. Many of the problems suggested or touched upon will be discussed more fully later in this study.

Summary

The following facts, developed in the present chapter, will be restated in summary form at this point.

1. Collegiate schools of business at leading universities organized, in 1916, for the promotion and improvement of higher

education for business in North America. The standards of admission formulated by this organization, known as the American Association of Collegiate Schools of Business, represent the current code of acceptable practice in this field of higher education. The Association had 42 members in 1930.

2. Four distinct objectives are mentioned in the formal announcements of these schools. These are: (a) training in the general fundamentals of business; (b) training in various specialized phases of business; (c) training for business leadership; and (d) equipment with the cultural and ethical foundations for business life.

3. The various collegiate schools of business vary on the basis of the distribution and place of the business subjects. Most schools confine their plan of instruction to the undergraduate level. Several, however, are graduate schools, and still others combine the last undergraduate year with the first graduate year. The undergraduate schools differ, too, as to the length of the period covered by instruction in the business subjects. Some confine these subjects to the upper two years of the undergraduate course, but most of the schools distribute them over the entire four years. In business education, as formerly in engineering education, there has been a controversy between the two-two and the four-year plan. In both fields, experience seems to favor the latter plan.

*
* *

PART IV

THE CURRICULA OF THE COLLEGIATE SCHOOLS OF BUSINESS

* *
*

CHAPTER XI

THE ORGANIZATION OF THE BUSINESS CURRICULA[1]

The curricula of the collegiate schools of business represent the answer of the academic world to the demands of our business civilization. These curricula have been changing rapidly during recent years. They have evolved as the product of various forces and factors, other than that of rational judgment. These will be dealt with later in this study. At this point, certain data concerning curricula will be presented.

THE PROLIFERATION OF BUSINESS COURSES

Perhaps the most striking, certainly the most obvious, change in collegiate business curricula thus far has been the rapid growth in the number and range of courses. The extent to which this process of proliferation has proceeded varies from school to school. The longer range of its development can be seen best in the case of the older schools.

The Wharton School of the University of Pennsylvania

A tabulation of the catalogue offerings of this school by course topics and class hours by decennial years, 1890-1930, follows:

TABLE LXIV.* COURSE OFFERINGS, WHARTON SCHOOL OF FINANCE AND COMMERCE 1890–1930

Year	Course topics	Class hours	Average class hours per course topic
1890–91	28	1,188	42.4
1900–01	48	3,402	70.8
1910–11	52	4,032	77.5
1920–21	87	6,300	72.4
1930–31	118	8,262	70.0

* The number of credit hours for a course is obtained by multiplying the meetings per week by the number of weeks in a course. A semester is counted as eighteen weeks, as is the custom in academic reckonings.

Included in this are the data of the courses in political science and sociology, which at Pennsylvania are included in the school of business. Excluding these, there were offered in 1930-31, in economics and the business subjects, a total of 91 course topics and a total of 6,624 class hours.

---

[1] Prepared and written by J. H. S. Bossard.

Other Business Schools

These figures may be compared with those for other schools whose origin dates to the early years of the history of collegiate education for business. The College of Commerce, University of California, offered in 1928-29, thirty years after its founding, a total of 69 courses for a total of 4,068 class hours, of which 29 courses for 1,692 class hours are open exclusively to commerce students.

The School of Commerce, Accounts and Finance at New York University is the most striking illustration of the proliferation of courses. At the end of thirty years of its history (1929-1930) a total of 213 course topics for 10,512 class hours are announced, including only economics and the business subjects.

All of the above data are for undergraduate courses. The three schools selected are four-year schools. In each case the totals cited are for economics and the business subjects, combined. In view of the fact that all school of business curricula include a considerable number of liberal arts courses, the above figures must be thought of as the offerings which have been developed for a part of the student's undergraduate training. If the entire undergraduate curriculum comprises 60 semester hours, or 1,080 class hours, and if two-thirds of the entire curriculum, or 720 class hours be devoted to economics and the business subjects, then it is obvious that a number of the schools offer a profusion of courses far beyond the possible needs of their students. Clearly, there is a very considerable proliferation of courses based on factors other than the demands of undergraduate instruction. This is further indicated in the discussion and tables immediately following.

Relative Development of the Business Studies at the Several Schools

How have the various business studies fared in this process of proliferation? In which fields has the process gone farthest? How does one school differ from another in regard to the extent of instruction offered in a particular subject? How do schools differ in total offerings in the business studies or offerings in a given subject, on the basis of the size of the school?

Tables LXV and LXVI represent an attempt to answer these

TABLE LXV. NUMBER OF CLASS HOURS IN VARIOUS SUBJECTS IN 38 COLLEGIATE SCHOOLS OF BUSINESS

	Accounting	Banking and finance	Business cycles and forecasting	Business law	Business organization				Business and the public					Commercial teaching
					Business administration and management	Business organization	Business policy	Total	Business ethics	Social and economic reform	Trusts and combinations	Regulation of business, gen.	Total	
Alabama	612	306	108	108							54		54	108
Boston	684	360	36	252	36			36	8				8	144
California	612	288	108	216		54	60	120		54	54		108	
Chicago	480	360	60	240		60		60		120	60	60	240	300
Cincinnati	286	180		48			36	36						
Columbia	108	288		288						36		36	72	36
Denver	756	324	72	414	72		72	144						72
Florida	432	324	108	108	54	54		108			54		54	
Georgia	540	216		108						36			36	54
Georgia Tech	783	540	54	324										36
Illinois	774	486	54	216		54		54		54		54	108	
Indiana	378	270	72	180	36	54		90	18	36		36	90	198
Iowa	828	216	54	108		54	54	108		72	54	72	198	108
Kansas	432	252		108		36		36		54			54	
Kentucky	540	234	54	108			36	36			27		27	36
Marquette	540	342	54	180			36	36	54	54		54	162	
Minnesota	504	504	36	108								36	36	
Missouri	396	450	90	54	72			72		54			54	
Nebraska	486	342	108	126	72			72	36	54	54		144	
New York	1224	1404		216	30			30		72		72	144	468
N. Carolina	552	360	60	120		30		30		72	54	54	180	
N. Dakota	468	216	54	180		27	36	63		54			54	
Northwestern	748	540	108	144	24	162		186	108	54	108	54	324	
Ohio	696	840	96	216	54			54		54	54	12	120	
Oklahoma	882	468	108	306		36		36		72	36		108	
Oregon	528	444		144			60	60		96	48		144	
Pennsylvania	558	1350	72	450		72	108	180		72			72	
Pittsburgh	918	594	108	360			72	72	27	90	36	27	180	
So. California	612	522	54	324		54		54		36	54		90	
So. Methodist	684	324	54	108			54	54		54	54		108	
Syracuse	702	588	54	144	162	108		270		108		54	162	324
Texas	666	414	54	144	54	54	54	162		162	54		216	54
Tulane	270	288	54	72	54			54						
Virginia	324	324		108			60	60		108	108		216	36
U. of Wash.	960	636	120	168	108	72		180						120
Wash. Univ.	594	432	54	162	60			60		54	54		108	
Wash. and Lee	378	216	54	108										
Wisconsin	324	342	54	108	36	54		90	36	54		54	144	
Total	22,259	16,584	2,226	6,768	924	1,035	738	2,697	287	1,590	1,113	825	3,815	1,968

TABLE LXV (*Continued*)

	Distribution					Economics									
	Adver-tising	Market-ing	Sales	Retail store mgmt. and mer-chandis-ing	Total	Eco-nomic descrip-tion	Elemen-tary econo-mics	Eco-nomic problems	Adv. theory and hist. of eco-nomic thought	Eco-nomic history	Total	Foreign trade	Geogra-phy and resources	Insur-ance	Labor
Alabama	90	306	90		486	108	108	36	72	54	270	54	72	72	144
Boston	396	216	72	36	720	108	108	378	144	72	396	180	72	72	180
California	72	144	54	108	378	108	108		420	162	900	324	162	432	420
Chicago	60	360	60	60	540	60	180			400	1,060	240	420	180	66
Cincinnati		98	58	40	196		66			66	132		210		36
Columbia	108	144	108		360	36	108		72		72		108	216	54
Denver	72	54	54	36	216		108		72	144	324	36	36	216	54
Florida	108	108	54	54	324		108		36	108	216	162	216	162	54
Georgia	54	108	108	54	324		108			108	216	108	54	144	90
Georgia Tech	162	126	162	54	504	54	90			162	216			162	108
Illinois	162	198	72	108	486		108		36	72	342	162	252	108	162
Indiana	54	108	54	36	324		108		126	216	306	36	180	108	54
Iowa	36	108	18	36	198	90	54		162	90	486	54	108	72	108
Kansas	144	144		36	324		108		198	288	432	90	36	108	162
Kentucky		108	108	54	252		108	36	180	108	576	54	54		72
Marquette	72	180	36	36	342		60		54	432	270	36	72	54	90
Minnesota	144	204	36	90	420	180	90		144	108	852	36	96	72	144
Missouri	288	36	180	54	594		108	72	180	180	378	36	54	108	120
Nebraska	828	216	144	792	1,980	72	72		90	180	450	72	144	108	54
New York	60	126	120	60	420		120	162	72	144	360	252	324	216	162
N. Carolina	54	120	54	108	270	60	54		60	60	300	180	180	180	180
N. Dakota	324	54	198	36	666		90		108	54	378	162	324		108
Northwestern	108	108	48	132	588		120		108	108	306	306		72	264
Ohio	108	300	54	108	432		108	108	162	120	348	108	492		72
Oklahoma	156	162	120	72	384	108	90		144	90	450	54		108	108
Oregon	180	36	288	54	810		108		144		360	300			54
Pennsylvania	144	288	72	36	468		90	72	108	144	576	288	450	72	54
Pittsburgh	198	216	54	396	882	108	108	108	54	90	288	108		522	54
So. California	162	216	72	54	432		108	36		216	324	162		108	108
So. Methodist	324	162	72	72	450		54			108	396		240	162	108
Syracuse	108	144	72	108	612	54	108	144	36	162	540	288			108
Texas	54	36	198	54	378	54	108	108	108		180	252	324	252	312
Tulane	36	152	108	36	108	72	108			108	432		108	108	54
Virginia	210	36		396	1,056		120		216		444	108	108		108
U. of Wash.	108	390	60	108	450		108	84	240		108	540	60	108	54
Wash. Univ.	54	108			324		108			90	162	54	240	300	108
Wash. and Lee.	54	54	54	36	162		108		54		324	54	54	54	54
Wisconsin		54	36		198		144		90		306		108	72	90
Total	5,472	5,738	3,172	3,604	17,986	1,272	3,762	1,344	3,726	4,372	14,476	4,950	5,358	4,728	4,332

TABLE LXV (*Concluded*)

| | Office management | Personnel administration | Production | | | | | Public finance and taxation | Public utilities | Real estate | Secretarial science | Statistics and investigation of business problems | Transportation | Total | Number of graduates 1929 |
			Factory management	Production management	Manufacturing	Industrial management	Total								
Alabama		54				54	54	36	54	72		108	90	2,862	67
Boston		72				36	36	72	36			72	72	3,212	207
California	60	108		120	60		180	240		162	120	126	216	4,482	151
Chicago		180							108			300	240	5,980	73
Cincinnati	36	36						36		36		96	108	1,214	34
Columbia	36	36		36	54	72	72	54			144	252	36	2,070	62
Denver		36				36	36	108		36	234	54	108	3,312	20
Florida					54	54	108					54	324	2,556	26
Georgia		54				108	162	144	270	108		54	360	2,745	45
Georgia Tech		54	54			36	36	108	90	108	144	126	90	4,230	48
Illinois		36				108	108	36	108	72	108	60	226	3,006	292
Indiana		54						90	54	36		144	108	3,448	77
Iowa	36	54	54	54			54	108	54	72		126	54	2,520	113
Kansas	36	54	54				54			288		108	54	2,862	65
Kentucky	27	144	36				36	108	54		54	54	144	2,664	37
Marquette	36	54		168			168	144			192	276	54	4,128	38
Minnesota	36	54						144	108	108		154	108	2,466	134
Missouri	36	54	54				54	108	90	108		134	108	3,232	64
Nebraska	72	252	54			216	216	432	144	396	72	468	360	9,216	89
New York		60		144	72		96	120				60	132	3,180	631
N. Carolina	54	54				27	27	54	54			144	108	2,736	57
N. Dakota	36	72	108	36			162	108	360	108	54	126	198	4,852	53
Northwestern	36	54		36	54	204	240	168	168	54		36	276	4,974	144
Ohio		36			36			36	132	36	126	108	264	3,564	205
Oklahoma		54			144	252	132	48	72	288		168	612	3,618	87
Oregon	48	108		96	54	54	396	72				180	108	6,786	52
Pennsylvania		54			162	162	108	54	180	108		72	396	4,104	607
Pittsburgh	54	108		54	54		378	54	54	180	36	162	108	2,412	111
So. California	54		54			54	54	54	54	162	324	126	432	5,520	89
So. Methodist	162						54	108		108	216	108	54	3,978	40
Syracuse	36	260										108		1,790	190
Texas						180	180	108	180	60	156	60	216	2,484	98
Tulane								120				54	672	6,384	13
Virginia	60	60		54		54	54	54	54	180		54	270	2,616	20
U. of Wash.		54						54	108			54	108	1,728	144
Wash. Univ.		54						90				324	216	2,952	62
Wash. and Lee															44
Wisconsin															79
Total	**897**	**2,360**	**360**	**762**	**636**	**1,551**	**3,309**	**3,180**	**2,586**	**3,102**	**2,034**	**4,768**	**6,958**	**137,341**	**4,368**

TABLE LXVI.   ORDER OF SCHOOLS ACCORDING TO NUMBER OF GRADUATES, 1928–29, AND CLASS HOURS OFFERED IN VARIOUS BUSINESS SUBJECTS

	Number of Graduates	Rank of schools in order of graduates	Accounting	Banking and finance	Business law	Business organization and management	Business and the public	Distribution	Economics, including Economic history	Foreign trade	Geography and resources	Insurance	Labor and personnel	Production	Public finance and taxation	Public utilities	Real estate	Statistics and Business cycles and Forecasting	Transportation
New York	631	1	1	1	9	6	7	1	12	6	4	5	2	4	1	5	1	1	5
Pennsylvania	607	2	17	2	1	3	11	4	16	5	2	1	11	1	8	9	3	11	2
Illinois	292	3	7	10	9	9	9	12	14	9	5	9	13	7	4	2	6	18	5
Boston	207	4	11	16	7	7	15	5	10	8	14	10	16	13	3	4	6	15	18
Ohio	205	5	10	3	9	1	8	9	13	10	1	10	8	3	9	10	5	9	7
Syracuse	190	6	9	6	13	8	6	7	10	5	4	4	6	12	8	11	5	8	3
California	151	7	14	20	9	2	9	18	2	2	1	2	12		6	1	2	9	12
Northwestern	144	8	13	7	11	2	1	6	2	3	10	4	4	5	6	11	8		1
U. of Washington	144	8	2	4	1	4	13	8	19	1	15	3	9	6	5	1	6	11	14
Minnesota	134	9	21	2	16	9	13	2	16	14	13		10	9	4	3	8	18	11
Iowa	113	10	5	9	6	5	4	16	9	13	13	9	12	9	11	7	6	5	16
Pittsburgh	111	11	3	24	13	6	5	25	3	10	12	10	14	9	9	10		6	16
Texas	98	12	12	15	13	8	3	13	6	6	11	9	13	12	6	7	4	11	9
Nebraska	89	13	22	17	4	8	7	14	5	12	6	9	12	2	9	10	9	16	14
So. California	89	13	14	8	5	8	10	18	7	10		7	13		6	7	9	9	11
Oklahoma	87	13	4	11		9	9	3	5	6	12		12	12	11		4	2	12
Wisconsin	79	14	16	17	10	8	7	15	18	12	12	10	3	13	7	10	7	10	17
Indiana	77	15	27	21	8	9	2	21	7	13	9	9	2	5	6	7	7	3	16
Chicago	73	16	23	19	16	4	12	10	15	14	3	6	1	12	2			9	12
Alabama	67	17	14	16	16	9	12	12	16	17	14	9	1	12	11	10		18	17
Kansas	65	17	25	22	18	5	12	10	1	7	17	10	10		7	8	7	14	16
Missouri	64	18	26	12	6		11	12	19	13	16	9	14	13	2			20	19
Columbia Univ.	62	18	31	16	12	5	11	21	9	11	12	5	16	10				18	16
Washington Univ.	62	19	15	14	15		9	16	8	8	6	11	14	14	9	10	10	14	15
North Carolina	57	20	18	16	10	5	5	23	17	9	9	6	11	14	5	6	6	17	16
North Dakota	53	21	24	24	16	7	12	17	12	4	4	10	11	8	9	7		10	15
Oregon	52	21	20	13	4	10	7	11	12		4	7	14		7	8		12	9
Georgia Tech	48	22	6			7	13	11	20	10	16	10	18	9	6	10	10	18	6
Georgia	45	23	19	24	16	8	9	21	22	13	16	7	12	12	9	6	6	12	16
Wash. and Lee	44	24	27	24	16	5	6	15	15	14	14	10	17	13	9	7		21	17
So. Methodist	40	25	11	18	16	6	14	20	19	13	16	11	18	12	9	10		18	19
Marquette	38	26	19	17	10	8	12	22	4	9	8	6	9	9	9			9	
Kentucky	37	27	16	23	19	5		26	23	14	7	10	12	13	6	7	3	8	17
Cincinnati	34	28	29	25	2	5	3	21	20	13	17	11	17	12	9	10		18	19
Florida	26	29	25	18	16	6		24	15	9	14	7	15	13	9			13	16
Denver	20	30	28	18	17	8		25	24	14	17	5	14	12	9	10		18	20
Virginia	20	33	28	18	16	5		24	24	14	17	9	14	13	11			19	17
Tulane	13	34	30	20	17	3	3	18	21	10	12	9	7	11	6	10	10	13	12

questions in tabular form. In constructing these tables, it seemed essential that the data tabulated be entirely comparable. To include the course offerings in the evening schools of the institutions located in large metropolitan centers, and the large number of graduate courses offered at several similarly situated schools, would be to present a picture true neither of the undergraduate day school, the evening school, nor the graduate school. Accordingly, only the 38 undergraduate schools in the American Association of Collegiate Schools of Business are included in these tables, and the offerings tabulated are for the undergraduate day schools only.

In restricting the studies of the present and the succeeding chapters to the member schools of the American Association of Collegiate Schools of Business, there is no thought of depreciating or slighting the work of any collegiate school of business not included. The members of the Association are selected as representing the current practices and developments in collegiate business education. Unfortunately the limitations placed on the present study did not permit a more comprehensive summary.

Table LXV shows the undergraduate offerings in the various subjects of the 38 schools included, expressed in terms of class hours. As previously indicated, the number of class hours for each course is obtained by multiplying the meetings per week by the number of weeks in the course. A semester is counted as eighteen weeks; a quarter, as twelve weeks. Included in the table is the number of graduates of each school for the year 1928-29. Because of the administrative differences between the two and four year schools, the number of graduates rather than the number of students enrolled, is taken as the measure of the size of the school.

Table LXVI shows the 38 undergraduate schools arranged in order of size, based on the number of graduates during the academic year 1928-29, and the rank of each school in each of the business subjects according to the number of undergraduate class hours offered in that subject.

These tables show a highly irregular development. There seems to be a certain correlation between size of school, as indicated by the number of graduates, 1928-29, and the total development of business subjects. Other than that, there is a great irregularity from school to school, and from one subject to another. Obviously, the curricula of the business schools often have not been planned; they have just grown up. Here is an elaborate development with a relatively few students; there one finds more students and fewer courses. A school which is among the leaders in amount of work offered in one field lags in another field. This may indicate a certain specialization in development as between schools. In many cases, however, the explanation is to be

TABLE LXVII. TOTAL UNDERGRADUATE CLASS HOURS BY SUBJECTS ARRANGED IN ORDER OF NUMERICAL IMPORTANCE

Rank	Subject	Class hours
1	Accounting	22,259
2	Banking and finance	16,584
3	Transportation	6,958
4	Business law	6,768
5	Marketing	5,738
6	Advertising	5,472
7	Foreign trade	4,950
8	Statistics	4,768
9	Insurance	4,728
10	Economic history	4,372
11	Labor	4,332
12	Elementary economics	3,762
13	Economic theory and thought	3,726
14	Retail stores management and merchandising	3,604
15	Production	3,309
16	Public finance and taxation	3,180
17	Selling	3,172
18	Real estate	3,102
19	Business organization and management	2,697
20	Public utilities	2,586
21	Personnel administration	2,360
22	Business cycles and forecasting	2,226
23	Secretarial science	2,034
24	Commercial teaching	1,968
25	Social and economic reform	1,590
26	Economic problems, advanced	1,344
27	Economics, descriptive	1,272
28	Trusts and combinations	1,113
29	Office management	897
30	Regulation of business	825
31	Business ethics	287

found rather in the play of individual interests, regional demands, departmental ambitions, and the like.

Another aspect of the development of the business curricula, of particular interest from the standpoint of the particular subject, is a comparison of the total offerings in the various business studies. Table LXVII shows the total undergraduate offerings in the business studies included in the preceding tables, arranged in order of numerical importance. The totals are for the 38 undergraduate schools.

Influencing materially the above order is the relative inclusiveness or exclusiveness of the terms used. To utilize banking and finance as one category, and to group separately advertising, marketing, selling, and merchandising, presents a list not wholly comparable. Table LXVIII presents the offerings in the business studies arranged by general subjects of a more comparable nature.

The above list of business studies, while omitting several of secondary numerical importance as well as the subjects usually taught by the liberal arts faculty, does include the chief elements of the existing collegiate curricula for business, and serves to

TABLE LXVIII.   TOTAL UNDERGRADUATE CLASS HOURS BY GENERAL SUBJECTS ARRANGED IN ORDER OF NUMERICAL IMPORTANCE

Rank	Subject	Class hours
1	Accounting	22,259
2	Distribution	17,986
	Advertising	
	Marketing	
	Selling	
	Retail stores, etc.	
3	Banking and finance	16,584
4	Economics	14,476
	Descriptive	
	Principles	
	Problems	
	Theory and thought	
	History	
5	Transportation and public utilities	9,544
6	Management	9,263
	Business organization and management	
	Personnel	
	Production	
	Office management	
7	Statistics, business cycles, and forecasting	6,994
8	Business law	6,768
9	Foreign trade	4,950
10	Insurance	4,728
11	Labor	4,332
12	Business and the public	3,815
	Business ethics	
	Social and economic reform	
	Business regulation	
	Trusts and combinations	
13	Public finance and taxation	3,180
14	Real estate and land economics	2,940
15	Secretarial science	2,034
16	Commercial education	1,968

indicate, on the basis of a quantitative measure, the extent of their relative development.

THE LOWER CLASS CURRICULA

Following the foregoing analysis of business curricula in terms of their constituent elements, the distribution of these studies over the four years of the collegiate schedule seems logically the next step in the inquiry. Which studies, in other words, are pursued commonly during the freshman year, which during the sophomore year, which in the upper classes?

TABLE LXIX.   THE FRESHMAN YEAR IN 38 COMMERCE AND PRE-COMMERCE CURRICULA

	Accounting	Business Finance	Business Law	Business Organization	Economics, Descriptive	Economics, Elementary	Economic History	Elective	English	Geography	History	Language	Marketing	Mathematics	Office Management	Orientation	Psychology	Science, Natural	Science, Politics	Science, Social	Total
Alabama	108				108[k]		72	72	108	72		108		108		36					576
Boston	108		90			180[p]		36	108			180		72							504
California						66			108	120		120[m]		90						60[m]	522
Chicago	88								60	110											540
Cincinnati (n.)									44		66	108		134		198					508
Columbia	108		108			108			108	108				36		36					522
Denver					36		72		90					108	54			108	108		540
Florida							108		108			108		108							540
Georgia									108			108		108				72[a]			576
Georgia Tech	108								108												720
Illinois	72				54		108	144[b]	180			180						144			468
Indiana							54		144			54[b]					108				540
Iowa					108				180			90[a]		108		18		144			468
Kansas					90				108							18			54		450
Kentucky							90	36[c]	144	72				54				144			504
Marquette	60						108		180					60[a]				60[a]			612
Minnesota					180		108		108					180		72		90			540
Missouri	108				72	72	72	90	72			90[a]		54				54	108		450
Nebraska	72	72		48	60				60			120						72			504
New York(l)								54[d]	108	48[a]			48[a]	120				108			576
N. Carolina	36							72[e]	108	60	120										540
N. Dakota								60[f]	120	144	108	72[a]						144		72[a]	558
Northwestern									120			60[f]						120		120	540
Ohio									120	60		108		72[a]				90	54		540
Oklahoma	144					90	90	360[g]	(i)												558
Oregon	90		90						144							90			90		504
Pennsylvania	108				108				144	90				144							684
Pittsburgh	144						90	108[h]	108	36				108		18					504
So. California						108	108[o]		108					54							504
So. Methodist									108					108		36		108			486
Syracuse						108		108	108	108				108							576
Texas	36				54				108			108		108				108		108[j]	540
Tulane									108			108		108							522
Virginia						120		120	120	60		108		108				216			540
U. of Wash.								108	108					40[a]				40[a]			540
Washington U.									108			40[a]		54				54[a]			540
Wash. and Lee							108		108		108	108		108		108		108			540
Wisconsin									108		54	108		144				90			504
Total	390	72	288	48	870	852	1,188	1,368	4,166	1,088	456	2,194	48	2,712	54	630	108	1,966	522	360	20,380

a. An alternate elective.
b. The figure cited is the minimum. The maximum is 260 credit hours. These electives are rather circumscribed by university requirements.
c. For non-Catholic students only.
d. The figure cited is the minimum. The maximum is 144 credit hours.
e. The figure cited is the minimum. The maximum is 108 credit hours.
f. Equal to one-half of credit hours elective if foreign language requirements have been satisfied in high school.
g. Choice of general survey courses.
h. The figure cited is the minimum. The maximum is 162 credit hours.

k. This course, known as "Principles of Business," is listed in the catalogue under marketing. Because its purpose as well as its contents agree so largely with that of other courses in descriptive economics, it is listed here under that heading rather than as marketing.
l. The freshman curricula in Accounting is tabulated.
m. May be taken in freshman or sophomore year. Exact amount depends on entrance credentials.
n. The first of the four years in commerce is tabulated here. This is the second year of the co-operative plan.
o. Economic History only in part.

The Freshman Year

What is the nature of the freshman commerce and pre-commerce program among the 38 undergraduate schools of the American Association? What does a composite of the first year of these schools look like? There are difficulties in the way of obtaining such a picture. A number of schools, for example, have lower class or lower division requirements in which the freshman and sophomore years are not clearly distinguished. Another problem is the distribution of class hours in the case of alternate requirements. Also, there are schools where the work of the first two years turns on the entrance credentials.

In constructing Table LXIX, these difficulties have been met as follows: Where the lower class or division requirements are grouped with no hard and fast division between the requirements of one year against the other, representatives of these schools were asked to designate which subjects were taken customarily in the freshman year, and which in the sophomore year. In the case of alternate requirements, i.e., where one of two, or two of three, designated subjects were required, the total number of class hours constituting the requirement were distributed among the specified subjects. Where, however, a large number of subjects were enumerated as constituting the range from which one subject was to be taken, such requirement was listed among the electives. Finally, in those cases, like Chicago, where the work

TABLE LXX. THE FRESHMAN YEAR

Subject	Number of schools	Class hours
Accounting.........................	15	1,390
Business finance.....................	1	72
Business law........................	3	288
Business organization................	1	48
Economics, background for...........	23	2,058
Economics, descriptive.............	10	870
Economic history..................	13	1,188
Economics, elementary principles......	8	852
Electives...........................	13	1,368–1,664
English............................	37	4,166
Geography, chiefly commercial.........	13	1,088
History............................	5	456
Language...........................	21	2,194
Marketing..........................	1	48
Mathematics........................	28	2,712
Office management...................	1	54
Orientation.........................	10	630
Psychology.........................	1	108
Science, natural.....................	19	1,966
Science, political....................	6	522
Science, social......................	4	360
Total		20,380

TABLE LXXI. THE SOPHOMORE YEAR IN 38 COMMERCE AND PRE-COMMERCE CURRICULA

	Accounting	Business Administration and Organization	Business Finance	Business Law	Economics, Advanced	Economics, Descriptive	Economics, Elementary Prin.	Economic History	Electives	English	Ethics	Geography	History	Insurance	Language	Logic	Marketing	Mathematics	Money and Banking	Orientation	Psychology	Religion	Science, Natural	Science, Political	Sociology	Statistics	Total
Alabama	108					108	108	54	144	54		108	54ᵃ		108			36			72		54	108			540
Boston	72						108		180	36					144		18	54ᵃ			60		120i	54ᵃ			612
California	60			90						60		108						180ᵇ					112	72			612
Chicago	66	72	66					66	108	44		100					13		54	108	36		54ᵃ		60i		540
Cincinnati (j)										72		108															472
Columbia	108			108			108			72		54	72		108								180	54			486
Denver	108						108	108		216					108				108					108			540
Florida	108						108	108	144ᵇ	36			54		108			54	54				72	90			504
Georgia	108	54					90	72	54ᶜ		54				54ᶜ	54		90			90		90	54			504
Georgia Tech	108	54					108		18				54								72		108				648
Illinois	36						108		144	108			30ᵃ											30ᵃ	30ᵃ		668
Indiana	108						54	36ᵃ	156	36		30ᵃ	108					54ᵃ					90	90		36	486
Iowa	108						54	60	126						54ᶜ			54ᵃ					54ᵃ				540
Kansas		54					108	54									54										504
Kentucky	54	54					60	36ᵃ	72	108						54		54	108		72		90				612
Marquette	144	72					90	60	120ᵈ	120			20ᵃ		120			60					54ᵃ				486
Minnesota	144						108	54	90ᵈ	60				90					54								576
Missouri	36ᵃ	72							216	90					108						54					60	540
Nebraska (j)	36ᵃ		90						g	72									108		54		120	90			486
New York (j)										72												108					576
N. Carolina	108						120			120			108		108			54			54						540
N. Dakota	108			108			108			144											54ᵃ		144				576
Northwestern	120						90			60								60			54ᵃ		108ᵉ				558
Ohio	90						120		120ᵈ	90			20ᵃ								54ᵃ		54ᵃ			54	540
Oklahoma		108					90		216	72					108				108				54ᵃ				468
Oregon		108					108		90ᵈ	72							108										504
Pennsylvania					24ᵃ		108		g	108			108											24ᵃ	24ᵃ	54	540
Pittsburgh							108		108	72											54	108	144	108			540
So. California							108			108					108		108	54			54ᵃ		108ᵉ				486
So. Methodist	144			108			108		144	108			108		108				108		54ᵃ		144	108			576
Syracuse	54						108		108	108		108			108			54	54		54ᵃ		54ᵃ				540
Texas	144						108			108			108		108						54ᵃ		54ᵃ			54	576
Tulane	144			108			108			108					108						54ᵃ		54ᵃ				576
Virginia	108						108			108					108						108						540
U. of Wash.	180						108		144	108		108			108									108			540
Washington U.	108			108			108		108	108			108		108			54						108			540
Wash. and Lee	108						108		72	108		108	108		108												540
Wisconsin	108						144			72														108			504
Total	**2,946**	**486**	**156**	**414**	**24**	**108**	**2,856**	**450**	**2,004**	**2,372**	**54**	**616**	**662**	**90**	**1,398**	**54**	**180**	**690**	**452**	**108**	**762**	**108**	**1,594**	**1,163**	**161**	**204**	**20,112**

a. Alternative elective.
b. Circumscribed by university requirements.
c. Alternate, dependent on high school preparation.
d. The figure cited is the minimum. The maximum is 144 credit hours.

h. Exact amount dependent on entrance credentials. Above amount strongly advised.
i. May be taken in freshman or sophomore year, exact amount depends on entrance credentials.

of the first two years depends somewhat on the entrance credentials, representatives of the institution were asked to indicate the customary schedules.

The next table summarizes Table LXIX. It shows the various subjects included in the freshman year, the number of schools scheduling each subject, and the total number of class hours offered.

The Sophomore Year

What is the nature of a composite sophomore year? The second year of the schedules of the member schools, similar to that presented for the freshman year, is shown in Table LXXI.

TABLE IXXII. THE SOPHOMORE YEAR

Subject	Number of schools	Class hours
Accounting	29	2,946
Business administration and organization	7	414
Business finance	3	192
Business law	4	414
Economics, background for	8	558
Economics, descriptive	1	108
Economic history	7	450
Economics, elementary principles	28	2,856
Economics, advanced	1	24
Electives	17	2,004
English	27	2,372
Ethics	1	54
Geography	7	616
History	9	662
Insurance	1	90
Language	13	1,398
Logic	1	54
Marketing	4	216
Mathematics	10	690
Money and banking	6	452
Orientation	1	108
Psychology	12	762
Religion	1	108
Science, natural	16	1,594
Science, political	16	1,163
Sociology	5	161
Statistics	4	204
Total		20,112

Table LXXII presents in summary form the totals shown in Table LXXI. It shows the various subjects included in the sophomore year, the number of schools mentioning each subject, and the total number of class hours offered.

The Lower Class Studies

By combining the composite schedules of the freshman and sophomore years, one gains an idea of the constituent elements of the work of the lower classes, as well as the relative emphasis placed upon various subjects, in so far as a comparison of class hours is of value as an objective measure. Such addition shows the following result.

TABLE LXXIII. DISTRIBUTION OF SUBJECTS, SOPHOMORE AND FRESHMAN YEARS, BY CLASS HOURS

Subject	Total class hours
Accounting	4,336
Business administration and organization	462
Business finance	264
Business law	702
Economics, background of	2,616
Economics, elementary principles	3,708
Economics, advanced	24
Elective	3,668
English	6,538
Ethics	54
Geography	1,704
History	1,118
Insurance	90
Language	3,592
Logic	54
Marketing	264
Mathematics	3,402
Money and banking	452
Office management	54
Orientation	738
Psychology	870
Religion	108
Science, natural	3,560
Science, political	1,685
Science, social	360
Sociology	161
Statistics	204

The studies of the first two years, in the order of their importance on the basis of the total number of class hours required, are as follows:

TABLE LXXIV. FRESHMAN AND SOPHOMORE SUBJECTS, BY CLASS HOURS, IN ORDER OF NUMERICAL IMPORTANCE

Rank	Subject	Class hours
1	English	6,538
2	Accounting	4,336
3	Economics, elementary principles	3,708
4	Language	3,592
5	Science, natural	3,560
6	Mathematics	3,402
7	Economics, background of	2,616
8	Geography	1,704
9	Political science	1,685
10	History	1,118
11	Psychology	870
12	Orientation courses	738
13	Business law	702
14	Business administration and organization	462
15	Money and banking	452
16	Social science	360
17	Business finance	264
18	Marketing	264
19	Statistics	204
20	Sociology	161
21	Religion	108
22	Insurance	90
23	Ethics	54
24	Logic	54
25	Office management	54
26	Advanced economics	24
27	Electives	3,668

Conclusions and Comments on Lower Class Curricula

A study of the above table seems to warrant at least the following conclusions.

1. The first two years of the collegiate scheme for business education show a wide range of subjects. More than the 27 listed aspects are represented, for the above enumeration of subjects takes no notice of the differences in the titles and content of courses in the same subject from school to school. Does this range mean a lack of agreement on curriculum content? Does it mean an accumulation of "hangovers" and experiments? Does it mean a considerable number of deviations on the basis of personal whims or academic compromises? Undoubtedly the answer varies from school to school.

2. There is a general agreement upon the importance of English. The margin in the number of credit hours between English and any other subject is considerable. A similar agreement, only to a lesser extent, prevails concerning the first ten subjects. Obviously, this is the traditional liberal arts curriculum, plus accounting and economics.

The elective hours introduce a somewhat indefinite element, but such information as was obtained indicates that lower class electives are distributed largely among the natural and social sciences, thus tending to equalize more nearly the distribution of class hours among the first ten subjects in Table LXXIV.

3. The other 16 subjects constitute what might be termed the departures from the normal. Several of them obviously are concessions to denominational colleges; several more can be attributed to the influence of outstanding faculty members, either as teachers or as politicians; and the remaining ones represent experiments, wise and otherwise, to teach business subjects to students in the lower classes.

4. One cannot but be impressed with the lack, in these lower years, of subjects and courses which might be termed the fundamentals of business training. The term fundamentals is used in the sense that mathematics and the physical sciences are fundamentals in engineering education. Such fundamentals undoubtedly exist in business education as they do in other fields of education. No serious attempt to discover them has yet been made. The composite lower class schedule, shown above, clearly indicates

this. Not even does the approach to business education by way of the liberal arts curriculum represent a reasoned judgment. It is purely a matter of historical accident. Just as natural, and perhaps more logical, would have been the emergence of business curricula out of an engineering background.

The identification of the fundamentals of business training, objectively arrived at on the basis of an analysis of the demands of the upper class curricula and of the business world, and the placement of such fundamentals in the lower class curricula of the schools, would seems to be an immediate and imperative task of business education.

5. Another serious omission in the lower class curricula is the frequent lack of a course or of courses giving the student a general introduction to, or survey of, the field of business. Boys and girls of sixteen to eighteen, except for the few who have had very unusual opportunities, know rather little of the economic life of society in general, and of the business world in particular. For half of them, still, the community background has been devoid of big business and of most of the evidences of modern industrialism. Deficiencies of the kind indicated above seem to exist even among some teachers in collegiate schools of business.

Certain developments in this direction, through the medium of introductory courses in economics, and some incidental gestures by way of other courses, are now being made. Few schools, however, have faced the task directly and seriously. The development of a descriptive interpretative introduction to modern business and an emphasis upon the training that business requires, to the end that the further studies of the student may be motivated properly, would seem to be another immediate and imperative task of collegiate education for business.

A course called "Principles of Business," given by Professor Leo D. O'Neill at the School of Business Administration of Boston University, might be cited in connection with this discussion. The course is given to first-year students and grew out of experience in teaching elementary economics. Beginning the course is a discussion of the meaning and functions of business, relating it to the economic structure as a whole. Business concerns itself, however, with more than inanimate objects. It deals also with human beings. Business must be looked at, then, not abstractly but in an intensely human way. This leads to a discussion of the qualifications of the business man. What does the student, who has come to college to be a business man, need to know? What sort of training ought he to get? This leads to an analysis of the catalogue of the school of business administration, and the possibilities which it includes for training along the different lines which have been considered. Other topics considered in the course are the fields of business endeavor, necessity of a broad education, elements of a successful enterprise, external factors affecting business, forms of business enterprise, organization of production and manufacture, present importance and development of marketing, the marketing functions, classification of goods in relation to distribution, buying and patronage motives, the channels of distribution, etc.

This course appears to be unusually successful, not only in leading students at the beginning of their course to face the realities of the business world, but also to see their relationship to the work offered by the school, thus tending to motivate their effort.

Recent Plans and Programs Involving Lower Class Curricula

Lower class curricula are receiving a good deal of attention today, both in colleges of liberal arts and in colleges of commerce. It is a hopeful sign—this going back to the beginning. Numerous faculty committees for study have been appointed, and various changes and experiments have been and are being undertaken. Particularly does this healthy sense of dissatisfaction prevail in regard to the first two years of the commerce program.

Recently emphasized plans concerning lower class curricula in collegiate schools for business center around two main ideas: first, that the fundamental studies in business education be identified and emphasized; and, second, that certain composite survey courses be included, such courses to be determined objectively by analyzing the foundation needs of the upper class courses, and developed regardless of departmental lines.

There seems to be a growing conviction that the reorganization of the first two years must be fundamental in character, and must begin *de novo*. That is to say, it must free itself from the onus of thinking in terms of departments of instruction and of certain traditional categories and compartments of subject matter.

It is a matter of considerable significance that virtually every comprehensive change in lower class curricula in American colleges and universities in recent years has involved the elimination of departmental lines and a reorganization of the material considered essential into broad functional units. The recent vogue of orientation and survey courses, and their apparent success in those institutions where they have been tried seriously, are illustrations in point. Even more often than such developments have occurred have they been recommended by investigating committees of faculty members who have studied the problems of lower class curricula.

There are many advantages in favor of such a reorganization of the first two years. It would enable the inclusion of much material without giving it the status of a separate course. It would facilitate, certainly, the exclusion of much material not immediately pertinent. It would eliminate much duplication, for the plan calls for the careful co-ordination and integration, perhaps under an assistant dean, of the work of the first two years. It would enable the more efficient co-ordination of instructional staff, and avoid a too narrow specialization in teaching. It would do away with much of the jealousy between departments. It would avoid the race for large departments. Departmental heads would be relieved of many details of administration of lower class work, in which they are often not interested but which they are loath to forsake.

Against these advantages is—the disarrangement of existing vested interests.

In the discussion of orientation courses in the next chapters, examples of courses organized on this basis and with this purpose in view will be presented.

THE UPPER CLASS CURRICULA

The upper two years constitute the part of the curricula of the collegiate schools of business devoted in most schools to meeting the specific business requirements and to specialization in some restricted part of the business field. It is pertinent, then, at this point to present these two groups of facts: first, the upper class requirements; and second, the fields of specialization.

TABLE LXXV. UPPER CLASS COMMERCE CURRICULA

	Accounting	Advertising	Business Admin. and Management	Business and Government	Business Cycles and Forecasting	Business Law	Business Organization	Business Policy	Business Talks	Corporation and Business Finance	Economic History	Economics, Advanced	Economics, Principles of	English, Business	Ethics	Financial Admin. and Management	Foreign Trade	Geography	History	Income Tax Law	Industrial Organization and Mgmt.	Insurance	Investments
Alabama, (gen.)	108	54				108				54	54	120		108							54	72	36
Boston, (core)	105					180				48				104								45	
California	132					180				72	54	72											42
Chicago, (core)	108	72	54			180		18		54													
Cincinnati, (core)						48	54																
Columbia, (core)	108					108	54					108		54						54	108		
Denver, (B.A.)	108	54	36		36	36		72		108					54								
Florida, (core)		18	54			108				54													
Georgia, (B.A.)	108					108				108													
Georgia Tech, (core)						108				54		108		36		45							
Illinois, (gen.)						108				54				36		72							
Indiana, (gen.)	108[a]					108				54				12									
Iowa, (core)						108										108							
Kansas, (gen.)						108																36	
Kentucky, (gen.)					54	54		36		36			54					54					
Marquette, (gen.)		18				108		36		54				36									
Minnesota, (core)	36				36	54				54	54	72				72							
Missouri, (core)	198					54	60			54				72									
Nebraska, (core)			54	60		108	108	54		54						72							
New York, (B.A.)	120			54		120	108	60		60													
N. Carolina				12		108	54																
N. Dakota, (gen.)	180[a]					72																	
Northwestern, (gen.)	60	108				72			36					36					72				
Ohio, (gen.)																			54				
Oklahoma[b]						144																	
Oregon[c] (core)					54	108			72	54									108				
Pennsylvania, (gen.)	108	108				108	54			54	108			36		60	54				60		
Pittsburgh, (core)						108	108			54													
So. California, (core)	108					72	54			54		60		72		72			108				
So. Methodist, (core)						108																	
Syracuse, (gen.)						108																	
Texas, (core)	108					108				108				60									
Tulane, (core)						108																	
Virginia, (core)						108				108													
U. of Wash., (core)						108																40	
Wash. Univ., (core)	18	18	54			108				108		60		54				18			18		
Wash. and Lee, (B.A.)	108		36			108				54		18		36		54							
Wisconsin, (core)																							
Total	1,497	324	288	126	180	3,210	492	276	108	1,350	216	450	54	752	54	555	54	72	234	54	240	193	78

TABLE LXXV. (Cont.) UPPER CLASS COMMERCE CURRICULA

	Labor Problems and Management	Language, Foreign	Marketing	Mathematics of Business	Money and Banking	Natural Science	Office Management	Personnel Administration	Political Science	Production Management	Psychology	Public Finance	Public Utilities	Research	Retail Merchandising	Salesmanship	Social Reform	Sociology	Statistics	Transportation	Traffic Management	Trusts and Combinations	Totals
Alabama	54		54		54				36					36					108	54		54	792
Boston		144			72														72				504
California	66										60			64	40	58			105				450
Chicago					24														96				840
Cincinnati			45					45		45									54		45		802
Columbia, (B.A.)	108		80		108														108				504
Denver, (B.A.)			54					56	108	36	108					36			54				540
Florida			216		72		36			108					54					54			792
Georgia, (B.A.)	54		54		72											108							864
Georgia Tech			54		54																		432
Illinois			54		54															54			468
Indiana			54		36											36							540
Iowa	54				90																		504
Kansas	54				54			54			54	54							108	54			576
Kentucky					120			54											54				522
Marquette	36		108		54					36		36	36			18		18	54		36	54	522
Minnesota			36	54	60			56									30		36				624
Missouri			54							36	108								54	54			612
Nebraska, (B.A.)						108																	378
New York, (B.A.)																			60				144
N. Carolina			54													54			54				660
N. Dakota			54													54			72				594
Northwestern	36		60		60														36				900
Ohio														72									612
Oklahoma					60				60	60		60				60				60			504
Oregon	60	108ᵈ	108																				288
Pennsylvania			108		108			108						72					108				360
Pittsburgh								108						72					72				288
So. California			108						108														324
So. Methodist			72		108			54	60										72				468
Syracuse								54											108				450
Texas																			108				466
Tulane	60																						432
Virginia	60		40		40																		360
U. of Wash.	54		108		54								54			54			54				648
Wash. Univ., (B.A.)			54		54								54						108				810
Wash. and Lee, (B.A.)	18		54		54								54						54	54			396
Wisconsin																			54				
Total	624	252	1,683	54	1,348	108	36	519	372	285	330	150	144	316	94	478	30	18	1,701	384	81	108	19,972

a. Accounting, if not taken in sophomore year.
b. Varies from one major to another.
c. Considerable flexibility in upper years. The courses listed are taken quite
d. Science or mathematics may be substituted.
e. The last two years of the cooperative course are tabulated.

The Upper Class Requirements

Table LXXV has been constructed for the purpose of showing the common core of the upper class curricula of the business school, i.e., those subjects which are required of all students, regardless of their field of specialization. The table shows the total class hours for these core requirements. In the case of

TABLE LXXVI. UPPER CLASS REQUIREMENT, BY CLASS HOURS, IN ORDER OF NUMERICAL IMPORTANCE

Subject	Credit hours	Number of schools
Business law	3,210	30
Statistics	1,701	23
Marketing	1,683	24
Accounting	1,497	14
Corporation and business finance	1,350	21
Money and banking	1,348	21
Business English	752	14
Labor problems and management	624	13
Financial administration and management	555	8
Personnel administration	519	8
Business organization	492	7
Salesmanship	478	9
Advanced economics	450	6
Transportation	384	7
Political science	372	5
Psychology	330	4
Advertising	324	6
Business administration and management	288	6
Production management	285	5
Business policy	276	6
Industrial organization and management	240	4
History	234	3
Economic history	216	3
Insurance	193	4
Business cycles and forecasting	180	4
Public finance	150	3
Public utilities	144	3
Business and government	126	3
Trusts and combinations	108	2
Traffic management	81	2
Investments	78	2
Geography	72	2
Principles of economics	54	1
Income tax law	54	1
Mathematics of business	54	1
Ethics	54	1
Office management	36	1
Social reform	30	1
Sociology	18	1

several schools, where core requirements were not stated, the requirements of the general course were included instead. The particular requirements tabulated for each school are specified. The two groups of data, while not entirely comparable, are sufficiently so for the purpose intended, namely, that of indicating the common core of the upper class curricula. In certain cases, specific courses rather than general subjects are listed in the table. The purpose of doing so is to show the importance of these specific courses.

The total number of class hours required, shown in the line at the bottom of Table LXXV are presented in Table LXXVI, arranged in the order of numerical importance.

No discussion of collegiate education for business is likely to proceed far before reference is made to the fundamental business subjects and their importance in the training of the student. Table LXXVI seems to reveal the judgment of the schools as to the identity of these fundamentals.

Six courses stand out as of primary importance. These are business law, statistics, marketing, accounting, money and banking, and finance.

The courses known as corporation finance, business finance, financial administration or management, may be taken as different approaches to the same field. The data on these six courses, coupled with those concerning their development in the lower class schedule, show their status and the general emphasis in collegiate education for business.

Six additional subjects might be mentioned, on the basis of Table LXXVI, as being of secondary importance as upper class requirements. These are business English, labor problems, business organization and management, economic theory, salesmanship, and personnel administration.

It is significant, too, to notice in Table LXXVI the wide range of requirements. The list includes thirty-nine different courses and subjects, sixteen of which are mentioned at less than four different schools.

Specialization in the Business Curricula

The facts about the extent, nature, and time of specialization in the curricula of the undergraduate schools of business are given in Table LXXVII. These facts are significant in several ways. They serve, in a sense, as a measure of the development of collegiate business education. Obviously, they indicate how far the subdivision of the subject matter of business has gone, how extensive the range of interests of students and teachers of business are at the present time. Summarized, they represent somewhat of a composite judgment of the leaders of collegiate education for business as to which aspects of business present opportunities or need emphasis.

TABLE LXXVII. DATA ON SPECIALIZATION IN 38 UNDERGRADUATE
SCHOOLS

School	Year in which Specialization begins	Number of fields of specialization	Names of fields of specialization
Alabama	Junior	11	Accounting and statistics, advertising, banking and finance, business and law, commercial teaching, foreign service, general business, merchandising, production and personnel, real estate and insurance, transportation and public utilities.
Boston	Sophomore	6	Accounting, banking and finance, advertising and selling, business management, foreign trade, commercial education.
California	Junior	9	Accounting, actuarial work, advertising, banking, government foreign service, foreign trade and shipping, hotel management, real estate, transportation.
Chicago	Junior	11	Accounting, production, finance, personnel, transportation and communication, risks, marketing, law, management of meat packing industry, business teaching, secretarial work.
Cincinnati	Senior	4	Accounting, production, sales, traffic.
Columbia	Senior	10	Accounting, banking and finance, commercial teaching, foreign trade and consular service, insurance, labor administration, merchandising, statistics, transportation, general business.
Denver	Freshman	4	Accounting, business administration, commercial teaching, and secretarial science.
Florida	Junior	10	Accounting, banking and finance, general business, marketing, production, management, transportation and communication, risk bearing and insurance, personnel management, foreign trade and consular service, business and law.
Georgia	Junior	7	Accounting, banking and finance, business administration, economics, industrial management, marketing, and public utilities.
Georgia Tech.	Junior	3	Accounting, banking and finance, merchandising and advertising.
Illinois	Sophomore	12	Accounting, banking and finance, commerce and law, general business, commercial teaching, foreign commerce, trade and civic secretarial service, insurance, general railway administration, railway transportation, industrial administration, public utilities.
Indiana	Sophomore and senior	8	Accounting, banking and finance, commercial education, business and law, insurance, marketing and merchandising, personnel management, secretarial training.
Iowa	Junior	6	Accounting, banking and finance, management, merchandising, transportation, teacher training.
Kansas	Junior	7	Accounting, commercial organization, production, personnel, finance, marketing, general business.
Kentucky	Junior	8	Accounting, business and law, general business, foreign service, banking, merchandising, manufacturing, commercial education.
Marquette	Junior	8	Accounting and statistics, banking and finance, commercial teaching, general business, marketing, personnel administration, real estate, business and law.

TABLE LXXVII (*Cont.*)

School	Year in which specialization begins	Number of fields of specialization	Names of fields of specialization
Minnesota	Junior	14	Accounting, advertising, agricultural business, finance, foreign trade, general business, personnel management, merchandising, real estate, secretarial, industrial administration, statistics, traffic and transportation, insurance.
Missouri	Junior	7	Accounting; banking and finance; manufacture, trade, and transportation; government service; foreign service; industrial relations and personnel management; social service.
Nebraska	Junior	21	Accounting, banking and finance, business and law, economics, commercial education, insurance, real estate, building and loan management, statistics, retail merchandising, sales management, advertising, industrial administration, personnel management, secretarial work, commercial arts, chamber of commerce secretarial service, public utility administration, foreign trade and consular service, agriculture, commercial engineering.
New York	Freshman	23	Accounting, banking and finance, banking, corporation finance, credits and collections, investment banking, real estate, real estate and insurance, insurance, taxes, business administration, economics, journalism, management, office management, marketing, advertising, salesmanship, economic geography, foreign trade, transportation, retailing, labor problems and personnel administration.
North Carolina	Junior	13	Accounting, banking and finance, business law, business and law, advertising and salesmanship, marketing, retail merchandising factory organization and management, personnel management, risk bearing and insurance, transportation and shipping, foreign trade and consular service, general course.
North Dakota	Junior	11	Accounting, banking and finance, commercial secretaryship, economic theory, foreign trade and consular service, insurance, merchandising, public administration, secretarial work, commercial education, business and law.
Northwestern	Junior	12	Accounting, general business, advertising, commercial teaching, finance, foreign trade, insurance, real estate and land economics, manufacturing and production, public utilities and transportation, sales administration and merchandising, secretarial.
Ohio State	Sophomore	11	General business, public accounting, industrial accounting, finance and banking, foreign commerce, industrial and personnel organization and management, marketing, municipal administration, social administration, journalism, business and law.
Oklahoma	Junior	5	Accounting, business law, business administration, economics, finance.
Oregon	Senior	8	Accounting, finance, foreign trade, business administration and household arts, business and law, marketing, transportation, and labor management.
Pennsylvania	Sophomore	15	Accounting, banking and real estate, brokerage, commerce and transportation, corporation finance and investments, foreign trade service, general business, insurance, journalism, labor management, manufacturing, merchandising, preparation for law, public service and civic work, social economy.

TABLE LXXVII (*Concluded*)

School	Year in which specialization begins	Number of fields of specialization	Names of fields of specialization
Pittsburgh	Junior	7	Accounting, business law, economics, finance, commerce industry, statistics.
Southern California	Junior	6	Accounting, banking and finance, management, marketing, trade and transportation, business and law.
Southern Methodist	Junior	5	Accounting, banking and finance, general business, marketing, statistics.
Syracuse	Junior	14	Accounting, advertising and selling, domestic commerce, economics, finance, foreign trade, insurance, organization and management, political science, real estate, traffic and transportation, secretarial science, business education, journalism.
Texas	Junior	13	Managerial accounting, public accounting, banking and finance, insurance and real estate, foreign trade, manufacturing, hotel administration, marketing, cotton marketing, public utilities, business statistics, secretarial training, commercial teaching.
Tulane	Junior	5	Accounting, banking, foreign trade, retailing, wholesaling.
U. of Washington	Junior	14	Accounting; business finance; commercial teaching and secretarial training; foreign trade and consular service; economics; management; insurance; marketing, merchandising, and advertising; transportation; maritime commerce; labor; public utilities; statistics; business and law.
Virginia	Junior	9	Accounting, banking, business organization, economics and labor, finance, foreign trade, insurance, marketing, statistics.
Washington U.	Junior	7	Production, marketing, finance, labor, social regulation, accounting and statistics, business and law.
Washington and Lee	Junior	5	Accounting, banking and finance, business administration, public administration, business and law.
Wisconsin	Junior	8	Accounting, commercial teaching, finance, labor and personnel, marketing, public utilities, risk, and insurance, statistics.

Data are presented for 38 undergraduate schools. At Cincinnati, the specialization indicated is in the work which the student does in business establishments under the co-operative plan, rather than in any selection of courses. It should be added that there are several other schools were specialization to any appreciable extent is disclaimed. However, the possibility of specialization exists at these schools, and it has been deemed proper to include them in the present tabulation. The information has been taken in most cases from the published announcements of the schools. In those cases where doubt existed, a statement from the dean or other officer of instruction at the school was obtained. Combined commerce and law curricula are counted as fields of specialization, although not all schools so specify them.

Year when specialization begins. Undergraduate specialization in the commerce curricula usually begins with the junior year. This is the case in 28 out of the 38 undergraduate member schools. Only two schools, Denver and New York, distinguish their curricula over the entire four years. Four schools begin specialization with the sophomore year—Boston, Illinois, Ohio State, and Pennsylvania. Indiana begins some specialized curricula in the sophomore year, and others are postponed until the senior year. In the case of three schools, all specialization is delayed until the senior year.

Most institutions recognize the first two years of a college or university course as concerned primarily with the development of a broad foundation. This fact, coupled with the desirability of postponing for another year or two the selection of one's chosen field of specialized preparation, leads one to consider with grave misgivings any academic arrangement which involves such a decision before the end of the sophomore year. Were it not that so large a proportion of students avoid the necessity of making the decision by selecting the general business curriculum, even that time might be challenged with good cause.

Extent of specialization. A total of 356 specialized curricula are indicated in the announcements of these 38 schools, or an average of more than nine per school. The range in the number of fields offered in any one school varies from three to 23. The number of schools offering each number of fields of specialization are shown in the following table.

TABLE LXXVIII. NUMBER OF SCHOOLS AND FIELDS OF SPECIALIZATION

Number of schools	Number of fields of specialization
1	3
2	4
4	5
5	6
3	7
5	8
2	9
2	10
4	11
2	12
2	13
3	14
1	15
1	21
1	23

From this table it will be seen that seven schools offer from three to five fields, inclusive; 13 schools from six to eight, inclusive; ten schools from nine to 12, inclusive; and eight offer 13 or more. Twenty-three of the 38 schools offer eight or more fields of specialization.

The range and distribution of fields of specialization.

Table LXXIX shows the fields of specialization arranged by titles used in the announcements or statements of the respective schools. After each title or term used is indicated the number of times such curricula or fields of specialization are offered. It will be observed that there is a range of 132 in the terms or titles used.

TABLE LXXIX. FIELDS OF SPECIALIZATION: RANGE AND DISTRIBUTION

Field of specialization	Number of schools offering
Accounting	31
Accounting, industrial	1
Accounting, managerial	1
Accounting, public	2
Accounting, banking and finance	1
Accounting and statistics	3
Acturial work	1
Advertising	6
Advertising and salesmanship	1
Advertising and selling	2
Agriculture	1
Agricultural business	1
Banking	5
Banking and finance	19
Banking and real estate	1
Brokerage	1
Building and loan management	1
Business, general	13
Business and law	14
Business administration	5
Business administration and household arts	1
Business education	2
Business finance	1
Business law	4
Business management	1
Business organization	1
Business statistics	1
Chamber of commerce secretarial service	1
Commerce	1
Commerce, domestic	1
Commerce, maritime	1
Commerce and law	1
Commerce and transportation	1
Commercial arts	1
Commercial education	5
Commercial engineering	1
Commercial organization	1
Commercial secretaryship	1
Commercial teaching	8
Commercial teaching and secretarial training	1
Corporation finance	1
Corporation finance and investment	1
Credit and collections	1

TABLE LXXIX.   (*Cont.*)

Economic geography	1
Economic theory	1
Economics	7
Economics and labor	1
Factory organization and mgmt.	1
Finance	1
Foreign commerce	2
Foreign service	3
Foreign service, government	1
Foreign trade	9
Foreign trade service	1
Foreign trade and consular service	6
Foreign trade and shipping	1
Government service	1
Hotel administration	1
Hotel management	1
Industrial administration	3
Industrial management	1
Industrial and personnel management and organization	1
Industrial relations and personnel management	1
Industry	1
Insurance	12
Insurance and real estate	1
Investment banking	1
Journalism	4
Labor	2
Labor administration	1
Labor management	2
Labor problems and personnel administration	2
Labor and personnel	1
Management	4
Management of meat packing industry	1
Manufacture, trade, and transportation	1
Manufacturing	3
Manufacturing and production	1
Marketing	15
Marketing, cotton	1
Marketing and merchandising	1
Marketing, merchandising, and advtg.	1
Merchandising	7
Merchandising and advertising	1
Municipal administration	1
Office management	1
Organization and management	1
Personnel	2
Personnel administration	1
Personnel management	5
Political science	1
Preparation for law	1
Production	4
Production and personnel	1
Production management	1
Public administration	2
Public service and civic work	1
Public utilities	5
Public utilities and transportation	1
Publicity utility administration	1
Railway administration	1
Railway transportation	1
Real estate	6
Real estate and insurance	2
Real estate and land economics	1
Retail merchandising	2
Retailing	2
Risk	1
Risk and insurance	1
Risk bearing and insurance	2

TABLE LXXIX. *(Concluded)*

Sales administration and merchandising	2
Sales management	1
Salesmanship	1
Secretarial	2
Secretarial science	2
Secretarial training	2
Secretarial work	3
Social administration	1
Social economy	1
Social regulation	1
Social service	1
Statistics	7
Taxes	1
Teacher training	1
Trade and civic secretarial service	1
Trade and transportation	1
Traffic	1
Traffic and transportation	2
Transportation	6
Transportation and communication	2
Transportation and public utilities	1
Transportation and shipping	1
Wholesaling	1

Main fields of specialization. It is evident, of course, that a good deal of this seeming variety of specialization is really one of terminology instead of subject matter or emphasis in content. In Table LXXX the different terms are grouped together under the heading of the subjects or functional fields generally recognized in collegiate schools of business, and arranged in the order of numerical importance. The number after each general heading,

TABLE LXXX. MAIN FIELDS OF SPECIALIZATION, IN ORDER OF NUMERICAL IMPORTANCE

Distribution—including advertising, marketing, merchandising, wholesaling, retailing and selling	47
Management—including business organization and management, industrial organization and management, manufacturing, production, labor management and personnel administration	45
Banking and finance—including brokerage, building and loan management, credits and collections, corporation finance, etc.	44
Accounting—including curricula in accounting and statistics, and accounting, banking and finance	40
General business—including business administration and economics	28
Foreign trade and service	24
Business and law	20
Insurance—including curricula in insurance and real estate, actuarial work, risk and risk bearing	18
Transportation—including curricula in transportation and traffic, transportation and public utilities, etc.	18
Commercial education	17
Public service—including social service, social economy, commercial secretaries, etc.	14
Statistics—including curricula in accounting and statistics	11
Real estate—including curricula in real estate and insurance	10
Secretarial training	10
Public utilities—including curricula in public utilities and transportation	8
Journalism	4
Hotel management	2
Agriculture	2
Economic geography	1
Taxes	1
Total	364
Duplications	8
Total	356

it should be noted, gives the number of times a given subject or functional field is represented in a curriculum or field of specialization cited. A curriculum in insurance and real estate is counted both under insurance and under real estate. Repititions within

TABLE LXXXI. SCHOOLS, NUMBER OF GRADUATES, AND FIELDS OF SPECIALIZATION

School	Graduates 1928–29	Number of fields of specialization
Alabama	67	11
Boston	207	6
California	151	9
Chicago	73	11
Cincinnati	34	4
Columbia	62	10
Denver	20	4
Florida	26	10
Georgia	45	7
Georgia Tech	48	3
Illinois	292	12
Indiana	77	8
Iowa	113	6
Kansas	65	7
Kentucky	37	8
Marquette	38	8
Minnesota	134	14
Missouri	64	6
Nebraska	89	21
New York	631	23
North Carolina	57	13
North Dakota	53	11
Northwestern	144	12
Ohio State	205	11
Oklahoma	87	5
Oregon	52	8
Pennsylvania	607	15
Pittsburgh	111	7
Southern California	89	6
Southern Methodist	40	5
Syracuse	190	14
Texas	98	13
Tulane	13	5
Virginia	20	9
U. of Washington	144	14
Washington University	62	7
Washington and Lee	44	5
Wisconsin	79	8
Total	4,368	356

a field separately noted, as within management for example, are not counted.

Specialization in relation to the number of graduates. Another angle from which to consider specialization in business curricula is to compare its range at each institution in relation to or in comparison with the number of students, as indicated by the size of the graduating class for the academic year, 1928-29. Table LXXXI shows the schools, the number of graduates for 1928-29, and the number of fields of specialization at each.

In considering Table LXXXI, it is important to recall that in most of the collegiate business schools, half, if not more, of the students are enrolled in the general curriculum, whatever its name may be at any particular institution. The total number of graduates for the 38 schools in this table is 4,368, and the total number of fields of specialization is 356. Allowing one general curriculum for each school, and assuming that half of the students are enrolled in those generalized curricula, it follows that there are 318 specialized curricula for a total of 2,184 graduates, or an average of seven students per field of specialization. This, of course, is an average which is mathematically correct but actually misleading. Allowance for two additional factors need to be made. One is the relatively large proportion of students who specialize in accounting, and the other is the fact that the large enrollment at several institutions raises the mathematical average. In view of all the ado about these specialized curricula and the wide range of choices available, it is all the more remarkable that half and more of the students have enrolled in the general business course. This would seem to buttress the statement already made: that business *per se* constitutes sufficient specialization in the judgment of most students and their parents.

General considerations. It must be clear from the foregoing analysis that many of the specialized curricula announced by colleges of commerce are but expressions of a wish or professions of faith. One wonders whether much of the purported specialization in the collegiate business schools, most of it perhaps, is not mere window dressing, designed to impress students and business men. It may be that it does serve these purposes. Conceivably it has a value in making concrete the different aspects of business activity. Undoubtedly, the announcement of these various specialized curricula has been thought necessary to satisfy the ambitions of members of business school faculties. This factor has been particularly important at certain institutions. For the most part, the real reasons for the development of any extensive specialization have to do with matters other than that of the educational interests of the students.

The reader will recall at this point Table XVIII which shows that in the case of 1,322 Wharton School graduates, but 38 per cent are now holding positions in the field in which they specialized as undergraduates.

SPECIALIZATION AMONG THE FACULTY PERSONNEL

Another interesting and objective measure of the range and distribution of specialization in collegiate business education is

TABLE LXXXII. SPECIALIZATION AMONG MEMBERS OF
COLLEGE OF COMMERCE FACULTIES

Field of specialization	Number of times reported
Accounting	257
Economics	195
Business finance	141
Marketing	103
Banking	93
Business law	80
Business organization and management	72
Statistics	72
Public finance and financial history	63
Advertising	60
Transportation	52
Commercial geography	50
Economic history	50
Insurance	49
Foreign trade	48
Labor	48
Business English	45
Merchandising	43
Investments	35
Public utilities	35
Real estate	35
Personnel administration and management	31
Salesmanship	26
Journalism	25
Research	25
Business cycles and forecasting	22
Psychology	21
Credits and collections	16
Business administration	15
Secretarial training	15
Industrial relations	14
Office management	14
Political science	13
Mathematics	12
Trusts and their administration	9
Business education	8
Monopolies and trusts	8
Teaching of commercial subjects	8
History of economics	7
Stock and produce exchanges	7
Commerce	6
Government and business	6
Public speaking	6
Business policy	5
Brokerage	4
Civic and trade association work	4
International law	4
Business ethics	3
Traffic management	3
Factory management	2
Risk and risk bearing	2
Library (business school)	1

to be found in the data on the faculties of the schools. There has appeared recently (February, 1930), a new edition on the faculty personnel of the members of the American Association of Collegiate Schools of Business. A total number of 1,398 instructors are included. The names of teachers of foreign languages, mathematics, and other subjects not closely related to business subjects are not included. Among the data concerning each faculty member are the fields of his specialization. Since many instructors indicate more than one field of specialization, the num-

TABLE LXXXIII. FACULTY SPECIALIZATION, BY MAIN PHASES OF BUSINESS

Field of specialization		Number of times reported	Per cent
Banking and finance.................................		352	17.2
Banking..................................	93		
Brokerage................................	4		
Business finance.........................	141		
Credits and collections...................	16		
Investments..............................	35		
Public finance and financial history...........	63		
Accounting...................................		257	13.0
Economics....................................		252	12.8
Economic history...........................	50		
Economics................................	195		
History of economic theory.................	7		
Distribution..................................		232	11.7
Advertising...............................	60		
Marketing................................	103		
Merchandising............................	43		
Salesmanship.............................	26		
Management..................................		108	5.4
Business administration....................	15		
Business organization and management........	72		
Business policy...........................	5		
Factory management.......................	2		
Office management........................	14		
Statistics....................................		94	4.7
Business cycles and forecasting..............	22		
Statistics.................................	72		
Labor and personnel administration.............		93	4.7
Industrial relations........................	14		
Labor....................................	48		
Personnel administration and management.....	31		
Business law.................................		80	4.0
Transportation and traffic management...........		55	2.8
Transportation............................	52		
Traffic management.......................	3		
Business English and public speaking...........		51	2.7
Business English..........................	45		
Public speaking..........................	6		
Insurance and risks...........................		51	2.7
Insurance................................	49		
Risks and risk bearing.....................	2		
Commercial geography.........................		50	2.6
Foreign trade................................		48	2.4
Public utilities...............................		35	1.7
Real estate..................................		35	1.7
Research....................................		25	1.2
Unclassified.................................		150	7.7

ber in this respect exceeds the number of instructors. The total number of fields of specialization indicated is 1,968, as shown in Table LXXXII.

For purposes of comparison, the various fields listed in Table LXXXII are grouped together under the more general divisions usually recognized in discussions of business education. Table LXXXIII shows these main groupings in the order of numerical importance.

It has been pointed out that the total number of "specializations" indicated is 1,968. Of these, 352, or 17.8 per cent are in banking and finance; 257, or 13 per cent are in accounting; 252, or 12.8 per cent are in economics; and 11.7 per cent are in the general field of distribution. These four fields account for slightly more than 55 per cent of the total number.

The Predominance of the General Course

It was not possible, unfortunately, to secure accurate data to any appreciable extent concerning the distribution of students in the various fields of specialization. Inquiry in this direction did reveal, however, one fact of outstanding importance; viz., the predominance of the general business course. Whatever the term applied to this more generalized curriculum—general business, business administration, or economics—apparently close to one-half of the students at such schools make it their field of choice.

To this number another somewhat similar group of students should be added. These are the majors in economics in the liberal arts colleges. At a number of universities, students in the liberal arts college may major in economics under circumstances which permit a reasonably wide choice of business subjects. The resultant curriculum differs little at times, if at all, from that of the general business course in the school of business. At institutions where there is possible a free expression of this trend, the number of such majors is relatively quite large.

This situation seems highly significant, and one cannot but wonder whether its implications have been grasped fully by the leaders who are shaping collegiate education for business. Its fundamental meaning seems to be that a large proportion of students find business *per se* enough by way of specialization for their college education. Faculty members in business schools in all parts of the country who act as advisers to students emphasize this fact. They point out that a large proportion of the students in collegiate schools of business today are young men, and, to a less extent, young women, who have no definite objectives such as students in law and medical schools have, who are not interested primarily in specialization in any one field, but who have come to the business school for the purpose of obtaining a general education, with a business background, and stripped of the traditional requirements of the liberal arts college.

From the standpoint of the student, his background and his family's interest, a general business course developed along conservative lines implies in itself a high degree of specialization. It seems safe to assume that, so far as the interests and wishes and needs of many of the students in the business schools go, they might as well have gone to a liberal arts college with provision for liberal electives in economic and business studies. Because of the lack of such liberal provisions in the liberal arts college and their rigid inclusion of certain vestigial[2] studies, these students find in the more general curriculum of the collegiate school of business the opportunity they seek.

FACTORS IN THE EVOLUTION OF BUSINESS CURRICULA

No one familiar with the academic world would be so naïve as to assume that curricula represent wholly rational developments to meet definite and clear-cut objectives. More particularly would one not expect to find this situation in a group of schools whose history has covered a brief span of years, and whose development has been hampered by many unfriendly or modifying influences. The curricula of the business schools are a product of many factors, and the particular pattern of these factors varies to some extent from school to school. The history of the school, the time of its origin, the background of the pioneers in its development, the varieties of local demand, the financial resources available, the personalities of the instructional staff, their relation to each other, the relation to the arts college and to the administrative head of the institution, the type of leadership of each—all of these factors have played their rôle in addition to the judgment of faculties concerning the needs of the students. Several factors which seem of primary importance will receive more extended discussion.

1. Curricula, like men, elephants, and ant eaters, are what they are because of their ancestry. Business curricula are descendants of that imperious dowager of academic life—the liberal arts col-

---

[2] The term vestigial is used to mean those studies in the liberal arts curriculum which remain chiefly for sentimental and traditional reasons.

lege. This, as has been pointed out previously, was largely a matter of accident, and it might conceivably have been as logical if business education had made its advent via the engineering school. But the fact of this lineal descent from the arts college remains, and perhaps no factor has been so persistently important in shaping the curricula of the collegiate schools of business, as well as in other phases of their development.

Business curricula have been developed in a certain measure to meet the demands or to avoid the antagonism of the arts faculty; sometimes such demands having been given more consideration than the obvious needs of the students. In other words, these curricula are a compromise between liberal arts insistence and the business school judgment. The result is an academic structure lacking, in some cases completely and in other cases in certain respects, in coherence from either point of view.

It is unfortunate that some of the business schools have been manoeuvered, temporarily at least, into the position of attempting to offer a liberal education as excellent as that of the liberal arts college, and at the same time a professional training equivalent to that of the law and medical schools. The former pretension is made to justify their existence to their academic competitors; the latter, to win their clientele and the support of the business world. It should be obvious that it is impossible to do both.

The problem of the relationship of the school of business to the college of liberal arts is a difficult one. "These two units cannot serenely go their own separate ways." As Marshall has pointed out, "Not only is the school of business the off-spring of the liberal arts college, but also its subject matter and the traditional outlook of its instructors lead to close relationships with the arts college."[3]

It is a problem which exists to some degree at each institution. Almost no conference held in the course of this study proceeded far without reference to it. Happily, at some of the older schools, the earlier animosities are dying out, and gradually schools of business are being left more free to develop their work in their own way to meet their own peculiar needs. To the extent that the arts colleges have done their work well, present day instructors

---

[3] Marshall, L. C., op. cit., p. 39-40.

in the business schools, who have been trained so largely in arts colleges, will inject enough of the arts influence into business curricula, without the promptings of coercion.

This unconscious slant of arts trained instructors in the business schools is an important factor. Even where the schools of business function as independent units, with relatively free reign, this influence of the arts training of the instructors can easily be discerned.

2. If the liberal arts college is the grandmother, then the department of economics has served "in the dual capacity of father, and midwife" to the collegiate school of business. The attitude of the economists has constituted a second factor of primary importance in the evolution of the business curriculum, and the relation of the business school to the department of economics is one of the outstanding problems in the development of collegiate education for business. This problem is discussed in a later chapter.

The attitudes of the economists toward the business schools are not so clear cut as those of the liberal arts faculties. At some institutions, they are in nebulous form, at others, they seem to have crystallized more definitely. To the extent that there is anything like a common or typical attitude, it may be likened to that of a petulant father who is partly proud of, partly envious of, partly skeptical of, or even antagonistic toward his offspring, who has outgrown him or is threatening to do so.

There are various results of this tension. One could name four or five schools where the development of the business subjects seems to lag because of a petty domination by the economics group. There are institutions where the relationship is described as one of "more or less constant tension between two groups working in fields not sharply distinguished." At other institutions, the economists appear almost peevish, preferring the non-business atmosphere of the college of liberal arts, or, if within the fold of the business school, longing to resume their liberal arts connections. And finally, at some schools there is a clear-eyed vision of the importance of a constructive integration of the work of both business and economic departments, in which each profits by service through critical co-operation with the other. This is the relationship obviously to be desired, and which happily, seems to be developing to an increasing extent.

A real difficulty is that so many economists are not really "sold" on business education. These are mostly liberal arts men in training and background and sympathy who, under pressure of demand, have become teachers of commerce subjects. In many cases they are confronted with demands for "practical" courses which they are not wholly qualified to give. Defense mechanisms of various sorts can be discerned. Of course, the particular reaction depends upon age and temperament. The young (in spirit) and the adaptable are adjusting themselves to the demands of business; those less so, growl about the "acquisitive" trend in business education, and sigh for the sheltering folds of the liberal arts college. And yet, one finds the growth of an inductive spirit. Many thoughtful economists realize that their science has developed as far as possible without a rigorous application of the inductive method. Furthermore, this inductive spirit is being carried over into their teaching. Many are frankly experimental, dissatisfied with their courses and existing texts.

Considerable emphasis has been given to the attitudes of large portions of present faculties because it seems clear that the successful building up of any profession, or professional school, or professional spirit involves, among various other things, an abiding faith in the values inherent in that field and in its cultural possibilities. It has been a sort of fad to abuse the American business man, with his homely habits, his Main Street prejudices, his Rotarian playfulness, etc., but as one moves about the length and breadth of this country, there isn't a town, a city, a college, a scholarship fund, a community chest, a home for tubercular children, but what evidences concretely his communal interests. It just may be that culture abides in management studies as well as in classic mythology, in advertising courses as well as in nineteenth century poetry, in business research as well as in the artist's easel.

3. Some of the business schools and their curricula obviously are but lengthened shadows of some dominant faculty figure. When one considers departments within a school this is still more often the case. It happens not infrequently, and perhaps not unnaturally, in the early history of a school or a department that some capable or vigorous person, thoroughly imbued with the idea involved, translates that idea into reality, and then maintains

dominance too completely and retains it too long for the best interests of his creation. This is apt to lead to an unfortunate and painful situation much as exists in families where the parent tries to dominate the child too much and too long. The results often are disastrous for both.

4. Another factor in the development thus far of some collegiate schools of business and of their curricula has been the attitude of the general university administration, particularly with reference to financial support. Certain schools of business have been considered too much in the light of a good thing, financially. They have been utilized in a number of cases to make a net financial contribution to the general university budget. At places they have been exploited specifically for the benefit of the liberal arts college. At other places, they have been starved, consciously and purposively, to prevent their development as competitors to other schools and programs of the university.

It should be evident that this is a short-sighted policy, educationally and financially. Educational institutions are not the only undertakings that have failed because they have maintained traditional supply in the face of changing demand. A university cannot be conducted successfully in the long run, any more than a department store, by disregarding changes in the vogue.

Moreover, such manipulation of funds is apt to affect adversely financial gifts from persons interested in business education. The needs of a school of business make a peculiarly attractive plea to many business men of substantial means, but no large amount of money can be brought into a school of business through its front doors, to be let out the back door for the support of an overstaffed department in a remote part of the university's work. What has just been said is not meant to imply in any sense that a university should maintain only such schools and departments as are self-supporting or produce a surplus. The matter at issue is entirely one of degree and of deliberate policy.

5. The constant factor in the development of the curricula of the collegiate schools of business, of course, has been the judgment of its leaders as to what they ought to be, i.e., what kind of training a student preparing for business ought to receive. In determining this, the business schools have had to "start from scratch." There were no models to follow, no experience from

which to profit, no precedents, no text books. The situation was like that which prevailed in the early stages of the history of other professional schools. What is amazing, as one views the subject in retrospect, is not that there should have been hesitance, bewilderment, blundering, and the like, but that so much progress should have been made in the face of so many difficulties in so brief a time. Some of the aspects and trends in this development will be considered later. It is meant, here, only to emphasize the factor of judgment along with the others which have determined the development of the curricula of the collegiate business schools.

SUMMARY AND CONCLUSIONS

Ten points would seem to stand out from the data and discussion of this chapter. For the sake of greater clarity and emphasis, they will be restated in summary form.

1. The history of the curricula of collegiate schools of business is one of rapid growth in the number and range of courses. The larger and older schools show offerings of more than five thousand class hours in the business studies, the total in one case approximating seven thousand, and in another case, ten thousand class hours, open to undergraduates alone. The number of separate undergraduate courses in some of the older schools varies from 60 to 100, and in one case exceeds 200.

2. This process of proliferation of courses, however, has developed rather unevenly. It varies considerably from school to school, somewhat, but not entirely, on the basis of size of school. Even more pronounced are the variations from one subject to another within the same school. It would seem that there is developing a certain degree of specialization between schools in the development of the business field, some emphasizing one, some another, aspect.

3. The business fields which have been most extensively developed, on the basis of class hours of undergraduate instruction offered, are accounting, distribution (including advertising, marketing, selling, and retail merchandising), banking and finance, economics, transportation and public utilities, management, statistics and business law, in the order named. Courses dealing with the foreign field, insurance, labor, business and the public, public finance and taxation, real estate, secretarial science and com-

mercial education, show a less extensive development, also in the order named.

4. In the lower class commerce and pre-commerce curricula, English, accounting, economics, language, natural science, mathematics, geography, political science, and history predominate. Obviously this is the liberal arts lower class curriculum, plus accounting and economics. No fundamentals of business seem to have been identified.

5. There is lacking, in large measure an introductory survey of business, presumably the student's chief interest, nor is the student given any understanding of the relation of the various elements of the curriculum to his chief interests. The attitude is "take it or leave it." There is no appreciation of the psychology of the situation.

6. The problem of a reorganization of the work of the lower two years is raised. There is a considerable body of opinion that such reorganization ought to proceed independently of traditional department lines, and ought to concern itself with the fundamentals of business education rather than a transference from the liberal arts college. Further consideration of this problem will be given in the next chapter.

7. Upper class core requirements, while showing a wide range, center rather definitely upon certain courses. Six of these seem to be recognized as of primary importance. They are business law, statistics, marketing, accounting, money and banking, and business or corporate finance. Six additional courses are widely emphasized, whatever the particular titles may be. They are business English, labor problems, business organization and management, economic theory, selling, and personnel administration.

8. Specialization in the business curricula runs riot—at least so far as differentiated curricula and faculty preferences are concerned. Of a total of 353 curricula announced by 38 undergraduate schools, 132 different titles appear. Twenty-three of these 38 schools offer eight or more fields of specialization.

9. Much of the specialization is window dressing. Half, if not more of the students in undergraduate commerce schools are enrolled in the general business curriculum. Business seems to be sufficient specialization for most undergraduates—an obvious

fact that commerce faculties, in the enthusiasm of their own particular interests, are so apt to forget.

10.   The commerce curricula are the product of factors other than the careful analysis and rational judgment of the commerce faculties as to the needs of their students.   Desire to conciliate the arts college faculties, the predilections of the economists, the dominance of pioneers, and the attitude of university administrators have played their rôle in varying degree from school to school.

CHAPTER XII

CERTAIN GENERAL STUDIES[1]

The selection of the title of this chapter calls for brief comment. The particular grouping of studies involved, and reference to them as general studies, both are assumptions made for purposes of organization of material. It is not meant that these are the foundation studies which will be identified ultimately as such, nor that they can be distinguished clearly from the business studies, which form the subject of the next chapter. For economics, here included among the general studies, would be designated as one of the business studies by most business school students; and conceivably certain of the business studies, included in the following chapter, may come to be used for general educational purposes. The title of the present chapter is used, then, in a very general sense to include certain broadly educational studies, usually pursued during the first two years, but not confined to them. Explicit reference is made to this matter of title, since there is every wish to avoid becoming involved in questions of terminology or classification of courses at this point.

ECONOMICS IN THE BUSINESS CURRICULA

It has been pointed out that the collegiate school of business is an outgrowth largely of the subject of economics. In the building of business curricula, the general assumption has been that economics is, in a peculiar sense, the foundation or basic subject to be studied. Some work in economics is required of all commerce students. In fact, no other subject is so generally and so extensively required of commerce students. It would seem pertinent, then, to present the data concerning some of the more important problems which concern the rôle of economics in the curricula of the business schools. Table LXXXIV presents the data concerning the development and status of economics in the 38 undergraduate schools.

The Introduction to Economics

The introduction of the student to the science of economics is one of the outstanding problems of the collegiate school of busi-

---

[1] Prepared and written by J. H. S. Bossard.

TABLE LXXXIV.   ECONOMICS IN THE UNDERGRADUATE BUSINESS SCHOOLS

Schools	Undergraduate credit hours offered						When required			Courses required				Field of specialization
	Economic description	Elementary economics	Economic problems	Adv. theory and history of economic thought	Economic history	Total	Freshman	Sophomore	Upper class—core or general	Economic description	Elementary economics	Adv. theory and hist. of economic thought	Economic history	Field of specialization
Alabama	108	108			54	270		162		108	108		54	
Boston	108	108	36	72	72	396	180	108		108b	108		72	
California	108	108	378	144	162	900		108	54		180d		54	
Chicago	60	180		420	400	1,060	180	108	120			120		
Cincinnati		66			66	132	66	66	72	36	66		66	
Columbia				72		72						72		
Denver	36	108		36	144	324	108	108			108			
Florida		108			108	216	108	108			108		72	
Georgia		108			108	216		216			108		108	Economics
Georgia Tech		108			108	216					108		108	
Illinois	54	90		36	162	342	216	90		54	90		54	
Indiana		108		126	72	306	108	180	108		108	108		
Iowa		108		162	216	486		108			108			
Kansas	90	54		198	90	432	108	54		90	54		90	
Kentucky		108		180	288	576	180	54			54		108	
Marquette		108		54	108	270	108	108			108		108	
Minnesota	180	60	36	144	432	852	108	60	72	180	60	72		
Missouri	72	90		180	108	450	180	90		72	90			
Nebraska		108		90	180	378	72	144			108		36a	Economics
New York	60	72	72	72	144	360	144	180	54	60	72		72	Economics
N. Carolina		120		60	60	300	60	162	54		120			
N. Dakota		54		108	54	378		90			108		60	Economic theory
Northwestern		90	162	108	108	306		120			144		108	
Ohio		120		108	120	348		90			120			
Oklahoma	108	90	108	162	90	450		108		108	90		90	Economics
Oregon		108		144		360	90	108			108			
Pennsylvania	108	90	72	144	144	576		24		108	90	24a		Economics
Pittsburgh		108	108	108	90	288	90	108			108			
S. California		108	36	54	216	324	108	108			108		90	
S. Methodist		108			108	396	90	108			108		108c	
Syracuse	54	54	144	36	162	540	108	108			108			Economics
Texas	54	108	108	108		180		108			108			
Tulane	72	108				432	162	108		54	108			
Virginia		108			108	444		108			108		108	
U. of Washington		120	84	216		108	120	108	60		120	60		Economics and labor
Washington U.		108		240		162		108			108			Economics
Wash. and Lee		108		54	108	324	108	108	18		108	18	108	
Wisconsin		144		90	90			144			144		108	
Total	1,272	3,762	1,344	3,726	4,372	14,476	2,910	3,438	720	978	3,762	474	1,854	

a. Alternate electives.
b. Listed in catalogues under marketing. Listed under Economics because contents agree with other courses in descriptive economics.
c. Economic History only in part.
d. Part of this course is descriptive. Many economic problems are included.

ness. No other pedagogic problem was alluded to more frequently in the course of the visits to the member schools made in connection with this study.

1. At what place in the curricula of the schools is the student introduced to the field of economics? The answer to this question depends on the interpretation one gives to the term economics. If it be taken to mean the elementary course in the principles of economics, then the usual place of first contact with the student is the sophomore year. Only eight schools place this course in the freshman year—Chicago, Cincinnati (first commerce year), Georgia Tech, New York, Pennsylvania, Syracuse, Tulane, and the University of Washington. Moreover, several of the schools which attempt to teach this course in the freshman year place considerable emphasis upon the problem aspect. There seems to be a considerable body of opinion that the principles of economics cannot be taught to advantage to first year college students.

If, on the other hand, the term economics is used to include the various descriptive and historical courses of a general economic nature, then the place of contact with the student is for the most part in the freshman year. Only eight of the 38 undergraduate schools fail to include some courses of a general economic nature in the freshman year. These schools are Alabama, California, Georgia, Indiana, Missouri, North Dakota, Texas, and Virginia. In two additional schools—Northwestern and Oregon—such courses in the freshman year are not absolutely required.

The customary manner and place of introduction of the student to economics, then, is apparent. In the freshman year are scheduled the descriptive or historical or background courses, and in the sophomore year are placed in most cases the courses which deal with principles and theory.

2. What is the nature of the courses in the general field of economics which precede the study of principles and theory? Three types of courses should be mentioned here. While these courses are not always given by the department of economics, they contain material directly pertinent by way of background to the study of economic principles.

a. To begin, there are those elementary economic courses which are primarily descriptive by nature. Boston's course on "The Principles of Business" has been alluded to. Denver's elementary course describes "the major phases of business activities: intended as a background for the study of economic principles." Iowa, Kansas, Nebraska, North Carolina, Pittsburgh, and Tulane each give courses to freshmen which are largely surveys of the present economic order or system.

Special mention might be made of a course given five hours a week throughout the year to pre-business freshmen at the University of Minnesota. The first quarter deals with marketing organization; the second, with production; the third, with the financial organization of society. The course is chiefly descriptive, although there is some instruction in fundamental concepts. Its purpose is to give to freshmen a sort of orientation to the business world as a foundation for subsequent study.

Of interest in this connection, too, is a course on "Modern Industry," required of all freshmen enrolled in the college of commerce at the University of Illinois. The following statement concerning the course and its purpose has been furnished by Prof. M. H. Hunter, who is in charge of the course:

> The discussions are built around the material contained in the book, "Modern Industry," written by Bogart and Landon. I may say that instead of two lectures we have presented motion picture reels, one illustrative of the steel industry and one of the coal industry. In addition to this, we have required at least one piece of independent investigation of some industry, usually one in the home community of the student.
>
> I would say the primary purpose of this course is one of orientation and preparation for a study of principles of economics. . . . . I have felt from my experience in teaching principles, that the biggest handicap of the student is that he has never experienced any economic environment. The occasional student who may have worked in some capacity either as truck gardener, clerk in a store, or somewhere else, has always seemed to have a much better advantage in grasping the principles since he has had some background upon which to build. It seems to me that if we can somehow give the freshmen some contacts with the economic environment which surrounds them and yet which, because he has been pushed so rapidly through his preliminary education that he has had no chance to experience, we will have done him a great service in preparing him for his future studies in economics. Such is the ideal which I have in mind but just how it can best be accomplished I am not certain.

b. A second type of background course in economics is to be found in those of an historical nature. Usually these courses are known as economic history, dealing either with economic evolution in general, or with the economic development of some specific region such as England, Western Europe, or the United States. Such courses are frequently, but not always, given in the department of economics. Economic history will be given fuller consideration elsewhere.

c. A number of the schools now offer general "gateway" or orientation courses to freshmen, and some of these courses contain a good deal of descriptive material of an economic nature. Obvious instances are Columbia's course on "Contemporary Civilization in the West," Ohio State's "Introduction to Social Science," Oregon's "Background of Social Science," and Washington University's "American Political and Economic Institutions." Teachers of economics have cooperated in the development of these courses. The subject of orientation courses is discussed more fully elsewhere.

It should be added here that the courses in commercial geography and resources also serve in a measure as a foundation for, or preface to, the study of economic principles. This field also is discussed elswhere.

Taking the undergraduate schools of the American Association as a whole, the prevailing arrangement concerning the introduction of the student to the study of economics is as follows: The freshman year is devoted to the development of a foundation or background of concrete and factual material. The means commonly utilized to achieve this end include courses describing the economic order, structure, or institutions; courses in economic history; and courses of the gate-way or orientation type, with economic material constituting a substantial part of the courses. The sophomore course in the theory or principles of economics is then built upon this factual foundation.

To attempt to teach principles of economics before the student is given such a concrete factual foundation is, in the opinion of many students, like putting the cart before the horse. It involves an attempt "to build up a body of sweeping abstractions in the minds of students, interesting enough as reflecting a stage in the development of economic thought, but vitally related neither to current economic or business life nor to the needs of students who have still to acquire those facts and experiences which must form the raw material of effective generalization."[2]

Recently, the introductory descriptive courses in economics being offered to business students show signs of the ferment of change. In the past, and still in large measure, such descriptive courses seem to have been very broad and general, with little pointing toward modern business, and designed for miscellaneous classes of commerce, arts, social science majors, and home economics students. There now seems to be crystallizing the idea that such courses should be pointed more toward business, that they should give the student a picture of the changing structure of modern business and of the practices which have been so greatly emphasized in recent years. Teachers of economics seem to be handicapped because these obvious needs of beginning students in business schools in present day America do not seem to fit into the mold of the traditional economics courses. On the other hand, it appears that some considerable new wine is being served through the medium of old bottles.

Advanced Courses in Economics

All of the undergraduate member schools require all of their students to take at least one elementary course in economics, such course or courses being taken in the freshman or sophomore years. In view of these facts, it seems particularly pertinent to ask to what extent further or advanced courses in general economics play a rôle in the curricula of the business schools.

One index of this rôle is the extent to which such advanced courses are announced in the offerings of the schools. The total offerings in economics in undergraduate credit hours, by main divisions of material, are as follows:

Economic description	1,272
Elementary principles of economics	3,762
Economic problems	1,344
Advanced theory and history of economic thought	3,726
Economic history	4,372

From these figures it appears that more credit hours are offered

---

[2] McCrea, Roswell C., "The Place of Economics in the Curriculum of a School of Business", *Journal of Political Economy*, Volume XXXIV, No. 2, April, 1926, p. 219.

in advanced courses dealing with problems than with introductory descriptive courses, and almost as many credit hours in advanced theory and history of economic thought as in courses dealing with elementary principles.

A second measure of the rôle of advanced courses in economics is the extent to which such courses are found among upper class requirements. Here the list is a rather restricted one. Chicago requires business economics of all upper classmen, a course which "presupposes familiarity with the policies and operations of business units, an acquaintance with the main features of our economic order," and which "involves both the generalizations of orthodox theory and some of the more recent contributions, especially those of a quantitative character."

Columbia requires business economics of all seniors. This course is largely a synthetic course, binding together the fragments of the economic training of the students, and emphasizing the importance of the social viewpoint.

Minnesota requires advanced general economics of all seniors. This course is "a study of some of the more important theoretical problems of economics; competitive and monopoly prices; equilibrium prices and costs; theories of valuation of producers' goods; capital earnings and interest rates; profits."

Nebraska includes among the alternate requirements for all seniors a course in advanced economics, being a "review of economic theory together with a history of economic thought, ancient, medieval, and modern; recent economic theories in relation to industrial conditions."

The University of Washington requires a five hour, one quarter course on advanced economics of all seniors. This course is "a study of economic thought centering about the neo-classical theories of value and distribution and the validity of this thought under present conditions."

Widely elected, but not required, is a course given to seniors in the Wharton School of the University of Pennsylvania. Its title is "The Theory of Business," and it "views the business process as a whole," emphasizing "the significance of theory in the various applied fields which the students have surveyed in other courses."

It would seem that some discussion of economic theory has its place at the end of the business curriculum, even as it has now at the beginning. Concerning its nature, place, and the factor determining the value of such a course, Professor McCrea has well written: "Conceived as a mass of descriptive data in slightly sublimated form, it may have little result, either positive or negative, other than waste of time. Conceived in analytical and philosophical spirit, and given at the end of the general course of study, a course of business economics may well serve to integrate and focus what has been learned in earlier years. But the value of analytical and philosophical courses is peculiarly dependent upon the capacity of the instructor who gives them. They may make for clarity or for confusion. They have a place in a well-rounded plan of business education, but that place is a subordniate one. The essential thing is that every business course shall have its analytical and philosophical phases, and that these shall be permeated with economic influence."[3]

Departments of Economics and Schools of Business—The Problem of Their Administrative Relationship

Should the department of economics be in the school of commerce or in the college of liberal arts? There is keen and general interest in this question. What are the facts? What are the possible relationships? What is the prevailing arrangement? Here again, one finds all sorts of situations from the school where little if any differentiation of groups exists to those where their development and administrative relationship is a matter of engrossing preoccupation.

Four kinds of relationship exist. First, economics may be a department in the school of business; second, it may be in the college of liberal arts; third, the school of business may be a sort of secondary organization comprehended by the department of economics; and fourth, the two may overlap or be interrelated in an inexplicable, illogical, indefinite, but apparently workable arrangement. The first two are the more prevalent, the location of the department of economics in the school of business being the more customary of the two.

This problem has been discussed at length with many persons in the course of the survey. There seems to be a general agree-

[3] McCrea, R. C., Ibid., p. 220.

ment that under ordinary circumstances the arrangement of an economics department outside of the school of business is not satisfactory. The phrase "under ordinary circumstances" is emphasized, because to place the department of economics in the college of liberal arts with the dean of the business school as its head is an unusual, even if satisfactory, arrangement.

Deans of schools of business rather generally express dissatisfaction with any organization which leaves economics out of the school of business. Economics has formed so fundamental and so extensive a part of the training of commerce students in the past, and has been so intimately connected with subsequent courses that the conduct of this work beyond the jurisdiction of the school of business hardly seems wise. One finds institutions where more than three-fourths of the students in the courses in economics are commerce students, yet these courses are planned and controlled outside of the administration of the college of commerce, and without complete recognition of its needs. Such procedure is indefensible from the standpoint of sound educational policy. In view of the relative importance of economics in the existing educational programs of colleges of liberal arts, and in colleges of commerce, the weight of these considerations seem to be in favor of the latter. So far as this investigation has revealed, the location of the department of economics in the school of business seems to be the more satisfactory arrangement—on the basis of educational considerations.

Another problem of relationship has to do with the line of demarcation between those courses offered in the department of economics and those offered in the other departments in the school of business. A survey of the situation reveals that institutional considerations and practical expediency have led to various and diverse arrangements. No educational principle of division has been accepted generally nor honored except in the breach. The nearest approach to a principle has been to assign to the department of economics those courses which emphasize broad public and social policies, and to the commerce departments those in which the approach is primarily from the acquisitive or private standpoint.[4]

---

[4] Heilman, Ralph E., "The Relation Between Departments of Economics and Collegiate Schools of Business." *The American Economic Review,* Supplement, Vol. XVIII, No. 1, March, 1928, p. 73, f. The same distinc-

While this seems at first glance an obvious and logical line of cleavage, certain questions do persist. Is it meant to imply that good business is bad economics? Is a sound acquisitive policy necessarily unsocial? San public policy which is unbusinesslike succeed? Do the meek never inherit the earth? May it not be that sound social wisdom is also good business? Furthermore, is the school of business merely to turn out technicians? Is the facility to get an immediate job the primary purpose of a professional school? Is it not the earmark of the older professional schools, and the lesson of their experience, that the broader implications of the tasks trained for be considered? Even the law schools are beginning to translate law into terms of society, out of which it originally developed. Also, is it the purpose of science to understand or to pass judgment? Is it not true that an understanding of business in its private aspects and in its social aspects are but two aspects of the same scientific task?

The last question suggests what seems to be the one element of certainty in the situation, and that is that the future of economics and the business school do not lie apart, nor consist in the making of distinctions. Uncomfortable as economists and teachers of business subjects may make each other for the next several decades, such discomfort is the price of the development of both. "Both business and economics need to be saved from themselves," McCrae has pointed out.

> Without the presence of economics in some vital form, the work of a school of business is likely to degenerate into detail description of business organization and procedure, with no organizing principle other than the possible one of search for effective competitive devices, and with no clear vision of the social goal of business activity. And economics, divorced from business, is too likely to spend itself either in closet philosophizing by traditional modes, altogether too little affected with a present interest, or in fortifying predilections regarding public policy with broadly garnered data too remote from the intimate, work-a-day world of fresh experience to yield more than a crop of articles, books, and book reviews. If schools of business realize their opportunities, the economic theory of the future will grow out of their researches and will be formulated by their teachers. The joining of socially

---

tion is also implicit in McCrea, R. C., "The Place of Economics in the Curriculum of A School of Business," op. cit.

motivated thinking with a knowledge of concrete, shifting reality, such as can be effected in a school of business, may well escape the puttering of the strict vocationalist on the one hand, and the futility of the closet philosopher on the other. The foundations of wise business policy can be laid in this as in no other way.[5]

The Teaching of Economic History

The curricula of the collegiate schools of business show a general recognition of the importance of an historical approach to the study of economic phenomena. Formal evidence of this fact is to be found in the courses in economic and industrial history. It is evident, of course, that the historical approach is not confined to separate courses in economic history. Nevertheless, the facts concerning such courses and their place in the curricula are the best available objective measure of the emphasis upon such an approach.

1. To what extent is economic history required in collegiate schools of business? Half of the 38 undergraduate schools make a course in economic history an absolute requirement for all students, (Alabama, Boston, California, Cincinnati, Denver, Florida, Georgia, Georgia Tech, Illinois, Indiana, Kansas, Kentucky, Marquette, North Carolina, New York, Oklahoma, Southern California, Virginia, and Washington and Lee.) To this number should be added Pennsylvania and the University of Washington, which require work in history from all students, and with some emphasis in these requirements on economic aspects. Furthermore, orientation courses at Columbia and Washington universities, required of all students, have a relatively large economic-historical content. It should also be noted that the descriptive introductory course at Iowa has a substantial economic history content. In short, a total of twenty-four of the undergraduate schools require courses wholly or in substantial part of this nature. In addition, several other schools strongly urge its election.

2. At what place in the curricula are courses in economic history scheduled? In most cases such courses are required in the freshman year, apparently to serve the purpose of a back-

---

[5] McCrea, Ibid., p. 222.

ground course for the subsequent study of the principles of economics. At fourteen schools where economic history is required or strongly advised, it is scheduled for the freshman year (Boston, Denver, Florida, Georgia Tech, Illinois, Iowa, Kansas, Kentucky, Marquette, New York (usually), Northwestern, Oklahoma, Southern California, and Washington and Lee.) The two orientation courses important in this connection are also scheduled for the first year. Seven schools place it in the sophomore year. (Alabama, Georgia, Indiana, Minnesota, Nebraska, North Carolina, and the University of Washington). At only five schools where economic history is required or widely taken is it placed among the upper class subjects (California, Cincinnati, North Dakota, Pennsylvania, and Virginia).

3. What is the nature of these courses in economic history? Four varieties of courses are found: (a) those dealing with the economic history of the United States; (b) those including the United States and part of Europe, chiefly England; (c) those attempting a general survey of our economic evolution; and (d) those dealing only with the economic history of Europe. Of these the first two are by far the most frequent, indicating an overwhelming emphasis upon the economic and industrial development of the United States.

4. Are courses in economic history given customarily by the department of history or by the department of economics? This question has agitated internal administrative circles from time to time. So far as the facts go, the customary arrangement is for such courses to be given by the department of economics. This seems to be necessary for the proper integration of such work. It is much more vital, from a pedagogic point of view, that courses in economic history be integrated into the work of the economics department than into the academic program of the historians. Only nine schools offer these courses through the medium of the history department (Alabama, Cincinnati, Georgia, Georgia Tech, Minnesota, Missouri, Pennsylvania, University of Washington, and Washington and Lee).

Economic history, as a factor in the curricula of the business schools, consists chiefly of one course, dealing wholly or largely with the economic and industrial development of the United States, offered ordinarily in the freshman year, and having as a purpose the laying of a foundation for subject courses in economics as well as in other business subjects.

Of the value of the historical approach, there can be no argument. Concerning its particular place, its utilization in the curricula, and its specific relation to other materials, one question might be raised. Is it pedagogically sound to rely as largely as is done in certain schools upon a course in economic history to give the student a background of economic data? Is not the plan of a survey of the contemporary scene, followed by a tracing out of its historic roots, a better motivated teaching arrangement? There is some evidence of a trend in this direction. This may involve the merging of the present elementary descriptive courses with the historical ones into one broad introductory course, ostensibly designed for the freshman year.

THE TEACHING OF ENGLISH

The importance in our educational system of a thorough training in the use of the English language, and of an intelligent appreciation of English literature, have long been recognized. More recently, much emphasis has been placed upon their commercial value. As the medium of business activities, training in the use, written and oral, of the English language must be recognized as a fundamental in business training. Business leaders, employers of graduates of commercial schools of every grade, the graduates themselves, all agree in placing very great value in a direct way in the business world upon the ability to express oneself, both on the written page and in direct relationships.

It becomes pertinent, then, to inquire as to the manner in which collegiate schools of business recognize the importance of such training. To what extent is work in English required in business curricula? Where, in the make-up of the curriculum, is it required? How much is required? What is the nature of the work offered? To what extent have teachers of English adapted their offerings to the special needs of commerce students? These questions will now be considered.

1. To what extent has English been required in the curricula of business school graduates? It is necessary to put the question in this manner since English is so largely a lower class study and some of the business schools comprehend but the upper two years.

The four year curriculum is made the basis of study, regardless of whether all four years have been spent within the administrative control of the school or not.

Considering the curricula of the 38 undergraduate schools, it is found that English is either required or largely elected by the students in all of these schools. At Oregon, for example, where the freshman has his choice of certain designated survey courses, English is selected by three-fourths of the business school freshmen.

The students at most schools are required to take at least two years of work in English. At California, Chicago, Georgia, Indiana, and New York, there is a minimum requirement of one year. On the other hand, business students at North Carolina, North Dakota, Texas, and Wisconsin find English required during three years of their curricula, while Boston and Cincinnati require four and five years each, respectively. At all other schools the required spread covers two years.

2. What is the nature of the courses usually taken by business students? While the titles of the courses in English show some diversity, an examination of their content indicates a decided convergence upon a limited number of offerings.

a. All of the undergraduate schools emphasize a course in English composition. This is usually scheduled in the freshman year and constitutes the freshman requirement, wholly or in part. Instruction consists in drill in writing, in some institutions with reference to business subjects, in others without it.

b. The survey of literature type of course is also very common in the lower class curricula, for commerce students as well as for students in other fields. Since the amount of time that can be devoted to the study of literature by commerce students is somewhat limited, a broad survey type of course for such students seems logical and is frequently included. Such courses have taken several different forms. The most frequently found form surveys the field of English literature, somewhat fewer deal with American literature, and several deal in general with "types of literature."

c. "Argumentation," "speech," and "public speaking" are terms used to indicate another kind of course frequently found. These courses aim to train in the effective utilization of spoken words. At nine schools, such courses are required in the training of commerce graduates and a number of additional schools are now considering such a step. The importance of training of this kind is being emphasized increasingly in higher business education circles.

d. Courses in business or commercial correspondence represent a specific development in the field of English in the business schools. More than half (23) of the undergraduate schools require such a course, usually but not necessarily in the upper years.

e. Perhaps one more type of English course found in collegiate curricula for business ought to be mentioned. This is the course on "report writing." It represents another attempt to give specific training in a task constantly required in business, namely, the organization and presentation of business reports. Four schools require such courses of all commerce students, and others include them in the offerings open for election.

3. Who controls the courses in English offered to commerce students? The administrative control of courses in a field which plays so important a rôle in the education of commerce students is an important problem. Two aspects of that problem are outstanding and will be considered here.

Should the college of commerce have its own English department? This question is less pressing in the two year colleges. It is rather in the four year schools, and particularly in the case of certain relationships with the college of liberal arts, that the problem seems more imminent. A survey of the facts shows that a minority of schools have this arrangement, but that such as do are very much pleased with the results. This arrangement obtains, for example, at Boston, Denver, New York, Tulane, and several others.

The purpose of such control of courses is primarily that of securing English courses which are adapted more fully for the purpose of commerce students. This is the second problem involved. Should such adapted courses as "commercial correspondence," "report writing" and the like be included in the offerings to students in the business schools? Two-thirds of the undergraduate schools think so, judging by the inclusion of these courses in their curricula, and most of the others think so, judging by the professions of their leaders. But such adaptation of work is not always easy to obtain. Professors of English, often not friendly to the atmosphere of business and knowing little of particular business English needs, rationalize both deficiencies by insisting that such courses are neither necessary nor English.

The situation which actually exists is something like this : where English departments cooperate and consent to the selection or designation of some member of their staff to develop courses adapted to business needs, such an arrangement obtains; on the other hand, where English departments have shown no interest in such courses, the adapted courses are given by the school of business, sometimes openly and by mutual consent of all concerned, and sometimes surreptitiously by offering such courses under somewhat flexible titles.

FOREIGN LANGUAGES

Foreign languages are the prohibition problem of college administration. Certainly they are the source of much acrimonious debate, and hectic maneuvering by academic politicians to avoid or compromise the issue.

The arguments concerning the value of foreign languages in the educational process are a delight in wishful dialectic. Originally, foreign languages were studied in order to be mastered. They were the vehicles to the treasure store of knowledge. With the decline of their need for such purposes, scholars contrived a new argument: that their study was indispensable as a mental discipline. This argument sounded impressive and perhaps plausible until the 19th century brought with it the development of obviously and directly useful studies of equal, if not superior, disciplinary value. Whereupon the ingenious versatility of the linguists discovered a new virtue in their academic stores: that elegance and facility in the native tongue was gained by the mastery of a foreign tongue.

The present study is concerned with one aspect of this issue: the teaching of foreign languages in the curricula of commerce students. What rôle do they play in these curricula? What is the reason for their inclusion? What seems to be their future in higher education for business? Each of the questions will be discussed in the light of the data gathered in the course of the present investigation.

The Rôle of Foreign Languages in the Business Curricula

There is a considerable variety of arrangement concerning the teaching of foreign languages to commerce students. Nor have these arrangements always been made by, or with the consent of, the schools of business. In certain cases, the teaching of foreign languages is a matter of university regulation, regardless of the program of any particular school.

First, there are the schools which make no mention or requirement of foreign languages. Students may be given the opportunity to go on with their work in language if they so desire, but such courses are not considered as an element in the plan of instruction of the students in the school of business. Such cases include Cincinnati, Denver, North Dakota, Minnesota, Nebraska, Pittsburgh, Southern Methodist, and Texas. In the case of North Dakota, the curriculum in foreign trade and consular service includes language.

In the second class are those schools in which foreign languages are not generally required, but are included among the electives, with perhaps some recommendation of selection. Illustration of such schools are Illinois, Kansas, Marquette, Oregon, Washington University, and the University of Washington. In certain cases, there is little difference between this type of arrangement and the one preceding, except such significance as may be attached to enumeration among certain possible choice of electives. An exception to be noted at several of the above institutions is the requirement or strong recommendation of language in a particular field of specialization such as foreign trade.

The third type of arrangement is where foreign language is not required if the student has presented a designated amount of language credit in his entrance credentials. Chicago, for example, requires "a total of (high school plus college) credits" of four majors in language other than English. Iowa waives its language requirement if a student presents four units in one foreign language, or two units in each of two foreign languages. Kentucky requires one year of foreign language of any student who has not had at least two years of foreign language before entering college. At Ohio State, "students who have had three years of foreign language in the high school are not required to take a foreign language . . . . except in the case of those specializing in foreign commerce." The catalogue of the College of Commerce and Business Administration at the University of Southern California states that "it is presumed that entering students have successfully completed two units of a foreign language. In case they have not completed two units in high school, they will be required to complete ten semester units of a foreign language in their freshman year." At these schools, the election of foreign language may be urged, even when the minimum requirement has been met.

The next group of institutions are those which have a definite minimum of a year's work in foreign language after entering college. This includes Georgia Tech, Indiana, Missouri, Northwestern, and Pennsylvania. Probably the University of California should be added to this group because of the stipulation which reads: "Students must pass an examination designed to test their ability to read one of the following languages . . . . unless they have completed one year of collegiate instruction in French or German with a minimum grade of C, or unless excused by vote of executive committee of the College of Commerce."

The final type of arrangement is where two years of foreign language is required. These two years usually are the freshman and sophomore, although in two cases the sophomore and junior years are utilized. Among the institutions where this requirement still holds are Alabama, Boston, Columbia, Florida, Georgia, North Carolina, Tulane, Virginia, Washington and Lee, and Wisconsin.

In most institutions where there are language requirements, modern languages are implied. French, German, and Spanish are designated most frequently. Such institutions as Chicago, Georgia, Iowa, Ohio State, Southern California and others include a wider range of languages. Tulane limits her language requirement to commercial Spanish.

Reasons for Foreign Languages in the Business Curricula

John Locke, in 1692, railed against wasting time and money in teaching Latin to a pupil intended for a trade: "Wherein he, having no use of Latin, fails not to forget that little which he brought from school, and which 'tis ten to one he abhors for the ill usage it procures him."[6]

---

[6] Quoted by Brigance, William Norwood, "The Foreign Language Grindstone," *The American Mercury*, Vol. XIX, No. 76, April, 1930, p. 438.

More than two centuries later, in constructing college curricula to educate American youth for business life, foreign languages are included to a considerable extent as a requirement, whereas whole fields of business activities have but achieved the status of "included among the electives." Why has this been done? The question is particularly important in view of the substantial protest against, and dissatisfaction with, the presence of foreign language requirements in the older academic curricula.

Except in those schools where the issue has been settled negatively, no discussion of college of commerce curricula proceeds far without reference to the foreign language issue. This problem has been talked over widely, during the course of this study, with faculty members of business schools. These opinions, carefully recorded and now tabulated, show the operation of four rather well defined factors in the situation. These will be discussed briefly.

1. Foreign languages are included in the curricula pursued by commerce and pre-commerce students at certain institutions because they are a part of the general undergraduate requirements. Where such blanket provisions exist, their inclusion in the commerce and pre-commerce curricula may represent nothing more than an adjustment to a general requirement. Such university requirements may go back in turn to the attitude of a state board of regents, or to other factors of outside pressure or influence.

2. There are two or three cases where the inclusion of foreign languages in commerce and pre-commerce offerings is attributed quite frankly, and apparently almost wholly, to tradition. Foreign languages represent a sort of traditional hangover, to which one remains faithful, albeit with a smile on the face and a tongue in the cheek. It is safe, at places, to let sleeping dogs lie.

3. One finds four or five schools where, apparently, the inclusion of foreign language in a business curriculum is believed to be of value. The reasons given differ somewhat from school to school. Here there is insistence that the mastery of foreign languages facilitates usage of one's own, there is the belief that they serve to open to the student the outside world. One dean speaks of their necessity for purposes of foreign trade, another includes them to the end that the students may become genuinely "international-minded." Where the right hand points out their

very great cultural value, the left is used to operate a foreign language sieve to weed out the weak students. It may be significant to add that various college of commerce administrators of the present generation are products of the classical curricula of yesterday's liberal arts college.

4. In by far the larger number of schools of business where the foreign language requirement is retained it is an arrangement frankly representing a compromise with or a concession to the liberal arts college. Foreign languages have constituted so large and fundamental a part of the arts college curriculum, and for so long a period of time, that denials of its importance in any scheme of higher education resembles in a peculiar sense the laying of sacrilegious hands upon the arc of the academic covenant. There seems to be this great fear among the cultured devotees of the classical tradition lest students receive the opportunity of obtaining approved education without contact with this dread juggernaut of the schools.

Schools of business have had to make their way. During the period of their struggling infancy, they have had to make compromises. Thus it happens that the foreign language requirement in commerce and pre-commerce curricula is there almost wholly as a price of academic peace, and not as the result of any generally recognized value in business education.

The Future of Foreign Languages in the Business Curricula

Of the changes in curricula contemplated by the schools of business included in this study, few were mentioned more frequently than the removal of the foreign language requirement. While some of these expressions of prospective change may be but the embodiments of a wish, there is reason to think that a number of schools will make such changes in the not altogether remote future. Colleges of commerce are maturing and acquiring a status as a result of which their curricula may embody increasingly the judgment of their leaders as to what their particular students need.

There is also to be found in certain quarters the not unbusinesslike demand that if foreign languages be included in the commerce curricula, they be taught in a manner and to an extent that they may be a readily usable tool by the student. Several rather positive expressions were encountered during the progress of this study to the effect that a more favorable attitude toward foreign languages would be taken provided schools could so function in this respect as to give students a reading and speaking knowledge of a particular language.

It might be added that this revolt of the college of commerce against foreign languages comes at a time when psychologists and educators, approaching the problem with the inductive methods of science, are assaulting freshly and vigorously the legitimacy of the historic defenses of their importance in the whole scheme of education. This larger subject, while pertinent to this discussion, lies somewhat outside of the immediate province of this report. The reader is referred to Michael Best's *Bilingualism,* Charles Judd and Guy Buswell's report on *Silent Reading, A Study of the Various Types,* or E. L. Thorndike's *The Mental Discipline in High School Studies.*

GEOGRAPHY

The study of geography may be approached from several different angles, with a corresponding difference in the selection and emphasis of material content. These emphases include the economic, the physical, the ecological, the commercial, and the geological. The particular emphasis at any one institution seems to be influenced profoundly by its academic connection or setting, and to be somewhat less a matter of its adaptation to a particular purpose.

Of importance in this connection are the data concerning its rôle in college of commerce curricula. To what extent is geography included in these curricula? Where is geography placed in the sequence of studies? What is its relation to the introductory course in economics? By whom is the work in geography customarily given? Answers to these questions, based on the undergraduate schools of the American Association, will be presented at this point.

1. To what extent is geography included in the curricula of the business schools?

a. At 18 of the 38 schools, geography is required of all commerce or pre-commerce students—Alabama, California, Chicago, Cincinnati, Columbia, Florida, Georgia, Marquette, Missouri, North Carolina, North Dakota, Ohio, Pennsylvania, Southern

California, Syracuse, Virginia, University of Washington, and Wisconsin. In addition, geography is required at certain other schools, in specialized curricula such as in foreign trade or commercial education.

b. At nine schools, geography is named or urged as an elective —Iowa, Kansas, Kentucky, Minnesota, Nebraska, New York, Oregon, Southern Methodist, and Washington University.

In the case of the other schools not included above, geography does not seem to be considered, as such, in the work of the school. Departments of geography may exist within the university, and courses within the business schools may include a partial discussion of economic resources, but there is no inclusion of courses in geography in the curricula of the business school or in the course offerings to which they refer.

2. Where is geography scheduled in the curricula? Geography has been considered by the business schools, with but one exception, as a lower class study, at least so far as any general utilization is concerned. Eleven of the 18 schools making geography a general requirement place it in the freshman year, six in the sophomore year, and one in the upper classes.

Consideration of the nature of such courses in the business schools and of their purpose point toward their location in the freshman year. Certainly there seems to be no justification for their postponement to the junior or senior year, except in the case of advanced courses included in specialized curricula. General courses in geography are included in business school curricula to serve as a background or foundation for courses in general economics as well as for the business courses. To serve such a purpose, they need to come early in the commerce set-up, preferably during the freshman year.

3. By whom is the work in geography given? At those institutions where courses which may be labelled geography are utilized in the commerce curricula, a variety of academic arrangements involving these courses seem to exist.

To begin with, there are those cases where separate departments of geography exist. Such departments generally are located in the college of liberal arts. This is the arrangement in 12 cases, where the courses in geography are utilized in the commerce curricula.

A second type of administrative arrangement is where geography is combined with geology. Courses in geography may either be given by the geology department, or geology and geography may be combined in a department in which both developments are definitely recognized. This type of arrangement is found in seven cases.

Courses dealing with the commercial and economics aspects of geography are given at seven of the member schools as a part of the offerings in economics or business administration and at another seven schools, the work in geography is connected administratively with courses in trade or industry. In both of these types of arrangement, geography courses are a part of the work of the business school.

Geography, like the other non-business subjects discussed, plays its chief rôle in business education as a lower class foundation course. Although considered essential in this connection by a substantial proportion of the business schools, the subject has usually found its place in the university organization outside of these schools. As a separate department in the college of liberal arts or as a part of a department of geology, there does not seem to be always an abiding interest in the needs of commerce students. Confronted with this fact, and yet impressed with its importance in business education, schools of commerce have met the situation by developing their own courses in geography. At one or two schools, still other situations obtained.

On the whole, then, the problem of geography, as far as the business school is concerned, is one of the adaptation and of coordination: adapatation of the content of geography courses to the needs of commerce or pre-commerce students and coordination of such content with other courses designed for descriptive, background purposes.

MATHEMATICS

Training in the measuring function has been recognized as a basic element in most programs of education. In the development of curricula for commerce students, it was natural to turn for help to departments of mathematics in the liberal arts colleges. The extent to which mathematics has been incorporated in commerce and pre-commerce curricula, the nature of its development, the sequence of such courses, and other aspects of its relation to collegiate education for business will be considered here.

Its Rôle in the Curricula of Commerce Students

Twenty-four of the 38 undergraduate schools require mathematics of all commerce or pre-commerce students—Alabama, Boston, California, Chicago, Cincinnati, Denver, Florida, Georgia, Georgia Tech, Indiana, Kentucky, Marquette, North Carolina, North Dakota, Oklahoma, Pittsburgh, Southern California, Southern Methodist, Syracuse, Texas, Tulane, Virginia, Washington and Lee, and Wisconsin.

At seven institutions, mathematics is required in some but not in all of the commerce curricula—Illinois, Kansas, Minnesota, Missouri, New York, Ohio, and the University of Washington.

At Columbia, Nebraska and Northwestern, mathematics has the status of an alternate elective so far as commerce or pre-commerce students are concerned; while in the remaining four cases—Iowa, Oregon, Pennsylvania, and Washington University, it is a possible elective.

Kinds of Courses Offered to Commerce Students

In most cases (31 out of the 38), departments of mathematics have adapted to some extent courses given to commerce and pre-commerce students. Three course titles are found most frequently among these adapted courses: mathematical theory of investment, mathematics of finance, and business mathematics. At 14 institutions courses are offered under the first named title, 11 utilize the second, and eight give courses under the third. In addition, there are courses in commercial algebra and the mathematics of insurance at four schools each, in actuarial methods at two, and in secretarial mathematics at one.

Mathematical theory of investment and mathematics of finance are two terms applied to substantially the same material. This is a fairly standardized course, including the mathematical theory of compound interest, annuities, amortization, perpetuities, evaluation of bonds, sinking funds, depreciation, building and loan associations, probabilities, etc.

Business mathematics, as given by the institutions named, has a fairly definite content. It includes short methods of computation, interest, percentage, profit and loss, partial payments, commission and brokerage, investments, insurance and exchange, graphical representation of business data, logarithms with commercial applications, etc. In one or two cases, the term is used to imply material usually included in the next two named courses.

In addition to these adapted courses, departments of mathematics offer one or more courses dealing with the mathematics of statistics at 15 of the institutions where undergraduate member schools are located. They are Boston, Cincinnati, Florida, Illinois, Indiana, Minnesota, Missouri, Nebraska, Northwestern, Ohio State, Oregon, Syracuse, Texas, University of Washington, and Wisconsin.

The course usually given is most generally referred to as mathematical theory of statistics. Other terms used at times are mathematics of statistics or mathematical statistics or mathematical background of statistics. The customary content of this course includes a consideration of errors and numerical computation, interpolation, averages, applied graphics, the normal curve, binomial series, etc.

Not all of the mathematics courses given to students in our schools of business are adapted courses in finance or statistics, or commercial algebra. Algebra, intermediate and college; trigonometry; and geometry are given frequently even in institutions where departments of mathematics have developed adapted courses. In these cases, a combination of the two is usually offered.

Sequence of the Mathematics Courses

Courses in mathematics given to business students, either when required or elective, are invariably placed in the freshman year. In a few institutions, they may be taken either in the freshman or the sophomore year. This is the case particularly in those institutions where the requirements of the first two years are grouped without being differentiated by years. Cincinnati and the Georgia Institute of Technology extend their mathematics requirements over both the lower years, and several others have alternate requirements in mathematics extending over a similar period.

The typical or most frequently found arrangement is the combination in the freshman year, of algebra during the first term and an adapted course, like the mathematical theory of investment or the mathematics of finance, during the second term. Fifteen institutions make this arrangement: Alabama, Boston, California, Florida, Georgia, Georgia Tech, Indiana, Kansas, Kentucky,

Minnesota, Nebraska, Southern California, Syracuse, Tulane, and Wisconsin. In other cases, the adapted courses are upper class electives or particular group requirements, usually in the junior year.

Departments of Business Mathematics in Business Schools

It has been pointed out that colleges of commerce have turned as a rule to departments of mathematics in liberal arts colleges for the training of their students in mathematics. At a few schools, however, such as Syracuse and Tulane, such work has been developed within and by the school of business. The courses developed in these cases should approximate most completely the possible contributions of mathematics to the education of commerce students.

The courses offered in business mathematics in the college of business administration at Syracuse University will be summarized briefly by the way of example of such development.

1. Secretarial mathematics—some of the elementary applications of mathematics that a secretary may be called upon to make.

2. Algebra—for students presenting only one unit of algebra and one unit of geometry for entrance.

3. Introductory business mathematics—including topics selected from algebra and business arithmetic which are frequently used in business.

4. Mathematics of investment—explaining the methods of computation involved in such topics as interest, annuities, amortization, valuation of bonds, sinking funds, and insurance.

5. Mathematics of statistics—a study of the methods of collecting, classifying, presenting, and interpreting statistics. It includes such topics as tables, graphs, averages, approximation, probability, deviation, and correlation.

6. Actuarial mathematics—the preparation and use of life insurance and annuity tables, together with the mathematics involved.

7. Statistical problems—designed to meet the needs of students who are doing research work, includes a plan for investigation, collection of data, arrangement and correlation, and graphical presentation.

Inductive Determination of Mathematics for Commerce Students

A criticism of mathematics courses offered to commerce students which one frequently encounters is that they have been constructed too much as the result of deductive reasoning and too little as the result of inductive analysis. What has happened quite generally in the development of the business curricula is that the department of mathematics, being asked to give a course to college of commerce students, surveys its offerings and, on the basis of some vague knowledge of business, selects those which it would seem logical for future business men to study. This procedure, when done carefully and honestly, represents the situation at its best.

The other method of approach is through inductive analysis. What mathematical concepts and processes are utilized in the subsequent courses in the business schools, in accounting, in marketing, in finance, in investment banking? Such facts can be gathered and tabulated. What sort of a course emerges as a result? Has this been done? Can an introductory course in mathematics for commerce students be built up in this inductive manner?

At the College of Commerce and Administration at Ohio State University, such an experiment is being made. Representatives from the department of mathematics, various commerce departments, and from the school of education are co-operating in an effort to determine a course in this manner.

NATURAL SCIENCES

The natural sciences constitute another group of studies which the colleges of commerce took over bodily from the liberal arts curriculum, which are emphasized as of fundamental importance in the training of business executives, and which under the particular needs of business students are showing signs of adaptation. The several aspects of the relation between the natural science and collegiate education for business will be discussed briefly in turn.

The Rôle of the Natural Sciences

Reference to the tables showing the freshman and sophomore requirements and that showing the studies in the lower class schedules in the order of numerical importance will show the relatively important position held by the natural sciences.

It will be observed that 26 of the 38 undergraduate schools make natural science a general lower class requirement for all students, nine mention it is an alternate requirement or urge its election, and three mention it as a possible upper class elective.

There are these further facts in this connection: that at 11 institutions, there are, in addition to the minimum requirement of a year's work, additional requirements for the second year or the suggestion of a possible second year. At the other 16 schools where natural science is a general requirement, such requirement is limited to a year's work, with no further emphasis other than the inclusion of the natural sciences among the free electives.

Seldom have these requirements specified which of the natural sciences should be pursued by commerce students. Chemistry, physics, geology, geography (in several cases), biology, and evolution have constituted the range of choice. Inquiry reveals that where complete freedom of choice has prevailed, geology has been taken more frequently than any of the other sciences.

Reasons for the Inclusion of Natural Science

Five reasons are commonly cited for the inclusion of natural science courses in the curricula of commerce and pre-commerce students. The importance attached to each of these varies from one institution to another.

To begin with, there are those cases where natural science is one of the general undergraduate university requirements. In such cases, the school of business has no choice. Second, there are the schools where it has seemed wise to satisfy a substantial element of the liberal arts faculty by including natural science in the commerce or pre-commerce curricula. Third, there is the emphasis upon their selective value in weeding out weak students. A fourth reason places great value upon keen habits of observation and the natural sciences as the proper media to develop such habits. The fifth reason grows out of a widespread conviction that all students in higher institutions of learning, whether in schools of business or not, should be given a fairly thorough training in the scientific method of approach. Many educators seem to believe that such training is synonymous with a laboratory course in the natural science.

In actual practice, the natural science requirement has failed to a considerable extent in accomplishing the last three objectives, which have to do with educational policy. The wide latitude of choice allowed usually in satisfying the requirements has led quite frequently to a hunt on the part of the student for easy credits. One who knows college students at first hand cannot but regard with some suspicion the singular and widespread interest of future business executives in courses in geology at so many institutions, particularly where there is no adaptation of course content to the specific needs of the aforesaid executives-to-be.

Experiments in Adaptation of Science Courses

Dissatisfied with the results of a wide latitude of electives and no adaptation of courses in natural science, yet convinced of the importance of some scientific background for the college of commerce student, several schools have developed science courses of a different kind. These courses, it should be noted, have been developed not by natural science departments, but within the schools of business. Five of the member schools have taken such a step within recent years. They are Boston, Chicago, Marquette, New York, and Pennsylvania. It is a curious fact that at several of these schools, the suggestion for such courses has come from the students themselves.

The offerings of courses by the College of Business Administration at Boston University include two courses of this kind. Elements of Science is a "broad survey of the nature of the sciences and their relation to modern life," Science in Industry is "a survey of the nation's industries with reference to the laws of science that control them. . . . . About 25 specific industries controlled largely by science are considered and each of these industries is chosen as illustrating a particular chemical or physical process."

At Chicago, in addition to the pre-commerce requirements in science, the school of business offers two specially adapted courses: "introduction to the study of technology," and "special studies in technology and production." More extended reference to these courses has been made in another connection.

The College of Business Administration at Marquette offers "industrial chemistry," the purpose of which is "to give the students . . . . some appreciation of the importance of chemistry to modern industry."

New York offers three courses of this general kind to its commerce students. "Outlines of science" is "a general survey of such major sciences as astronomy, anthropology, geology, physics, chemistry, biology, etc., and their relation to one another and to industry." "Physics in industry" deals with the science of physics as applied in modern industry. Topics include color in advertising and sales, office and plant lighting; standard weights and measures, tare and shrinkage; new applications of electricity; photo-electric cells and other devices for automatic control; photography, motion pictures, phonographs, and talking pictures in business." "Chemistry in industry" surveys "the science of chemistry as applied in modern industry. Topics include the chemistry of iron, steel, aluminum, and other metals; fuels, oil, and gasoline; acids and alkalis; fertilizers; drugs; dyes, dyeing, textiles and rayon; fats and soaps, foods, beverages, and canning; paints and varnishes; paper and inks; municipal and governmental chemistry, railway chemistry in general business; chemical accounting, sales and advertising."

The Wharton School of Finance and Commerce of the University of Pennsylvania requires of all freshmen a course which covers the general field of science and the application of the facts of science to economic and social phenomena. More than half of this course, more detailed reference to which is made elsewhere, deals with the natural sciences.

Science and the Business World

Of all the achievements of science, those of a material nature have been the most outstanding and the most emphasized. The exploitation of natural resources by means of scientific knowledge is the most conspicuous feature in the history of civilization during the past two centuries. This exploitation of nature constitutes the basis of modern business.

Not only have the historic foundations of business been scientific, but science is constantly revising business. The Industrial Revolution has proved thus far to be a continuing process, and science has been the chief factor in man's increasing productivity. Furthermore, science is constantly creating new business. Many new industries have been created within recent decades as a result of progress in scientific knowledge and its application to the business world. Research has been called the mother of industry.

Not only do the material achievements of science have far-reaching business consequences, but the application of the scientific method is revolutionizing the conduct of modern business. Purchasing, for example, is ceasing to be done on a hit or miss basis. A single bad purchase may cause the failure of a company, or, at least, a multitude of lesser ills. Buying is more and more done after comprehensive investigation, with complete statistical and technical data and careful interpretation and study over a long period of time.

The study of costs on the basis of standard cost accounting, the development of industrial budgeting, the analytical study of production jobs, the control of production operations through scientific planning, personnel work, vocational guidance, the whole development of industrial management—these and many other features of modern business bespeak the increasing application of scientific method to the daily conduct of business operation.

In summary, it is safe to say that, as a result of the experience of the past hundred years, and of the last fifty years in particular, business has come to see that "science, in its industrial applications, is as intensely practical as a market report or a balance sheet. It represents the accumulated experience and organized knowledge concerning the behavior of things, which thousands of the world's best minds have acquired by the incessant questioning of nature for more than a hundred years. As such, the manufacturer ignores it at his peril."[7]

What has been said about the rôle of science in business is not meant, of course, to imply that business men must attain specialized command or understanding of the various sciences. It would be folly to entertain such a hope, however desirable this might be. But it is equally true that the modern business man who does not realize that science and her facts and ways are of great import to him, who does not realize the possibility or value of research to science, is hopelessly antiquated and seriously handicapped in competition with his fellows.

---

[7] Little, Arthur D., *Annals of the American Academy of Political and Social Science,* May, 1925, p. 9.

It appears that students in collegiate schools of business should receive as part of their equipment thorough training in the method of science, an appreciation of the continuing achievements of science, and an understanding of the utilization of the facts of science in business and in social life.

It must be clear that these ends will not be achieved by enrolling business students in first-year courses in college science which are designed as introductory courses to continued study and specialization. Departments of science have not been interested as a rule in the development of courses to meet the needs of students from the business schools. It is this failure of co-operation which has led schools of business to develop their own courses in science. The future of this development lies in the lap of the gods—and of the science departments.

POLITICAL SCIENCE

Some knowledge and understanding of the structure and functioning of the government under which business is conducted is recognized quite generally as a fundamental element in collegiate education for business. Data on the status of political science in the curricula of the schools of business, on their relative place in the curricula, and on the kinds of courses offered to business students will be presented at this point.

The Rôle of Political Science in Business Curricula

An analysis of the data concerning political science courses in the 38 undergraduate schools shows the following facts.

1. All but three of these schools make some mention of political science in their announcements. The exceptions are Cincinnati, Tulane, and Wisconsin.

2. Twenty-four schools make it a requirement for all or virtually all students—Alabama, California, Columbia, Florida, Georgia, Georgia Tech, Indiana, Kansas, Kentucky, Marquette, Missouri, Nebraska, New York, North Carolina, North Dakota, Northwestern, Oklahoma, Pennsylvania, Pittsburgh, Syracuse, Texas, Virginia, University of Washington, and Washington and Lee.

3. At two institutions, political science material is incorporated

extensively into orientation courses—which are required of, or open to all students—Oregon and Washington University.

4. At six institutions, political science is one of several alternate electives for business students—Chicago, Illinois, Iowa, Minnesota, Ohio, and Southern Methodist.

5. Two schools mention it among the general electives, but with no special emphasis—Boston and Denver.

6. One school—Southern California—mentions it as an upper class requirement in a specialized curriculum.

It is clear, from the foregoing, that some instruction in political science is included quite generally in the curriculum of the business student.

Sequence in the Business Curricula

Considering the 24 schools which generally require political science, its place in the curriculum most frequently is in the sophomore year. Only six schools require it in the freshman year. They are Georgia, Marquette, Nebraska, North Dakota, Oklahoma, and Pennsylvania. At the other schools, the first course in political science is scheduled for the sophomore year. In a few cases, where a second course is required, or the requirement consists of a course of any advanced nature, it is placed in the upper half of the curriculum.

Kinds of Courses Offered to Commerce Students

Three types of courses prevail among the offerings by political science departments to commerce students. The following summary is based upon an analysis of the courses in the 24 schools generally requiring work in political science.

1. Most frequent are those courses, which consist chiefly of descriptive analyses of the American government system. Fifteen of the 24 schools emphasize this type of course for business students. In several, attention is directed chiefly to the national government, but in most cases the effort is made to survey the entire governmental system—national, state, and local.

2. At six of the schools, the required course in political science is comparative in its approach, contrasting our system of government with that of the principal countries of Western Europe. Here

the field covered seems more extensive, and the emphasis apparently is more upon principles.

3. The general political science requirement at five schools includes a course devoted to the relationship between government and business. In addition, there are quite a number of schools where courses on this subject are offered, even if not generally required. Consideration of this aspect of the work of government is given in some of the courses included in the first group. At still other schools, the problem is one that is dealt with at some length in the courses in economics. In other words the relationship between government and business is given a good deal more attention than would appear from a mere statement of the number of schools requiring a particular course by that name.

Other political science courses included in particular business curricula are courses in international law and parliamentary government, frequent in foreign trade curricula; and courses in municipal government, included in trade and civic secretarial and public utility curricula. Courses dealing with the regulation of public utilities have been developed at a few schools by the department of political science.

Departments of political science have not developed as a rule within the administrative organization of the business schools. Only at Boston, Denver, Georgia Tech, Marquette, Missouri, North Dakota, and Pennsylvania are the courses alluded to above given by members of the business faculty. In these cases, this arrangement seems entirely satisfactory to the business schools. Elsewhere, political science is located in the liberal arts college.

Courses in political science constitute, as has been intimated, an integral part of the commerce curricula. They are intended to serve three purposes primarily: first, an understanding of the American system of government under which business is done; second, in certain cases, an understanding of foreign governments under which business may be done; and, third, problems of the interrelationships between business and government.

The two general facts stated in the preceding paragraphs constitute, in combination, the problem concerning political science courses in commercial curricula. Here again, the problem is one of adaptation. Courses describing the American government at work may be taught so that commerce students see the direct relationship of such a course to their chief interest or so that they fail completely to sense the connection. All other factors being equal, this depends upon the extent to which the content selected, the cases cited, the illustrations used, are taken from that vast body of material which touches the business interests of the nation. Professor James T. Young, of the Wharton School of Finance and Commerce of the University of Pennsylvania, has been signally successful in thus adapting a course on the American government to the needs of commerce students. Such adaptation appears to be destructive neither of the political nor scientific aspects of the course.

It is not meant to imply, however, that all of the courses in political science are to be dressed in commerce colors. Departments of political science, like sociology, English, natural science, and the like, are university departments and must always conceive of their functions in broad university terms and must be regarded in this light by administrative heads. The adaptation of courses for commerce students is one of their functions, but it is a very important one, and one that is not everywhere recognized.

The development of political science points ultimately toward the creation of schools of public administration, public service, or citizenship. Such schools have crystallized already at a number of institutions, and are in process of formation at still others. The emergence of schools of business out of departments of economics, of schools of social work out of departments of sociology, and of schools of public administration out of departments of political science, represent substantially the same general process and tendency.

PSYCHOLOGY

There are few business men or psychologists who will deny the importance of applied psychology in the successful conduct of business operations. It is particularly pertinent, then, to inquire to what extent courses in psychology have been incorporated in the curricula of the business schools, to what extent psychologists have adapted courses to meet the special needs of commerce students, and what the nature of such courses is. Certain problems growing out of the relationship of psychology and business education will also be discussed.

The Rôle of Psychology in the Business Schools

At 13 of the 38 undergraduate schools, psychology is a general requirement for virtually all commerce students—Boston, Chicago, Denver, Florida, Indiana, Kansas, Kentucky, Nebraska, New York, North Carolina, Northwestern, Minnesota, and Southern California.

Four additional schools—Alabama, Illinois, Missouri, and Ohio State—require one or more courses in specific curricula, without making the requirement a general one. The specific curricula are commercial teaching, trade and civic secretarial service, marketing, industrial relations, and personnel management.

In nine cases, psychology is an alternate or recommended elective. These schools are Illinois, Iowa, Oklahoma, Oregon, Southern Methodist, Syracuse, Texas, Tulane, and Washington University. Seven schools mention psychology as one of the general electives and at several of these it is elected extensively. These schools are California, Columbia, Georgia Tech, North Dakota, Pennsylvania, University of Washington, and Washington and Lee.

In the case of those schools not mentioned, courses in psychology may be taken by commerce students, but no mention is made of such courses in the announcements of the curricula for business or pre-business students.

Where psychology is required, it is usually scheduled in the sophomore year; where it has the status of an elective, it is usually mentioned in connection with the junior year. Only one school places it in the freshman year.

Extent of Adaptation of Psychology Courses

An examination of the offerings by departments of psychology at the 38 institutions where these undergraduate schools of business are located reveals that thirty of them have adapted one or more courses for commerce students. These schools, together with the number of adapted courses, follows:

Alabama	1	Indiana	4
Boston	10	Iowa	2
California	1	Kansas	2
Chicago	2	Kentucky	3
Columbia	2	Michigan	2
Denver	4	Minnesota	4
Florida	2	Missouri	2
Georgia Tech	1	New York	4

North Carolina	2	Stanford	1
Northwestern	3	Syracuse	4
Ohio State	8	Texas	3
Oregon	1	Tulane	1
Pennsylvania	1	University of Washington	1
Southern California	1	Washington and Lee	1
Southern Methodist	2	Wisconsin	2

From one point of view, such a list indicates a considerable and satisfactory program. When one considers, however, the proportion of undergraduates who are commerce or pre-commerce students, the total number of courses in psychology offered, and the obvious opportunities for the science of psychology which business offers, the development indicated above is somewhat disappointing, if not perplexing. One finds, for example, a department of psychology at an institution considered which offers 26 undergraduate courses, and adapts one for the purposes of the commerce school; another with 24 undergraduate courses adapts one; another with 21, adapts one. Situations similar in kind if not in degree exist at additional institutions.

It is not meant to imply that the responsibility for this rests entirely upon the psychologists. There are those cases where commerce school administrators and faculties are indifferent or skeptical or even antagonistic. In general, however, one cannot escape the conviction that psychologists have been much more prone to grasp the opportunities for their science in, or adapt their courses to the needs of, schools of education and social work than schools of business.

The Nature of the Adapted Courses

1. The most frequently found adapted psychology course has to do with advertising and selling. At fifteen schools, the departments of psychology give courses concerned with these subjects —Boston, Denver, Indiana, Iowa, Kansas, Kentucky, Michigan, New York, North Carolina, Northwestern, Ohio, Minnesota, Southern Methodist, Syracuse, and Texas.

2. Business psychology. This is usually a general psychology course with business illustrations and applications. Thirteen institutions announce such a course—Alabama, Boston, Chicago, Columbia, Denver, Florida, Georgia Tech, Indiana, Michigan, Northwestern, Tulane, Texas, and Washington and Lee.

3. Personnel problems are emphasized by psychology courses

at 11 schools—Columbia, Indiana, Iowa, Kansas, Kentucky, Minnesota, New York, Northwestern, Ohio, Southern Methodist, and Texas.

4. Vocational aspects of psychology are considered in courses of psychology at eight schools—Columbia, Indiana, Kansas, New York, Ohio, Minnesota, Syracuse, and Wisconsin.

5. Employment psychology is dealt with at seven schools—Boston, Columbia, Florida, Missouri, North Carolina, Oregon, and Syracuse.

6. Applied psychology is the name of a course referred to at California, Ohio, Southern California, University of Washington, and Wisconsin—a total of five.

7. Industrial psychology is given at four schools—Pennsylvania, Syracuse, Ohio, and Indiana. This may be the same as the course called business psychology. It is essentially the introductory course in psychology with industrial applications.

Other courses mentioned include the psychology of working conditions, psychology for business executives, psychology of motives, and social psychology.

The Trend of the Development Concerning Psychology

Inquiries conducted in the course of the present study indicate a growing appreciation of the importance of psychology in business education. Business is peculiarly a matter of applied psychology. Particularly is there a reliance upon sound psychological principles where such activities as advertising, personnel work, management, and selling are being developed on a scientific basis.

It appears, however, that persons, engaged in these activities are interested in a psychology somewhat different from that generally taught in university departments of psychology. Their insistence is upon a more practical psychology, functional in its approach, concerned primarily with mind in action, and stripped of academic verbiage and refined abstractions. It is highly significant that a similar demand is coming from various other groups who deal professionally with human problems, such as social workers, physicians, teachers, and the like.

The result of these demands has led to the development of a "new psychology," based on the experience of these various groups in dealing with human problems. Many, perhaps most, of the orthodox academic psychologists, however, have rejected this "new psychology," wholly or in part, which fact, coupled with the insistent demand for it, has created a problem in schools of business, as well as in other professional schools. These schools have been in the position of wanting more psychology in their curricula, but less of the kind that academic psychologists offer. As a consequence, a good deal of psychology has come to be taught in courses otherwise labelled. The situation has been complicated further by the invasion of the field by charlatans who have injured its repute and handicapped its healthy growth, but who, fortunately, have not wholly succeeded in obscuring its inherent values.

Concretely, the problems which schools of business have faced are these : how shall psychology be taught, for example, to students in advertising? Shall the professor of advertising turn psychologist, or shall the psychologist turn advertiser? There is much crimination and recrimination. Advertising specialists insist that they cannot get the kind of psychology they need from the college departments of psychology, and that they (the psychologists) attempt to teach advertising, they are beyond their depth. The psychologists reply in kind, depreciating the psychology which advertising teachers include in their courses.

The situation seems most fortunate in those cases, as at Columbia, where the professor of advertising, for example, is a trained psychologist, with subsequent specialization in the industrial and commercial application of his subject. It would of course be equally satisfactory if advertising teachers would also master the psychological foundations of their field.

Concerning this whole question, Dr. H. K. Nixon, professor of advertising in the Columbia University School of Business, has written as follows:

> My major course in business psychology is one covering the psychology of advertising. I believe that in a business school of any size there is room for such a course and it perhaps should follow a general course in the principles of advertising. In my experience the chief value of this course to the student is that it may serve as an introduction to the use of laboratory and test methods applied to the study of human problems in business. That is, I feel that from such a course, well taught, a student ought to carry away a clear

idea of the necessity for finding out what the public thinks and methods evaluating and dealing with these reactions of the public. This knowledge and the attitude engendered by it, is, I believe, of considerable importance not only in advertising but at every other point where business touches the public. Expressing this idea in a slightly different form, I am far more interested in this particular course in teaching what might be called the "psychology of the public" than I am in teaching facts about the psychology of advertising. That being the case, it might be more logical not to call this course "psychology in advertising" at all but to label it "public psychology."

A second course which I give as "principles of selling" has running through it a strong backbone of personal psychology or individual psychology, as opposed to the psychology of the public dealt with above. I feel very strongly that this course can be made extremely useful—again not so much because of its application to a specific field such as selling, but because of its general bearing on human problems in business. Frankly I think that we are apt to become so immersed in giving our students a good background in economics and banking and accounting and other important subjects, and we tend to minimize and perhaps ignore the very important fact that the student's success or failure will depend much more on his personality and temperamental adjustments than on the knowledge that we have been able to give him. Now, of course, I do not pretend that I am doing a very effective job in helping my students on this matter of personality and human relationships, but I at least insist on the importance of study and of the necessity for more research to discover better methods of teaching in this most difficult of all fields. The mere fact that we do not know very much about the psychology of making men more effective in their human relations in business is no reason why we should underestimate its importance, as I sometimes feel that we do.

At present I am giving a third course, called "Psychology in Banking," open to members of the American Institute of Banking. It is a rather informal course in which I try to give these mature students a picture of modern ideas and theories in psychology and try to tie up as closely as possible with their own personal problems, the psychological problems involved in their relationship to the bank, and the psychological problems involved in the relationship of the bank to the public. I feel that this course is not perhaps as scholarly in its content as might be desired, but I have discovered that the students are better pleased and are perhaps served better by a somewhat popular and informal approach. As a matter of fact I am not sure that it is a good thing in any of our courses to try to bring in too much of the point of view of the professional academic psychologists. I have been through the psychological mill myself and I realize that we are very apt to fall into the habit of teaching our courses on the assumption that our job is to turn out more personal psychologists rather than remembering that what we want to do is to give business people a useful insight into their own mental life and that of the public with which they deal.

If I summarized these rather rambling ideas, it would be something like this: I believe we are in a transition period with "psychology in business," walking rather unsteadily between the too academic abstractions of the highly trained psychologists and the utter quackery of the charlatan. I think we have yet to learn how to give our business students a helpful picture of human nature without dehumanizing it or romanticizing it.[8]

Objective Determination of Courses in Business Psychology

In view of the agreement concerning the general importance of psychology as an element in business education and its extensive utilization in various commerce courses, the problem resolves itself into the organization into courses of the psychological data most useful for commerce students and their effective introduction into the curricula of the business courses.

Here again one gains the impression that most courses in business or industrial psychology have been organized on the basis of deductive reasoning rather than inductive analysis. It would seem that one of the first steps in the satisfactory solution of the problem of psychology courses for commerce students would be for representatives of all fields involved to co-operate in an objective analysis of the psychological implications of business activities. At least it would be an exceedingly important experiment for some school to make.

SOCIOLOGY

Historically, the relationship between sociology and collegiate education for business has been a close one. As has been pointed out, collegiate schools of business have sprung from an economics and social science parentage, so that sociology may be considered

---

[8] From a personal letter, January 15, 1930.

as a sort of paternal uncle to the business school. It will be interesting, therefore, to see to what extent this relationship has been maintained, and to what extent their development has been in differing directions.

The Rôle of Sociology in the Business Curricula

The rôle of sociology in the business curricula needs to be considered both from the standpoint of lower class general requirements and of the specialized upper class curricula.

Except as an alternate elective in the general group of social sciences, or as a part of a composite or orientation course, sociology receives no specific emphasis in the lower class curricula developed for commerce students. On the other hand, sociology has figured prominently at a number of schools among the general electives open in the lower classes. It will be recalled that liberal provisions of this sort frequently exist, so that sociology plays a somewhat more important rôle as a general study in the lower class curricula than formal tables are likely to show.

Turning to the specialized curricula, chiefly in the upper two years, sociology appears as a requirement, or among the suggested electives, in at least 13 of the undergraduate schools. Alabama requires it in the commerce teaching course. Boston makes it a requirement in business management, foreign trade, and commercial education. Columbia refers to its importance in the preparation of business students preparing to teach commercial subjects in secondary and special schools. Denver makes it a junior requirement for commercial teachers. At Illinois, it is a part of the trade and civic secretarial science course. Indiana includes it for commercial teachers; Missouri, for students in industrial relations and personnel management; Northwestern suggests it in the production and personnel curricula; North Dakota, for commercial secretaries and public administration; Ohio, in management and public administration courses; Pennsylvania, as an alternate elective in the sophomore year in all specialized curricula; Virginia, in the courses in labor and insurance; and Washington and Lee in the course in public administration. Obviously, it is elected widely at schools and in various curricula where it is not specifically mentioned. Most of the business schools definitely specify sociology among the general electives.

Concluding Comments

There seems to be little if any coordination of these various courses, although all four groups deal largely with the same fundamental problem. Still more striking is the almost complete divorce of courses on the regulation of combinations or business in general from the work in business law. Here, apparently is another of the situations which one finds particularly in growing curricula, with four or five distinct groups making as many approaches to the same basic problem, each covering in part the material of the other, but emphasizing one particular aspect of that problem.

It may be that such a situation is helpful and even necessary in the early development of a field, but it seems equally clear that, once a given stage of development has been reached, much duplication of effort can be avoided by their better co-ordination.

The School of Commerce and Administration of the University of Chicago, in developing a curriculum based on functional fields rather than traditional departments, accepts "social control of business" as one of these fields. The titles of the courses included in this grouping indicate its nature and its scope. They follow: "public regulation of business," "introduction to government finance," "industrial combinations," "international trade and finance," "international economic policies," "types of economic organization," and introduction to the study of law and business, the law of market practices and financing, the law of risk-bearing, labor, and business associations, special studies in legal aspects and business problems, government finance, state and local taxation, research in government finance, research in state and local finance.

If it is on business that one focusses attention, there is much in such a grouping to commend itself. If, on the other hand, one is influenced by the vested rights of departmental organizations, there are many grounds for objection.

THE FIELD OF DISTRIBUTION

The term distribution is used in this study to include work in marketing, advertising, selling, and retailing or merchandising. While there is no complete agreement among students concerning the particular usage of some of these terms, their meaning in this connection will at least be understood. Avoiding then, any ques-

TABLE XC. ADVERTISING, MARKETING, SALESMANSHIP AND RETAIL STORE MGMT., AND MERCHANDISING IN THE UNDERGRADUATE SCHOOLS OF THE AMERICAN ASSOCIATION

School	Undergraduate Credit Hours Offered					When Required			Courses Required				Field of specialization
	Advertising	Marketing	Selling	Retailing and Merchandising	Total Distribution	Freshman	Sophomore	Upper Class Core or General	Advertising	Marketing	Selling	Retailing and Merchandising	
Alabama	90	306	90		486	(b)		108	54	54			Advertising
Boston	396	216	72	36	720								Advertising and Selling
California	72	144	54	108	378								Advertising
Chicago	60	360	60	60	540							40	Marketing
Cincinnati		98	58	40	196		18	45		45	58		Selling
Columbia	108	144	108		360			178		98	36		Merchandising
Denver	72	144	54	36	216			162	72	54	108		Marketing
Florida	108	108	54	54	324			54		54	36		Marketing
Georgia	54	108	108	54	324			324		216			Merchandising and advtg.
Georgia Tech	162	126	162	54	504			108		54		54	
Illinois	162	198	72	54	486			144	54	54			Marketing and merchandising
Indiana	54	108	54	108	324			54		54			Merchandising
Iowa	36	108	18	36	198			54		54			Marketing
Kansas	144	144		36	324		54	54		54			Merchandising
Kentucky		108	108	36	252			36	18	108	18		Marketing
Marquette	72	180	36	36	342			108		36			Merchandising
Minnesota	144	204	36	36	420			36					Merchandising
Missouri	288	36	180	90	594								Retail mdsing.; sales mgmt.; and advtg.
Nebraska	162	126	36	54	378			54		54			Marketing; advtg.; salesmanship; retailing
New York	828	216	144	792	1,980	48[a]				48[a]			Advtg. and salesmanship; marketing; retail merchandising
N. Carolina	60	120	180	60	420								Merchandising
N. Dakota	54	54	54	108	270			108			54		Advertising; sales admin. and merchandising
Northwestern	324	108	198	36	666			216	108	54	54		Merchandising
Ohio	108	300	48	132	588			60		54			Marketing
Oklahoma	108	162	54	108	432			60		60	60		Commerce
Oregon	156	36	120	72	384		36	(c)		36			Marketing
Pennsylvania	180	288	288	54	810					36			Marketing
Pittsburgh	144	216	72	36	468			108		108			Marketing; advertising and selling
S. California	198	162	72	396	882								Marketing; cotton mktg.
S. Methodist	162	162	54	54	432								Retailing; wholesaling
Syracuse	324	144	72	72	612			108		108			Marketing; merchandising and advertising
Texas	108	36	198	108	450		108	72		72			Marketing
Tulane	54	162	108	54	378		108			108			Marketing
U. of Washington	210	390	60	396	1,056			40		40			Marketing
Virginia	36	36		36	108								Marketing
Washington U.	108	108		108	324			108		108			Marketing
Washington and Lee	54	54	54		162			126	18	54	54		
Wisconsin	72	54	36	36	198			54		54			Marketing
Total	5,472	5,738	3,172	3,604	17,986	48	216	2,579	324	1,947	478	94	

a. An alternate elective.
b. A course known as "Principles of Business," required of all freshmen, has a large marketing content.
c. One course in this general field must be taken by all students

Data From the Sociologists

In addition to the data secured from the business schools, as evidenced in their curricula offerings, letters of inquiry were addressed to, or direct visits were paid to, a selected number of heads of departments of sociology at universities which also included undergraduate collegiate schools of business. No effort was made to secure data on a comprehensive scale. Information of the nature sought was obtained from departments of sociology at Chicago, Iowa, Kansas, Minnesota, North Carolina, Oregon, Pennsylvania, Pittsburgh, Southern California, and Wisconsin.

At six of these universities, a large proportion of the commerce students come in some way or other to include sociology in their courses. The courses taken by business students at these schools include the background of social science, introduction to sociology, social psychology, industrial sociology, criminology, social problems, and social institutions. At all but one of these schools, students elect extensively among the sociology courses at the recommendation and with the approval of their business school advisers. On the other hand, at four of these universities, there is a selection of sociology courses by business students, even though such selection is discouraged in several instances.

The rôle of sociology in the business schools at this time may be summarized somewhat as follows. Being a relatively new field of study, its general status is that of an elective. Where a good teaching job is being done by the sociologists, where there are no personal or course rivalries, and where sociologists seem interested in the academic establishment of their work, sociology is extensively elected by business students. Where sociology has not proven itself through sufficient emphasis upon good teaching, or where modifying circumstances of some other kind have existed, sociology has had little relation with the work of the business schools.

Administrative Connections Between Sociology and Schools of Business

Because of its bearing upon subsequent, as well as the preceding, discussion, it seems pertinent to recall the administrative connection between departments of sociology and schools of business at a number of universities. At Iowa, Missouri, Ohio State,

Pennsylvania, Washington University, and Washington and Lee, sociology is a department or division within the school of business. In addition the schools of business at Boston and Denver have developed their own courses in sociology. At Indiana, North Dakota, and Wisconsin, the relationship administratively has been very close, either through overlapping of personnel, or because of the formal combination of economics and sociology.

Schools of Public Administration or Social Work

In these cases where the development of sociology has occurred within the school of business, there have been organized usually schools or curricula of social work or public administration. Iowa is on the verge of a development in this direction. The name of the Missouri school includes business and public administration, and includes a curriculum in social service. Ohio offers curricula in public service, municipal administration, and social administration. Pennslyvania includes a curriculum in social economy, and Washington University has developed a course in social work within the school of business and public administration.

Schools of social work, or courses for training in that work, have grown up rather generally out of or in connection with departments of sociology which are administered outside of colleges of commerce. It would seem, on the basis of the above, that administrative connection with a school of business need not preclude such a development.

The Adaptation of Sociology Courses for Business Students

Because of the close relation in many cases between sociology and schools of business during the period of their respective developments, it is particularly pertinent to inquire to what extent courses in sociology have been adapted to the interests and needs of commerce students. This question was raised rather widely in the course of the present study, both with business school administrators and with representatives of departments of sociology. The information obtained was largely negative. To a large number of the sociologists, the question seems not to have presented itself before. Of these who have considered it, only three or four seem to have made any move in the direction of such adaptation. On the other hand, deans of schools of business, confronted with

the needs of a specific kind of training, made frequent references to this lack of adaptation and to the dissatisfaction of business students being placed in the same course with household arts majors, social work apprentices, and liberal arts electives.

There are two basic problems confronting each of the modern social sciences; one is its development as a science, the other is its academic establishment. The former of these has been emphasized almost exclusively in the councils of the guild, yet, paradoxical as it may appear, the former is possible in part only as the latter is achieved. At any rate, sociologists seem to have failed signally in realizing the opportunities which the collegiate schools of business have offered for the academic establishment of their science. The reasons for this statement should be obvious. Collegiate commercial education has been the most rapidly growing field in the province of higher education during the past several decades. Coupled with this is the fact that many of the phenomena of the business world and their implications are wholly or largely sociological. There is the further fact that in many instances, as has been pointed out, departments of sociology have been peculiarly close, in point of place, history, and organization, to these rapidly growing schools of business. The combination of these circumstances would seem to have created an opportunity for academic establishment and social usefulness amazing in its promise and unlimited in its scope. It seems well nigh incredible that sociologists should have failed so universally in taking advantage of this opportunity. The rôle of social relations in the field of production, the sociology of fashions and fads and fancies with their tremendous importance in demand for consumers' goods, arbitration—these and other problems, fundamentally sociological as present concepts go, are tempting fields rich in promise of reward to the social scientist with imagination enough to sense their possibilities and ability sufficient to understand them.

Concerning the importance of these aspects of the training of the future business executive, there should be little difference of opinion. Business is a part of the larger life of society. Business is administered under the conditions which the social environment imposes. The two are inextricably bound up with each other, and at innumerable points and in every conceivable way. This would seem to justify clearly an emphasis, not only upon sociology but

upon all of the social sciences, in the training of business executives.

Moreover, the need for courses emphasizing the social aspects of business would seem to be increasing, due to certain changes that are taking place in the personnel of the faculties of collegiate schools of business. The older teachers in these schools started their academic careers in a large proportion of cases as social economists or sociologists, subsequently diverting their efforts into the direction of the growth of the schools. Such teachers naturally emphasized the social implications of their courses. Now, as the result of a marked increase in specialization and courses wholly business in content, and with the development of technically trained teachers in the business schools who are not interested *per se* in the social aspects of their particular phase of business, one is led to speculate as to where and how this part of the business executive's training will be given the necessary emphasis. This again would seem to indicate a particularly excellent opportunity for the social sciences at this stage of the development of business education.

Training in Personal Traits

It is a matter of common observation that the ability to please, and to adjust one's self to other people, is one of the most important factors in the achievement of happiness and success in life.

The analyses and opinions presented in Part I bear eloquent witness to the very great importance attached in business circles to the possession of desirable traits of personality and to the capacity of the individual to work effectively with other persons. Business does not disregard scholarship, but it supplements it with emphasis upon personal traits, attitudes, habits of work and thought, understanding of human nature, and ability to co-operate in the achievement of common ends.

A survey of the life sciences, using that term in its most general sense, indicates that the one common point toward which they have been converging in recent years is the development of human personality. This seems to be particularly true in the case of such sciences as psychology, sociology, psychiatry, biology, and education. The emphasis upon case work in the various fields

of professional practice where the principles of these sciences are being applied is a further illustration of this tendency in modern thinking, for the essence of case work is the differential treatment of human personality.

Recognition by the Business Schools

Some consciousness of the business importance of personal traits is penetrating into the colleges of commerce. It is significant to note that few conversations with leaders in collegiate business education held in the course of the present study concluded without some reference on their part to this aspect of the work of the business school. Such conversations invariably indicated an awareness of the problem, of its importance, of some responsibility of the school in dealing with it, and an intent but uncertain groping toward some successful method of doing so.

Here and there a teacher in the commerce faculties has called attention to it. Under the title of "Neglected Elements in a Business Education," Dr. Edward S. Mead, Professor of Finance of the Wharton School of Finance and Commerce, has called attention to the increasing frequency of the large corporation form of business and the added premium which this change in business organization is placing upon personal qualities. "The modern corporation," writes Professor Mead, "especially when it has reached a substantial size, is independent of individuals. Rules of procedure, traditions of policy, and established lines of business conduct based on long and successful experience grow up for the guidance of the company. These great organizations are like the trees of the primeval forest. They are widely and deeply rooted in the desires and necessities of mankind, and in preferential opportunities to supply human wants. . . . . Their methods and machinery are standardized. The directing members of their personnel are interchangeable. . . . ."

> Let me enumerate the qualities and abilities which carry a man to success in a large corporation. In these large organizations, promotion is not only by ability, but also by favor. The lower ranks are filled with hundreds of bright, intelligent, aspiring young men, and only a minority of these can expect rapid advancement. The importance of their positions in rank and salary depends largely on the favor of their superiors. And this favor is obtained not only by punctuality,

diligence, accuracy, and enthusiasm (the virtues which have always been held up as guiding stars to youth), but also by personal qualities, including robust abounding health, revealing itself in good nature and affability; careful attention to the intimate minutiae of personal appearance, together with an evident spirit of loyal co-operation.[9]

Experiments Concerned With Personal Traits

Concrete evidence of the interest among business educators in the development of the personalities of their students can be found in the courses that have been offered and the other experiments that have been made for this purpose. Grouped on the basis of the method of approach, three distinct types of effort can be distinguished.

First are those efforts whose approach is rather direct. An illustration of such effort is a course given by Dean Everett Lord, of the College of Business Administration of Boston University, under the title of "Personal and Business Efficiency." The course is described in the announcements of the school as follows:

> The application of the principles of efficiency to daily life in college and in business.
> Personality; its nature, determinants, and expression. Scales and tests for the analysis of traits. Sound health as the foundation of a vigorous individuality. The social influences which make for mental balance.
> Personal development and its objective control. The value of routine and habit; system in action and thought. The preparation and use of records, plans, schedules, files, and standardized equipment. Scientific management in personal affairs.
> The place of recreation in a program for efficient living. Varieties of recreation; their evaluation and relative attractiveness.
> Aims and ideals; the attainment of coherence in a plan of living, through the proper subordination of minor interests to a leading motive. The objective study of interests with an analysis of their vocational significance.[10]

A course largely similar in nature and purpose, is given by the School of Business Administration at the University of Oregon,

---

[9] Mead, Edward S., "Some Neglected Elements in a Business Education", *The Wharton News*, Vol. I, No. 1, February, 1928, p. 4.
[10] Boston University Bulletin, Vol. XVIII, No. 13, April 29, 1929, p. 88.

under the title of "Personal Efficiency Management." This course deals with the "methods of finding personal interests and qualities necessary to successful management. Outline of individual characteristics needed for specific kinds of position. Possible improvement of present or undeveloped personal traits."

Other direct methods which have been attempted or suggested include the utilization of small senior research groups for such purposes; the establishment of professional psychiatric service for students, such as has been done at Dartmouth and in the Harvard Graduate School of Business; and the division of the entire student body into small groups and their allotment to individual members of the faculty, who would then become responsible, not only for the scholarship but for the personal appearance, habit patterns, and personal adjustments of their charges. This latter suggestion would involve a rather intimate and personal relationship between a student and some particular faculty member, presumably during the entire period of the student's course. The serious acceptance of such a responsibility on the part of the instructor would involve, undoubtedly, a considerable amount of time and some adjustment of teaching load would have to be made. Considerable care would have to be taken that such a plan would not be pointed solely toward the promotion of scholarship—important though that may be—to the neglect of its primary purpose, which is the development of the entire personality of the student.

The second type of efforts to deal with the problem of personal traits are those more indirect in their approach. Courses in social adjustment, in management, or in personnel, lend themselves most readily for such purposes. Here the student is led to consider traits of personality objectively, from the standpoint of their social desirability or business value. Although couched wholly in terms of discussions of the "other fellow," such courses, if handled deftly, may be made to serve, unconsciously in large measure, as mirrors in which the student comes to see his own personal assets and liabilities. Particularly does it seem that by establishing the fiction of teaching the student the art of managing others, he may be taught something about managing himself; by way of emphasizing the traits necessary for advancement in those whom he presumably will manage, he may be led quite un-

consciously to regard his own, and in a way that neither hurts nor opens the opportunity for campus ridicule. Several experiments of this nature, both from the standpoint of sociology and of management, report unusual success.

A third contribution to the achievement of development of personal traits in students is suggested by experiments made by Dr. James T. Young, professor of political science in the Wharton School of Finance and Commerce of the University of Pennsylvania. Professor Young emphasizes what he terms the "by-products" in teaching. "By the by-product method is meant the selection of certain mental powers or habits which are of special importance and the conscious direction of the student's attention to the development of these mental powers."[11] From experiments in his own classes in which concentration was on a single mental process, i.e., analysis, Professor Young reports increases in the average grade per student of nine per cent in one year and of 14.9 per cent the second year. In the former year, the training was less extensive, with only one-half as much attention devoted to the by-product.[12]

Elsewhere, Professor Young suggests the possibility of the conscious cultivation of other mental traits or habits, such as inductive reasoning, clearness of expression, etc., and infers that the conscious cultivation of such traits as by-products of teaching any particular subject does not interfere with but rather accelerates progress in that subject.[13]

In large measure, Professor Young's experiments are but the concrete application of a conviction which many experienced teachers have expressed, namely, that *what* a student is taught is not nearly so important as *how* he is taught. There are those members of the teaching guild who are convinced that colleges and universities, in tolerating habits of carelessness, lack of promptness, absence of precision, and serious application, do almost irreparable damage to many young people entrusted to them. To be indulged in habits of work, dress, and speech which modern busi-

---

[11] Young, James T., "An Experiment in By-Product Teaching," *The American Political Science Review*, Vol. XXIII, No. 4, November, 1929, p. 1002.

[12] Ibid., p. 1004.

[13] "By-Products in the Teaching of Government," *The General Magazine and Historical Chronicle of the University of Pennsylvania*, July, 1928.

ness will not permit is a very poor preparation for business. Traits are not developed by postponing attention to them. It may well be that the by-products of teaching, like those of certain industries, are really of primary importance.

There is not a teacher in our collegiate schools of business who cannot identify numerous students who would profit immeasurably from individual attention of a corrective sort, with reference to personal habits, traits, and peculiarities. Many a student might be benefited more in a business way from liberal doses of homely wholesome psychiatry than from all the technical and professional instruction that any school of business can hope to give him. It may be that the time is near at hand when this omission in our educational approach will be considered a serious weakness. Certainly there is nothing illogical in this suggestion, since it is the defects in the attitudes, habits, and traits of college and university graduates which business most frequently emphasizes.

A business school is a business enterprise. Its object is the training of business men, and it should seek to achieve this object in a business-like manner. Recognition of the personnel problems in the organization and the operation of a school is just as important as those problems in the conduct of a business.

Academic leaders are so apt to consider their work in comparison with that of other institutions instead of in terms of the possibilities of the situation. Or, they think in terms of the very good student, or the negative work of salvaging some rather poor ones. Yet the real job of any academic institution ought to be the positive promotion of the possibilities of the great group of students who will profit most from constant and constructive supervision. While it is true that there are all kinds of experiments and programs for intensive work with small groups of students, these are aimed almost wholly at the more effective mastery of academic content or method, and very little at the development of personality of students. The fact of the matter is that higher institutions of learning have paid somewhat less attention to the revolutionary developments resulting from the scientific discovery of personality than have certain other fields of professional activity. This is curiously strange since the scientific foundation for this new development has come from university scientists in many cases.

There are those who hold that the business school which will come forward today with a new program of training centering about the development of personality, and pointed toward a business career, will be as much of a pioneer as the Wharton School was in 1881. This would involve an extensive development of the by-products of teaching. It would widen, of course, the breach between the university teacher and the research student. It would mean that the stone which the builders rejected would become the head of the corner. Such a project would have to be built upon the effort of many interested teachers, alive to the possibilities involved. It would mean a great deal of experimentation and a constantly open mind, while such experiments were in progress. It would necessitate the slow accretion of a technique to achieve the end in view.

Such a project ought sometime to intrigue a donor who had the imagination to conceive its possibilities, and the means to enable progress toward their achievement.

Certainly we can agree with the spirit of the utterance of the late secretary of the interior, Mr. Lane: "We are quickly passing out of the rough and ready period of our national life, in which we have dealt wholesale with men and things into a period of more intensive development in which we must seek to find the special qualities of the individual unit, whether that unit be an acre or a desert, a barrel of oil or a mountain canyon, the flow of a river, or the capacity of the humblest of men."

Orientation Courses in Commerce and Pre-Commerce Curricula

The recent emphasis upon specialization within university curricula, combined with the growing heterogeneity of student bodies, have intensified considerably the need for guidance, both academic and personal, of students, particularly in the lower years. To this problem, new in degree if not in nature,

> The reaction of many institutions naturally has been one of impatient irritation. Too many, as high as 50 per cent of the students now in college, we are told, do not belong there. The colleges are educating "a lot of youngsters who ought to be left illiterate for the benefit of the unskilled labor market." The logic of such an attitude leads its advocates inevitably to the acceptance of one or both of two policies: first, the merciless elimination of poorer students; and second, to the

principle of limited and selective admission. It would seem unnecessary to add that not all limitations upon size of student bodies are to be thus construed. There is a difference between arbitrary fixing of members on the basis of available facilities, i.e., its advocacy as a matter of educational facilities, and its advocacy as a matter of educational policy.

Other institutions do nothing. Their responsible leaders fail to recognize changing conditions, or, doing so, rationalize away any responsibility on their part. They are apt to depreciate the efforts of their more progressive fellows as forms of collegiate quackery, influenced by the aggressive activities of edu-experts who are dismissed as "glib fellows away from home."

Fortunately there are those in the field of higher education who recognize the factors which are transforming collegiate populations as well as collegiate curricula, and appreciate the importance of constructive adaptation. Confronted with new situations, man has recourse to the trial and error method. Thus there results experiments of various kinds and with differing success. This is what has been happening in the colleges and universities, particularly in more recent years. The orientation project is an experimental gesture of the higher institution of learning in the direction of the educational guidance of its new students.

The history of the orientation project is a short but varied one. It was in 1915-16 that Brown University took the first step in this direction with a series of lectures upon the scope and aims of college education. Other institutions followed with experiments similar in name, if not altogether so in content or intent. All of such projects now under way are, of course, still in the experimental stage. The objectives to be sought and the details to be employed for their achievement are being worked out slowly on the basis of exerience. In view of the shortness of the time that has elapsed since the pioneer development at Brown University, and of the inherent difficulties which are involved, progress, to such as are fully informed, would seem to be entirely satisfactory.

The earlier orientation courses were developed for the most part outside of the formal curriculum of the college or university. Their aim seems to have been chiefly that of orientating the student to his new situation—to the administrative requirements and routine of the institution, to the effective utilization of its resources and to the life of the campus community. In some cases an effort was made to advise students constructively with respect to their later careers. The emphasis, in other words, was upon the problems which the freshman faced personally and as a student.

The more recent orientation work, on the other hand, has developed within the curriculum, as an integral part of it or an introduction to it. The aim here is to orient the student to the life and thought of the modern world. The emphasis is upon curriculum content, fields of knowledge, life's problems in their largest aspect.

Some of these courses deal with the general field of contemporary life and science, some seek to survey the range of the social sciences, some confine themselves to the physical sciences, while still others attempt to achieve an introduction to several or all of these provinces of synthetic study. Different situations and needs prevail at different institutions, and this fact, plus the personal interests and qualifications of the men associated with these projects, has dictated their particular emphasis and form at any one institution.[14]

Both types of orientation courses are found in the commerce and pre-commerce curricula of the members of the American Association of Collegiate Schools of Business. Courses or series of lectures of the first type are given at Boston, Denver, Georgia Tech, Iowa, and Syracuse. As indicated, these courses are confined to the freshman year, and usually to an hour a week, either for the first term or throughout the year. They deal with college life and its problems, and aim to orient the student to the university, its problems, its resources, and its opportunities. There is, of course, considerable variation in the content and emphasis of these courses.

Courses of the second type alluded to, seeking to orient the student to the life and thought of the modern world, or to some well defined aspect of it, are given at Boston, Columbia, Missouri, New York, Ohio State, Oregon, Pennsylvania, Southern California, and Washington University.

1. The course in "Principles of Business" at Boston University has been alluded to already, and it has been deemed proper to include it among these courses.

2. The course on contemporary civilization, given at Columbia University since 1919, is particularly well known. Confined originally to the freshman year, it has been extended recently (1928) to the sophomore year.

The course is an introduction to some of the social problems of the present—economic, governmental, national, and

---

[14] Bossard, James H. S., "Educational Guidance and the Orientation Course," *School and Society*, Vol. XXX, No. 764, August 17, 1929.

international. It is also an introduction to some of the intellectual trends of the present—scientific, religious, and cultural. The development of our present civilization from the Renaissance through the industrial and intellectual revolutions to the World War and after is given in sufficient detail to throw into relief the chief characteristics of our age. It is a machine age, an age of mass production for world distribution. It is a democratic age in which each economic group is more or less integrated and effective in its participation in the determination of public policy. It is an age in which the application of investigation and exact methods of discovery and control are spreading to the whole of man's activity.

Some of these present characteristics are so strikingly illuminated by contrast that enough medieval thought and life is introduced at the outset of the course to show the new against the background of the old.

Put briefly, the course is an attempt to ask: What are our social and intellectual worries; how do we come to have them; what attitudes shall we take toward them; what promising solutions can we find for them?[15]

3. The course at Missouri is called "Problems of Citizenship." It includes the theory of evolution, man's physical environment, geologic survey, the development of life, man's history and antiquity, race, and elements of man's social heritage.

4. The School of Commerce, Accounts and Finance of New York University has a group of "general courses," which include outlines of literature, outlines of history, outlines of science, general mathematics, general sociology, general psychology, etc., designed for the average business man's need for or interest in these fields.

5. Ohio State requires "Introduction to Social Science" of its freshmen. "This course is designed to give students an appreciation of the social and economic forces of present day life. The departments of sociology, economics, and business organization join in the presentation of material which will give the student a background of information and will develop an interest in and prepare for further studies in these fields. Topics presented are built around a consideration of the theory and evolution of society and its problems; the economic relations growing out of the development of wants for material goods and the means taken

---

[15] Coss, John J., "A Report of the Columbia Experiment with the Course on Contemporary Civilization," in *The Junior College Curriculum*, University of Chicago Press, Chicago, 1929, Chapter X.

to satisfy these wants; and a description of the organization and functioning of modern business."

6. The University of Oregon is now following the plan of organizing the work of the first two years into broad survey courses of a general introductory type. There are four main divisions of work—(a) language and literature group, (b) social science group, (c) mathematics and physical science group, and (d) biological sience group. These general survey courses are open as electives to commerce students.

7. The general survey course in science, given at the Wharton School of Finance and Commerce at the University of Pennsylvania, has been alluded to in Chapter X. This is a course about science and the sciences designed, not for purposes of further specialization in a particular science, but for the needs of commerce students. It is a non-laboratory course, emphasizing somewhat more the spirit of science than the details of its method, more its achievements and their significance to business and to society, than its mechanics.

8. Southern California is now working on the project of a broad survey course for the freshman year, with the departments of history, philosophy, political science, and sociology co-operating. There is also the suggested plan there of reorganizing the entire work of the first year or two on the basis of three broad general courses.

9. Washington University requires a course in American political and economic institutions of all commerce freshmen. This combines elementary concepts and fundamental data from the fields of economics and political science, chiefly.

LOWER CLASS ELECTIVES

Examination of the tables in Chapter XI of the lower class curricula shows that in a considerable number of cases provision for electives exists, and that at certain schools, such provisions are rather liberal. It will be recalled that the total number of class hours designated as elective ranks fourth in order of numerical importance among the studies of the lower two years.

These electives seldom are wholly free in the complete sense of the word. Usually they serve to introduce an element of leeway or flexibility into the curricula, to be utilized as circumstances

dictate. Their immediate purposes vary from one institution to another. Brief reference to some of these follows.

There are, for example, those schools where the electives are rather circumscribed by general university requirements. A definite number of credits in certain specified subjects must be taken. The purpose of the electives is to avoid the designation of particular courses in those specified objects, or to allow, perhaps, some small range of choice between subjects.

At other institutions under discussion, particularly in the case of the two-year undergraduate schools, the first two years include provision for electives to the end that the curricula may be pointed somewhat toward the work of the upper two years. That is to say, the first two years of general training may be pointed somewhat toward commerce, or at some other specialized upper class kind of training.

Other schools seem to utilize lower class electives to a considerable extent to project business studies, supposedly limited to the upper years, into the curricula of the first two years. In other words, specialization in some aspect of the business field may begin earlier than appears on the surface, since the upper class specialized curricula reach down to dictate the lower class electives.

A goodly portion of the elective class hours are apportioned to the general field of the social sciences, without any particular one being mentioned. Reference has been made already to the fact that the social sciences figure more prominently in the curricula of the first two years than the enumeration of specific requirements would indicate. In the development of collegiate curricula what has happened is that the older studies, such as language, natural science, mathematics, etc., have established their priority as a rule by acquiring the status of requirements. With the advent of the newer and in a sense competing social sciences, a certain number of designated hours have been set aside as electives to allow some opportunity to students to pursue these newer studies. This has resulted in a sort of competitive race among the social sciences which has put them on their mettle. There have been undoubted advantages to the arrangement.

Reference should also be made to such schools as Oregon, for example, where the work of the first two years has been

organized into several broad survey or background courses, with the student having a certain choice as to which of these courses he will take. Here, electives are a necessary part of a new and intensely interesting experiment in university education.

Finally, it should be noted that at a few institutions lower class electives are utilized, in part at least, to adjust student schedules to their entrance credentials. This has been noted in the case of various schools in regard to the foreign language requirement. At the University of Chicago, the program of the first two years turns in large measure upon the student's entrance credentials.

THE PROBLEM OF ADAPTED COURSES

In discussing the various studies included in this chapter, two facts stand out clearly.

1. Each of the specific subjects discussed in this chapter plays an important rôle in the lower class commerce and pre-commerce curricula. Some are required more generally and to a greater extent than others, but if the actual distribution of electives is taken into account, the difference in total class hours among these various subjects would be somewhat less pronounced.

2. In most schools, the departments responsible for instruction of commerce and pre-commerce students in these subjects are located outside of the school of business. The exceptions to this statement in the case of each subject have already been noted. These two facts in combination create what is undoubtedly one of the outstanding problems in collegiate education for business, namely, that of the adaptation of these studies to meet the needs of commerce students.

The problem of the adaptation of courses is not peculiar to the colleges of commerce. It is emerging in all of the specialized undergraduate schools—commerce, education, social work, etc. All of these schools, in the development of their curricula, have had to draw upon departments much older than they; departments usually located in the college of liberal arts, and identifying themselves, in varying degrees, with the arts college.

When the demand for courses has come from the more recently established schools these departments at first are pleased. They interpret the demand as a recognition of their importance.

And the arrangement which these departments usually make in meeting the demand is that which is least burdensome. They simply repeat courses which they already give, or combine the students from these specialized schools with classes already existing.

Dissatisfaction speedily arises. Students rebel. With differing backgrounds, differing interests and different concrete material in mind, students from the various specialized curricula begin to demand courses particularly adapted, by illustrative material and through concrete application, to their particular objectives. Sometimes these demands are articulate, sometimes the dissatisfaction expresses itself through complete disapproval of the subject rather than the particular form of the course. Ultimately the faculties of these specialized schools reiterate these demands, in some form or other.

Such demands usually precipitate a problem for the particular department involved. The adaptation of courses necessitates instructors who have knowledge of the field to which they are adapting and applying. This involves a dual background which unfortunately, many teachers do not have. Nor, frequently, are persons trained in one field interested in the relation of their chosen specialty to another specialty.

The result of all this has been quite natural. Particular departments confronted with this situation rationalize their inability. The wish of convenience becomes father to the philosophy of defense. Adaptation of work, they say, is undesirable, unnecessary. English is English, science is science, mathematics is mathematics, sociology is sociology, no matter where given or to whom. The department members insist that, being specialists in their field, they are the best judges of what students should be taught.

This is one situation. Others obtain. For example, department X may have developed a course particularly adapted or pertinent for a specialized group of students. But it is an advanced course, the path to which is dotted with hurdles in the form of prerequisites. In order to take adapted course 46, the student is expected to elect courses 1, 14, 28, and 35 in the same field as prerequisites. This removes course 46 from the range of possibility.

This problem has been discussed thus far in general terms.

Specifically, the problem of the college of commerce in this respect is to persuade liberal arts departments usually, and engineering school faculties to a lesser extent, to adapt their work to meet the needs and to fit in with the purposes, of commerce curricula. It is a real and very important problem. Everywhere, in the course of the investigations attending this study, has it been emphasized as one of the most important aspects in the improvement of collegiate education for business.

There is, of course, much adaptation. The facts concerning such adaptation have been set forth in the analysis of each subject. On the whole, there has been more in mathematics, psychology, and geography, than in English and political science, and more in these two than in natural science or sociology. On the other hand, because of the failure of departments to co-operate, there are those schools of business which have developed wholly or largely as isolated and self-sufficing units.

On the whole, one cannot but be surprised at the lack of interest in many quarters in the integration of specialized fields of knowledge, and their adaptation to the objectives of whole undergraduate schools. These intermediate fields are usually rich in possibilities. It is a fact well-known to farmers that the richest soil is to be found in the fence streams which formerly divided fields. Ultimately, when the diminishing returns of continued specialization will become more apparent the richness of the academic fence streams will come to be appreciated—and exploited.

Problems in Lower Class Curricula Changes

In the preceding chapter, some current tendencies in the reorganization of the lower class curriculum were discussed. The plan described involved the development of general composite or survey courses, organized independently of departmental lines.

What are the constituent elements in a foundation for business life? What are the fundamentals of business training? Objectively, these have not been determined. Much inductive analysis over long periods of time and in many quarters must precede their ultimate determination. In the meantime, a reorganization of the work of the first two years along the line described above, and including the following elements, seems to be in process of development.

General Aspects of Business Curriculum

1. Every collegiate business curricula might begin with an introduction to modern business—its forms, its practices, its interrelations, its changing patterns. The object here would be interpretation. Business needs first to be understood, not evaluated. Instruction should be visual, so far as possible. Field trips might be utilized, whenever possible. Business can be brought to co-operate intelligently with this project, if intelligent and constant effort is made to secure such co-operation. English themes developed in connection with such work might emphasize observation and verbal reproduction. Such themes could be as helpful in a course in English composition as those on "How I Spent My Vacation"—provided the English instructor accompanied the field trips.

2. Modern business is conducted in an economic setting. This larger economic background is made up of various factors. It is partly a matter of history, the result of a long process of development of ideas and institutions; it is partly a matter of resources and geography; it is partly a matter of certain concepts and principles which are operative, or believed to be.

3. The intimate and pervasive relationships between natural science and the business world have been alluded to. Reference has been made also to adapted courses in science at several schools. It seems clear that the scientific and technological background of modern business should be an element in each business student's training.

4. Business is conducted within and between territories which are organized into governments. Business must operate within the laws and rules which these governments impose. The relationship between governmental agencies and modern business is constant and pervasive. The politico-legal setting of business, it would seem, should be a part of the training of every business man.

5. There is the general social setting of modern business. Business, as has been said previously, does not exist in a vacuum. It is a part of the larger life of society. It is profoundly influenced by social psychology, as many business men have learned, some to their advantage and others to their very great grief. A true understanding of modern business must proceed hand in hand

with a true understanding of modern society—its forces, its processes, and their business significance.

6.   The element of human behavior in business is of the first order of importance and, as happens so frequently in matters of primary importance, is largely neglected, both in the operation of business and in the training of business students.   Here is a virgin field, fruitful beyond the imagination of most persons, waiting for exploitation by the collegiate school of business that is to come.

7.   All students probably would agree upon the importance of preparation and drill in the measuring functions of business.   With the increasing size and complexity of business, this function becomes increasingly important.   It is basic in the control and scientific operation of business.

8.   Finally is the medium of business—language.   Enough has been said in this study concerning the value in business of facility in the use of both spoken and written word.   Much is being said by students in the business schools of this need; much, by faculty members.   The verdict of business itself is clear; its demand, sharp and direct.

These elements which have been mentioned are not to be thought of as representing so many courses.   They do not coincide with departmental divisions or distinctions.   To conceive of them as such is to misunderstand the basic idea involved.   There are many mature students who believe that it is time to rescue education from the departmental incubus.   Certain thoughtful students of modern education emphasize this as the next price of progress in the field of higher education.   Only in this way, they contend, can the duplication of materials and emphases, which specialization has produced, be reduced; only in this way can students be educated in the terms of life problems.

The modern orientation course is blazing the trail.   Two, three, perhaps six, departments cooperate in the development of such courses, or they involve the material of so many departments. A similar pooling of interests and materials is implied in the reorganization here suggested.   Economics, geography, geology, and economic history must be pooled to develop the economic setting of business.   All of the natural sciences will be called upon to understand the scientific setting of business.   Business law and political science are basic in furnishing the legal setting of busi-

ness; and all of the social sciences, in its social setting. The measuring function of business involves mathematics, accounting, and statistics; the human element, psychology and the life sciences.

Business education learns constantly from business. Business has learned the possibilities of mergers. May it not be that the day of departmental mergers is at hand?

Summary and Conclusions

By way of conclusion, certain outstanding facts concerning the general studies and problems dealt with in this chapter, will be restated in summary form.

1. The study of economics is required of all commerce students. Introductory courses, either descriptive or historical in nature, are usually offered in the freshman year, followed by the study of economic principles in the sophomore year. Frequently, too, advanced courses in economic theory are required at the end of the four year course, synthesizing the plan of instruction. The relationship between schools of business and departments of economics, as well as between the teachers of the more purely business subject and the economists, raise important problems.

2. Training in the written and oral use of English is receiving increasing emphasis as a fundamental in business training. Courses in English composition, public speaking, argumentation and the like are generally required. There is a tendency to increase these requirements, particularly in training in oral English. Commercial correspondence courses are also popular. A problem exists in convincing teachers of English to adapt their courses to the needs of commerce studies.

3. Coincident with the increasing emphasis upon English, college of commerce faculties are growing more and more restive with the foreign language requirements, where they still persist. There are indications that a number of schools will remove these requirements in the not remote future.

4. Courses in geography and resources are included in the lower class curricula in many schools, serving as a foundation for subsequent economic and business courses. The problem confronting college of commerce administrators is that of securing courses properly adapted to the needs of business students.

5.   Training in the measuring function is recognized as a basic element in most programs of education. Nearly all of the schools of business require or encourage students to pursue courses in mathematics during the first two years. Adapted courses in the mathematics of finance, or the mathematical theory of investment are frequent.

6.   Natural sciences are generally included as requirements in the lower class curricula of commerce students. Although some interesting and apparently successful experiments have been made in recent years in developing science courses especially adapted for commerce students, most natural science teachers are rather indifferent to such projects. As a result, colleges of commerce have developed their own adapted science courses.

7.   Some knowledge of and understanding of the structure and functioning of the government under which business is conducted would seem to be another fundamental element in education for business. Most commerce programs include courses in political science to achieve this purpose. Should such courses be chiefly national, or local, or international in scope? The problem of adaptation, too, is important, as well as the further integration of such courses with those in business law and with those dealing with various aspects of the relation of business and the public.

8.   Applied psychology is a constant element in the conduct of business operations. To train commerce students in this respect, courses in psychology have been added frequently to commerce curricula. There is some difference of opinion between academic psychologists and persons actively engaged in business as to the nature and scope of the psychology that should be taught. Where schools of business have been able to secure teachers in this field who combine training in psychology with subsequent specialization in its industrial and commercial afflictions, the results are very successful.

9.   Although sociology is not a general requirement in any school of business, it has become an important element in the curriculum in commerce as an elective, partly because of its close relation to economics and partly because of its popularity with students. There is need, and opportunity as well, for the adaptation of sociology courses to the needs of business students.

10.   Training in the personal traits which make for success is

at once the most rudimentary and the most intriguing of proposed curricular activities for schools of business. Experiments indicate that real achievements in this field can be obtained. These involve an extensive development of the by-products of teaching. Further efforts in this direction are likely to be made by farsighted business educators.

11. The recent efforts to "humanize" the curriculum have produced among other things, the orientation course. Starting in 1915 as an effort to meet the personal problems of the freshman it has grown steadily in popularity and scope. Its shares with the attempt to inculcate desirable personal traits the view that the curriculum is for the student and not the student for the curriculum. Courses given a panoramic view of many fields of study, presenting the essentials of each branch of human knowledge in its proper perspective, appear likely to become established, not only in schools of business but in all departments of higher education.

12. The more general courses in commerce curricula are usually taught by teachers connected with divisions or schools of the university other than the college of commerce. For the most part, they are from the liberal arts faculties. The resultant problem, which is of outstanding importance at this stage of the development of collegiate education for business, is the adaptation of these general courses to the needs of commerce students. The orientation course suggests a method for the adaptation and combination of courses and course content. A well organized and well integrated curriculum for business training may conceivably be compelled to organize the fundamental elements of such training without regard to departmental divisions and traditions.

CHAPTER XIII

THE BUSINESS STUDIES[1]

ACCOUNTING

Accounting is, undoubtedly, the most fully developed subject or field of study in our collegiate schools of business. The objectives of accounting departments are usually well-defined and clear; the courses in accounting and their content are relatively standardized. Accounting is usually the first "business" subject to be introduced in college curricula. In fact, to many persons accounting stands in a peculiar sense as the Alpha of business education.

Table LXXXV presents in tabular form the data concerning the development and status of accounting in the 38 undergraduate schools. In the following discussion, the data included in this table are summarized, and other facts gathered in the course of the study also are presented.

The Rôle of Accounting in the Undergraduate Curricula

In determining the rôle which accounting plays in business education the following facts are significant.

1. All of the schools offer courses in accounting. It is generally recognized as an essential and integral element in business education.

2. In 22 of the member schools, there are separate departments of accounting. In schools where there are no or few lines of departmentalization, one finds the work in accounting set off and given a somewhat separate and distinct recognition.

3. In all of the member schools, accounting is a field of specialization. In the case of three of the schools, accounting is combined with statistics as a field of specialization, and in one case with banking and finance.

4. Not only is accounting generally recognized as a distinct specialty in collegiate schools for business, but it is widely selected as such by students. While it is not considered feasible to present in tabular form data on the distribution of students in various

---

[1] Prepared and written by J. H. S. Bossard.

fields of undergraduate specialization, such information as was obtained would indicate that the proportion of students majoring in accounting is usually first or second on the list.

TABLE LXXXV. ACCOUNTING IN THE UNDERGRADUATE SCHOOLS OF THE AMERICAN ASSOCIATION

Schools	Total credit hours offered	Credit hours required			Field of specialization	Separate department
		Freshman	Sophomore	Upper class		
Alabama...............	612	108	108		Yes with statistics	Yes
Boston................	684	108	72		Yes	Yes
California.............	612			108	Yes	No
Chicago...............	480		60	105	Yes	Yes
Cincinnati.............	286	88	66	132	Yes	No
Columbia..............	108			108	Yes	Yes
Denver................	756	108	108		Yes	Yes
Florida................	432		108		Yes	No
Georgia...............	540		108		Yes	Yes
Georgia Tech..........	783		108	171	Yes	No
Illinois................	774	108	108		Yes	No
Indiana...............	378	72	36		Yes	No
Iowa..................	828		108[b]	108[c]	Yes	No
Kansas................	432		108		Yes	Yes
Kentucky..............	540		144		Yes	No
Marquette.............	540		144		Yes, with statistics	No
Minnesota.............	504	60	72	36	Yes	Yes
Missouri...............	396		36[a]	198	Yes, with banking & finance	No
Nebraska..............	486	108	36[a]		Yes	No
New York..............	1,224	72[d]			Yes	Yes
North Carolina.........	552			120	Yes	No
North Dakota..........	468	36	108		Yes	Yes
Northwestern..........	748		108	180[c]	Yes	Yes
Ohio..................	696		120	60	Yes, in both public and industrial accounting	Yes
Oklahoma..............	882		90		Yes	Yes
Oregon................	528	144			Yes	No
Pennsylvania..........	558	90			Yes	Yes
Pittsburgh.............	918	108			Yes	Yes
Southern California......	612	144			Yes	Yes
Southern Methodist.....	684		144		Yes	Yes
Syracuse..............	702		54	108	Yes	Yes
Texas.................	666		144		Yes, in both managerial and public accounting	Yes
Tulane................	270	36	144		Yes	No
Virginia...............	324		108		Yes	No
University of Washington	960		180		Yes	Yes
Washington University...	594		108		Yes, with statistics	No
Washington and Lee.....	378		108	18[a]	Yes	Yes
Wisconsin.............	324			108	Yes	Yes

[a] An alternate elective.
[b] Strongly urged.
[c] If not taken in sophomore year.
[d] In most curricula.

5. What is the nature of the specialized curricula in accounting in the several schools? What courses are included? A tabulation of the various set-ups reveals a somewhat striking similarity. First, with the exception of a few institutions where the number

of courses in accounting is too large, all of the courses in accounting offered by the department are included. An accounting major, in other words, includes a good deal of accounting. In fact, accounting curricula are more narrowly specialized than those in any other offered in the business schools. Second, courses in mathematics (adapted to business students) and statistics are usually included. Third, courses in business law are mentioned rather generally. Beyond these is a scattering of courses, usually just one or two, in finance, marketing, management, investment, or insurance.

6. To what extent is work in accounting required of students in the member schools? Twenty-seven of the 38 undergraduate schools require one year of accounting of all business students. Nine require a year and a half or two years of all students. Two schools require more than two years in accounting of all students —Minnesota and Cincinnati. The latter institution requires four years. It needs to be emphasized, however, that this tabulation is of requirements in accounting for all students. In addition to these general requirements, further courses in accounting are an important part in other group requirements. On the other hand, in more than half of the schools, no further work in accounting beyond the introductory courses is required. This raises the question as to what kind of an introductory course should be given. Introductory courses in accounting usually are large. Many of the students will major in that subject, even more are taking the course as one element in their business education. Does this imply two separate introductory courses?

7. Where is the study of accounting started? Examination of the curricula of the member schools shows that most of them include it now among the lower class requirements, as the following summary shows:

a. Fourteen include accounting in the curricula of the freshman year—Alabama, Boston, Denver, Illinois, Indiana, Minnesota, Nebraska, New York (in most courses), North Dakota, Oregon, Pennsylvania, Pittsburgh, Southern California, and Tulane.

b. Nineteen begin the study of accounting in the sophomore year—Chicago, Cincinnati, Florida, Georgia, Georgia Tech, Iowa (frequently), Kansas, Kentucky, Marquette, Northwestern, Ohio State, Oklahoma, Southern Methodist, Syracuse, Texas, Virginia,

University of Washington, Washington University, and Washington and Lee.

c. Five schools postpone the first course in accounting to the junior year—California, Columbia, Missouri, North Carolina, and Wisconsin. In several of these institutions, there is the stipulation that work in accounting begins in the sophomore year for students expecting to major in that field.

There is considerable discussion at some of the institutions which schedule accounting in the freshman year concerning the advisability of so doing. There is objection on the ground that the work is too difficult for freshmen, and that its requirement prejudices students against the subsequent pursuit of commerce studies. On the other hand, vigorous defense is made on several scores. In the first place, the concrete and precise nature of the subject is pointed out, and its pedagogic value is emphasized. Second, reference is made to its value in orienting the student in the field of business. Finally, there is considerable significance in the psychological or motivating value of having the student take a "practical business course" early in his academic career, thus giving him the idea that he is "solving business problems." Argumentation aside, the differences in the experiences of the several schools scheduling accounting in the freshman year would suggest that its successful conduct at that place in the curriculum is one largely, if not wholly, of teaching personnel and course content.

In this connection, considerable interest attaches to a course in "constructive accounting" required of freshmen in the School of Business Administration at the University of Oregon. This course is in charge of Professor A. B. Stillman, and has found expression in a text by Folts, F. E. and Stillman, known as *Interpretive Accounting*. This course is really an interpretative survey course based on the manager's use of accounting, instead of a routine bookkeeping course. The results obtained seem quite satisfactory. It is a large and popular course, taken by many non-commerce students, but is not considered in any way as a "fresh-air course." Different members of the staff carry different sections, indicating that the personality of the professor in charge is not its sole attraction. Two values in particular seem to be served by this course; first, that the student gains some general introduction to the field of business, chiefly from the managerial viewpoint, in addition to the accounting that is involved; and second, the students' interest is stimulated and his progress in commerce studies facilitated by this first interesting contact with the field.

It seems not amiss to emphasize the particular aspect of the introductory course in accounting which has just been mentioned. In the curricula of many schools as now constituted, the students' first contact with "business" studies is through the introductory course in accounting. This again emphasizes the importance of the content and teaching personnel of this course.

Nature of the Courses Given in Accounting

An examination of the course offerings by the member schools shows a considerable diversity and range of material. A total of 42 different course titles are mentioned. Undoubtedly, different institutions announce the same course, in substance at least, under different titles. Certain customary offerings, however, can be identified.

a. Each school has an elementary course, variously referred to as elements of accounting, principles of accounting, accounting I, first year accounting, etc., the purpose of which chiefly is to introduce the student to the kinds of recording and types of analysis which accounting involves.

b. Every member school has an advanced course of this general nature, usually referred to as advanced accounting, which carries forward the general development of the introductory course.

c. Each school offers a course in cost accounting. The terminology and general content of this course seems fairly well standardized. Considerable emphasis upon the determination of standard costs is given to the development of accounting at the University of Pittsburgh, through the work of Professor Charles Reitell. Various departments and courses in management also are interested in the subject of cost accounting, because of its relation to budgeting and operating control.

d. Auditing is another division of the field of accounting to which most (34) of the schools devote a separate course.

e. Income tax problems and procedure constitute a part of the work of the accountant separately considered in 31 schools.

f. Accounting systems of various types of business loom next in order of importance on the basis of separate attention. Twenty institutions offer a course under this title.

g. The problems of the certified public accountant are considered separately at 15 schools.

h. Fourteen schools offer courses in accounting problems, in which particular aspects of accountancy are considered through the case method.

i. A number of schools (12) consider in a separate course the various systems of governmental accounting—state, city, county, and federal.

j. Nine schools consider separately the problems of accounting from the managerial standpoint.

k. Nine schools offer courses in the analysis of financial state-

TABLE LXXXVI. ACCOUNTING IN GRADUATE SCHOOLS

School	Total class hours graduate	Field of specialization
Dartmouth	270	yes
Harvard	540	yes
Michigan	432	yes
Stanford	not given	yes
Columbia	1,134	yes
Illinois	1,080	yes

ments, and in eight of these cases the course is given by the accounting group.

As previously intimated, a number of other courses in accounting are to be found. In most cases, these are of a specialized nature, involving the application of the principles of accounting in some restricted field, such as retail accounting, public utility accounting, investment accounting, fiduciary accounting, and the like.

Accounting in the Graduate Schools

Accounting is a basic element in the work of the graduate schools of business. It should also be noted that several of the larger institutions included in the preceding table show very substantial graduate offerings in accounting for graduate students. Table LXXXVI presents certain data concerning courses in accounting in graduate schools.

The titles of the courses offered in those schools to graduate students do not differ from those of the undergraduate schools.

TABLE LXXXVII. BANKING AND FINANCE IN THE UNDERGRADUATE SCHOOLS OF THE AMERICAN ASSOCIATION

Schools	Credit hours required				Money and banking	Distribution of requirements			
	Total credit hours under-graduate	Freshman	Sophomore	Upper class		Corporation or business finance	Finance: administration and management	Investments	Field of specialization
Alabama	306			144	54	54		36	Yes
Boston	360			72	72				Yes
California	288			45^a					Banking
Chicago	360			114			45^a		Finance
Cincinnati	288		66	144	90	48		42	No
Columbia	324			54	72	72			Yes
Denver	216		54	108	54	54	54		No
Florida	324			108	54				Yes
Georgia	216			108	108	108			Yes
Georgia Tech	540		108	54	108	54			Yes
Illinois	486		54	180	72	108			Yes
Indiana	270			54	72	54			Yes
Iowa	216			126	54	54			Yes
Kansas	252			108	54	54			Finance
Kentucky	234			108	54	54			Banking
Marquette	342			126	54		72		Yes
Minnesota	504			72	36	36			Finance
Missouri	450			144	90	54			Yes with Accounting
Nebraska	342			108	54	54			Yes
New York	1,404	72^b		72^e		72	72		Yes several Curricula
N. Carolina	360			120	60	60			Yes
N. Dakota	216			108	54	54			Yes
Northwestern	540		54	54	54	54			Finance
Ohio	840			120	60	60			Yes
Oklahoma	468		36	c		36			Finance
Oregon	444		90	120	60	90	60		Finance
Pennsylvania	1,350		108	54	108				Yes several Curricula
Pittsburgh	594			108	54^e	54			Finance
S. California	522			54	108				Yes
S. Methodist	324		54	108	54				Yes
Syracuse	588			126	72				Finance
Texas	414			108		54			Yes
Tulane	288			40^a	54	108			Banking
U. of Washington	636			108	40^a				Business Finance
Virginia	324			108	108				Banking
Washington U.	432			108		108			Finance
Wash. and Lee	216			162	54	108			Yes
Wisconsin	342			54	54	54	54		Finance

a. Alternate elective.
b. In most of the first year curricula.
c. Varies from one major to another.

d. The courses listed are generally taken.
e. In most upper class curricula.

BANKING AND FINANCE

Banking and Finance constitute another well defined and well developed field in collegiate business curricula. All of the 42 Association schools offer courses, and about half of the schools have separate departments or groupings of courses, under this general heading. Banking and finance or finance are the names usually given to such departments or groupings. Table LXXXVII brings together certain data concerning the development and status of banking and finance in the 38 undergraduate schools.

Rôle in the Undergraduate Curricula

The questions most likely to be raised concerning the development of this field in the business schools will be answered at this point, on the basis of the announced offerings of the member schools.

Extent of Specialization

Every one of the Association schools offers opportunity for some degree of specialization in banking and finance. Thirty-six of the 38 undergraduate schools indicate definite curricula in this general field. The two schools not included are Cincinnati and Denver. It must not be inferred that the subject is neglected at these institutions. Cincinnati, with a prescribed program, requires more credit hours in this subject of all students than any other member school. Although there is no announced curriculum in banking and finance at Denver, liberal upper class (usually senior) electives do permit some specialization in this as well as in other fields.

Most of the schools combine banking and finance into one specialty; 11 speak of finance; five of banking; Missouri combines banking, finance, and accounting into one curriculum; New York distinguishes between banking and finance, and offers other specialized curricula in the field; and in the Wharton School of the University of Pennsylvania offers separate groupings in (a) banking and real estate, (b) brokerage, and (c) corporation finance and investments.

General Requirements in Banking and Finance

Thirty-four out of 38 have an absolute requirement of some work in this field for all commerce students. The other four—

California, Chicago, Oklahoma, and the University of Washington —make it an alternate requirement with many of the students selecting it.

Of the 34 schools, there are nine—Boston, Georgia, Pennsylvania, Pittsburgh, Southern Methodist, Syracuse, Tulane, Virginia, and Wisconsin—that require but one course of all students. The other nineteen require more than one course of all students. In other words, not only is banking and finance a general requirement, but there is a considerable amount of it generally required.

Particular Courses Required

a. Money and banking is the commonly accepted introduction to this field. Thirty-one schools require this course of all students —Alabama, Boston, Cincinnati, Columbia, Denver, Florida, Georgia, Georgia Tech, Illinois, Indiana, Iowa, Kansas, Kentucky, Marquette, Minnesota, Missouri, Nebraska, North Carolina, North Dakota, Northwestern, Ohio, Pennsylvania, Pittsburgh, Southern California, Southern Methodist, Syracuse, Texas, Virginia, University of Washington, Washington and Lee, and Wisconsin. Florida's course is known as the financial organization of society; Texas' course as short-term finance; Pennsylvania's course on finance, five hours, one semester, is in part (about half) a discussion of money and banking. This course is usually given in the sophomore year.

b. Next to money and banking in frequency is the course in corporation finance. Fourteen schools require this course of all students—Alabama, Columbia, Georgia Tech, Illinois, Iowa, Kentucky, Minnesota, Missouri, North Carolina, North Dakota, Northwestern, Ohio, Southern California, Texas. In addition, much of the material in Chicago's course on the manager's administration of finance, Florida's financial management, and Marquette's financial administration is similar to that included in corporation finance. This course is usually given in the junior year.

c. A third generally found requirement is in business finance which ten schools require of all students—Cincinnati, Denver, Indiana, Kansas, Nebraska, New York, Pennsylvania (part of course), Tulane, Washington University, and Washington and Lee. The course is given usually in the junior year.

Business finance, in some institutions, includes the field of cor-

poration finance, in others it differs in that it is the general and introductory course while corporation finance is the subsequent, more specific, and more specialized course.

Courses in banking and finance are required in various specialized curricula in many of the schools, in addition to the general requirements noted above. These curricula usually are in real estate, insurance, accounting, management, and marketing.

In summary, it may be said that a substantial amount of work in banking and finance is required in virtually all of the schools of all students, that the most frequently found courses are in money and banking and in corporation or business finance, and that these courses are usually given in the junior year.

Nature of the Courses Offered

It must be noted that departments of banking and finance often include courses other than those directly a part of that field. Courses in insurance, real estate, and public finance are most often the ones included. Since these groups are separately dealt with, they are not included in the discussion at this point.

As to what the courses in the field of banking and finance should be there seems to be considerable agreement. There are several standardized courses which are given at most institutions.

a. Money and banking. Virtually very member school devotes a separate course or a well defined part of a course to this general descriptive analysis of our financial institutions and organization. This invariably constitutes the introductory course in the field, unless there is a general survey introductory course of a more comprehensive nature.

b. The study of the financing of business enterprises and the problems which arise constitute a second field very generally covered. Twenty-seven schools give courses dealing wholly or in part with corporation finance. Seventeen schools give courses dealing with the general field of business finance.

c. The field of investments, together with investment banking, is dealt with in separate courses at 37 different schools.

d. Banking is dealt with separately at 27 institutions. Courses are usually listed under the terms banking, banking management, banking administration, and the like.

e. Credit is another subject whose importance is rather gener-

ally recognized. Nineteen institutions give separate courses in credit management or credit collections; six give separate courses in bank credit.

f. The international aspects of financial operations are considered in separate courses at a number of schools. Eighteen give courses in foreign exchange. Six give courses in international finance or banking. Three give courses on foreign banking systems.

g. Research as an undergraduate venture in banking and finance is provided for definitely at 11 schools.

h. The Federal reserve system, the money market, and a consideration of trust funds are each recognized as subjects for special courses at seven schools, while eight schools offer a course on the financial history of the United States.

i. Outside of these, there is a considerable range of other specialized courses—co-operative banking (1), bank portfolios (3), stock and produce exchanges (6), bond salesmanship (1), bond house organization and management (1), investment analysis (4), comparative finance (1), ocean shipping finance (5), law of banking (1).

j. In addition to these courses more or less directly in the field; courses such as business cycles (4), mathematics of finance, and analysis of business and financial statements are, at certain schools, developed by the banking and finance group.

A Service Course in Banking and Finance

One other course that has come to be offered in this field calls for special comment. It might be called a course in personal finance, developed as a service course for general university purposes. Since it is generally recognized that the so-called educated classes furnish an undue proportion of victims to unscrupulous investment agencies, a course of this nature offered generally to college students may render a uniquely valuable service to them.

Several schools have sensed this opportunity. The School of Business Administration at the University of Michigan offers a course called "personal budgeting, savings and investments." Its general purpose is to give a foundation for the intelligent management of one's personal financial affairs. It is designed and offered

for students entering the professions of law, engineering, medicine, dentistry, farming, and education.

The course is given in two parts. First, there is a brief introduction to the elements of corporation finance, leading up to an analysis of corporation bonds and stocks as media for investment. The different types of investments or savings funds are analyzed; the relative merits of savings accounts, local mortgages and bonds, government bonds, municipal bonds, foreign government bonds, real estate, railroad, industrial, public utility bonds and stocks. Some attention is also given to fraudulent securities and how to detect them. The second part is devoted to an analysis of the

TABLE LXXXVIII. BANKING AND FINANCE IN GRADUATE SCHOOLS

School	Total class hours graduate	Field of specialization
Dartmouth	234	yes
Harvard	432	Commercial banking
		Investment banking
Michigan	396	yes
Stanford	not given	yes
Columbia	918	yes
Illinois	900	yes
Pennsylvania	432	yes

proportion of each individual's income which should be devoted to insurance, savings, and the various elements of personal expenses.

The School of Business Administration at Oregon offers a course dealing with "the principles governing the proper investment of savings in building and loan associations, savings banks, insurance, real estate mortagages, stocks and bonds."

Banking and Finance in the Graduate Schools

Courses in banking and finance loom large in the offerings of the business schools to graduate students. Table LXXXVIII indicates the development of this field in certain graduate schools.

Of the above, Harvard distinguishes between commercial banking and investment banking to the point of establishing differentiated groups of courses. The commercial banking group is planned to give to the student a knowledge of industrial management and corporate organization and methods, a knowledge needed by the commercial bank executive in order to maintain sound relations between corporations and the bank. The investment group, on the

other hand, concerns itself with the problems of the investment banker, his relations to industry and to investors, and to internal problems of management.

BUSINESS LAW

In the conduct of large scale operations, carried on over long periods of time, rules of the game come inevitably to develop. In certain aspects of society, these rules become institutionalized in the form of laws. Business is an illustration in point, and its institutionalized rules constitute the field of business law. Since its implications touch virtually every business and every business man, instruction in business law has come to be recognized as an integral part of business training. To what extent courses in business law have been developed, the sort and variety of courses offered, the extent to which these courses are required and at what place in the curriculum—these are the questions to be considered at this point, basing the answer on the facts as found in the 38 undergraduate member schools, some of which are presented in tabular form in Table LXXXIX.

Extent of Development in the Business Schools

Table LXXXIX shows the development of the subject in the separate schools, as measured in terms of undergraduate credit hours. Pennsylvania, Denver, and Pittsburgh lead, in the order named, in amount of instruction offered in business law. The Georgia Institute of Technology, Southern California, and Oklahoma also show heavy offerings in this subject. Most of the other schools offer from two to four semesters of work.

Other criteria of its development are to be found in the fact that 13 schools (Alabama, Boston, Chicago, Columbia, Denver, Georgia, New York, Northwestern, Oklahoma, Pennsylvania, Pittsburgh, Southern California, and Texas) have separate departments of business law. It will be noted that 15 schools (Alabama, Florida, Illinois, Indiana, Kentucky, Marquette, Nebraska, North Carolina, North Dakota, Ohio, Oregon, Southern California, University of Washington, Washington University, and Washington and Lee) have set up separate six-year curricula combining the work of the commerce and the law schools. The first three years are spent in the schools of commerce, and the second three in the law school.

The commerce degree is usually given at the end of the fourth year (occasionally at the end of the fifth) and the law degree at the end of the sixth year. In addition to these schools, Pennsylvania offers a four-year course in its school of commerce known as the "preparation for the law" curriculum, and Chicago, North

TABLE LXXXIX. BUSINESS LAW IN THE UNDERGRADUATE SCHOOLS OF THE AMERICAN ASSOCIATION

Schools	Total credit hours under-graduate	Credit hours required			Field of special-ization	Combined law and commerce curriculum
		Freshman	Sophomore	Upper class		
Alabama	108			108		Yes
Boston	252			180		
California	216			180		
Chicago	240			180	Yes	
Cincinnati	48			48		
Columbia	288			108		
Denver	414	90	90	36		Yes
Florida	108			108		
Georgia	108			108		
Georgia Tech	324	108	108			
Illinois	216			108		Yes
Indiana	180			108		Yes
Iowa	108			108		
Kansas	108			108		
Kentucky	108			108		Yes
Marquette	180			108		Yes
Minnesota	108			108		
Missouri	54			54		
Nebraska	126			108		Yes
New York	216					
North Carolina	120			120	Yes	Yes
North Dakota	180			108		Yes
Northwestern	144			72		
Ohio	216			72		Yes
Oklahoma	306			*	Yes	
Oregon	144			144		Yes
Pennsylvania	450	90			Yes	
Pittsburgh	360			108	Yes	
Southern California	324		108			Yes
Southern Methodist	108			108		
Syracuse	144			72		
Texas	144			108		
Tulane	72					
University of Washington	168		108			Yes
Virginia	108			108		
Washington University	162			108		Yes
Washington and Lee	108			108		Yes
Wisconsin	108					

* Some business law must be taken by all commerce students.

Carolina, Oklahoma, and Pittsburgh offer specialized curricula in business law.

General Requirements in Business Law

All but two of the 38 member schools require instruction in business law of all students. The exceptions are Tulane and Wisconsin. Business law is among the elective courses at Tulane specified in the upper years.

Thirty-three schools confine their requirement in business law to one year or a part thereof. The exact amount of this particular requirement is rather uniform. Twenty-four of the 33 schools require a three-hour per week course throughout the year; four schools, a two-hour course throughout the year; three schools a five-hour course throughout the year; one school a five-hour course for one semester; and one school a three-hour one term course. Three schools—Boston, California, and Georgia Institute of Technology—extend their business law requirements for all students over two years. One school—Denver—extends it over four years.

Place in Curricula of Business Law Requirements

At what place, or year, in the curricula of these schools is instruction in business law required? In the case of those schools extending the required work over more than a year, where does it begin?

Business law is primarily an upper class study. Of the 36 schools, 32 begin business law in the upper two years. Only three schools attempt generally to teach business law to freshmen—Denver, Georgia Insititute of Technology, and Pennsylvania. New York University also includes it in some of the freshman curricula. Two schools—Southern California and the University of Washington—place it in the sophomore year. Fifteen schools particularly specify the junior year—Boston, California, Columbia, Indiana, Minnesota, Nebraska, Northwestern, Ohio State, Oregon, Pittsburgh, Syracuse, Texas, Virginia, Washington University, and Washington and Lee. Nine schools indicate the senior year—Cincinnati, Florida, Illinois (usually), Iowa (usually), Kansas, Kentucky, Marquette, North Carolina, and Southern Methodist. Eight schools indicate it as an upper class study without specifying the year—Alabama, Chicago, Georgia, Missouri, North Dakota, Oklahoma, Tulane (elective), and Wisconsin.

There is a general consensus of opinion that courses in business law should be given to upper classmen—that lower classmen, particularly freshmen are not sufficiently informed as yet concerning the organization or structure of the business world to discuss intelligently questions of the legal regulation and control of the details of its functioning. Such justification, pedagogically speaking, as is urged for its inclusion in the freshman year and to a

certain extent in the sophomore year, is based on the contention that it serves an orientation purpose, i.e., that students become familiar with the business world because of such a course. The obvious reply is that, important as such orientation to the business world is, this is no more the function of a course in business law than of any other course, and naturally somewhat less than that of some other courses.

It is interesting, and perhaps significant to add that in the graduate and undergraduate-graduate schools, business law is an advanced study. At Dartmouth, it is given the second year; at Harvard, the second year; at Michigan, the second year.

Nature of Business Law Courses

Most of the schools offer one or two general courses in business law. What are the subjects covered in this course or two? The content is rather standardized. It includes elementary studies of law, contracts, agencies, partnerships, corporations, bailments, sales, negotiable instruments, bankruptcy. That is, such instruction deals with those ordinary business relations, business forms, business organizations, and points of litigation in business with which business men come in contact.

Beyond these general courses, there are a variety of courses, chiefly dealing with the law in specialized fields such as property, banking, market practices, insurance, railway law, maritime law, public utilities, audits and collections, traffic, poverty, labor, and income tax. Of these, the most frequently found are those dealing with the field of insurance, marketing, and property.

To what extent is the law of labor recognized in these courses? At two schools, courses or parts of courses dealing with the law of labor are offered by the department or teachers of business law. A number of other schools include courses dealing with labor legislation, but given as a part of the work in general economics or personnel administration.

To lawyers, the law of labor is not a promising field for practice nor an alluring field for specialization. Perhaps this explains largely its lack of development in both business and law schools. To students of commerce, on the other hand, the situation is completely reversed. To a large extent it is true that any appreciable success of the business school graduate will result in his becoming

an employer of labor, and a substantial part of present day legislation deals with the problems growing out of the relations of employer and employee. Moreover, the law of labor becomes particularly important because it is on these legal questions that the employer is least likely to consult professional advice.

The general lines of development of such a course for business students are indicated in two texts of recent years. *A Selection of Cases and Other Authorities on Labor Laws* by Francis B. Sayre, Harvard University Press, 1922, includes such topics as: legality of combination, federal jurisdiction over labor disputes, legality of means used by labor organizations, lockouts, boycotts, black list, union label, use of injunction against labor organizations, trade agreements, regulatory labor legislation, compulsory arbitration and the industrial court, and workmen's compensation laws.

Selected Cases and Other Authorities on Industrial Law by E. F. Albertsworth, Northwestern University Press, Chicago, 1928, includes relations between employer and employee, personal injury, disease and death of employees; relations between producer and consumer; the producer in combination with other competitors; relations between industry and the state, involving relations between employer and employee, and the relations of producers and the state.

Albertsworth uses the term "industrial law." He says:

> The present era is one of industrialism . . . . . By industrialism is meant the organized effort of human society thru machine methods to master and employ physical and natural phenomena in order to meet human wants. In truth, it may be said that the civilized world is in the throes of a second industrial revolution. It is at a turning point in history, due to the tremendous transformation in the conditions of human life and in the relations of human societies to each other (p. ix) . . . . Attention on the part of the legal order to those legal phenomena that are symptomatic of industrialism, that are concomitants or by-products of it, is imperative. (p. ix)
> Industrial law would seem to be both the most convenient and at the same time inclusive term which unifies the various legal phenomena of industrialism. (p. ix) . . . . From a broad standpoint, the term is inclusive of all economic and legal activities of modern industry, whether based upon the manifold situations in industry out of which the economic problems arise for solution by the legal order, or regarded

from the viewpoint of the legal doctrines, dogmas, and institutions that are applicable to industrial society. (pp. ix and x) In view of the economic factors which are coefficients of industrialism, the following legal phenomena may be justifiably considered as embraced within the convenient term of 'industrial law.'

A—Application of unique or special legal principles in making recompense for injuries sustained by the employee growing out of the industry in which and during which he is engaged.

B—The mass of statutes and court decisions dealing with the trade disputes element in the picture of industrialism.

From the functional standpoint, it is believed that the field of industrial law properly may be divided into three broad divisions; (1) relations between employer and employee; (2) relations between producer and consumer; and (3) relations between industry and the state. (p. xiii)

Dean John H. Wigmore, in the introduction of this book, calls it "A symbol of the transitional epoch, now with us, in juristic studies." It is based on the view that a single broad complex of economic interests and conflicts may be made the subject of an analysis of all the legal rules, however varied and separate in legal principle, that may have attached themselves to that group of economic facts. (p. xv)

It is a trend of the times—to compel "a study of law in the light of the background in Economics." (p. xv) This trend is to get away from the consideration of branches of science as separate compartments, with insistence that each compartment be studied by itself, with no one looking into any compartment but the one to which he was professionally committeed. Now, all that is past. The partitions of the compartments are all broken down. The distinct spaces are there yet; but no one can devote himself to a particular one without having an intelligent acquaintance with the adjacent ones. It is an era when Form, in the philosophical sense, has ceased to be decisive—an era of Formlessness in science and philosophy (and of Informality in behavior!). The mathematician must also be something of a logician, a chemist, and a physicist. The chemist must also be a physicist and a biologist. The biologist must be something of a chemist and a geologist. And the jurist must be something of a philosopher, a sociologist, an economist—and what else? (p. xv)

The Larger Aspects of Business Law Teaching

An unusually broad conception of business law and its function in the collegiate school of business, making it a part of the larger

problem of social control, has been emphasized by Dean W. H. Spencer, of the University of Chicago. In the preface to his *Law and Business*[2] he writes:

> Speaking in general terms, the real purpose of teaching law in a school is, or should be, to bring to the future business man a certain awareness of the larger problem of social control. Whether he likes it or not, he must play the game according to the rules. He must therefore be brought to a realization that one of the conditions of carrying on business in our present economic order is that he submit himself and his business to the control of society. Law is one of the most important instrumentalities of social control and it is for this reason that students preparing for business should be given instruction in it.
>
> More specifically, there are several objectives which should be reached by a proper presentation of these materials. (1) This study should introduce the student to the whole field of the law, giving him a working knowledge of legal phraseology, and prepare him for the study of case material. (2) It should assist him in visualizing more clearly the structure of modern society, by showing him the part which law and legal institutions have played in its development. (3) The study should give the student a practical knowledge of the legal devices which business men use in the administration of their affairs. (4) It should give him an appreciation of certain portions of the law which directly and intimately throw around him the lines of social control. These rules of law, commanding this, prohibiting that, and permitting the other, are important because they mark out definite limits within which business men must formulate their policies. (5) It would seem not too much to hope that upon the completion of the study of these materials the student will have become fairly skillful in analyzing court decisions. This desideratum, if realized, should prove to be of the greatest value to the future business man. The power to analyze a court decision will not only open up and make available for him the whole field of reported cases, but will also give him a certain mental outlook and resiliency which will aid him in adjusting himself to his social environment.

To the student of business curricula, Dean Spencer's contention raises an important problem, *viz.*, that of the integration of the work in business law with the larger field of the interrelations

---

[2] Spencer, W. H., *Law and Business,* Volume I, University of Chicago Press, Chicago, 1921, p. xii.

between business and social control. Unless one thinks within rather narrow departmental lines, this problem cannot be avoided indefinitely.

BUSINESS AND THE PUBLIC

Business operations are a part of the larger life of society. Its activities influence that larger life in diverse ways and at many points. The relation of business and society constitutes a problem fundamentally important to both.

Collegiate schools of business have developed out of a social science background. Because of the social interests of these parent studies, it was natural that some consideration should be given in the curricula of these schools to the public or social aspects of business.

Table LXV in Chapter XI, showing the total undergraduate credit hours by general subjects, shows the courses listed under the heading of "Business and the Public" as twelfth on that list with a total of 3,815 class hours. Four more or less distinct kinds of courses are grouped under that general heading. Their enumeration will indicate the general meaning given to the heading as used. In the order of numerical importance these four kinds of courses are: first, those covering the general field of economic and social reform, constituting 41.6 per cent of the total number of class hours; second, those which concern themselves with the problems presented by trusts and various combinations of business units, accounting for 29.1 per cent of the total; third, those dealing with the general problem of the relationship between business and government, comprehending 21.6 per cent; and, finally, those courses dealing with the self-regulatory aspects of business, usually labelled as "business ethics," and amounting to 7.5 per cent of the total.

Courses in the Field of Economic and Social Reform

The customary titles of the courses in this group are such as these: "contemporary theories of social reform," "types of economic organization," "socialism and economic reform," "economic and social reform movements," "the distribution of wealth and income," "economic institutions," etc. Where there are some differences in the content of these courses, the chief thought underlying their development is a consideration of various business and industrial phenomena from the standpoint of the play of economic

forces, or social ideals, or public interest. Not infrequently, current practices are considered in relation to primary factors of economic organization.

Courses on Trusts and Business Combinations

This group consists of courses concerning themselves somewhat specifically with the regulatory problems of big business. Different kinds of economic concentration are surveyed, competitive methods of big business are analyzed, and considerable attention is given to the attitude of law and government. The titles of these courses are fairly well standardized, being usually something like "corporation and trust problems," "industrial combinations and trusts," "industrial consolidation," or "monopolies and trusts."

Courses on the Public Regulation of Business

This type of course seems to have gone out of those in the preceding group, from which they differ in being more broad and comprehensive. Such growth has come, in some instances, by way of the department of economics, considering regulation as a problem in business development. In other cases, these courses have developed by way of the department of political science, viewing regulation of business as one of the problems and trials of government. The latter source seems to be the more prevalent.

The customary titles of these courses include "public regulation of business," "social control of business enterprise," "business and government," and "the public control of business."

Courses on Business Ethics

It is a significant fact that a number of schools have come to develop formal instruction on the ethical aspects of business conduct. Such instruction varies from a few lectures to a fully developed course. These courses are given under various terms such as "business ethics," "business procedure," "business conduct," and "business standards." In content, they deal with such matters as standards of right and wrong, and of good form as applied to business, sanctions under which business institutions and methods have developed, ideals of justice in the distribution of wealth—in short, an examination, wholly or in part, of the self-regulatory functions of business.

tion of terminology, the facts concerning the development of these subjects in the Association schools will be summarized.

Rôle in the Curricula of the Business Schools

The relative importance of distribution, on the basis of the total number of undergraduate class hours of instruction offered, is shown in Table LXVIII, as ranking second, being exceeded only by accounting. All of the 42 member schools have courses in this field. Half of them have separate departments or groupings of such courses. These developments are listed under various terms. Marketing easily is the most popular, and the development of the field at 17 schools is under that term. Other schools use the terms commerce and merchandising to indicate the work in distribution. At 14 schools, all such courses are listed under economics, or business administration, or business organization and management. Table XC indicates the development of the field of distribution as a whole, as well as of its divisions in the 38 undergraduate schools.

Examination of the Table XC will show that courses in some phase of distribution are generally included among the requirements. For the most part, such requirement is in the upper years. Boston, in its "Principles of Business" course, explanation of which has been made, Cincinnati, Kentucky, New York, and Tulane are the only schools which have placed such work among the lower class requirements. For the most part, required courses in this field are taken in the junior year.

This required work, it will be observed, generally is in the field of marketing, involving ordinarily a descriptive analysis of the channels of trade and distribution of goods between producer and consumer. Marketing also is a core course in the curricula of the four graduate schools.

The extent to which some one or more aspects of the field of distribution are recognized as fields of specialization is another measure indicative of its rôle or status in the present development of business education. It will be observed that all but five of the 38 undergraduate schools make distribution a field of specialization. At 27 of the schools, there is but one specialized curriculum in the field, and in most of these cases the term marketing is used.

Other terms are advertising, advertising and selling, merchandising, merchandising and advertising, and commerce.

At five schools, there are two fields of specialization—Alabama (advertising and merchandising); Minnesota (advertising and merchandising); North Carolina (marketing and retail merchandising, and advertising and salesmanship); Southern California (marketing and retail merchandising); and Syracuse (advertising and selling, and commerce). At three schools there are three fields—Nebraska (retail merchandising, sales management, advertising); Northwestern (advertising, sales administration, and merchandising); and the University of Washington (marketing, merchandising, and advertising). At one school, New York, there are four—marketing, advertising, salesmanship, and retailing.

Nature of the Courses Given in Distribution

More class hours of instruction are offered in marketing than in any other phase of distribution. The courses generally given in marketing include the following:

1. Marketing. An introductory descriptive course, dealing with the elements, functions, structure, and organization of the field of marketing. Twenty-three schools give such a course.

2. Principles of Marketing. In a number of schools, this course is similar to the one above. In other cases, it combines the introductory description of the market with a survey of the entire field. It is either a basic course or a general survey course, depending on the stage of development of the subject. Eleven schools have such courses.

3. Market Analysis is given at eight schools. This usually is a course emphasizing methodology (technique, principles of analysis) with reference to different types of problems and products. Its purpose usually is a measuring or analysis of the effectiveness of distribution methods, using the analysis as a basis for the determination of distribution policies and methods, estimating and analyzing consumer demand, discovering new sources of demand.

4. A seminar or research in marketing is specified as a separate course in 11 schools. This is a relatively high percentage. Such courses deal with a variety of problems, including the matter of market analysis, just referred to.

5. Market management or administration is separately considered at eight schools.

6. Marketing methods are dealt with separately at four schools.

7. Eleven schools give separate courses on the marketing of specific products or group of products such as the marketing of agricultural products, perishable food products, raw materials, products of the northwest, etc.

Other separate courses include: co-operative marketing, marketing policies, the market as a social institution, terminal marketing, marketing campaigns, the law of marketing, export marketing, etc.

The field of selling is fairly well standardized at its present stage of development. The courses now given follow:

1. Salesmanship or principles of salesmanship as an introductory or survey course is given at 19 schools.

2. Sales management or sales administration is dealt with separately at 29 different schools.

3. There seems to be but one research course in the field, and that is at North Carolina—research in sales relations.

Advertising is widely developed, but apparently less standardized than the other fields, both in content and terminology. Some of these courses deal with advertising as a business, with consideration of the technique, others, more with the principles of the subject, considered from the standpoint of the business executive.

1. Thirty-three schools give a general introductory or survey course in advertising in the school of business. In several other schools, such as Missouri, the developments in this field are not in or by the school of commerce.

2. Advertising campaigns are dealt with separately at ten schools.

3. Retail store advertising is a separate course at six schools.

4. Copy writing is separately dealt with in nine schools—Boston, Marquette, Minnesota, Nebraska, New York, Northwestern, Oregon, Southern California, and Texas.

5. Other specialized courses deal with such subjects as direct mail and mail order advertising, advertising design, advertising agency procedure, advertising to women, newspaper advertising, evaluation of advertising media, space selling, business paper advertising, advertising in other countries, window and store display advertising, etc.

Retailing or Merchandising. It is in this division of the field of distribution that questions of terminology and delimiting of subject matter have arisen. Retailing, retail stores management, retail merchandising, and merchandising are terms used at various schools to mean the same or different courses. Being a relatively new field, there is less unanimity and standardization concerning these matters. An examination of the catalogue offerings shows:

1. Retail merchandising is easily the most emphasized aspect of this field. Twenty-eight schools offer courses in retail merchandising, retailing, and retail store management.

2. Eight schools offer general courses in merchandising. These are conceived of either as courses in the general organization of selling effort, with special reference to sales policies, sales planning, and sales control; or as courses dealing with the principles and problems of retail store management—buying, planning, control, sales promotion, pricing, stock turnover, personnel administration, etc.

3. Other scattering courses offered include import merchandising, export merchandising, real estate merchandising, economics of consumption, economics of fashion, economics of retailing, trade investigations, analysis and interpretation of consumer demand. Credit and collections, and credit management are included in some schools in the merchandising offerings.

Interrelations Between Distribution and Other Specialized Curricula

What curricula in other fields of specialization require courses in distribution?

a. Foreign trade at eight schools—Alabama, Boston, Columbia, Marquette, North Carolina, Northwestern, Southern California, and Virginia.

b. Banking and Finance at six schools—Alabama, Boston, Georgia, Georgia Tech, Northwestern, and Pennsylvania.

c. Insurance at five schools—Alabama, Illinois, North Carolina, North Dakota, and Pennsylvania.

d. Real Estate—Alabama and Pennsylvania.

e. Accounting—Boston and Northwestern.

f. Transportation—Alabama and North Carolina.

g. Industrial Management—Alabama and Georgia.

What other courses are drawn upon by the distribution curricula?

An examination of the curricula in distribution shows them to be unusually broad and liberal, i.e., on the basis of the range of other courses and departments included; contrasting decidedly in this respect with the curricula in accounting, for example.

a. Departments of Psychology are drawn upon for courses in the psychology of advertising and selling at fourteen institutions—Boston, Denver, Indiana, Iowa, Kansas, Kentucky, Michigan, Minnesota, North Carolina, Northwestern, Ohio, Southern Methodist, Syracuse, and Texas. New York University should also be included, the course being given in the department of marketing.

b. Statistics is required, either elementary statistics or business cycles, at eleven schools—Columbia, Harvard, Iowa, Kansas, Marquette, North Carolina, North Dakota, Ohio, Southern California, Texas, and the University of Washington. It is usually in connection with specialization in marketing that these courses are required.

c. At eleven schools, banking and finance are required. They are Alabama, Georgia, Georgia Tech, Iowa, New York, North Carolina, North Dakota, Pennsylvania, Southern California, Syracuse, and University of Washington. These courses are usually required where the emphasis is upon merchandising.

d. Courses in journalism are required in connection with courses in advertising at nine schools—Alabama, Indiana, Kansas, Michigan, Missouri, Nebraska, Northwestern, Syracuse, and University of Washington. At Indiana, Kansas, Missouri, all of the work in advertising is developed by the department or school of journalism, which are outside of the school of commerce.

e. Eight schools require transportation courses usually in connection with specialization in marketing. These schools are Alabama, Columbia, Iowa, Kentucky, Marquette, Pennsylvania, Syracuse, University of Washington.

f. English courses of an advanced and adapted nature are required at eight schools, usually in connection with work in advertising and selling. These schools are Boston, California, Kansas, Marquette, New York, Northwestern, Syracuse, Texas. It is curious how little public speaking is emphasized in these courses.

g. Law is included at eight schools, usually in connection with marketing—Georgia, Kansas, Kentucky, Marquette, New York, North Carolina, North Dakota, and Ohio.

h.   Seven schools require work in foreign or international trade, usually in connection with marketing—Florida, Georgia, Harvard, Iowa, Northwestern, Syracuse and Texas.

i.   Four schools require geography in connection with marketing—Florida, Michigan, Nebraska, and Ohio.

j.   Accounting is required in connection with merchandising at five schools—Georgia Tech, Harvard, Kentucky, New York, and North Carolina.

Courses in art (advertising) at California; insurance (merchandising) at Pennsylvania; management (merchandising) at Alabama; sociology (merchandising) at Nebraska; and the economics of consumption at Columbia, Michigan, and the University of Washington are also included.

Summary

Surveying the field of distribution as a whole, one is impressed with a certain lack of co-ordination. Economists generally offer the courses in marketing; psychologists seem to predominate in selling; journalists and psychologists abound in the field of advertising; and to all of these is added the viewpoint of the retail store executive. One is particularly impressed with differences in personnel, in viewpoint, in sympathy and approach, of the marketing group on the one hand, and the advertising and selling group on the other.

It seems especially undesirable to increase this lack of coordination by having these courses given in several departments, or even schools, as at Kansas and Missouri. There may be an element of strength in the diverse approaches of the present situation. This is particularly true in view of the newness of the field and its undoubted present importance. It does seem, however, that the time for a higher degree of co-ordination is here.

FOREIGN TRADE AND SERVICE

A total of 128 colleges and universities offered one or more courses in foreign trade and foreign service in 1928, according to a report of the Federal Bureau of Education. This report shows further that 240 members of the instructional staffs are assigned to these courses; and that 372 such courses are offered. There are 7,524 students, including duplicates, enrolled in these courses in the 82 institutions that reported their enrollments. In 4 additional institutions that did not report enrollments by courses, there are 779 students majoring in the foreign trade and foreign service curricula, making a total of 8,303 students, including duplicates.

Of the 128 institutions reporting courses in foreign trade and foreign service, 65 reported only one course in this field; 27, 2 courses; 8, 3 courses; 8, 4 courses; 2, 5 courses; 5, 7 courses; 2, 8 courses; and 9 reported 10 or more courses.

The compliation shows further that in each of 99 of the 128 institutions only 1 instructor offers courses in foreign trade and foreign service; in 11 institutions, 2 instructors; in 3 institutions, 3 instructors; in 7 institutions, 4 instructors; in 3 institutions, 5 instructors; and in 5 institutions there are 6, 7, 11, 14, and 29 instructors, respectively, of foreign trade and foreign service courses.[3]

Rôle in Business School Curricula

The present study is concerned particularly with the rôle played by courses in foreign trade in the curricula of the member schools of the American Association. An examination of their offerings shows that 33 of the undergraduate and three of the graduate schools offer courses in this field. The chief offerings, on the basis of credit hours are at the University of Washington, California, Northwestern, and Oregon.

There is a separate department in foreign trade at three undergraduate schools. Elsewhere such courses are grouped with transportation, industry, merchandising, commerce, or general economics. The latter is the more prevalent arrangement, indicating usually a development not sufficient for separate differentiation.

Opportunity for specialization in the foreign field is rather general. Ten schools offer opportunity for specialization in foreign trade; six in foreign trade and consular service; four in foreign service; and three in foreign commerce. The number of students specializing in this field has not been large in the past.

Courses in foreign trade are not required as a rule in the curricula of other fields of specialization, nor do they constitute a general requirement.

---

[3] Malott, J. O., *Commercial Education Circular, No. 28.*

Nature of Courses Offered

Analyzing the various courses offered in the field of foreign trade in the member schools, eight rather definite kinds can be found.

Of these, general survey courses are the most frequent. This is natural, since about half of the schools giving work in the field offer but one course. Akin to these are the courses which deal with the "principles" of foreign trade.

Next, in order of frequency, are courses which deal with regional markets. Ten schools offer courses of this nature. The regional markets dealt with are the Far East, Latin America, Europe, etc. There is considerable emphasis upon South American trade and its significance to the United States.

Studies in foreign trade practices, techniques, or methods are offered as separate courses at nine schools, as are also courses dealing with importing and exporting.

Courses in the financial aspects of foreign trade, dealing with the principles and practices of foreign exchange; marketing methods, involving the study of channels of foreign trade; and export traffic management are considered separately at four schools each.

Foreign service or trade curricula rather generally require considerable training in foreign languages. This seems to be the one field which emphasizes the importance of language equipment.

INSURANCE

A compilation of data on collegiate courses in insurance, 1928, shows "that 105 colleges and universities offer one or more courses in insurance; that 157 members of the instructional staffs are assigned to these courses; and that 238 such courses are offered. There are 5,950 students, including duplicates, enrolled in these courses in the 94 institutions that reported their enrollments.

Only 18 of the institutions reported that they offer curricula in insurance in which students might major. These institutions reported an average of five courses, three instructors, and 209 students enrolled in insurance courses. The numbers of students majoring in this curriculum in the various institutions are reported in parentheses in column No. 4.

Of the 105 institutions, 53 reported only 1 course in insurance; 21, 2 courses; 14, 3 courses; 10, 4 courses; 2, 5 courses; 2, 7 courses; 1, 9 courses; 1, 13 courses; and 1, 15 courses.

The compilation shows further that in each of 84 of the 105 institutions only 1 instructor offers courses in insurance; in 12 institutions, 2 instructors; in 4 institutions, 3 instructors; in 1 institution, 4 instructors; in 2 institutions, 7 instructors; in 1 institution, 8 instructors; and in 1 institution, 11 instructors.[4]

Further data on courses in insurance will be confined to the undergraduate member schools of the American Association and will center about two main topics; first, insurance as a factor in the curricula of these schools; and, second, the nature and number of courses given.

Insurance as a Factor in the Business School Curricula

There are four objective tests by which the rôle of insurance in business school curricula may be measured: the extent to which it is a general requirement, its extent as a field of specialization, the extent to which separate departments of insurance exist, and the extent to which it is specified as a subject in other specialized curricula.

1. Only one school requires a course in insurance of all students. This is at Pennsylvania, where a five hour, one term course in the principles of insurance is required of all sophomores. It might be added that at all other schools insurance is scheduled above the sophomore level.

2. Fifteen schools make insurance a field of specialization— California, Chicago, Columbia, Florida, Illinois, Minnesota, Nebraska, New York, North Carolina, North Dakota, Pennsylvania, Syracuse, Virginia, University of Washington, and Wisconsin; three more offer curricula in insurance and real estate—Alabama, New York, and Texas.

3. Eight schools indicate insurance as a separate department or grouping of courses—Alabama (with real estate), Chicago, Columbia, Denver, Minnesota, Pennsylvania, Texas (with statistics), and Wisconsin.

4. Insurance courses receive rather general emphasis in the makeup of other specialized curricula. For example, nineteen

---

[4] Malott, J. O., *Commercial Education Circular*, No. 33.

schools require courses in insurance in specialized curricula. Such requirements are distributed rather evenly among curricula in accounting, banking and finance, real estate, personnel, and transportation. Eleven schools specify insurance among the recommended general business electives.

On these four objective bases, insurance would seem to be a fairly well developed, generally utilized, upper class specialized study.

The Number and Nature of Insurance Courses

The range in the number of courses or semesters of work offered in insurance by the member schools vary from one to 15. Most of the schools (25) offer from two to four semesters.

Of insurance courses given, two easily outdistance all the others: (a) personal or life insurance, and (b) property insurance. Each is offered at 23 different undergraduate schools.

Next in importance on the basis of frequency are the general courses on insurance. Twelve schools offer such courses. They are known usually as "principles of insurance," "economics of insurance," and "general insurance." Whatever their name, they are of two kinds: (a) omnibus courses, attempting to cover the entire field of insurance, given usually at smaller schools; and (b) introductory courses, dealing with common elements and principles, to serve as a basis for subsequent and more specific courses.

Separate courses on actuarial science are given at ten schools—California, Illinois, Minnesota, Missouri, Nebraska, Ohio, Pennsylvania, Syracuse, Texas, and Wisconsin.

Casualty insurance is mentioned as the subject, wholly or in large part of courses at nine schools—California, Columbia, Indiana, Nebraska, New York, Minnesota, Pennsylvania, Southern California, and University of Washington.

"Risk and risk bearing" is the title of a course at six schools—Chicago, Iowa, North Carolina, North Dakota, University of Washington, and Wisconsin. In this connection, mention should be made of the course in "stock and produce exchange markets" by the insurance department at Pennsylvania.

Social insurance is the theme of a course at six schools—California, Columbia, Georgia, Georgia Tech, Kansas, and Ohio.

Other courses given less often than the above include insurance, accounting, the law of insurance, insurance salesmanship, insurance carriers and contracts, and loss prevention activities of insurance companies.

TABLE IXC. INSURANCE IN THE UNDERGRADUATE SCHOOLS

Schools	Total under-graduate offerings	Distribution of requirements		Total require-ments	Field of specialization
		Sopho-more	Upper class core or general		
Alabama	72		72	72	Real Estate and Insurance
Boston	72				
California	432				
Chicago	180		45	45	
Cincinnati					
Columbia	216				Insurance
Denver	216				
Florida	162				Risk Bearing and Insurance
Georgia	144				
Georgia Tech	162				
Illinois	108				Insurance
Indiana	108				Insurance
Iowa	72				
Kansas	108		36	36	
Kentucky	54				
Marquette	72				
Minnesota	108				Insurance
Missouri					
Nebraska	108				Insurance
New York	216				Real Estate and Insurance
					Insurance
North Carolina	180				Risk Bearing and Insurance
North Dakota					Insurance
Northwestern					Insurance
Ohio	72				
Oklahoma	108				
Oregon	72				
Pennsylvania	522	90		90	Insurance
Pittsburgh	108				
Southern California	162				
Southern Methodist					
Syracuse	252				Insurance
Texas	108				Insurance and Real Estate
Tulane					
Virginia	108				Insurance
University of Washington	300		40	40	Insurance
Washington University	54				
Washington and Lee	72				
Wisconsin	72				Risk and Insurance
Total	4,728	90	193	283	

Summary

Insurance is a subject of great importance, both from a personal and from a business standpoint. It is not unlikely that there will be increased demand for insurance courses in collegiate schools of business, both for general business training and for the more specific purpose of the training of leaders in an important and developing field of business activity.

Business Organization and Management Courses

"The art of management, in almost all its aspects and activities, turned a corner in 1921. During the up-swing with which the century started, sheer power and drive could win almost every time over finesse. At the turn of the tide, amid the confused cross-currents, more depended upon skillful understandings of the whole situation and nice adjustment of means to the immediate environment. The art of management today is in large part the progressive adjustment and integration of conflicting needs, conflicting influences, and conflicting purposes."[5]

The schools of business have been prompt to recognize this new field emerging into the front rank of importance. A compilation by the Federal Bureau of Education of "collegiate courses in business organization and management, 1928" shows the extent to which this has occurred. It is learned that 329 colleges and universities offer one or more courses in this field, that 805 instructors are assigned to these courses, that 1,256 courses are offered. There are 20,689 students, including duplicates, enrolled in these courses in the 176 institutions that reported their enrollments.[6]

This study is concerned primarily with the development of this field in the member schools. The subject is approached with considerable caution, since the field is not clearly defined as yet, and there seems to be some careless use of terms. The Federal report, referred to above, states that eighty-three different curriculum titles in business organization and management are reported. The various divisions in this study are made tentatively, and primarily on the basis of the nature and interrelations of the courses given.

Business Organization and Management

Organization and management are rather general terms to which various shades of meaning may be given, and to preface them with the term business in no way tends to clarify them. For the moment, the confusion may be increased by including under

---

[5] Dennison, Henry S., "Recent Economic Changes," McGraw-Hill Book Company, New York, 1929, Vol. II, Chapter VII, pp. 544-545.

[6] Malott, J. O., Circular No. 13, Office of Education, U. S. Department of the Interior.

this general heading courses in business administration and business policy.

Their rôle in the business curricula. Most of the member schools have developed some one or more courses under the titles indicated above. Thirty-two of the 38 undergraduate schools and the four graduate schools offer one or more courses under the above terms.

Twenty-two schools require such a course or courses of all students. Eight additional schools required it of some appreciable proportion of their students. In the undergraduate schools, such course or courses are given usually to upper classmen. Where offered below the junior level, they are usually of an elementary and descriptive nature. The particular sequence in the curricula of these courses depends, of course, upon the nature of the course, which subject will next be discussed.

The nature of the courses. The courses under this general heading are of four main kinds, representing perhaps as many stages of development of the particular field.

a. One well defined group consists of those courses which deal with the various types of business organization, such as the sole proprietorship, partnership, joint stock company, corporation, etc. The approach usually is historical and expository. Consideration is given to the external relations and setting of these various forms. At several institutions only the corporate form is considered. In short, these courses consist chiefly of an analysis of the structure of the business organization.

b. A second fairly definite kind of course is that which, while describing the various forms of organization proceeds to deal with the various elements and processes of administration within a business, i.e., with the administration or internal coordination of the factors in a business unit. These courses not infrequently partake of the nature of a buisness orientation course, with the flavor of administration added for good measure.

c. Third are the courses which interpret the phrase business organization wholly in terms of the integral parts of a business unit and their administration and coordination. They are concerned, in other words, with the organization of the various phases of business activity—production, marketing, finance, personnel, risk bearing, etc.

Once the internal functioning of the business is considered, the technique of the manager comes to be emphasized. Accordingly, at the present moment, a number of business schools are approaching this field from the standpoint of the organization and management of a business with reference to the problems of the executive. Excellent statement of this point of view is contained under the title of business organization in the catalogue of the Graduate School of Business at Stanford University. It says:

> The central management of a business has the task of knitting departments together and of keeping the business functioning as an organic whole. Management determines the common ends toward which effort shall be directed and maintains co-ordination between departments.
>
> Study will be made of the way management is organized, by the way line, staff, departments, and functions in a highly organized business co-operate in making and executing decisions, and of the way authority is delegated and controlled. Attention will be given to the influence of historical and personal considerations in determining organization policy and procedure, especially in cases in which concerns are undergoing reorganization.
>
> Emphasis will be placed upon the applications and limitations of standardization, upon means of preserving flexibility in an organization, and upon ways of making provision in the structure of a business for its orderly development and growth. Distinction throughout will be drawn between scientific and rule-of-thumb methods of dealing with organization problems. The aim will be to foster a habit of regarding business problems primarily from the viewpoint of general, as distinguished from divisional, management.

Courses with this conception of their purpose are given at Boston, Dartmouth, Illinois, Ohio, Stanford, Texas, Tulane, University of Washington, and other schools.

d. The fourth type of course follows rather naturally in this process of evolution. This is the course which as a rule goes by the name of "business policy." About a dozen schools offer such courses.

In purpose, these courses essay the task of coordinating other and more specialized business courses which the student has pursued, emphasizing the interdependence between different functional departments of a business. The point of view is that of the chief executive. Problems are considered "not in terms of one phase of management, such as production, sales or finance, but in terms of a combination of two, or more of these phases and with careful attention to the underlying economics of the situation."[7]

Business does not exist in a vacuum. The administrative problems of business operation raise broad questions involving fundamental and far reaching questions—the relation of a specific business policy to the general economic situation, its relation to public policy, etc. As a result, these courses in business policy are related to, and in certain cases apparently overlap, advanced courses in economics which seek to integrate business and its broader economic setting. Courses of this latter kind are given at Columbia, Michigan (Part II of Business Policy), Pennsylvania (Theory of Business), and other schools.

By way of summary, then, these courses, recognizing the growing complexity of modern business activities, emphasize the essential unity of management problems, and the fundamental necessity of coordinating all business activities in terms of an inclusive, consistent policy.[8]

Management in the Field of Production

Scientific management in America had its origin in engineering practices in the field of production. To many persons, the concept of management is still confined to production. Courses in collegiate schools of business dealing with management deal more frequently with this aspect than with any other.

Thirty-four of the member schools offer courses in management which emphasize the production aspect. Some of these courses are announced under the name of "industrial organization and management," some under the term "factory management," and some as "production management." Of these the first named is used most frequently.

In content, these courses consist of studies of the forms and plans of the organization and equipment of industrial plants and of systems and methods of management. Concrete topics considered are plant location, buildings, plant layout, plant design,

---

[7] Catalogue, School of Business Administration, University of Michigan, p. 26.
[8] Catalogue, Stanford University, op. cit., p. 26.

functions of different departments, production control, incentives, systems of wage payments, and development of production standards.

In addition to the above, eight schools offer courses which are descriptive studies of manufacturing plants or processes. An interesting experiment in this direction is a course known as introduction to the study of technology, given by Professor Mitchell at the University of Chicago. This course includes a consideration of basic raw materials, with their relation to connected sciences; of the basic technological processes; the tools of industry; and the industrial applications of the above in various groups of industries and resulting commodities of commerce. As a part of the work of the course each student makes a technological study of a selected industry.

Management courses in the field of production play an important rôle in the curricula of the business schools, considering the recent development of these courses. Twenty schools offer specialized curricula which may be classified under this particular heading. The terms used and the schools follow:

Commercial Engineering...Nebraska.
Industrial Management.............. Georgia, Illinois, Minnesota, Nebraska, Ohio,
Manufacturing and Production......... Alabama, Chicago, Florida, Kansas, Missouri,
        Northwestern, Pennsylvania, Pittsburgh,
        Texas, Washington University.
Management....................... Iowa, New York, Southern California, Syra-
        cuse, and the University of Washington.

In the undergraduate schools, these courses are offered almost exclusively in the upper classes. Less than a quarter of these schools make these courses a general requirement.

Office Management

Courses in office management represent another of the phases of operating management. Such courses have found their way into 20 of the member schools—Boston, Chicago, Denver, Florida, Georgia Tech, Iowa, Kansas, Kentucky, Marquette, Minnesota, Nebraska, New York, North Dakota, Northwestern, Ohio, Oregon, Southern California, Syracuse, Texas, and the University of Washington.

In general, these courses deal with the theory and practice of office procedure from the viewpoint of management, considering such topics as functional organization, office planning and layout, standardization and simplification of method and functions, equipment, and personnel.

Personnel Management

Personnel represents another established phase of the modern management movement. Thirty-four member schools offer courses of this general nature. A variety of course titles are used—personnel management, personnel administration, labor management, employment management, etc. Inasmuch as it serves as an index of the development of the subject, it might be noted that 20 of the 34 schools offer one course, ten offer two courses, two offer three courses, one offers four, and one offers six courses. Together with labor, it is a field for specialization at fifteen of the undergraduate schools.

Some of the schools have a professor of personnel, but most combine these courses with those in other fields. Instructors teaching these courses come from varying backgrounds. Some are general economists, interested in labor problems. In other institutions, the psychologically trained have been selected. To the extent that a group of technically trained teachers in personnel courses is developing, they seem to represent a combination of training in psychology and economics, coupled with industrial experience. The psychological influence has loomed particularly large in recent years.

The content of courses in personnel management seems to be fairly well standardized. They deal with the problems confronting the manager of a business enterprise in the coordination and direction of human energy—job analysis, selection of employees, trade tests, intelligence tests, vocational histories, labor turnover, absenteeism, withheld effort, wage classification, health and safety, etc.

This increased recognition of the human factor in management is one of the most striking changes in the management movement. "Men who a few years ago were talking and writing such subjects as plant layout, planning, routing, job analysis, time study, and the rest, are now discussing means of bringing workers, organized and unorganized, into the management picture."[9]

---

[9] Hotchkiss, W. E., "Education for Management in American Universities," *International Management Congress*, Paris, June, 1929.

Labor Problems

Courses in labor problems are related closely to those in personnel management. In fact, these two groups of courses represent two different but not unlike approaches to labor as a factor in economic life. Personnel courses imply the approach of the manager, and in relation to an individual business or group of business activities. Courses in labor problems represent the approach of the socio-economist, and from the standpoint of labor and society.

Courses of the latter type constitute one of the most comprehensively recognized elements in commerce curricula. All but two of the undergraduate schools offer some work of this kind, or their students have already access to them in the offerings of departments of economics in the liberal arts college.

A survey of the current offerings indicate three different courses dealing with labor problems, and excluding the personnel aspect. First, there is a general course, usually called labor problems, and covering the customary material found in the traditional textbooks published under that title; second, are the courses which emphasize the organization of labor and its efforts in its own behalf; and, third, are the courses dealing with labor legislation, comprehending the social efforts in behalf of labor as expressed through legislation. In addition, there is a sprinkling of isolated courses dealing with specialized aspects of the labor situation—unemployment, women in industry, European labor movements, history of labor, etc.

The courses on labor problems are usually a part of the offerings of the economics department, and are taught by economists with social interests.

Other Management Courses

Management as a problem is not confined to the field of production. Recently the principles of management have been introduced into other aspects of the business process. The collegiate schools of business evidence this change. Various courses in marketing management, financial management, sales management, traffic management, credit management, public utility management, etc., have been introduced during the last few years. These courses have been included in the tabulations under the particular subject involved, but they are significant in this connection, and might conceivably be listed as courses in management quite as justifiably as in the particular subject involved.

Management as a Business School Objective

Management has been made the central idea or objective around which several collegiate schools of business have organized their entire curriculum.

The graduate school of business at Stanford University in California offers a striking illustration. The fundamental plan of that school, as contrasted with that of other schools, is stated in its general bulletin in the following words:

> Business schools came into the system of higher education at a time when specialization in professional study was at its height. It was natural therefore for the scientific study of business to be directed largely toward the functional divisions of business—accounting, production, finance, marketing, advertising—rather than management as a whole. It is essential in the further study of business that especial emphasis be placed on management as a unifying and co-ordinating force.
>
> Throughout its program of study the Graduate School of Business emphasizes the essential unity of management. Without neglecting the problems that arise in the several divisions of business, effort is made to develop such habits of mind that students instinctively will think of a business as a unit, and work out the solution of problems with the requirements of the whole business in mind.[10]

In further explanation of the Stanford plan, Dean Hotchkiss has written:

> We are trying the experiment of starting our course as far as possible at the center instead of the periphery of business. We set apart a considerable portion of the student's time during the first year for work which bears the caption "Business Organization." The data employed in this work, even when they have to do with the functional divisions of business, are handled from the standpoint of general management policies; much of the material is drawn from current experience of business executives whose plants the students visit.
> These visits are in no sense sightseeing tours. The cri-

---

[10] Stanford University Bulletin, op. cit., p. 15-16.

terion for deciding what concerns to visit is the educational significance of the business and the prospect of fruitful participation on the part of responsible executives. Before a visit is made the teacher in charge works out a program with executives providing for informal discussion of specific problems. Written reports after the event crystallize the student's impression of the business, stimulate his imagination concerning its significant management problems, and develop his power to express himself discriminatingly on a business subject.

The balance of the work required during the first year has been set up under two main captions—"Aspects of Management" and "Accounting, Financial and Legal Problems of Management." Divisions under the second caption are suggested by the title. Throwing these three divisions together means that the marshalling of material and the scheduling and giving of instruction are worked out co-operatively by the teachers who participate. The caption "Aspects of Management" includes economic, psychological, geographic, and engineering aspects, each subject being handled by an appropriate authority.

During the second year, under the captions "Operating Problems of Management" and "Marketing Problems of Management," students go more deeply than they have previously done into the functional aspects of production and distribution. Such subjects as plant location, plant engineering, simplification, standardization, production control, labor policy, and practice are studies with a view to developing a philosophical grasp of management and a scientific attitude toward it. Forms, charts, formulas, and other mechanisms are presented as tools of management but not as its substance.[11]

PUBLIC UTILITY COURSES

The interrelationships between public utilities and institutions of higher learning are considered in a comprehensive study made recently under the direction of Professor C. O. Ruggles, of Harvard University.[12] This survey considers the extent of instruction in public utilities in colleges and universities as well as industry's interest in college graduates, and the ability and willingness of the industry to cooperate with higher educational institutions in the training of college men for the industry and in the study of utility

---

[11] Hotchkiss, op. cit.

[12] *Public Utilities,* published by the National Electric Light Association, 1929.

problems. It is with the extent of instruction in this field as well
as its nature, that we are concerned at this point.

The Rôle of Public Utilities in Business Curricula

Results of an earlier study. The report of a commission of the
American Association of collegiate schools of business for 1925-26
showed that courses in public utilities, other than railroads, were
then given in 22 of the 38 member schools, with a total of 1980
credit hours. The subject ranked twenty-first in a list of 27 fields
on this basis. In regard to hours of class instruction, it ranked
twenty-sixth in a group of 34; on the basis of books published
in 1926 by faculty members of the association schools it ranked
thirty-second in a list of 40; considering monographs and periodical articles, it ranked fourteenth in the same list.

Data on the present rôle of the subject. An examination of the
catalogue offerings of member schools in 1929-30 shows a total
of 23 undergraduate schools offering courses in public utilities
for a total of 2,586 credit hours. For purposes of comparison
with the earlier study just referred to, it is necessary to include
the developments in the graduate schools. This results in a total
of 25 member schools and 2,802 credit hours.

Before comparing the data of the two studies, recognition must
be given to the fact that the number of member schools increased
since 1925-26 from 38 to 42. If public utility courses at schools
admitted since 1925-26 be excluded, it is found that in 1929-30,
the total number of schools is 23 and the total credit hours is
2,694. This involves, then, in four years, an increase of one in the
same number of schools, and an increase of 36 per cent in class
hours of instruction.

Another index of the present rôle of the subject is to be found
in the fact that eight undergraduate and two graduate schools
recognize public utilities as a field of specialization—Alabama,
Georgia, Harvard, Illinois, Michigan, Nebraska, Northwestern,
Texas, University of Washington, and Wisconsin. At two of
these, it is combined with transportation—Alabama and Northwestern. In addition to these, New York and Ohio recognize
public utilities as a partial specialization in the last year of an
established curriculum.

The Nature of Public Utility Courses

An examination of the various courses offered reveals five kinds of courses or points of emphasis.

First, there are those courses which are general in nature, being apparently a descriptive survey of the field. The titles generally used are public utilities, principles of public utilities, public utility economics, and introduction to public service industries. Eighteen schools offer such courses.

The second group consists of those courses which concern themselves with control and regulation of public utilities. Eight schools give courses devoted wholly or largely to this aspect. This includes two schools where such courses are given by the department of political science, which in these cases are outside of the schools.

Third, are the courses dealing with rates and valuation. Five schools include courses of this nature. In the fourth group are those courses which deal with management or operation or administration of public utilities. Twelve schools emphasize this aspect of the field.

Finally, one finds a type of course which concerns itself largely with the business aspects of the utilities, such as their relation to field of investments. Six schools consider this aspect separately.

Summary

Certain conclusions of the study directed by Professor Ruggles, which seem particularly important in connection with the development of instruction in public utilities in collegiate schools of business, are included by way of summary at this point.

> 1. In the light of the fact that the new field of utilities other than railroads has developed at a very rapid pace within the past decade, there is urgent need for a more intelligent understanding of public utility problems both on the part of those engaged in the business and on the part of the public.[13]
>
> It ought to be evident that there can be no intelligent and effective regulation of the utility industry unless the nature of the problems to be regulated are understood. Those who may later become legislators, utility commissioners, and judges should have an opportunity while in our colleges and univer-

---

[13] Ruggles, op. cit., p. 8.

sities to obtain some understanding of the vital problems which affect the public in its relation to public service corporations. There should be, for example, a substantial increase in the number of experts along various lines on the staffs of our state public utilities commissions. It is vital that these men be trained not only in the engineering, business, and legal phases of the field but that they should have some appreciation of the problems which are involved in the relation of the public utilities to the public. It is obvious that graduates of our colleges and universities who, in turn, become instructors, should have an opportunity to obtain a perspective of these problems.[14]

2. The facts submitted show that an increasing number of the graduates of both schools of business and schools of engineering are entering the field of public utilities; also that even in the field of engineering there is a striking decrease in the number of graduates taking employment with the railroads. These statistics verify the conclusions reached in the Yale Survey on Transportation. The results of the Survey show that the demand is not only for graduates of engineering schools but that the need for non-engineering graduates is becoming a very important factor. Indeed the facts reported by the parent companies which submitted data on this phase of the Survey show that the greatest number of college men employed by them in 1927 were non-engineering graduates.[15]

3. In view of the fact that the utilities other than railroads are now absorbing an increasing number of college graduates, there might well be some consideration on the part of colleges and universities of more adequate instruction (not necessarily more courses) in this field. The business administration aspects of the industry deserve careful study.[16]

The demand of the industry for college men other than engineering graduates and for an increasing number of engineers who have taken accounting and business courses is merely one indication of the increasing importance of the business aspects of this industry. It is obvious, too, that the teaching material in accounting and business administration for schools of business and for schools of engineering ought to be secured through the laboratory method of obtaining actual cases from the industry itself.[17]

4. Educators appear to believe that there is a need for more effective coordination of the fields of engineering and

---

[14] Ibid., p. 7.
[15] Ibid., p. 2.
[16] Ibid., p. 8.
[17] Ibid., p. 8.

business, both for undergraduates and graduates in the training of men for the utility industry. There appears to be a disposition to recognize that students in engineering must be provided with instruction in economics and business administration which is much less specialized than that ordinarily given to students in the schools of business. To some extent there appears to be a willingness on the part of the schools of engineering to provide certain courses in engineering which students in schools of business may take which would given them a perspective that would enable them to work more intelligently with engineers in large public service corporations.[18]

5. The men in the industry are right in their contentions that the new and rapidly developing utility industry must be studied first-hand by graduate students and by instructors if there is to be a true reflection of the real situation in the utility industry in the work of our colleges and universities, and if we are to turn out graduates prepared to enter the industry. As has been previously stated an understanding of many of the problems which are of vital interest from a public point of view is sometimes essential in the teaching of courses dealing with the business problems of the industry.[19]

COURSES IN REAL ESTATE

The subject of real estate has found its way recently into the curricula of the business schools. As used here, the term includes also courses in land economics.

1. To what extent have courses in real estate been developed? Twenty-two of the undergraduate member schools offer courses in real estate, in the day school—Alabama, California, Denver Georgia Tech, Illinois, Indiana, Iowa, Kansas, Marquette, Minnesota, Nebraska, New York, Northwestern, Ohio, Oklahoma, Oregon, Pennsylvania, Southern California, Syracuse, Texas, University of Washington, and Wisconsin. In addition, Boston offers courses in connection with its evening work, as does also Michigan, among the "graduate" schools. Most of the schools offer a course or two, except New York, Northwestern, Marquette, and Pennsylvania, where the development of the field is somewhat more pronounced.

---

[18] Ibid., p. 2.
[19] Ibid., p. 708.

2. To what extent is real estate a recognized field of specialization? Since extent of specialization offers another index of the development and status of a subject, it is of significance to note that 11 schools recognize it in this manner, Michigan being included in this number—Alabama, California, Marquette, Michigan, Minnesota, Nebraska, New York, Northwestern, Pennsylvania, Syracuse, and Texas. It should be added that at Ohio the field is indicated as a possible senior sequence in the general course. In three cases, real estate is combined with insurance as a field of specialization and at one with banking.

3. To what extent is real estate recognized as a separate department? This is another index of status, although too much importance cannot be attached to it because the problem is bound up with the general plan of departmental organization. Six schools now have separate departments or groupings of courses in real estate.

Where there is no separate department, one finds courses in real estate developed in connection with insurance, as at Alabama; with management, as at Boston; with business law, as at Denver or Texas; or with banking and finance, as at New York, Ohio, Pennsylvania, or Southern California. These connections serve also to reflect the various angles from which the subject is approached.

4. What is the nature of the work in real estate offered at the various schools? The number of courses now offered in real estate is not large. Two or three term courses are the rule. Marquette offers nine two hour semester courses. Michigan lists seven semesters of work, including a course in landscape design, each three hours per semester. New York University offers 11 semesters of work, two hours per week. Northwestern offers nine separate semester courses for a total of 18 semester units. Pennsylvania has four semesters, each of three hours.

An examination of courses announced shows a predominance of such headings as real estate principles or fundamentals; real estate practice, or methods or transactions; land economics; and real estate valuation or appraisal.

The general subjects covered include such topics as real estate as a business, origin and development of real estate ownership, land classification and utilization, land tenure and land policy, spread of population, city growth, community analysis, city planning, zoning, subdividing, rural and national planning, local ordinances, law of real estate, relation of landlord and tenant, real estate boards, economic principles of real estate values, method and technique of appraising, listing and selling of property, renting and leasing, mortgages and financing, property management, real estate investments, etc.

5.   What other offerings are utilized in real estate curricula? In building up their specialty, real estate teachers have drawn upon resources of other departments of the business school and upon other schools of the university.   Economics, especially land economics, is perhaps most frequently called upon.   But law has furnished courses dealing with the legal aspects of real estate. Landscape design—California and Michigan—insurance, accounting, agronomy (Nebraska), finance, school of fine arts for agricultural appreciation (Syracuse), theory of surveying (Syracuse), are some of the other offerings utilized.   It is curious that there seems to be no connection or coordination with the work in population distribution and population changes which are so important to the sociologists.   Equally important to both groups would seem to be the study of numerous problems of urban life and development.

6.   To what extent is real estate included in other specialized curricula?   The subject has not yet been given much status outside of its own group.   Only four schools require or specifically suggest work in real estate in other than the real estate curriculum. Pennsylvania makes it a senior requirement in insurance, and a suggested elective in brokerage and corporation finance and investment.   Syracuse and Texas list it as an alternative general senior elective, and the University of Washington specifies is as a general upper class elective.

Summary

Because of its intimate relation to work in land economics, banking, business law, population studies, etc., the development of work in real estate would seem to present peculiar problems of coordination and integration of existing resources of a school, to the end that duplication of effort be avoided.

STATISTICS, BUSINESS CYCLES, AND FORECASTING

Every school in the American Association of Collegiate Schools of Business includes courses in statistics in its catalogue offerings for 1929-30. Its present development is the result of a very rapid

TABLE VIIIC. STATISTICS, BUSINESS CYCLES, AND FORECASTING IN THE UNDERGRADUATE SCHOOLS

Schools	Total undergraduate class hours		When required			Distribution of requirements		Field of specilization
	Statistics	Business cycles and forecasting	Freshmen	Sophomore	Upper class-core or general course	Statistics	Business cycles and forecasting	
Alabama	108	108			108	108		Accounting and Statistics
Boston	72	36						
California	126	108			72	72		
Chicago	300	60			105	105		
Cincinnati	96				96	96		
Columbia	90				54	54		Statistics
Denver	252	72			144	108	36	
Florida	54	108			54	54		
Georgia	54							
Georgia Tech	54	54						
Illinois	54	54						
Indiana	126	72		36		36		
Iowa	54	54						
Kansas	108				108	108		
Kentucky	54	54			108	54	54	
Marquette	54	54			54	54		Accounting and Statistics
Minnesota	276	36		60	72	96	36	Statistics
Missouri	54	90			54	54		
Nebraska	154	108						Statistics
New York	468							
North Carolina	60	60			60	60		
North Dakota	144	54		54	54	108		
Northwestern	126	108			72	72		
Ohio	36	96			36	36		
Oklahoma	108	108		54		54		
Oregon	168							
Pennsylvania	108	72						
Pittsburgh	180	108			108	108		Statistics
So. California	72	54			126	72	54	Statistics
So. Methodist	162	54						
Syracuse	162	54						
Texas	126	54			72	72		Business Statistics
Tulane	108	54			108	108		
Virginia	108				108	108		Statistics
U. of Washington	60	120						Statistics
Washington U.	54	54						Accounting and Statistics
Washington and Lee	54	54			54	54		
Wisconsin	324	54			54	54		Statistics
Total	4,768	2,226		204	1,881	1,905	180	

growth in recent years. Previous studies of offerings in statistics for the years 1910-11 and 1925-26 show an increase of credit hours from 1,836 to 15,645. "The data were gathered from the official catalogues of our colleges and universities, 392 institutions being represented in the 1910-11 tabulations and 571 in those for

1925-26."[20]   The total for 1925-26 is 8.5 times that of 1910-11.

Not only is statistics a study of the first order of importance in the colleges of commerce, but its development has presented important and peculiar problems of administration and of pedagogy. For these reasons it becomes important to examine the data concerning its development, as well as the various problems involved. These constitute the purpose of the present study.

Rôle in the Curricula

At 24 of the 38 undergraduate schools, statistics is a required course for all business students. At seven schools, it is required in some but not in all curricula. At six schools, it is elective. Twelve schools recognize statistics as a field of specialization, wholly or in part. Three schools combine it with accounting—Alabama, Marquette, and Washington University. At nine other schools it stands as a separate field—Columbia, Minnesota, Nebraska, Pittsburgh, Southern Methodist, Texas, Virginia, University of Washington, and Wisconsin. In addition, Ohio includes it among the senior sequences of the general course curriculum.

In view of the very general development of statistics in the offerings of the schools, together with its comparative general requirement, it is a rather striking fact that only nine schools should offer separate curricula in this field. This combination of facts, together with its association with accounting, indicate that the general conception of statistics is as a measuring aid in business control.

Place in the curricula.   Barring statistical aspects of courses in the mathematics of finance, as well as in other courses, the first point of contact with statistics for the student is customarily in the junior year. Only five of the schools require or recommend it as early as the sophomore year—Indiana, Minnesota, Oklahoma, North Dakota, and Oregon. Only one of two schools postpone the first course to the senior year. In all other cases, constituting the overwhelming proportion of the schools, the introductory course is scheduled for the junior year. This allows for an advanced course in the senior year which is required or recommended in a number of schools.

---

[20] Marshall, op. cit., p. 204.

Administrative Arrangements Concerning Statistics

The administrative arrangements involved in the development of statistics have presented quite a problem at a number of collegiate schools of business. It becomes pertinent, therefore, to summarize the facts concerning the location of statistics in the organization of the work of these schools.

Three types of administrative arrangements concerning statistics prevail in the business schools. First, there may be a separate department or professorship or grouping in statistics, singly or in combination with accounting or insurance. Twelve of the 38 undergraduate schools have this arrangement. It should be added, however, that this does not mean that all of the instruction in statistics at these institutions is given by this department. At several of them not even all of the instruction to business students comes from this source, the departments of mathematics also offering courses of a statistical nature.

The second type of arrangement is for some or all of the courses in statistics for business students to be developed within the department of economics. At 20 schools, this was the case in 1929-30. Obviously, and for the most part, this is a transitory arrangement, reflecting a certain stage of the development of the subject.

The third type of arrangement consists of some half a dozen cases where the work in statistics is given by some other department such as mathematics, insurance, accounting, business administration, or sociology. These are departures from the normal, based usually on peculiar institutional situations or concessions to some particular teacher.

Nature of Courses Given

An examination of the work in statistics offered to commerce students shows that four different courses are commonly found.

a. Most frequent is some kind of an elementary course, involving the use of the more simple statistical concepts, and their application to the field of business. The emphasis in the more successful courses seems to be more upon interpretation and analysis of business problems with statistics as a tool, and less upon statistical craftsmanship.

b. A course dealing with the business cycle is next in order of frequency. About two-thirds of the undergraduate schools give a course wholly or in part devoted to this subject.

c. Business forecasting is considered by a number of institutions, sometimes in a separate course, sometimes in combination with the business cycle.

d. A number of schools also offer courses which deal more largely with statistical technique or craftsmanship. Such courses usually are of an advanced nature and not infrequently are listed as "advanced statistics."

Three of the above courses figure rather generally in the curricula of the schools, either separately or as parts of courses. Following the work in mathematics in the first two years, reference to which will be made later, the elementary course in statistics is scheduled customarily for the junior year, and business cycles and forecasting for the senior year. Both of these courses are required rather generally for all students, or their election is strongly recommended.

In referring to the work in business cycles and forecasting, it should be added such courses are not always given by the teachers of statistics. At several schools, their development is in connection with the work in finance; at other schools, as a part of general economics; and at one school, in connection with the work in sociology. Whatever the justification for such arrangements, there seems no doubt but that this still further complicates the work of statistics as a definite unit in the curriculum.

The Teaching of Statistics

The problem of statistics in the collegiate schools of business, as in other undergraduate schools, is peculiarly a pedagogical one. In quite a few of the schools where statistics is a required study, there seems to exist a considerable antagonism toward it. While some of this antagonism may be due to the prejudices which students form against mathematical studies while still in the lower grades, and some to the apparent unwillingness of students "schooled" in the social sciences to meet the more onerous requirements of an exacting subject, the almost complete absence of such antagonism at certain schools indicates that factors other than those just mentioned are more important.

These other factors seem to be: first, the extent to which the mathematics of statistics is stressed—much emphasis of this sort being rather deadly, especially in the introductory course; second, the extent to which interpretation or analysis of problems is emphasized, with statistics as the somewhat incidental tool—students being considerably more friendly to this approach; and, third, the extent to which the instructor is familiar with data, examples, or problems from the business world. Perhaps these are but so many ways of saying the same thing, viz., that useful courses in business statistics need to contain more business than statistics, that the way to a student's interest in statistical craftsmanship is through his discovery of its value in the solution of the problems of his chosen field of work. This is not only putting the horse before the cart, but also hitching it there, thereby giving the student a sense of motion and direction before expecting any overwhelming interest in the vehicle that is transporting him. Such, certainly, is the experience of successful introductory courses in statistics, whether in business, education, biology, psychology, or sociology.

The proper basis for determining the character of an introductory course in statistics is the purpose which it is designed to serve, not the interest of the instructor or the availability of a textbook. For students aiming to be statistical experts or teachers of statistics, an emphasis upon the mechanics of statistics is entirely justifiable.

In a course in elementary business statistics, the purpose of which is to prepare the student for an active business career, emphasis should be placed upon the practical application of the elementary methods. Only incidental attention need be given to the theory underlying methods—to their mathematical demonstration—and only limited consideration to the more complex and exact mathematical methods. Too frequently the reverse is true. The more advanced mathematical methods are theoretically more fascinating and offer a great challenge to the academic mind. For the same reason the problems of forecasting have, at times, commanded greater attention than those of current analysis.

In our elementary college courses this situation is unfortunate and should be corrected. These more advanced and complex methods frequently carry us into the realm of pure theory and in many cases attempt a finer accuracy than usual business data warrant and than is generally required in practical problems faced in running a business organization. From the practical point of view, their use is often, on the one hand, somewhat like using a razor instead of a drawing knife to shave clapboards into shingles, or, on the other hand, like applying surveying instruments to enable the farmer to make straighter the furrow as he breaks his soil. The young college graduate who is so steeped in these more refined and complex methods is apt with tragic results to attempt to apply finer instruments than the raw material will stand and struggle for greater accuracy than the practical aspects of the situation require.

At a recent meeting of leading statisticians the discussion arose as to how much mathematical training is necessary for successful statistical work in business. One of the most successful statisticians, whose work has covered a wide field in the business world, stated that the usual school course in arithmetic was quite sufficient. While this statement may seem somewhat exaggerated it is certainly true in most such statistical work.[21]

In other words, the successful conduct of courses in statistics in collegiate schools of business demands teaching ability, understanding of economic and business phenomena, and statistical knowledge, the above rank seemingly being that of their order of importance.[22]

Statistics and Mathematics

The foregoing discussion has its bearing upon the problem of the relationship between departments of statistics and of mathematics. Widespread inquiries made in the course of this study seem to indicate that where the problems of the teaching of statistics have been faced honestly and worked out successfully, there has emerged a somewhat natural line of cleavage between the two. Since introductory courses are more a matter of content than of statistical technique, their allocation in the academic scheme would seem to be determined by the former consideration. That is to say, elementary courses in biometrics fall within the province of statistically minded biologists, courses in educational measurements to educators with a statistical background, and

---

[21] The Ronald Forum, 1926.

[22] Cf. Ayres, Leonard P., "The Dilemma of the New Statistics," *Journal of the American Statistical Association,* March, 1927, p. 1-8.

courses in business statistics to statistically trained students of business.

On the other hand, in work of an advanced and highly specialized nature, where the emphasis is more upon the refinements of statistical method, the mathematician may play some role. As a consequence, graduate instruction in statistics at certain schools has been entrusted to the department of mathematics. But here again, an eminent statistican has warned us against an over-weighting of the mathematical influence. "The fact is," writes Leonard P. Ayres, "that most of the mathematics called for by the Greek letters and strange symbols of the new statistics is plain arithmetic with sometimes a little elementary algebra added. The proof that this is so is found in the fact that most of it is being computed daily by clerks who are accomplishing their tasks by using the mathematics they had acquired by the time they reached the eighth grade. . . . . It is true that higher mathematics are needed for the derivation of some of the formulas in common use, and that in a larger proportion of cases they must be called upon for the demonstration of the validity of the formulas. But most statistical investigation does not require the development of new formulas, or the demonstration of the validity of the old ones."[23]

In short, statistics and mathematics seem to be two separate studies, and it appears to be to the gain of neither by pretending to be the other, unless it be in the higher realms of both.

The Future of Statistics

Discussion of the status of statistics with deans and instructors of the member schools indicates that statistics is scheduled to be given even greater emphasis in the fundamental or core training of all business students. At most schools where statistics is now but an elective, its requirement may be expected relatively soon. The two factors retarding this process seem to be the dearth of successful teachers and the cost of necessary equipment.

Students specializing in statistics seem to be of uniformly high grade. With the development of the work of bureaus of

---

[23] Ayres, ibid., p. 5-6.

business research in connection with collegiate schools of business, their number may be expected to increase.

TRANSPORTATION AND TRAFFIC IN THE BUSINESS SCHOOLS

Transportation is a subject of general culture, with its place in the curricula of schools of liberal arts; an engineering study, illustrating certain principles in that field; as well as a field of vocational or professional study .

The extent of its development in colleges and universities, comprehending these three lines of development, is evidenced by the compilation of the Federal Bureau of Education for 1928 which shows that "199 colleges and universities offer one or more courses in transportation; that 267 members of the instructional staffs are assigned to these courses; and that 410 such courses are offered. There are 5,748 students, including duplicates, enrolled in these in the 107 institutions that reported their enrollments."[24]

Instruction in transportation subjects has been more widely developed in the business schools than elsewhere, and it is with this aspect that the present study deals. To be considered at this point are the roll of transportation in the curricula of the business schools, and the nature of the courses given. It would seem pertinent, too, to refer here to the conclusions of the well known study of current methods of study and instruction in transportation, made under the auspices of Yale University.[25]

Rôle of Transportation in the Business Curricula

From the standpoint of the number of schools giving instruction in it, as well as on the basis of undergraduate credit hours offered, transportation is an important element in the curricula of the business schools. Table VIIC shows that 35 of the undergraduate schools offer 6,958 credit hours, which, with Harvard's 270 hours, makes a total of 36 of the 42 schools and of 7,228 credit hours. The heaviest offerings are at the University of Washington, Pennsylvania, Syracuse, Southern California, Illinois, and New

---

[24] Malott, J. O., *Circular No. 11, U. S. Department of the Interior, Office of Education*, G.P.O., Washington, March, 1930.
[25] Cf. Topping, Victor, and Dempsey, S. James, *Transportation*, Privately Printed, New Haven, 1926.

York, in the order named if undergraduate courses only are considered.

It is entirely an upper class study, except for incidental references in general survey courses. In seven schools transportation is one of the required studies in the general course or curriculum. In the other schools where there is any development in the subject, its role is confined to specialized curricula in transportation or public utilities, and inclusion among the available electives.

At 17 undergraduate schools, transportation is a field of specialization, either wholly or in part. At six of these, transportation stands by itself—California, Columbia, Iowa, New York, Oregon, and University of Washington; at two, it is combined with public utilities—Alabama and Northwestern; at two, with traffic—Minnesota and Syracuse; and at the other schools, with shipping (North Carolina), or commerce (Pennsylvania), or trade (Southern California), or trade and manufacture (Missouri), or communication (Chicago and Florida). Illinois offers two curricula, one in general railway administration and one in railway transportation. Among the graduate schools, Harvard and Michigan offer specialized curricula in transportation.

The Nature of the Courses in Transportation and Traffic

A rather wide range of courses dealing with transportation is found in the offerings of the business schools. Those found most frequently include:

1. The general survey or introductory courses, usually referred to as "transportation," "elements of transportation," and "principles of transportation." Thirteen of the undergraduate schools offer such courses.

2. Courses on "railroad transportation" are found at 13 schools. These consider the railroad as an agency of transportation, together with some of the problems involved.

3. "Railway traffic and rates" is another popular course. Fourteen schools offer this course, which deals in general with the classification of traffic and the prevailing rate system.

4. Traffic Management covers much of the material of preceding courses, but with more emphasis upon the executive or managerial aspects. Fourteen schools announce such a course.

TABLE VIIC. TRAFFIC MANAGEMENT AND TRANSPORTATION

Schools	Total under-graduate offerings	Upper class require-ments	Distribution of requirements		Field of specialization
			Trans-portation	Traffic manage-ment	
Alabama............	90	54	54		Transportation and public utilities
Boston.............	72				
California...........	216				Transportation
Chicago............	240	45		45	Transportation and Communication
Cincinnati..........					Traffic
Columbia...........	108				Transportation
Denver.............	36				
Florida.............	108	54	54		Transportation and Communication
Georgia............	324				
Georgia Tech........					
Illinois.............	360	54	54		{General Railway Transportation {Railway Transportation
Indiana.............	90				
Iowa...............	226				Transportation
Kansas.............	108	54	54		
Kentucky...........	54				
Marquette..........	90				
Minnesota..........	144	36		36	Traffic and Transportation
Missouri............	54				Trade and Transportation
Nebraska...........	108				
New York...........	360				Transportation
No. Carolina........	132				Transportation and Shipping
No. Dakota.........	108	54	54		
Northwestern........	198				Public Utilities and Transportation
Ohio...............	276	60	60		
Oklahoma..........	108				
Oregon.............	264				Transportation
Pennsylvania........	612				Commerce and Transportation
Pittsburgh..........	108				
So. California.......	396				Trade and Transportation
So. Methodist.......					
Syracuse...........	432				Traffic and Transportation
Texas..............	54				
Tulane.............					
Virginia............	216				
U. of Washington.....	672				Transportation
Washington U........	270				
Washington and Lee...	108	54	54		
Wisconsin..........	216				
Total	6,958	465	384	81	

5. The most frequently found course in the field is that which deals with the subject of ocean transportation. Fifteen schools give such courses. A variety of aspects of ocean shipping are emphasized to varying degrees—ocean transportation, ocean shipping finance, ocean shipping management, ship operation, shipping and consular regulations, etc.

In addition to the above, there are a number of other courses given by from one to six schools. The list of general subjects follows, the numbers after each indicating how many schools offer such courses.

Economics of transportation..	6
Railway economics...	2
Railroad administration, organization or finance.............................	5
Railway operation..	6
Railway regulation...	4
Ocean terminal problems..	5
Highway or motor transportation..	6
Air transportation..	5
Electric railway transportation..	1

Instruction Problems in Transportation

Reference has been made to the Yale study on transportation, with its emphasis upon current methods of study and instruction. Concerning any appreciable demand for general instruction or specialized curricula in transportation, this survey expresses extreme doubt. Although "practically every institution which has a department of economics offers an undergraduate elementary course in this subject," such course "is generally elective and, with few exceptions, the enrollment is decidedly small as compared with that of other subjects."[26] As for further study of the subject, the interest shown here, too, "is very meager," growing chiefly out of the requirements of curricula in other fields.[27] Even in the Harvard Graduate School of Business, where the curriculum in transportation is reported as unusually attractive, "there has been slight demand for the entire curriculum."[28] It is "very strongly emphasized that intensive specialization in such a subject as transportation should be relegated to the realm of post graduate courses" although it is recognized that "there is a debatable zone between those university years which are unmistakably preparatory in nature and those which may just as definitely be assigned to graduate specialization. The lower limit of such a zone will vary with the student and with the institution, but may generally be found in the senior or graduating year."[29]

Although "the necessity for a sound understanding of the real nature and importance of the various instrumentalities of transport to the advancement and improvement of the economic and social welfare of society," as well as the key responsibility of the university in so doing are clearly recognized, the greater part of existing instruction is given from "a distorted viewpoint,"[30] there is an "overemphasis of evils which existed in the past,"[31] there is "no scientific division of the field among the various institutions"[32] too much emphasis upon the railroads, and an "inadequate consideration of the phases which require

---

[26] Ibid., p. 49.
[27] Ibid., p. 50.
[28] Ibid., p. 55.
[29] Ibid., p. 119.
[30] Ibid., p. 112.
[31] Ibid., p. 112.
[32] Ibid., p. 112.

most attention".[33]   There is particular insistence upon an approach which includes "all instrumentalities of transport, a discussion of their proper position in the whole field, and the coordination of all forms of transportation to the best advantage of society in general"[34] with more stress "upon fundamental economic principles and less upon detailed historical recital of past developments."[35]

Reference has already been made to the offerings in transportation in the Graduate School of Business at Harvard.   In addition, it should be noted that Columbia offers six graduate courses in transportation and traffic for a total of 324 class hours; Pennsylvania offers five courses with a total of 360 class hours in connection with its graduate work in business administration, and four courses for a total of 288 class hours in the undergraduate school of the university.

THE PROBLEM OF COORDINATION AND A UNIFIED CURRICULUM

The present chapter summarizes the data on the development and present status of the business subjects.   Each of the main fields of business, as indicated by their relative frequency in the course offerings of the American Association schools of business, has been analyzed with particular reference to their rôle in the business curricula and to the kinds and range of courses offered in that field.

These details, tiresome and perhaps trivial as they may appear at first glance, constitute nevertheless the present picture of collegiate education for business.   Moreover, it is the details of the present picture which tell the story of its past development. For American higher education for business is not the story of the development of schools with unified programs of instruction nearly so much as it is the story of the growth of departments with their ceaseless proliferation of courses, their narrow specialized curricula, their needless duplication of material, and their frequent lack of coordination.   These various aspects will be briefly considered in this summary.

---

[33] Ibid., p. 112.
[34] Ibid., p. 113.
[35] Ibid., p. 118.

The Growth of the Business Subjects

The process of growth of these departments has been a sort of academic crocheting. It starts usually with a nucleus or solid center piece of a course or two. From this center there are "knitted" various lines of development, following the specific interests of the particular instructor. The specific line not infrequently begins with a doctor's dissertation. Having reached a certain growth, or degree of recognition, it is connected, sometimes naturally and sometimes as the result of considerable professional dexterity, with the centerpiece. Whereupon the process is repeated over again, and again, and again. The results of this process are those decorative academic fabrications which adorn and constitute our collegiate schools of business—and the rest of the universities as well. Professor Hoagland has described this process in scientific terms more pleasing to members of the guild. "Starting with neither suitable texts nor qualified teachers," he says, "these courses have been divided and subdivided, amoeba-like, until today Malthus, looking back from beyond, must find tremendous satisfaction in the verification of his theory, namely, that business courses will multiply indefinitely unless checked by a scarcity of students or a dearth of appropriations."[36] Whichever statement of this process be acceptable, it is the end product of this process which has been summarized in the foregoing sections.

Departmental offers usually consist of a substantial center of a course or two, with as many surrounding accretions as the ambition of the department or the size of the school or both seem to make possible. One finds school after school where from five to 30 courses are offered in a given field, yet but one of those courses is generally taken. And what seems still more striking from the standpoint of the education of students is that the particular course that is generally taken is apt to be developed, not as a contributing factor in the training of the students of the school, but as an introduction to the other four or twenty-nine courses which only a minority of students can pursue.

Some of the fields discussed do not even seem to have a core

---

[36] Hoagland, H. E., "An Era of Water-Tight Compartment Instruction in Business Subjects," The Ronald Forum, 1928, pp. 18-19.

of common importance. One finds, for example, a field which half of the schools recognize as deserving of a specialized curriculum, in which eight different courses generally obtain, yet which is given almost no recognition in the core requirements of the great majority of students. One cannot but contemplate with tongue in cheek the sight of earnest faculty members piling course upon course within a specific field, developing it as a separate department, with a separate curriculum for specialization, but with almost no coordination of their work with that of the rest of the school.

If some of these particular fields of specialization are anywhere so important as their advocates insist, and as the number of courses developed would seem to indicate, their students, especially those who wish to enter those particular fields, ought to devote four years to their mastery. To this program, New York University seems to have set itself resolutely, with four year standardized programs in a number of fields. If, on the other hand, the purpose of a university school of business is to give to its students (many of whom will have no other appreciable opportunity for higher academic instruction) a general training directed toward business, plus some facility in the use of business methods or tools, then to take those students, after spending two years largely in the pursuit of liberal arts studies, and direct them into two year curricula so specialized that business teachers do not recognize any general importance of that field, seems decidedly unwise.

It will be argued at once that the proliferation of courses within a field is necessary for the development of that field. There can be no doubt that certain universities conceive of themselves as carrying a peculiar responsibility to advance the bounds of knowledge in the subjects taught. All interested students of a subject are concerned with the general advancement of its understanding, and the conditions of academic labor prevailing at certain institutions make it possible for a selected personnel of the faculty to contribute from time to time to that end. But the undergraduate schools of business, and it is with undergraduate instruction that this study is concerned chiefly, owe their chief duty to the student. This cardinal fact is all too often forgotten or brushed aside.

Most schools of business require in the neighborhood of 120 semester hours of credit. If half of these credit hours are taken in the strictly business courses, it follows that ten six-semester-hour courses or twenty three-semester-hour courses constitute the "business" part of the student's entire course. The acid test, then, for any course of undergraduate instruction, under all ordinary circumstances, should be whether that particular course, let us say of three semester hours, is worth one-twentieth of a student's business education. Stripped of all verbiage, self-interest or other confusing factors, it is primarily by this test that developments in the various business fields should be judged. There may of course be other reasons for the existence of highly specialized courses which cannot possibly meet this test, but such reasons are beyond the problem of ordinary undergraduate instruction.

Notwithstanding the profusion of business courses, one finds but six courses, other than elementary economics, which are generally required of all students. These are elementary accounting, money and banking, corporation or business finance, business law, marketing, and statistics. Perhaps to this number a course dealing with some phase of management seems in process of being added. These appear to be the fundamentals of business. Adding the customary number of semester hours devoted to these, the result constitutes more than half of the "business" part of the students course. Viewed objectively, the schools seem to accept the plan of the general course, even as the majority of students select it when given a free opportunity.

The other fields of business not represented in these common core requirements present a problem. For example, if transportation is important enough to warrant the development of 6,958 credit hours of instruction (which is more than the total in business law, marketing, statistics, or elementary economics), and a customary range of five courses, then all students receiving a college training in business should gain some understanding of this particular aspect. If insurance is important enough to justify a total of almost 5,000 credit hours, and specialization at fifteen schools, then the schools not including some instruction in this field for all students offend seriously against them.

Duplication—The Inevitable Result

There is one important reason why this proliferation of courses and specialization of curricula is not so serious in some respects as would at first glance appear. The reason is that there is nowhere a corresponding proliferation or specialization of subject matter. There exists, in other words, a tremendous amount of duplication of material.

Extensive duplication of material has been inevitable in view of the circumstances under which this proliferation has occurred. In a large proportion of cases, courses seem to have developed regardless of the work done in other courses in the same field, and certainly of the work done in the courses in other fields. One of the most striking experiences in the field work of this study has been the frequency with which faculty members have shown a lack of knowledge of the plan and content of courses closely related to their own. Outlines of courses which teachers distribute to students are zealously guarded from the hands of colleagues, even in rather remotely related subjects. It is particularly serious when this situation exists between courses which follow in a given order of sequence.

The resultant duplication of course content is a serious matter. It wastes the student's time, and may dissipate his interest. It leads to overemphasis of certain aspects and underemphasis of others. Because it is unregulated, it lacks usually the merit of repetition. Because of the time element involved, it narrows the range of the student's instruction. There is an element of financial waste, from the standpoint of the school's budget. One can question also certain ethical aspects of the situation, with reference to the duty of a school toward its contributing clients. Finally, it is unbusiness-like, a peculiarly serious indictment to bring against the teaching of business subjects.

The Experiment at the University of Southern California

A number of schools of business, as well as other divisions of our universities, have shown an awareness of this problem, and various gestures have been made in the direction of dealing with it. Particular mention might be made in this connection of the work of Professor Frank C. Touton, vice-president of the University of Southern California and director of educational research and service. Believing that duplication in courses is not ethical, both to students and university, and that appreciable economies can be affected in the students' time and the university's budget, the administration of that institution has set itself the task, through Professor Touton, of eliminating such overlapping of courses. The method pursued is the detailed and objective analysis of each course with reference to its content, its objectives, and its relation to the program and purpose of the school.

It is an exacting task, calling for tactful yet vigorous executive leadership, patiently working out the problems involved through a mass of detailed difficulties. It is a sizeable job, calling for more than the incidental activities of a committee the members of which are occupied with their accustomed tasks. Faculty members are apt to construe such a movement as a threat to certain vested interests, and unless its sponsor or sponsors have the strong and continuous support of the administration, their efforts are doomed to failure.

The Emotional Aspects of the Departmental System

This whole problem of duplication, as well as the preceding process of proliferation and the subsequent problem of coordination are complicated by the personal elements involved. Collegiate education for business is still of a youth in which original heads of department, responsible for their development, are serving in this capacity. These persons not infrequently have been the pioneers in their particular fields. They retain the zealousness of the crusading spirit which enabled them in the earlier years to hew their fields out of the academic wilderness. Particularly in the older and more firmly established schools is one prone to find departments and subjects identified with personalities. These personalities in turn identify themselves with their fields.

This situation, at best offers peculiar difficulties. To many of these leaders, collegiate education for business owes a real debt. Beginning in a field in which there were no textbooks, no courses, no precedents, they have made contributions in many cases of lasting value. There is a natural reluctance to advocate changes in departments which are the lengthened shadows of outstanding faculty figures, no matter how desirable they may seem, lest such a policy be interpreted as indicating in any sense a lack of appreciation of their sterling worth.

Coupled with a natural zealousness for the subject matter which has been one's life work is the unfortunate ambition of some of these personalities to enhance their egoes by becoming employers of academic labor. It is a pathetically humorous circumstance, this overweening desire of some scholars to have as many intellectual laborers "under" them as possible. The inevitable result has been the growth of vested interests which motivate the maintenance of the *status quo,* if not its further fortification. The whole situation becomes tinged with emotion. Department heads transmit that emotion, in part at least, to their "retainers" within the department. It is the interjection of this emotional factor, reinforced with considerations of personal ambition and vested interests, into the situation which makes its adjustment so difficult even when its evils are current coin in the academic market places.

The Lack of Coordination

Another definite aspect of the development of the business subjects has been the lack of coordination in so many cases. Evidence of this can be found both as within the department or subject, and as between departments or subjects.

The development of many departments has been usually a growth by addition. Like the typical American city, departments have just accumulated. There seems to have been lacking often the semblance of any consistent plan or program or philosophy of instruction. This is particularly apt to be the case where changes in personnel have been rapid, where department heads have changed often, or are weak, or have little interest in teaching over against the specialized contributions by members of his staff.

A similar situation prevails frequently as between departments. There has been a general denunciation of water-tight compartments in business instruction, and a general functioning in terms of them. The development of business curricula has been in terms of departments, and each department has been prone to develop its field and its implications as though it could have no conceivable relation to any other field.

In order to avoid the evils of this rigorous departmentalization of the business school, there is a tendency now to think in terms of functional fields or aspects of business, or in terms of actual problems encountered. The arrangement of courses in the School of Commerce and Administration of the University of Chicago is an illustration of this tendency. It remains to be seen what the advantages of this arrangement will be.

One distinct step forward in this connection is the growing conviction of the sin of departmental thinking. It may be that the departmental emphasis has been a necessary phase of the development of the business schools in their early stages, particularly in view of the strong spirit of specialization that surround their pioneer period. Certain is it now, however, that this emphasis has been outgrown largely, and remains now only to plague where once it sought to serve.

Coordination and the Unity of the Curriculum

Underlying this entire discussion there is apparent what, in the judgment of very many careful students, is the outstanding present day need in collegiate education for business. This need is the effective coordination of the elements of the business curriculum into a structural unity. A very clear statement of such a need in the field of engineering education was made several years ago.

> To be sound, an engineering education must be more than the mere sum of its parts; it must be conceived and planned as a whole. While it is desirable to provide a reasonable degree of flexibility within an orderly curriculum structure through a moderate diversity of programs, some provision for the election of individual subjects and group options, and the gradual introduction of some more autonomous plan of work for selected upper-classmen, any tendency toward disintegration into a loose succession of un-coordinated subjects is to be vigorously opposed. The coherent, integral structure of the engineering curriculum at its best, with its logical sequences running from beginning to end, drawing on many fields of knowledge, but progressively bringing the student's efforts to a focus in a well-defined realm, is probably its most distinctive merit.[37]

This structural unity which has been a characteristic of engineering education throughout its history, is very definitely lacking thus

---

[37] The Society for the Promotion of Engineering Education, "Preliminary Report of the Board of Investigation and Coordination", November, 1926, pp. 1-2.

far in collegiate education for business. The need for such unity, with closely knit and logical sequence of subject matter throughout the entire curriculum, has come to be very much emphasized in the discussions of business school circles in the last few years.

SUMMARY OF CONCLUSIONS

Concerning the business studies, the following facts, brought out in this chapter, are restated here in summary form.

1. The business studies taught in present day curricula of collegiate schools of business include accounting, banking , and finance, business law, marketing, advertising, selling, merchandising, foreign trade and foreign service, insurance, business organization and management, labor and personnel, public utilities, real estate, statistics and business cycles, and transportation and traffic.

2. Accountng is the most fully developed of these subjects, on the basis of class hours of instruction offered. All the schools offer such courses, most of them have separate departments of accounting. All offer specialization in it. Accounting curricula usually are rather narrowly specialized. Generally required courses in accounting usually are placed in the lower classes.

3. Banking and finance also receive major emphasis in business education. Every school in the American Association requires courses in this field and enables specialization in it. Courses in money and banking and in business or corporation finance are very generally required. Courses in investments are increasing in popularity.

4. Business law, too, is recognized as a business fundamental. All schools include it among their requirements. It is usually scheduled for upper class students. Contracts, agencies, partnerships, corporations, bailments, sales, and negotiable instruments are the chief topics included. There is very little consideration of industrial or labor law.

5. Various kinds of courses dealing with aspects of the relationship between business and the public are offered. They include courses in economic and social reform, on trusts and business combinations, on the public regulation of business, and on business ethics. Such courses are not generally required.

6. The field of distribution ranks next to accounting in the number of class hours of instruction offered. Courses in market-

ing appear most frequently, but advertising, selling, and merchandising are also well represented. The introductory course in marketing is required rather generally of business school students. Considering the field of distribution as a whole, there is rather a lack of coordination. Economists generally offer the courses in marketing, psychologists predominate in selling, journalists and psychologists abound in the advertising aspects. Sometimes the courses in these several aspects are not all given in the school of business, thus increasing the lack of coordination as a rule.

7. Foreign trade and insurance both are fairly well developed, extensively utilized, upper class specialized subjects. Many schools offer specialized curricula in these studies, but neither subject is a general requirement as a rule.

8. Management is increasingly emphasized in the business schools. The courses in this field vary considerably, from mere description of organization to critical studies of business policy. Management studies in production appear most frequently, and specialized curricula in this phase of business are widely offered. Personnel management and labor problems account for another large part of the instruction offered in the field of management. Several schools have developed their entire program around the management objective.

9. Public utilities and real estate are two fields which have been developed in recent years in the business schools. Beyond a course or two, instruction and specialization in both subjects are still confined to a relatively few of the business schools. An increasing number of business school graduates seem, however, to find employment in these fields.

10. Statistics is a study of the first order of importance in the colleges of commerce. While generally required of all business students, statistics thus far has not been widely emphasized as a field of specialization, thus indicating that it is conceived of as a tool to be utilized in the control of business. The subject presents peculiar problems and pedagogy. Less emphasis upon higher mathematics and the refinements of statistical technique may be desirable in general required courses.

11. Transportation and traffic courses are widely offered in schools of business. These courses are pursued in the upper years usually. Specialization in the general field is offered in many

cases. Engineering schools also include courses in transportation, but the subject has been developed most in the business schools.

12. Numerous courses of instruction and specialized curricula are offered in each of the fields referred to above. These subjects have developed, for the most part, without regard each to the other, or the central project of the training of students for business. The result has been a multitude of courses, with considerable duplication of material and very little coordination. What the business schools have accomplished has been the development of certain phases of business much more than a unified program of business education. Coordination of the general and business subjects into a curriculum conceived and planned as a whole, seems to be a major need at this time in collegiate education for business.

CHAPTER XIV

REPORTED TRENDS IN THE CHANGING BUSINESS CURRICULA[1]

CHANGE AND THE BUSINESS SCHOOLS

The concept of change is fundamental in modern thinking. Everything is seen in process of development. That which has been yields to that which is, to be displaced in turn by that which shall be—this, applicable from electron to solar system and from amoeba to man, is the cornerstone of contemporary interpretation.

Consciousness of change leads naturally to interest in the direction of that change. Thus arises that earnest consideration of trends, again so characteristic of present day thought. A trend, scientifically conceived and determined, is a sign post on the highway of change. It indicates direction, it clarifies change, and it gives a sense or semblence of orderliness to it.

University curricula do not stand outside of the currents of our changing civilization. To the extent that they justify their existence, they remain abreast, perhaps even become leaders, of the changing order of things. Particularly is this true of collegiate schools of business. Modern industry, business in its various aspects, conceptions of the functions and objectives of business education—all have changed with such unusual rapidity during recent decades that the collegiate school of business which shows no capacity to adjust itself to these changes ceases, sooner or later, to receive serious consideration. As a matter of fact, collegiate education for business has been changing, and with amazing rapidity. One need only compare the developments of today with those of ten years ago to see how complete and sweeping these changes have been.

What is the nature of the changes which have taken place, particularly in the curricula of the colleges of commerce? Have there been any shifts in emphases, any additions or omissions in the curricula? Is there any direction in which these changes are moving? What, in other words, are the trends in collegiate education for business? These questions inevitably present them-

---

[1] Prepared and written by J. H. S. Bossard.

selves, and none were asked more frequently by persons interested in the present inquiry.

In attempting to answer questions of this nature, the proper procedure would seem to be that of objective, quantitative measurement. That is to say, the desirable method would be to record all changes in the curricula and work of the colleges of commerce, institution by institution and year by year, for the purpose of ascertaining the cumulative nature and direction of such changes.

Unfortunately, the circumstances controlling the present study did not permit the addition of a task of such proportions. Then, too, one questions whether the field of university education for business has matured as yet sufficiently for a study of this kind. There is some reason to think that it is still too much in the stage of beginnings; that the respective development of constitutent schools is still too uneven; that too many schools still seem in process of catching up with developments which other schools attained some time ago, and are now in process perhaps of discarding. Trends can be identified in particular schools, it is true, but for the situation as a whole, some considerable collective maturity must exist before any objective determination of trends is feasible.

In the meantime, this study seeks to make a possible step in this direction by attempting to deal objectively with opinions of existing trends. The method of the present inquiry has been to discuss with selected responsible members of the faculties of the several collegiate schools of business the question of trends in business education, both so far as their particular school was concerned and with regard to the situation as a whole. These are opinions, it is true, and represent subjective impressions rather than conclusions objectively determined. But opinions may be dealt with objectively. When a dean or faculty member in a school of business refers to a trend in his school, or in the field of university education for business as a whole, it may be taken to mean either that he actually sees that trend in operation or that he thinks it ought to be in operation. Declarations of trend, in other words, if not true statements of actual or impending changes, are significant as wish embodiments. That is to say, they indicate convictions, whether they represent observations or not. Projection of wishes into fancied facts is a very common mental habit. There is reason to assume, therefore, that the trends indicated in this chapter are in part declarations of future policy rather than conclusions of previous achievements.

Opinions, judgments and observations of representatives of 35 of the 42 schools in the American Association were obtained and recorded as nearly verbatim as possible. These statements were then classified and analyzed. Analysis of them shows a surprising agreement, both as to the points emphasized and the trends or conclusions stated. The remainder of this chapter will be devoted to a consideration of the main trends revealed. Effort is made to present them in general rather than specific form.

The Trend Toward Fundamental Business Studies

Statements of a trend toward the fundamentals of business were both direct and general. Constant reference was made to an increasing tendency to emphasize certain basic courses as being of outstanding importance, both for purposes of training in the habits and methods of work essential for business success and for the understanding of business processes. No point or trend was mentioned more frequently or with more positive assurance.

Considerably less clear and positive are the identifications of these fundamental studies. Reference to the data presented in Chapters XI-XIII is pertinent at this point. Of particular significance are Tables LXIX-LXXVI, and the discussion in the latter part of Chapter XII. The tables cited would seem to indicate the prevailing judgments of the schools concerning these fundamentals.

In general, the ideas expressed informally concerning these fundamental studies seem to imply the following conceptions; viz., that education for business involves certain fundamental studies, necessary and important as foundations for a second group of common or core studies, which, in turn, are essential to an understanding of business processes. In other words, from these discussions of trend toward the fundamentals of business education there emerges the idea not of one but of two groups of fundamental studies: one consisting of those which develop a foundation for business education and a setting for business life; and, second, a group of studies which comprehend the common core of business operations and processes. At any rate, the tendency seems to be to regard increasingly these studies as the common core of business education, to view them as constituting a standard curriculum, to be required of all business students, and with rather free electives in all other fields. The predominance of the general course, reference to which has been made previously, represents another aspect or evidence of the same tendency.

Decreasing Emphasis Upon Technical Instruction

Complementary to the trend toward the fundamentals, and as another aspect of the same general development, is the decreasing emphasis upon technical courses, i.e., courses which concern themselves with the "turning of the trick." A number, but not all, of the schools indicate this trend. Even the work in accounting has been brought in line at several schools with this general policy, courses in this subject concerning themselves primarily with its use as a measuring aid or tool in the conduct and control of business, rather than with the training of accountants.

The general contention underlying this expressed trend is that other agencies of commercial education, such as the business college, the corporation school, the evening school, etc., serve this function of giving specialized, technical, "acquisitive" training to persons who know usually directly what they want. It is urged further that if the collegiate school of business has any definitely distinctive place in the scheme of commercial education, it is to be found, not by competing with these other agencies in the production of technicians, but in the training of students in the larger aspects and situations which lie behind and beyond technique. The thought involved is not a depreciation of technique, but its relegation to a certain definite place in the general plan of education.

Something of the same idea inheres in the somewhat differently expressed argument, declared as a trend at several schools, of emphasizing the social or cultural or situational approach to business education. The chief thought here is that business places a premium upon the culturally trained men who can grasp the larger aspects and implications of business problems, and that even technical courses, so-called, must have some cultural flavor and background and value if they are to serve best their chosen purpose.

Whatever the particular guise of their appearance, the central thought in the two trends thus far stated would seem to be this: that business must be understood before it can be administered successfully, and that the fundamentals of business need emphasis more than training in technique.

Among the concrete aspects of the trend away from technical emphasis in the collegiate schools of business, these might be mentioned. There are several schools which have reduced arbitarily the number of so-called technical courses. Certain changes have been made, too, in the direction of restricting admission to such courses to students who are nearing the end of their undergraduate training, and after they have completed the more general and fundamental courses. Finally, there seems to be developing the idea that the evening, extension and graduate classes afford the more fruitful and desirable opportunity for instruction in administration and technique.

A Frowning Upon Further Specialization

There are signs on the academic sky portending that the summer of specialization is passing, at least so far as undergraduate curricula and instruction are concerned. Statements from responsible leaders in a number of colleges of commerce visited indicated that, despite the data on specialization presented in the previous chapter, university education for business does not stand outside of this trend. "We are aiming now," says one dean, "at a general training in those subjects which are considered fundamental, and with a decreasing attention to specialization." Another declares that "the tendency here is to emphasize the general course with a 'bias for business.'" A third declares: "We are getting away from specialization. The general business course in itself is sufficient specialization." Thus run the statements encountered.

On the whole, this trend, which may be designated as a frowning upon further specialization, is complementary to the two trends which have been noted. On the whole, they constitute a development in collegiate education for business similar to that reported recently in engineering education. "It is apparent," states the report of the Society for the Promotion of Engineering Education, "that the general trend since 1870 has been toward greater specialization and concentration that this movement has passed its peak and that a reaction to more general training is developing. ****

Undoubtedly the desires of students, teachers, practitioners and employers have all contributed in some measure to the use of specialization as well as the great expansion of engineering knowledge, and it is significant to note the turn of contemporary opinion away from early and extensive specialization for undergraduate students."[2]

The Emergence of Regional Specialization

While specialization in curricula among students in the same institution is being frowned upon, there are, on the other hand, various evidences of a growing specialization between institutions, particularly in the development of business and economic data and literature. This specialization, if so it may be termed, seems to accord with certain regional divisions of the United States. That is to say, one finds certain courses and research projects peculiar to the New England schools of business which deal specifically with problems peculiarly important to that region, and so likewise in the schools of the south, of the middle west, of the southwest and of the Pacific coast.

There is, undoubtedly, a growing appreciation in all of the social sciences of the fact that there are well defined regional areas in the United States whose existence and differences alike need receive recognition. A number of factors underlie or are responsible for these regions—physical background, economic resources, race, social heritage, psychology, collective experience, etc. These regional areas have their own peculiar problems and evolve their own particular ways of dealing with them. Although sharing certain common bases, each nevertheless develops its own superstructure upon this common foundation. An appreciation of both common foundation and distinctive regional superstructure is necessary for an understanding of the particular area.

This development of regional business and economic data may be interpreted as a step forward, involving a getting away from the broad generalizations which have characterized so generally our economic literature in the past, and a coming to grip with our problems at closer range. Naturally, this closer range con-

---

[2] Bulletin No. 11, pp. 4 and 11.

tact with problems brings into sharper relief the characterizing details of the picture and gives them a deeper meaning. In other words, the recognition of regional differences marks another aspect in the development of a more intensive educational policy, further reference to which is made in this chapter.

Individual members of commerce faculties are very positive in their conviction that it is the duty of the collegiate school of business to build up this more specific literature pertinent to the regional area which the school serves. To the extent, they point out, that any educational institution draws its clientele and support from a given area, it needs, in all phases of its work, to develop an intimate understanding of the values and problems of that area, to the end that it may instruct its students to the best advantage and serve it most adequately in all ways. In this connection, it is important to remember that with the increase in the number of colleges of commerce in different parts of the country, each school, under normal circumstances, is more likely than formerly to draw its students from restricted areas. Disavowing any gesture in the direction of provincialism, what is implied in these developments is the addition by the collegiate school of business, to the broad general work it may be doing, of a more intensive adaptation to the situation immediately at hand.

The Trend Toward Fewer Courses

There is much current discussion in college of commerce circles concerning the number and increases of courses, and certain institutions seem to have turned to the policy of reducing, or at least restricting, the number of business courses offered. In regard to this trend, there is considerable confusion between fact and fancy. There are schools which actually offer fewer business courses today than three or four years ago, despite the accumulative results of continuing research. Other schools have added courses in recent years, but attribute such increase to the growth of student enrollment and the development of peculiarly pertinent regional material. This much seems certain, that most of the 38 undergraduate member schools are now scrutinizing the proposal of new courses with very great care, and increasingly with negative decisions.

Behind this policy there seems to be a certain pressure on the basis of administrative economy, but for the most part it appears to be a matter of educational policy. The feeling appears to be widespread that the proliferation of courses, previously referred to in this study, has gone too far, that in running riot, as it undoubtedly has, much duplication of material and wastage has resulted.

The Trend Toward Better Courses

Whenever, in times past, there have been intimations that students have been prepared inadequately in a given field or subject, the tendency in academic circles has been to add new courses and more hours of instruction. Educational institutions have pursued, in other words, a policy of educational efficiency which might be called extensive, i.e., a policy of more and bigger courses.

There seems, now, to exist a trend in university education for business which involves a transition to a more intensive policy of education. This policy involves the development, not of more but of better courses, of courses more adequately organized, of courses pedagogically more sound, and of courses taught more intensively and more effectively.

Many evidences were found in the course of the present study of a general raising of standards of instruction, of a more rigid holding to requirements, and of an increased insistence upon the business value of a thorough drill in work habits. In fact, some of the emphasis upon certain basic courses seems to rest upon the belief that they were unusually valuable for such drill purposes. Accounting and statistics were mentioned most often because of their disciplinary worth in this respect. In fact, as was stated in the preceding chapter, there are not a few experienced teachers who hold that what is taught is seldom so important as how it is taught. One observes this curious fact in this connection; that as a rule the younger teachers, glowing with enthusiasm, place great store upon subject matter, crowning their particular bit with undue importance. Older and more experienced teachers seem much more likely to emphasize the method and effectiveness of instruction. Discussion of experiments in teaching methods appears in other chapters.

The Trend Toward the Engineering Viewpoint

Numerous references have been made recently to the penetration of the field of business by the engineer and by engineering ideals. There seems to be a belief, rather widely held in present day business circles, that when a task really needs to be done, the engineer is the person to be summoned. While his selection may be attributed at first glance to his technical preparation, closer examination reveals that what impresses the public mind about the engineer is not so much his knowledge of engineering, as the way in which he works. That is to say, the engineer is selected because he can be depended upon to work with such precision as to bring two and two together and dovetail them into a perfect four.

Careful students of university education for business have been aware of this increasing emphasis during the last few years upon the engineering viewpoint. While there are those who have mistaken this as placing a premium on the content of engineering education, the more discerning have been quick to see that the really significant thing is the method of the engineer—his precision, his exactness, his ability to analyze, his capacity to coordinate, etc. The trend toward engineering, both in business and in business education, is to be interpreted, then, as a symbolic demand for certain habits or methods of work by way of reaction to the loose thinking and easy generalizing which have characterized the social sciences from whose loins business education has sprung. As such, this trend is not dissimilar to the earlier emphasis upon the classics because of their reputed capacity of disciplining the mind and training it so as to enable it to grapple successfully with the problems of reality and everyday life.

Recognition that certain habits or methods of work adhere to certain professions leads naturally to the conclusion that they are to be viewed as the result of training rather than as traits inherent in the individual. From this it follows that such traits can be cultivated consciously in the schools. Reference has been made to the experiments reported by Professor J. T. Young, of the University of Pennsylvania. Such programs are in keeping with certain recent developments in the field of educational psychology.

While the trend toward the engineering methods of work is pronounced, it might be added that there are those leaders who fear lest the pendulum swing too far. These men agree that while business education needs an infusion of the disciplinary values of engineering education any undue amount of it must be avoided. For the curse of the engineering approach is that often it is too precise, too mechanical and not imaginative and speculative and understanding enough. Business education should find warning in the fact that its own progression toward engineering ideals comes at the very time when engineering education is moving toward the humanities, and when engineers are emphasizing that not all things can be reduced to quantitative measurement. Perhaps here too the path to progress lives in the middle of the road, and those collegiate schools of business that will combine the liberality in their present curricula with the precision and exactness of the engineering schools may make a real contribution to our academic development.

The Trend Toward Objective Determination of Curricula

Reference to the objective determination of curriculum and course content has been made in Chapter III. This process, a development of the past fifteen years, grew out of experience with training enterprises conducted in the United States during the World War. While applied originally to more simple and concrete jobs, there are those educational leaders who insist upon its general applicability, including the field of higher education.

Several, but by no means all, of the association schools of business, are committing themselves to such a policy of curriculum building. At the University of Pittsburgh the work of executives is being analyzed for purposes of curriculum construction. Harvard's program of developing concrete case material about business situations, treated from the viewpoint of the executive, is well known. At Ohio State the content of certain basic courses in the business school is being determined by objective analysis of subsequent courses.

Two aspects of this trend may be identified: one emphasizes the objective analysis of occupations in the field of business for the purpose of revealing the educational needs of university training for business; the other, a similar analysis of upper class courses to determine the necessary content and elements of the fundamental courses.

Although not clearly focussed everywhere, there seems to be a growing sentiment among faculties in the colleges of commerce that revisions of curriculum are too much based on traditional arrangements, emotional prejudice and the compromise of contending views of specialists absorbed in the importance of their particular subjects. This, obviously, is the negative background out of which may grow the alternate positive program of objective analysis. Difficult as such a process is when applied to the various professional branches of higher education, it is perhaps the only alternative.

The Tendency to Disregard Departmental Lines

"The social sciences are not merely theoretical disciplines," write Ogburn and Goldenweiser in their introduction to "The Social Sciences and Their Interrelations", "but also tools to be employed in the solution of the concrete practical problems of an existing and developing society. As tools they must constantly cooperate, with an all but complete disregard of academic and classificatory distinctions. The problems of living society do not range themselves so as to fit the artificial isolation forced upon the social sciences by differences of specific subject and method. These problems are what they are. If they are to be solved, whatever knowledge we possess about society must be called into service, wherever needed.

"The problem of poverty, for example, is related to biology because of a possible heredity factor. It also falls in the domain of psychology, for many cases of destitution are neurotic—a problem for the psychiatrist. Economics contributes to the solution, for the distribution of wealth, wages, and the business cycles are all factors in poverty. Sociology is related to the problem through population, migration, birth control, housing, city planning, old age pensions, public health measures, etc. From still other angles poverty enters the fields of political science, ethics, and education. Immigration, as a social problem, falls within the provinces of sociology, economics, anthropology, political science, jurisprudence, and education. Race problems are dependent upon information from biology, anthropology, history, economics, sociology, and statistics. A study of nationality means cooperation on the part of history, psychology, sociology, political science, economics, and anthropology. In dealing with crime one must use statistics, sociology law, psychology, political science, and economics. Taxation is the concern of political science and economics, as well as of other sciences.

"If one makes a list of research problems, even very specialized ones, and examines it with reference to the various social sciences to be consulted, one is often surprised to find how much they are interrelated in their pragmatic aspects. This is true today and will become increasingly so in the future, as changes in society, brought about by an efficient handling of social problems, become more frequent and thoroughgoing."[3]

As business educators come to grip increasingly with the problems of reality, less emphasis is bound to be given to the maintenance of traditional lines of departmental organization and more to the pooling of the materials and methods which the different sciences have placed at their disposal. Stated briefly, more concern with business problems means less interest in departmental distinctions.

Perhaps, too, teachers are coming to see that departmental divisions are not so important as has been supposed in recent years, and that their own best interests are not served by too restricted an interest upon any particular aspect of the field of education. Obviously no effective educational program, such as will determine ultimately the degree of success of the collegiate schools of business, is possible by simply combining the maximum development of individual departments, each regarding only itself.

Three aspects of this tendency to get away from watertight compartments in the work of the collegiate schools of business may be recognized. One of them is the development or contemplation of composite courses, reference to which has been made. This tendency is most pronounced in regard to the work of the freshman and sophomore years, and in the graduate courses of several institutions. Such composite courses go far to minimize domination by vested departmental interests.

A second aspect of this tendency is to found in the increasing emphasis upon the adaptation of non-business courses, so-called, to the purposes of the business school. Reference to this problem has also been made repeatedly in the course of this study. Until rather recently, very few teachers showed any interest in the adaptation of their courses to the needs of any particular group

---

[3] Ogburn, William F., and Goldenweiser, Alexander, *The Social Sciences and Their Interrelations,* Houghton, Mifflin Company, New York. 1927, pp. 7-8.

of students. English was English, chemistry was chemistry, and biology was biology. Moreover, no professional future was believed to exist in such adaptive development. Today, thoughtful students are seeing that the contention that chemistry is always the same is but a half truth. A man is a man, it is true, but sometimes he wears a dinner coat, sometimes a business suit, and sometimes a golfing outfit. Or, to change the illustration slightly, a man needs to be considered at one time as a father, at another as an employer, and a third time as a republican or democrat. Moreover, it is coming to be recognized that such adaptation of instruction, presuming as it does a primary interest in the interrelation of subjects, is as legitimate a field for professional exploitation as any particular subject, considered independently. In fact, effective teaching in any subject means emphasis upon it, not as an isolated unit, but as a center from which radiate filaments into various other fields of study.

A third aspect of this trend is to be found in the interchange or overlapping of teaching personnel, a policy consciously cultivated at several schools. This involves the assignment of instructors to several departments for the purpose of avoiding too restricted a professional interest and too premature and narrow a specialization. There is, of course, nothing new in the facts of such overlapping of teaching personnel, such a practice obtaining more or less generally, especially in the smaller colleges and universities. Reference is here made to the conscious cultivation recently of this policy, in certain larger schools of business, and to the significance of such a policy when considered in relation to other developments in the business schools.

Applying Science in Business Education

One of the outstanding facts in the recent history of science is its commercial vindication. Scientific research has been sold completely to modern business, principally because of the rôle it has played in increasing productivity, and in business pioneering. Partly because of its achievements in this respect, and partly as a result of other factors, schools of business are placing more and more emphasis upon research. In fact, this growing interest in scientific research constitutes one of the most pronounced trends in the field of university education for business. Considered in its larger meaning, it involves the growing application of scientific method to the problems of the business schools. At least three aspects or evidences of this trend, thus conceived, may be discerned. Brief reference will be made to each of these.

The bureau of business or economic research represents the most formal and obvious token of the scientific emphasis in business education. Twenty-one of the 42 schools belonging to the American Association of Collegiate Schools of Business have bureaus of business research. These bureaus, in addition to other services which they render, are an essential factor in a number of institutions in enriching and giving greater reality to the business courses. In addition to the bureaus of business research, some of the colleges of commerce maintain cooperative relationships with separately organized research agencies. The conduct of investigations by these research agencies of the current problems of the various business communities has, it is needless to add, a stimulating effect upon instructors and students participating.

Courses dealing with the methodology of business research constitute a second aspect of this scientific trend in business education. Courses in statistics, business forecasting and business research are obvious illustrations. A few schools seem to recognize the larger purpose of such courses, coordinating the various techniques that may be employed into "the investigation of business problems," which phrase is used as a course title at some six or eight member schools. One or two schools apparently have organized their entire program, at least so far as the upper classes are concerned, around the development of research projects.

A third aspect of the scientific movement in business education includes the various instances of the application of the scientific method to problems of curricula and methods of instruction. Reference has been made to the trend toward objective determination of curriculum and course content. The follow-up of college of commerce graduates, of which a part of this study is an illustration; the biographical study of various groups of business leaders and technicians; the scientific analyses of student failures; tests to measure the returns of various types of instructional effort; and the increasing willingness of members of the business school faculties to experiment, both in teaching methods and materials, all indicate the growth of a scientific attitude in the conduct of business educations. Particularly important is this interest in experimentation and the objective determination of results. Much improvement may be made in this manner, and even in those cases where experiments will but lead to a vindication of the original method or material, there has been a net gain. The more challenging of these experiments will be dealt with in the following chapter. The present reference has been merely by way of identification of a trend.

Summary and Conclusions

Other developments obtain in the colleges of commerce included in the present study which might conceivably be spoken of as trends. There are, for example, the recent requirements of business experience for graduation, the conduct of extension institutes for certain selected business groups, or the development of short and intensive curricula in technical subjects for those students who do not intend to graduate. The foregoing discussion of trends is not meant to be complete. Only those more generally emphasized, as evidenced by the tabulation of recorded comments and opinions, have been presented. They are ten in number, and these, together with the introductory discussion, will be summarized briefly by way of conclusion.

1. The concept of change is fundamental in modern thinking. Consciousness of change leads naturally to interest in the direction of that change. Thus arises that earnest consideration of trends also so characteristic of present day thought. A trend, scientifically conceived and determined, is a sign post on the highway of change.

2. Collegiate education for business has been changing, and with amazing rapidity. Interest is very general as to the nature of the trends in this field.

3. While an objective determination of the trends in university education for business was not possible in conection with the present study, opinions concerning these trends expressed by responsible members of business school faculties were obtained and treated objectively. These are significant, if not always as statements of actual or impending changes, at least as wish embodiments.

4. Statements of a trend toward the fundamentals of business were both direct and general. There seems to prevail a conception not of one but of two groups of fundamental studies: one consisting of those which develop a foundation for business education, and, second, a group of studies which comprehend the common core of business operations and processes.

5. Complementary to the above trend is a decreasing emphasis upon technical courses, i.e., courses which concern themselves with the "turning of the trick." The general contention underlying this expressed trend is that other agencies of commercial education can serve this function of giving technical training, and that if the collegiate school of business has any distinctive place in the scheme of commercial education, it is to be found in the training of students in the larger aspects and situations which lie behind and beyond technique.

6. Further specialization is being frowned upon, at least so far as undergraduate curricula and instruction are concerned. This trend again is complementary to the two previously expressed.

7. There are evidences of an emergence of regional specialization, i.e., between institutions in the development of business data and literature. Various schools accept this as a duty to the regional area from which they draw the majority of students, and in which their graduates most likely find their employments.

8. There seems to be a trend towards fewer courses, or, at least to the very careful scrutiny of new courses. This is partly a matter of administrative economy, and partly a matter of educational policy. There is a widespread belief that the proliferation of courses has run riot, resulting in much duplication.

9. The trend toward better courses involves, apparently, a transition to a more intensive policy of education. There seems to be considerable emphasis upon raising the standards of instruction, upon a more rigid holding to requirements, and upon the business value of a thorough drill in work habits.

10. The trend toward the engineering viewpoint, which seems quite pronounced, is mistaken at times as placing a premium upon the content of engineering education. Correctly interpreted, it is essentially a demand for certain habits of precision, of exactness, of analysis and coordination, by way of reaction

to the loose thinking and easy generalizing which have characterized the social sciences from whose loins business education has
sprung.

11. The trend toward objective determination of curricula content is new only in its application to the field of higher education.
It is urged increasingly in opposition to the traditional methods of
curricula construction which involve, as a rule and at best, but an
awkward compromise between the clashing demand of contending specialists.

12. The tendency to disregard departmental lines in recognized
as an inevitable consequence of concentration upon business problems. Obviously, too, no effective educational program, such
as will determine ultimately the degree of success of collegiate
schools of business, is possible by simply combining the maximum
development of individual departments, each regarding only itself.

13. The increasing application of science in business education has lead to the development of bureaus of business or economic research, to the addition of courses dealing with the
methodology of business research, and to the application of the
scientific method to many of the problems of curricula and of
methods of instruction.

PART V

PROBLEMS OF PERSONNEL AND TEACHING METHODS

CHAPTER XV

TEACHING METHODS AND PROBLEMS[1]

Problems of curriculum are of obvious and vital importance in developing a program for collegiate business education and there is doubtless much justification for the great amount of attention directed toward their solution. Continued and excessive concentration upon these problems, however, frequently obscures the fact that the content of the curriculum is a far less important determinant of the success or failure of university education for business—or of any other sort of education—than the quality of the teaching. With stimulating and effective teaching the most antiquated curriculum may become a successful educational medium; without it, the most carefully designed course of study fails to accomplish its purpose.

Equally obvious is the fact that, regardless of the curriculum content and of the instructional methods employed, effective teaching is impossible without effective teachers. Any careful appraisal of educational problems in the leading collegiate schools of business furnishes abundant confirmation of Professor Munro's contention that men, rather than measures, determine the effectiveness of teaching. "There is", he states, "no substitute for *men* in the process of education—for earnest, enthusiastic, capable men in the faculty and in the student body. It is men, not methods or measures, that determine whether a college shall be first-rate or second class. Or, to put it more accurately, first find the men, and the methods will take care of themselves."[2]

Any consideration of teaching methods and devices, therefore, must commence with recognition of the fact that the central problem of teaching is one of personnel. Most educational administrators would accept this assertion as a platitude concerning which there can be no shadow of a doubt, yet administrative practice frequently neglects the task of recruiting and training the instructional staff and fails to recognize and reward good teaching. These important questions are discussed at considerable

---

[1] Prepared and written by J. Frederic Dewhurst.
[2] William Bennett Munroe, "Quack Doctoring the Colleges", *Harper's Monthly Magazine,* April 1928.

length in the following chapter, but at this point it is important to emphasize the fact that until the problem of personnel is squarely faced, revision of the curriculum and experimentation with teaching methods will be of small avail in raising the standards of collegiate education for business. There is obviously no magic to be found in any particular system or method of teaching, nor is there magic to be found in any particular curriculum. Curricula and teaching methods are nothing more than tools for education, which depend for their effective use upon the imagination and skill of the teachers who employ them.

It is the purpose of this chapter to consider briefly some of the virtues and defects of traditional teaching methods commonly employed in business education and to examine certain experiments, such as the case method and the cooperative method, which appear to be especially well adapted to collegiate training for business. No attempt has been made to discuss extensively general questions of teaching methods which have been treated exhaustively and admirably elsewhere.

It may safely be assumed that the aims of collegiate business education, at least in the undergraduate field, are not greatly different from the aims of other forms of university education. "Education," as Abbott Lawrence Lowell says, "has many objects. One of them is mechanical training—as in the use of figures which must give speed and accuracy, and applies to all direct use of formulas that enter to some extent into most occupations. Another is to acquire what has been called codified knowledge, that is, facts and ideas generally recognized as true and valuable. A third, with which we are concerned here as one of the chief objects of education, is to give the power to deal with facts, conditions and ideas new to the person who confronts them."[3]

To these important aims could be added many others, as indicated by the opinions expressed by employers in Chapter III and by graduates in Chapter VIII. In addition to the acquisition of skill and knowledge and the capacity for their use in the analysis and solution of business problems, both business executives and former students are agreed upon the importance of training in

---

[3] Abbott Lawrence Lowell, "Self-Education in College," Forum Education Series IV. *The Forum,* April 1928.

effective oral and written expression, of facility in organizing and administering human activities and in persuading and influencing others, and of the possession of desirable personal traits and qualities which will enable the individual to become socially effective in his future environment.

Whether or not one can accept all of these *desiderata* as reasonable objectives of university training, it is clear that their attainment must depend not only upon the nature and content of courses studied, but to a very great extent upon the methods of instruction employed. Indeed, except for the matter of mechanical skill and basic knowledge of facts and principles, the content of the curriculum is of subordinate importance to the instructional technique. Almost any method of instruction followed diligently and persistently will be effective in imparting knowledge and routine skill to the student, but only a high order of teaching ability will develop in him a capacity to think independently and accurately and to express his thoughts clearly and forcefully. And in actual practice college training frequently fails to develop in any substantial degree the student's capacity for independent thinking and effective expression. Certainly the traditional methods of lecture and quiz, whatever their aims may be, frequently result in little more than the absorption and memorization of pre-digested information—facts and principles which should be the means rather than the ends of education. And naturally one finds these less effective teaching devices used somewhat more extensively in the newer fields of knowledge represented by the social sciences and the business studies than in the older disciplines where longer pedagogical experience has made possible the development of more effective teaching methods.

The Lecture System

Probably no other method of instruction in the undergraduate college has been so widely used and so severely criticized as the lecture system. Originally transplanted from Germany, it has flourished in American academic soil as Professor Richardson indicates, for two outstanding reasons. First, it is an economical system since it enables one man to reach as many students as can be seated within range of his voice—in some cases as many as five hundred or even a thousand. In view of the rapid growth of higher education in recent decades and especially of the collegiate schools of business, it is only natural that this method of enabling the most effective teachers to reach the largest number of students has been favored extensively by the administrators of these institutions. Secondly, the lecture system has found favor among teachers because it is a comparatively easy method of organizing and presenting material, especially material in newer fields of knowledge where adequate texts are not yet available. As Professor Leon B. Richardson aptly remarks, "To some teachers it is a most attractive idea that they can simply talk and talk with no interruption from anyone; with no necessity of concerning themselves with the difficulties of individuals, and with no chance that a smoothly working schedule, by which they calculate that they may 'cover the course' may, in any way, be impeded."[4]

In spite of its extensive use the lecture system finds few advocates even among the most successful lecturers. Moreover, formal lectures appear to be less well adapted to the large freshman and sophomore classes, where they are now used most widely, than to advanced courses in which the students are already familiar with the field of study. Criticisms of the lecture system center around the fact that the student, at best, is only a passive listener rather than an active participant in the learning process. "The simple fact is that, for the American student, the lecture system fails to embody the chief element in education, namely, the intellectual wrestling of the teacher and the student. The student is to be compelled to reason, to weigh evidence, to judge, to relate fact to fact, to infer a new truth. Each is to be made an active participant in the discussion. In the lecture system, one is a silent, or even a passive partner."[5]

As a matter of fact, under the lecture system the student is not altogether a passive participant in the process; but his activity is chiefly a physical one, that of feverishly taking notes which furnish him, too often, with only a garbled account of the lecturer's discourse. Where the lecture is used merely for conveying

---

[4] Leon B. Richardson, *A Study of the Liberal College*, A Report to the President of Dartmouth College, Hanover, N.H. 1924, p. 193.

[5] C. F. Thwing, *The American and the German University*, Macmillan Co., New York, 1928, p. 124.

to the student facts and principles which might be learned as readily through reading, this criticism is an entirely valid one, and there is little doubt that the lecture is much less effective than other methods of accomplishing the same result. Professor Richardson's investigation of the functioning of the lecture method in liberal arts colleges led him to the conclusion that:

> The system simply does not work. In those institutions where it most prevails, we find most evidence of the success of those academic camp followers who sell synopses, and who furnish private instruction. There we find on the part of the student least evidence of steady consecutive work during the course, and the greatest signs of feverish activity at the time of examinations and tests. If we examine the situation, we can come to no favorable conclusion as to the merits of the basic process involved. As long as the reaction of the American student to the lecture remains as it now is that system should have as a means of instruction but a restricted place in our colleges.[6]

There is no reason to believe that the lecture system is altogether ineffective, however, or that it is likely to be entirely abandoned as a means of undergraduate instruction. Certainly it possesses certain advantages not possessed by other methods of teaching which justify its limited use even in undergraduate schools. Since the lecture method has probably met with greatest success and found most extensive use in the German universities, from which it was introduced into American institutions, it may be of interest to quote at length the opinions expressed by Friedrich Paulsen, professor of philosophy in the University of Berlin, —a notable advocate of this system of instruction—as to its peculiar virtues. "Its object", he says, "is to give the hearer seeking an introduction into a subject, a living survey of the whole field, through a living personality, in a series of connected lectures. It should enlighten him concerning the fundamental problems and essential conceptions of this science, concerning the stock of knowledge acquired and the method of its acquisition, and finally concerning its relation to the whole of human knowledge and the primary aims of human life, and should in this way arouse his

---

[6] Op. cit. p. 197.

active interest in the science and lead him to an independent comprehension of the same."[7]

Several distinctive features wherein he believes the lecture system excels other methods of instruction are outlined by Paulsen as follows:

> (1) In the lecture the hearer is confronted with science in the form of a *personality* that possesses it and is devoted to it. In case the personality is equal to the occasion, he is at once inspired with a belief in the thing itself. A book, especially a systematic manual or text-book, is a lifeless object that cannot create a belief; all faith is transmitted from person to person. The fact that a man who is standing before me and speaking to me, a man whom I respect and in whom I have confidence, believes in science, and devotes his strength and life to it, that alone inspires me with the belief in its importance and reality.
>
> (2) The book is a fixed and finished product, the lecture is a living and moving growth; even in the outward form, for the book exists as a complete whole, while the lecture offers a small and comprehensible part of the subject from hour to hour. And even this is not presented to the hearer as a finished product, but is developed before his very eyes at the present moment. It is well known with what keener interest we watch the growth of a thing than we contemplate the finished product. . . Nor can the interest with which the hearers follow the development of the lecturer's thought be easily awakened by a text-book. And this interest is in turn communicated to the teacher. He comes into a mutual personal relation with his hearers and depends upon the moment for the effective phrase, and telling expression, and the illuminating comparison. And the word is assisted by the voice, the way in which it is spoken, the expression of the countenance, none of which things can be found in any book.
>
> (3) This outward flexibility of the lecture is accompanied by an inner *flexibility* and freedom. It can and does, for example, employ different methods of presentation. The text-book demands unity of style and form, it prefers to proceed systematically according to the deductive, synthetic

---

[7] Friedrich Paulsen, *The German Universities and University System.* New York: Charles Scribner's Sons, 1912. See also C. F. Thwing, op. cit. in which some of these quotations from Paulsen appear, and which contains an excellent description of the contribution of the German university to American higher educational methods.

method. The lecture course is more flexible, it is not compelled to adhere to a fixed plan, in one chapter it can adopt one method, in another another, if it seems pedagogically desirable. It will, on the whole, incline to the analytical method. It will not begin with an exhaustive discussion of the fundamental concepts and principles, but will start out with known facts and phenomena, rising to the general concepts. . . . The lecture will absolutely refrain from overloading the student with dates and details, which are presented by the reference book. Details will have for it rather the value of methodical examples and illustrations. For it would after all be a useless undertaking to attempt to burden the memory of the hearer with a mass of detail. The object of the lecture is not to cram his memory with facts or to furnish him with a note-book that will prepare him for the examination, but to help him to understand the great and essential features of the sciences, as they are seen through the living personality of the teacher.

(4) All this is, of course, doubly and trebly true where *perception* plays an essential part, for example where the experiment stands in the foreground, as in experimental physics and chemistry or in physiology, or where the speaker's word explains a perceived object, as is the case in the clinic, or in archæology, or the history of art.

(5) But there is still another side to the question. The lecture not only helps him who hears it, but him who delivers it. If the lecture system were not necessary for the students, it would be necessary for the sake of the *teachers*. Let us emphasize two points.

First, the systematic presentation of a science in lecture-form constantly directs the attention towards the *essential* and the *universal*. It consequently acts as a healthy counterpoise against the tendency of scientific research to *specialism*. Without the constraints, under which the teacher is placed by the lecture course, of getting a general view of his subject in its broad outlines and relations, many a man would be still more inclined than is the case at present to pursue his specialistic investigations to the exclusion of everything else, regardless of whether his work accomplished anything for the general conception of the subject or not. It cannot be doubted that he would thereby lose some of his ability and effectiveness as a teacher. I am also convinced that he would not gain anything as an investigator; nothing is better calculated to save the thinker from losing his way in the labyrinths of fruitless and senseless specialistic investigations than a contemplation of the whole of things, I should like to say, the philosophical element in every science. And every time the lecture course is repeated the demand is repeated to keep in view the whole and its inner connections, to accentuate the principles more sharply and distinctly, to systematize more clearly and definitely. . . . . . .

Secondly, the teacher immediately perceives in the lecture, in the personal contact with his hearers, what is living, what is effective, what is fruitful, and what is true. . . Paper is patient; it accepts the most laborious ruminations and compilations, the mediocre, the barren, and the dead forms, just as readily as the living and vigorous and fruitful. It is much harder to say unreal and inane things in a lecture; we feel the opposition of the hearer who is repelled by artificiality and sophistry. Thus the lecture with silent, but perceptible force, draws us to the essential, the real, and the true.

(6) Lastly, the lecture is the only form of instruction in which a teacher can communicate his thoughts to a large number at the same time. Only a few can take part in the exercises; the active participation of the individual, on which the superiority of the exercises depends, diminishes as the number grows; if the number becomes too large, the individual is here condemned to stupid passivity more than anywhere else. . . On the other hand, the effectiveness of the lecture is increased to a certain degree by the number of hearers. We are apt to speak in another strain to a hundred than to ten or five hearers; the many eyes that look up at the lecturer give wings to his thoughts, and lend his words such force and animation as cannot be attained within a narrower circle. It may be said that the great and far-reaching influences produced by university teachers have gone out from the large lecture halls.[8]

Patently, Paulsen has described the lecture system at its best, not at its worst, or even at its average level in American colleges and universities; and at its best the lecture undoubtedly possesses most of the virtues he attributes to it. Even at its best, however, the lecture can hardly be expected to serve more than an incidental function in undergraduate education. It is important that the student be informed and acquainted with "what is living, what is effective, what is fruitful, and what is true", and that he be inspired and stimulated to an eager interest in his field of study. But if the real aims of education are to be attained, if the student

---

[8] Ibid. p. 193 et seq.

is to acquire mastery in the manipulation of ideas and facts and principles, if he is to become effective and convincing in the oral and written expression of his thoughts, he must learn by doing, by becoming an active rather than a passive partner in the learning process.

Generally speaking, among the business schools there is widespread recognition of the limitations of the lecture system and a marked tendency to restrict its use and in many courses to abandon it altogether. In those institutions where it is still used extensively the primary reason for its retention is the comparative economy of this method whereby the ablest members of the faculty are enabled to reach and influence much larger numbers of students than would be possible in ordinary class room contacts. As rapidly as more ample funds have become available, making possible smaller classes and the employment of well-trained instructors, and as more of the instructional materials in the field of business appear in published form, the need for informational lectures has diminished. As a result of these factors, there has been a decided trend toward smaller classes and a reduction in the number and proportion of formal lectures.

In addition to the impelling reasons of economy, chiefly responsible for the continued use of the lecture system in large courses, lectures can perform a useful function in presenting new and important information not yet available in published form and in analyzing and interpreting significant current developments in various fields of business study. Limited use of lectures for this purpose is particularly appropriate in the social sciences and in business, where changes in conditions and in the theories explaining these changes are occurring with such extraordinary rapidity. Even this type of material, however, can be introduced and utilized more effectively in the smaller discussion groups if the instructional staff is mature and experienced and fully aware of the significance of recent developments and of their relationship to the materials of the course.

Finally, every faculty possesses a handful of rarely gifted individuals, brilliant and inspiring lecturers who possess the rare capacity for illuminating their subjects and arousing the enthusiasm of their students. These are the men who transmit faith in their science, who inspire their students with a "belief in its importance and validity", who perform what Paulsen describes as the most vital and essential function of the lecture. They are, to use the vernacular of the market-place, no mere "order-takers"; they are the "super-salesmen" of their subjects. Granted that these compelling and convincing lecturers are sometimes not profound scholars in the technical sense, that they frequently "oversell" their subjects, that their students often regard them in the nature of performers rather than teachers; yet they are all too scarce in our college faculties and the students should not be denied the advantage of their inspiring influence. Men of this type are usually widely known on the campus, and students flock into their lectures whatever their specialties may be, and whether their courses are required or elective.

There is some question, however, as to whether their talents should not be made more widely available through the medium of special lecture courses entirely separated from required class room work. The recent reorganization of the curriculum and teaching program at Columbia College offers an interesting example of this type of experiment. As a result of curriculum revision at that institution, formal lectures in the freshman and sophomore courses have been eliminated and the work of the first two years is now being conducted in small discussion groups. But during the last two years, when the student is working intensively in his field of concentration, a number of short elective lecture courses are offered by outstanding members of the faculty. For these courses, which are given two hours a week, only half credit is allowed; but attendance only is required, there being no examinations, lecture notes, outside reading, or other requirements.

This would seem to represent a situation ideal both from the standpoint of the student and that of the lecturer. The student engaged in specialized study in one field is thus enabled to gain a "rich but rapid survey" of the essential aspects of another subject under the guidance of an outstanding authority, while the lecturer presumably is assured of greater attention and interest on the part of a willing rather than an unwilling audience. While sufficient time has not yet elapsed to determine the effectiveness of this particular experiment, this general scheme or some modification thereof seems to provide the means of permitting outstanding lecturers to exert the widest possible influence among the student body under the most favorable conditions. Such a program would have to be undertaken cautiously and circumspectly, of course, and with full realization of its dangers. The chief advantages of the plan would be lost if these lectures were made required courses; on the other hand it would probably be desirable to limit the number of credits which each student might obtain in this fashion. Finally there should be a frank recognition that the content or subject matter of such upper-class lectures is secondary to the quality and capacity of the lecturer. In other words the lecturers should be selected on a personal rather than a departmental basis, as individuals who have demonstrated a capacity to make a unique and distinctive educational contribution. This last problem, however, would probably solve itself in a fairly satisfactory fashion if such lectures were maintained on a strictly elective basis with a requirement for a certain minimum enrollment before a given course might be offered.

The Work of the Class Room

The lecture system is rarely used exclusively as a means of instruction in the collegiate schools of business, but is usually closely correlated with the work of the class room. A three-hour course sometimes comprises two hours of formal lecture each week and one hour of recitation, but the more usual ratio is one hour of lecture and two hours of quiz, while in some instances, where the five-hour one semester course has been adopted, as at the Wharton School of Finance and Commerce, only one of the class hours is devoted to lecture. In general this latter plan reflects a growing tendency, since it involves not only a desirable reduction in the number of courses pursued by a student at any one time, but also a smaller proportion of formal lectures.

Here in the class room where the smaller groups make possible a closer and more intimate contact between teacher and student and the latter becomes an active participant in the learning process, the real teaching of the student should occur. Unfortunately the conduct of quiz classes, particularly in the elementary courses, is often regarded as drudgery and is usually entrusted to immature instructors. As a result, and because the instructor is held responsible for "checking up on" and "getting grades on" the student, an inordinate amount of time is apt to be spent in merely quizzing the student to discover how thoroughly he has memorized the current assignment or the previous day's lecture. This means that primary emphasis is usually placed upon memorization of facts and principles, and the poor student who is on the border-line of failure receives major attention. This is particularly true when classes are so large that the instructor feels himself under the necessity of spending the entire hour in asking questions to determine whether or not the students are "prepared", i.e. have read and memorized the day's assignment. Even under these unfavorable conditions, however, with large sections and relatively inexperienced instructors, the recitation is doubtless superior to the *average* lecture as a means of instruction, for here the student is, at least to some extent, actively participating in his own education.

All of which leads inevitably to the conclusion which, as Professor Richardson says, "is so platitudinous that it seems hardly worth stating: a conclusion to which most of those who have written on matters of education have come, but the logic of which is still neglected by many of those who have our colleges in charge —*that teaching is really effective only if sections are small and if instruction is so far as possible individual.*"[9] Given small sections of twelve or fifteen students conducted by enthusiastic and capable teachers, and everything else becomes secondary. Under these ideal conditions effective teaching is an inevitable result, regardless of what subject is studied and what teaching method is employed. Here the student, guided by his instructor, becomes the active agent in his own education; here he can be induced to think for himself, to draw inferences from facts, to discover significant relationships, to reach his own conclusions.

Another marked advantage of the small section is that it permits much greater flexibility in teaching methods than larger classes. Relieved of the necessity of spending most of the hour in finding out how much the students have already learned, the teacher can vary the method of instruction to suit the needs of the material or of the students. He can employ the problem or case method if that seems desirable, with the assurance that all members of

---

[9] Leon B. Richardson, *A Study of the Liberal College*, op. cit. p. 199.

the class can be led into discussion. The seminar and conference method can be utilized successfully with small groups, and more attention can be devoted to developing the student's personality, his facility in cooperative effort, and capacity for effective expression by means of formal written and oral reports. If the nature of the subject demands it, the laboratory and demonstration method, or field trips, can be employed more successfully with twelve or fifteen students than with larger groups. Whatever method is used it is safe to say that the small class permits the able teacher to secure creative participation by his students rather than the passive acceptance of knowledge gained from textbooks and lectures.

Although it is quite obvious that the most effective teaching, regardless of what method is employed, can be done in small classes, it is by no means true that teaching will be improved *ipso facto* by a reduction in the size of sections. The teacher is faced with a far more difficult and delicate task in successfully guiding the discussion of a small group than in conducting the more formal recitation of a large section. Meeting in small groups—even seated in easy chairs around a fire-place—does not mean that discussion has replaced recitation or that the quiz-master has become a discussion leader.

Consummate skill and constant vigilance must be exercised by the instructor in order that, as Henry Suzzalo says, "Bad logic in a class discussion should become as intolerable as discord in a musical studio . . . while guaranteeing intellectual freedom to think, we should insist on the discipline of a rigid connection between evidence and conclusions."[10] No instructor who has honestly endeavored to conduct a discussion group will fail to recognize the difficulties involved in securing really intelligent participation by his students and in preventing a "creative discussion" from degenerating into a "bull session" commencing anywhere and ending nowhere. Nor will he be unaware that almost every discussion group is afflicted by the presence of the loose-tongued student described by Professor Fulcher as "the worst pest of all, who never reads anything that is assigned but has half-baked views on every subject—views without any foundation

[10] Henry Suzzalo, "The Effective American University System," *The Educational Record.* October 1923.

except his own laryngeal processes and a few scraps overheard and misunderstood—remarks sired by prejudice out of conceit."[11] The necessity for skillful teaching and for high-grade personnel becomes vastly more important when classes are small and personal contact is great.

Individualized Instruction

Organization of instruction on the basis of small discussion groups is of course not an end in itself. Small sections do not ensure effective teaching, but they do make possible an escape from the traditional methods of lecture and quiz, which emphasize "docility and a reproductive memory" and little else. The aim of the discussion group is to achieve a greater individualization of instruction and differential treatment of students according to their natural abilities and aptitudes. More important still, this system makes it possible for the teacher to develop and test each student's capacity for individual work and independent thinking. The preceptorial plan, as employed at Princeton, and the tutorial method, in use at Oxford and at a number of institutions in this country, represent special efforts to attain the educational advantages resulting from close personal supervision and individual guidance of the student's efforts. The tutorial system, as applied in American institutions, follows no fixed scheme, but varies widely in its nature and effectiveness. At Harvard, where it has been used with great success for many years in the division of history, government, and economics, it is an integral part of the system of specialized study in the student's major field which leads to a comprehensive examination covering the work of the last two years. Indeed, at this institution the plan for a comprehensive examination is regarded as the very *raison d'etre* of the tutorial system.

At Princeton, on the other hand, the preceptorial plan was introduced by President Wilson to secure for students in other fields than physical science the special advantages of personal contact afforded by laboratory exercises in the latter subjects. At Swarthmore individual instruction along the lines of the

---

[11] Paul Fulcher, "Lectures—To Be or Not To Be," *Wisconsin Alumni Magazine*, Jan. 1930.

individualization of instruction by varying the quantity, quality, content, and method of work for each section (3) establishes a better basis of grading, a fair basis for praise and blame (4) creates better morale among students and increases the quantity and quality of output at each level (5) ensures more efficient and sympathetic attention to the needs of the poor student, and (6) serves as a means of encouraging and stimulating the superior student.[14]

However, there is by no means unanimous assent as to the advantages of segregation, even where the plan has been given extensive trial. Common criticisms are that conduct of the poor sections is unbearable drudgery for the instructor, and that, since the low section is frequently regarded as a penal colony, this discrimination is discouraging to the poor student, who most needs encouragement. Another objection to the plan is that, owing to lack of adequate student (and teacher) motivation, segregation frequently involves no real differentiation in the quantity, quality, and content of work required at the various levels of capacity and hence segregation of students fails to attain its main object.

Finally, serious doubt is expressed as to whether it is possible to separate even a large group of individuals accurately into several distinct levels of achievement. When it is remembered that the statistical distribution of learning capacity is such that only a very few students are found at the upper and lower extremes, while the large modal group in the middle is only slightly differentiated, it appears doubtful whether the various levels would represent appreciable differences in capacity. Thus, if a hundred men were divided equally into two sections the variations *within* each section would still be much greater than the average variation between sections, while the majority of the students in each of the two sections would be nearly equal in intelligence and scholarly capacity. On the other hand, if the same hundred men were divided into as many as five sections,

---

[14] For a more complete statement of the advantages of sectioning see various articles by C. E. Seashore and report of Committee G of the American Association of University Professors on Methods of Increasing the Intellectual Interest and Raising the Intellectual Standards of Undergraduates. Volume IX, No. 6 of *The Bulletin.*

ranging from lowest to highest, the three middle sections would be nearly equal in capacity.

It seems likely, therefore, that segregation of the extremes, i.e., the very superior, and the very inferior, students would be the most profitable procedure. Thus it has been found practicable in fairly large courses to form a special honor section of the unquestionably superior students comprising, perhaps, some ten per cent of the entire group. This section preferably should be small, so that the discussion method could be employed, and it would be desirable that this group be taught by the most effective teacher available—presumably the professor in charge of the course. Such a group, if properly motivated and led by an inspiring teacher, could undoubtedly attain a much higher standard of achievement and rate of progress than the average section. It is important, however, that the quantity, quality, and nature of work required of the honor section be on a distinctly higher level than that of the others. Also, unfortunate as it may seem, some more tangible reward than high grades and the glory of being in the honor section must be offered the student to induce his maximum effort. Usually the members of the honor section are allowed more freedom for individual study and they are frequently exempted from formal regulations and restrictions regarding attendance at lectures and quizzes. On the other hand, they should be required to do more work and work of a better quality, than the average student: they should not be allowed to rest on their laurels; otherwise they themselves will derive more harm than good from the experiment. Since the highly selected group of students included in the honor section should be able to perform a greater amount of work of a higher quality in less time than the average student, the suggestion has been made that they might be offered the very tangible reward of completing the given course in less time than is usually required. Thus the work of the honor section could be organized so that a year's course might be completed in six or seven months rather than the usual eight, with provision for a rigid examination at the end of the shortened period of study. Any student failing to pass this test with a high grade would then be required to repeat the remainder of the course with the lower sections and to submit to the final examination a second time.

This plan of speeding up the year's work would seem to offer no particular pedagogical difficulties in the typical undergraduate course. Each day's work would consist of a substantially longer assignment and a considerable amount of outside reading, while formal lectures could either be dispensed with altogether or could be given more rapidly in a condensed form by the instructor in charge of the honor section, who would generally be the lecturer in charge of the course. Whether or not such a program of honor sections would prove ultimately desirable, the experiment could be tried inexpensively on a small scale without any changes in the present organization of lectures and classes in large freshmen and sophomore classes. In the smaller sections of the upper-class courses, however, segregation of the superior students would probably not be feasible for reasons of economy.

Honors Courses

The last two years of the undergraduate course appear to offer the most inviting opportunities for individualized treatment of students according to their natural aptitude and intellectual capacity. After completion of the basic introductory courses the student enters upon a field of specialized study with a mature grasp of methods of work and study, and, presumably a heightened interest and higher motivation.

By the introduction of some form of "honors" work in the last two years of the college course many institutions in recent years have attempted to escape from the "lock-step" of lecture and quiz and to offer a suitable incentive to their superior students. The nature of these plans varies widely, involving in some instances merely a modification of grading systems, but in most cases they offer a much greater "scope for qualities of initiative and independent effort and permit the student to direct himself more fully to intellectual pursuits with the knowledge that he will receive official merit for his effort."[15] Generally the honors work is confined to the last two years and is limited to a small proportion of all students, to those who have given

---

[15] "Report on Honors Courses" prepared by Asst. Professor Amos E. Taylor as member of Committee on Incentives of the Wharton School of Finance and Commerce. This report constitutes the basis for the discussion of honors courses in this chapter.

distinct evidence of scholarly capacity, initiative, and interest during the work of the first two years. Since the key-note of honors courses is voluntary effort, students must take the initiative in applying for this work. At Swarthmore College, which has been a pioneer in the development of honors work, "The successful candidate is excused from all ordinary course requirements including class attendance and periodic examinations. He sets out more or less on his own initiative to master the field of his choice and the work in which he has shown special aptitudes. Should he care to attend any of the regular classes he may do so, but in such matters he is usually guided by the advice of the chairman of the division in which he is studying. He is provided with reading lists to guide him in working out a systematic plan of study. . . . The honors students pursue their tasks mainly through extensive reading and the preparation of weekly papers, which are read and discussed at weekly seminars of a somewhat informal nature attended generally by at least two faculty members. The limitation of the seminars to a membership of five tends to assure serious discussion and critical analysis."[16]

After completing his two-year course of study, the candidate submits to a comprehensive written and oral examination covering all of his work and given by examiners not identified with the college. The student is also required to complete a satisfactory thesis. Many modifications of the Swarthmore plan have been adopted at other institutions. Frequently the honors work is only partial, being limited to a few courses in the student's major field. In some instances, as at Antioch and Chicago, some form of instruction similar to honors work such as an informal or autonomous study plan is being adopted for all students.

Although it is probably too soon to form general conclusions as to the results of honors courses there can be no doubt that they constitute the means for permitting the real scholar to develop his own capacity for individual and creative study. They appear to be especially well adapted to the needs of students who expect to pursue graduate work of a scholarly or professional nature. There is some doubt, however, as to whether the

---

[16] Ibid. pps. 4, 5.

usual program of honors work is as well adapted to students who are pursuing semi-technical or semi-professional courses as undergraduates, such as engineering and business students.

It is notable, at any rate, that honors courses have not been introduced as widely in technical and commercial schools as in the liberal arts colleges. In the latter institutions the introduction of honors courses and the provision for junior and senior specialization in "fields of concentration", with a comprehensive examination covering this work, represent a reaction from the haphazard "go as you please" results of the free elective system. The business and engineering schools, on the other hand, almost from their inception, developed their curricula in the opposite direction—toward extreme specialization. And in these institutions there is a widespread feeling among faculty, students, and graduates that specialization has been carried so far as to lose much of its educational value.

Both business and engineering, in themselves, are fields of concentration, in some respects of narrower scope than the fields in which liberal arts students are expected to pursue their major studies. Thus, an important field of concentration at Harvard College, represented by the division of history, government, and economics, includes the work offered by these three departments. Students who major in this field complete seven courses in this division out of the sixteen required for graduation, and specialize further in the work of one of the three departments. When this is compared with the prevailing distribution of studies in the business schools, whereby the student generally takes fifty per cent or more of his work in business subjects (exclusive of social science), it is clear that the collegiate business curriculum, even that of the "general business" major, is already designed "to keep the intellectual activities of the student centered upon a definite field of learning." It would seem evident, therefore, that a system of fields of concentration superimposed upon the already specialized business curriculum would be of doubtful educational value.

Comprehensive Examinations

The advantages of a comprehensive examination covering the work of the last two years or of the entire business course are widely recognized, and a few of the business schools have already adopted this plan. The primary purpose of the comprehensive examination is to test the student's knowledge and understanding of facts and relationships in a broad field of knowledge rather than a restricted portion of that field. Theoretically the prospect of the comprehensive examination at the end of a two-year period of study will induce the student to think continually in terms of the entire field and to relate the subject matter of the individual course to the larger aspects of the subject. While the comprehensive examination is undoubtedly a useful device in helping to bring about this desirable result it is by no means certain that it will ensure it. The difficulty of preventing students from thinking primarily in terms of the courses they have studied is sometimes no greater than that of preventing teachers from taking a narrow view of their specialties.

Administrative problems involved in the preparation of questions and in the grading of papers are considerable, and in consequence the comprehensive examination frequently becomes nothing more than an assembly of course examinations. Administrative problems also arise in connection with the possibility of failing a student who may have completed all the course requirements and passed the term examinations satisfactorily, but who yet fails to give satisfactory evidence of having mastered the field as a whole. If the comprehensive examination is merely superimposed upon the existing course examinations, with no provision for tutorial instruction, the student who has completed his course with a good record feels that a cruel injustice has been done him if he is failed at the end of his final term. On the other hand, if course examinations are entirely abandoned and the student's fate is decided on the basis of the comprehensive test, and he fails in this, he is likely to feel that he should have been warned in advance of the approaching calamity. Under these conditions the comprehensive examination is in danger of becoming neither comprehensive nor an examination, but merely an extra yard of red tape, in the judgment of the students, and frequently of the faculty as well. The comprehensive examination, properly administered, can become a very effective pedagogical device, a useful means of providing motivation and incentive to the student, but poorly administered, there is danger that it will gradually be softened to the point where it will have only slight educational significance. Certainly, the comprehensive examination will be of slight effectiveness unless the upper-class courses which prepare the student for the final test are well integrated with each other and are truly comprehensive in their nature. The student can hardly be expected to acquire a comprehensive understanding of a broad field of human knowledge unless his instructors have the same broad comprehension of the relation of their courses to the entire major field of study.

Quality Grades

Many other devices and mechanisms for providing incentive and motivation to the student might be considered. In addition to the sectioning of large classes, honors courses, and comprehensive examinations in advance work, the quality or "point" system of grading might be mentioned. This device aims to establish a quality standard as well as a quantity standard by requiring each student to accumulate, in addition to the units for graduation, a certain minimum number of quality points based on the grades received in each course. A common form of quality grading is to grant three points for the grade of "excellent", two points for "good," one point for "fair", with no quality credit for a barely passing grade and sometimes with negative points for a condition or failure. Under this system the student might be required to secure 120 units of credit and also 120 quality points, or an average grade of "fair" for his entire course of study. Whether or not the quality-point system of grading would have any appreciable effect upon the efforts of the good student, who normally tries to achieve a high standing in his courses, is questionable, but there is little doubt that it does serve as a stimulus to the indifferent and mediocre student who aims merely to "get by" in all subjects.

The objection so frequently raised against the point system of grading, that it makes "bookkeeping" more complicated, can be dismissed as of little importance. More serious, however, is the contention that under this system students are impelled to search diligently for "pipe" courses in which high grades are easily obtained, especially if they find themselves near the end of their college career with sufficient units, but below par in honor points.

It requires no great amount of mathematical knowledge on the part of the man who sometimes fails to achieve even the "gentleman's C" to realize that one "gravy" course which yields an "A" with little effort is the equivalent, so far as honor points are concerned, of three courses barely passed. Thus, the problem of the "snap" course, and indeed the entire question of grading, becomes even more important under a system which requires quality points, as well as units, for graduation. It may seriously be questioned whether an institution should inaugurate the honor point system without first eliminating the notoriously easy courses from the curriculum and making some provision for a scientifically standardized system of grading, particularly in the larger courses. For the latter there is ample statistical justification despite the opposition usually encountered among certain members of the teaching staff.

Contemplation of these and other formal mechanisms and systems leads one inevitably to the realization that many of them function chiefly as *external* stimuli to greater effort, and presumably greater interest, on the part of the student. They are either in the nature of prods to keep the idler from getting too far behind the procession, or of extra pats on the back to encourage the willing student to still greater effort. Serving primarily as external incentives they do possess limited value, even though none of them appears to provide an absolutely fool-proof automatic mechanism for ensuring superior work on the part of inferior students.

But at best these systems are by no means a substitute for effective teaching. The really successful motivation of the student comes from within himself, arising from an impelling interest in the content of the course and in the way it is taught and not from an abstract interest in grades, honor points, dean's lists, interfraternity competition, and other types of awards and prizes. Thus the problem of student motivation narrows down to the question of student and teacher; again it depends upon "men rather than measures."

The Case and Problem Method

The highly successful use of the case system during the past decade as the standard method of instruction at the Harvard

Graduate School of Business Administration has attracted the widespread attention of educators to the use of problems and case materials in business teaching. The introduction of the case system at Harvard by Dean Wallace B. Donham was based primarily upon his belief that "practically all business not of a routine nature may be reduced to the solution of problems, the making of decisions", and that the study of actual problematic business situations furnished the best means for giving the student "command over new concrete situations, ability to reason back from these situations to the principles involved . . . and to apply to new facts the lessons of similar events in the past".[17]

Originally introduced in the field of labor relations, the case method has since been extended to include practically all of the subjects of instruction. At first the instructors and students attempted to discover and develop cases suitable for class room use, but this method was soon found to be impracticable and since 1920 the Bureau of Business Research, through an elaborate and heavily financed organization, has collected several thousand authentic business cases. These and many other cases collected by members of the faculty have since been published as the "Harvard Business Problem Series" by the A. W. Shaw Company. The material presented in these volumes contains not only a statement of the specific business problem or situation in its essential details, but a wealth of descriptive background material which enables the student, in some measure at least, to see the problem in its natural setting.

The pedagogical procedure followed under the case system is quite similar to that in other courses where the discussion method is employed. One or more cases are assigned for the class meeting and the students are expected to prepare their own solutions to the problems involved, basing the preparation upon a knowledge and understanding of the stated facts in the case and additional information obtained from library source materials, from other cases, from discussion with other students, and frequently from first-hand observation and investigation. During the group meeting the instructor, functioning as a discussion leader rather than as an inquisitor, guides and assists the student

---

[17] "Business Teaching by the Case System," *American Economic Review* Vol. XII., No. 1.

in applying his own mental processes of analysis and synthesis in arriving at a solution to the problem. Primary emphasis most distinctly is not placed upon "getting the right answer",—since it is frankly recognized that business cases, unlike legal cases, frequently admit of more than one reasonable solution—but upon the development of sound judgment based upon accurate observations of the facts and logical analysis of their implications.

The pedagogical advantages of this system of instruction, at least as applied at Harvard, must be apparent to anyone who has witnessed the method in operation. In the class meetings one finds few students who are not keenly alive and actively interested in the problems under discussion. Moreover, the enthusiasm and eagerness of the students appears to reflect much more than a mercenary interest in "right answers" and grades. There is little evidence of "yes" men; on the contrary the student apparently relishes the opportunity of differing from the views of his instructor, and the latter rarely is guilty of dogmatism. Apparently the nature of the case material, involving the study of problems rather than the memorizing of assignments, provides a far more powerful incentive and motivation to the student than any number of purely external stimuli.

It must be admitted, however, that conditions at Harvard are nearly ideal for the development of high standards of teaching and learning. The student body is highly selected, consisting moreover of men who have already served a college or university apprenticeship. Most of the students live together in dormitories where the opportunity for free discussion and access to ample library facilities aids them in preparation for the class room work. The faculty staff are of high calibre, enthusiastically interested in the problems of teaching under the case system, and are not too heavily burdened with instructional and administrative duties. To the outsider one defect appears to be the large size of the recitation groups which makes it impossible for all students to participate in the discussion each day.

The success of the case system at Harvard, however, by no means indicates that it would be equally successful elsewhere, particularly in the earlier years of the undergraduate business course. The undergraduate business curriculum as a whole has a somewhat different purpose than the graduate course in business administration. In the first place the latter curriculum is offered to mature students who have already completed four years of preparatory work involving, in addition to English and the general or cultural courses, considerable study of economics and related subjects, and presumably a familiarity with methods of study and investigation. The formal general education of these students has been completed and they are prepared to devote their time exclusively and intensively to professional study. The undergraduate student, on the other hand, enrolls in the business school for the purpose of obtaining a general college education with substantial emphasis upon the study of economics and business. Whether or not the compromise between cultural and professional interests is a wise one, it is clear that the typical business course will continue to offer a "mixture" of business and general college courses in each year of the entire period. General introductory or survey courses appear to be necessary to acquaint the beginning student, who enters college at the age of seventeen or eighteen, with the nature of business and to orient him for more specialized study. It is doubtful whether these introductory courses, which are usually offered during the first two years, are well adapted to the case method of instruction. Despite the undoubted pedagogical advantages of the case or problem method as a means of developing the student's active interest and his power of analysis, it is apparent that it is not a rapid and economical method of presenting facts and principles in a subject with which he is relatively unfamiliar.

But in the advanced and more specialized business subjects, cases or problems can undoubtedly be used with great effectiveness. Certainly their use, where they have been given a fair trial, results in a heightened interest and increased mental activity on the part of the student, a result which goes far to offset the failure to acquaint him with all of the details of business practice. It may be recalled in this connection that the testimony of employers and of former students of the Wharton School is overwhelming to the effect that the capacity to exercise sound judgment in attacking and solving the concrete problems of business is of far greater importance than a detailed knowledge of routine business procedure. And this result is unquestionably attained to a far greater extent by the use of the case system than by ordinary methods of instruction. As Dean Donham says, "it is clearly impossible by any method of training to transmit to the student more than a comparatively small fraction of the facts of business . . . the adoption of the case approach to teaching any subject will rapidly and inevitably change the emphasis from giving the student a content of facts to giving him control of the subject."[18]

Moreover, it is clear that the intelligent use of the case method in advanced courses does give the student a real and vivid knowledge of the essential facts and principles of business gained in an incidental but natural way as a part of the process of solving the problem. It is important in this connection, however, to distinguish between what appears to be the primary educational value of the case method—the training of the mind in solving problems—and the value which business cases are sometimes alleged to possess as precedents for future business decisions. In this respect the business case is hardly analagous to the legal case. The law case constitutes a description of a legal situation, or problem, and a statement of the judicial decision, or solution. The decision rendered is, ordinarily, final; the problem with its solution becomes in a very real sense a precedent; it becomes a part of the law. Through the study of law cases, therefore, the law student learns the law directly, and not incidentally. It can hardly be said that the business student learns business in the same way through the study of a business case, for the solution of a particular business situation does not constitute a reliable precedent for the future solution of a similar problem. As indicated by Dr. L. S. Lyon, "while business remains, as at present, a matter of individual initiative, and business action essentially a matter of judgment, obviously a case in business can recite *what was done*. But what was done in business does not, as in law, establish a rule. Very often the fact that something was done in a certain way in business, is the best possible business reason for doing it differently."[19]

As a matter of fact, business cases, as they are used at Harvard

---

[18] Ibid.

[19] L. S. Lyon, Proceedings of the Seventh Annual Meeting of the American Association of Collegiate Schools of Business, *The Ronald Forum*, May 1925.

and elsewhere, are really business problems and their undoubted educational value is similar to that possessed by the use of problems in other fields of study. The problem method has long been of basic importance in teaching physical science, statistics, mathematics, and engineering; indeed the importance which employers attach to engineering training can be attributed to a great extent to the mental development derived from the solution of problems. In a somewhat different field, the problem or "situation" method has long been used at the United States Military Academy and at the Army staff and line schools as a means of training in the principles of military strategy.

Introduction of the problem method into business education, however, is of comparatively recent date, and Harvard still remains the only institution which uses the method almost exclusively. Many of the undergraduate schools have found the method effective in upper-class courses, not only for illustrative purposes, for which problems are widely used, but as a substitute for lectures and text books. Questions of expense have undoubtedly deterred other institutions from using the method more extensively, while the difficulty of securing suitable teaching personnel is doubtless more serious than with the usual methods of instruction. It is clear that the free play of class discussion necessitates wider experience and a higher order of teaching ability than the usual instructional methods. On the other hand, while use of the problem method places a heavy responsibility on the instructor, most teachers who have used the method agree that it is a more stimulating and interesting task than the conduct of lectures and quiz classes. Whatever the administrative or other difficulties may be, it is clear that any school which aims to fit its students for business leadership "for the handling of new business facts and new relationships" cannot fail to recognize the educational advantages to be derived from a more extended use of problems and cases.

The Natural Setting in the Study of Business

Educators in professional fields have long recognized that the older systems of apprenticeship possessed one outstanding virtue: that the student learned the principles and practice of his profession in the natural setting, by doing rather than by being told how to do. And despite the cumbersomeness and wastefulness of the apprenticeship system it must be admitted that in this respect it possessed advantages not easy to duplicate in the modern professional school. The necessity of some measure of practical experience, of contact with reality concomitant with theoretical training, has been recognized in most branches of professional study. In legal training, the use of the case method and the postgraduate apprenticeship in a law office; in medicine, the clinic and the interneship; in engineering and technology, the laboratory method, field work and observation trips, all are devices which attempt to provide the student with an atmosphere of reality in which he can learn to apply and evaluate the knowledge gained in the class room.

The use of problems and cases in business instruction also represents at least partially an effort to acquaint students with the realities of business situations. In the same way, field trips, visits to industrial and mercantile establishments, the presentation of lectures and problems by business executives, and similar devices help to furnish a practical background for theoretical study. Plant visits and observation trips, even at their worst, when they are merely sightseeing tours, serve to provide a natural setting, an air of reality to the student's thinking about business problems. When these inspection trips, as at Stanford, are coupled with the discussion of organization and management problems with executives, the results approach those of the project method of study, with creative participation by the student. At many of the undergraduate business schools junior and senior students are organized into small groups which make weekly visits to a number of representative business establishments for the purpose of observation and investigation of the particular phases of management practice which are exemplified in the various plants visited. If this work is carefully organized, with written reports and class room discussion following the visits, it serves a useful purpose in vitalizing the concepts and principles presented in lectures and text books.

A few of the business schools also offer a research course in the senior year in which students investigate actual problems of management in industrial plants. As this work is organized at the Wharton School, the student is placed in a plant where he spends several hours each week during the year, under the joint super-vision of the plant executives and his instructor, investigating a specific problem. At the end of the year he must submit a report based upon his research topic which is satisfactory to the school and to the business establishment.

An interesting course which combines the advantages derived from the study of business problems with the realism found in the project method is the course in business policy offered to senior business students at the University of Pennsylvania under the direction of Professor J. H. Willits. In this course the natural setting of the problem is provided not only by having it described in great detail with full attention to the "background" factors so important in reaching any business decision, but by having the case presented to the class by the responsible executives. This individual first presents the situation to the class and, after he has examined the written solutions submitted, again discusses the problem at a subsequent meeting. The students are thus pre-sented with an actual business problem as it arises in its natural setting and are required to participate in and witness the steps in its solution.

The Cooperative Plan

Probably the most elaborate system for providing the natural setting of business practice to students in engineering and com-merce is the cooperative plan which has been in successful operation for many years at the University of Cincinnati and other institutions. First introduced in engineering at Cincinnati in 1906, the plan has since been extended to include commerce students at that institution and has also been adopted by the business schools at New York University, Georgia Institute of Technology, and a few other universities.

Under the cooperative plan the student alternates between periods of study in the university and employment in a business or industrial establishment. Although there are many minor variations from the program followed at Cincinnati this school can probably be considered as fairly representative of the most successful practice. At this institution the cooperative course covers five years instead of the usual four and the summer vaca-tion is about a month instead of the usual three. The student commences his work as a freshman at the very bottom of the ladder, being first employed as a laborer or in a minor clerical position in some industry in which he is interested. Inasmuch as nearly 250 firms, in a large number of industries, are now cooperating with Cincinnati, the students obviously have a wide choice of interests. After working for a period of four weeks at his job, the student is replaced by his alternate, and returns to the university for his class room instructions. By this system of alternation the plants are assured of stability in their working force, while the student retains the same job over a considerable period of time. As the student progresses at the university he is likely to be promoted into a more responsible position at the establishment where he is employed. Thus study and work, theory and practice, are taught concurrently in preparing the student for the responsibilities which he will eventually assume in his business career.

Obviously, the successful functioning of the cooperative plan presents serious operating problems. Therefore, the function of the coordinator, who is the contact man between the school, the employer, and the student is a very important one. This individual, a regular member of the faculty, is responsible for placing the student and for supervising in a general way his work at the plant and his relations with his employer. The coordinator also conducts classes in which the students report upon and discuss their industrial work. In the regular class room work, as well, there is careful coordination of plant experience with theoretical study. It is clear that the success of the plan at Cincinnati depends to a very great extent upon the effective work of the coordinators in ensuring satisfactory personnel relations and in aiding in the effective integration of university study and employment. That the plan has been thoroughly successful at Cincinnati, there can be no doubt. Students, employers, and faculty are almost unanimous in their enthusiastic approval of the system. Applicants for admission to the cooperative course are many times larger than the number accepted and the plan is now being extended as rapidly as conditions will permit to other branches of instruction. Credit for the success of the plan can be assigned very largely to the imagination and persistence of Dr. Herman Schneider, for many years dean of the engineering college and now president of the university.

Despite the undoubted success of the plan at Cincinnati and at more than twenty other institutions there is by no means general agreement as to its merits. Moreover, it must be remembered that the plan has been applied primarily to engineering and only to a limited extent to students of commerce. It seems probable that the physical and mechanical aspects of industry, which are the province of the engineer, can be more readily witnessed in their natural setting than can the less visible commercial aspects of business. Much longer experience is needed before any decision can be reached as to the possibilities of the cooperative plan in business education. It is significant in this connection that the Society for the Promotion of Engineering Education in their report upon the plan emphasize particularly its advantages in preparing engineers for operating positions in industry. "The attributes of the cooperative plan in developing particular personnel traits and points of view, together with the orientation to industrial organization which it affords, would seem to indicate that it is particularly advantageous as a means of developing personnel for the administrative and operating side of industry. This, indeed, seems to be the peculiar merit of the system which is indicated most clearly."[20] This would seem to suggest that in the business school as well, the advantages of the plan should be considered most carefully as a means of training men for executive and operating positions in industry.

As for the educational merits which are claimed for the plan the Society for the Promotion of Engineering Education concluded that "there is no proof that the effort to coordinate industrial experience with instruction received in college results in greater learning efficiency or a better grasp of fundamental principles."[21] The Society did, however, note two outstanding effects of the plan, first "it should be credited with tending to develop, through actual trial, the student's stamina, resourcefulness, and sense of responsibility at an early age" and second, "that the cooperative plan provides a means of acquainting the student with the importance of the human element in practical affairs . . . and the point of view of the working men and thus equip him

---

[20] *A Study of the Cooperative Method of Engineering Education,* Bulletin No. 12, S.P.E.E., May 1927, page 51.
[21] Ibid., page 50.

better to deal with the labor problems which he is likely to encounter in later years."

The economic features of the plan, both as they affect the school and the student, also deserve consideration. If the plan is used during the entire course the school can accommodate twice as many students, so that despite the increased expense for the employment of coordinators the cost of education per student is substantially reduced. As for the student, the plan is financially attractive despite the fact that it requires five years instead of four, since he is enabled to earn a considerable proportion of his expenses. It must be recognized, of course, that this feature may result in attracting a preponderance of students from poor families.

It may be assumed that some form of industrial experience such as that involved in the cooperative plan would go far toward developing in the student what the employer most frequently finds lacking, a cooperative spirit and attitude and the capacity to lead and influence others. For the student, it would seem that this type of experience would help to lessen the shock involved in adjusting himself to his first job after graduation. It must be remembered of course that many students gain some experience and facility in working with others, through campus activities, while a very considerable proportion of students in business schools earn some part of their expenses through outside employment. Owing to the importance of these activities in preparing the student for his future responsibilities it may well be questioned whether the university should not concern itself to a greater degree than at present with their control and supervision.

While few of the collegiate schools of business have adopted the cooperative plan *in toto* a number have experimented with it in a modified form. At the University of Minnesota students in accounting are employed in alternating periods of three months during their senior year, for which work they receive regular pay as well as credit toward graduation. At Boston University students do not receive degrees until they have completed one year of supervised employment with some firm satisfactory to the vocational department of the school. During this extra year the students are supervised by the school, are required to perform their work to the satisfaction of the employer, and to submit written reports on various phases of their work. Only after completion of this year of supervised employment is the student granted his degree. At other institutions there is a requirement that students find satisfactory employment during one or more of their summer vacations.

It is safe to say that all of these plans recognize the responsibility of the school to test in some way the capacity of the student to work successfully with others in mutual enterprises. More than that they reflect a belief that a demonstrated capacity for cooperative effort is an essential requisite for graduation. Whether or not such a requirement for outside work should be imposed it is impossible to decide. Based upon purely mercenary considerations there is little statistical evidence that the student's future earning capacity is increased by such practical experience. The Society for the Promotion of Engineering Education found that the average earnings of regular engineering graduates were practically the same as those of cooperative graduates. And it may be recalled in this connection that the study of earnings of Wharton School graduates showed that the average for students who earned some part of their expenses (constituting nearly half of the entire group) was somewhat less than that of students who were not employed during their college term.

Summary and Conclusions

1. The quality of the teaching, upon which the success of collegiate education for business depends far more than upon the content of the curriculum, is primarily a matter of securing suitable faculty personnel, and only superficially a matter of devices and mechanisms. Both curriculum and teaching methods are necessary and valuable tools, but their effective use in the educational process depends solely upon the skill and spirit with which they are employed.

2. Although there is no general agreement among educators as to the primary aim of education, it may safely be assumed that collegiate training for business aims to accomplish several purposes, involving the acquisition by the student of (a) routine skill and facility in the use of certain facts, figures, formulæ, and commercial phraseology; (b) a knowledge of generally accepted fundamental facts and principles regarding the nature and func-

tioning of business and our economic institutions; (c) the capacity for disciplined thinking, for logical analysis and reasoning, particularly with respect to the problems of business and society; (d) facility in oral and written expression; and (e) personal effectiveness, involving the development of personal traits and attitudes which enable the individual to become effective in working with and influencing others. It is clear that the relative importance of these several purposes is not in the order named.

3. The lecture system, which, for reasons of economy and administrative simplicity, is still the most widely used method of instruction in the undergraduate schools of business, possesses one distinct virtue and one outstanding defect. Its chief advantage is that it enables the few brilliant and inspiring lecturers to reach and influence a larger number of students than would otherwise be possible; its outstanding weakness is that even under ideal conditions the student is a passive listener rather than an active participant in the learning process. Recognition of the pedagogical ineffectiveness of lectures is leading to their gradual elimination in the collegiate schools of business.

4. Accompanying the decline in the use of formal lectures there is a growing tendency to reduce the size of recitation classes in recognition of the fact that the most effective teaching is possible when the discussion method is employed with groups of fifteen or less.

5. The aim of the small discussion group is to achieve greater individualization of instruction by assuring participation of the students in the learning process according to their natural aptitudes and abilities. The advantages of personal contact between teacher and student can undoubtedly be attained more completely under the tutorial and preceptorial plans than by other methods of instruction, but the costliness of these plans and the difficulty of securing suitable personnel has prevented their extensive use in the schools of business.

6. The failure of mass education to recognize various levels of student capacity has led to many experiments aiming to keep each student at his highest level of achievement. Sectioning of classes on the basis of ability appears to offer considerable promise in this direction, especially when it is applied to the small group of distinctly superior students who, when offered

a sufficiently powerful incentive, are able to do much more work of a substantially better quality than the average.

7. By means of honors courses in the last two years superior students are given the opportunity to do independent work on their own initiative under the personal guidance of the teacher and freed from the lock-step of lecture and quiz. This method of instruction, which is usually conducted under some form of the tutorial plan, involves intensive study in a field of concentration the results of which are tested by a comprehensive examination at the end of the entire period of study.

8. Despite the proven merits of honors work in liberal arts colleges there is some question as to whether all the usual features of the plan are as well adapted to business students. Certainly the provision for intensive study in a field of concentration would appear unnecessary, as the typical business curriculum is already designed to keep the student's "intellectual activities centered upon a definite field of learning". The comprehensive examination can become a highly useful device which compels the student to think in terms of his entire field of study and to integrate what he learns in the separate courses of the curriculum, but there is always danger that in practice the comprehensive examination will be softened to the point where it has slight educational significance.

9. Another stimulant to greater student effort is the point system of grading whereby the student is required to accumulate a certain number of quality points based on the grades received in each course, in addition to the units required for graduation. If the problem of snap courses and standardized grading can be solved satisfactorily, the point system of grading does possess limited value although, like other external stimuli, it appears to be unsuccessful in ensuring superior work on the part of inferior students.

10. The educational advantages to be derived from the use of case and problem materials in the teaching of business are forcefully demonstrated by the success of the case system at the Harvard Graduate School of Business Administration. While the exclusive use of the case system in the undergraduate business school would probably be impracticable and uneconomical, there can be no doubt that in the more advanced and specialized

subjects this method is far more effective than ordinary methods in developing the student's capacity for exercising sound judgment in attacking and solving the concrete problems of business.

11. The necessity of providing the students with some measure of practical experience, some contact with the natural setting, has long been recognized in most branches of professional study. In the business schools these efforts have taken the form of observation and inspection trips, problems presented by business executives, supervised employment, and field investigation and research. Probably the most elaborately organized plan for providing the natural setting and for correlating class room study and practical experience is afforded by the cooperative plan in engineering and business first introduced at the University of Cincinnati. This plan, which involves alternating periods of paid employment in a business establishment and study at the university during a period of five years, helps to develop in the student an understanding of business problems, an appreciation of human relations and a cooperative spirit and attitude. Its value in business education has not yet been fully demonstrated, but it seems probable that some form of the cooperative system should be particularly effective in training students for operating positions in industry.

CHAPTER XVI

PROBLEM OF FACULTY AND STUDENT PERSONNEL[1]

What is it that makes a university? Obviously, there are many things that suggest themselves—buildings, equipment, students, athletic teams, curricula, traditions, administrative regulations, faculty, etc. Manifestly, a university is each of these, it is all of these, and it is the special relation of these constituent elements to each other at any particular time and place.

Which of these elements are of primary importance? Who shall say? Most persons familiar with university problems no doubt would single out its personnel—its faculty, officers and students. In a peculiar way they are the life blood of an academic institution. Back of problems of curricula, academic requirements, teaching methods and materials, is the human equation, made up of persons with differing aptitudes, attitudes, interests and relations to each other. A university, then, is essentially an organization of personalities, with certain selected common interests and relationships; from which it follows that the problems of personnel are in many ways its primary concern. Of this personnel, the faculty is the relatively permanent directive and responsible part; but recognition of the problems of student personnel is also essential. There is, then, a peculiar fitness in the discussion of these problems of personnel by way of conclusion of the present study.

THE FACULTY PERSONNEL

Before turning to a discussion of faculty problems, it seems pertinent to present, by way of background, certain data concerning the teaching personnel of the collegiate schools of business. In keeping with the limitations of the foregoing part of the study, such data will be confined to the 42 members of the American Association of Collegiate Schools of Business. The topics considered include the number of business teachers and their distribution by rank, degree, and certain professional experience other than in teaching.

---

[1] Prepared and written by J. H. S. Bossard.

TABLE VIC.   BUSINESS SCHOOL FACULTIES: BY DISTRIBUTION OF RANK

	Total	Professor	Associate Professor	Assistant Professor	Instructor	Assistant	Lecturer	Other or No Rank
All Schools	1398	355	175	248	381	55	166	18
Alabama, University of	12	4	2	2	4	—	—	—
Boston University	57	16	7	9	20	1	2	3
California, University of	18	7	6	3	—	—	1	—
Chicago, University of	29	9	11	6	2	—	—	—
Cincinnati, University of	48	6	4	4	7	—	27	—
Columbia University	36	13	2	10	6	—	5	2
Dartmouth College	12	6	—	6	—	—	—	—
Denver, University of	31	7	4	4	7	—	9	—
Florida, University of	12	3	5	1	3	—	—	—
Georgia School of Technology	13	3	3	4	3	—	—	—
Georgia, University of	8	3	2	1	2	—	—	—
Harvard University	68	19	13	10	14	4	3	5
Illinois, University of	80	11	8	8	13	40	—	—
Indiana, University of	16	5	1	6	3	—	—	—
Iowa, University of	28	7	3	6	6	3	3	—
Kansas, University of	19	5	2	3	7	2	—	—
Kentucky, University of	9	4	1	2	2	—	—	—
Marquette University	18	3	4	2	—	2	7	—
Michigan, University of	20	5	3	6	4	—	—	—
Minnesota, University of	35	12	3	6	12	—	2	—
Missouri, University of	13	6	1	5	1	—	—	—
Nebraska, University of	18	7	4	—	6	1	—	—
New York University	175	21	16	25	88	—	24	1
North Carolina, University of	22	5	9	5	3	—	—	—
North Dakota, University of	10	2	1	3	4	1	—	—
Northwestern University	123	16	8	18	18	—	63	—
Ohio State University	56	19	7	10	17	—	2	—
Oklahoma, University of	12	4	6	7	1	—	—	—
Oregon, University of	12	4	4	3	1	1	—	1
Pennsylvania, University of	134	28	4	36	65	—	1	—
Pittsburgh, University of	44	10	1	9	23	—	—	—
Southern California, University of	29	12	4	3	2	—	8	—
Southern Methodist University	5	2	1	2	—	—	—	—
Stanford University	10	8	1	—	1	—	—	—
Syracuse University	43	10	3	12	17	—	1	—
Texas, University of	34	18	3	—	7	—	—	6
Tulane University	6	4	2	—	—	—	—	—
Virginia, University of	7	4	3	3	1	—	—	—
Washington and Lee University	10	4	2	2	8	—	—	—
Washington, University of	28	9	4	—	2	—	5	—
Washington, University of	12	4	5	6	1	1	—	—
Wisconsin, University of	20	10	2	6	—	—	1	—

TABLE VC. BUSINESS SCHOOL FACULTIES: DISTRIBUTION BY DEGREES

	Total	Ph.D.	C.P.A.	L.L.B.	M.B.A.	M.A.	M.S.	B.A., B.S. and other Bachelor	Other	No Degree
All Schools	1398	368	124	95	118	279	65	240	35	74
Alabama, University of	12	2			5	11	1	1		7
Boston University	57	5	9	5	1	1		14		
California, University of	18	14	1			4		1	J.D.-3	
Chicago, University of	29	13	4	6	1	5	3	5		10
Cincinnati, University of	48	7	10	3		3	4	9		1
Columbia University	36	23	2	1		2	4	1		5
Dartmouth College	12	2	1	5	1	2	1	2		
Denver, University of	31	3	5	2	2	2		7		
Florida, University of	12	2	2	2	2	4	1	3		2
Georgia School of Technology	13		2		22	13	18	5		
Georgia, University of	8	1	0			18	2	6	M.E.-1	1
Harvard University	68	19	7	4	2	3	2	13	J.D.-2	1
Illinois, University of	80	18		4	2	7		3	J.D.-2	
Indiana, University of	16	8	3			4	1	1	J.D.-2	4
Iowa, University of	28	9	1	1		4		6		
Kansas, University of	19	5	1	1	5	4		2		
Kentucky, University of	9	3	1	1		3		6		
Marquette University	18	2	1	1		11	5	2		
Michigan, University of	20	8	1		1	2	3	6		
Minnesota, University of	35	16	1	1	1	10	1	2		24
Missouri, University of	13	7	1		11	24		1		
Nebraska, University of	18	6	15	18	1	10		48	12	13
New York University	175	18	2	1	24	3	5	3	J.D.-1	
North Carolina, University of	22	5	1		4	13	3	24	3	
North Dakota, University of	10	2	23	3	1	18	1	4	J.D.-1	
Northwestern University	123	19	5	2	5	6	2	3		13
Ohio State University	56	21	2	1	1	32	1	22	LL.M.-2	
Oklahoma, University of	18	3	4	20	2	11		10	J.D.-2	
Oregon, University of	12	2	2	7	4	5		3		3
Pennsylvania, University of	134	55	1	2		1	10	2		1
Pittsburgh, University of	44	10	1		2	12	1	1		
Southern California, University of	29	8			2	4	1	12		2
Southern Methodist, University	5	1	6	1	9	1		1	J.D.-1 (J.D.-1) (Ph.M-2)	
Stanford University	10	6	1	2	2	5	1			
Syracuse University	43	6				5		3		
Texas, University of	34	12	3	1	6	3	1	2	J.D.-1	2
Tulane University	6	1	1	2		5		2		
Virginia, University of	7	5				5				
Washington and Lee University	10	2		1						
Washington, University of	28	7								
Washington, University of	12	6								
Wisconsin, University of	20	11								

The Number of Business Teachers

A total of 1398 faculty members are listed in the third edition of the directory of the American Association of Collegiate Schools of Business, published in the spring of 1930. This directory, unlike the previous editions, omits the names of teachers of foreign languages, mathematics, and other subjects not closely related to business subjects. It is well to keep this fact in mind, particularly in considering subsequent tabulations involving faculty personnel.

Distribution by Rank

Table VIC shows the distribution of the business faculty personnel by rank, for each school and by totals. Of the total of 1398, it will be noticed that 355, or 25.4 per cent, are full professors; 175, or 12.5 per cent, are associate professors; 248, or 17.7 per cent, are assistant professors; 381, or 27.2 per cent, are instructors; 166, or 11.9 per cent, are lecturers; and 73, or 5.3 per cent, are assistants or unclassified. Expressed in general terms, two out of every five are full or associate professors, one out of every six is an assistant professor, and one out of every three is an instructor or assistant.

Study of the table will show considerable variation from school to school in regard to this distribution by rank. Certain schools apparently make it a policy to conduct their work chiefly with mature and experienced teachers, while other schools show an undue proportion of instructors, assistants and the like. Unless there are peculiar circumstances justifying such a situation, such as a very large number of part-time teachers who have the rank of instructor regardless of maturity, its existence would not seem to be desirable.

Distribution by Degrees

Inasmuch as the advanced degree is now recognized almost universally as the key to the teaching profession, especially on the collegiate level, it is interesting, and perhaps of some significance to examine the facts concerning such degrees among commerce teachers. Table VC gives this information, by ranking degrees, school by school, and by totals. For purposes of easy comparison, the totals and percentages for each ranking degree are given in Table IVC.

Marked variations from this general distribution will be found to exist in the case of individual schools.

Professional Experience Other Than Teaching

Data on the professional experiences of commerce teachers, other than in teaching, is important in more ways than one. Table IIIC represents an effort to summarize and to tabulate such experience. It is based on the statements contained in the sketches furnished by faculty members and recorded in the third edition of the directory of the Association schools. While these statements manifestly are not complete in all instances, it may be assumed that no undue amount of humility has been exercised

TABLE IVC. COMMERCE TEACHERS, BY RANKING DEGREES

Degree	Number	Percent
Ph.D.	368	26.3
C.P.A.	124	8.7
LL.B.	95	6.8
M.B.A.	118	8.5
M.A.	279	20.0
M.S.	65	4.6
Bachelors	240	17.2
Others	35	2.5
None	74	5.3
Total	1398	99.9

by individual faculty members to the exclusion of any professional, non-teaching, experience of importance.

Upon examination, it was found that these professional experiences divided themselves into two main groups, one of which was commercial or administrative by nature, and the other primarily of a research character. In slightly more than a hundred cases, experience of both kinds by the same person was indicated. In virtually all of these cases, however, the experience was predominantly one or the other and was so classified. Accordingly, all cases have been tabulated under these two headings. Table IIIC summarizes this information by schools and by totals. For the sake of convenience, table IIC summarizes the data by rank and percentage. It will be observed that 891, or 63.7 per cent, of the faculty personnel indicate professional experience other than teaching, and that such experience was chiefly commercial and administrative, rather than research, in character. Interesting variations occur from school to school and from rank to rank.

TABLE IIIC. BUSINESS SCHOOL FACULTIES: PROFESSIONAL EXPERIENCE OTHER THAN TEACHING

	Total All Ranks	No Experience All Ranks	With Experience All Ranks	Professors C&A¹	Professors R²	Professors C&A	Professors R	Assistant Professors C&A	Assistant Professors R	Instructors C&A	Instructors R	Assistants C&A	Assistants R	Lecturers C&A	Lecturers R	No Rank C&A	No Rank R
All Schools	1398	507	891	148	89	83	19	115	31	209	31	15	1	123	12	11	4
Alabama, University of	12	9	3	1	0	0	0	1	1	1	0	0	0	0	0	0	0
Boston University	57	22	35	8	0	3	0	2	1	15	2	0	0	2	0	2	0
California, University of	18	8	10	2	5	0	2	0	1	1	0	1	0	0	0	0	0
Chicago, University of	29	9	20	2	4	6	1	2	2	6	1	0	0	1	1	0	0
Cincinnati, University of	48	8	40	0	2	1	1	3	2	2	3	0	0	24	2	0	0
Columbia University	36	11	25	3	6	1	0	3	0	6	0	0	0	1	2	0	0
Dartmouth College	12	3	9	5	1	0	0	4	2	1	0	0	0	0	0	0	0
Denver, University of	31	5	26	3	1	3	0	4	0	6	0	0	0	7	0	2	0
Florida, University of	12	7	5	1	0	2	0	1	0	1	0	0	0	0	0	0	0
Georgia School of Technology	13	4	9	0	0	2	0	3	1	1	0	0	0	0	0	0	0
Georgia University	8	3	5	1	0	1	0	3	0	1	0	0	0	0	0	0	0
Harvard University	68	30	38	8	5	3	3	5	1	6	3	1	0	3	0	5	0
Illinois, University of	80	50	30	8	0	3	0	1	0	1	1	8	1	0	0	0	0
Indiana, University of	16	6	10	2	1	1	3	4	0	3	0	0	0	3	0	1	0
Iowa, University of	28	16	12	1	0	1	0	1	1	3	1	2	0	0	0	0	0
Kansas, University of	19	8	11	1	3	1	3	1	0	4	0	0	0	3	0	0	0
Kentucky, University of	9	8	1	1	0	0	0	1	0	0	0	0	0	0	0	0	0
Marquette University	18	2	16	1	1	1	0	2	0	0	0	0	0	8	0	0	0
Michigan, University of	20	4	16	3	2	1	0	5	0	2	0	2	0	0	0	0	0
Minnesota, University of	35	21	14	3	2	1	0	2	1	3	0	0	0	1	0	0	0
Missouri, University of	13	9	4	1	1	0	0	2	0	0	0	0	0	0	0	0	0
Nebraska, University of	18	13	5	1	0	1	0	2	0	2	0	0	0	0	0	0	0
New York University	175	41	134	14	2	11	1	15	4	57	10	0	0	15	4	1	1
North Dakota, University of	22	10	12	3	1	3	1	2	0	1	0	0	0	0	0	0	1
North Dakota, University of	10	2	8	0	1	0	2	3	0	1	0	0	0	0	0	0	0
Northwestern University	123	28	95	9	3	3	1	10	4	2	2	1	0	44	3	0	0
Ohio State University	56	31	25	2	11	3	2	4	1	14	2	0	0	0	0	0	0
Oklahoma, University of	18	6	12	2	1	4	0	2	1	4	0	0	0	0	0	0	0
Oregon, University of	12	5	7	2	1	2	0	3	1	1	0	0	0	1	0	0	0
Pennsylvania, University of	134	48	86	10	9	3	0	15	7	36	5	0	0	0	0	0	0
Pittsburgh, University of	44	18	26	4	2	1	0	3	0	15	1	0	0	1	1	0	0
Southern California, University of	29	9	20	6	2	3	0	1	0	1	1	0	0	6	0	0	0
Stanford University	10	1	9	4	4	0	0	0	0	0	0	0	0	1	0	0	0
Syracuse University	43	14	29	8	0	3	0	7	1	8	0	0	0	0	0	0	0
Southern Methodist University	5	2	3	0	1	0	0	1	0	0	0	0	0	1	0	0	0
Texas, University of	34	11	23	10	5	1	0	2	1	3	0	0	0	0	0	3	3
Tulane University	6	1	5	1	2	2	0	0	0	0	0	0	0	0	0	1	0
Virginia, University of	7	4	3	1	2	0	0	0	0	0	0	0	0	0	0	0	0
Washington and Lee University	10	5	5	0	1	0	0	0	0	1	0	0	0	4	0	0	0
Washington, University of	28	5	23	7	4	3	0	2	0	6	0	0	0	0	1	0	0
Washington, University of	12	7	5	1	0	1	0	2	0	0	0	0	0	4	0	0	0
Wisconsin, University of	20	3	17	6	4	1	2	1	1	1	0	0	0	1	0	0	0

¹ Commercial and Administrative.
² Research.

TABLE IIC. BUSINESS SCHOOL FACULTIES: PROFESSIONAL EXPERIENCE SUMMARIZED BY RANK

Rank	Total		No Experience		Experience		Commercial and Administrative		Research	
	Number	Percentage	Number	Percentage	Number	Percentage	Number	Percentage	Number	Percentage
All Ranks	1398	100.0	507	100.0	891	100.0	704	100.0	187	100.0
Professors	355	25.4	118	23.2	237	26.6	148	21.0	89	47.6
Associate Professors	175	12.5	73	14.4	102	11.5	83	11.8	19	10.2
Assistant Professors	248	17.7	102	20.1	146	16.4	115	16.3	31	16.6
Instructors	281	20.1	141	27.8	240	26.8	209	29.7	31	16.6
Assistants	55	4.0	39	7.7	16	1.8	15	2.1	1	.5
Lecturers	166	11.9	31	6.1	135	15.2	123	17.5	12	6.4
No Rank	18	1.3	3	.6	15	1.7	11	1.6	4	2.1

THE SELECTION OF FACULTY PERSONNEL

"It is the unanimous and evidently heart-felt testimony of university presidents," writes Richardson in his enlightening analysis of the problems of the liberal college, "that the greatest problem of their position is to secure teachers of competence—to say nothing of those who are of marked excellence. Most presidents are frank to admit that their best efforts in this direction fail to gain the desired success, nor do they believe a large degree of success possible so long as conditions remain as they now are. One president expressed himself as utterly discouraged by the 'anaemic' character of the product of the graduate schools, and another administrative officer considered that the chief difficulty of the college comes from the preponderance of 'mud turtles' on the faculty. Picturesque language of this kind is not to be taken with entire seriousness, but it is none the less true that, as a class, those who are preparing themselves for the work of college teaching do not present, as much as could be desired, those characteristics of personality and breadth of viewpoint which are indispensable if a large measure of success is to be attained."[2]

In view of the very rapid growth in recent years in the number and size of collegiate schools of business, and the resultant marked increase in the number of teachers needed, it may be appreciated readily that the above mentioned problem is a particularly keen one in the field of university education for business. While there are those who hold that the situation has improved in the last few years, it is still perplexing and important enough to warrant most serious consideration.

The Recruiting Process

In analyzing this problem, it becomes apparent that faculty personnel is recruited on the basis of a series of selective processes and factors, each of which plays its own particular rôle. To begin with, the personnel of teaching, like that of all professions, is, in the first instance, largely self-selective. Since prolonged training is necessary for a professional career, and since increasingly that training must be of a specialized character, it follows that only those who have chosen that particular pro-

---

[2] Richardson, L. B., op. cit., p. 246.

fession and prepared themselves for it will be in line for admittance to it.

It is obvious, too, that this original selective process is influenced to a considerable extent by current and popular attitudes toward that profession. Of the utmost significance in this connection is that decline of prestige in the eyes of the community which the teaching profession has suffered in recent years. Whatever the contributing factors have been, and whatever the differences in the extent of the decline in various parts of the country may be, there can be no doubt but that

> "the process which for years has applied to the clergy is also at work with the college teacher, although it has by no means gone so far. With the public at large the term 'professor' as applied to an individual is in itself an argument against any principle which he advances unless the discussion be one in which his specialty is directly involved."[3]

Upon analysis, this attitude toward the college teacher seems to rest upon the notion that he is a "mere theorist," that he is not a "practical person," and that in anything that has to do with the administration of important affairs, he is not to be trusted. Curiously enough, this attitude prevails at a time when colleges and universities are overrun with students, when big business proclaims a premium upon scholarship, and when the so-called practical value of a higher education is shouted from the house tops. There is a humorous lack of logic in this depreciation of those persons who are to carry on and direct these important and responsible tasks.

Another factor in this self-selective aspect of recruiting faculty personnel is to be found in the reputed prospects of financial reward. Probably no person influenced wholly by mercenary considerations will enter the professions, and certainly not the teaching profession. On the other hand, few persons of ability will choose any occupation which does not promise at least a reasonably good living. Moreover, there is this peculiar problem for the teacher of the business subjects, in that the field of his interest offers such particularly contrasting prizes. The opportunities of business itself are in constant competition with

---

[3] Ibid., p. 247.

the teaching of business subjects. The fact of such competition makes the problem of a livelihood of particular importance in the building of an effective faculty personnel in collegiate schools of business. Subsequent and more detailed consideration will be given to the problem of faculty salaries.

Once these self-selective factors, such as degree of prestige in the eyes of the community and prospects of financial reward have had their effect, the next selective agency is that of the nature and demands of professional training. Since the problem of training will be discussed separately in this chapter, reference is made here only to indicate its importance as a selective agency, and to point out that the particular qualities and virtues which it emphasizes will have something to do with the type of personnel ultimately found in the faculties of our universities.

Finally, there is the selection of the particular teacher for the particular job in the particular school. Here, in other words, is the process of personal selection. Many factors enter into this process. One, of undoubted importance but apt to be disregarded, is the organization of the teaching labor market. What every college and university administrator knows is that this market is not organized with the completeness and intelligence which he has the right to expect for and from his guild. While various schools do placement work with their own graduates, and while the rôle of the commercial teachers' agencies is not to be disregarded, the present situation leaves much to be desired, particularly from the standpoint of teachers and positions in the collegiate business schools. The whole field of business education has grown so rapidly and has become so large, and the intelligent organization of demand and supply has so lagged, that the good job and the good man are far too often like the proverbial ships that pass each other in the night.

Building a Faculty

Some faculties are built; some, like little Eva, merely attain a certain (or is it uncertain?) state of growth. In passing from one collegiate school of business to another or from one large department to another, one becomes conscious of rather striking differences in this respect. Certain business school faculties give every indication of the operation of a guiding hand in the not too remote background. Such schools or departmental groups constitute a purposive combination of selected men, consciously picked on the basis of their academic training, their specific interests, personal traits and capacity to cooperate in common projects, and carefully dovetailed into a functioning unit. Even the differences which exist between individual members seem to have been the result of conscious planning. For whether a certain type of teacher is desirable or not is a relative matter, depending on the character of those about him, and how many individuals like him are members of the group. At the other extreme, there are business school faculties or departments that show a preponderance of time servers and mediocre neophytes who have just drifted or been shifted together.

These are things which, in the final analysis, constitute the spirit of an academic institution. They are difficult, in fact impossible, of statistical determination. Yet they are very real and very important. There are schools, some well financed but others not, which do their jobs in an outstanding way, largely because a well balanced faculty has been built up and functions effectively. On the other hand, the problems of several schools seem to be chiefly those of personnel, the present dilemma of these schools being the price for long continued carelessness or defective judgment in the selection of teaching material. Such schools squabble or stagnate or both. The time server is too fearful, even to achieve; and mediocrity always acts defensively.

The selection of individual members of a departmental or school faculty is a highly important matter. It should be regarded as such. Provisions, including finances, should be made to enable administrators to make personal contacts and familiarize themselves with applicants. Selection of personnel on the basis of a sight unseen policy will never build an effective school or department—save by the grace of a kindly providence.

There seems to be a disposition in certain quarters to minimize the importance of careful selection of personnel except in the cases of additions of teachers of professional rank. This again involves that peculiar disregard of the rights of the student, repeated evidences of which have been pointed out in this study. For the lowly lower classman, whose faculty contacts are apt to be confined largely to these instructors, is as much a part of the student body as the half dozen graduate students in Professor Blank's seminar.

It is perhaps a pertinent question to raise whether university education for business calls for a distinctive type of teacher. Can the collegiate school of business tolerate the unprepossessing type of teacher? There may appear nothing amiss to the student in the presence of an odd looking, eccentric sort of genius as instructor in the class in ancient philosophy. Is the situation different in a course on investment selling? Do business schools need teachers who, whatever the other requirements common to their guild may be, are also typical of business life? Such questions may suggest invidious comparisons that edge upon delicate grounds, but they do present themselves in the analysis of problems of selection of business school faculty personnel.

The Problem of Training

The college teacher is a product primarily of the graduate school. Its advanced degrees are accepted as the keys for admission to and promotion within the ranks of the teaching profession. The training which it affords is well standardized, and combines two main emphases. One has to do with the giving of a wide knowledge of a particular subject, the other with training in the methods of its further mastery, i.e., research. The assumption is that these are the essential requirements of the teacher, and the degrees which it grants are supposed to symbolize this dual preparation. Whatever its other pretensions and achievements, the American graduate school has become a professional school for the training of college teachers.

On the credit side of the present plan of training are certain results upon which there is rather general agreement. To begin with, the student does receive an improved grasp of, and often a fair mastery of, his chosen field. This is the natural consequence of his concentration of effort. In the second place, he obtains some training in research. That the masters' and doctors' theses often make no definite contribution to knowledge is all too true, but that the working out of a project and the formal organization and preparation of a report thereon involves a valuable training and discipline is perhaps equally true. Finally, the graduate school does lift the veil for most of its students, revealing vistas of new fields beyond, and developing quite generally an interest in the further extension of knowledge in some one or more fields. These are the things which the graduate school seeks to do, and these, even by consent of its critics, it succeeds reasonably well in doing.

There are other results, however, of the present method of training college teachers, that are somewhat less satisfactory. Four of these, each partaking somewhat of the nature of a by-product, can be identified. It will be understood, of course, that reference to these results is intended only insofar as the educational process involved is responsible.

(1) A limited knowledge of things outside of the field of specialization. The spirit of the graduate school is almost overwhelming in its narrow intensity, and its products are prone to be rather lacking in general culture. There is a pathetic humor in the fact that many graduate students look forward to the completion of degree requirements in order that they may resume their education.

(2) A distorted view of the appeal, importance and implications of the particular specialty. In the intensity of his application, the graduate student is apt to get too close to his subject, with results that are inevitable. Viewed too closely, a sparrow may hide the near-by eagle, and the new born camel may assume the proportions of a dinosaur.

(3) Lack of interest in teaching. Since the emphasis of his graduate training is so largely upon research, the student is prone to develop a set of professional values in which the "mere" imparting of knowledge is given a rather low rating. Thus arises that certain contempt for teaching, subconsciously held by the well trained graduate student. Since research is not the whole or even the main part of the job which he is called upon to do, the immediate post training period calls for a rather complete and often rather painful readjustment of values.

(4) Ignorance of the art of teaching. There is this strikingly curious contrast in actual practice between secondary and higher education, in that the former has come to emphasize methods of teaching to the near exclusion of material, whereas the latter has emphasized material with an almost complete disregard of method. Although the graduate school is utilized

mainly for the training of teachers it has paid absolutely no attention to their training as teachers. As has been pointed out, the assumption underlying its work is that a thorough knowledge of the subject to be taught is sufficient by way of preparation, yet every college professor who has learned to teach knows that this is not true. The total lack of preparation which it gives in this respect constitutes, in the opinion of certain keen observers, the major deficiency of the graduate school.

The real truth of the matter is that the graduate school has not yet faced the facts of its own situation. It has not accepted the purpose which the evolution of higher education has assigned to it. It insists upon living in a world of make believe. It has accepted its responsibilities and done its work only in part.

> "We may . . . conclude," says Richardson, "that no part of our educational system is in greater need of reappraisement, of examination of purpose and method, or reorganization in view of the needs of the time. But if such suggestions are made, we find that in no part of our educational system are those who have it in charge more confident that both principles and methods are valid, and more sure that the results represent the deciding word in educational progress. Nor do we find elsewhere such intolerance of objection, and such inclination to regard the objector either as mentally defective or as inspired by motives far from creditable. Nevertheless, as a training school for college teachers, the institution is justly subject to the criticism of doing only incompletely those things which it ought to do."[4]

Two recent trends give particular point to this criticism so far as collegiate education for business is concerned. One is to be found in the increasing insistence that what is taught is not nearly so important as how it is taught, and the other is the growing conviction that the teaching job has not been done nearly so effectively as it could be. The whole field of higher education seems to be more and more concerned with the technique of teaching, which fact, of course, involves the admission that there is more to teaching than knowledge of the subject. A majority of the administrators of business schools with whom contacts were made in the present study indicated an awareness

---

[4] Ibid., p. 265.

of this whole problem. They seem to agree that there ought to be developed some way of training instructors in the problems of teaching procedure, but there was equal agreement that it shall not be done in the spirit of the pedagogy whose formal exactness now characterizes its application in the field of secondary education. Several schools are making gestures in the direction of rudimentary training of their own instructors. Other and more ambitious experiments in this direction would seem to be in order. While no one seems inclined to think that it should constitute a large part of the training of the college teacher, it is reasonable to conclude that some preparation for this part of his work would be of very great value.

Important as this part of its work is, nothing that has been said should be interpreted to mean that the function of the graduate school shall be confined to the training of teachers. Obviously, graduate training may be directed toward other objectives, particularly so far as the field of business education is concerned. Conceivably, the main task of the graduate school or business may come to be the advanced training of business executives or business specialists. These are matters for future determination. But insofar as a large proportion of its students will continue to enter the teaching profession, it should face this fact and develop adequate training for this particular function.

The Problem of Financial Remuneration

The circumstances of the present survey did not permit a comprehensive study of salaries in collegiate schools of business. It was found possible, however, to secure data for 23 of the 42 members of the American Association of Collegiate Schools of Business. The 23 are as follows: Boston, California, Chicago, Columbia, Dartmouth, Harvard, Illinois, Indiana, Iowa, Kansas, Marquette, Michigan, Minnesota, Missouri, Nebraska, North Carolina, North Dakota, Oregon, Pennsylvania, Pittsburgh, Southern California, University of Washington, and Wisconsin.

Much more difficult than the collection of data on teachers' salaries is the problem of their organization so as to avoid obvious misrepresentation. There are, for example, those differences in purchasing power which minimize materially the meaning of a mere mathematical comparison of salary scales. A salary of

$5,000 in Pittsburgh is somewhat different from a like amount at Grand Forks, North Dakota. There is the further importance of differences in the age make-up of any particular faculty group. To compare salaries obtaining in the Wharton School of the University of Pennsylvania, where one-fourth of the full professors have held that title for more than 20 years and one-half for more than 10 years, with those prevailing in an institution where the professors are much younger, is not a fair comparison. This fact is often lost sight of.

The data obtained are those for salary schedules or ranges for each rank. This may be considered as a satisfactory measure, if it will be remembered that the majority of salaries actually paid in each rank are usually nearer to the minimum than to the maximum, and that the latter is the prize obtained by the few and dangled before the eyes of the many.

In a number of cases, the information obtained was given on condition that its use in this report should not be such as to permit its identification with the particular institution where it prevails. For purposes of preserving this anonymity and yet to furnish some reasonable basis of comparison, the 23 schools from which data were secured are classified into four groups. Group I consists of those schools located in or near metropolitan centers, and with relatively large endowment. Chicago, Columbia, and Harvard are placed in this class. Group II is made up of certain large state universities, such as California, Illinois, Michigan, Minnesota and Wisconsin. Group III includes privately maintained institutions, not included in Group I. These schools are Boston, Dartmouth, Marquette, Pennsylvania, Pittsburgh, and Southern California. Group IV consists of state universities not included in Group II—Indiana, Iowa, Kansas, Missouri, Nebraska, North Carolina, North Dakota, Oregon, and the University of Washington. For the sake of brevity, the above mentioned numerals will be used in the subsequent summary.

Salaries of Instructors

Teachers with the rank of instructors constitute 27.2 per cent of the faculty personnel of the business schools. What are the prevailing salary ranges for this rank? Table IC presents information concerning minimum and maximum rates for each school, with the foregoing classification into groups. The arrangement by schools in each group is not alphabetical.

TABLE IC. INSTRUCTORS' SALARIES BY SCHOOLS AND GROUPS

Group I	Group II	Group III	Group IV
1.* 2200–4000	1. 2000–3000	1. 2400–3500	1. 2000–2600
2. 2500–3500	2. 2000–2600	2. 2000–3000	2. 1800–2400
3. 2400–3200	3. 1800–2700	3. 1800–3000	3. 1800–2200
	4. 1800–3000	4. 2000–2800	4. 1700–2500
	5. 1800–2500	5. 1800–2500	5. 1600–2400
		6. not given	6. 1500–2400
			7. — –2000
			8. aver. 2250
			9. not given

* The numbers (1, 2, 3, etc.) are merely for purposes of identification in compiling the table. They have no significance for the reader, and do not represent the same schools in subsequent tables

In summary, it would seem that the customary range of instructors' salaries is between two and three thousand dollars, and generally nearer to the former than to the latter limit.

Salaries of Assistant Professors

Teachers with the rank of assistant professor constitute 17.7 per cent of the faculty personnel. Table C presents information concerning the salary ranges for this rank by groups and schools. It shows that the most frequent range is between three and four thousand dollars. Group I is somewhat in advance of this; and Group IV, with two exceptions, barely attains it.

TABLE C. ASSISTANT PROFESSORS' SALARIES· BY SCHOOLS AND GROUPS

Group I	Group II	Group III	Group IV
1. 4500–7500	1. 3000–4000	1. 3500–4500	1. 2750–3750
2. 3600–4500	2. 3000–4000	2. 3000–4000	2. 2600–3200
3. 3500–5000	3. 3000–4000	3. 3000–4000	3. 2500–4000
	4. 2700–3000	4. 2500–4000	4. 2500–3300
	5. 2500–3600	5. 2500–3300	5. 2500–3000
		6. aver. 2700	6. 2500–2600
			7. 2300–2800
			8. 2200–3000
			9. 2250–2750

Associate Professors' Salaries

Not all of the colleges of commerce maintain the rank of associate professor, yet 12.5 per cent of the entire personnel listed in the directory of the Amercian Association falls under this head. Table CI presents data on the salary ranges for this rank. They show considerable variation. The maximum figure in nine out of 19 schools reporting fails to exceed $4,000. Six schools reach or exceed $5,000.

TABLE CI. ASSOCIATE PROFESSORS' SALARIES BY GROUPS AND SCHOOLS

Group I	Group II	Group III	Group IV
1. 6500–8000	1. 4000–5000	1. 4000–4500	1. 3500–4500
2. 5000–6000	2. 4000–5000	2. 3000–3500	2. 3300–3600
3. 4000–6000	3. 3500–5000	3. aver. 3000	3. 3200–3800
	4. 3500–4100	4. not given	4. 3000–3600
	5. 3000–4000	5. not given	5. 3000–3600
		6. not given	6. 3000–3500
			7. 3000–3500
			8. 2900–3400
			9. not given

Full Professors' Salaries

A quarter (25.4 per cent) of the business school teachers have the rank of full professor. Table CII shows the range of salaries for full professors at 23 schools.

TABLE CII. SALARIES OF FULL PROFESSORS, BY GROUPS AND SCHOOLS

Group I	Group II	Group III	Group IV
1. 8000–10,000	1. 5000–10,000	1. 5000–7500	1. 4000–6500
2. 7500–12,000	2. 5000–6000	2. 5000 —	2. 4000–6500
3. 5500–10,000	3. 5000 —	3. 4500–6000	3. 4000- 6500
	4. 4000–8000	4. 4000–7500	4. 3900–4800
	5. 4350–6750	5. 3700–3800	5. 3800–5000
		6. 3500–4800	6. 3600–4500
			7. 3500–4500
			8. 3500–4500
			9. 3500–4000

It will be observed that in eight of the 23 schools included, the minimum is $5,000. On the other hand, in seven schools the maximum is $5,000, or less. The salaries in Group I represent, of course, the highest in the field of university education for business. It is significant to add that the total of full professors in these three schools is 41, which is slightly less than three per cent of the combined faculties of the 42 business schools.

Supplementary Earnings

Information concerning the extent to which college teachers supplement their salaries through activities outside of the class room is included in the study of teachers' salaries, made by the General Education Board. This study showed that seven out of ten (69.2 per cent) of the teachers in men's coeducational institutions supplemented their salaries; that the percentage in urban institutions was higher than in those classified as rural, the percentages being 74.9 and 66.7 respectively; and that the higher the rank, the larger the percentage so doing. The percentages for professors is 78.8; for associate professors, 73.7; for assistant professors, 64.3; and for instructors, 54.8. The chief kinds of supplementary work are writing, extra teaching or services, outside lectures, and consulting work. That much of this outside work is done because of economic pressure seems to be borne out by the differences in percentage between married and single teachers. While 77.6 per cent of the married teachers in men's and coeducational institutions thus supplement their salaries, the percentage among single teachers is but 49.7 per cent.[5]

The question naturally arises as to the amounts of these supplementary earnings.

"There is a general impression, even within the University," reports the Yale Committee on "Incomes and Living Costs of a University Faculty," "that many members of the faculty earn large sums for extra teaching and lectures and for other outside work such as magazine articles, technical advice, royalties on books and inventions, and payment for other activities."[6]

A study of the facts for the Yale faculty shows

"that 32 per cent of the members of the faculty replying to the questionnaire have no supplementary earnings; another 23 per cent earn less than $500 a year each, over and above their salaries; 75 per cent earn less than $1,000; 89 per cent less than $2,000; 95 per cent less than $4,000."[7]

These facts deny

"the widely held belief that many members of the faculty are easily able to supplement their salaries to large amounts. Even the highest paid expert rarely receives more than $100 a day, and such days in any one year are few. In

---

[5] Arnett, Trevor, "Teachers' Salaries in Certain Endowed and State Supported Colleges and Universities in the United States, with Special Reference to Colleges of Arts, Literature and Science, 1926-27," Publications of General Education Board, Occasional Papers, No. 8., pp. 70-76.

[6] Henderson, H., and Davie, M. R., *Incomes and Living Costs of a University Faculty*, Yale University Press, New Haven, 1928, p. 31.

[7] Ibid., p. 33.

most cases outside work involves a large expenditure of time and strength to earn a rather small amount of money. Not only is it usually poorly paid, it is frequently of a tedious, or otherwise unpleasant, character. It often interferes with University work in respect to productive scholarship, although rarely in respect to teaching. Yet if it were not done, a considerable percentage of the faculty would be forced to leave the University. The suggestion that supplementary earnings should be limited is therefore now impracticable; for under present conditions this income is as essential to the support of the University as if it figured in the treasurer's report."[8]

Opportunities for teachers in the colleges of commerce to supplement their academic salaries do not seem to be lacking. Reference is made in an earlier chapter to an extensive development of evening school work at eight schools; as well as to the large number of students enrolled in extension courses in the commercial studies. Also, certain of the more technical fields which have developed in the business curricula present excellent opportunities for the acquistion of supplementary earnings. In fact, there are several institutions, unusually favored by location for the development of these sources of supplementary income, where it is said to have created a problem for the university administration.

Obviously, a university administration has the right to be informed of all such tasks outside of the ordinary schedule of academic duties, and such work must be considered in relation to the program of the particular faculty member involved. Evening and extension work usually partake of the nature of an extra teaching load, with separate additional compensation. There are, however, instances where such teaching is integrated into the general program, or where much of it is done by persons specially selected for that purpose and who are not members of the day school faculty. It is a pertinent question to inquire whether these supplementary earnings within the university should be regarded as separate items, or whether they should be integrated with, and considered as part of, a single unified salary. This question will be considered more fully in connection with the problem of the teaching load.

---

[8] Ibid., p. 34.

From an idealistic point of view, any considerable amount of work outside of the regular teaching load, should be tolerated only as it fits into the program of the individual faculty member and contributes to his professional development and then only to the extent that it does not compete or interfere with the requirements of his customary work. Several schools have committed themselves to this principle.

There is no doubt but that any considerable amount of outside work interferes with the work of the teacher. It drains his nervous energy, it lessens his productiveness, and it prevents often those additional applications of effort which account for the difference between conventional and very good teaching. And yet, until such supplementary earnings shall cease to be essential in enabling persons of ability to remain in academic life, who is there that will lay the hand of restriction upon them?

Significance of Salary Scales

Reference has been made to the selective influence which prospects of financial remuneration exercise upon the recruiting of the teaching profession. As President Angell, of Yale University, has pointed out, there are many competent men who are quite willing to live on extremely modest stipends in return for the intrinsic rewards which they find in a scholarly life. "But they rightly hesitate to subject their wives to the prospect of hard and unremitting physical drudgery, and their children to the limitations of the under privileged in a time of general financial prosperity."[9] Few persons will deny the relation between rate of financial reward and quality of personnel in other professions, or in almost any other calling, and to assume that this correlation does not exist in the teaching profession is but to cherish an illusion. One can find no rational grounds to suppose that universities enjoy any special dispensation from the laws of cause and effect.

But there are at least two other ways in which economic conditions affect the teaching profession. Obviously, they play a rôle in determining who, of those entering the profession, will

[9] Angell, James R., in the foreword to *Incomes and Living Costs of a University Faculty*, Yale University Press, New Haven, 1928, p. vii.

remain in it. Here again, reference must be made to the particular circumstances which exist in the case of teachers of the business subjects. The very nature of their teaching experience creates contact with, and affords a certain mastery of, types of business activities in which the prospects of financial reward are very great. In other words, to put the matter concretely, for the professor of investments, or insurance, or marketing, there is the constant temptation of a competition which the professor of Sanskrit is not likely to face. It will be remembered, too, that the growth of collegiate education for business since 1914, with the parallel increase in the demand for teachers of the business subjects, has corresponded in point of time with the period which has offered unusually high rates of remuneration to the personnel of business management. "Something may be credited to idealism, something to the balance of advantages in the scholar's life; but accessory support of a more material character must also be available if the household bills are to be met. Unless the material conditions of academic life are comparable with what men of ability can command in other callings, it is useless to expect that such men will give up that mode and level of living in order to serve a university."[10] Finally, there is the effect which the rate of compensation has upon the quality of the academic work done by the individual teacher. The relationship here is less obvious, perhaps, but by no means less important. Industry has learned the economy of high wages, and ultimately, perchance, universities may make the same discovery.

Inadequate compensation affects the efficiency of teaching in many ways. Worry over finances is destructive of nervous energy, and nervous energy in abundance is indispensable for effective teaching. Underpaying lessens self respect. It warps judgment, personal and academic. It eliminates leisure, through the necessity of obtaining supplementary earnings. It lessens the prestige of the professor with his students. Students cannot be expected to have much respect for the teachings of the apparently unsuccessful. Wealth respects wealth, and poverty rationalizes its longing for it. Especially is this observation pertinent for the business schools. The picture of an instructor unravelling

---

[10] Ibid., pp. 1-2.

the intricacies of corporation finance or business forecasting with frayed cuff showing as he gesticulates before the class is incongruous, even to the point where students recognize it.

Data enabling a comparison of average salaries of teachers in colleges of commerce with those in colleges of liberal arts and in other professional schools or departments is contained in the report of the General Education Board on Teachers' Salaries for 1926-27. Table CIII presents this information together with the rate of increase in average salaries over that for 1919-20.

TABLE CIII. AVERAGE SALARIES, 1926–27, BY DIVISIONS OF UNIVERSITIES, AND PERCENTAGE OF INCREASE SINCE 1919–20*

Division of University	Average Salary, 1926–27 Full-time basis	Percentage of Increase Since 1919–1920
College of Arts, Literature and Science	2958	29.8
Class A	3162	23.8
Class B	2751	40.4
Class C	2443	45.7
Agriculture	3149	34.6
Commerce	3307	23.2
Education	3438	28.4
Engineering	2989	27.2
Fine Arts	2633	29.
Law	5197	32.1
Medicine	3391	29.
Music	2388	29.5
Theology	3889	25.8

* Arnett, Trevor, op. cit.

The average salary in commerce for 1926-27 is based on data for 818 persons reduced to a full time basis in a total of 38 different institutions. Comparison shows that the average salaries in five university divisions—arts, agriculture, engineering, fine arts and music—were lower than in commerce. On the other hand, those in education, law, medicine and theology were higher. It appears, too, that the rate of increase in average salary for 1926-27 over that in 1919-20, was lower in commerce than in any other university department or school. This would seem to substantiate the contention of college of commerce teachers in various parts of the country to the effect that university administrations have been prone to exploit them in a financial way.

One further aspect of this comparison of salaries would seem to warrant emphasis. Teachers in the business subjects, and in the economic and social sciences as well, are dealing with material which cannot well be reduced to routine. Their subject matter is constantly changing, and is distributed over an area that is world wide. Many of the problems which it presents call in a peculiar way for the application of very able minds, for ripeness of scholarship, and for relative experience and maturity. There exists, in other words, the somewhat unusual necessity for able, well trained, well travelled, mature teachers in these fields. Obviously, the inadequate training of future bankers is at least of equal seriousness with the effects of poor scholarship and personnel in the training of specialists in medieval philosophy or the contemporary drama.

Academic salaries, like other facts, are relative. In the last analysis, the test of the adequacy of salaries in the teaching profession in general and of the collegiate schools in particular is the ability to secure the type of personnel necessary to render the maximum in service to the youth of America. By this test, too, the salary schedule of each school must be measured. Schools that are constantly losing their best men are paying inadequate salaries, no matter what the numbers of dollars may be, and their personnel will inevitably come to resemble the inhabitants of fished out ponds. And these are said to consist mainly of bullheads and suckers.

It is not too much to say, by way of summary, that the problem of academic salaries is as important as any now confronting American education. While it is true, of course, that the problem of improving the personnel in the teaching profession involves a good deal more than an upward revision of salaries, such a step would seem to be an indispensable first step.

The Problem of Employment Conditions

The Teaching "Load"

There are problems of employment conditions in teaching just as there are in any other occupation. First, and in a sense foremost, is that of teaching hours. By way of preface to more extended discussion of this problem, certain data need to be presented. Table CIV summarizes the information obtained from 34 of the schools belonging to the American Association of Collegiate Schools of Business. To enable comparison with the data on salaries, the four fold classification of schools utilized in Tables IC—CII is retained here. Section A represents the teaching hours of the schools included in the tables dealing with salaries, while Section B represents those for whom data on teaching hours are available, but not on salaries. Asterisks indicate cases where hours given include evening and extension classes. In all other cases, the number of hours indicated is for the day school only.

Considering only the minimum number of hours, which are usually carried by the faculty members of professional rank, it

TABLE CIV. TEACHING HOURS BY GROUPS AND SCHOOLS

SECTION A

Group I		Group II		Group III		Group IV	
School	Hours	School	Hours	School	Hours	School	Hours
1	4-5	1	7½	1	6-11	1	8-12
2	6	2	7-9	2	8-12	2	9-11
3	8	3	8-12	3	8-15*	3	10
		4	9-12	4	10-14*	4	10-12
		5	9-12	5	12-14*	5	11
				6	not given	6	12
						7	12
						8	12-14
						9	12-16

SECTION B

6	9-12	7	10	10	10	9	
7	9-12	8	12	11	11	9-11	
		9	12	12	12	12	
		10	12	13	13	15	
				14	14	15-18	

* Figures include evening and extension classes.

appears from Table CIV that in 10 of the 34 schools the number of hours is eight or less, and in 17 of the 34, or exactly one-half of the schools, it is nine or less. It will be observed, too, that there is some tendency for the number of teaching hours to vary inversely with the size of salaries.

It is a curious fact that thus far no effort has been made to determine objectively what constitutes a full-time teaching job. Most teachers probably will rise in their wrath to insist that by no stretch of imagination could this be done. And yet the fact remains that it has not been tried. Manifestly, such an effort will have to proceed in terms of units of energy rather than in hours spent in class room instruction. And many facts will need to be taken into consideration. Much more important than the number of hours is the number of courses carried or preparations involved. To carry an eight hour schedule by repeating one course under four different sets of circumstances is far different from offering four different courses of two hours each. To carry the administrative responsibility for a course is different from carrying a section in it, even though the number of hours of class room instruction is alike. To give a new course is different from repeating an old one. Some teaching materials change less frequently, some courses require more exacting preparation than others.

It has been alleged that evening and extension teaching should be made a part of a unified teaching program, with a single unified salary, i.e., that such courses should be added to those of the day school and carried as part of the regular teaching program. This is being done at several institutions. But here, too, are factors that need to be recognized. Those who carry extension and evening courses know from experience that these classes make different and heavier demands upon them than an equal number of morning hours in the day school. As a matter of fact, extra credit is given for evening courses at those schools where such work is integrated into the rest of the teaching program.

In addition to these factors which have been mentioned, various others such as administrative responsibilities, committee commitments, extent of secretarial aid, research projects, etc., need to be included in any equitable determination of the teaching load.

In a majority of the schools a good deal of flexibility in regard to teaching load already exists, chiefly on the basis of the number of different courses, administrative responsibilities and participation in research projects. There is little or no standardization; existing arrangements differ from institution to institution and even from individual to individual. However, since the number of teaching hours normally is standardized, it is a fair question to raise whether the exceptions and deviations could not be similarly dealt with. But it must be admitted that to a certain extent the problem is a local one, peculiar to each school, and perhaps even an individual one. At any rate, it is an important problem which needs particularly to be faced at the larger schools, and there remains the suggestion of a truly scientific attempt to measure objectively the teaching load.

Conditions of Intellectual Stimulation

Other employment conditions have to do chiefly with the morale and intellectual stimulation of the teaching personnel. In passing from one institution to another, one comes to be impressed with striking differences of this kind between schools, as well as with the rôle which certain factors play in the determination of these differences.

The spirit of a faculty depends, for one thing, upon the extent to which its members are thrown together during periods of freedom and relaxation. Always and everywhere do differences dissolve when men have the opportunity for frank and informal discussion of their differences of opinion. This is, in a large measure, a matter of physical facilities. Every experienced teacher of graduate students, for example, knows that seminars can be made or unmade by the presence or lack of proper room, table and chairs. In like manner, one finds certain schools which have fine facilities for faculty members to get together, such as faculty clubs, faculty dining service, the institution of four o'clock tea, a small town setting, or an isolated campus community. Under such circumstances, other things being equal, common interests are more apt to be discovered, conflicting viewpoints to be resolved, and incipient animosities to be scotched. Some schools consciously create such opportunities through periodic smokers and other social devices. This problem of physical facilities seems particularly important in the case of schools located in metropolitan areas where faculty residents are scattered, differences of viewpoint are accentuated by other than academic influences, and where impersonality of relationship is so likely to be taken for granted.

No faculty, however, should live by itself, nor should it be expected to elevate itself by its own intellectual boot straps. Individual teachers need stimulation from the outside, as do departments and universities. Some schools enter whole-heartedly into the current intellectual stream, others stand on the shore, still others remain contentedly in the hinterland. In this connection are to be considered such important matters as exchange professorships, lecturers from the outside, attendance at scientific meetings, and participation in current intellectual projects. Many of the influences important in this connection do not make glaring headlines for the market place. One school, for example, secures a noted European authority to come—and simply visit with the faculty, individually and in small groups, at the faculty club house. These are things of the spirit, hard to measure, and immeasurably important.

Teaching vs. Research

Two interests supposedly lure the members of university faculties—one, the imparting of knowledge in their chosen subject; the other, the enlargement of its boundaries. Teaching and research, in other words, constitute the dual task of the university professor, and ability in both is stated commonly as essential for academic advancement. As a matter of fact, however, a changing emphasis has been manifesting itself, constituting a real problem of faculty efficiency. One of the outstanding developments in American academic life in recent years has been the very great emphasis upon research. In fact, this development has reached a point where certain universities are centering their whole work about their research programs.

A number of factors seem to have contributed to this vogue of research. There is the continuance of the earlier influence of the German universities. There is the pedagogic contention, partly a matter of logic and partly rationalization, that a subject must be known thoroughly to be taught successfully. The extension of science is opening new vistas and stimulating the search for new gains. With the growth of the inductive attitude, teachers are less and less willing to dogmatize their instruction. Also, and this is a very important factor, large amounts of money are being made available for research purposes. Research has proved its value in business, and there is the natural implication that it may prove itself similarly in other fields of activity. Other factors seem less worthy, but by no means less effective. Publications produced by research workers are easy to measure and have an advertising value for the institution. Promotion follows production, and the reward for reprints comes often through calls from other universities.

The results of all this have been all too evident to the observer of academic life. Teaching comes to be neglected, relegated to the plane of a bothersome incident. The term "good teacher" becomes a phrase of damaging praise. Especially is this true if he is a teacher of lower class men and in elementary courses. Prestige and the more material rewards go to the research man. The good teacher is "also" promoted. Students who come to be taught remain to be utilized in research projects. Obviously, this again is fitting the student to the institution. It is contrary to the purpose of the undergraduate school, and in the end it must defeat its own purpose.

Moreover, a good deal of the research work done in American universities is of rather questionable value. Some of it consists largely of exercises in arithmetic, with the statement of conclusions (if any) in footnotes. Other research projects, while excellent in conception and execution, result but in crowning a triviality with the dignity of a monograph. Much of both kinds of work is the result of the pressure under which faculty members have been placed in recent years. There is a good deal of truth in the charge recently made that

> "from the beginning to the end, scientists in universities, museums, state and federal bureaus are lashed into publication either to hold their jobs or to obtain better ones. If they make a hasty observation or venture a theory that proves fallacious, they are lashed again. Between the desire for recognition and the fear of ridicule they must choose a middle course. They are not all geniuses, and it takes a genius to find three of four new things of real significance to say each year. It is not at all remarkable that so many are devoted to the insignificant.
>
> "Trivial experiments proving something new which nobody ever thought worth trying to prove before, observations and catalogues of obscure and trivial phenomena, even occasionally cleverly manipulated old data and cleverly disguised old results—these are an all too plentiful portion of the output of our scientific presses today. They are the logical result of the loss of the amateur spirit which came with the standardization of the instinct of curiosity, and the natural human desire of the individual to rise in the mummery of his group."[11]

Certain aspects of the situation seem clear, and will be stated by way of summary.

---

[11] Bradley, John H., "Good Little Boys of Science," *The New Republic*, Volume LXIII, No. 815, July 16, 1930, p. 224.

1. All faculty members should continue to study. This is what research implies. The modern university has no room for the person who retires intellectually upon completion of the doctorate. Security of tenure leads, at times, to unfortunate results.

2. Modern universities must offer opportunities for research if they expect to retain their most promising men. This is particularly true of such departments of the university as the college of commerce. The harvest is too great and the rewards too alluring for men of the first rank to overlook, constantly. Furthermore, every university worthy of its name must attempt to carry some part of the responsibility for the general advancement of the boundaries of knowledge.

3. If ability to teach and to conduct research be represented by two lines each ranging from zero to a hundred, it is evident that any particular individual may occupy any one point on either line. This means that all sorts of possible combinations exist, from the man with very high rating on both lines to the individual who has the ability to do neither task acceptably. Since a university has both responsibilities, it seems apparent that ability of either kind should be recognized. Which is chiefly what the problem now is—one of a more evenly balanced recognition. Specifically, this means more recognition for good teaching.

The Way of the Instructor

One third of the members of the business school faculties, it has been shown, have the rank of instructor or assistant. This is an important fact to remember in any discussion of the problems of faculty personnel. To many persons, reference to the faculty of an academic institution immediately calls forth a picture of Professor Blank, whose contributions to finance or insurance are so widely and favorably known, or to Professor Dash, whose antics and eccentricities have been a tradition for a quarter of a century. But to the student, and this is the utmost reality to consider here, the faculty is the newest instructor of the smallest freshman section. This is his contact with the university, his personal touch with a large organization. And for a substantial part of his course, his contacts with that organization will be made chiefly through faculty members who have the rank of instructors.

The way of the beginning instructor is hard. Perhaps it would be more to the point to say that the way of the student in his class is hard. At any rate, the matter of importance is that *their* way is *unnecessarily* hard. These unnecessary hardships arise because of an almost complete lack of guidance by the instructor from his superiors. Perhaps a majority of teachers in the business schools, as in other divisions of the university, begin their teaching by working toward ends that have not been defined, and with few hints in their professional training concerning the means to be employed. Under the pretense of academic freedom, the young instructor is left to sink or swim, and while, in most cases, he seems to learn to swim, it is by dint of experience that is unnecessarily bitter, wasteful and prolonged.

Sympathetic guidance, now attempted at several of the business schools with every indication of success, may be given by the dean or by department heads. The chief reliance must be upon the latter, for the professional development of the individual instructor turns upon so many factors, all of which are departmental in nature and scope. These include the organization of the work of the department, group discussions of teaching methods, helpful personal hints, and the general atmosphere of the department. On the other hand, autocratic control of a department, its domination by persons not interested or adept in teaching, and the tendency to utilize the younger personnel as intellectual serfs, are the chief obstacles in the departmental way of the instructor.

The Problem of Leadership

As a complement to virtually all of the problems discussed in this chapter, and the entire study as well, rises the problem of faculty leadership. Because of the very rapid growth and development of the collegiate schools of business, and the problems which this has created, both within the schools and in their relations to other divisions of the university, the problem of leadership of these schools is peculiarly important.

Two aspects of this problem will be referred to in this connection—that of the deanship and that of the departmental head. The deanship of a college of commerce calls for men of ability who combine varied experience and interests. Obviously, they need to know business, they need to know the field of education, and they need to be interested in both and in their effective integration. Fortunately, the importance of leadership in the dean's office has been generally recognized. The majority of collegiate schools of business have been fortunate apparently in the type of persons selected as dean and a part of their satisfactory growth may be attributed to this fact.

There is some reason to conclude, on the other hand, that the situation is not so fortunate with reference to the department heads. As in the case in American political life, so in the organization of American universities, the least satisfactory and weakest point is the local one, i.e., the departmental relationship. This is particularly unfortunate because of the important rôle played by the department. With few exceptions, the organization of higher educational institutions, both for many administrative purposes and for curriculum building, is in terms of departments; and no question involving the reorganization of university work can go far without being confronted by the problem of departmental autonomy.

The very important problem of departmental organization is seldom faced in university circles. A variety of forms exist, and in differing stages of development. Three systems of selection of departmental heads usually prevail. One is selection by order of seniority, one by election of the group, and one by appointment from above. Each of these has its own advocates—and critics. The weight of considered opinion favors the third method. It must be clear, however, that wisdom in such matters, as well as in the type of person needed as head, varies from department to department, and from time to time within the same department. Where, for example, a department is in process of development, one type of arrangement is needed. The building-up of a department calls for long range planning, for careful selection of additional personnel, for cordial contacts with other departments, and for other aspects of continuous constructive leadership. These things demand continuity of policy and personnel, and perhaps a more autocratic form of control. Where, on the other hand, departments have been developed, where the staff is relatively stable, and the division of the university in which the department is located has reached a certain stage of growth, the headship of a department involves more of the details of administration than of the foresight of constructive leadership. In such cases, leadership will gravitate to the ablest member of the group, regardless of nominal headship.

In the ultimate analysis, all that has the right to prevail in any community of scholars is the preeminence of the more capable, not the power of the passing poseur. There is too much talk of "headship" of departments, and too little conception of the obligations and responsibilities involved. What university departments need are leaders, not "heads"; builders, not autocrats; servants, not tyrants.

Problems of Student Personnel

Two factors have complicated and multiplied in recent years the problems of collegiate student personnel. One of these is the growth in the proportion of young people going to college; the other, the increasing heterogeneity of our student bodies. Both of these have been unusually operative in regard to the collegiate schools of business.

The facts of student enrollment and its marked increase during recent years have been set forth in Chapter IX. It has been shown that the percentage of young people in the age group, 19 to 22 years inclusive, going to colleges, universities and professional schools in 1928, was more than five times that in 1890, almost three times that in 1915, and almost twice that of 1920. Considering collegiate education for business, it will be recalled that growth here has been more phenomenal than in any other division of our universities, that the student enrollment in commerce in 1926 was more than six times that of 1915, and that the number of first degrees granted in commerce in 1927-28 was more than ten times those granted in 1917-18.

The significance of these facts to the problems of student personnel should be obvious. The very increase of student enrollments has involved changes in the character of those admitted. When twelve are selected where formerly only two were taken, changes in the make-up of the group are inevitable. These changes will be most marked naturally where the rate of growth has been most rapid. This means, again, that the student personnel of the school of business have been affected to an unusual extent.

Not only have student bodies in American colleges and universities grown in size, but they have become markedly more heterogeneous. Until a generation or less ago, our academic hosts would seem to have been recruited chiefly from rather restricted social, economic and occupational levels, and their careers subsequently were confined to circles fairly well defined. Speaking somewhat more specifically, they were drawn in large measure from the professional classes of the Anglo-Saxon element in our population. Two decades have changed this situation completely. Our college students today are drawn from virtually every occupational group and every economic level, and upon the completion of their courses will return to a wide range of activities.

Racial Heterogeneity

This heterogeneity of present-day student bodies is a reflection, to a large extent, of the cosmopolitan nature of our population. It is well to remember, in the discussion of any problem in this country, that more than one third (34.4 per cent) of our population is enumerated by the census (1920) as of foreign stock, recruited from a half a hundred nations of the world. There are, for example, five nations (Germany, Ireland, Russia, Italy and Austria) which have contributed each more than three million persons to the foreign stock in the United States, as enumerated in 1920; seven nations who have contributed more than a million; and twelve nations, more than a half million, each. Census data on school attendance attest the presence of six million children of foreign stock. In 1930, one half of the children in the schools of Philadelphia were of foreign white stock; in Chicago, two thirds; and in New York City, three fourths.

In citing such data in this connection, a possible point of criticism must be anticipated in that this heterogeneity of our population is not of recent development, that as large a proportion of the population was of foreign stock in 1890 as in 1920. By way of answer, attention is called first, to the change in the racial character of the foreign stock from north and west European to south and east European origins, as a result of which actual heterogeneity has been increased; and, second, to the fact that only in recent years have developments in the economic circumstances of this element in the population made possible to any appreciable extent the attendance of their children in college or university.

Psychological Diversity

Modern student bodies are characterized by marked psychological diversities. This is due in part, no doubt, to the racial heterogeneity to which allusion has just been made. Different racial groups do exhibit distinctive traits and particular patterns. Successive generations within the same racial strain differ psychologically, too. All other things being equal, the attitudinal pattern of a third-generation Russian is somewhat different from that of one just making the transition from an old to a new world culture.

Then, too, American youth lives in a rapidly changing, a daringly dynamic world, with excessive stimulations and variegated distractions. Not all parts of the United States, however, have been affected to the same degree and manner by the influences of modern life. Since different community situations produce different personal patterns, it follows, from the present wide range in territorial origin of college populations, that there will be found a corresponding psychological diversity among the members of our respective student bodies.

Changing curricula, with the widening scope of academic pursuits they present, constitute another factor making for psychological diversity among college students. Colleges, in other words, no longer limit their admissions to students with identical ambitions, but seek to attract a student body whose members have many unlike interests. This, of course, is more true of some institutions than of others. All of these and other factors combine to create a very wide diversification of attitudes among students entering college at the present time.

Educational Unevenness

How marked are the differences in the educational background of present-day students, and to what extent such differences are greater than a generation ago, are somewhat problematical. On the one hand, the influence of the college upon the preparatory and high schools has tended, among other things, to standardize the training of those expecting to enter college. On the other hand, there has developed an increasing flexibility of college entrance requirements which "has all but reduced the common preparation—common in nomenclature of studies only—to the single subject of English. In the quality of the preparation a wide range of variability exists."[12]

The Selection of Student Personnel

Both of these factors—the increase of student enrollments and the increasing heterogeneity of student bodies—have resulted, among other things, in a marked increase of attention to the selection of students to be admitted to college. The traditional basis for such selection has been that of scholastic proficiency, expressed in grades and measures in terms of units. Progress in selection has been conceived as consisting of refinements of this method of selection, and of upward revisions of the score of proficiency. There have been no special features of the selective process peculiar to collegiate schools of business. That is to say, students expecting to prepare for business careers have been selected on the same basis as prospective clergymen, professional translators, and architects.

Over against the prevailing methods are several groups of stubborn facts, unearthed by research and proved by experience, which are precipitating fundamental changes in the process of selection. Chief among these is a growing emphasis upon the importance of the student's personality, his emotional background and organization, his attitudes and vocational interests, and the nature of the individual differences which constitute his particular personality. Evidence is being accumulated to show that these factors are of the utmost importance in determining the student's success or failure in college, as well as in his subsequent pursuits.

All of this is of particular interest and importance to collegiate schools of business because of the corresponding stress upon traits of personality as factors in business life. Enough has been said in Chapters III and VII to make clear the relatively important role which these traits play in the achievement of business success. It is of particular significance to recall that, at least so far as the data for the alumni of the Wharton School of Finance and Commerce of the University of Pennsylvania

---

[12] Much of the foregoing discussion is reproduced from an article by the author, published in School and Society, op. cit.

show, most of the business school graduates go into executive positions and into selling, that it is in these fields that levels of scholarship are somewhat lower and the importance of personal traits is somewhat higher than in other well defined fields of business activity. In view of their undoubted importance, in academic and in business life, should not these other qualifications be recognized in the admission of students to collegiate schools of business? If so, how much importance should be assigned to them?

It seems needless to add that such suggestions in no way seek to convey any depreciation of scholastic standards in the admission of students. Rather do they imply the recognition of additional qualifications to supplement those which now prevail. As has been pointed out in the earlier chapters, emphasis upon desirable personal traits and qualities in no way involves the abandonment of scholarship as a goal, but seek rather to make it more effective through a selected and trained personnel. There is some reason to think that there has been too indiscriminate an admission to the colleges of commerce. Hundreds of boys and, more recently, girls, are taking the business course because it is the novel and popular thing to do. This is not meant to say that university education for business is a fad. Rather is it true that the business schools, engrossed in the process of establishing themselves, have set too much store in a mere growth of numbers, and without determining whether many of the students they accepted were fitted by temperament or otherwise for business careers. By adding emphasis upon personal qualifications for business to those of intelligence and scholarship in the selection of commerce students, not only will business education profit thereby, but youth and business as well.

The foregoing discussion suggests a related question. What is a school's responsibility for the number of students admitted particularly in any chosen field of specialization? Concretely speaking, does a school have any responsibility to measure the existing frequency of certain positions for which it prepares? Particularly does this question arise in view of the fact that the graduates of most institutions locate within a rather restricted local area. If, for example, the field of accounting is obviously overcrowded in a particular area, do the schools training accountants in that area have any responsibility to restrict the number of students specializing in that field?

The present inquiry might be pursued to the point of asking about the responsibility of a school to conduct researches in the objective determination of the qualities necessary for success in definite fields of business activity. What are the traits required in banking that are peculiar to that field? This suggests the relationship between job analysis and the future selection of students. Here is a striking opportunity for business interests to cooperate in making a real contribution both to their own business and to business education. Such objective tests are being made in certain fields, and the general idea involved has been accepted. There is a curious lag in its application to certain occupations peculiarly able in a financial way to support experiments of this kind.

Another question which presents itself has to do with the extent to which a school of business should distribute its admission of students on the basis of the outstanding qualifications of individual applicants. It will be recalled from the discussions in Chapters III and VII that, within limitations, distribution among certain main occupational divisions turns upon the student's preeminence in scholarship, or of personality, or in regard to other traits. If it is true, as has been pointed out in Chapter III, that men of highest scholarship tend to gravitate toward research and analytical work, and those with certain traits of personality largely enter selling or executive positions, should the number of students admitted to a school be apportioned on the basis of such considerations? Should the school interested primarily in research select its men chiefly on the basis of scholarship? Should the school seeking to train executives weigh unduly the personal qualifications of its student applicants? Should the bases of selection of students be determined largely by the objectives of the school?

Another problem of student personnel directly related to the policy of admissions involves the distribution of students admitted on the basis of racial and psychological differences. The growing heterogeneity of student bodies has created problems which cannot be ignored permanently, with impunity. This is a matter which is particularly important to schools interested in the personality development of its students. A school, like a country, can absorb so much that is different from its accepted pattern or mode. Beyond that point, only confusion and negation result.

Student Personnel and the Continuing Responsibility of the University

A transformation almost revolutionary in its ultimate significance has been taking place recently in the conception of the university's responsibility toward its students. Instead of conceiving of its task solely in terms of a four (or more) year training period for the student before his entrance upon his chosen occupation, the modern university has now come to regard this training period as but a part of a responsibility which needs to be continued after graduation and for an indefinite period of time. While the obvious symbol of this new attitude is the placement bureau, and the immediate task is the student's placement in a position, the relationship between institution and graduate is being extended, both in point of time and scope of development, until it comprehends nothing short of the continuous satisfactory adjustment of the graduate to his life work.

With the acceptance of this principle of continuing responsibility, the problems of student personnel take on at once an added importance. There are a number of reasons for this. To begin with, it means that an institution which accepts a lot of poor material, speaking academically or in terms of personality, correspondingly increases its difficulties when these students complete their courses. Again, it means that a division of a university, such as the college of commerce, which accepts a large number of students who, no matter how promising in other ways, are not fitted for business careers, will have to bear a corresponding burden. Furthermore, it is clear that a division of a university that trains large numbers of students for positions the ranks of which are already overcrowded, must pay subsequently the price for it.

It might be noted incidentally that the continuance of responsibility for students has profound implications for curriculum building. It means that a school of business, to consider the aspect of our specific interest, must integrate its work rather carefully with the requirements of business. Since it is the permanent adjustment of the student that is sought rather than his temporary placement, the student needs to know more about the concrete requirements of jobs and the school needs to know more about particular business offerings, as well as about particular students. Vocational guidance, needs to be done, not in general terms and as an incident, but as an integral part of the curriculum. Courses, particularly in the upper classes, must be developed in terms of business functions instead of the abstract and arbitrary classifications of the schoolmen of yesteryear. The closer integration of the products of the schools into the processes of business necessitates a more intimate understanding and a more discerning appraisal of business and education, each by the other. And this closer integration, as illustrated in the lives of unnumbered, eager young people, must be the abiding task of university education for business.

Summary and Conclusions

1. There are 1398 teachers of business subjects in the faculties of the 42 schools in the American Association of Collegiate Schools of Business. This does not include those who teach the business students in the non-business studies.

2. Of this total, 25.4 per cent have the rank of full professor; 12.5 per cent, the rank of associate professor; 17.7 per cent are assistant professors; 27.2 per cent are listed as instructors; 11.9 per cent are lecturers; and 5.3 per cent are assistants or are unclassified. Interesting variations in distribution of rank exist from school to school.

3. A study of the ranking degrees of these teachers shows that 35 per cent possess a Ph.D or C.P.A. degree; 33.1 per cent, one of the master's degrees; and 17.2 per cent, the baccalaurate degree. The remaining ones are scattered among various other degrees, of which the bachelor of laws degree is the most frequent. Here again there are interesting variations from school to school.

4. Statements furnished by individual teachers and listed in the business school faculty directory indicate that 63.7 per cent, or two out of every three, have had professional experience other than in teaching. Such experience is either administrative and commercial, or of a research character. The former is reported more frequently.

5. Faculty personnel is recruited on the basis of various selective factors, chief among which are the degree of prestige of the

teaching profession in the eyes of the community, the reputed prospects of financial reward, the nature and demands of professional training, and the organization of the teaching market.

6. Some faculties are built, others merely attain a certain state of growth. There are faculties which obviously are purposive combinations of selected teachers, there are others made up chiefly of time servers and mediocre neophytes. These are things which, in the final analysis, constitute the spirit of an academic institution. The problems of several schools are chiefly those resulting from continued carelessness or defective judgment in the selection of teaching personnel. The time server is too fearful, even to achieve; and mediocrity always acts defensively.

7. The college teacher is a product primarily of the graduate school. The training which he receives is now relatively standardized, and combines two main emphases. One has to do with the giving of a wide knowledge of a particular subject, the other with training in the methods of its further mastery, i.e., research. While the graduate school does reasonably well that which it seeks to do, other results of its training are somewhat less satisfactory. Among these are (a) a limited knowledge of things outside of the field of specialization; (b) a distorted view of the appeal, importance and implications of the particular speciality; (c) a lack of interest in teaching; and, (d) an ignorance of the art of teaching. There is urgent need that the graduate school face the facts of its own situation, and reorganize its work in view of the needs of the time. Recent emphasis upon the inefficiency of much current college teaching and upon the importance of better teaching give particular point to this demand.

8. Data on salary scales of 23 of the 42 Association schools of business show that instructors generally receive between two and three thousand dollars per year; assistant professors, between three and four thousand; associate professors, from three to five thousand; and full professors, from thirty-five hundred on up, with five thousand the figure of greatest frequency. Salary scales at the highly endowed school, located in metropolitan centers, show higher scales, especially for full professors. The range for these extends to $12,000. However, only three per cent of the total faculty personnel fall within this group.

9. Studies of supplementary earnings show their wide prev-

alence, especially in the upper ranks. That this work is done under economic pressure is evidenced by the marked difference in the proportion of those so doing between married and single teachers. There is no doubt but that any considerable amount of outside works interferes with the work of the teacher. It drains his nervous energy, lessens his productiveness, and prevents that extra application of effort necesary for very good teaching.

10. Recent data show that college of commerce teachers are not paid as well as teachers in education, law, medecine and theology, and that the percentage of increase in average salary for 1926-27, over that in 1919-20 was lower in commerce than in any other division or school of our universities.

11. Data on the number of hours taught by business school teachers show that, on the whole, they vary inversely with the size of salaries. That is to say, long hours and low pay go together here, as in the exploiting industries.

12. It is a curious fact that thus far no effort has been made to determine objectively what constitutes a full-time teaching job. Most teachers insist that this cannot be done. The fact remains that it has not yet been tried. Manifestly, such an effort must proceed in terms of units of energy rather than in terms of hours spent in class room instruction, and must allow for the differing circumstances under which university teaching may be done, such as number of preparations involved, new courses carried, time of hours taught, etc.

13. The efficiency of a faculty depends, furthermore, on the prevailing conditions of intellectual stimulation. These include such factors as opportunity for frank and informal discussion between faculty members, contact with current intellectual movements, exchange professorships, travel, outside lectures, etc. These are things of the spirit, hard to measure, but immeasurably important.

14. Emphasis upon research is one of the outstanding features of American academic life. Certain universities are centering their entire development about their research programs. While the extension of knowledge is one of the commonly accepted functions of our leading universities, there is reason to believe that the emphasis upon research has gone too far in certain quarters, leading to a neglect of the teaching function and to the

exploitation of students, in the furtherance of research projects. Moreover, under pressure to produce, much research is inane in conception or crowns a trivality with the dignity of a monograph.

15. One-third of the business school faculties are of the rank of instructors, and for a substantial part of his course, the student's contact is with these. Yet there is an almost complete lack of guidance and constructive help for instructors from their academic elders. The ways of the young instructor, and of his students, are both unnecessarily hard.

16. The problem of faculty leadership is of fundamental importance. While this fact is generally recognized in regard to the dean's office, the situation is less fortunate in regard to department heads. There seems to be too much talk of "headship" of departments, and too little conception of the obligations, responsibilities, and opportunities involved.

17. Two factors have complicated and multiplied in recent years the problems of collegiate student personnel. One of these is the growth in the proportion of young people going to college; the other, the increasing heterogeneity of our student bodies. Both of these have been unusually operative in regard to the collegiate schools of business.

18. One result of these factors has been a marked increase of attention to the selection of students to be admitted to college. In addition to the traditional basis of scholastic proficiency, there is a growing emphasis upon the student's personality, his emotional background and organization, his attitudes and his vocational interests. This is of particular interest to collegiate schools of business because of the corresponding stress upon traits of personality as factors in business success.

19. Further questions of the responsibility of colleges of commerce in the selection of students present themselves. Does a school have any responsiblity to measure the existing frequency of positions for which it prepares? Should a school conduct researches in the objective determination of the qualities necessary for success in selected fields of business activity? Should a school make up its quota of students admitted on the basis of their outstanding qualifications, admitting a certain proportion because of proficiency in scholarship, another proportion because of unusual personal traits, etc? To what extent should

admissions be distributed on the basis of racial and psychological differences?

20. A transformation almost revolutionary in its ultimate significance has been taking place in the conception of the university's responsibility toward its students. Instead of conceiving of its task solely in terms of a four (or more) year training period for the student before his entrance upon his chosen occupation, the modern university has now come to regard this training period as but a part of a responsibility which needs to be continued after graduation and for an indefinite period of time. While the obvious symbol of this new attitude is the placement bureau, and the immediate task is the student's placement in a position, the relationship between institution and graduate is being extended, both in point of time and scope of development, until it comprehends nothing short of the continuous satisfactory adjustment of the graduate to his life work.

CHAPTER XVII

CONCLUSIONS

During the past three decades the United States has risen to a position of economic world leadership, a position in which the leaders of our industries have come to exercise a potent and pervasive influence upon the social and economic life of the entire world. The extraordinary advances in the application of science to modern life which have made possible the remarkable economic progress and vast improvement in human well-being during the present century have created a multitude of economic and social problems for the solution of which our business leaders must assume primary responsibility. Hence the task to which the collegiate schools of business have addressed themselves, that of training young men for the heavy responsibilities of the business leadership of the future, constitutes an educational problem of paramount importance.

Development of an adequate program for such training, it is clear, must aim to prepare the student for the broad responsibilities, rather than the narrow routine, of this new profession. Graduates of business schools, the faculties of these institutions, and business executives themselves are in agreement that a broad background of general and economic knowledge, a disciplined capacity for independent thinking, a facility in oral and written expression, and an instinctive appreciation of ethical values and responsibilities should constitute the primary goals of professional training for business.

Although it is apparent that the attainment of these ends can best be achieved in the field of the student's interest and motivation, it is clearly recognized that courses and curricula are but .means to the end rather than the end itself. Successful business management, it is true, demands adequate technical knowledge of business practice and procedure, but it is by no means certain that the undergraduate business school is the proper place for the acquisition of such knowledge. Certainly there is a growing tendency on the part of employers of college labor to deplore the further development of specialized "practical" courses in the undergraduate curriculum. There is general agreement that a mere knowledge of business facts and principles gained at second hand is of far less importance in preparing the student for a business career than the development of his capacity for applying imagination and intelligence in attacking and solving concrete problems.

Moreover, it is apparent that the student's oportunity for achieving a successful and socially useful career in business is greatly enhanced by the possession of certain personal traits and attitudes which enable him to work effectively with others in mutual enterprises. These traits of personality, which involve the capacity for influencing human behavior, may be in large part innate but insofar as they are susceptible of conscious development this also would seem to be among the responsibilities of the school. The extent to which such formal courses as psychology, labor relations, public speaking, and salesmanship can be effective in developing the student's facility in human relationships is uncertain, but it should be emphasized that these personal traits and skills are an important by-product of the entire university environment. Moreover, it appears that they are to a great extent unrelated to superior intelligence and high scholarship. Of course it would be most unwise to assume on the basis of this evidence that the school should abandon its traditional aims and devote its energies exclusively to the development of "personality", but it is equally obvious that the maintenance of high standards of scholarship should not be the sole aim of an institution which attempts to prepare young men for successful and socially useful careers in business.

Study of the occupational experience and of the expressed opinions of Wharton School graduates, in the light of their undergraduate careers, furnishes abundant confirmation of the testimony of executives as to the qualities necessary for success in business. Here there is found additional evidence that scholarship is by no means the sole determinant of success particularly in managerial and selling occupations, in which a large majority of graduates become engaged. Nor is there much reason to believe that highly specialized courses of a so-called practical nature are particularly effective in preparing students for specific occupations in view of the fact that a large proportion of those following specialized curricula eventually find work in fields other than those for which they prepared themselves.

Generally speaking the opinions of former students regarding the content and method of undergraduate business training coincided with those expressed by business executives. Almost unanimously graduates agreed that the study of English should be of primary importance in the business curriculum, while there was a similar preponderance of opinion that foreign languages were the least valuable subjects in the course of study. Courses which aim to instruct in the practical administration of business affairs were generally believed to be of subordinate importance to those which furnish a descriptive analysis of business activities and to those which treat of the social setting of business and economic life.

There was also a widespread belief among graduates as to the fundamental purposes of university education for business, which may be expressed briefly as follows. The collegiate business course should aim primarily to train students in habits of work and methods of thought and oral and written expression. Information regarding business facts and practices is useful, not as an end in itself, but as a means of training the mind and strengthening the judgment of the student. The content of the curriculum and the methods of teaching should be organized to accomplish these two ends—training in analysis and training in expression. Informational lectures and memorization and class room repetition of factual material are of little avail in achieving these purposes. On the contrary, primary emphasis in teaching should be placed upon seminar and research work, field and laboratory investigations, the use of cases and problems, and other individualized methods of instruction involving the investigation and critical examination of original material and the formal written and oral presentation of results.

To achieve these results the curriculum should not consist of scattered and unrelated subjects, but should comprise a core of integrated and coordinated studies required of every student, with only a moderate number of elective subjects to be studied chiefly in the later years. More important than either the content of the curriculum or the method of instruction as a determinant of the success or failure of undergraduate instruction is the character and training of the teaching staff. The most effective instructors are those who not only are thoroughly familiar with their own and related fields, but who are fitted by sympathy and temperament to serve as guides and counsellors to their students.

Approximately a million students in our educational institutions are today definitely preparing to enter business occupations. The various educational activities which prepare specifically for an understanding of the relationship and the performance of activities in business constitute the field of commercial education. Its chief forms include the private commercial school, better known as the business college; the commercial departments of the high schools, public and private; the private schools of commerce; the corporation schools, conducted by business enterprises; and the collegiate school of business, or college of commerce. Close to a hundred thousand students are now receiving instruction for business at the latter, or university, level. On the basis, then, of the number of persons involved, the problems of commercial education in general and of collegiate education for business in particular are relatively very important.

Collegiate education for business covers a scant half century, the first collegiate school of business having been established in 1881 by Joseph Wharton at the University of Pennsylvania. The movement grew slowly, however, for a number of years. Most of the university schools of business have been organized since 1910; many, since 1920. All judgment of their work and every analysis of their problems must take into consideration constantly the relative newness, not only of any particular school, but of the entire movement of education for business at the university level.

One evidence of this lack of maturity perhaps is the lack of clear-cut objectives. Shall the collegiate school of business aim primarily to give training in the general fundamentals of business? Shall they attempt a vocational preparation in various specialized phases of business? Shall they seek to prepare selected students for business leadership? There is considerable confusion and uncertainity on this score. Obviously, consciousness and definiteness of purpose are prerequisite to their achievement. Collegiate schools of business need to define their objectives more definitely and more specifically.

In preparing for business, shall the student spend the first two years in pursuing the conventional academic studies, and devote the last two years to business studies, or shall the entire course be devoted to a unified four year plan in which business and non-business studies are integrated? The same problem has long agitated the engineering schools. In both fields, experience favors the latter plan. An increasing majority of collegiate schools of business operate on the basis of a four year curriculum. The university curriculum seeking to prepare for business should be considered as a four year unit.

These facts stand out preëminently in the past development of collegiate business curricula.

(a) A number of conventional academic studies have been retained. Chief among these are English, foreign language, science, mathematics, history and the social sciences. In fact, taking the situation as a whole, the curricula of the business schools for the first two years consist of accounting, economics, and the customary lower class liberal arts studies. To a large extent, the latter are taught with little or no adaptation or consideration for the purposes of the college of commerce. This arrangement is the result generally, not of the judgment of commerce faculties, but of the necessity of making concessions.

(b) There has been a rapid growth in the number and range of courses in the business studies, some schools offering a hundred and more. The business fields most extensively developed are accounting, distribution (including advertising, marketing, selling and retail merchandising) banking and finance, economics, transportation and public utilities, management, statistics, and business law, in the order named. This development, which represents the interests of specialists rather than the educational needs of students, has resulted in much duplication of material.

(c) These various business courses have been made available to students, as a rule, not as parts of one unified, coordinated curriculum, but they have been distributed among various specialized curricula, usually offered in the upper two years. In 38 leading collegiate schools of business, the average number of specialized curricula is more than nine per school. Specialization, in other words, has been running riot.

The great difficulty in the past has been that college of commerce curricula have been the product of factors other than the careful analysis and rational judgment of commerce faculties as to the needs of their students. Once there is both freedom and willingness to construct commerce curricula on the basis of the needs of students and the demands of business, and these factors only, the following problems would seem to require immediate and careful attention. (a) The identification of the fundamentals for business training. The term fundamentals is used in the sense that mathematics and the physical sciences are fundamental in engineering education. Such fundamentals undoubtedly exist in business education as they do in other fields of education. No serious attempt to discover them has yet been made. Perhaps these must be identified as the result of a long inductive process of job analysis. More and more is being said in favor of this form of scientific approach. (b) To the extent that these fundamentals or other courses for commerce students are outside the more purely business studies, there is the problem of the adaptation of these courses to the fundamental purpose of the curriculum of which they are a part. This problem of adaptation of courses is not peculiar to colleges of commerce. It is emerging in all of the specialized undergraduate schools which, in the development of their curricula, have had to draw upon departments older than they and historically identified with other divisions of the university, usually the college of liberal arts.

The particular departments involved usually are not favorably disposed to these demands; first, because the adaptation of courses necessitates instructors who have a knowledge also of the field to which they are adapting, a dual background which many of them do not have; and, second, such intermediary fields have not been conceived of in the past as having any professional future or status. Rationalizing their wishes, they insist that such adaptation is undesirable and unnecessary. English is English, science is science, mathematics is mathematics, no matter where given or to whom. The department members insist that, being specialists in their field, they are the best judges of what students should be taught.

This view seems fallacious; first, because it fails to utilize the motive of the student's interest in the related field; second, because if the teacher cannot make and clarify the relationship between studies, the student is even less able to do so; and, third, while the elements of any subject are the same, their form of concrete expression or aspect of application can and do vary profoundly. (c) Based on the foundation studies are the essentials of or common core of a business education. What business studies should all commerce students pursue before specialization is tolerated? Upper class core requirements now emphasized include business law, statistics, marketing, accounting, money and banking and business or corporation finance. Are these the elements of a well-rounded business education such as each graduate of a collegiate school of business should receive?

Certainly each student should receive this common core of business studies: first, because so many students do not yet know what particular field of business they will enter; second, because of those who have definite fields in mind and prepare for them, so many will not remain permanently in those fields; and, third, because each business man, no matter what his particular specialty may be, needs an understanding of business in its larger aspects if he is to make any appreciable progress in his chosen field. (d) Of the utmost importance is the effective coordination of the elements of the business curriculum into a structural unity. A business education should consist of more than the mere sum of its parts; it should be conceived and planned as a whole. While this does not preclude a reasonable degree of flexibility, with provision for electives and group options, such latitude must always be limited so that the program for the student shall not degenerate into a loose succession of uncoordinated subjects. The need for such structural unity, with coherent integration and logical sequence of subject matter, is coming to be much emphasized in business education circles.

Business curricula, however, are in process of change. Opinions of prominent educators as to the direction of recent changes would indicate a trend toward the fundamentals of business, a decreasing emphasis upon technical instruction, a frowning upon further specialization except in a sort of regional adaptation of business literature and courses, a trend toward fewer courses, an insistence upon a more intensive pedagogy, a trend toward the precision and exacting analytical methods of the engineer, a growing belief that curricula need to be built on the basis of objective analysis, an increasing suspicion that departmental lines must be disregarded, and a rapidly growing emphasis upon the importance of research.

All of these factors grow perhaps out of two primary considerations. One of these is the principle that the curriculum should be fitted to the student and to business, instead of the reverse; and, second, the inductive spirit of modern science which considers nothing, either in teaching method or material, as fixed or settled.

Business places a particular premium upon personality. The analyses and opinions presented in Part I bear eloquent witness to this fact. The life sciences are all, from their respective viewpoints, seeking to understand the processes and problems involved in the formation and possible constructive development of personality. Colleges of commerce, sensing both the demands of business and the promise of science, are awakening to this very important aspect of their work.

There are those who hold that the college of commerce which will come forward today with a new program of training centering about the development of personality, and pointing toward a business career, will be as much of a pioneer as was the Wharton School of Finance and Commerce in 1881. This would involve an extensive development of the by-products of teaching. It would widen, of course, the breach between the university teacher and the research student. It would mean that the stone which the builders rejected would become the head of the corner. Such a project would have to be built upon the effort of many interested teachers, alive to the possibilities involved. It would mean a great deal of experimentation and a constantly open mind, while such experiments were in progress. It would necessitate the slow accretion of a technique to achieve the end in view. Such a project ought sometime to intrigue a donor who has the imagination to conceive its possibilities, and the means to enable progress toward their achievement.

While formal lectures and large recitation classes still constitute the standard methods of instruction in collegiate schools of business, there is growing a realization of their inadequacy. Granting that the development of the student's capacity for independent thinking and effective expression should be the primary aim of education, it is clear that methods which ensure his active participation in the learning process are best designed to attain these ends. Among the more promising experiments of this sort in the field of business education are the use of actual business cases and problems in the class room and the participation by the student in some form of practical work concurrently with theoretical instruction. Whether or not these methods can be employed extensively, it must be recognized that they fill a distinct need in this branch of professional education similar to that supplied by clinical and experimental methods in medical and engineering training. Inherent in these and other plans for improving the quality of the teaching are the basic ideas of participation by the student in the learning process, greater individualization of instruction, and of recognition of different levels of student capacity. Whatever the means employed to achieve these results it is apparent that both curriculum and teaching methods are merely tools; their effectiveness depends primarily upon the skill and spirit of the teaching staff.

A university is essentially an organization of personalities, with certain selected common interests and relationships; from which it follows that the problems of personnel are also essential.

Of outstanding importance in the development of an effective university faculty are the following factors: careful selection of personnel, both with reference to task and other personalities in the group; teachers well qualified not only with a mastery of subject, but also an interest in and a knowledge of the art of teaching; a salary scale adequate for a plane of living commensurate with other professions and which does not compel undue outside activities to secure supplementary earnings; a teaching load which permits effective teaching and continued study; conditions of more or less constant intellectual stimulation of faculty members; academic recognition for effective teaching as well as for productive research; and constructive educational leadership, both in departments and in the larger academic units.

The problem of faculty personnel in the collegiate schools of business is of peculiar importance; first, because of the rapid growth in the number of schools and students enrolled; and, second, because of the constant competition of business itself with the business schools for the services of personable, well-trained business students.

Finally, it must be remembered that collegiate schools of business exist for the training of students, from which it follows that the problems of student personnel are of fundamental importance. Because of the growth in recent years in the proportion of young men and women going to college and of the increasing heterogeneity of student bodies, these problems are of particular importance at this time. There is increasing attention to the selection of students to be admitted to college, with the possible development of certain new bases of selection. There is some evidence, too, of the growth of a revolutionary transformation in the conception of the responsibility of universities to their students comprehending ultimately nothing short of the continuous satisfactory adjustment of the graduate to his life work.

INDEX OF SUBJECTS

INDEX OF NAMES

32142

Date Due			